# Vancouver
## The Complete **Residents'** Guide

Passionately Publishing...

**EXPLORER**

**Vancouver Explorer 1st Edition ISBN 978-9948-03-384-4**

Front Cover Photograph: Coal Harbour – Pamela Grist

Printed and bound by Emirates Printing Press, Dubai, United Arab Emirates.

**Explorer Publishing & Distribution**
PO Box 34275, Dubai
United Arab Emirates
**Phone**      +971 (0)4 340 8805
**Fax**          +971 (0)4 340 8806
**Email**       info@explorerpublishing.com
**Web**          www.explorerpublishing.com

## Welcome...

You've just made living in Vancouver a whole lot easier by buying this book. In the following pages you'll find out everything you need to know to get settled into – and then get the most out of – your new life in one of the world's most liveable cities. From finding an apartment to embarking on a wilderness hike or sampling some sushi, we can tell you how and where to do it.

The **General Information** chapter (p.1) fills you in on Vancouver's history, geography and culture, and provides details of how to get around and where to stay when you first arrive, plus a round-up of the city's annual festivals.

The **Residents** chapter (p.61) takes away all the headaches involved in setting up your new home. With information on visas, residential areas, schools, health and red tape, this section will tell you how to deal with all the formalities.

After settling in, take a look at **Exploring** (p.183). This chapter guides you through Vancouver's different neighbourhoods, telling you all about its museums, galleries, parks and beaches, and detailing where to go to see more of Canada and beyond. There's also a checklist of must-do experiences to work your way through.

If you've still got time on your hands, move on to **Activities** (p.271). Here you'll find out where to practise tai chi, how to join a drama group, and where to learn to ice skate or ski. If you'd prefer to indulge, there's also a wealth of well-being options to digest, from acupuncture to yoga, with a bit of spa in between.

Now that you're living in Vancouver, you'll also have full access to all the retail that one of Canada's best **Shopping** (p.359) cities has to offer. We've got a whole chapter dedicated to helping you discover the top markets, malls and high streets in which to splash the cash, as well as picking out some of the more quirky independent outlets.

Don't spend all your dollars in the shops though – save some for the evening. **Going Out** (p.419) gives you a detailed run-down on Vancouver's premier places for eating, drinking and partying

Nearly all of the places of interest have references that correspond to the detailed **Maps** (p.481) in the back of the book – use these for everything from planning your route to work, to finding the quickest way out of town and on to the mountains.

And if you think we have missed something, please let us know. Go to www.explorerpublishing.com, fill in the Reader Response form, and share the knowledge with your fellow explorers.

**The Explorer Team**

**Explorer's Vancouver**
*A fantastic mix of cosmopolitan city and the great outdoors, Vancouver is an active urbanite's dream. You can live Downtown but in no time at all be hiking the North Shore Mountains (p.324); skiing or biking world-class Whistler Blackcomb (p.264); kayaking False Creek or Indian Arm (p.258); and walking, cycling or blading around the city's many green spaces (p.241). The food's not bad either, with fantastic west coast fare (p.446) and the best sushi outside of Asia (p.437). There are some fascinating creative ventures too – check out the Museum of Anthropology (p.231) and the Eastside Culture Crawl (p.220). Finally, every true or aspiring Canadian must take in an ice hockey game (p.337) – go Canucks go!*

**Aefa Mulholland** Hotel school graduate and former restaurant manager Aefa has been surveying the Vancouver scene since arriving in BC in 2003. Now a travel writer for publications including *The Irish Times* and *The Miami Herald*, when she's not sashaying through airports or staying at plush hotels, she checks out bands, concocts cocktails and hunts for the ultimate izakaya. **Best city memory:** Discovering a rocky river beach near Lynn Canyon Bridge (p.243). **Reason to never leave:** The sushi (p.437).

**Anya Levykh** Writer and editor Anya has lived in Vancouver for over 20 years, contributing to titles including *The Vancouver Sun*, *Metro Vancouver* and *Good Life Connoisseur*. Originally from Russia, she loves the city's varied dining scene. Upcoming projects include a Russian cookbook and a foodie's guide to Vancouver. **Best view:** From Jericho Beach (p.238): ocean, mountains and city – it's got it all. **Best place to drink with locals:** At the Opus Hotel (p.463), for the orange julius martini.

**David Tycho** David is a Canadian Literary Award winning writer, internationally exhibited artist and dedicated English teacher who has lived in Vancouver for all but five years of his life. In his spare time, David can be found cycling or running the trails and byways of the city, stopping at seaside bars and restaurants along the way. **Vancouver must-do:** Sip wine on Spanish Banks at sunset (p.239). **Favourite cultural experience:** Nipping into the galleries on South Granville Street (p.220).

**Isabelle Groc** A freelance writer and photographer who has lived in Vancouver for 10 years, Isabelle's work covers environmental issues, urban affairs, conservation and wildlife. Rain or shine, you're likely to find her angling her camera at the birds in Stanley Park or along the Seawall. **Best city memory:** Watching a coyote cross West Georgia Street on a Saturday morning. **Vancouver must-do:** Take your bike to a Critical Mass event every last Friday of the month (p.43).

*Having trouble navigating your way around the streets and avenues of Vancouver? Look no further than the **Vancouver Mini Map**, an indispensable pocket-sized aid to getting to grips with the city's roads, areas and attractions.*

**Janet Gyenes**  After a decade working with slow-moving provincial government bureaucrats, this longtime Vancouverite traded red tape for the fast-paced magazine industry where she now works as an editor and writer – although her background in officialdom came in handy when researching part of the Residents chapter.
**Favourite cultural experience:** FUSE nights at Vancouver Art Gallery (p.224).
**Favourite daytrip:** Shopping in Seattle (p.262).

**Kristine Thiessen**  A journalism graduate from UBC, Kristine currently works as a reporter for the *South Delta Leader*. She entered Vancouver's world of basement suites during university and delved into everything the city has to offer, from improv shows to weekday 'ultimate' games.
**Favourite Vancouver restaurant:** Sunday Brunch at Havana on Commercial Drive (p.427). **Vancouver must-do:** Summer night markets in Chinatown and Richmond (p.413).

**Leah Buchan**  Leah has travelled the globe, but it's not just an expired visa that draws her back home. When tuk-tuk drivers were ripping her off in Bangkok, and wild pigs were sniffing at her tent in Tanzania, she dreamt of Jericho Beach and the Pacific lapping at the foot of the mountains. **Best thing about Vancouver:** The views, and the smell after it rains. **Best city memory:** Watching fireworks with friends on English Bay Beach (p.238).

**Lori Henry**  Lori is a globetrotting travel writer who calls Vancouver her home. When shopping, she always tries to find the best deal while sticking to high quality – and is the authority on locating both. Looking for a left-handed hockey stick or the hippest sustainable dress? She'll find the perfect store. **Vancouver must-do:** Main Street shopping, for the talented and fresh designers (p.407). **Worst thing about living in Vancouver:** The Seawall (p.211) gets too crowded in summer.

*Now that you've moved to Vancouver, it won't be long before you're playing host to wave upon wave of visiting family and friends – and we've got the perfect guide to help them get the most out of their sightseeing. Packed with info on Vancouver's shops, restaurants and tourist spots, you can't go wrong with the **Vancouver Mini Explorer**.*

**Marty McLennan**  Marty has worked as a freelance photojournalist for more than 30 magazines, including *Canadian Geographic*, *Ski Canada*, and *Explore*, and has written several travel guides. When not on assignment, he enjoys exploring BC and watching soccer matches at Abruzzo Cafe. He also teaches at Simon Fraser University. **Favourite Vancouver restaurant**: Hapa Izakaya (p.213). **Favourite daytrip:** Kayaking in Indian Arm (p.258).

**Rob Mathison**  Rob came to Vancouver in 2004 from Scotland via a stint in magazines in Toronto, and now works on a freelance basis to give him more time to explore. He loves rising early on a wet January morning, fuelling up at Tim Hortons and driving up Cypress Mountain, marvelling at the transition from drizzle to winter wonderland. **Best view:** The Cut ski run on Grouse Mountain (p.242) at night. **Best thing about living in Vancouver:** People live Downtown, meaning 24 hour vibrancy.

**Tara Thorne**  Tara was born in Toronto, grew up in Australia, and now lives in Vancouver, where the city's mountainous backdrop and alluring seaside satisfies her desire for adventure. Since becoming a freelance writer, Tara has written for various magazines and websites as well as ghostwriting books for a trailblazing doctor. **Best place to drink with the locals:**  Malone's on Kitsilano Beach (p.238). **Favourite cultural experience:**  Stumbling across Inukshuk art in Yaletown (p.194).

**Thanks...**  As well as our star authors, a number of other people have made invaluable contributions to this book. In Vancouver, massive thanks go to Anne Duke and Lawrence Lowe, and Stuart Wales, Mia Olsson and Jake Cheung for hospitality and hijinks; Marko Ferenc for lending his insider knowledge of the Vancouver dining scene; Jim Hoy, Tony and Vicki Grist, Mark Grist, Andreas Seppelt, Katy Chamber for her Garibaldi Lake picture (p.189), John Baldwin for his skiing photo (p.323), Wendy Underwood, Brenda Meikle, Lynn Gervais and Tamara Almas. Closer to home, thanks to the whole team for weighing in when needed, and Hannah Jordan for everything.

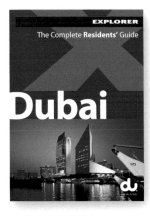

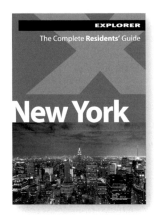

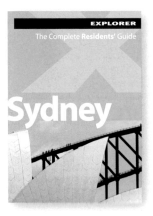

# Tired of writing your insider tips…

## …in a blog that nobody reads?

The Explorer Complete Residents' Guide series is growing rapidly, and we're always looking for literate, resident writers to help pen our new guides. So whether you live in Tuscany or Timbuktu, if writing's your thing, and you know your city inside out, we'd like to talk to you.

Apply online at www.explorerpublishing.com

# Where are we exploring next?

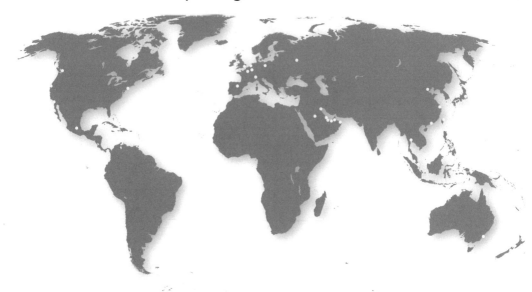

- Abu Dhabi
- Amsterdam
- Bahrain
- Bangkok*
- Barcelona
- Beijing
- Berlin
- Brussels

- Dubai
- Dublin
- Geneva
- Hong Kong
- Kuala Lumpur
- Kuwait
- London
- Los Angeles

- Mexico City*
- Moscow*
- New York
- New Zealand
- Oman
- Paris
- Qatar
- San Francisco*

- Saudi Arabia*
- Shanghai
- Singapore
- Sydney
- Taipei*
- Tokyo
- Vancouver

* Available 2009

## Where do you live?

Is your home city missing from our list? If you'd love to see a residents' guide for a location not currently on Explorer's horizon please email editorial@explorerpublishing.com.

## Advertise with Explorer…

If you're interested in advertising with us, please contact sales@explorerpublishing.com.

## Make Explorer your very own…

We offer a number of customisation options for bulk sales. For more information and discount rates please contact corporatesales@explorerpublishing.com.

## Contract Publishing

Have an idea for a publication or need to revamp your company's marketing material? Contact designlab@explorerpublishing to see how our expert contract publishing team can help.

# Online

Life can move pretty fast, so to make sure you can stay up to date with all the latest goings on in your city, we've revamped our website to further enhance your time in the city, whether long or short.

## Keep in the know...

Our Complete Residents' Guides and Mini Visitors' series continue to expand, covering destinations from Amsterdam to New Zealand and beyond. Keep up to date with our latest travels and hot tips by signing up to our monthly newsletter, or browse our products section for info on our current and forthcoming titles.

## Make friends and influence people...

...by joining our Communities section. Meet fellow residents in your city, make your own recommendations for your favourite restaurants, bars, childcare agencies or dentists, plus find answers to your questions on daily life from long-term residents.

## Discover new experiences...

Ever thought about living in a different city, or wondered where the locals really go to eat, drink and be merry? Check out our regular features section, or submit your own feature for publication!

## Want to find a badminton club, the number for your bank, or maybe just a restaurant for a hot first date?

Check out city info on various destinations around the world in our Residents' info section – from finding a pilates class to contact details for international schools in your area, or the best place to buy everything from a spanner set to a Spandau Ballet album, we've got it all covered.

## Let us know what you think!

All our information comes from residents which means you! If we missed out your favourite bar or market stall, or you know of any changes in the law, infrastructure, cost of living or entertainment scene, let us know by using our Feedback form.

# Contents

# Contents

**Expat Women**

Helping Women Living Overseas

Our mission is to help you succeed overseas by providing you with a first-stop website to share stories, network globally, develop personally and find the best resources!

Visit Now: www.ExpatWomen.com

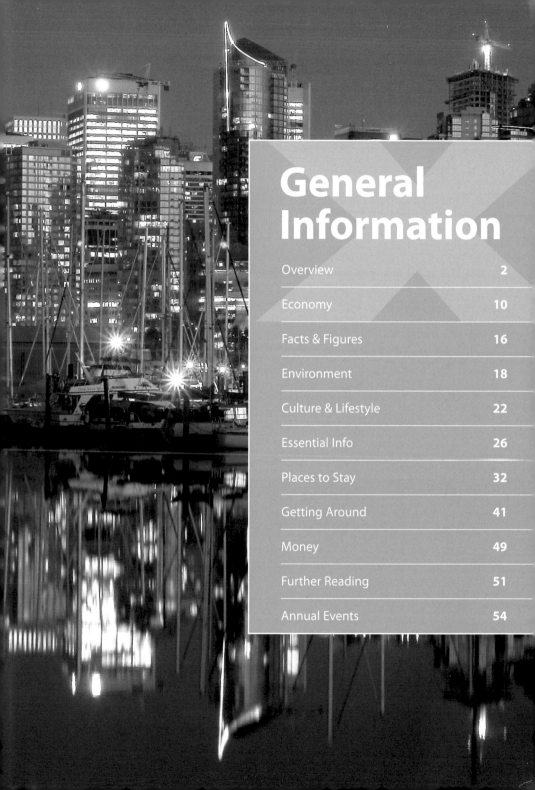

# General Information

# General Information

## Geography

Canada is the second-largest country in the world, after Russia; it's a vast and geographically diverse land that covers 9,984,670 square km – 40 times the size of the UK.

Canada touches three oceans: the Atlantic in the east, the Pacific in the west, and the Arctic in the north. The country's only physical neighbour is the US, and the two share the longest common border in the world (8,890km), known as the International Boundary. Canada and the US also share four of the five Great Lakes – Superior, Huron, Erie and Ontario, with one third of their total surface area residing in Canada. Almost 9% of Canada is covered by fresh water, and the Northwest Territories and Nunavut alone contain 9.2% of the world's total freshwater supply.

The country is split into 10 provinces (Alberta, British Columbia, Manitoba, New Brunswick, Newfoundland and Labrador, Nova Scotia, Ontario, Prince Edward Island, Quebec and Saskatchewan) and three territories (Northwest Territories, Nunavut and Yukon).

Large tracts of Canada remain thinly populated due to a combination of climate, terrain, and the vast distances between major settlements. The 2006 census found that nearly two in three Canadians, from a population of 33.4 million, huddle less than 100km away from the southern Canada-US border. Four out of every five Canadians live in large metropolitan areas, particularly the three largest cities, Toronto, Montreal and Vancouver.

**Big Country**

*If you're up for a stroll and have a couple of years to kill, the 18,000km Trans Canada Trail (www. tctrail.ca) will let you experience the full variety of Canada's landscape up close and personal. Or you can drive along the Trans-Canada Highway, one of the longest national highways in the world (www.transcanada highway.com).*

## Physical Geography

Canada is commonly sub-divided into the North (Northwest Territories, Nunavut and Yukon), Central Canada (Ontario and Quebec – confusingly not in the centre of the country), the West (BC, and increasingly Alberta), the Prairies (Alberta, Manitoba and Saskatchewan) and the Maritimes (New Brunswick, Nova Scotia, Prince Edward Island and Newfoundland and Labrador). Each region has its own distinctive physiographic characteristics. The North features vast areas of frozen tundra, the Canadian Shield – a massive area made up of an ancient rock base mostly covered by a hilly, forested landscape – and the western shores of the enormous Hudson Bay, which drains much of Central Canada and the Prairies. Canada's highest point, Mount Logan, is in the Yukon. Mount Logan is also North America's second tallest mountain, and is said to have the largest base circumference of any mountain in the world. Just over 100,000 people live in the North, most of who are of aboriginal descent. Gold, silver, zinc and copper are all mined in areas of the Canadian Shield.

To the east, the Maritimes was the first area to be settled by Europeans. The landscape features wild coastline, undulating hills, forests, and mining, farming and fishing communities, including the oldest city in Canada, St John's. Central Canada incorporates part of the Canadian Shield, the Great Lakes, Niagara Falls and Canada's most populated area, around Toronto and Montreal, which forms the industrial and commercial centre of the country. Moving west, the incredibly flat Prairies make up Canada's largest agricultural area, including wheat and cattle farms. They also feature the oil rich Athabasca Oil Sands and the rocky Canadian Badlands of Alberta, which is renowned for its dinosaur fossil finds. The jagged peaks of the Canadian Rockies are found here too. The Rockies are home to some of Canada's most scenic spots, including Lake Louise and the Columbia Icefield, which contains eight glaciers. Continuing through the Rockies is the heavily forested region of British Columbia. BC's Okanagan Valley features wine country and Canada's only desert, surrounding the town of Osoyoos. Finally, the west coast features the temperate rainforests of the Coast Mountains, Vancouver Island and the Queen Charlotte Islands.

*False Creek*

## Canada Fact Box

**Coordinates:** Canada's geographical centre is at 62° 24 minutes north, 96° 28 minutes west.

**Bordering countries:** USA

**Total land borders:** 8,890km

**Total land area:** 9,093,507km

**Total coastline:** 202,080km

**Highest point:** Mount Logan, 5,959m

### Vancouver

Vancouver's location is what gives the city much of its unique appeal and character. Cypress Mountain, along with Grouse Mountain and Mount Seymour (the tallest at 1,449m), are part of the North Shore Mountains to the north of the city. These mountains belong to the Coast Mountain Range, and they form Vancouver's scenic backdrop. On the western portion of the North Shore lies West Vancouver, containing many of the city's most expensive homes. Beyond West Vancouver, across the Strait of Georgia, lie several pretty Gulf Islands and Vancouver Island. The islands form a protective barrier between the Pacific Ocean and Vancouver.

Downtown Vancouver sits on a thumb of land that marks the entrance to the Burrard Inlet, connected to the City of North Vancouver by the green spans of Lions Gate Bridge. The bridge allows access to the city through the dense forest of Stanley Park. Beyond the park, Downtown's gleaming skyscrapers rise up from the landscape. The young city's winking glass condominium towers contrast with the cobbled streets of Quebec City's old town and the clapboard houses of St John's on the other side of the country.

The Burrard Inlet wends its way east past Downtown to Port Vancouver, under the Second Narrows Bridge towards North Vancouver's Deep Cove neighbourhood and Belcarra Regional Park. Port Moody and Coquitlam also lie ahead. The rest of Greater Vancouver, including the cities of Burnaby and Surrey, stretch south-east to the fertile agricultural area of the Fraser Valley and the cities of Langley and Abbotsford.

South-west of Downtown, English Bay provides safe anchor for large tankers before they enter the inlet. Across the bay sit the beaches of Kitsilano and Point Grey. These neighbourhoods connect to Downtown via the Granville and Burrard bridges that span False Creek, where Granville Island is located. On the westernmost point of the Burrard Peninsula, where the City of Vancouver sits, the University of British Columbia and Pacific Spirit Park can be found. Greater Vancouver then stretches south of the peninsula to Vancouver Airport and the City of Richmond. Further south is the US border and the state of Washington.

## History

With the 2010 Winter Olympics approaching fast, Vancouver is experiencing a significant period of growth and has gained an international reputation for trying to promote sustainable urban expansion. With so much gleaming glass around, it's easy to forget that none of it existed 120 years ago.

### The First Inhabitants

The earliest recorded inhabitants of what is now Greater Vancouver are the Coast Salish First Nations people, who are thought to have settled in British Columbia as much as 10,000 years ago. The different bands that make up the Coast Salish include the Squamish and the Musqueam, who both inhabited many areas of today's Vancouver, including Kitsilano, Point Grey, Stanley Park and English Bay. There they lived comfortably off the land and sea for many generations before European settlers arrived. The ancestors of those first inhabitants now live mainly in band reserves around Vancouver. First Nations art and culture is preserved in institutions like the Museum of Anthropology, and in city references, such as the Kitsilano neighbourhood (named after Squamish chief, Xats'alanexw, or August Jack Khatsahlano).

# Canada Overview

## The Europeans Arrive

The Spanish were the first to explore the waters of Canada's west coast, with Lieutenant Jose Maria Narvaez being the initial European to see the area, in 1791. An Englishman whose name would later be given to the city, Captain George Vancouver, followed him one year later. He sailed in through an inlet he named Burrard, after a member of his crew, but left after just one day, having realised the Spanish had already discovered the area. He did however stop long enough to chat with two more Spaniards, captains Valdez and Galliano, on a beach now named Spanish Banks in honour of that friendly meeting.

In 1808, another explorer, Simon Fraser, sailed the length of what is now called the Fraser River before being chased away by the Musqueam. In 1827, another Scot, fur trader James McMillan of the Hudson's Bay Company, sailed up with a small band of men and built a fort next to the Fraser River, later named Fort Langley. To this day, you can still shop at a Hudson's Bay department store in Vancouver.

## Fraser River Gold Rush

It wasn't until 1858 that things really started happening in the area, when gold was discovered around the Fraser River and more than 25,000 American prospectors flooded the region in search of their fortune. This 'invasion' prompted James Douglas, the governor of Vancouver Island (a British colony since 1849), to move fast to also claim the mainland for Britain, naming it British Columbia after the Columbia River that flows through the province. From that moment on, everything changed for Vancouver as people started moving in and settling down (unfortunately at the expense of the First Nations people). In 1862, three Englishmen – immortalised as the 'Three Greenhorns' – started the Downtown peninsula's first development, a failed brickworks, in what is now the West End. Logging activity quickly increased in the area, including in the now protected Stanley Park, and Captain Edward Stamp built the Hasting Mill sawmill in 1867, near the area that became known as Gastown. That neighbourhood, the origins of today's City of Vancouver, featured another important local business – a pub built by one 'Gassy' Jack Leighton, whose statue now sits nearby.

In 1871 British Columbia officially joined New Brunswick, Nova Scotia, Ontario, Quebec, Manitoba and Northwest Territories in the Canadian Confederation, and, in 1886, the City of Vancouver was incorporated. Not long afterwards, the Great Fire (p.204) destroyed almost all of Vancouver's 1,000 or so wooden buildings.

Rebuilt by the end of the year, Vancouver finally felt connected to the rest of Canada when the first Canadian Pacific Railway train to steam into town arrived in 1887, at the end of its first cross-country trip. That train, Engine 374, can now be seen at the Roundhouse Community Arts & Recreation Centre (see p.275).

## Rapid Growth

The railway fuelled Vancouver's growth, and by the end of the century its population was greater than BC's capital, Victoria; by 1901, the population was 29,000. The early part of the 20th century was scarred by a large city riot in 1907, when resentment about an influx of cheap foreign labour – mainly from Asia – led to a mob attacking local Chinese and Japanese businesses.

However, progress continued on through the roaring 20s. The city's first skyscraper appeared, the University of British Columbia opened its doors and, by 1928, Vancouver was the third largest city in Canada – a status it still holds. In fact, Vancouverites were so excited during the 20s that some of them decided to jump into the

### Memorable Mayor

Incumbent mayor Sam Sullivan's (p.15) predecessor is another interesting character in the city's history. The highly popular Larry Campbell, easy to spot in his distinctive fedora hat, was previously BC's chief coroner, and this role inspired the popular Vancouver-based TV series *Da Vinci's Inquest*. Campbell put much of his energy into trying to solve Vancouver's problems with drug use, and he once famously said of legalising marijuana: 'Legalise it, control it and tax the livin' hell out of it.'

freezing water off English Bay on the first day of the decade as part of the first ever Polar Bear Swim – an annual tradition ever since. While the Great Depression between 1929 and 1939 slowed progress somewhat, by the end of the 30s present-day Vancouver landmarks Lions Gate Bridge, Hotel Vancouver and Vancouver Art Gallery had all been built.

**Terry Fox, Local Hero**
*One of Canada's most enduring and inspirational characters is Terry Fox. After being diagnosed with cancer leading to the loss of his leg at the age of 18, Terry created the Marathon of Hope – a coast-to-coast run he would undertake to raise money for cancer research. He set out from Newfoundland on 12 April, 1980, but was forced to give up after 143 days and 5,373km. A subsequent telethon raised millions for charity, and Terry's determination made him a Canadian hero. He died in 1981, and the annual Terry Fox Run in aid of charity takes place around the world in his honour. In Vancouver, the Terry Fox Memorial near GM Place commemorates his achievements.*

## The Post-War Years

By 1941, Greater Vancouver's population had soared to more than 400,000, the vast majority in Vancouver itself. The second world war saw Vancouver's economy begin to recover as local shipyards contributed to the war effort. And by the time the 5th British Empire and Commonwealth Games came to town in 1954, the city was on another upwards trajectory. The games featured the famous Miracle Mile when Roger Bannister and John Landy both broke the four minute barrier in an event beamed around North America to an increasing television audience. The post-war years were heady times. Vancouverites could now shop six days a week and drink at Vancouver's first cocktail bar, in the Sylvia Hotel. Even Elvis came to town.

The 60s swung into Vancouver in style as it did elsewhere around the world, and the city began to take on important aspects of its present-day identity. Kitsilano gained its reputation as the city's hippy hang-out. The anti-Vietnam war protests predated Vancouver's eventual declaration as an official 'nuclear free city', environmental protests were successful at halting a planned freeway through Strathcona, and Greenpeace took root in the city.

## Vancouver Welcomes The World

While fans of the Vancouver Canucks and Vancouver Whitecaps (which made their National Hockey League debut and won the North American Soccer League championship respectively in the 70s) may disagree, the most important event of the next 20 years was Expo 86.

Held during Vancouver's 100th birthday year, the six-month Expo 86 world fair brought the city to the attention of the globe. Attracting more than 22 million visitors, the event represented a giant step forward in Vancouver's journey from a small and unremarkable, if scenic, city to a desirable tourist and expat destination.

Not only did Expo 86 change the way many outsiders viewed Vancouver, but it also changed the way many Vancouverites saw their own city and generated immense civic pride, which can still be detected today. Expo 86's physical legacy includes Science World, the SkyTrain, Canada Place and BC Place – the world's largest air-supported sports stadium.

## The World Moves To Vancouver

The decade following Expo 86 saw Vancouver's population take another dramatic upswing. While the population of the City of Vancouver increased by just over 20,000 between 1976 and 1986, the next 10 years saw a jump of more than 80,000. This number included a surge in immigrants arriving from Hong Kong in advance of the country's handover to China by Britain.

Vancouver had attracted large numbers of Chinese immigrants before, and has continued to do so since, but never on this scale. While there was some resentment of the newcomers, even among the existing Chinese-Canadian community, there was no repeat of the 1907 anti-Asian riots, and this period helped establish the city's Asian-Pacific feel and cemented its place as one of the most multicultural cities in the world. A lot of money also flowed into the city from Hong Kong, giving the economy a boost and helping drive the orgy of development that continues to transform the city skyline. This includes the redevelopment of the old Expo

# Canada Overview

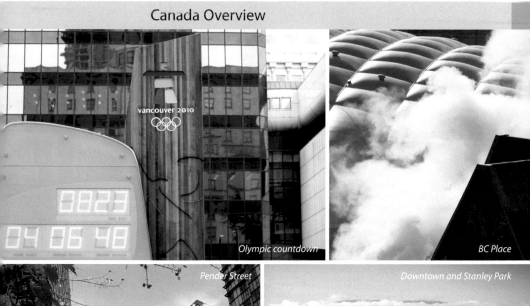

Olympic countdown

BC Place

Pender Street

Downtown and Stanley Park

View from Cypress Mountain

86 site by Hong Kong businessman Li Ka-Shing, who bought the land from the government, and the transformation of an old warehouse district nearby into the shiny new Yaletown neighbourhood.

The 90s also saw Vancouver begin to establish itself as a major film production centre – now North America's third largest, behind Los Angeles and New York.

Perhaps recognising how the city benefited from Expo 86, and to a lesser extent due to the arrival of attention-grabbers like the Molson Indy and the Vancouver Grizzlies NBA team in 1990 and 1995 respectively, Vancouver ended the 20th century by forming a team to bid for the 2010 Winter Olympics.

### Modern Vancouver

Vancouver has started the new millennium well. In 2003, it was awarded the 2010 Winter Olympics, meaning the eyes of the world will again be on the city – at least for two wintry weeks.

An extra pat on the back was to follow. In 2005, Vancouver was declared the best place to live in the world after a livability survey by the Economist Intelligence Unit placed it top in a list of 127 global cities.

Of course, there has to be a down side to Vancouver's speedy growth. Vancouver's Downtown Eastside – the oldest part of the city and where it all started – is one of the poorest neighbourhoods in North America. Wander a block or two east of Gastown and you'll see open drug and alcohol abuse, prostitution, and scenes of abject

## Vancouver Timeline

| | |
|---|---|
| 1791 | Spanish explorer Lieutenant Jose Maria Narvaez becomes the first European to reach what later becomes Vancouver. |
| 1792 | Captain George Vancouver sails into town. |
| 1808 | Simon Fraser sails the length of the Fraser River. |
| 1827 | James McMillan builds the Hudson's Bay Company's first trading post on the Fraser River, named Fort Langley. |
| 1858 | Gold is discovered around the Fraser River, prompting thousands of American prospectors to head north. |
| 1886 | The City of Vancouver is incorporated into the Confederation, and then burns to the ground in the Great Fire. |
| 1887 | The first Canadian Pacific Railway train steams into Vancouver, connecting the city to the rest of the country. |
| 1907 | An angry mob attacks Chinese and Japanese businesses in protest at the influx of cheap labour from abroad. |
| 1938 | The Lions Gate Bridge is opened to traffic. |
| 1954 | The Fifth British Empire and Commonwealth Games are held in Vancouver, featuring the 'miracle mile'. |
| 1964 | The BC Lions win their first CFL Grey Cup. |
| 1970 | The Vancouver Canucks play (and lose) their first NHL match. |
| 1971 | The first Greenpeace voyage sets sail for Amchitka Island to protest against US nuclear testing. |
| 1979 | The Vancouver Whitecaps win the North American Soccer League championship. |
| 1983 | BC Place Stadium becomes the world's largest air-supported dome. |
| 1986 | The Expo 86 world fair is held during Vancouver's 100th birthday year, attracting millions of visitors and bringing the city to the international stage. |
| 1988 | The first Vancouver Gay Pride Festival is held. |
| 1994 | The Vancouver Canucks lose game seven of the Stanley Cup Final, sparking riots from unhappy fans in Downtown Vancouver. |
| 1996 | The 1996 census shows that Vancouver's population has enjoyed unprecedented growth, mainly due to an influx of immigrants from Hong Kong. |
| 2003 | Vancouver is awarded the 2010 Olympic and Paralympic Winter Games. |
| 2005 | Vancouver is declared the best place in the world to live by the Economist Intelligence Unit. |

poverty on the streets day and night. Drug-related crime and health problems are, not surprisingly, serious concerns.

During the 80s and 90s, the neighbourhood was allowed to degenerate into its present state. While shiny new condos were being built everywhere, a lack of good social housing saw less fortunate people forced on to the streets, many with serious drug addictions. The good news is that the area is a source of serious debate in the city, with the public, police, charities and the council constantly discussing ways to solve the problems. One man who tried to tackle the issue of drug abuse head-on was Vancouver's mayor between 2002 and 2005, Larry Campbell. Campbell presided over the opening of a ground-breaking safe injection site and promoted a 'Four Pillars Drug Strategy' to solve the problem.

Now, with the Olympics on the horizon, gentrification is slowly creeping into Downtown Eastside. A number of new condo developments, including the old Woodward's site, are prompting concerns among social groups that Vancouver's low stock of social housing will reduce even further. The hope is that the neighbourhood, which is also home to good restaurants, pubs, shops and many creative and arts-related businesses, will revitalise itself through an influx of new residents. The Vancouver Whitecaps soccer club has also put forward plans to build a new 15,000 seat mixed-use waterfront stadium in the neighbourhood.

## Looking Ahead

A lack of affordable housing in the city as a whole, not just social housing, is a major issue, in particular for first-time buyers. The average house price outstrips the average salary by some distance and there are concerns, especially among younger and lower-income people, that the city has become a victim of its own success.

This being Vancouver though, innovative plans are afoot to remedy the situation. The current mayor, Sam Sullivan, coined the term 'ecodensity' to describe his vision of sustainable growth for Vancouver through higher-density, mixed-use neighbourhoods (see p.13). The plan is to build up and increase the amount of affordable housing, with a view to accommodating continued growth as well as meeting the needs of new immigrants and future generations.

Meanwhile, the 2010 Olympics has given the city a degree of economic security for the next few years, and Vancouver keeps growing. As well as new sporting facilities, including a speed skating oval and increased ski terrain on Cypress Mountain, the Sea to Sky highway to Whistler has been upgraded and the expanded Convention Centre, with its grass roof, is expected to open in 2009. The Shangri-La Hotel will, at 62 storeys, become Vancouver's tallest building when completed in 2008, and the new rapid transit Canada Line between Vancouver Airport and Downtown is scheduled to open in 2009.

Amid all the growth, one thing remains certain: however quickly Vancouver expands in the future, nothing beats its whirlwind transformation from tiny lumber town to internationally renowned city in little over 120 years.

## Online Communities

There are numerous expat-focused websites offering advice and advertising services specially for expatriates. See p.52 for a list. And check out www.explorerpublishing.com, where you can join an online community for your city, share tips, get updates, ask questions and make friends.

## Sporting Shenanigans

The 90s saw Vancouver's sports scene crank it up a notch. In 1990, the first Molson Indy Vancouver car race blasted into town, coming back every year until 2004. Then, in 1994, the Vancouver Canucks made it to the NHL Stanley Cup Final, only to lose the last game in the seven-game series. The fans took it badly and infamously rioted in Downtown Vancouver. There was better news for the BC Lions football team, who won the CFL Grey Cup the same year. To top it all off, Vancouver got its own NBA team in 1995, the Vancouver Grizzlies – at least until 2001 when the team was sold.

## Canada Overview

Canada's unemployment rate was 5.9% in November 2007. The healthy job market is the main reason why the number of immigrants attracted to Canada has grown during the last few years. With an aging workforce and low birth rate, the government sees its immigration policy as an important driver of future economic growth. Many Canadian companies actively recruit overseas, although the message has not quite hit home with all businesses and industries. While the country's workforce is certainly very diverse, some immigrants are often surprised to encounter barriers to finding work. Those in professions like medicine or engineering, who have been through the application process and therefore believe they have the necessary qualifications and experience, can have difficulty due to a lack of Canadian training or work experience. In fact, it's commonly heard that cities like Vancouver and Toronto have the best-educated taxi drivers in the world, and there's every chance that the person selling you your morning coffee could be a trained doctor or engineer. Therefore it's a good idea to research the training you may need in order to upgrade your qualifications before arriving. Once in Canada, volunteering is a good way to get around the lack of Canadian work experience. Visit www.govolunteer.ca for opportunities.

### Economic History

Canada's economy wasn't always so buoyant. In the early 30s, the country was mired in the Great Depression, triggered by the global stock market crash of 1929, and 25% of people were out of work. The second world war was the catalyst for an economic transformation driven by a huge increase in manufacturing output and trade. By 1944, the jobless rate was less than 1% and Canada enjoyed a thriving post-war economy driven by a skilled workforce.

The post-war baby boom fuelled further growth, and the economy received another leg-up in 1947 when the Leduc oil discovery in Alberta transformed the rural province into a major oil producer. This led to the find of Canada's large reserves, which continue to fuel Alberta's current boom. The next major event was the signing of the Canada-US Free Trade Agreement (Cusfta) in 1989, closely followed by the North American Free Trade Agreement (Nafta) in 1994. With Mexico joining as the third trade partner, Nafta became the largest free trade area in the world. Canada is now the US's largest trading partner, with almost 80% of Canadian exports heading south to the US, including motor vehicles, industrial machinery, timber, crude petroleum and natural gas.

In 2001, Canada's economy, like much of the rest of the world, was thrown into uncertainty by the events of September 11 and its aftermath. While the economy has since recovered, increased security at the Canada-US border still causes some trade problems and delays. Currently, Canada's economy is being boosted by Alberta's oil boom and strong growth in BC.

## Vancouver Overview

Vancouver makes an important, and growing, contribution to Canada's economy. The province of British Columbia contributes around 12% of the country's GDP – about the same as Alberta, but behind Quebec and Ontario. Vancouver itself contributes more than 50% of that total, making it a major economic hub, along with Calgary, Montreal and Toronto (Canada's largest city). Although the economy of the region as a whole relies heavily on natural resources such as forestry, mining, and oil and gas, Vancouver has developed a thriving service and knowledge-based economy. With few large corporate head offices calling Vancouver home, many small and medium-sized companies operate in the city. Consequently, there is quite an entrepreneurial spirit in Vancouver, particularly in the vibrant technology sector.

# Great things can come in small packages…

Perfectly proportioned to fit in your pocket, these marvellous mini guidebooks make sure you don't just get the holiday you paid for, but rather the one that you dreamed of.

## Explorer Mini Visitors' Guides
Maximising your holiday, minimising your hand luggage

## Vancouver Salaries (Average Weekly Earnings)

| | |
|---|---|
| All industries | $741.05 |
| Construction | $814.93 |
| Educational services | $894.53 |
| Finance and insurance | $843.40 |
| Forestry, logging and support | $903.44 |
| Healthcare and social assistance | $736.54 |
| Information and cultural industries | $917.60 |
| Manufacturing | $770.83 |
| Mining and oil and gas extraction | $1,329.16 |
| Professional, scientific & technical services | $1,022.71 |
| Retail trade | $493.36 |
| Wholesale trade | $818.57 |

Source: Vancouver Economic Development Commission, July 2006

### Leading Industries

A major component of the local economy is the film industry, which generated $1.2 billion and created 25,000 jobs in BC in 2005, with most of the activity revolving around Vancouver. Dubbed Hollywood North, the city is the third-largest film location in North America, after Los Angeles and New York, although it rarely features as itself. The technology and new media sectors are also major players in Vancouver. More than 800 small and medium-sized new media companies operate in the city, providing work for 15,000 people. This means laptops are a familiar sight in coffee shops and there is a vibrant blogging and internet community. Video game production is a growing area, with EA Canada now a major employer. Another growing sector is biotechnology. BC is home to Canada's largest biotech community, with most of the activity based around Vancouver. Tourism is also a major employer, providing work for around 100,000 people. The city is an environmental hub within Canada, particularly in the growing area of fuel cell and alternative fuel technologies, environmental research and development and related services. This sector employs around 18,000 people. Cranes are a prominent feature of the Vancouver skyline, and the city's construction boom, including housing and 2010 Olympic Games projects, has created thousands of new jobs in the industry.

### Trade

Port Vancouver is a major international port and a significant gateway for trade with the far east, particularly Japan, China and South Korea. As Canada's largest port, Port Vancouver handled 79.4 million tonnes of cargo in 2006. The main exports are wood pulp and lumber.

### New Developments

Major new developments in Vancouver revolve around 2010 Winter Olympics projects that provide contracting and employment opportunities for both businesses and individuals. Visit www.vancouver2010.com for information on specific Olympic-related opportunities. The Olympics has spawned a number of high-profile construction projects, including improved roads, new facilities and housing, and a new light rail line from Vancouver Airport into Downtown. That aside, Vancouver is a growing city, and new construction in general shows little sign of slowing. The technology sector is expected to continue to grow, and Microsoft announced plans to open a new software development centre in the area in 2007. A good employment

### Canada's Main Industries

Canada is an overwhelmingly service-based economy, with its two historical cornerstones, manufacturing and agriculture, now trailing far behind. A large percentage of the services sector is government services. Other major contributors include a strong financial services sector, retail and wholesale trade, and professional, scientific and technical services. The automobile industry forms the largest manufacturing segment, concentrated in Ontario, although the recent downturn in the US economy has led to job losses. Fuelled by a housing boom, the construction industry is very strong, particularly in BC, and tourism is important across the country, especially in Vancouver and Toronto. Alberta's oil boom has created rapid growth and prosperity in that region, with mining, fishing and agriculture prominent in parts of the North, the Maritimes and the Prairies.

# Economy

*Waterfront industry*

resource for Vancouver tech jobs is www.techvibes.
com. Opportunities in tourism will grow, particularly
in the run up to the Olympics. Tourism Vancouver
(www.tourismvancouver.com) and Tourism British
Columbia (www.tourismbc.com) carry news of
major developments. For news and opportunities in
biotechnology visit Life Sciences British Columbia
(www.lifesciencesbc.ca).

## Tourism

As well as being popular with expats, Vancouver is
also a much-loved tourist destination. The city was
voted 'best city in the Americas' by *Conde Nast Traveller*
readers for three years in a row between 2004 and
2006, narrowly losing out in 2007, while *The Economist*
ranked Vancouver as its top business travel destination
in 2006.

According to Tourism Vancouver, the city welcomes
more than 500,000 visitors a month on average, the vast
majority between June and September. In 2006, 60%
came from elsewhere in Canada, 25% from the US, almost
9% from Asia-Pacific and the rest from Europe (almost half
of those from the UK). By October 2007, tourist numbers
were already significantly up on that total.

These figures make tourism a major part of Vancouver's economy. Around 100,000
people work in the sector and visitors contribute upwards of $4 billion to city
coffers. Nearly one million of these visitors come by cruise ship, with more than
250 of the floating buffets arriving each year. As well as cruise ship passengers and
business travellers, Vancouver attracts the full spectrum of tourists – from families to
backpackers to adventure sports enthusiasts. They stay in B&Bs, hostels or one of the
city's 97 hotels (see p.32).

It's not hard to see why Vancouver is an appealing destination. The city enjoys a mild
climate, is very easy to get around and its location ticks all the boxes. Ocean beaches:
check. Snow-capped mountains: check. Sparkling city skyline: check. If you arrive in
Vancouver on one of its many good days, the city can be breathtakingly beautiful. Even
when low grey clouds obscure the mountains and blanket the city for a spell, spectacular
sunsets often make up for it by day's end. And whatever this young city may lack in
history it makes up for in the huge range of activities on offer. Numerous cultural,
sightseeing and recreational activities, as well as a healthy sprinkling of well-attended
annual festivals and events, let visitors immerse themselves in Vancouver and its environs
for the duration of their stay. With the 2010 Winter Olympics poised to be the next big
show in town, Vancouver looks set to remain a well-travelled-to destination for the
foreseeable future.

## International Relations

Canada is a member of the G8, the UN, the Commonwealth and Nato. In addition,
along with the US and Mexico, the country is part of Nafta, which allows free trade
between the three nations. Culturally, Canada has close ties with the US, Britain and
France. Economically, Canada's closest ties are with the US and, increasingly, with
Pacific Rim countries such as China. Vancouver itself is home to a large number of
foreign consulates, including the US, UK, Australia, France, China and Japan.
The country has gained an international reputation for playing prominent roles in

**Ecodensity**
One legacy of Sam
Sullivan's tenure as
mayor will be the term
'ecodensity', which he
and his staff came up
with to describe their
vision of sustainable
growth in Vancouver
by accommodating
more people in
denser, mixed-use
neighbourhoods. The
Vancouver Ecodensity
Planning Initiative
(www.vancouver-
ecodensity.ca) is still at
the consultation stage.

UN peacekeeping missions around the world for more than 50 years, and this contribution is a source of much pride among Canadians. In Ottawa, the Reconciliation Peacekeeping Monument honours the thousands of Canadians who have served in UN peacekeeping forces in Rwanda, Bosnia, Somalia and many other countries. Canada's peacekeeping role is now much reduced, mainly due to the country's military playing a major part in Nato's International Security Assistance Force (ISAF) in Afghanistan – something that continues to be a source of much debate across the nation (see Afghanistan Conflict, left).

The other major foreign affairs issue currently occupying Canada is an environmental one. Although Canada's Liberal government ratified the Kyoto Protocol, the current Conservative government says it cannot and will not attempt to meet Kyoto's targets for reducing greenhouse gas emissions. Instead it supports the alternative Asia-Pacific Partnership on Clean Development and Climate, which sets voluntary targets, as well as announcing a 'Made in Canada' approach, through which the most concrete initiative so far has been a proposed Clean Air Act.

In 2007, Canada was criticised at home and abroad for joining the US, Japan and Saudi Arabia in opposing the setting of firm emission reduction targets at the UN Climate Change Conference in Bali.

## Queen Who?

In 2002, an EKOS poll found that only 5% of Canadians could correctly identify Queen Elizabeth II as their country's head of state. In general, the attitude towards the role of the monarchy in modern Canada ranges from ignorance to mild curiosity or complete indifference. There are no real calls for Canada to become a republic, and the issue is not a matter of any real public or political debate. One reason for this could be that this historical link to the UK and Commonwealth helps Canada retain its sense of independence from the cultural, economic and political behemoth next door – the US. Another is that Canadians simply aren't really that interested. In a country that includes a large number of new immigrants with no real ties to or knowledge of the British monarchy, the Queen is essentially a symbol, an occasional visitor and a face on coins and bank notes.

### Afghanistan Conflict

Canada's high-profile role in Afghanistan is currently the country's major foreign affairs issue. Although Canada did not support the 2003 US-led invasion of Iraq, in line with the feeling in the country as a whole, it plays a major role in Afghanistan, particularly in Kandahar province. More than 13,500 troops served in the country, suffering 60 casualties, up to June 2007. This has led to debates in Canada, with many people preferring a return to its traditional peacekeeping role. Canada's troops are set to withdraw from Afghanistan in 2009.

## Government & Politics

In order to manage the diverse needs of such a large country, Canada is run by a combination of federal and provincial/territorial governments, with municipal governments, such as Vancouver City Council, operating at a local level.

Canada is also a constitutional monarchy. Britain's Elizabeth II is the current queen of Canada, with her powers being limited by the Constitution of Canada. The monarch holds the position of head of state, whose representative in Canada at a federal level is the governor general – currently Michaelle Jean.

The head of the government, called the prime minister of Canada, is the leader of the party with the most seats in the House of Commons. The current prime minister is Stephen Harper of the Conservative Party, which secured a minority government in the 2006 elections – winning 124 out of 308 seats in the first-past-the-post voting system. The Liberal Party, which won 103 seats in 2006, had been in charge since 1993. The other main political parties in Canada are the New Democrat Party and Bloc Québécois.

The federal government is responsible for matters that affect all Canadians, including defence, foreign policy and criminal law. The prime minister appoints a cabinet of ministers who each have responsibilities relating to specific areas of government, such as finance, defence and foreign affairs. There are currently 27 cabinet ministers. An elected party can govern for a maximum of five years before a general election must be called.

### The Parliament Of Canada

The parliament of Canada sits at Parliament Hill in Ottawa. It is made up of the Sovereign, the Senate and the House of Commons. The main action occurs in the House of Commons, which contains elected members of parliament who each represent one constituency, or riding, in Canada. The Sovereign, in the form of the governor general, and the Senate, consisting of 105 senators appointed by the governor general on the advice of the prime minister, have no real influence on the running of the country.

### Provincial & Territorial Governments

The 10 provincial governments (Alberta, British Columbia, Manitoba, New Brunswick, Newfoundland and Labrador, Nova Scotia, Ontario, Prince Edward Island, Quebec and Saskatchewan) preside over local affairs, such as provincial and municipal courts, education and health services. Responsibility for some areas, such as transportation, agriculture and natural resource management, are shared between federal and provincial governments. The three territorial governments (Northwest Territories, Nunavut and Yukon) have pretty much the same powers as the provinces, but do not manage land and natural resources. Provincial and territorial governments are decided through public elections, with the elected party allowed to govern for a maximum of five years before a provincial election must be called.

In the province of British Columbia, the BC government sits in the Legislative Assembly of British Columbia in Victoria. The current head of the BC government is Gordon Campbell.

### The Mayor Of Vancouver

In Vancouver, the municipal government is the Vancouver City Council, consisting of the elected mayor and 10 elected councillors. Elections take place every three years. The council operates out of the historic Vancouver City Hall on West 12th Avenue. Its areas of responsibility include garbage disposal, building permits, parks and property tax.

The current mayor of Vancouver is Sam Sullivan. A quadriplegic since the age of 19 following a skiing accident, Sullivan cuts a distinctive figure. A consummate self-promoter, Sullivan enjoys being in the limelight. He attracted international attention when accepting the Olympic flag on behalf of Vancouver at the 2006 Turin Winter Olympics closing ceremony, and a documentary about his successful 2005 mayoral campaign, *Citizen Sam*, further boosted his profile. His stint in the hot seat has not been without its struggles, including a lengthy city workers' strike in 2007.

### Roméo Dallaire

The best-known figure in Canadian peacekeeping is Lieutenant-General Roméo Dallaire. In 1993, Dallaire became Force Commander of UNAMIR (the United Nations Assistance Mission for Rwanda). After his appeal for more UN forces was turned down, Dellaire was unable to prevent the subsequent genocide in Rwanda. However, under his command, the forces available to him saved the lives of thousands of people. Despite being widely praised for his efforts, Dellaire blamed himself for failing to stop the genocide, and his book *Shake Hands with the Devil* details the episode.

## Population

Canada's official 2006 census found that some 2.24 million people live in metropolitan Vancouver – more than half of British Columbia's population. That makes the area, known as the Lower Mainland, home to Canada's third-largest population, behind Toronto (5.41 million) and Montreal (3.67 million). With a 6.5% increase since 2001, it's also one of the fastest growing areas. The population of the City of Vancouver itself, incorporating Downtown and surrounding environs, is 578,041 (an increase of 5.9% since 2001). The average household contains 2.6 people, slightly above the national average of 2.5. In Vancouver, women make up 51% of the population and enjoy a province-wide average life expectancy of 85.2 years. Men in BC live longer than men anywhere else in the world, with an average life expectancy of 79.2 years. A national birth rate of 10.8 per 1,000 people means Canadians are not making babies fast enough to fuel the country's continued growth. And with a provincial birth rate of just 9.8 per 1,000, Vancouver's projected population growth of more than 30,000 people a year between 2006 and 2011 will be largely due to immigration. Already, 39.6% of Vancouver's population is foreign-born, up from 37.5% in 2001. As with the rest of Canada, that number is likely to rise as more expats continue to arrive from around the globe hoping to make their home in this multicultural city.

### Vancouver Population – Age Breakdown

*Source: Statistics Canada 2006 Census*

### Vancouver Population by Ethnic Origin

*Source: Statistics Canada 2001 Census*

### Education Levels

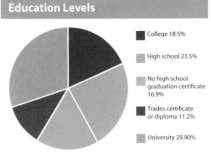

- College 18.5%
- High school 23.5%
- No high school graduation certificate 16.9%
- Trades certificate or diploma 11.2%
- University 29.90%

*Source: Statistics Canada 2001 Census*

## National Flag

The distinctive national flag of Canada is known as the Maple Leaf. The flag consists of a large red maple leaf on a white background, bordered by two thick red stripes at either side. The maple tree is native to Canada, and the distinctive maple leaf itself has been a Canadian icon for nearly 300 years. However, the leaf has not always featured on the Canadian national flag. In 1964, prime minister Lester B Pearson instigated a process of replacing the Red Ensign (which featured the British Union Jack) to find one that better reflected Canada. A special flag committee considered three proposals and, after much debate, chose George FG Stanley's maple leaf design. The Maple Leaf was first raised, in Ottawa, on 15 February, 1965 – a day that is now recognised annually as Flag Day, although not with a public holiday.

## Local Time

Vancouver observes Pacific Standard Time (PST), which is eight hours behind Universal Coordinated Time (UCT) – formerly known as Greenwich Mean Time (GMT). In relation to the rest of Canada, Vancouver wakes up one hour behind Calgary, three hours behind Toronto and Montreal, and four hours behind Halifax. In 2007, Canada changed its approach to Daylight Saving Time (DST) to bring it

## Time Zones

| | |
|---|---|
| **Vancouver** | **12:00** |
| Dallas | 14:00 |
| Denver | 13:00 |
| Dubai | 00:00 (next day) |
| Dublin | 20:00 |
| London | 20:00 |
| Los Angeles | 12:00 |
| Mexico City | 14:00 |
| Moscow | 23:00 |
| Mumbai | 01:30 (next day) |
| Munich | 21:00 |
| New York | 15:00 |
| Paris | 21:00 |
| Perth | 05:00 (next day) |
| Prague | 21:00 |
| Rio de Janeiro | 18:00 |
| Rome | 21:00 |
| Sydney | 07:00 (next day) |
| Toronto | 15:00 |
| Wellington | 09:00 (next day) |

in line with the US. DST begins at 02:00 on the second Sunday in March, when clocks go forward an hour, and ends at 02:00 on the first Sunday in November.

## Social & Business Hours

For most people, Vancouver's working week runs from Monday to Friday. Most offices operate standard 09:00 to 17:00 business hours, although the time lag behind the rest of Canada means it's not uncommon for people to start and finish slightly earlier. That's not the only reason. Many people with flexible employers choose an earlier start to avoid traffic or to take advantage of life outdoors after work. It's not uncommon to see cars streaming out of the city at 15:00 on a sunny Friday afternoon, or after a heavy snowfall on the local mountains. In general, Vancouverites take their recreation time seriously, and many of the city's employers understand and actively encourage a life outside work.

Most people take up to an hour for lunch, usually between 12:00 and 13:30, and eat dinner between 18:00 and 21:00, with the majority of restaurants staying open until around 23:00. While Vancouver doesn't have the strong pub scene of some cities, bars near offices fill up to varying degrees after 17:00, especially if there's a Vancouver Canucks hockey game on TV. Bar opening hours tend to be from 11:30 until as late as 01:00. Nightclubs generally stay open until 03:00.

Bank opening hours vary. In general, banks open between 09:00 and 10:00 and close between 16:00 and 17:00, Monday to Friday. Many operate extended hours at selected branches on Thursdays and Fridays. Some branches also open on Saturdays. Government offices, such as the passport and tax offices, open between 08:00 and 09:00 and close at 16:00 or 17:00, Monday to Friday. Most shops and malls are open for business seven days a week, from around 09:00 to between 17:00 and 20:00. Some convenience stores stay open 24 hours. BC Liquor Stores allows the purchase of alcohol between 07:00 and 23:00, six days a week, with some stores also opening on Sundays.

## Public Holidays

Of the nine official Canadian holidays, British Columbia only fails to recognise Boxing Day as a statutory holiday. However, many Vancouver companies give their employees this day off as a goodwill gesture. British Columbia residents also get an extra holiday in the form of BC Day. People who work for US companies may get US Thanksgiving off as well as, or instead of, Canadian Thanksgiving.

The only official religious public holidays are Christmas Day and Good Friday. Victoria Day marks the anniversary of the birth of Queen Victoria; Canada Day celebrates the birth of Canada; Labour Day recognises the achievements of workers; Remembrance Day commemorates Canada's war dead; and British Columbia Day is in honour of the province's early settlers. Apart from Christmas Day, New Year's Day, Remembrance Day and Canada Day, official holiday dates are not set in stone. Instead, they fall on the nearest Monday or Friday, such as the first Monday in September, to create a long weekend.

The legal minimum for non-statutory holidays in Canada is 10 days a year, usually rising according to the length of time you spend at a company or how good you are at negotiating. Generally, public sector employees get more holidays, but private companies are free to hand out more days off above and beyond the legal minimum.

## Public Holidays

| | |
|---|---|
| New Year's Day | 1 January |
| Good Friday | Friday before Easter Sunday |
| Victoria Day | Monday on or before 24 May |
| Canada Day | 1 July |
| British Columbia Day | First Monday in August |
| Labour Day | First Monday in September |
| Thanksgiving | Second Monday in October |
| Remembrance Day | 11 November |
| Christmas Day | 25 December |

## Climate

Thanks to a moderate year-round climate, Vancouver is spared the sub-zero winters and baking hot summers endured by most other Canadian cities, such as Calgary, Toronto and Montreal. What Vancouver does endure is rain. Not as much rain as you might have heard, but certainly more than other parts of Canada. And more than enough to make an umbrella and waterproof jacket an essential piece of kit.

The close proximity of the ocean and coastal mountains means Vancouver gets an average of 115.5cm of rainfall every year. Most of the rain falls between November and February, with areas nearer the mountains, such as North Vancouver, getting the heaviest soaking. These winter months also tend to be on the dark and grey side, with low-lying clouds sometimes hiding the sun for several days. Usually the worst that happens during long stretches of rainy days is that driving can become hazardous, especially when drains clogged with leaves cause slick road conditions, but more serious problems can arise. In November 2006, 25.5cm of rain fell over 16 days straight, causing landslides in higher areas that affected the city's water supply. The frequent rain also means home buyers must check carefully for water damage and beware of leaky condos.

The upside for skiers and snowboarders is that rain in the city often means snow in the mountains. Vancouver itself gets an average of 4.8cm of snow a year, with the temperature during winter averaging 5°C and rarely falling below freezing. In summer, June through to August enjoy the lion's share of sun and average more than eight hours of sunshine a day. The average summer high is a comfortable 21°C. Spring and autumn (fall) are more unpredictable, offering an equal chance of rain, sun or low-lying clouds.

Recently, Vancouver, like much of the world, has experienced some extreme weather events. Following on from record rainfall and an unusually heavy deposit of snow, a brutal storm ripped through the city in December 2006, destroying thousands of ancient trees in Stanley Park and closing much of the hugely-popular Seawall for a year.

## Temperature

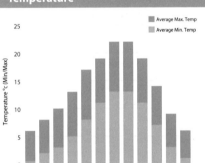

## Rainfall

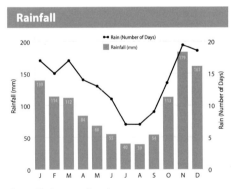

*Source: Environment Canada*

## Flora & Fauna

You don't have to go far to get back to nature in and around Vancouver. Green spaces are legion and the city's trademark cherry blossom trees line many streets in spring. The most famous green space in Vancouver is Stanley Park. Although a major storm cut large swathes through the park's forest in 2006, towering douglas fir, cedar and hemlock trees still dominate the landscape. Stanley Park satisfies all the senses during summer, showcasing a variety of plants and flowers including rhododendrons, magnolias, azaleas and roses in a riot of colour. And if you think you can smell a skunk, it's most likely the distinctive aroma of the park's skunk cabbage plants. (Although it could quite possibly be a skunk – see Fauna, p.19). Another urban oasis is the Dr Sun Yat Sen Classical Chinese Garden, where seasonal displays of water lilies, bamboo, orchids and other plants help create a welcome retreat from the hubbub of Vancouver's Chinatown. Not as well known as the

*Cherry blossoms*

previous two spots, Queen Elizabeth Park (p.244) contains an extensive arboretum, several small gardens and the Bloedel Floral Conservatory (p.245), which houses exotic plants, birds and fish. Outside the city, the forest-blanketed coastal mountains contain all manner of plant life, and provide plenty of opportunities to pick wild fruits such as huckleberries and blackberries.

## Fauna

While English Bay on summer evenings is a great place to spot almost every breed of dog you can think of within Vancouver's city limits, the only wildlife you're likely to encounter are raccoons, skunks and perhaps the odd coyote. Further afield, residents of North Vancouver have been known to encounter black bears rummaging for scraps or, in one case, relaxing in an outdoor hot tub. Black bears are native to the coastal mountains around Vancouver, and there's always the chance you'll run into one of the generally shy animals while out hiking. You are far more likely to see chipmunks, rabbits and squirrels in the area. Cougars also inhabit the region, but are rarely encountered.

**Emissions Mission**
*Vancouver takes the environment seriously. Tiny Smart cars and scooters are familiar sights on city streets, and Vancouver's taxi fleet is the most environmentally friendly in Canada, with 50 out of 477 taxis being hybrids. Local car-sharing schemes, such as the Co-operative Auto Network (www.cooperativeauto. net), are increasingly popular, and the electric buses and iconic SkyTrain light rail system also play their part in moving Vancouver forward in a green manner.*

## Birds

In and around Vancouver, you can easily spot blue herons, especially at the large Stanley Park rookery, loons (which gave the Canadian dollar coin its nickname – the loonie) and bald eagles. Eagles often make their nests in city parks, and, for a truly awe-inspiring sight, visit the Brackendale Winter Eagle Festival near Squamish (see p.54). This is where a world record 3,769 bald eagles were counted in 1994.

## Marine Life

Vancouver Aquarium (p.219) offers an excellent overview of marine life around the region, and exotic fish lovers will enjoy the Bloedel Floral Conservatory (p.245) and Dr Sun Yat Sen Classical Chinese Garden (p.246). Out in the ocean, harbour seals are common visitors to False Creek near Granville Island and off the beaches in Kitsilano and Point Grey. Bigger marine life in the shape of porpoises and whales inhabit the waters further out, and whale-watching tours from Vancouver will take you to see them. Back in the city, a small pond next to the children's playground at the entrance to Granville Island is home to sunbathing turtles in summer.

## Environmental Issues

Driven by Vancouver's close proximity to natural beauty and its status as a young city with the advantage of being able to learn from others' mistakes, the city's governors and residents have a real sense of responsibility towards the environment. Particularly in light of the recent attention given to climate change, many Vancouverites are rather proud of their reputation as 'tree huggers'. After all, Greenpeace took root in Vancouver, and Canada's most prominent tree hugger of all, David Suzuki of the David Suzuki Foundation, was born and bred in the city and still lives here.

That's not to say Vancouver doesn't face the same problems as other cities around the world when it comes to environmental issues. It does; namely how to reduce greenhouse gases, and its environmental footprint in general, while at the same time fuelling a growing economy and accommodating large numbers of new residents. It's just that Vancouver is a city that genuinely aspires to, and in many cases succeeds in, being a model of urban sustainability. One example of this is the fact that there is no large highway running through its city limits – something of a rarity in car-fuelled North America.

## Greenpeace Takes Root

On 15 September, 1971, a boat called the Phyllis Cormack, but christened Greenpeace for the voyage, set sail from Vancouver, bound for Amchitka Island off the Alaskan coast – an area teeming with endangered wildlife. On board was a small group of environmental activists from Vancouver's Don't Make a Wave Committee, armed with a mission to increase public awareness of underground nuclear testing being carried out by the US in Alaska. The voyage generated huge public interest and nuclear testing ended in the area that year, with the island eventually declared a bird sanctuary. So began the story of the most famous environmental organisation in the world.

### Ecosystems

In a city of many parks, Stanley Park (p.244) and Pacific Spirit Regional Park (p.243) stand out as two of the most important natural areas within Vancouver. While Stanley Park has a number of buildings and facilities within its limits, Pacific Spirit – a 90 hectare ecological reserve – remains a true wilderness in the city. In 2007, the BC government proposed to hand over a section of the park to the Musquem First Nations Band, who claim aboriginal rights and title to the land, as part of a lands transfer deal. This raised concerns that some of the park could be developed. A group called the Friends of Pacific Spirit Park (www.friendsofpacificspiritpark.com) formed to help preserve the area.

### Pollution

Vancouver's air quality is generally high, and for 98% of the time it achieves or betters the 'good' Air Quality Index rating (www.gvrd.bc.ca/aqi). The city's air has actually improved during the last 20 years, despite the huge growth of its economy and population. However, as more and more people commute into town, vehicle emissions are becoming increasingly threatening to quality levels.

Various official emissions programmes are in place and, in 2007, BC premier Gordon Campbell announced an ambitious plan aimed at cutting the province's greenhouse gas emissions by 33% by 2020. As well as encouraging use of alternative fuels and more efficient vehicles, the scheme hopes to increase the take up of alternative energy sources and develop a 'green building code'.

### Recycling

The city runs a programme that provides a free recycling kit to homeowners (available from www.city.vancouver.bc.ca), and most apartment buildings provide different waste bins that let residents separate out recyclable materials.

### Water

Vancouver's water is perfectly drinkable, although many people filter it at home. The city's water flows from the region's watersheds in Coquitlam, Capilano and Seymour, before being treated. Occasionally in winter, tap water becomes discoloured when silt gets into reservoirs after heavy rainfall or snowmelt. If there are concerns with drinking the water, the city will issue a 'boil water advisory'.

### Environmental Organisations

There are a number of organisations concerned with the environment in Vancouver. As well as being the birthplace of Greenpeace (www.greenpeace.org), Vancouver is home to the prominent Canadian non-profit organisation the David Suzuki Foundation (www.davidsuzuki.org), which is dedicated to promoting a sustainable planet.

Two active issue-based environmental groups are the Eagleridge Bluffs Coalition (www.eagleridgebluffs.ca) – concerned with protecting Eagleridge Bluffs from disruption caused by 2010 Winter Olympics-related highway expansion – and the Citizens Concerned with Highway Expansion group (www.cche.vcn.bc.ca), which opposes the twinning of a major bridge into the city.

# Life in the fast lane?

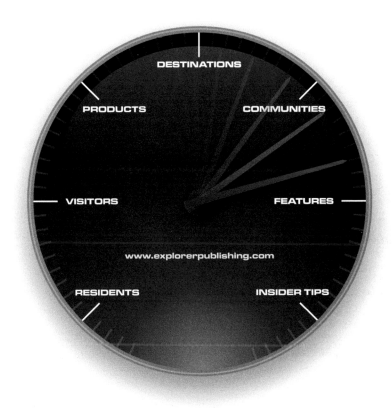

Life can move pretty quickly so make sure you keep in the know with regular updates from **www.explorerpublishing.com**

Or better still, share your knowledge and advice with others, find answers to your questions, or just make new friends in our community area

**www.explorerpublishing.com** – for life in real time

**EXPLORER**
www.explorerpublishing.com

## Culture

Vancouver's culture and lifestyle is very much tied to its coastal location and multicultural population. Compared with other Canadian cities, Vancouver's more relaxed, health-conscious west coast lifestyle – typified by crowded city beaches in summer and the year-round stampedes of lycra-clad joggers pounding the Seawall, is a large part of the city's unique identity. It's an identity that can make it seem, on the surface at least, that Vancouver has more in common with California than Toronto. As well as a love of the outdoor lifestyle, Vancouverites are crazy about coffee. The city is home to the most Starbucks franchises in Canada, as well as numerous other chains and independent coffees shops, making 'meeting for a coffee' Vancouver's cultural alternative to Britain's 'going for a pint'.

However, aside from the agreeable, if soggy, weather and the Seattle-like level of coffee consumption, Vancouver is still a very Canadian city. From the totem poles in Stanley Park to the choice of the Inuit inukshuk as the 2010 Vancouver Olympics logo, First Nations culture is more prominent in Vancouver than Toronto and Montreal. That most Canadian of sports, hockey, is a consuming passion in the city and, like Canada's other big cities, Vancouver is a liberal, cosmopolitan place, and a tapestry of different cultures. That diversity is reflected in the city's festivals and arts, fashion and music scenes.

Almost 40% of the city's population is foreign-born, and Asian cultural influences in particular are everywhere – from the abundance of sushi restaurants to the absence of the number four (considered unlucky in parts of China) in many addresses in predominantly Chinese-Canadian neighbourhoods. In fact, while remnants of Vancouver's British colonial origins remain in day-to-day culture (vinegar, for example, is offered as a condiment with fish and chips, and many people have recent British ancestry), the 2007 revelation that the surnames Lee, Wong and Chan are more common than Smith in the Lower Mainland phone directory illustrates the city's modern-day ties to the Pacific Rim.

### Multiculturalism

Whether you take in an Italian soccer match in a Commercial Drive cafe or window-shop the colourful sarees in Main Street's Punjabi Market stores, a stroll through the different areas of the city reveals the vibrant communities that make Vancouver one of the most comfortably diverse cities in the world.

In the main, as with much of the rest of Canada, each new arrival to Vancouver appears to be seamlessly integrated into society with the minimum of fuss. There have been no racial riots or anti-immigrant protests in Vancouver since the 1907 anti-Asian riots against Japanese and Chinese immigrants (see p.6). The city has come a long way since then; in fact, Vancouver's only other real riot occurred in 1994, not as a result of any racial tension, but because the Vancouver Canucks lost the Stanley Cup Final.

## Language

| Local Lingo | |
| --- | --- |
| BC Lions | The Lions |
| Commercial Drive | The Drive |
| Kitsilano | Kits |
| Port Coquitlam | PoCo |
| Stanley Park Seawall | The Seawall |
| Vancouver Canucks | The Canucks |
| Vancouver Island | The Island |
| Vancouver Whitecaps | The Caps |

| Slang | |
| --- | --- |
| 24 pack of Beer | Two-Four |
| A Canadian | Canuck |
| Beer keg party | Kegger |
| Couch | Chesterfield |
| Fries/chips with cheese curds and gravy | Poutine |
| One-dollar coin | Loonie |
| Toronto | Hogtown |
| Two-dollar coin | Toonie |
| Vancouver | Raincity |
| Woolly hat | Toque/tuque |

## Language

Other options **Language Schools** p.307

The sound of conversation in Vancouver often reflects the multicultural make-up of the city. While Canada is officially bilingual, with English and French being the two languages, Vancouver is unofficially multilingual. English is the dominant language, but Chinese, Punjabi, German, Italian, French, Filipino and Spanish are all common mother-tongue languages in the city.

You will usually hear these languages being spoken in city neighbourhoods that contain a concentration of a particular ethnic group, such as Chinatown, the Punjabi Market, Greektown (a few blocks of West Broadway) and areas of Commercial Drive that have traditionally been home to Italian immigrants.

While Chinatown is the second-largest Chinatown in North America, after San Francisco, other ethnic neighbourhoods are smaller. The Punjabi Market, for example, is an area of five blocks on Main Street to the east of the city. However, even within these neighbourhoods, it's common to see bilingual street signs and shop fronts written in the mother tongue of local residents.

*First Nations Inukshak*

*Downtown*

*Beach life at English Bay*

*Kitsilano*

## Religion

Vancouver residents, like British Columbians as a whole, are not especially religious. In the 2001 census, BC was second only to the Yukon in terms of respondents who answered 'no religion' to the question on faith – representing 35% of the population. Although nominally a Christian country by tradition, there is no dominant, all-encompassing religious culture. The most prominent religions in Vancouver are the Catholic and Protestant strands of Christianity. Tolerance is the main attribute here, and most other main faiths are represented, reflecting the city's multicultural mix, with Buddhists, Sikhs, Hindus and Muslims making up the fastest growing religions in the city.

The only recognised religious holidays occur at the Christian festivals of Christmas and Easter, although in Vancouver, as elsewhere in Canada, many people now send cards and offer greetings that say 'happy holidays' rather than 'merry Christmas'. This is a trend that recognises the growing multiculturalism and secular nature of the country's largest cities, although it's not one that curries favour with everyone. However, you won't insult anyone by saying 'merry Christmas', but you should be aware that a significant proportion of the population may not celebrate the holiday. And, as you'd expect of an integrated, multicultural city, other religious holidays are marked in their respective communities and respected by the population as a whole.

### Places of Worship

| | | | | |
|---|---|---|---|---|
| Akali Singh Sikh Temple | 1890 Skeena St | Burnaby | 604 254 2117 | Sikh |
| Christ Church Cathedral | 690 Burrard St | Downtown | 604 682 3848 | Anglican |
| Fuji Hindu Temple | 5460 Gladstone St | Oakridge | 604 324 8359 | Hindu |
| Holy Rosary Cathedral | 646 Richards St | Downtown | 604 682 6774 | Catholic |
| Richmond Jami'a Mosque | 12300 Blundell Rd | Richmond | 604 270 2522 | Islam |
| Vancouver Buddhist Temple | 220 Jackson Av | Hastings East | 604 253 7033 | Buddhist |

## National Dress

The iconic Red Serge – the formal uniform of the Royal Canadian Mounted Police – is the clothing most commonly associated with Canada. Although the humble toque (woolly hat), or even the hockey jersey, seem to be ubiquitous items of clothing across Canada, the country has no official national dress. In Vancouver, the unofficial get up of choice tends to be GORE-TEX and fleece jackets, or, for some, yogawear from Vancouver-founded lululemon (p.395).

That said, the multicultural make-up of the city means you will often see people wearing the traditional dress of their native countries, particularly around events such as the Chinese New Year celebrations in Chinatown, the Powell Street Festival (a celebration of Japanese culture) and the Baisakhi Day Parade, celebrating the Sikh Indian New Year.

## Food & Drink

Other options **Eating Out** p.420

It's not surprising that Vancouverites reportedly dine out more than residents of any other Canadian city when you consider the sheer volume, variety and quality of its eating establishments. As well as providing excellent fine dining options, the city's many ethnic restaurants serve up culinary delights from around the world. Whether you're in the mood for Indian, Chinese, Thai, Japanese, Italian, French, Greek, Afghan, Moroccan, or almost any other type of cuisine, Vancouver caters to pretty much all tastes. While the Downtown core is packed with restaurants, you can also find many gems slightly off the beaten track, and a culinary tour of the city is a great way to get to get a flavour of the different neighbourhoods. Plenty of Vancouver's restaurants will empty your wallet as fast as they fill your belly, but there are also many good quality budget establishments. In fact it's almost cheaper to go to somewhere like Jolly's Indian Bistro (www.jollysindianbistro.com) in Kitsilano for a tasty butter chicken dinner than to buy the ingredients in the supermarket and make it yourself.

However, Vancouver has also gained plaudits in the more expensive area of fine dining. Perhaps it's the climate and lifestyle, or the abundance of local produce to work with, but a number of top chefs call Vancouver home. Well know names have included Rob Feenie, who took Canada's fine dining reputation to new heights in 2005 when he won a prestigious televised 'Iron Chef America' battle.

There are a few 'must-eats' when in Vancouver. Wild BC salmon is often found on menus in a variety of forms, and a salmon burger at the outdoor Go Fish seafood stand (p.429) at Fisherman's Wharf is a great introduction to this local favourite. Another feature of the Vancouver culinary landscape is the large number of sushi restaurants. *Maclean's* magazine reported in 2006 that Vancouver has three times as many sushi restaurants as McDonald's, with Tojo's (p.437) on West Broadway being perhaps the best known. Dim sum is also popular in a city with a large Chinese population, and the ones served by the Pink Pearl Chinese Restaurant (www. pinkpearl.com) on East Hastings Street receives rave reviews.

With such a cultural mix in the city, it's not surprising that fusion food is often on the menu. The Indian fusion eatery Vij's (p.434) – which doesn't take reservations, meaning you should get there early to join the queue – is one of the most popular in town. But perhaps the strangest food fusion can be found at the annual Chinese New Year meets Scottish Burns Night event, Gung Haggis Fat Choy (www. gunghaggisfatchoy.com), complete with haggis wontons.

For classic North American burger and fries, Vera's Burger Shack (www. verasburgershack.com) is a Vancouver institution. 'You can't beat Vera's meat' is the slogan, and the regular queues suggest that's true. And for dessert, True Confections (www.trueconfections.ca) is another local fixture that lives up to its name.

The best way by far to sample the huge variety of restaurants in Vancouver (particularly some of the pricier ones) is by participating in the annual Dine Out Vancouver festival (p.54). For a few weeks in January and February you can munch your way through special three-course menus from many of the city's best restaurants at prices ranging from $15 to $35 per person.

## Drink

While Vancouver doesn't have the same kind of pub culture as, for example, the UK, Vancouverites still enjoy a cocktail, beer or glass of wine. Most pubs offer a range of Canadian beers like Alexander Keith's, Molson Canadian, Moosehead and Sleeman's Honey Brown, as well as imports such as Heineken and Stella Artois.

There are also several excellent microbreweries and brewpubs, with Steamworks Brewing Company (p.465) and the Yaletown Brewing Company (p.465) being two to try. A favourite cocktail, renowned for its recuperative powers, is a 'bloody caesar', and fans of the grape can choose from a variety of excellent wines produced in BC's Okanagan Valley. The annual Vancouver Playhouse International Wine Festival (www. playhousewinefest.com) is now a major city event.

The most popular drink in Vancouver, however, has to be coffee. There are more Starbucks franchises in Vancouver than any other city in Canada. They are joined by several other chains, such as Blenz and Tim Hortons, as well as local independents including Caffè Artigiano (p.455), which recently introduced the country's first $15 cup of coffee.

### Eat Local

As awareness of the harmful effect of food transportation on the environment grows, a pair of Vancouver writers earned worldwide attention for introducing the concept of the '100 mile diet' (www.100milediet.org). JB MacKinnon and Alisa Smith decided to only eat food originating within 100 miles of their home in Vancouver for one year. Their resulting book, The 100-Mile Diet: A Year of Local Eating became a bestseller and started a global trend of eating local. If you want to give it a go, a good start is to buy produce at the farmers' markets around the city in summer. Your Local Farmers Market Society (www.eatlocal.org) lists dates and places.

# In Emergency

The freephone number to call in an emergency is 911, and the police, fire and ambulance services are normally quick to respond. It's advisable for non-residents to take out travel and medical insurance, and everybody must have valid insurance documents when driving or renting a car. All Vancouver residents must buy car insurance through ICBC (see Residents, p.178). If you are involved in an accident, the ICBC 24 hour Dial-A-Claim number is 604 520 8222.

## Police

For situations that are not an emergency and don't require an officer to attend the scene immediately, such as car theft and vandalism, the number of the Vancouver Police Department is 604 717 3321. Petty crime is the most common variety in Vancouver, with car theft being particularly rife in certain areas of town around the Downtown Eastside. Due to the large volume of cases, it can take a while to report small crimes and even then there's very little chance police will have time to follow up. It's faster to report smaller, non-violent crimes, such as theft from your car, online at www.city.vancouver.bc.ca/police.

## Medical

Vancouver's major hospitals, such as Vancouver General and St Paul's, have 24 hour accident and emergency wards (see p.152 in Residents for more information). Drop-in medical centres are also located around the city – the most central being the Ultima Medicentre in the Bentall Centre on Dunsmuir Street. While healthcare is free for Canadian residents, non-residents should make sure they have medical insurance to cover emergencies and a range of treatments as they will be billed and then have to make a claim. There is a 24 hour pharmacy in the Shoppers Drug Mart in the city's West End.

## Lost Or Stolen Property

You should report lost or stolen property to the police so that you can receive a report for insurance purposes and see if someone has handed it in. If you lose something on the transit system, TransLink's lost property office is open at Stadium SkyTrain station, Monday to Friday from 08:30 to 17:00.

# Crime & Safety

Like the rest of Canada, Vancouver is generally a very safe place. The overall crime rate fell during 2005 and 2006, although Vancouver still finished second in the list of Canadian cities with the most criminal offences committed during 2006 – 10,609 per 100,000 people. Those crime statistics showed that Vancouver experienced 2.5 homicides, 153 robberies, 5,874 instances of property crime and 1,121 break-ins per 100,000 people during 2006.

The homicide rate increased during 2007, due to a series of what police take to be tit-for-tat gang shootings – often drug-related. These incidents included several shootings in public places, which alarmed the general population somewhat. Police are concerned about the flow of illegal weapons over the border from the US, but shootings that don't involve criminal gangs are rare.

Public transit is generally safe, although care should be taken at SkyTrain stations at night. The stations have well-lit designated waiting

| Emergency Numbers | |
|---|---|
| Emergency services (police, fire, ambulance) | 911 |
| ICBC Dial-A-Claim | 604 520 8222 |
| Shoppers Drug Mart (24 hour) | 604 669 2424 |
| St Paul's Hospital | 604 682 2344 |
| TransLink Lost Property | 604 682 7887 |
| Ultima Medicentre | 604 683 8138 |
| Vancouver General Hospital | 604 875 4111 |
| Vancouver Police Department | 604 717 3321 |

# Essential Info

## Embassies & Consulates

| | |
|---|---|
| Australia | 604 684 1177 |
| Austria | 604 687 3338 |
| Bangladesh | 604 736 6770 |
| Brazil | 604 696 5311 |
| Chile | 604 681 9162 |
| China | 604 734 0704 |
| Croatia | 604 871 9170 |
| El Salvador | 604 732 8142 |
| Estonia | 604 408 2673 |
| Finland | 604 687 8237 |
| France | 604 681 4287 |
| Germany | 604 684 8377 |
| Greece | 604 681 1381 |
| Hungary | 604 730 7321 |
| Iceland | 604 922 0854 |
| India | 604 662 8811 |
| Indonesia | 604 682 8855 |
| Ireland | 604 683 9233 |
| Italy | 604 684 7288 |
| Jamaica | 604 515 0443 |
| Japan | 604 684 5868 |
| Jordan | 604 685 9200 |
| Korea | 604 681 9581 |
| Malaysia | 604 685 9550 |
| Mexico | 604 684 3547 |
| Netherlands | 604 684 6448 |
| New Zealand | 604 684 7388 |
| Norway | 604 682 8376 |
| Peru | 604 662 8880 |
| Philippines | 604 685 7645 |
| Poland | 604 688 3530 |
| Portugal | 604 685 7042 |
| Serbia | 604 940 3838 |
| Seychelles | 604 261 3737 |
| Singapore | 604 669 5115 |
| Slovakia | 604 682 0991 |
| South Africa | 604 688 1301 |
| Sweden | 604 683 5838 |
| Switzerland | 604 687 1143 |
| Thailand | 604 687 4434 |
| UAE | 613 565 7272 |
| United Kingdom | 604 683 4421 |
| USA | 604 685 4311 |

areas, while the trains themselves are fitted with silent alarms and speakerphones in case of emergencies. Transit police also patrol the transport system.

The most common crimes in Vancouver tend to be petty property or car crimes. Particular care should be taken in the Downtown Eastside, and you should never leave valuables in your car there or anywhere else. Other areas of town to be extra careful in are the streets surrounding Pacific Central Station (at all times) and the Granville Street strip (on weekend nights).

### Traffic Accidents & Violations

If you are involved in a serious traffic incident, you should obtain a police report for insurance purposes and, if you are a resident, make a claim via ICBC (www.icbc.com) – the body through which all Vancouver residents must buy their car insurance (see Residents, p.61). If you are stopped for a driving infraction, you must produce a valid driver's licence, vehicle registration and insurance documents. Your car can be impounded immediately for 24 hours if you fail a breathalyser test, and penalties for doing so range from a one-year driving suspension and fine for a first offence up to a two-year suspension and imprisonment for future offences.

If you cause a crash, you can be charged and convicted of impaired driving. All impaired driving convictions increase your insurance premiums – often dramatically. A points system is in place, and the more points you accrue on your licence for each ticket or penalty, the more your insurance premium rises.

As a side note, do take care when driving in Vancouver. Accidents caused by careless, impatient and sometimes downright dangerous driving are all too common. Be especially careful in wet conditions and at junctions, where the amber light seems to mean speed up rather than slow down to many Vancouver drivers. For that reason, pedestrians should always look both ways when crossing the road. This applies even if you have the right of way as cars are allowed to turn right on red lights in Vancouver, and some do so with little consideration for the safety of crossing pedestrians.

### Getting Arrested

If you are arrested in Vancouver, you have the right to phone calls; how many is at the discretion of the police. You also have the right to a lawyer, and an interpreter if needed, and the police are obligated to help you find one or put you in touch with your own lawyer. You shouldn't be held for more than 24 hours without going in front of a justice of the peace to assess if you can be released and bail can be posted for you.

### Prison Time

There are nine federal prisons, known as correctional institutions, in British Columbia, and the emphasis is on rehabilitation, with visitors and telephone and written contact allowed. Some inmates can qualify for private family visits, and there is a parole system. Since 1997, the prison population in Canada has fallen by 12% for men, to 12,158 inmates in 2006, and increased by 22% for women, to 403 inmates in 2006. In 2002, the Supreme Court ruled to allow all inmates who are Canadian citizens to vote in federal elections.

The death penalty is not implemented in the country, and there is no desire among Canadians for it to be introduced.

### Victims Of Crime

Report any non-urgent crimes to the Vancouver police on 604 717 3321 or through the online reporting system at www.city.vancouver.bc.ca/police. The Vancouver Police Department operates a 24 hour Victim Services Unit (604 717 2737) for victims of more serious crimes. The service includes emotional care and general criminal justice system information.

## Police

Policing in Vancouver is undertaken by both the Royal Canadian Mounted Police (RCMP) and the Vancouver Police Department (VPD). The Vancouver Transit Police Service supports the VPD and RCMP in policing the transit system. As well as being Canada's national police force, the RCMP is often contracted to perform provincial and municipal policing duties around Canada – either as the sole law enforcement agency or alongside other forces – and it has a number of detachments in Greater Vancouver.

*Fire engine*

However, the VPD is the main police presence in Vancouver itself, with its dark-blue uniformed officers mostly seen around town in distinctive white cruisers. On-foot officers are not in abundance, apart from in Downtown Eastside, where they are forced to spend most of their energy trying to stem the tide of incidents – mostly drug-related – resulting from the area's well-documented social problems. Officers on mountain bikes also patrol the city, particularly in summer. The police in Vancouver are armed, but incidents involving shootings are rare. The VPD website is www.city.vancouver.bc.ca/police, and you can report small crimes, such as small-scale theft, online.

## Gay & Lesbian

Vancouver has twice been ranked the top gay leisure travel destination in Canada – fourth in the world – in Community Marketing's 2006 and 2007 surveys of US gay and lesbian travellers, cementing its growing international reputation as a gay-friendly city. Same-sex marriage was legalised in BC in 2003, and Vancouver has reaped the benefits of the lucrative gay and lesbian travel market ever since.

The hugely popular Vancouver Pride Parade & Festival (see p.57) has been a prominent date in the city's calendar every summer since it debuted in 1978. Vancouver's large gay and lesbian community is centred in the West End neighbourhood around Davie Street, helping to make the area one of the most vibrant parts of the city (for more information visit www.gayvan.com). See also Going Out, p.420.

---

**Mounting Concerns**

*Mounties – the Royal Canadian Mounted Police – are famous worldwide for their iconic uniform and for always getting their man. However, in the past few years the force has been in the public eye for all the wrong reasons, most recently in 2007 when Polish immigrant Robert Dziekanski died after being tasered by RCMP officers in Vancouver International Airport. The event received global attention and led to an RCMP review of its taser policy following overwhelming public condemnation of the incident. In late 2007, a government taskforce recommended that a major restructuring of the RCMP was needed to regain the trust of the Canadian public.*

## Female Visitors

Vancouver is generally a safe city and women should feel free from restriction. However, it is advisable that women on their own should take care at night, especially around Pacific Central Station and the Downtown Eastside. There have been isolated instances of women being attacked while walking or jogging alone in Stanley Park, but, on the whole, Vancouver is a very safe city for females. Public transport is a safer option than walking, although care should be taken on the SkyTrain at night, particularly at stations. SkyTrain stations have well-lit designated waiting areas, while the trains themselves are fitted with silent alarms and speakerphones that let riders alert the control centre in an emergency. In addition, Transit Police patrol the transport system.

## Travelling With Children

Vancouver and its environs are not just a giant playground for adults; the city is also geared up for kids. If the clean, safe beaches fringing the West Side and West End aren't enough to keep children happy, the Kitsilano and Stanley Park Second Beach open air swimming pools are always busy on sunny days. Other attractions sure to elicit squeals of joy (and the kids will like them too) include the Vancouver Aquarium and Children's Farmyard and Miniature Train in Stanley Park, Granville Island, Telus World of Science and the HR MacMillan Space Centre (see Exploring, p.233), while the annual Pacific National Exhibition and nearby Playland amusement park are firm favourites with kids of all ages. The annual Vancouver International Children's Festival in May is another date for the calendar. Throughout the year, Vancouver's excellent community centres offer many programmes for parents and children, including school holiday activities. Restaurants are generally welcoming to children, and more family oriented establishments often provide high chairs. Many large malls and department stores have play areas and baby-changing facilities. The large Oakridge Shopping Centre on West 41st Street, for example, hosts an 800 sq ft children's play area. Parents can find more resources and information on amenities for children, including health services and playgroups, at www.kidsvancouver.com.

## Accessible Outdoors

One of the joys of living in Vancouver is easy, year-round access to the great outdoors, and people with disabilities can also take advantage of everything the region has to offer. The city's 'recreation for all' policy means that municipal community centres, ice rinks and swimming pools all cater to the needs of disabled people through the provision of special elevators and equipment (www.city.vancouver.bc.ca). Two of Vancouver's finest natural attractions are also fully accessible: a free wheelchair-accessible trolley ride tours Stanley Park (604 801 5515), and the Grouse Mountain gondola provides wheelchair access with 24 hours' notice (604 984 0661). Other sports activities can be arranged through the BC Sport and Fitness Council for the Disabled (www.disabilitysport.org) and the Mobility Opportunities Society (www.disabilityfoundation.org/bcmos). With Vancouver due to host the Paralympic Winter Games in 2010, awareness of sport for people with disabilities has never been higher in the city.

## People With Disabilities

As you would expect of a city where the mayor, Sam Sullivan, is quadriplegic, Vancouver is a very accessible city. Vancouver International Airport initiated its Airport Barrier Free programme in 1980 to make it as accessible as possible, including installing adapted washrooms and information monitors, and providing a range of services for the visually impaired and hard of hearing. As for getting around the city itself, Vancouver was the first Canadian city to introduce scheduled bus services for disabled people, and the transit system as a whole, including the SeaBus, SkyTrain and buses, is very accessible. The HandyDART service caters to disabled residents who register through TransLink (www.translink.bc.ca). Disabled drivers can apply for parking permits through Sparc BC at www.sparc.bc.ca, and disabled parking is plentiful.

When it comes to accommodation, the Hotel Association of Canada runs an access Access Canada programme to encourage hotels to look after the needs of people with disabilities. Visit its website at www.access-canada.ca to find member hotels in Vancouver, including Accent Inns Vancouver Airport, Hyatt Regency Vancouver, Quality Inn Downtown Vancouver and Westin Bayshore.

## What To Wear

Vancouver is a very casual city, and business suits, or even shirts and ties, are a relatively rare sight on the streets and in workplaces. Offices that do enforce a dress code often have 'casual Fridays'.

Outdoors, the city's relatively mild year-round climate makes it unique among the other large Canadian cities. This means that acquiring clothing to protect you from the elements is not as important as elsewhere in the country. In winter, while most other Canadians shovel snow and hunker down for the duration, Vancouverites simply zip up their waterproof jackets a little higher and open their umbrellas more often. In summer, Vancouver rarely experiences the baking hot temperatures of, for example, Toronto and Montreal.

However, essential clothing does include a good waterproof jacket. Wear layers in winter as it can get very chilly (although rarely falling below zero), and have an umbrella on standby year-round. Fleece and GORE-TEX clothing is as common on city streets as on the local mountains, and shorts and flip-flops (or thongs) are standard summer attire. And if you want to forgo clothes altogether, there's always the popular nudist hangout at Wreck Beach (see p.240).

## Dos & Don'ts

Despite being a liberal, generally laissez-faire city, Vancouver has a number of bylaws you should be aware of. Smoking is banned in pretty much all public places, including workplaces, bars and restaurants (apart from on patios and in separate smoking rooms). And, despite many people's belief that cannabis use is legal in Vancouver, it is not. However, personal use of the drug is tolerated in the main and is widely accepted as part of Vancouver's sub-culture.

While the city's strict licensing laws that led to it being dubbed 'no-fun city' have been significantly relaxed in recent years, public drinking is banned, and the police, and public, generally frown on overt displays of drunkenness. Other bylaws worth keeping in mind include a new idle-free ruling, which means you risk a fine of $50 for sitting in your car with the engine running. Jaywalking is not permitted and, although not strictly enforced, you could get a ticket for crossing the street through moving traffic. And if you are a dog owner, you must observe Vancouver's dog-related bylaws, including keeping your pet on a leash, aside from in specified park and beach 'off-leash' areas.

## Photography

There are virtually no barriers to taking photographs in Vancouver, although it's always polite to ask before snapping a close-up shot of a passer-by. Vancouver is an incredibly scenic city and many locals also carry cameras around to capture that perfect mountain or sunset shot. And, despite the need to be wary when openly toting a camera in the Downtown Eastside area of the city, the only real hazard facing photographers in Vancouver is likely to involve bumping into a fellow shutterbug.

## Tourist Information

Vancouver TouristInfo Centre is conveniently located in the Downtown Waterfront area near Canada Place. The large facility is open seven days a week, from 08:30 to 18:00, and gets very busy during peak summer periods, particularly when cruise ships arrive at the terminal nearby. As well as picking up several trees' worth of maps and information leaflets on things to do in and around

| Vancouver Tourism Offices Overseas | | |
|---|---|---|
| Australia | Sydney | +61 2 9571 1866 |
| China | Beijing | +86 10 8529 9066 |
| France | Paris | +33 1 4312 8042 |
| Germany | Dusseldorf | +49 211 8285 5367 |
| Japan | Tokyo | +81 3 5408 1039 |
| Korea | Seoul | +82 2 733 7751 |
| Mexico | Mexico City | +52 55 5514 4849 |
| United Kingdom | London | +44 20 7389 9980 |
| United States | Portland | +503 777 2608 |

the city, you can get advice from the multilingual staff and book accommodation, tours and activities in Vancouver and elsewhere in British Columbia. Don't forget to pick up a copy of the *Official Visitors' Guide* to take advantage of discounts and special offers in shops, restaurants and attractions in Vancouver. If you're looking for something to do at short notice, one service in the TouristInfo Centre well worth taking advantage of is the Tickets Tonight kiosk that lets you buy half-price tickets for cultural and sporting events, including hard-to-come-by Cannucks ones, on the day of the event. Visit www.ticketstonight.ca for more information. You can access tourism information online at the official Tourism Vancouver website, www. tourismvancouver.com.

*False Creek*

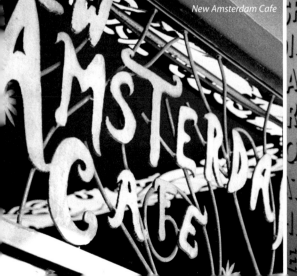

*New Amsterdam Cafe*

*False Creek art*

## Places To Stay

Vancouver's glorious setting has long attracted droves of visitors, and the city offers every echelon of accommodation to cater to this demand. Gracious and elegant properties abound, hip boutique spots pop up with increasing regularity, and charming guesthouses entice those wanting more intimate surrounds. Moderate and budget hotels also flourish throughout the city and the impressive selections of hotel apartments, motels and hostels help round out the picture. Visitors to Vancouver should note, however, that there is a non-refundable hotel tax of 10% and a goods and services tax (GST) of 6% added to all hotel bills.

Perhaps surprisingly for a city that attracts so many outdoor aficionados, there is a dearth of campsites within Greater Vancouver. However, those who have experienced the wilds that sit on the city's doorstep flock to the real thing rather than pitching camp amid the condos.

◄ *Hotels With Altitude*

*Take your visit to new heights and check in to one of the four penthouse suites at Sheraton Vancouver Wall Centre where floor to ceiling windows on the 27th floor offer stunning views. A lower star rating, but higher hotel floors, lure those looking for highs to the 42 storey Empire Landmark.*

## Hotels

Other options **Landmark Hotels** p.34, **Weekend Break Hotels** p.265

Vancouver's hotels are of a high standard compared with many other cities of a similar size, with some of the country's finest among Downtown's cluster of high rises. With its proximity to Stanley Park, False Creek and Coal Harbour, the West End is another popular location. Hotels are classified by both a star rating system and by the joint American and Canadian automobile associations' diamond ratings. Vancouver boasts one of Canada's two five-diamond hotels; the award-winning Sutton Place attracts deep-pocketed business travellers and a galaxy of visiting film and TV stars.

With more than 24,000 rooms in Metro Vancouver and 13,000 of those Downtown, you would think rooms would be easy to find, but during July and August, as well as in cruise season (May to September), accommodation in the City of Glass is at a premium. Tourism Vancouver (604 682 2222, www.tourismvancouver.com) is an excellent resource when rooms are scarce. Average room rates are slightly over $120, but accommodation prices ascend sharply from $60 a night to as much as $1,000. As a general rule, the higher the price, the better the views, but in a city that looks good from so many angles, even more moderate hotels can come up with dazzling vistas. Facilities at the city's budget level usually include basics such as coffee makers, mini fridges and sometimes continental breakfast. Moderately priced properties offer newer, higher quality amenities in rooms and often a pool and bar or restaurant on property. At the high end, you can expect turndown service with artisan chocolates, doting attention from 24 hour concierges, oodles of amenities, renowned restaurants on the property and impeccable health and fitness facilities.

### Bargain Beds

It's hard to beat the price, and the beachside location, of The Sylvia Hotel, a venerable old dame built in 1912. Nearby, The Buchan Hotel is a budget gem in the West End. The hotel apartments in The Meridian at 910 Beach, a contemporary favourite less than a block from False Creek and Granville Island ferries, win fans with their sparkling clean suites and generous continental breakfasts.

### Pamper Palaces

For those who want more than just a room and a robe, several of Vancouver's top hotels offer enticing onsite spas. The city's most luxurious hotels have truly decadent spas. The Sutton Place is home to Vida Wellness, Pan Pacific has Spa Utopia and The Fairmont Hotel Vancouver is the setting for Vancouver's 'first spa for men', Absolute Spa. If you want top quality pampering but at a slightly lower price, many other hotels offer appealing spa menus, from the bright and cheerful MBody Fitness and Wellness Spa at the Pacific Palisades to the diminutive Spa at the Wedgewood at The Wedgewood Hotel. For more spa options, see Well-Being, p.347.

## The Right Address

A good starting point for shopping at Granville Island Market is The Granville Island Hotel. For easy strolls to Stanley Park, The Buchan Hotel, The Sylvia Hotel and The Westin Bayshore Resort & Marina all share top honours. Pan Pacific wins the prize for proximity to cruise ship departures. Hockey fans wanting to keep close to the action can check into the nearby Westin Grand. Super stylish Opus Hotel is the one to saunter to if you want to be able to nip back to your room and change between social bookings in chic Yaletown. If Grouse Mountain and Capilano Suspension Bridge are high on your to-do list, snap up a suite at Holiday Inn Hotel & Suites North Vancouver.

## Hotels

### Four & Five Star

| | | |
|---|---|---|
| Century Plaza | 604 687 0575 | www.century-plaza.com |
| Delta Vancouver Suites | 604 689 8188 | www.deltahotels.com |
| The Fairmont Hotel Vancouver | 604 684 3131 | www.fairmont.com |
| The Fairmont Waterfront | 604 691 1991 | www.fairmont.com |
| Four Seasons Hotel Vancouver | 604 689 9333 | www.fourseasons.com |
| Georgian Court Hotel | 604 682 5555 | www.georgiancourt.com |
| Hilton Vancouver Metrotown | 604 438 1200 | www.hilton.com |
| Hyatt Regency Vancouver | 604 683 1234 | www.hyatt.com |
| Le Soleil Hotel & Suites | 604 632 3000 | www.lesoleilhotel.com |
| The Listel Hotel | 604 684 8461 | www.listel-vancouver.com |
| Loden Vancouver | 604 669 5060 | www.lodenvancouver.com |
| Metropolitan Hotel | 604 687 1122 | www.metropolitan.com |
| Opus Hotel | 604 642 6787 | www.opushotel.com |
| Pacific Palisades | 604 688 0461 | www.pacificpalisadeshotel.com |
| Pan Pacific | 604 662 8111 | www.panpacific.com |
| Sheraton Vancouver Wall Centre | 604 331 1000 | www.sheratonwallcentre.com |
| The Sutton Place | 604 682 5511 | www.suttonplace.com |
| Vancouver Marriott Pinnacle Downtown Hotel | 604 684 1128 | www.marriott.com |
| The Victorian Hotel | 604 681 6369 | www.victorianhotel.ca |
| The Wedgewood Hotel | 604 689 7777 | www.wedgewoodhotel.com |
| The Westin Bayshore Resort & Marina | 604 682 3377 | www.westinbayshore.com |
| The Westin Grand | 604 602 1999 | www.westingrandvancouver.com |

### Three Star

| | | |
|---|---|---|
| Coast Plaza Hotel & Suites | 604 688 7711 | www.coasthotels.com |
| The Granville Island Hotel | 604 683 7373 | www.granvilleislandhotel.com |
| Holiday Inn Hotel & Suites North Vancouver | 604 985 3111 | www.ichotelsgroup.com |
| Lonsdale Quay Hotel | 604 986 6111 | www.lonsdalequayhotel.com |
| Plaza 500 | 604 873 1811 | www.plaza500.com |
| Rosedale On Robson | 604 689 8033 | www.rosedaleonrobson.com |
| Sandman Hotel Vancouver City Centre | 604 681 2211 | www.sandmanhotels.com |

### Two Star

| | | |
|---|---|---|
| Empire Landmark Hotel | 604 687 0511 | www.asiastandard.com |
| The Park Inn & Suites On Broadway | 604 872 8661 | www.parkinn.com |

### One Star

| | | |
|---|---|---|
| The Sylvia Hotel | 604 681 9321 | www.sylviahotel.com |

### No Rating

| | | |
|---|---|---|
| The Buchan Hotel | 604 685 5354 | www.buchanhotel.com |
| The Meridian at 910 Beach | 604 609 5100 | www.910beach.com |

## Landmark Hotels

**1015 Burrard St**
*West End*
*Map 7 D4* **1**

### Century Plaza

**604 687 0575** | www.century-plaza.com
Popular both for its luxurious, contemporary guest suites and its celebrity-magnet spa, this hip address also offers cutting edge design in the lobby and sleek restaurant. Helpful staff and a convenient location add to the allure of this 30 storey hotel.

**550 West Hastings St**
*Downtown*
*Map 7 F3* **2**

### Delta Vancouver Suites

**604 689 8188** | www.deltahotels.com
Subtle hues feature throughout this upscale 225 full-service suite property. Guest suites were designed with business travellers firmly in mind and star ergonomic chairs, expandible desks and doors or partitions to divide work and sleep areas. The central location adds yet more appeal for business travellers.

**900 West Georgia St**
*Downtown*
*Map 7 E3* **3**

### The Fairmont Hotel Vancouver

**604 684 3131** | www.fairmont.com
From the Scottish baronial style green copper roof to the cavernous lobby where Vancouver's most affluent congregate, the city's grand dame exudes old world elegance and style, alongside a slew of top notch, modern amenities. Acclaimed restaurant 900 West is another reason to check in to one of the 556 rooms.

**900 Canada Place
Way**
*Downtown*
*Map 7 F2* **4**

### The Fairmont Waterfront

**604 691 1991** | www.fairmont.com
Mountain and harbour views abound, courtesy of this luxurious 439 room hotel's strategic location on the water's edge at Coal Harbour. Floor-to-ceiling windows in elegant guest rooms gaze on sea planes and the bustle below. Terraced gardens and the excellent Herons Restaurant are added enticements to stay on property.

**791 West
Georgia St**
*Downtown*
*Map 7 E3* **5**

### Four Seasons Hotel Vancouver

**604 689 9333** | www.fourseasons.com
Although this 376 room edifice in the heart of Downtown appears rather nondescript from the outside, the interior more than makes up for that. Extremely generous, airy rooms contain all possible amenities, staff are smiling and knowledgeable, and health and fitness facilities are outstanding.

### 773 Beatty St
*Downtown*
*Map 7 F4* **6**

## Georgian Court Hotel

*604 682 5555 | www.georgiancourt.com*
Traditional elegance stars at this low-key, 180 room boutique property, housed in a modern building a short walk from Robson Street. Rooms feature dark wood and brass fittings, an impressive array of business amenities and complimentary high speed internet access.

### 1253 Johnston St
*False Creek*
*Map 9 C3* **7**

## The Granville Island Hotel

*604 683 7373 | www.granvilleislandhotel.com*
A modern hotel a stroll from Granville Island's market, theatres and restaurants, this 85 room charmer has a popular restaurant and bar. Rooms are spacious and straightforward without being bland. Something of a secret, Granville Island Hotel always seems calm, even when the rest of the island is overrun by tourists.

### 655 Burrard St
*Downtown*
*Map 7 E3* **8**

## Hyatt Regency Vancouver

*604 683 1234 | www.vancouver.hyatt.com*
The 644 ample-sized rooms, with floor-to-ceiling windows, are a key attraction for this well-known international chain. The hotel also boasts a heated outdoor pool area and hot tub. Guestrooms have been newly refurbished and feature a modern, sophisticated decor that appeals to a mixture of business travellers and holidaymakers.

### 567 Hornby St
*Downtown*
*Map 7 E3* **9**

## Le Soleil Hotel & Suites

*604 632 3000 | www.lesoleilhotel.com*
Demure on the outside, baroque and lush on the inside, Le Soleil welcomes guests with rich reds and gilded flourishes. The decadence continues in the 112 cosy suites with their feather beds and down duvets, Godiva chocolates at turndown and Aveda products in the bathrooms.

### 1300 Robson St
*West End*
*Map 7 D2* **10**

## The Listel Hotel

*604 684 8461 | www.listel-vancouver.com*
An uninspiring exterior masks one of the city's most interesting hotels. Choose a room on the Museum or Gallery floors and share your space with art and artifacts from the Museum of Anthropology, hemlock and cedar furniture, and a colour palette evocative of forestscapes of the Pacific Northwest.

**645 Howe St**
*Downtown*
*Map 7 E3* **11**

## Metropolitan Hotel

*604 687 1122* | *www.metropolitan.com*

When you want to balance work, play and feng shui, the former Mandarin Oriental is an excellent choice. The 197 room Met manages to be grand without overdoing it. Marble bathrooms, glass showers and soaker tubs allow guests to unwind. Some appealing extras include stellar squash courts and acclaimed restaurant Diva.

**322 Davie St**
*Yaletown*
*Map 9 E1* **12**

## Opus Hotel

*604 642 6787* | *www.opushotel.com*

The sultry Opus is a magnet for scene-seekers. The ultra-hip design hotel has held court on its Yaletown corner since 2002, seeing a stream of beautiful people and celebrities sashay past the lobby's fabulous melee of style statements. Rooms boast luxurious L'Occitane toiletries, Frette robes and bold colour schemes.

**1277 Robson St**
*West End*
*Map 7 D2* **13**

## The Pacific Palisades

*604 688 0461* | *www.pacificpalisadeshotel.com*

Cheerful and attentive staff start off any visit to this quirky, modern hotel on a good note. The only things brighter than the sunburst yellow guestrooms are the turquoise and crimson penthouses on the 23rd floor. The Palisades has an innovative restaurant and lounge, Zin, and an enticing pool and spa, MBody.

**300-999 Canada Place**
*Downtown*
*Map 7 F2* **14**

## Pan Pacific

*604 662 8111* | *www.panpacific.com*

All 504 rooms and suites at this elite waterfront address have spectacular Stanley Park, mountain, city or harbour views. Rooms feature flat-screen TVs, pillow-top beds and Frette robes. Popular with a pre and post-cruise crowd, Pan Pacific is renowned for its excellent health club, Five Sails Restaurant and the Cascades Lounge.

**845 Burrard St**
*Downtown*
*Map 7 E3* **15**

## The Sutton Place

*604 682 5511* | *www.suttonplace.com*

Flower arrangements so large you could lose the rest of your party in them welcome you to the opulent lobby of The Sutton Place. A 397 room hotel on one of the city's busiest streets, The Sutton Place features high-tech amenities, warm hues and impeccable service.

### The Sylvia Hotel

**1154 Gilford St**
*West End*
*Map 7 A2* **16**

*604 681 9321 | www.sylviahotel.com*

The Sylvia Hotel, which opened in 1912, is an old-fashioned historic hotel just yards from the water's edge at English Bay. Behind the somewhat faded exterior of this budget gem, the hotel is clean and atmospheric. Bay-view rooms offer thrilling sunset views.

### Vancouver Marriott Pinnacle Downtown Hotel

**1128 West Hastings St**
*Downtown*
*Map 7 E2* **17**

*604 684 1128 | www.marriott.com*

A popular choice with both business and leisure travellers, the Marriott Pinnacle is a pet-friendly option, situated adjacent to Downtown, Stanley Park and the Cruise Ship Terminal. Most of the 430 spacious and relaxing rooms offer views of the city's stunning surrounds.

### The Wedgewood Hotel

**845 Hornby St**
*Map 7 D4* **18**
*Downtown*

*604 689 7777 | www.wedgewoodhotel.com*

There are just 83 rooms in this intimate, traditional property, steps from Robson Street. A member of the elite Relais & Chateau group as of 2008, the warm, antique-filled hotel offers ample rooms, lively colour schemes and fresh cookies every night.

### The Westin Bayshore Resort & Marina

**1601 Bayshore Dr**
*West End*
*Map 7 C1* **19**

*604 682 3377 | www.westinbayshore.com*

The 510 room Westin Bayshore Resort & Marina is the city's only resort. Set on the water's edge by Stanley Park, guests can arrive by boat as well as road, and the floor-to-ceiling windows in the main building offer breathtaking views of Coal Harbour.

### The Westin Grand

**433 Robson St**
*Downtown*
*Map 7 F4* **20**

*604 602 1999 | www.westingrandvancouver.com*

The undulating green glass of the 26 storey Westin Grand hides a tranquil escape from Robson Street's hectic pace. An all-suite property with Heavenly Beds, deep soaker tubs and excellent views, it's a stylish address, popular with film production crews. Don't miss the Garden Terrace and the heated outdoor pool and hot tub.

## Hotel Apartments

Vancouver offers a plethora of short-term and extended-stay apartments, with a particular concentration of them in the largely residential West End. They can usually be rented for anything from a day to years, with reductions often being offered for stays of 30 days or more. Some properties waive the additional 15% tax for bookings of more than 30 days. Many better-known hotel apartments are classified by the same star rating as hotels. Apartments in this category come fully furnished and most buildings will offer additional facilities, from parking and a gym to a concierge, pool, private lounge and business centre. Monthly rates for studio apartments in the West End start at around $2,100, and at around $3,200 for two-bedroom suites.

### Hotel Apartments

| | | | |
|---|---|---|---|
| Aston Rosellen Suites At Stanley Park | West End | 604 689 4807 | www.rosellensuites.com |
| Carmana Plaza | West End | 604 683 1399 | www.carmanaplaza.com |
| Lord Stanley Suites On The Park | West End | 604 688 9299 | www.lordstanley.com |
| Meridian At 910 Beach Avenue | Yaletown | 604 609 5100 | www.910beach.com |
| Pendrell Suites | West End | 604 609 2770 | www.pendrellsuites.com |
| Sandman Suites On Davie | West End | 604 681 7263 | www.sandmanhotels.com |
| Sunset Inn & Suites | West End | 604 688 2474 | www.sunsetinn.com |
| Times Square Suites | West End | 604 684 2223 | www.timessquaresuites.com |
| Viva Luxury Suites | Downtown | 604 669 6686 | www.vivaluxurysuites.com |
| West Coast Suites At UBC | UBC | 604 822 1000 | www.ubcconferences.com |

## Guest Houses & Bed & Breakfasts

Antiques and gourmet breakfast feasts have become the norm for many of the stellar array of guesthouses that sprung up in the heady days of Expo 86. Housed in brightly painted Victorian homes and Arts and Crafts mansions, Vancouver's guesthouses and bed and breakfasts are not budget options; luxurious linens, elegant accommodation and genteel charm come with a price, but inn rates are usually slightly less expensive than nearby hotels. There are guesthouses scattered throughout the city and surrounding areas, but notable clusters occur in residential West End streets and along leafy avenues in the West Side. Tourism Vancouver (604 682 2222, www.tourismvancouver.com) offers an extensive database of bed and breakfasts and guesthouses. The Canadian Bed & Breakfast Guide (www.canadianbandbguide.ca) is another excellent resource.

### Guest Houses & Bed & Breakfasts

| | | | |
|---|---|---|---|
| Barclay House In The West End | West End | 604 605 1351 | www.barclayhouse.com |
| Beachside City View B&B | North Vancouver | 604 922 7773 | www.beach.bc.ca |
| Hamersley House | North Vancouver | 604 988 1101 | www.hamersleyhouse.com |
| Kenya Court Ocean Front Guesthouse | Kitsilano | 604 738 7085 | www.bbcanada.com/kenyacourt |
| Nelson House B&B | West End | 604 684 9797 | www.downtownbedandbreakfast.com |
| O Canada House | West End | 604 688 0555 | www.ocanadahouse.com |
| Penny Farthing Inn | Kitsilano | 604 739 9002 | www.pennyfarthinginn.com |
| Ten Fifteen West Sixteenth Avenue | Fairview | 604 730 0713 | www.tenfifteen.ca |
| Thistledown House | North Vancouver | 604 986 7173 | www.thistle-down.com |
| Treehouse Bed & Breakfast | Kerrisdale | 604 266 2962 | www.treehousebb.com |
| West End Guest House | West End | 604 681 2889 | www.westendguesthouse.com |

Vancouver's West End is home to a large number of the city's gay and lesbian residents, in addition to the bars, restaurants and clubs of its Gay Village. As a result, accommodation in the area is among the city's most gay popular. Of the many lovingly refurbished and renovated, brightly painted guesthouses around Davie and Denman streets, O Canada House, West End Guest House and Nelson House B&B are especially popular with gay and lesbian visitors.

## Motels & Rest Houses

In addition to a scattering of motels on the roads leading Downtown, there are several right in the heart of the city, allowing visitors to steer clear of costly hotel parking charges while enjoying a central location. Motels are no-frills options when compared with hotels, usually offering basic amenities such as parking and complimentary coffee. A good budget option when travelling with the whole family, some also boast full kitchenettes and separate living rooms. Some Downtown addresses, including The Greenbrier Hotel, also offer additional amenities, including free wireless internet. The Grouse Inn's North Shore location allows room for extras such as continental breakfast, a children's playground, a car wash area and a heated, seasonal outdoor pool.

### Motels & Rest Houses

| | | | |
|---|---|---|---|
| Bosman's Vancouver Hotel | Yaletown | 604 682 3171 | www.bosmanshotel.com |
| Burrard Inn | Downtown | 604 681 2331 | www.burrardinn.com |
| City Centre Motor Inn | Mount Pleasant | 604 876 7166 | www.citycentermotorhotel.com |
| Days Inn Vancouver Metro | Victoria | 604 876 5531 | www.daysinnvancouvermetro.com |
| The Greenbrier Hotel | West End | 604 683 4558 | www.greenbrierhotel.com |
| The Grouse Inn | North Vancouver | 604 988 7101 | www.grouseinn.com |
| Palms Motel | Collingwood | 604 435 3347 | www.palmsmotelvancouver.com |
| Robsonstrasse Hotel & Suites | West End | 604 687 1674 | www.robsonstrassehotel.com |

## Hostels

Vancouver contains a solid selection of hostels, several with fully equipped kitchens and welcoming common areas, and all offering both same-sex and mixed dormitories, as well as private rooms. The exception is the superb YWCA, which only offers private rooms – it's a great option for families, business travellers and older people. Younger, party-minded visitors gravitate towards Granville Street's Same Sun and Hostelling International Vancouver Central, close to Granville's boisterous nightlife scene. Those wanting to be close to Downtown distractions, but not kept awake by them, prefer Hostelling International Downtown (604 684 4565) in the quieter West End. Families and beach lovers opt for Hostelling International Jericho Beach (604 224 3208, summer only), mere steps from the water.

No matter how close they seem to Downtown's delights, stay clear of hotels and hostels in Chinatown and the seedier fringes of Gastown, as they tend to be dingy, down at heel, long stay or residential options. Properties near Pacific Central bus and train station should be avoided for similar reasons.

### Hostels

| | | | |
|---|---|---|---|
| Hostelling International Vancouver | Various Locations | 604 685 5335 | www.hihostels.ca |
| Same Sun Backpacker Lodge | Downtown | 604 682 8226 | www.samesun.com |
| YWCA | Downtown | 604 895 5830 | www.ywcahotel.com |

## Campsites
Other options **Camping** p.282

June to September provides the best weather for camping. You should book well in advance if visiting during the peak summer months of July and August. Camping in public places is not allowed in Vancouver. Most campsites adjacent to Vancouver offer coin-operated laundries and swimming pools. Several boast enticing extras, including Jacuzzis, children's playgrounds and all manner of hookups for those travelling by RV.

### Campsites

| | | | |
|---|---|---|---|
| Burnaby Cariboo RV Park | Burnaby | 604 420 1722 | www.bcrv.com |
| Capilano RV Park | North Vancouver | 604 987 4722 | www.capilanorvpark.com |
| Dogwood Campgrounds Of BC | Surrey | 604 583 5585 | www.dogwoodcampgrounds.com |
| Fort Camping | Langley | 604 888 3678 | www.fortcamping.com |
| Hazelmere RV Park & Campground | Surrey | 604 538 1167 | www.hazelmere.ca |
| Parkcanada RV Park & Tenting | Delta | 604 943 5811 | www.parkcanada.com |
| Seacrest Motel & RV Park | White Rock | 604 531 4720 | www.seacrestmotel.bc.ca |

Those wanting to pitch their tent within sight of Downtown should hammer their pegs in at 208 site Capilano RV Park, right beside the graceful Lions Gate Bridge. Other camping options are in further flung corners of the city, such as near the beach in White Rock or, closer in, at Burnaby Cariboo RV Park, an RV and tent option with all the bells and whistles from wireless internet and cable hookups to a fitness room and indoor pool.

Downtown traffic

SeaBus station

## Getting Around
Other options **Exploring** p.184

Unlike other major cities, there is no comprehensive rapid transit subway system in Vancouver – but then why would you want to travel underground in a place as attractive as this? Take the SeaBus ferry across Burrard Inlet, or a bus over Burrard Bridge, and you will start to understand why Vancouverites love their city.

Historical choices and suburban growth have made Vancouver largely car dependant, and residents pay for this with traffic congestion and parking costs. However, Vancouver's public transit system is pervasive, affordable, well-used, and more reliable than most. TransLink operates the entire public transit network so buses, SkyTrain, and SeaBus all use the same zones and fares. A $2.50 ticket will get you around Vancouver, and $3.75 will get you to the airport and most surrounding suburbs. The SkyTrain light rail system connects Downtown with eastern parts of the city and suburbs, with much-needed plans in place to expand to the south and west. Cycling is generally safe, though it can be a struggle to share the roads with so many other users. Vancouver cyclists regularly take to the streets en masse to promote the greenest option, pressuring TransLink and the city to develop new biking strategies. Taxis pick up where transit leaves off in the early hours, so expect to set aside around $20 to get home if you are out past about 01:00.

Vancouver was planned on the classic North American grid system and is easily landmarked, with the mountains to the north and the Pacific Ocean to the west. Incrementally numbered avenues run east-west from 70th Avenue in the south to 1st Avenue in the north. Streets run north-south. Marine Drive hugs the coastline from south-east to north-west, approximating a half-ring road. The main thoroughfare is Granville Street, with six lanes connecting Vancouver north to south. Oak Street, Cambie Street, Main Street and Knight Street are also major north-south routes. Broadway is a major east-west thoroughfare, as are 41st Avenue, King Edward Avenue, and 4th Avenue.

Downtown, Robson Street is Vancouver's version of a high street. Georgia Street and Davie Street run parallel and are also important routes north-west to south-east on the peninsula. Granville Street maintains its importance Downtown and runs perpendicular to Robson Street. Burrard Street is parallel to Granville Street and Denman Street in the West End. The famous Lions Gate Bridge connects the Downtown peninsula to North Vancouver through Stanley Park. Burrard Bridge and Granville Bridge connect Downtown with the trendy Kitsilano and Fairview (also known as South Granville)

| Airlines | | |
|---|---|---|
| AeroMexico | na | www.aeromexico.com |
| Air Canada | 1 888 247 2262 | www.aircanada.com |
| Air China | 604 685 0921 | www.airchina.com.cn |
| Air New Zealand | 1 800 663 5494 | www.airnewzealand.com |
| Air Pacific | 1 800 227 4446 | www.airpacific.com |
| Air Transat | 1 877 872 6728 | www.airtransat.com |
| Alaska Airlines | 1 800 252 7522 | www.alaskaair.com |
| All Nippon Airways | 1 800 235 9262 | www.ana.co.jp/eng |
| American Airlines | 1 800 433 7300 | www.aa.com |
| British Airways | 1 800 247 9297 | www.britishairways.com |
| Cathay Pacific | 604 606 8888 | www.cathaypacific.com |
| China Airlines | 604 682 6777 | www.china-airlines.com |
| China Eastern Airlines | 604 689 8998 | www.ce-air.com |
| Continental Airlines | 1 800 231 0856 | www.continental.com |
| Delta Airlines | 1 800 221 1212 | www.delta.com |
| Japan Airlines | 1 800 525 3663 | www.ar.jal.com/en |
| KLM | 1 800 447 4747 | www.klm.nl |
| Korean Air | 1 800 438 5000 | www.koreanair.com |
| Lufthansa | 1 800 563 5954 | www.lufthansa-ca.com |
| Mexicana | 1 800 531 7921 | www.mexicana.com |
| Northwest Airlines | 1 800 225 2525 | www.nwa.com |
| Qantas | 1 800 227 4500 | www.qantas.com |
| Singapore Airlines | 604 689 1223 | www.singaporeair.com |
| Thai Airways | na | www.thaiairways.com |
| United Airlines | 1 800 241 6522 | www.united.com |
| WestJet | 1 800 538 5696 | www.westjet.ca |

neighbourhoods, and the Cambie Bridge crosses False Creek further east. Further south, the Arthur Laing Bridge links Vancouver to the airport on Sea Island.

## Air Travel

Vancouver's relatively remote location means most international travellers arrive by air. To give an idea of distance, Calgary, the nearest major Canadian city, is 10 hours away by car, or 90 minutes by plane. Vancouver is a five hour flight from Toronto, a three hour flight from Los Angeles, a nine-and-a-half hour flight from London, and a 13.5 hour flight from Hong Kong. As Canada's gateway to the Pacific, the city is well serviced by direct flights from most major Asian, European and North American cities. It is also a hub for Canada's national airline, Air Canada, which flies to a wide range of international and domestic destinations, and is a member of the Star Alliance network.

### Vancouver International Airport

Located 15km south of Downtown, Vancouver International Airport (YVR) is Canada's second-busiest airport, serving 17 million passengers annually. It provides all the amenities you would expect from a world-class airport. Food courts, gift shops, large duty free shopping areas, convenience stores, pharmacies, ATMs, currency exchanges, spas and visitor information abound, and the free and plentiful baggage trolleys are an added bonus. The international and domestic terminals are joined by the shiny new Link Building, which has increased the airport's capacity for checking in and screening passengers and handling baggage, and will eventually serve as a hub for visitors travelling to and from YVR once it is connected to the future Canada Line transit station (see Airport Transport, below). In addition to their practical amenities, the terminals showcase an impressive collection of First Nations art. These carved wood pieces and the use of stone and water features complement the architecture's bright, modern, airplane-hangar style. Check out Bill Reid's Jade Canoe sculpture in the international departures area – it is featured on the $20 bill (see p.223). For more information about the airport, including real-time flight information, see www.yvr.ca.

### Airport Services

YVR FasTrack self-service check-in kiosks are a quick and easy way for passengers of any airline to check themselves in to their flight and avoid queues. After checking in at the kiosk, you simply need to take your luggage to a bag-drop location and proceed to security with your newly printed boarding card. The green kiosks are located throughout the terminals and in the car park. The Fairmont Vancouver Airport Hotel, Delta Vancouver Airport Hotel, and the Delta Vancouver Suites, as well as the Vancouver Touristinfo Centre next to the Fairmont Waterfront Hotel, have YVR FasTrack kiosks as well. The FasTrack premium check-in lounge is available for business class and first class passengers on British Airways, Cathay Pacific, China Airlines, Mexicana and Singapore Airlines. The airport also has Green Coat Ambassadors to point people in the right direction, and customer service counters throughout.

### Airport Transport

Bus number 424 will take you from the ground level of the domestic terminal to Airport Station, where you can transfer to the 98 B-Line to Downtown. As the cheapest alternative, the bus will cost you $3.75 for a two zone fare (the fare is $2.50 on evenings after 18:30, weekends, and holidays). The mint-green Airporter shuttle (604 946 8866, www.yvrairporter.com) leaves every 20 minutes between 09:00 and 21:30 from the arrivals level of the international and domestic terminals to major Downtown hotels. Tickets are $13.50 one way, $21 return for adults and can be purchased at the Airporter counter (located at the Tourism BC booth, in international arrivals), directly from the

---

*Growing Planes*

*Vancouver International Airport's ongoing expansions are funded by the traveller-paid Airport Improvement Fee (AIF). This fee – $5 if travelling within British Columbia and the Yukon, and $15 for all other destinations – is added on to all flight prices when you purchase your ticket. The growing airport is predicted to handle 19 million passengers in 2010, with a nine gate expansion set to be completed in 2009. Phase One was finished in spring 2007, with two of the four new gates able to accommodate the new Airbus 380 behemoths. The additional five gates in Phase Two will be completed over the next few years and will feature a giant aquarium full of indigenous marine life.*

---

driver on the shuttle itself, and at pick-up locations. Taxi ranks are located outside both terminals and the trip to Downtown Vancouver costs roughly $30 (including tax and tip), taking between 30 minutes to an hour depending on traffic. Sedans, minivans, and models with wheelchair access are available.

For a little luxury, leg room and luggage space you could indulge in Limojet Gold's chauffeur-driven sedans and limousines (604 273 1331, www.limojetgold.com). It offers flat per-vehicle rates to Downtown and ranges between $39 for a three person sedan and $45 for a six person limousine, not including tax or tip.

The eagerly anticipated Canada Line rapid transit system is scheduled for completion in late 2009, linking the airport to Downtown via Richmond and the Cambie Street corridor. Trains will run every eight minutes on a SkyTrain-like system of above-ground tracks and underground tunnels, with the entire end-to-end journey taking only 25 minutes. Sixteen stations are being constructed along the length of the new line to address the transport needs of Vancouver's ever-expanding population and lessen road congestion throughout the city.

## Bicycle

Other options **Cycling** p.288

*Biker Droves*

*Those who opt to be car-free unite outside the Vancouver Art Gallery in the evening of the last Friday of every month to take over the streets during 'Critical Mass' (www.velolove.bc.ca). The event sees cyclists touring Downtown to promote the greenest form of transportation available. Vancouver Area Cycling Coalition (VACC) promotes cycling as an integral part of transportation in the area and provides education and advocacy for Vancouver cyclists. Visit www.vacc.bc.ca for more information. A free course on bicycle safety and the rights of cyclists is offered by VACC and comes highly recommended by avid Vancouver cyclists.*

Cycling is as much a political statement as a means of transport in Vancouver. Supported hugely by the alternative, eco-friendly crowd that grows more and more mainstream every day, cycling trips into the Downtown core have more than doubled in the past 10 years, and cycling and walking have increased as a means of transport by roughly 30% throughout the city.

In terms of safety, about 100 car accidents per year involve cyclists. These are rarely fatal and drivers are generally considerate, but sharing the road with motorists can be dangerous, especially around intersections, stop signs, and small roundabouts on neighbourhood streets. Helmets are mandatory, and bicycles must have front and rear lights when travelling at night. It is important to know your hand signals to alert drivers and other cyclists when you are changing direction or stopping. It is also worth noting that bikes are not permitted to be ridden on the pavement, except on bridges, and that bike theft is unfortunately quite common in Vancouver, so a good lock is a must.

TransLink accommodates cyclists who use transit for part of their journey through front-loaded bike racks on buses and permitting bikes on SkyTrains and the SeaBus during off-peak times. It has also installed bike lockers at many SkyTrain stations for those who bike to and from transit, and is currently asking for feedback from cyclists to help design a cycling route planner. Plans are also being mooted for a city-wide bike-sharing programme with a possible launch in summer 2009, modelled on Paris's 'Velib' system, where users pay short or long-term subscriptions for access to a network of self-serve bicycle hire pick-up and drop-off locations throughout the city.

### Bike One, Get One Free

The City of Vancouver offers a free detailed Bicycle Route Map that can be downloaded from www.city.vancouver.bc.ca, and found in local library branches and community centres. TransLink's Regional Vancouver Cycling Map can also be downloaded for free from www.translink.bc.ca or purchased for $3.95 in gas stations, supermarkets, pharmacies, convenience stores and book shops across the city. It shows designated on and off-street routes, as well as alternative routes throughout Vancouver, pinpointing busy intersections, steep hills and other areas of caution.

## Boat

SeaBus is a popular 400 seat catamaran passenger ferry service between Downtown's Waterfront Station and Lonsdale Quay in North Vancouver. At 12 minutes a crossing, it's usually a much quicker and easier way to get to the North Shore than by road. The fare is the same as a two zone bus trip ($3.75, or $2.50 after 18:30 or at weekends and during holidays) and the tickets are transferable to the rest of the TransLink network buses and SkyTrain. On weekdays, the SeaBus leaves Downtown every 15 minutes during the day from just after 06:00, and every 30 minutes in the evening until about 01:00. The schedule is slightly less frequent at weekends.

Another popular water route is the Aquabus from Granville Island around False Creek. This mini-ferry makes quick trips to the bottom of Hornby Street Downtown, and longer ones to Yaletown, Science World and other spots around False Creek. Fares range between $2.50 and $12.00. The Aquabus departs every five minutes to Hornby Street from 06:40 to 21:30, and every 15 minutes to Yaletown from 08:45 to 19:15. Services to Science World run every 30 minutes at weekends. The Aquabus permits dogs on a leash and collapsible strollers to board, and its sister ferry the Cyquabus transports cyclists during the summer.

### Ferry Good Service

A fixture of the coastal landscape for more than 40 years, BC Ferries operates services to almost 50 destinations along the shores of British Columbia. The most popular routes are between the mainland and the Gulf Islands, Vancouver Island, and the Sunshine Coast. BC Ferries also runs the Discovery Coast Passage, Inside Passage, and Queen Charlotte Island routes along north-western BC. The ferries are a scenic and indispensable part of life on the coast, and are packed during the summer and on holiday weekends throughout the year. Tsawwassen terminal, 45 minutes south of Vancouver, and Horseshoe Bay terminal, 25 minutes north-west of Vancouver, are the mainland points of departure for trips to the local islands and Sunshine Coast.

## Bus

*Deals On Wheels*

*To accommodate cyclists, most buses have bike racks on the front that can hold up to two bikes during daylight hours. A soon-to-be-corrected design flaw should soon allow bikes at night as well. Most buses are also equipped with adjustable ramps for passengers with wheelchairs, strollers and mobility issues.*

Unlike most major cities where the subway system is key, Vancouver's buses are its main form of public transport. TransLink's Coast Mountain Bus Company operates Vancouver's buses. The service is well used and generally reliable, but can become crowded with commuters at peak times, so be prepared to get very close to your fellow passengers during weekday rush hours. The main bus routes are the 98 and 99 B-Line services that cross the city north-south and east-west, and meet at Granville and Broadway. The 98 B-Line heads north from Airport station along Granville, all the way to Downtown's Waterfront. The 99 B-Line is popular with students and travels the length of Broadway (9th Avenue), beginning at Commercial Drive in the east, all the way to the University of British Columbia in the west. Both pick up and drop off only at designated stops and run at high frequency.

Vancouver is divided into three zones for fare-paying purposes. A regular adult fare for travel in zone one (which includes Downtown and most of Vancouver) is $2.50. Travel over two zones (to or from the airport) costs $3.75 and three zones (outer suburbs) costs $5. After 18:30 on weekdays, and all day weekends and holidays, travel anywhere in Vancouver costs just $2.50. Transfers are issued with fare payment and are valid for 90 minutes within the selected zones. Fares can be paid in exact change or with bus tickets, available in FareSaver books of 10 at any 7-Eleven store, or anywhere with the FareDealer sign. A day pass for unlimited travel between all zones is $9. For more information about monthly passes and concession prices, visit www.translink.bc.ca.

*City of Glass*

## Car

Other options **Transportation** p.172

Getting around Vancouver's crisscrossing streets and avenues is relatively easy by car. However, as the city grows, driving is becoming more and more frustrating. Trip times double during peak congestion, and parking can be expensive or hard to find. In residential areas like Kitsilano and the West End, on-street parking is at a premium and highly regulated. Navigating Downtown's one-way streets and finding affordable parking is also a challenge. Vancouver, like other major Canadian cities, has flirted with the idea of a London-style congestion charge, but will have to contend with intense public opinion and a lack of viable transport alternatives. The city's growing pains are being addressed by future transportation projects such as the Canada Line (p.43) to get more cars off the road.

Like the rest of North America, Canadians drive on the right-hand side of the road and circulate in a grid system, with traffic lights at intersections. Major road signs for highways and bridges are in English and French. Seatbelts are mandatory, as are daytime headlights. The speed limit is 50kph on main roads, 100kph to 110kph on highways, and 30kph in lanes and school zones, unless otherwise posted. Due to public pressure, Vancouver ended the use of fixed speed cameras on its roads in 2001. However, cameras have been installed at most intersections, and police set up speed traps using photo radar on a regular basis. Right turns are permitted at red lights unless indicated otherwise, and you will find left-turning lanes and advanced left turning lights at some major intersections. It is important to note that it can be illegal to turn left on busy main roads, especially during peak times (07:00 to 09:00 and 15:00 to 18:30). Pedestrians have right of way at junctions, even if there is no pedestrian crossing.

Driving in Vancouver is not cheap. Petrol (or gas) is highly taxed and prices currently hover between $1 and $1.20 per litre depending on octane level (87, 89 and 91 octane, with 91 being the most expensive and cleanest burning fuel). Including insurance, maintenance and fuel, it is estimated that running a car in Vancouver costs around $9,000 per year. City-wide parking meters cost $2 per hour. Privately run surface lots and multi-level car parks can cost as much as $28 per day in Downtown, though some have good evening and weekend rates.

*Routes & Highlights*
*The TransLink website (www.translink. bc.ca) is an invaluable tool for planning routes and obtaining schedules for all modes of transport.*

Several major highways connect Vancouver and its surrounding areas. Highway 99 starts at the US border heading north and west into Surrey, through the George Massey Tunnel under the Fraser River into Richmond, over the Oak Street Bridge into Vancouver. Highway 99 becomes Granville Street and continues over Granville Bridge and Lions Gate Bridge, eventually leading up to Whistler. Highway 1, the Trans-Canada Highway, links Vancouver to the rest of Canada in the east. From Abbotsford, south-east of the city, Highway 1 crosses over the Port Mann Bridge into Burnaby, and over the Second Narrows Ironworkers Memorial Bridge into North Vancouver where it joins Highway 99 heading up the coast. The Lougheed Highway splits off from Highway 1 near Hope, roughly five hours north-east of Vancouver. It journeys along the Fraser River through Mission, Maple Ridge, Coquitlam, and Burnaby, before entering Vancouver at East Broadway Avenue. Highway 99 links with Highway 17 in Tsawassen to take you to the BC Ferries terminal, with services to Vancouver Island and the Gulf Islands. Highway 99 connects to Highway 91 which crosses the river on the Alex Fraser Bridge between Delta and Richmond, and Highway 91A which crosses the north arm via the Queensborough Bridge into Burnaby and New Westminster.

## Subway

Vancouver does not currently have an underground subway system, and some say this limits its growth as a world-class city. The SkyTrain's Downtown service to Burrard, Waterfront and Granville stations runs underground, and the forthcoming Canada Line expansion will run below Cambie Street connecting to Downtown. This phase will add eight subterranean stops to its route. For more information on Canada Line progress, in time for the 2010 Olympics, visit www.canadaline.ca.

**Grab That Cab**
When hailing a cab during peak times it's not the driver you need to worry about, but the other would-be passengers. Stand on the pavement facing the oncoming cab with your arm in the air, make eye contact and find a spot where the driver can pull over easily. On busy nights as the clubs spill out, it's best to jump in quickly as there's always someone who would be happy to snatch the ride out from under you.

## Taxi

Vancouver's taxis are independently operated but regulated by civic bylaws and licensed by the city. Taxis have a standard metering system that increases gradually from the $2.75 minimum depending on distance travelled and traffic conditions. This generally translates to a $5-$10 journey around the Downtown core, and a $15-$25 journey over the

| Taxi Companies | |
| --- | --- |
| Black Top | 604 683 4567 |
| Checker Cabs | 604 731 1111 |
| MacLure's | 604 683 6666 |
| Vancouver Taxi | 604 871 1111 |
| Yellow Cab | 604 681 1111 |

bridge into the residential and shopping areas of Vancouver. A taxi from the airport to Downtown, or vice versa, should cost roughly $30 (including tax and tip). If you are not carrying cash, most taxis conveniently accept credit card payment as long as you let them know at the start of the journey.

Taxis are easiest to find Downtown near hotels, and are familiar with all the popular destinations; the only time you'd need a map or directions is if you are heading to distant residential suburbs. Taxis can be flagged down from the pavement when their roof-top sign is lit, and are generally a hassle-free way to get around. If you are not in a popular area however, it would be best to phone and book one. Cabs are hardest to come by on Friday and Saturday nights when they do a roaring trade of shuttling people to and from bars and clubs and home again. They are also difficult to snag during busy holidays and major events when public transport can be more reliable. Each licensed vehicle is equipped with a surveillance camera for the safety of the passengers and driver and women should have no problem taking taxis on their own as they are all clearly marked and controlled.

**Station Safety**
The SkyTrain is generally very safe, with its transit police-patrolled trains and well-lit, camera-monitored platforms. Though rare, it is worth being mindful that when problems occur it is usually in the areas surrounding the station, most recently near 29th Avenue station and Surrey Central station. As with most places, it is best to be aware of your surroundings and avoid dark and isolated areas when walking by yourself.

## Train

Vancouver's signature public transit option is the SkyTrain. Serving Downtown, East Vancouver, and suburbs to the east, the SkyTrain is 'the world's longest automated light rapid transit system', stopping at 33 stations on almost 30km of track. The service is very popular with commuters and is packed at peak times. The Expo Line runs from Waterfront to King George station every two to four minutes at peak times, Monday to Friday, and every six to eight minutes off-peak and weekends. Service for the Expo Line departs Waterfront from 05:35 to 01:15 Monday to Friday, 06:50 to 01:15 on Saturdays, and 07:50 to 00:15 on Sundays. The Millennium Line runs from Waterfront to VCC Clark station every five to six minutes during rush hour, Monday to Friday, and every six to eight minutes at other times and at weekends. Millennium Line service starts at Waterfront at 05:54 and runs until 00:31, Monday to Friday, and continues from 06:54 to 00:31 on Saturdays, and 07:54 to 23:31 on Sundays. The journey on either line end to end takes only 40 minutes, and the majority is elevated, though Downtown is underground. The Canada Line expansion to the airport along the Cambie Street corridor is scheduled for completion in late 2009, and, though not compatible with the SkyTrain system, will offer another light rail route in Vancouver that connects to Waterfront Station. Standard TransLink zones and fares apply to the SkyTrain and are fully transferable to buses and the SeaBus. Fares cost $2.50 for one zone, $3.75 for two zones, and $5 for three zones at peak times ($2.50 for all zones after 18:30 on weekdays, and all day weekends and holidays). Tickets can be bought at SkyTrain stations, 7-Eleven stores and anywhere displaying the FareDealer sign, where daily and monthly passes can also be purchased. The stations do not currently have barriers, but transit police are known to check for proof of payment and could ruin your day with a $173 fine if you do not

*SkyTrain*

produce a valid ticket, transfer or pass. The transit police are part of the SkyTrain's larger network of security initiatives, including CCTV cameras that monitor all platforms and stations, and emergency silent alarm strips and speaker phones on the trains. Cyclists can bring their bikes onboard the SkyTrain during off-peak times (avoid 07:00 to 09:00 and 16:00 to 18:00). There are bike racks at every station, and about half of the stations offer bike locker rental (see www.translink. bc.ca for more information about SkyTrain schedules, fares, routes and services).

The West Coast Express is a TransLink-run commuter train service connecting the eastern suburbs and neighbouring cities to Downtown. Via Rail passenger trains (www.viarail.ca) to the rest of Canada and Amtrak trains to the US (www.amtrak.com) arrive and depart from Pacific Central Station at Main Street and Terminal Avenue. The Rocky Mountaineer (www.rockymountaineer.com) is a luxury scenic train with trips to Whistler, the interior of BC, and over the Rockies into Alberta. It departs from its own station across the street from Pacific Central Station on Terminal Avenue.

### Trolley Good

*Trolley buses run on the city's classic bus routes, like the 5 (Robson-Downtown), the 6 (along Davie Street), the 17 (Downtown-UBC-Oak), and the 3 (Main-Downtown). The city's most important thoroughfares – Arbutus Street, Broadway Avenue, Granville Street, Oak Street, Main Street and Kingsway – are all still linked to the overhead wire grid. For more information about trolley bus routes, visit www.translink.bc.ca.*

## Tram

Vancouver is one of many cities that abandoned tram systems in the 1950s in favour of cars. However, TransLink still runs over 200 electric trolley buses on 15 city routes – the second-largest fleet in North America, after San Francisco. The trolleys are part of the regular bus network and are identical to normal buses except for the roof-top rods that connect them to overhead electrical wires, and the fact that they run cleanly and quietly (with the occasional popping and crackling sound). Fares are interchangeable with the rest of the TransLink network's buses, SkyTrain and SeaBus, at $2.50 for an adult travelling in a single zone (most of Vancouver) with a 90 minute option to transfer. An additional 228 emission-free trolley buses will be added in 2008.

## Walking

Scenic Vancouver is enjoyable to walk around – just don't forget your umbrella. The sidewalks (pavements) are safe and there are pedestrian crossings and controlled intersections to get across the roads. Walking is a great way to get around Downtown; most people who live and work on the peninsula use it as their main means of transport, while many who live in Kitsilano choose to walk to work over the Burrard Bridge into Downtown. Walking around neighbourhoods in Greater Vancouver is also easy, especially along the shopping and transportation corridors of West 4th Avenue, West Broadway, Fairview, Cambie Street, Main Street and Commercial Drive, where the streets cater to pedestrians.

On foot, depending on your fitness and determination (and whether you are carrying anything), the distances in Vancouver seem much greater, so walking is often supplemented by bicycle, bus, or car for longer than about 10 avenue blocks. In terms of safety, it is always wise to avoid walking by yourself at night in dark or isolated areas, particularly Downtown and in the Downtown Eastside (near the intersection of Main Street and Hastings Street). Generally though, walking in Vancouver is a safe and easy mode of transportation for shorter distances.

## Money

Debit cards, credit cards and cash are widely used in Vancouver. Most people use cash for smaller purchases, such as coffee and lunch, and debit and credit cards for larger amounts. US dollars are accepted in some locations (mainly tourist places), but usually at a worse exchange rate than that offered by banks.

## Local Currency

The Canadian dollar is a lot like the US dollar, but more colourful. The denominations are identical – 1 cent penny, 5 cent nickel, 10 cent dime, 25 cent quarter – but Canada has a $1 coin, called the 'loonie' after the loon, a water bird on the coin's face, rather than a note, and a $2 coin, aptly named the 'toonie'. The $5 bill is blue, the $10 bill is purple, the $20 bill is green, the $50 bill is red, and the $100 bill is brown. Thousand dollar bills have been steadily removed from circulation since 2000 to combat money laundering, and Canada has some problems with counterfitting. Many smaller stores do not accept $50 or $100 bills, and some have a bill-checking machine at the sales counter.

*Win Sum Churchill*
*Canadians were asked to vote on the name of the polar bear that appears in the centre of the 'toonie' to commemorate its 10 year anniversary in 2006. The name Churchill won over Wilbert, Makwa, Sacha, and Plouf.*

### Canada Versus America

The Canadian dollar is linked to the US dollar due to the vast amounts of trade between the countries. Canadian currency has struggled against the US dollar since the 1980s, hovering between US$0.61 to US$0.87 over the past 20 years, but has rallied recently to levels unprecedented in modern times. In November 2007, $1 peaked at US$1.10, sending Canadians flocking south of the border on shopping sprees, and buoying up the US economy. Ironically, the strong Canadian dollar has a negative impact on the country's own economy, and the Bank of Canada has been correcting the surge through interest rates. Canadian and US dollars are currently roughly on par, but everyone expects Canada to be polite and start slipping again.

## Banks

Banks are located all over the city and are easy to find in main shopping areas. They offer the best foreign exchange rates, in addition to all the regular banking, lending and insurance services. Local credit unions include VanCity and Coast

### Exchange Rates

| Foreign Currency (FC) | 1 Unit FC = $x | $1 = xFC |
| --- | --- | --- |
| Australia | 0.9 | 1.12 |
| Bahrain | 2.71 | 0.37 |
| Bangladesh | 0.01 | 67.65 |
| China | 0.14 | 7.26 |
| Croatia | 0.2 | 4.9 |
| Cyprus | 2.55 | 0.39 |
| Czech Republic | 0.06 | 17.47 |
| Denmark | 0.2 | 4.99 |
| Euro | 1.49 | 0.67 |
| Hong Kong | 0.13 | 7.68 |
| India | 0.03 | 38.72 |
| Israel | 0.26 | 3.86 |
| Japan | 0.01 | 110.34 |
| Jordan | 1.43 | 0.7 |
| Kuwait | 3.71 | 0.27 |
| Malaysia | 0.31 | 3.27 |
| Mexico | 0.09 | 10.68 |
| New Zealand | 0.8 | 1.25 |
| Norway | 0.19 | 5.33 |
| Oman | 2.65 | 0.38 |
| Pakistan | 0.02 | 60.33 |
| Philippines | 0.02 | 40.53 |
| Qatar | 0.28 | 3.59 |
| Russia | 0.04 | 24.08 |
| Saudi Arabia | 0.27 | 3.67 |
| Singapore | 0.7 | 1.42 |
| South Africa | 0.15 | 6.63 |
| South Korea | 0.001 | 912.69 |
| Sri Lanka | 0.01 | 107.38 |
| Sweden | 0.16 | 6.32 |
| Switzerland | 0.9 | 1.12 |
| Taiwan | 0.03 | 31.89 |
| Thailand | 0.03 | 29.9 |
| United Arab Emirates | 0.28 | 3.62 |
| United Kingdom | 2.08 | 0.48 |
| USA | 1.01 | 0.99 |

*\* Rates from January 2008*

Capital Savings, and national banks include Royal Bank, TD Canada Trust, CIBC, Bank of Montreal, and Scotia Bank. HSBC is well represented in Vancouver, but very few international banks have offices outside of Toronto, Canada's financial centre. Banking hours are generally 09:30 to 16:30 Monday to Friday, but they vary widely as they compete to offer better customer service. In many areas banks are now open later and on Saturdays. Non-Canadians with work visas, student visas, or permanent residency can easily obtain bank accounts and credit cards with the presentation of the correct identification. For more information on banking in Vancouver see Residents, p.62.

## ATMs

ATMs are easily found throughout Vancouver. They are attached to banks and credit union branches, in convenience stores, supermarkets, malls and gas stations. The Cirrus (MasterCard) and Plus (Visa) networks are common. HSBC and BC credit unions are part of the Exchange and Acculink network and do not charge ATM access fees to members. Similarly, Scotiabank is part of the Global ATM network and does not charge Bank of America, BNP Paribas, Barclays, Deutsche Bank, and Westpac cards. However, these networks still apply account fees and exchange rate fees. All other ATMs add on access fees from $1.50 to $3. In terms of ATM security, it is best to be aware of your surroundings and always conceal your PIN. A few high-profile scams have involved tampering with the card slot, so if you notice anything strange, report it to the bank or ATM operator.

## Exchange Centres

| | |
|---|---|
| Cash 4 Cash Currency Exchange | 604 647 2274 |
| Central Currency Exchange | 604 263 0086 |
| Gastown Currency Exchange | 604 633 0860 |
| Granville Currency Exchange | 604 609 0666 |
| Money Flow Capital | 604 684 2226 |
| Moneyway Currency Exchange | 604 648 2000 |
| Pacific Cambio Coin and Currency | 604 687 7442 |
| Thomas Cook Foreign Currency | 604 713 7341 |
| Vancouver Bullion Currency Exchange | 604 685 1008 |

## Money Exchanges

Independent money exchanges are dotted around Vancouver, with several in Gastown and Downtown on Granville Street. It is worth shopping around for the best rate, but with several in close proximity you won't have to go far. Generally these businesses do not charge commission, but some have a $1 transaction charge. They have roughly the same hours as banks, generally open 09:00 and 17:00, Monday to Friday. To find the going exchange rates before you buy or sell, visit www.xe.com.

*Swiping Swindles*

*According to an Ipsos-Reid independent survey, 17% of Canadians have been personally affected by credit or debit card fraud. Because of this, people are becoming more savvy about protecting their personal information and putting more pressure on retailers to ensure their privacy.*

## Credit Cards

Visa and MasterCard are accepted almost everywhere in Vancouver. American Express is slightly less popular. Some smaller shops and cafes have a minimum charge for debit and credit card transactions or charge a small percentage to use the system. Credit and debit cards are so pervasive now that you will very rarely find a business with a 'cash only' sign at the till. If your card is lost or stolen, contact the financial institution that issued it and have it cancelled immediately. Your card issuer's customer service phone number is usually found on the back of the card, on your account statement, and online. Be sure to notify police if you believe you have been a victim of fraud.

## Tipping

Tipping is the norm in Vancouver. A standard tip for good service is 15% of the total amount. You will be expected to tip your taxi driver, bartender, waiter, hairdresser, hotel attendants and maid. If a service charge has automatically been added to a bill in a restaurant you need not tip extra. Tips are often shared between staff members at smaller establishments, but generally your server in a restaurant will receive the majority of his or her tips, and will 'tip out' the bar and kitchen staff a portion of their tip earnings that night. Tip functions are usually present on debit and credit card systems in restaurants so you can input the tip amount and adjust your total payment.

## Newspapers & Magazines

Vancouver has two daily newspapers, *The Vancouver Sun* and *The Province*. They both cost $1 on weekdays and $1.50 at weekends and are available in self-serve stands across the city, as well as in convenience stores and supermarkets. They cover local, regional and international news supplemented by lifestyle sections and classifieds. You can also find Canada's national newspapers, the *National Post* and *The Globe and Mail*, in the same locations throughout the city. These generally have a more east coast bent, and cost $1 on weekdays and $2 for their thick weekend editions. Though Vancouver has no overt censorship issues, it is worth noting that both the *Sun* and *The Province* are owned and published by the same company, CanWest, which also publishes the *National Post* and most community newspapers in the local area.

The ubiquitous *Metro* and *24* papers are free dailies offering snippets of news, sports and entertainment. They can be found at most bus stops, SkyTrain stations, coffee shops, and under every commuter's arm. *The Vancouver Courier* is a community newspaper published four times per week featuring local news, editorials and classifieds. *The Georgia Straight* is Vancouver's favourite free news and entertainment weekly. It independently reviews local and international arts, culture and politics, and provides complete entertainment listings. It also produces the popular Best of Vancouver readers' choice annual survey, offering great insights into the city as reported by its citizens. You can pick up a copy on the street and in cafes, bars and shops all over town.

## Books

Other options **Websites** p.52

Bookstores are well stocked with photo-filled coffee table books on modern Vancouver, but few have the peculiar authenticity of prodigal son Douglas Coupland's *City of Glass*. His nostalgic photo-essay commentary lends a real insight into Vancouver, appreciated 'from the inside looking out'. Michael Kluckner's *Vancouver Remembered* contains old photos and beautiful watercolours of quainter times in the city's history prior to its rebirth after the 1986 World Expo. Pauline Johnson's collection of First Nations Legends of Vancouver describes the area's natural landmarks according to oral traditions, and Paul Yee's *Saltwater City* offers an intimate portrait of the struggles of Vancouver's Chinese immigrants and their community over the past century. *The Vancouver Stories* is an excellent volume of short tales about

*Local newspapers*

the city by local writers spanning the last century, with contributions from authors as varied as Ethel Wilson through to Douglas Coupland. *The Stanley Park Companion* by Paul Grant and Laurie Dickson provides an interesting insight into Vancouver's favourite outdoor space. Former mayor of Vancouver and premier of BC Mike Harcourt candidly describes the past decisions in regional planning and urban management that have made Vancouver what it is, and set the tone for the future, in *City Making in Paradise: Nine Decisions that Saved Vancouver*, co-written with Ken Cameron and Sean Rossiter and published in 2007. In terms of practical local guidebooks, Vancouver's Touristinfo Centre offers a free visitors' guide at its Downtown location near Canada Place (200 Burrard Street). The Vancouver Park Board also provides a free Parks and Recreation Map and Guide, and the biannual *Leisure Guide*, available at its Beach Avenue office.

## Websites

Virtually every major publication in town runs an online operation as well, but some websites stand alone. Craigslist, an international free forum phenomenon, has an incredibly popular Vancouver site (www.vancouver.craigslist.ca) connecting every facet of people's lives. You can find jobs, mates, apartments, cars, furniture and even lifestyle discussion forums at this one-stop shop. CanWest Global's www.canada.com is a prominent news and entertainment site covering all media-related topics. The City of Vancouver also has helpful sites with practical information for newcomers and long-time residents (www.city.vancouver.ca).

### Blogs

Vancouver has plenty of blogs discussing the latest media headlines, personal dilemmas and providing occasional insightful editorials on politics and culture. The www.beyondrobson.com forum leans to the provocative and political side. The www.thevancouverite.com blog spot offers sharp and self-described 'snarky' commentary. Rebecca Bollwitt's popular www.miss604.com blog has been mentioned in *Wired* magazine. For an insight into Vancouver's green movement, visit the particularly good Green Print blog at www.greenprintevents.wordpress.com.

## Websites

| Business & Industry | |
|---|---|
| www.bcbusinessmagazine.com | Website of *BC Business* monthly magazine |
| www.biv.com | Online version of *Business in Vancouver* weekly newspaper |
| www.boardoftrade.com | Official website of Vancouver's Board of Trade |
| www.city.vancouver.bc.ca/business | Guide to business licences and links to relevant sites |

| City Information | |
|---|---|
| www.canada.com/cityguides/vancouver | CanWest Media's guide to Vancouver |
| www.city.vancouver.bc.ca | City of Vancouver's official website |
| www.tourismvancouver.com | Tourism Vancouver's official website |

| Culture | |
|---|---|
| www.vancouverplus.ca | Guides to concerts, nightlife, movies and shopping |
| www.vancouveruserguide.com | Excellent site combines city info with links to entertainment |

| Directories | |
|---|---|
| www.vancouver.areaconnect.ca | Local directory of people and businesses |
| www.gvrd.com | Greater Vancouver online directory |
| www.yellowpages.ca | Business listings by type and location |

| Living & Working | |
|---|---|
| www.bcpassport.com | Covers every aspect of discovering Vancouver |
| www.vancouver.ca | City information, including a newcomer's guide |

| News & Media | |
|---|---|
| www.canada.com | Headlines and entertainment news from the CanWest Global network |
| www.cbc.ca/bc | Canadian Broadcasting Corporation's focus on British Columbia region |
| www.cknw.com | News and talk radio station website |
| www.news1130.com | All-news radio station website |

| Nightlife | |
|---|---|
| www.dose.clubzone.com | Posts nightclub event profiles and photos |
| www.clubvibes.com | Guide to Vancouver hot spots |

| Online Shopping | |
|---|---|
| www.buyitcanada.com | Extensive directory for everything from pets to wedding cakes |
| www.ebay.ca | Canada's eBay auction site |

| Other | |
|---|---|
| www.vancouver.craigslist.ca | Popular free forum for finding jobs, renting apartments, buying and selling |

*Pacific living*

## Annual Events

*English Bay*
*Bathhouse*
*January*

### Polar Bear Swim
*www.vancouver.ca/parks/events*

For a brisk start to the new year, join the Polar Bear Swim at English Bay on January 1. Vancouverites have been taking the chilly plunge since 1920, with a record 2,128 participants in 2000. If you aren't brave enough to splash around in the 6°C water of the Pacific in midwinter, you can stay warm and dry on the beach and enjoy the atmosphere, the costumes, and the impressive 100 yard Peter Pantages Memorial swim race in honour of the event's founder.

*Brackendale Art*
*Gallery*
*January*

### Brackendale Winter Eagle Festival & Count
*www.brackendaleartgallery.com/Festival*

On the first Sunday in January, scientists and volunteers gather in Brackendale (one hour north of Vancouver, near Squamish) to tally the bald eagle population of this winter salmon-feeding ground. This annual event is a great excuse to get out and explore the natural wonders in the region. Walking tours leave from the Brackendale Art Gallery (which also serves as a theatre, tea house and community centre) in the morning.

*Various Locations*
*January-February*

### Dine Out Vancouver
*www.tourismvancouver.com/visitors/dining*

More than 180 restaurants participate in Dine Out Vancouver during the last few weeks of January and beginning of February. Diners enjoy special three course set menus from the best local restaurants for $15 to $35 per person. In addition to showcasing some of Vancouver's best cuisine and BC wines, partial proceeds support local charities.

*Chinatown*
*January or February*

### Chinese New Year Festival
*www.vancouverchinatown.ca/events.html*

This popular celebration is held on the first Sunday of the lunar calendar, which can fall in January or February, and features traditional Chinese music, crafts, and activities in and around the Dr Sun Yat Sen Classical Chinese Garden. The vibrant and colourful parade through the streets of Chinatown is a definite highlight, with dragons, lions and firecrackers stealing the show.

*Granville Island*
*February*

### Winterruption
*www.coastaljazz.ca*

Winterruption is an arts and cultural weekend celebration on Granville Island showcasing local artists, musicians, writers, dancers, chefs and performers. Many of the events are free and cater to all ages.

*Roundhouse*
*Community Centre*
*March*

### Vancouver International Dance Festival
*www.vidf.ca*

This month-long event in March features workshops and cutting edge performances by international dance troupes and Vancouver's dance community at venues across the city. Many events take place at the Roundhouse Community Centre in Yaletown.

*Ross Street Temple*
*April*

### Vaisakhi Day

The Sikh New Year is celebrated in April with festivities beginning at the Ross Street Gurdwara near South East Marine Drive, the biggest Sikh temple in North America. Everyone is welcome to enjoy the parade and taste the food along Main Street's Indian neighbourhoods.

**Various Locations**
*April*

## Vancouver Sun Run
*www.sunrun.com*

More than 50,000 runners participate in the biggest 10km race in Canada, held annually on the third Sunday in April. This hugely popular event is preceded by community running clinics in the spring and has been successful for over 20 years. The picturesque race route is lined by entertainers and runs through Downtown, Stanley Park, English Bay, over Burrard Bridge, and back across the Cambie Bridge into BC Place Stadium.

**Various Locations**
*May*

## Vancouver International Marathon
*www.bmovanmarathon.ca*

The largest marathon in the country is run on the first Sunday in May. It is a Boston marathon qualifier with a scenic regulation course through the streets of Downtown, Stanley Park and Kitsilano, finishing at BC Place Stadium. You can participate as a walker, in a wheelchair, as a team relay, in a half marathon, or in an 8km run.

**Various Locations**
*May*

## New Music West
*www.newmusicwest.com*

Hundreds of emerging rock and pop bands perform at 30 venues across the city during this music festival and industry conference in mid-May. The event brings exposure to new artists and is the largest of its kind on the west coast.

**Vanier Park**
*May*

## Vancouver International Children's Festival
*www.childrensfestival.ca*

Children's entertainers from around the world converge on Vanier Park in May bringing music, theatre, stories and puppets to life. The annual event has been amusing local kids for 30 years and is put on by a non-profit society.

**Cloverdale Exhibition Grounds**
*May*

## Cloverdale Rodeo & Exhibition
*www.cloverdalerodeo.com*

Get your bronco-busting, calf-roping, bull-riding fill at the second-largest rodeo in Canada. The exhibition is a 100 year old tradition that includes an agricultural showcase and all the fun and entertainment of a county fair.

**VanDusen Botanical Garden**
*June*

## Vancouver Sun Garden Show
*www.vancouversungardenshow.com*

The VanDusen Botanical Garden on Oak Street is the site of North America's biggest open air garden show in early June. The beautifully landscaped gardens feature exhibitions, events and contests for green enthusiasts.

**Concord Pacific Place**
*June*

## Alcan Dragon Boat Festival
*www.adbf.com*

More than 180 teams race across False Creek in brightly painted Chinese canoes during the largest event of its kind in North America. Appropriate to Vancouver, the festival celebrates the dragon, the ancient Chinese deity of water, rivers and rain, and has been enjoyed for 20 years as a weekend of multicultural celebrations.

**Vancouver Art Gallery**
*June*

## National Aboriginal Day Community Celebration
*www.aboriginalday-van.com*

National Aboriginal Day promotes aboriginal art and culture in Canada. The Vancouver Art Gallery and various Downtown venues host modern and traditional music and dance performances during this First Nations community celebration.

## Francophone Summer Festival

**Vancouver Francophone Cultural Centre**
*June*

*www.lecentreculturel.com*

The Vancouver Francophone Cultural Centre sponsors this summer festival showcasing music, art and culture from Quebec, France, and other French-speaking nations, proving that Vancouver can throw a party in both official languages.

## Vancouver International Jazz Festival

**Various Locations**
*June*

*www.coastaljazz.ca*

Jazz musicians from all over the world perform over 400 concerts throughout the city during one of Vancouver's favourite festivals. This world-renowned event attracts half a million people each year during the last week of June.

## Bard On The Beach

**Vanier Park**
*June-September*

*www.bardonthebeach.org*

Vancouver's summer-long Shakespeare festival is a perennial favourite. Shakespeare's work may take centre stage, but Vancouver's natural beauty steals the show, providing a backdrop of mountains and sea views through the open-ended stage.

## Canada Day

**Canada Place**
*July*

*www.canadaplace.ca/canadaday*

The first day in July is to Canadians what 4 July is to Americans. Vancouver celebrates Canada's birthday in style with all-day entertainment at Canada Place. Highlights include Canadian bands, a 10km run, a national anthem singing contest, and a traditional citizenship ceremony. A patriotic fireworks display in Burrard Inlet caps off the night.

## Steveston Salmon Festival

**Steveston**
*July*

*www.stevestonsalmonfest.ca*

Steveston Salmon Festival is a Canada Day celebration on 1 July in Richmond's historic fishing village, 30 minutes south of Vancouver. Highlights of this community celebration include a parade, carnival rides, arts and craft fairs, and the always sold-out wild salmon barbecue.

## Vancouver Folk Music Festival

**Jericho Beach Park**
*July*

*www.thefestival.bc.ca*

This weekend of folk and world music is held in beautiful Jericho Beach Park and set among a community village with food, crafts, and children's' entertainment.

## Tour De Gastown

**Gastown**
*July*

*www.tourdegastown.com*

Tour de Gastown is an elite cycling race through historic Gastown's cobblestone streets. There are $15,000 worth of prizes on offer, and cycling celebrity Lance Armstrong is a past champion. Visitors can also enjoy the cycling-themed festival and stunt shows surrounding the main event.

## Harrison Festival Of The Arts

**Harrison Hot Springs**
*July*

*www.harrisonfestival.com*

Harrison Hot Springs, on the shores of lovely Harrison Lake two hours from Vancouver, hosts the week-long Harrison Festival of the Arts in mid-July. Visitors can enjoy concerts, workshops, exhibits, an art market and a children's day.

# Annual Events

**John Hendry Park**
*July*

## Illuminares Lantern Festival
*www.publicdreams.org*

The Illuminares Lantern Festival is an atmospheric event surrounding East Vancouver's Trout Lake on the third Sunday in July. This community-crafted neighbourhood ritual involves music and dance performances at sunset, and a glowing paper lantern procession.

**North Vancouver**
*July*

## Caribbean Days Festival
*www.ttcsbc.com*

Waterfront Park in North Vancouver sways to the rhythms of the Trinidad and Tobago Cultural Society's Caribbean Days Festival at the end of July. The event includes plenty of music, a parade, tasty food, and arts and crafts, all celebrating Caribbean culture in Canada.

**English Bay**
*July-August*

## HSBC Celebration Of Light
*www.celebration-of-light.com*

More than one million people descend on Vancouver's extensive waterfront for this spectacular international fireworks competition each summer. The show lights up the sky at 22:00 every Wednesday and Saturday night during the last week of July and the first week of August. The fireworks are launched from a barge in English Bay and are best seen from the West End, Kitsilano, Vanier Park, Burrard Bridge and West Vancouver. Bring a blanket and picnic to the beach, and get there early to stake out a spot.

**Various Locations**
*August*

## Festival Vancouver
*www.festivalvancouver.bc.ca*

Festival Vancouver fills concert halls with the best choirs, orchestras, opera singers, jazz artists and world musicians around. National and international acts treat the city to more than 50 performances during the first two weeks in August.

**Powell Street**
*August*

## Powell Street Festival
*www.powellstreetfestival.com*

The Powell Street Festival celebrates Japanese Canadian arts and culture and is one of Vancouver's oldest community festivals. Come for the amateur sumo competition and martial arts demonstrations, and stay for the great food, and arts and crafts.

**West End**
*August*

## Vancouver Pride Parade & Festival
*www.vancouverpride.ca*

Vancouver's gay, lesbian, bisexual and transgender community has been celebrating with a parade and festival for the past 30 years. Street parties spill over into the nightclubs during this hot holiday weekend in August.

**West Vancouver**
*August*

## Harmony Arts Festival
*www.harmonyarts.net*

West Vancouver's waterfront hosts the North Shore's Harmony Arts Festival during the first two weeks of August. The event features open studios, exhibitions and concerts showcasing the local arts community.

**Abbotsford Airport**
*August*

## Abbotsford International Air Show
*www.abbotsfordairshow.com*

Highlights of this popular air show include the Canadian Forces aerobatics team the Snowbirds, and the Skyhawks parachute team, F16s, warbirds – including Spitfire replicas – and aerial comedy routines involving wing walkers and other death-defying stunts.

**Hastings Park**
*August-September*

## Pacific National Exhibition

*www.pne.bc.ca*

Carnival rides, concerts, demolition derbies, petting zoos, agricultural demonstrations and fried foods have been enjoyed by generations of Vancouverites. This huge and enduring event in East Vancouver runs during the last two weeks of August and marks the end of summer on Labour Day weekend, a national holiday on the first Monday in September.

**Various Locations**
*September*

## Vancouver Fringe Festival

*www.vancouverfringe.com*

The Fringe Festival is a dynamic mix of alternative theatre and comedy consistently voted the city's best arts festival by Vancouverites in *The Georgia Straight* newspaper. The 10 day event is part of an international circuit of Fringe festivals, with performances in venues around Granville Island, Commercial Drive and Yaletown during the first two weeks of September.

*Fringe Festival*

*Dr Sun Yat Sen Classical Chinese Garden*

*Paddlers on the water*

# Annual Events

**Various Locations**
*September*

## Global ComedyFest
*www.comedyfest.com*

Vancouver's Global ComedyFest brings in the big names in Canadian and American stand-up and improv, packing multiple venues across the city for 10 days in mid-September. The event is part of the international comedy circuit and draws thousands each year.

**Dr Sun Yat Sen Classical Chinese Garden**
*September*

## Mid-Autumn Moon Festival
*www.vancouverchinesegarden.com*

Vancouver's Chinese community celebrates the Mid-Autumn Moon Festival at Dr Sun Yat Sen Classical Chinese Garden around the fall equinox. When the moon is at its brightest and fullest during this open-air harvest festival it symbolises harmony and infinity, and visitors enjoy moon cakes, mahjong, tai chi and lanterns to commemorate the annual event.

**VanCity Theatre**
*September-October*

## Vancouver International Film Festival
*www.viff.org*

The Vancouver International Film Festival is a major event in the city's calendar. More than 150,000 people watch hundreds of film screenings from over 40 countries during this popular event at the end of September and beginning of October.

**Granville Island**
*October*

## International Writers & Readers Festival
*www.writersfest.bc.ca*

The International Writers & Readers Festival is a long-running and well-respected event centred on Granville Island. It features intimate public readings and workshops and has attracted the likes of Margaret Atwood, Michael Ondaatje, JK Rowling and Salman Rushdie, among many others.

**Britannia Community Centre**
*October*

## Parade Of Lost Souls
*www.publicdreams.org*

Shrines and altars of remembrance transform Britannia Community Centre and school fields during this Halloween-like festival as an eerie parade wends its way down Commercial Drive.

**Coal Harbour & English Bay**
*December*

## Carol Ship Parade Of Lights Festival
*www.carolships.org*

Join nearly half a century of festive tradition on these sparkling cruises around the harbour, English Bay and False Creek. The waterfront is also lit up throughout December with shoreside bonfires and carol singing in Burnaby, North Vancouver and West Vancouver when the boats stop by.

**VanDusen Botanical Garden**
*December*

## Festival Of Lights
*www.vandusengarden.org*

VanDusen Botanical Garden is illuminated with thousands of tiny bulbs during the Christmas season's Festival of Lights. Take a stroll through the park in the evening to enjoy holiday-themed displays and visits from Santa Claus.

**Stanley Park**
*December*

## Bright Nights
*www.city.vancouver.bc.ca/parks/events*

Visitors can support BC Professional Fire Fighters' Burn Fund charity by visiting Stanley Park's Bright Nights event in December. Ride the mini-train through a twinkling winter wonderland, and enjoy roasted chestnuts in the Children's Farmyard.

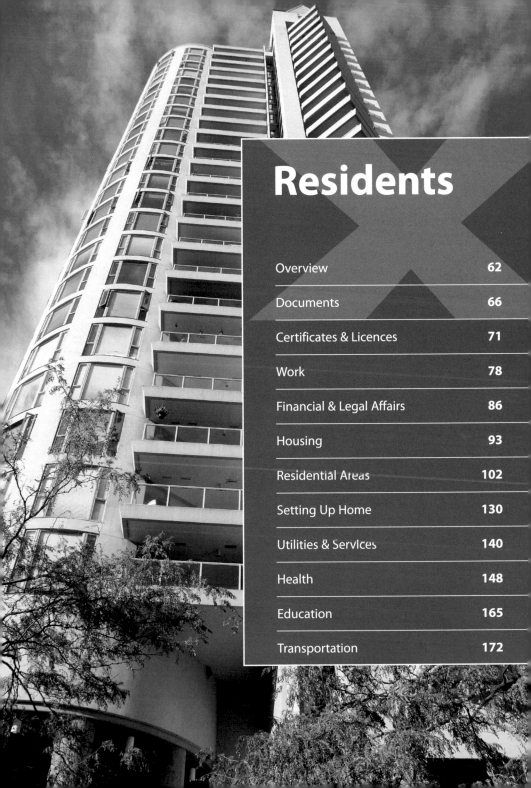

# Residents

# Residents

**Beautiful BC** ◄

*Lush forests, sweeping mountainscapes, undulating vineyards, deep fjords, and even a 'pocket' desert, comprise the geographic diversity of British Columbia. It is a massive province, encompassing a whopping 925,000 square kilometres of land (England could fit into BC seven times). Though there's plenty of room for people seeking wide-open spaces, about half of BC's four million residents live in Metro Vancouver, which is comprised of 22 separate municipalities.*

*Downtown*

## Overview

Vancouver isn't known for glitz and glamour, but rather for its diverse population of immigrants, top-notch cuisine, profound natural beauty, and the virtually limitless recreational opportunities right on its doorstep. Hemmed in by the Strait of Georgia and the Coast Mountains, Canada's most populated west coast city has earned a reputation – and deservedly so – for its laidback 'left-coast' lifestyle. Sure, there's a healthy mix of wacky politics (you can vote for the Marijuana Party), coffee swillers and GORE-TEX-clad outdoor types in this city of 600,000 (2.24 million in Greater Vancouver), but this youthful and sometimes idealistic locale is growing into its cosmopolitan side as it prepares to host the world during the 2010 Winter Olympic Games. With a skilled labour shortage and record levels of employment, Vancouver's doors are wide open, making it an ideal time to head west to this emerging city.

## Considering Vancouver

If you're ready to pull up stakes, immerse yourself in the outdoors and acquire an addiction to caffeine and sushi, then Vancouver is for you. You'll soon know whether you're ready to settle in and embrace the laidback pace for the long term, or if itchy feet will lead you to a city with a heartbeat that's a little less lethargic.

Time and again, Vancouver has been touted as one of the world's most liveable cities because of its cultural diversity, good access to healthcare and education, natural environment, political stability, low crime rates and excellent infrastructure.

Despite the city's casual atmosphere, Vancouverites work hard to afford a lifestyle that involves $4 per-day latte habits, skyrocketing real estate prices and increasing transportation gridlock. But when it comes to worldwide cost-of-living comparisons, Vancouver ranked 89th in 2007, making it a bargain for expats from pricier cities abroad, especially those from Pacific Rim cities such as Seoul, Tokyo and Hong Kong.

Vancouver's densely populated Downtown and beachfront Kitsilano neighbourhoods are the preferred places to live, but can be out of reach if you're earning the minimum wage ($8 per hour). If you have skills to offer or are entrepreneurial, you can make your mark. Before you wing your way out west though, it is best to see if

you can secure a job offer first, which is the easiest way to gain entry to the country. If you want to stay permanently, there are many ways to do so, but it can take time and some ingenuity.

## Before You Arrive

The vacancy rate in Downtown Vancouver is very low, so it's a good idea to at least have a temporary place to stay before you arrive. Most rentals only require a month-to-month lease, or you may be able to sublet until you get settled in.

**Documents** – gather all necessary identification and documentation for you and your family members (birth certificates, passports, job offers), especially if they also plan to work or to attend school.

**Visa** – apply for a temporary resident visa and work permit to gain entry into the country (p.66).

**Finances** – make sure your finances are in order, and find out if leaving your home country has implications for pensions, taxes or other investments.

**Address** – arrange to have your mail forwarded to your new address or set up a temporary mailbox until you get settled in.

**Work** – find out which industries have a critical labour shortage in BC (see p.78), as these are your best options for gaining a work permit quickly.

**Schools and daycare centres** – understand the requirements and restrictions for international students before trying to enrol your kids in school (see Education, p.165). Daycare is expensive and can be difficult to come by, so it's a good idea to secure a spot before you arrive.

**Medical** – it is best to bring any prescriptions and medication with you. You may not be eligible for coverage under the provincial plan for a couple of months, so look into travel insurance if your home country's coverage isn't sufficient.

**Belongings** – some local companies will receive the items that you shipped and store them for you until you're ready to move in (see p.130).

## When You Arrive

Now that you've arrived, it's a good idea to get that bureaucratic red tape out of the way so that you can start exploring and enjoying your new home. Most government offices are open weekdays from 08:30 to 16:30 and many have comprehensive websites, so do your homework and start gathering forms and information before you visit the offices.

**Consulate** – no matter how long you decide to stay, it's a good idea to register with your home country's consulate in case of emergency.

**Social Insurance Number (SIN)** – before you can be permitted to start work, your employer will require a SIN from you, so get the paperwork under way if you haven't already (see p.68).

**Accommodation** – if you plan to rent, the best time to look for a place is at the end of the month. Skip the newspapers, though, and walk or drive around and look for vacancy signs instead. The good places go quickly and don't need to advertise in the paper.

### Immigration Services & Advice

| | | |
|---|---|---|
| Affiliation of Multicultural Societies & Service Agencies of BC | 604 718 2780 | www.amssa.org |
| Immigrant Services Society of British Columbia | 604 684 7498 | www.issbc.org |
| Multilingual Orientation Service Association for Immigrant Communities (MOSAIC) | 604 254 9626 | www.mosaicbc.com |
| Pacific Immigrant Resources Society | 604 298 5888 | www.pirs.bc.ca |
| S.U.C.C.E.S.S. | 604 684 1628 | www.successbc.ca |

**Utilities** – whether you've bought a place or continue to rent, contact local utility companies to set up electricity, heating, internet and cable television. Many apartment rentals include heating and hot water, and sometimes cable, in the monthly rate.

**Language** – if your English isn't strong, brush up on your skills at one of the many local language schools (see p.307).

**Driving licence** – convert your licence if you're eligible, or explore options to get a BC driving licence if you plan to stay for longer than six months.

**Explore the outdoors** – it is exciting to venture into BC's backcountry, but it's not a good idea to go alone. Join a local club or team and meet like-minded people so you can share the thrill together.

*En Route*

*Even if you're just passing through Canada en route to another country and plan to stay for less than 48 hours, you'll still need to apply for a transit visa and provide proof of your travel plans. Make sure to arrange this before you fly out. Simply fill in and submit a TRV form to the visa office responsible for your area before you leave your home country; there's no fee.*

## Essential Documents

Before you leave home, photocopy all essential documents and keep a copy or two in a safe place; you never know when they'll come in handy. Photographic identification is frequently needed so keep your passport and other relevant documents with you (such as Social Insurance Number, certificates, and driving licence) when applying for government services. It makes good sense to keep these other essentials close at hand:

- Birth certificates for all family members
- Marriage certificate
- Driving licence
- Prescriptions for medication and glasses or contact lenses
- Bank account information (including credit and bank cards); you may need to provide proof of your ability to support yourself or family
- Work permits and job offer letters, if applicable
- University, college or technical school certificates and transcripts (for children, too)
- Insurance papers
- Children's school records
- Pet vaccination forms and certificates signed by a licensed veterinarian

## When You Leave

Once you're ready to pack up your things and say goodbye to friends and colleagues, make sure that you've tied up any loose ends, including:

**Utilities** – leave a forwarding address in case you're due a refund for pro-rated payments.

**Rent** – get your half-month damage deposit back, with interest, and make sure you're not charged for 'wear and tear' (such as nail holes and paint nicks).

**Furniture and household goods** – have a weekend garage sale; tape signs to telephone poles and set up shop on a pavement or grassy area. Otherwise, donate unwanted items to some of the local charity groups in need.

**Shipping** – send the big stuff home first, so it has plenty of time to arrive before you need it. Then, enjoy that last bite of Vancouver's bargain-priced sushi at one of your favourite haunts.

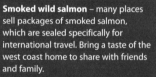

### Gifts For Home

**Smoked wild salmon** – many places sell packages of smoked salmon, which are sealed specifically for international travel. Bring a taste of the west coast home to share with friends and family.

**Ice wine** – frozen grapes are pressed to make the Okanagan Valley's decadent ice wines, with Riesling a popular choice.

**Aboriginal art** – bring back an authentic carving, paddle or mask fashioned by one of the many BC artisans that practice traditional art.

**Pure maple syrup** – though it's not made in BC, a maple-leaf-shaped bottle or old-fashioned can of maple syrup is a quintessentially Canadian gift.

# Are you always taking the wrong turn?

Whether you're a map person or not, these pocket-sized marvels will help you get to know the city – and its limits.

## Explorer Mini Maps
Fit the city in your pocket

# Documents

Canada was built on the skills and hard work of immigrants, and that sentiment holds true today, now perhaps more than ever before. With British Columbia's estimated labour shortage of 350,000, changes have been made to various policies and legislation to make working and living here easier. Sure, there are still a number of hoops to jump through, forms to fill out and general bureaucracy to endure, but many people, especially skilled workers, will find the welcome mat rolled out once they start a new life in Canada, whether temporary or permanent.

## Entry Visa

*Entry Denied*

*If you're not in good health, can't prove that you have enough money to support your stay, or you've been convicted of a crime in your home country, you might be refused entry into Canada. Many people, including high-profile American rap artists, and domestic diva Martha Stewart, have been turned back at the border thanks to their criminal convictions.*

If you're one of the 35 million people who head to Canada each year to work, study or visit as a tourist, you'll need to apply for a Temporary Resident Visa (TRV) before you arrive, unless your home country is on Canada's visa waiver list. When you enter, your passport must be valid for the period of your stay, so it's a good idea to have it renewed if it's going to expire within six months. If you don't have the proper documents or if you violate the conditions of your permit once you're here, you'll be asked to leave the country.

You'll find the forms that you'll need (see options below) at a Canadian visa office (high commission, embassy or consulate) in your home country. It is important that you include all relevant documentation so your application isn't rejected because it's incomplete. If you decide you want to stay longer once you've settled in, you can change or extend your visa; just make sure you do so before it expires (by filling in form IMM 1249E). All forms can be downloaded from the Citizenship and Immigration Canada website (www.cic.gc.ca). To speak to someone, call the office toll-free (1 888 242 2100) from anywhere in Canada, Monday to Friday between 08:00 and 16:00.

### Temporary Resident Visa (IMM 5257)

If you plan to visit Canada and your country is not on the waiver list (see Visa Waiver List, opposite), you'll need to apply for a temporary resident visa (TRV). You will then need to provide a reason for your visit, two valid passport photos, and the fee ($75 for single entry or $150 for multiple entry). It can take about a month for your request to be processed by your local embassy and there's a chance that a visa officer will want to interview you first, or ask you to prove that you have enough money to support your visit (and return home). You can apply for TRVs for your spouse, common-law partner or children on the same form; the fee for a family application is $400. Keep in mind that each person will need to meet the same TRV requirements.

A TRV is usually valid for six months, but unfortunately it doesn't guarantee entry into Canada. Once you arrive, an immigration officer can still reject you if your paperwork is incomplete, if your circumstances have changed since you applied for the TRV or if you weren't truthful on your application. Be prepared to convince the officer that you'll actually leave the country when the time comes for you to do so. If you decide you want to stay in Canada permanently, you can apply for a resident visa at any time if you meet the qualifications (see Residence Visas on p.68).

### Temporary Work Permit (IMM 1295)

An estimated 90,000 foreign workers come to Canada each year to find temporary employment, and most people require a work permit. If you're one of the lucky ones who can take advantage of Canada's labour shortage, you might be able to move ahead in the line and get a permit quicker (see Working in Vancouver, p.78). You can still apply for permanent residency once you arrive, which can be easier to attain when you already have a job and a solid source of income.

You can apply for a work permit either before you arrive in Canada or once you're here (you must have a TRV that's valid for six months or more to apply for a temporary work permit), but you must prove you have a job offer from a Canadian employer. That prospective employer may need to get a Labour Market Opinion (LMO) from Human Resources and Social Development Canada (www.hrsdc.gc.ca), which confirms that the company has been permitted to hire a foreign worker. This is part of a 'Canadians first' policy that ensures citizens have the first crack at the job market. You'll need to fill out an application form, prove that you have enough money to support yourself and your family, pay a $150 fee, and be able to convince a visa officer that you'll pack up and leave the country once your work permit expires.

**Calling The Government**
Call Enquiry BC on 604 660 2421 for quick, free access to provincial government information and services. You can also ask to be connected directly to government offices anywhere in the province (many head offices are in Victoria), which will save you the long-distance charge. There's a similar call centre line for federal government services (such as getting a visa, work permit and Social Insurance Number). Just call 1 800 O Canada (1 800 622 6232).

## Spouses, Common-Law Partners & Children

If you already have a work permit, your spouse, common-law partner and children may be able to work in Canada. They will, however, each need to apply for their own work permit and satisfy the same requirements. In general, the skills and education required for you to do your job must fall into a skill category defined by the National Occupational Classification (NOC) before you can qualify. For example, the NOC classification for physicians, dentists and registered nurses fall under Major Group 31 (the '3' designates this as a health occupation) and these jobs are categorised as skill level A professions. Level A professions usually require university education, while professions that fall under the skill level C classification usually require secondary school and/or occupation-specific training. The NOC number given to a specific job is generally four digits (a specialist physician is 3111, while a dentist is 3113).

## Health Requirements

Those who plan to visit Canada for more than six months will have to provide a medical certificate if they are from, or have travelled extensively to, a place that's on Canada's designated country and territory list. The certificate must be from an authorised medical practitioner and should prove that you don't have a mental disorder or chronic illness that could endanger the health of Canadian citizens, or make you a significant burden on the healthcare system. Your temporary resident visa form will include additional questions that will specify whether you or your family members have had tuberculosis (or have been in contact with someone who has) in the past two years. Visit Citizenship and Immigration Canada's website (www.cic.gc.ca) to find a list of designated countries and territories and a searchable list of approved medical practitioners worldwide.

## Study Permit (IMM 1294)

If you plan to enrol in a programme of study that's going to take at least six months to complete, you'll need to apply for a study permit, which involves filling in an application form from Citizenship

### Visa Waiver List

If you're visiting Canada as a student, tourist or temporary worker and you're a citizen of one of the many countries on Canada's visa waiver list you don't need to apply for a temporary resident visa (but you may still need to get a study or work permit). Once you arrive, a Canada Border Services Officer will ask to see your identification (a valid passport or travel document and work or study permits, if applicable), stamp your passport (the stamp is valid for six months) and ask you some general questions.

The list includes some members of the EU and former British colonies, British and US citizens, and those who can prove they are lawfully permitted to reside in the US for permanent residence. Since the list is subject to change at any time, it is best to check if your country features by visiting the Citizenship & Immigration Canada website (www.cic.gc.ca).

and Immigration Canada (you can download one from its website, www.cic.gc.ca), paying a $125 fee (this includes the TRV, you don't need to apply separately or pay an additional fee), providing two photos, a medical form, the original letter of acceptance from the university or college you plan to attend, along with other details such as tuition costs and living costs and expenses.

**Work permits for students** – if you're going to college, university or another educational institution and decide to get a job, you may need to get a work permit. Guidelines vary depending on whether you plan to work on or off campus or in your field of study. To find out if you need to apply for a work permit, check out the requirements on Citizenship and Immigration Canada's website (www.cic.gc.ca). Click the 'studying in Canada' link on the left.

**Young worker programmes** – Canada has a variety of programmes designed to enable young travellers to work for six to twelve months. The Working Holiday Programme, Student Work Abroad Programme (SWAP) and various young worker's exchange programmes are generally for those between 18 and 30, depending on which country you're from. In most cases, you'll need to have employment prearranged before you qualify. For general information, visit WorkBC's website (www.workbc.com). Note that requirements vary from programme to programme and country to country, so it's best to contact the Canadian high commission or embassy in your home country for comprehensive details.

## Residence Visa

More than a million people arrived in Canada between 2001 and 2006 to start new lives. In recent years the majority of immigrants (60%) came from countries in Asia and the Middle East, but European immigration (16%) was also significant. An estimated 70,000 made their new homes in Metro Vancouver. If you're a skilled worker and want to move to Vancouver permanently, the chances are you'll be successful. There are many avenues – some less circuitous than others – through which you can apply to become a permanent resident.

### Social Insurance Number

If you plan to work in Canada, you must apply for a Social Insurance Number (SIN) by filling out a form and providing some basic details, including a document that proves your status in Canada (such as a citizenship card, permanent resident card, work permit or study permit). There is no fee, and you can download the form from Service Canada's website (www.servicecanada.gc.ca). It is a good idea to apply in person at a Service Canada office if you can; there's one in the Sinclair Centre (757 West Hastings Street) or phone 1 800 206 7218. The centre is open on Mondays from 08:00 to 15:00 and Tuesday to Friday from 08:30 to 16:00. Peak hours are from 12:00 to 15:00, so it's a good idea to arrive early.

### Permanent Resident Card (IMM 5444)

By becoming a permanent resident of Canada, you and your family members will enjoy almost all the benefits and services afforded to citizens. If you want to travel outside the country, though, you'll need a permanent resident card to gain re-entry.

If you have applied for immigration in one of the ways outlined above, you'll be issued with a permanent resident card as part of the immigration process (once you're accepted). You'll need to pay a $490 fee (protected persons are exempt) and the card will be mailed to you within a month of your arrival in Canada. If you're already working or studying in Canada, you will need to fill out an application form detailing your education and work history for the past five years, provide two passport photos (one signed by a guarantor) and pay a $50 processing fee before mailing your application

**Accepting Visitors**
*Friends or family members visiting from home countries that are not on Canada's visa waiver list might need to find a Canadian visa office in their home country and apply for a visa before they arrive. The process can be tricky, but you can help by providing them with a letter of invitation. You'll need to include many details, such as the purpose of their visit and where they'll be staying, along with information on your own status and occupation. Some countries are considered to be at 'high risk' of violating Canada's visa rules, hence the strict requirements.*

to the PR Card Processing Centre. Once you qualify you'll need to pay the $490 fee before your card will be mailed to you.

## Protected Persons (IMM 5202)

Many refugees come to Canada to start a new life in the safe confines of a democratic country. But if you're here without permission, you could be deported. If you plan to apply for permanent residency as a protected person (refugee) or protected temporary resident, you must do so right away either at a point of entry (an airport or border) or at a Citizenship and Immigration Canada office. Generally speaking, you may be eligible under Canada's Immigration and Refugee Protection Act if you cannot return home for fear of persecution based on your religious or political beliefs, race or sexual orientation, or if you risk torture or even death. The Immigration and Refugee Board of Canada (www.irb-cisr.gc.ca) and Citizenship and Immigration Canada will review your claim, but the process can take up to a year. You can stay in Canada during this time, and are free to apply for a resident visa under one of the programmes below. You'll have to pay a fee of $550 for your application, plus additional costs for anyone accompanying you. While you're waiting for the outcome, you can apply for work or study permits.

**Dual Intent** ◀

*Applying for a resident visa can take a long time, so some people apply for a temporary work or study permit at the same time. This is called 'dual intent', and although it's legal, you must leave Canada after your visit or work permit expires unless you renew it.*

## Family Class (IMM 1344A, IMM 1344B)

Once you're a permanent resident of Canada and have a valid permanent resident card, you can sponsor your relatives, but you'll have to agree to support them financially for a period of three to 10 years. Spouses (including those of the same sex), common-law partners, conjugal partners and children qualify for sponsorship (they are classified as Family Class). Each person you sponsor will need to apply to become a permanent resident. You can also sponsor parents, grandparents and adult siblings, but the requirements are slightly different. There is a range of fees that you'll have to pay: $75 for yourself as the sponsor, as well as between $75 and $150 for family members under 22 and between $475 and $550 for family members over 22 who are married or in a common-law relationship.

## Citizenship (CIT 0002)

Once you've become a permanent resident, you may be eligible to apply to become a fully fledged Canadian citizen and exercise your right to vote during elections. There are some basic requirements, but the process is fairly straightforward. Just be prepared to brush up on your knowledge of Canada – you will be tested.

Anyone over 18 who has been a resident of Canada and has spent at least three of the past four years – the equivalent of 1,095 days – living anywhere in Canada is eligible to apply for citizenship. You'll need to fill out a form, provide proof of permanent residence, two passport photos (one signed by a guarantor), pay a $200 fee and send everything to Citizenship and Immigration Canada's Case Processing Centre.

If you qualify, you'll have to take a test and prove your proficiency in either English or French (Canada's two official languages). A citizenship judge may also interview you. If all goes well you'll then be invited to a ceremony where you and other participants will take an oath of citizenship (and you'll probably have to sing the national anthem, *O Canada*).

Citizenship only applies to the individual who has applied and not, for example, the rest of their family. Canada allows its citizens to have multiple citizenships, but some countries (the Netherlands, for example) require you to relinquish your citizenship once you acquire a foreign nationality. It is a good idea to find out your home country's rules before you apply for Canadian citizenship.

*Types Of Work Visas*

**Federal Skilled Worker Class – Simplified (IMM 0008SW)** If you meet certain professional or technical skill requirements and have worked full time for at least a year, you can apply to become a permanent resident in Canada before you move. Your job's National Occupational Classification (NOC) must be a specific skill type (skill level O, A or B) in order for you to qualify (see Work Permits for Spouses, Common-law Partners & Children on p.67).

*Permanent Residents*

*Becoming a permanent resident gives you a number of rights in Canada, but also some responsibilities. To keep your status as a permanent resident, you must live in Canada for a minimum of two years within a five-year period. If your pass expires while you're away, you can renew it at a Canadian visa office.*

Most people use the simplified application process, which involves filling in several forms. You can download the application kit, which includes a guide (Application for Permanent Residence: Federal Skilled Worker Class Simplified Application Process – IMM ESAP7000) and forms (Application for Permanent Residence in Canada – IMM 0008SW and Use of a Representative – IMM 5476) from the Citizenship and Immigration Canada website (www.cic.gc.ca), or pick one up at a visa office in your home country.

Your suitability is assessed using a points system (you will need to score a minimum of 67 out of 100 points) that takes your skills, experience, age and language abilities into consideration. Your family members are also considered, whether they are accompanying you or not, along with your ability to support yourself and your family financially. You must provide two photos of yourself and any family members accompanying you, information on your finances, and possibly a police certificate (as part of criminal records and security checks), and have a medical examination. You will also have to pay a $550 fee for yourself, plus $550 for your spouse, common-law partner or dependant child over 22 ($150 for children 22 and under).

**Federal Skilled Worker Class – Regular Application (IMM 0008)** If you have already arranged employment in Canada, or have been living in Canada for more than a year, you must apply for permanent residence using the regular application process, which is very similar to the simplified process outlined above. The requirements and points assessment still applies, but having prearranged employment can give you an extra 10 points. You also may be able to bypass the financial requirements. Fees and most requirements (such as photos and medical certificates) are as outlined above.

**Provincial Nominee Program (PNP) (IMM 0008)** This programme is designed to fast-track the process of filling labour shortages in Canada's various provinces and territories with skilled workers and entrepreneurs. In order to apply, you'll need to find an employer or 'nominee' that will submit a joint application under the PNP. The province that nominates you will send a certificate of provincial nomination directly to the visa office. Then you'll need to apply to Citizenship and Immigration Canada to become a permanent resident, providing medical and police certificates and clearances, two photos of yourself (and any accompanying family members), information on your finances and pay a $550 fee for yourself, as well as $550 for

*A New Canadian*

*If you're a resident, but not a citizen, and you have a baby in Canada, the baby is automatically a Canadian citizen (see Birth Certificate & Registration on p.74).*

your spouse, common-law partner or dependent child over 22 ($150 for children 22 and under). To find out more about BC's programme, visit the Ministry of Economic Development website (www.ecdev.gov.bc.ca) and select 'Provincial Nominee Program' from the menu on the left.

**Business Class (IMM 0008BU)** If you're self-employed, a business entrepreneur or business investor, you can apply to be a permanent resident, but you'll need to show how you'll contribute financially to Canada's economy. There are various criteria, points systems and financial requirements you'll need to meet. An investor, for example, must have a minimum net worth of $800,000, while an entrepreneur must have a net worth of $300,000. The definition of a 'self-employed person' strangely only applies to people who can support themselves by participating in cultural activities (such as music or fine arts), world-class athletics or buying and managing a farm. The primary applicant will need to pay a $1,050 fee, plus $550 for each additional applicant.

## Driving Licence

Other options **Transportation** p.172

If you plan to spend most of your time in Vancouver's Downtown core and nearby neighbourhoods, public transport is a reliable way to get around. Once you want to go further afield, driving becomes the best option, especially if you can take advantage of the city's innovative car-sharing programmes.

You have to be at least 16 to get a driving licence in BC. It can either be a quick and easy process or a complicated endeavour, depending on where you're from and how long you've been driving. BC has agreements with a handful of jurisdictions, so with the proper identification, a valid licence and a bit of paperwork, you can be on the road in no time.

You must carry your licence with you whenever you drive. If you're stopped by police and fail to produce it when asked you can be fined ($80). If you get caught driving without a valid licence, expect a fine ($138) and three driver penalty points (DPPs). Those points translate into fines that have to be paid before you can renew your annual car insurance. Once you have accumulated four or more points in a 12 month period your licence may be suspended (the 'assessment period' applies to DPPs accumulated during the 12 month period that ends five months before your birthday; for example, if your birthday is 7 June, in 2008 your DPPs are calculated from 7 January 2007 to 7 January 2008).

Driver licensing is regulated by the Insurance Corporation of BC (ICBC). Laws and regulations are complicated and they have changed drastically in recent years, so it's a good idea to check with ICBC at one of its offices, or online (www.icbc.com) for the latest information and office locations.

BC has driving licence exchange agreements with other Canadian provinces and territories, the United States, Britain, Austria, Germany, Switzerland, Japan and South Korea. But these are dependent on the type or class of licence you have, and you must have had a full-privilege licence for two years. If you meet these guidelines you can get a full-privilege Class 5 licence to drive a passenger vehicle. You'll need to bring three documents to an ICBC driver licensing office to apply for a BC licence:

**Driving licence** – must be either in date or expired less than three years ago. If your licence isn't printed in English you'll need to provide a translated version. Contact the Society of Translators and Interpreters of British Columbia (604 684 2940, www.stibc.org) to access a directory of professional translators. Costs vary, but, on average, same-day translation services cost $50.

**Primary identification** – should show your legal name and date of birth (such as a Canadian citizenship certificate, Permanent Resident Card, study or work visa).

**Secondary identification** – virtually any card that shows your full name and signature (including a passport, bank card or birth certificate).

Once you've gathered the relevant documents, applying for a driving licence is relatively cheap ($31) and pretty easy. Simply fill out some forms, answer some general road-safety questions, take an eye test, and respond to some basic questions regarding your medical fitness. Someone will take your photo at the office and then you just have to sign the documents and pay your fee. In the space of an hour, you're set to drive. Your licence is valid for two years, but once it expires it can be renewed for $75 at any ICBC driver licensing office for a period of five years.

If you're registered at one of the designated institutions as a full-time student, or if you're visiting BC for six months or less, your current driving licence allows you to drive anywhere in the province, even if your home country is not on the exchange agreement. But once you decide to stay longer, you'll need to get a BC driving licence.

## Need Some Direction?

The Explorer Mini Maps pack a whole city into your pocket and once unfolded are excellent navigational tools for exploring. Not only are they handy in size, with detailed information on the sights and sounds of the city, but also their fabulously affordable price means they won't make a dent in your holiday fund. Wherever your travels take you, from Europe to the Middle East and beyond, grab a mini map and you'll never have to ask for directions again.

*Driving Test*

Experienced drivers (meaning recent learners who have more than 24 months full-privilege driving; see below), and those from areas that are not included on the licence exchange agreement, who would like to obtain a BC licence need to pass a written knowledge test, which will cost $15, and a driving test ($50). You'll have to have your eyes tested (no appointment is necessary; it's done at the office), and you will be asked some questions to determine if you are medically able to drive a car or ride a motorcycle.

You don't need to make an appointment to take the knowledge test; just go to an ICBC driver licensing office. The test is multiple choice. To pass you must answer 40 of the 50 questions correctly. If your English isn't that proficient you can also take the test in French, Arabic, Cantonese, Croatian, Farsi, Mandarin, Punjabi, Russian, Spanish or Vietnamese. Though the test will only take you about 30 minutes to complete, it can be tricky (especially for drivers with bad habits), so brush up beforehand by reading ICBC's RoadSense for Drivers guide. You can pick one up at any ICBC office, or read it online (www.icbc.com). Once you pass the knowledge test, you need to make an appointment with ICBC for a driving test. You can book it online or on 604 661 2255. During the Class 5 road test you'll be asked to execute certain manoeuvres, which may include parallel parking, changing lanes and reversing. The examiner who accompanies you may also ask you to name any hazards that you encounter, such as an obstacle, or children crossing the street. And, of course, you'll be tested on your steering and ability to keep to the speed limit. Once the test is over, the examiner will let you know if you have passed. If you were successful, you can fill in the paperwork, pay your $50 fee (plus an additional $17 for your licence if it will take over six months to expire, or $75 if it will take less) and you're ready to drive away with your Class 5 driving licence. If you fail, you can take the test again, but you'll need to wait for at least seven days and pay the test fee once again. If you fail a second time, you'll need to wait 14 days before trying again.

New drivers (those who have never driven or have less than 24 months full-privilege driving) and people who haven't held a full-privilege driving licence are subject to the

*Lots of cars, lots of parking*

province's stringent Graduated Licensing Program (GLP). GLP involves passing a learner's stage and novice stage, each with driving restrictions. It can take up to 36 months before you can even take the driving test to obtain a full-privilege Class 5 licence.

Getting a learner's licence is pretty easy. You'll need to pass a written knowledge test first ($10). If you fail the test, you can try again the next day (and pay the fee again). If you pass, you'll need to have your vision tested and answer some medical questions. Afterwards, someone will take your photo and you'll be issued with a temporary learner's licence ($10) that's valid until your photo licence arrives in the mail – about a week later. A learner's licence offers some mobility, but there are many restrictions. You can only drive between 05:00 and midnight, and a licensed driver who's at least 25 years of age

## Driving Schools

| | | | |
|---|---|---|---|
| Alex's Driving School | 569 East 22nd Av | Fraser | 604 512 8008 |
| Alpha Driving School | 4-4424 Main St | Fraser | 604 808 7997 |
| Broadway Driving School (Young Drivers Of Canada) | 201-1690 West Broadway | Mount Pleasant | 604 739 0329 |
| Carmel Driving School | 3275 East 46th Av | Killarney | 604 439 9168 |
| Excellent Driving School | 1841 East Hastings St | Strathcona | 604 216 6718 |
| Fraser Driving School | 1662 East 12th Av | Main | 604 454 9337 |
| Johnston's Driving School | 101-4867 Main St | Fraser | 604 875 6026 |
| Loyal Driving School | 5644 Melbourne St | Collingwood | 604 432 9433 |
| New Drivers Driving School | 1778 Upland Dr | Victoria | 604 671 8130 |
| Vantek Driving School | 719 East 18th Av | Main | 604 872 6886 |

must accompany you at all times. You must also display the 'L' learner's sign on your vehicle and you have a zero blood-alcohol content when driving. After driving safely for 12 months you can take your first road test ($35), which involves performing various manoeuvres (such as changing lanes, parking and merging into traffic) and get a novice permit ($75), which is valid for five years. During the novice stage, you'll face three restrictions: you must display the 'N' novice sign on your vehicle at all times, maintain a zero blood-alcohol content, and you can only carry one passenger (unless a supervisor is with you who holds a valid Class 1-5 licence and is over 25). Once you qualify for a Class 5 driving licence you have full privileges and the restrictions mentioned above are lifted. If you take driver training from an ICBC GLP-approved programme at this stage, you can shave six months off the 24 month novice training period. You must complete a combination of 32 hours of driving and classroom instruction before you take your final road test, and this costs between $800 and $1,000. To find a GLP-qualified driver training school go to www.dtcbc.com.

### Motorcycle Licence

If you already have a valid BC driving licence, you still need to apply for a Class 6 motorcycle licence (which takes at least 30 days, or longer), unless you plan to drive a limited speed motorcycle (a 55cc motor scooter or moped). You'll need to provide identification (see Driving Licence, p.71), fill in some forms and pass a written motorcycle knowledge test ($15). Once you pass, fill out the appropriate forms, pay a licensing fee ($10) and you'll be issued with a motorcycle learner's licence, which is valid for one year. There are many restrictions, but after a minimum of 14 days you can take the motorcycle skills test. Once you pass and you've had your learner's licence for at least 30 days, you're eligible to take your final road test, which costs $50. You then qualify for a full-privilege Class 6 motorcycle licence, which costs $50 and is valid for five years.

If you don't have a valid BC driving licence you'll need to take the longer graduated licensing route and apply for a learner's licence (as described above) and, later, a novice licence (Class 8), before finally qualifying for a full privilege Class 6 motorcycle licence a minimum of 24 months later. The fees are the same as those for the passenger vehicle GLP programme outlined above.

# Birth Certificate & Registration

In Canada, roughly 106 boys are born for every 100 girls. The law requires every birth to be registered. British Columbia is one of only two provinces in Canada that has a Newborn Registration Service, which gives parents a convenient way to register a birth, obtain a birth certificate, and apply for the child's Social Insurance Number (SIN).

The process is straightforward. The Registration of Live Birth form is included in a birth package given to parents at the hospital. You can also download the form from the internet (www.vs.gov.bc.ca) or pick one up at the Vital Statistics Agency Downtown (605 Robson Street, 604 660 2937) weekdays from 08:30 to 16:30.

Fill in the form and submit it to the Vital Statistics Agency within 30 days of the child's birth. If the child's father isn't registered on the form, the mother must state the reason and in some cases she may need to sign a legal declaration. In these instances, a co-parent can be registered on the form instead. In BC, same-sex partners can be co-parents. A co-parent is defined as an individual who is in a spouse-like relationship with the mother of the child, but isn't the child's father. The mother and co-parent must have agreed to be the parents of the child.

When filling out the registration form, you can apply for the child's SIN at the same time. Although it's not required, the child's SIN allows parents to access government benefits and services. Any child born in Canada automatically becomes a Canadian citizen regardless of the nationality of the parents. The parents do not need to apply for residency. The child can be a dual citizen in Canada, however its home country may not recognise dual citizenship.

You can then apply for your child's birth certificate. Fill in and mail the application form, along with a $27 fee, to the provincial Vital Statistics Agency. This form can also be found online or picked up from the Vital Statistics Agency. Your child's birth certificate is a crucial form of identification and you'll need it in order to get a passport for them.

If you plan to fly anywhere, it's recommended that your children have their own passports. You can download a form from the internet (www.passportcanada.gc.ca), pick one up at Vancouver's passport office located Downtown in the Sinclair Centre (757 W Hastings Street, www.sinclaircentre.com), or at any Canada Post office (www.canadapost.ca). Make sure you have the correct form. If your child is under 16 years of age, you must apply for a passport on their behalf using the PPTC 155 form (note that children 11 or older must sign their own passport). Children 16 and older use the same form as adults, PPTC 153.

You can apply for a passport by mail, but it's quicker to apply in person and you'll have the opportunity to ask questions. Make sure you have all the proper documentation with you before you apply. You need to provide two passport photos of your child, your child's original birth certificate, any relevant documents relating to custody and access to the child, and a

*Avoid The Queues*
*When applying for a passport in person, you can avoid lengthy queues at the Downtown passport office by going to a Service Canada office instead (1 800 567 6868, www.servicecanada.gc.ca). These federal government offices can be found in Burnaby, Coquitlam, North Vancouver and Richmond.*

| Top 10 Baby Names In BC (2006) | |
|---|---|
| Boys | Girls |
| Ethan | Emma |
| Jacob | Emily |
| Matthew | Ava |
| Joshua | Olivia |
| Nathan | Hannah |
| Liam | Sarah |
| Benjamin | Sophia |
| Ryan | Ella |
| Logan | Isabella |
| Daniel | Madison |

fee ($22 for children under 3, $37 for children who are between 3 and 15). You'll also need a guarantor's signature. If the applicant or parent is a Canadian citizen, he or she can act as the child's guarantor. A guarantor is someone who has known the child's parent(s) – the applicant(s) – for at least two years, and who has knowledge of the child. They also need to be a Canadian citizen with a valid Canadian passport (or one that expired no longer than a year ago). If there isn't anyone that can meet the criteria, parents will need to fill in a Statutory Declaration in Lieu in Guarantor form and have it notarised.

Both parents need to be involved in the passport application process. If the parents are divorced, the parent who has custody of the child must apply. When parents have joint custody, either can apply. In both cases, the appropriate legal documentation, such as court orders or divorce agreements, must also be provided.

**Citizenship Of Adopted Children**
*In December 2007, the national government made it easier for children adopted outside Canada to attain citizenship without first becoming a permanent resident. Although the parents of the adopted child do not need to be Canadian citizens, at least one must be a permanent resident, and the child must live in Canada once the process is complete.*

## Adoption

BC has one of Canada's most progressive adoption systems. Any person who is over 19, whether married, single, in a same-sex relationship or divorced, can potentially adopt a child. There are many children in the care of the Ministry of Children and Family Development (1 887 236 7807, www.mcf.gov.bc.ca) who are waiting to be adopted. Only a few are infants and some have special needs, but each child needs a loving home. You'll need to complete an exhaustive list of forms, meet with a social worker, and submit to a criminal record check, but this is the quickest way to adopt in BC. There are also licensed adoption agencies that assist families who want to adopt local infants or children from another country. Only 40 to 50 local infants are placed each year, with almost 300 children from other countries adopted in BC over the same period. Most children are from China but many come from Haiti, Korea, Russia and, surprisingly, the United States. Intercountry adoption is very complex. In essence, parents must go through two processes: the adoption process and the immigration process, which can take up to two years to complete.

The Adoptive Families Association of BC (604 320 7330, www.bcadoption.com) provides information and support to parents who are considering adoption, or have already adopted a child.

# Marriage Certificate & Registration

With its sandy beaches, dramatic landscapes and mild weather, Vancouver is a popular place to tie the knot. Drive up to Queen Elizabeth Park (p.244) or stroll past the Rose Garden in Stanley Park (p.244) on a Saturday afternoon and you are likely to bump into several bridal parties posing for photographers. From grooms dressed in kilts and red Royal Canadian Mounted Police serge to brides decked in bejewelled saris, kimonos or traditional white gowns, you'll see all variations of attire and religions represented at the city's weddings. There are countless wedding planners, boutiques and venues that cater to the occasion (see Wedding Items, p.404).

## The Paperwork

Getting married in BC is easy. The whole affair can be as simple or as elaborate as you like. Depending on a couple's beliefs, many will opt for a religious ceremony officiated by a spiritual leader in a church, mosque, synagogue or temple. Others may choose a civil ceremony that's solemnised by a marriage commissioner. Whatever you choose, you'll need to adhere to some basic requirements.

You don't have to be a resident to get married in BC, but you must be at least 19 years of age, unmarried and unrelated to the person you plan to marry. If either person has been divorced recently you may need to provide proof. Couples planning to marry will also need to apply for a licence. You can download an application online from the

Vital Statistics Agency (www.vs.gov.bc.ca), but you'll need to bring the form, along with identification (for both parties) to a Marriage Licence Issuer (MLI). The Vital Statistics Agency has a searchable database of MLIs on its website, or you can phone the office in Victoria (250 952 2681) and ask for a list of Marriage Licence Issuers in your community. Various notary publics and insurance companies issue marriage licences, as do some London Drugs stores that provide insurance services. Check the website (www.londondrugs.com) and search the insurance department to see what services it provides.

Fill in the appropriate paperwork, pay the fee ($100) and you can get married right away. There's no waiting period, but the licence is only valid in BC and it expires after three months.

Vancouver is a city of many cultures and interfaith marriages, so it's not uncommon for couples to have two ceremonies – a civil one and a religious one – to satisfy family traditions. Religious or not, the ceremony must be solemnised by a person registered with the Vital Statistics Agency under BC's Marriage Act, so make sure your religious representative or marriage commissioner has the appropriate credentials. You'll also need two people to witness the ceremony. Afterwards, the person who performed the ceremony will ask you to fill in a Marriage Registration form, which will be sent to the Vital Statistics Agency within 48 hours. Then you're officially married. Once the registration is completed, the Vital Statistics Agency will send you a legal marriage certificate for your records.

Marriage to a Canadian doesn't give a non-Canadian automatic citizenship. The Canadian spouse can apply for a permanent resident visa on behalf of the non-Canadian spouse, but there are many requirements and the process can take time. For the most part, if an expatriate gets married in Canada, the marriage is valid in other countries, but there are some exceptions. Many countries and individual states in the US don't recognise same-sex marriage, which is legal in Canada.

After a couple get married, there's no requirement for either person to start using their spouse's surname, but they can if they want to. The process is simple: you assume your spouse's surname and provide a copy of your marriage certificate when requested. A legal name change is not necessary and you can continue to use either surname. When tax time comes around, you'll need to indicate if your marital status has changed since you last filed your taxes and you may be eligible for additional benefits. If you have been living in a common-law relationship with your partner for at least 12 months, you'll already enjoy many of the same benefits as a legally married couple in BC.

## Death Certificate & Registration

When a loved one passes away it can be a difficult and confusing time. If a physician isn't already present during the time of death, or if prior arrangements weren't made for an at-home death, the best thing is to call the BC Ambulance Service (911) for assistance. A physician or coroner will need to gather detailed information about the death in order to fill out a medical certificate.

### Registering A Death

As part of the registration process, a medical certificate needs to be completed by a physician or coroner and forwarded to a funeral director within 48 hours of the death. The funeral director needs this information in order to obtain a burial permit. During this stage of the process, the funeral director may contact an immediate family member (preferably someone who was present at the person's death or during the period of illness) to gather details (such as the history of the illness, and the date of birth), for the death certificate. If a relative isn't available, a friend or adult who was present during the death, or who knows the circumstances surrounding the death, can provide information. Once all the information is gathered, the funeral director can issue a death certificate and funeral arrangements can be made.

A death certificate (and possibly even proof of birth) is a vital document that will need to be supplied, along with an insurance claim form, before the deceased's policy can be paid out to the beneficiary. Anyone can order a death certificate; you don't need to be a family member, but you do need to include a reason for your request when you fill out the application form. You can pick up the form from the Vital Statistics Agency Downtown (p.74), or you can download it from the internet (www.vs.gov.bc.ca). There is a $27 fee, which you'll need to pay when you submit the form. If you need to speak to someone, call the main office in Victoria (250 952 2681).

**Giving Back**

*Registering as an organ and tissue donor is a common practice in BC. Almost 650,000 British Columbians are registered with the British Columbia Transplant Society (60% are women). If you have a BC CareCard you can register online (www.transplant.bc.ca) and specify which organs you want to donate.*

## Investigation & Autopsy

If you don't know how the person has died, or if there are suspicious circumstances (including an accident or suicide), call the police immediately (911). The police and coroner or medical examiner will investigate further to determine the cause of death and collect any relevant information or evidence. In some cases, an autopsy may be conducted, but only at the request of a coroner if the medical cause of death can't be determined. A pathologist performs the procedure in hospital. The process is concluded quickly, so families can make funeral arrangements. In some cases, a coroner might investigate further or order an inquest to determine additional facts, but it's the role of the police to determine who's at fault if the death is suspicious.

If a crime remains unsolved, you can hire a private investigator to work on your behalf, but make sure the investigator is someone who is licensed under the Private Investigators and Security Agencies Act.

## Returning The Deceased To Their Country Of Origin

Funeral directors can be a great source of knowledge and comfort at a difficult time and can help you understand your options when someone has died. In BC, all funeral providers are required by law to supply you with an itemised price list of the products and services they offer. Funeral directors can provide complete burial and cremation services or arrange for a body to be transported back to its country of residence for repatriation. The logistics and legalities are complicated, but funeral directors are well versed in the requirements and can make arrangements with the 'receiving' funeral home to ensure all needs are met. International shipping costs are around $500, but that doesn't include the cost of a container, flights or any additional services that you might request.

### Green Burials

Given Vancouver's penchant for preserving the environment, it comes as no surprise that eco-friendly burials, complete with biodegradable caskets, are gaining popularity. There's no law that specifies that people need to be embalmed or cremated and many people have expressed the desire to take their eco-ethics to the grave. Most cemeteries are happy to accommodate. Concrete grave liners are still mandatory, but plans for 'natural' burial sites within cemeteries are in the pipeline.

# Working In Vancouver

Too much work and too little play is a common complaint of Vancouverites trying to make it up the corporate ladder while resisting the lure of the golf course and other leisure pursuits. Despite Vancouver's soaring real estate market and ever-increasing cost of living, you can do very well here if you have a strong work ethic, are particularly entrepreneurial, or happen to be able to fill a void in a specific industry. BC is experiencing a profound labour shortage as baby boomers retire in droves and immigrants or temporary foreign workers have been heavily recruited to fill the gaps. With the Vancouver 2010 Olympic and Paralympic Winter Games around the corner, BC's billion-dollar construction industry is working non-stop to build the necessary infrastructure. Massive projects, which include a light-rapid transit line expansion and the redevelopment of the Vancouver Convention and Exhibition Centre, have led the construction sector to look to European countries such as Germany and Britain for skilled trades people.

**A United Front**
*If you work as a tradesperson, or for the government, you will probably belong to a union. You often join a union when you start a new job and monthly union dues are deducted from your pay. You can opt out but, you may not enjoy the same benefits as your co-workers. Some of BC's biggest unions are the BC Government and Service Employees' Union (www.bcgeu. bc.ca), BC Nurses' Union (www.bcnu. org) and the BC Teachers' Federation (www.bctf.ca).*

## Salaries

If you find work within Vancouver's skilled industries you may be able to achieve a comfortable lifestyle and even put money away for a rainy day, despite rising rent and real estate costs. Compared to many high-priced European and Asian cities, Vancouver can be a relatively cheap place to live. But if you're working part-time or earning the minimum wage, you might have to get a roommate or look further out of the city to find affordable accommodation.

## Speaking English

Canada's most recent census (2006) revealed that more than 200 languages are spoken throughout the country. In Vancouver, however, English is the common language in which most companies do business. Unless your English skills are up to scratch, you may struggle to find jobs in the higher income level of the market. There are dozens of language schools in Vancouver, with some offering English classes especially for academics or executives. In fact, many students specifically come to Vancouver from Asia to learn English. In some industries it can be very helpful to speak Cantonese or Mandarin.

# Working Hours

Unless you're a contractor or you work in the service industry, expect to clock in for the standard nine to five, 40 hour week. It can be a grind, but more offices are going 'casual', so you can toil away in your jeans instead of a suit or skirt. In some cases you can even bring your dog to work. And if you belong to a union you might get 'flexitime' (where you work extra time each day and get every second or third Friday off), not to mention higher pay, more vacation time and better benefits.

BC has set out some strict rules for hours of work, which vary from industry to industry. If you work in the high-tech sector, though, the BC government has made some exceptions to the rules. For example, you can average more than 40 hours a week, but once you've worked more than 12 hours in a day you must be paid overtime.

## Overqualified & Underemployed

Many expats who have worked in high-level positions in their home country find themselves overqualified and underemployed when they try to resume their careers in Canada. It is a huge issue, particularly in highly regulated industries such as finance, engineering, healthcare and IT. In an effort to remove these barriers, provincial and federal government programmes have been launched to develop foreign credential equivalency standards.

BC has nine statutory holidays – 'stats' – and most people, except those in retail and some in finance, enjoy these long weekends. There's usually one per month, except during the long stretch between New Year's Day and Easter. Though December 26 (Boxing Day), Easter Sunday and Easter Monday are not official stats, most employers, especially government and unions, give their employees the days off (see p.17).

## Holiday Time

Along with statutory holidays, companies are required to give new recruits just two weeks off. This goes up to a meagre three weeks after five years. It's certainly worth negotiating extra vacation time when someone has offered you a job. If you leave your job before you have taken all your holidays, the remaining days are usually included in your final pay cheque.

## Business Councils & Groups

| | |
|---|---|
| British Canadian Chamber Of Trade And Commerce | www.bcctc.ca |
| Business Council Of British Columbia | www.bcbc.com |
| Canada China Business Council | www.ccbc.com |
| Canada-India Business Council | www.canada-indiabusiness.ca |
| Canadian Australian New Zealand Business Association (CANZBA) | www.canzba.org |
| German Canadian Business Association | www.germancanadianbusinessassociation.com |
| Japan External Trade Organization | www.jetrovancouver.org |
| Malaysia Canada Business | www.malaysia-canada.com |
| Trade Commission Of Mexico | www.bancomext.com |
| Vancouver Board Of Trade | www.boardoftrade.com |

## Finding Work

Many people are lured to Vancouver for its natural splendour, but the opportunity to work in a myriad of sectors is also an attraction. Hovering just under 5%, the province's unemployment rate is low. If you want to find a part-time job that allows you to work a little and play a lot, answer the call of the many restaurants and retailers begging for staff. Getting seasonal work at one of the local ski mountains is also a great way to enjoy some adventure and meet new people while earning.

If you're interested in making some serious money and have a university degree, technical skills or a trade, you're a red-hot commodity. Some companies will pay for your relocation expenses, help you get settled and offer a decent salary, but you may need to agree to be a loyal employee for a length of time (or have to pay back your relocation costs if you leave early). They'll still need to cut through the appropriate red tape to get you here and many companies are very motivated to do so. In these cases, it's an employee's market and the power

*Situations vacant*

is in your hands. Practise the fine art of negotiation to ensure that you get what you want. Just remember to be realistic as there are plenty of other people who would jump at the chance to work in Vancouver's spectacular playground. Although a top-notch CV might get you in the door, while a little humility and a winning personality will bring you back for a second interview, and ultimately land you the job.

### Finding Work Before You Leave

**When You're 65**
*As of 1 January, 2008, changes to BC's Human Rights Code mean that workers who turn 65 are no longer required to retire. This is a huge relief to employers who are trying to retain the decades of skills and experience of these employees. And people who have thriving careers can continue to enjoy the challenges of their day-to-day work, no matter what their age.*

The quickest way to become a permanent resident in Canada is to go the 'immigration through employment' route. Again, because of the country's labour shortage, government programmes have been developed to speed up the immigration process (see Residence Visas, p.68). The federal government's Temporary Foreign Worker Program, operated by Human Resources and Social Development Canada (www.hrsdc.gc.ca), and WorkBC (www.workbc.ca), has identified a veritable laundry list of occupations considered to be 'under pressure'. For example, certain jobs in information technology, private live-in caregivers (for children or adults), engineers, senior managers, and architects are in demand. Registered nurses, psychiatric nurses, physicians and pharmacists are also needed. And the list goes on.

Health Match BC is a local recruitment service that's funded by the provincial government to help healthcare practitioners find work and match their skills with hospitals and facilities. There are job postings and requirements on its website (www.healthmatchbc.org), along with BC employment and licensing requirements; no fees are charged for its services. You can also call (604 736 5920) or visit the office at 1333 West Broadway.

If you don't fall into any of these categories, don't despair, just point and click your way to job-hunting sites such as www.workopolis.com and www.monster.ca, while www.canada.com offers job listings represented in the city's two major newspapers, *The Vancouver Sun* and *The Province*. Craigslist (vancouver.craigslist.ca) can also be a good source, while recruitment agencies usually post jobs on their websites (see Working as a Freelancer Or Contractor, p.82).

Some international companies recruit skilled workers directly from abroad, especially in sectors where there are labour shortages (including the high-tech and healthcare sectors). All companies, however, still have to adhere to Human Resources and Social Development Canada (www.hrsdc.gc.ca) requirements. In some cases they may need to get a Labour Market Opinion (LMO) (see Temporary Work Permit, p.66). International companies often have human resources professionals who are highly skilled in wading through the red tape and paperwork required to recruit foreign workers. Some will access skilled workers by liaising with immigration lawyers or firms that specialise in foreign recruitment.

### Finding Work When You Arrive

While there's an advantage in having a job in hand before you arrive, meeting prospective employers face to face can have many added benefits. After all, if you're skilled, likeable and require little training, you might be able to secure a three to six-month contract and jump into the job market right away. Don't be tempted to pass up a good opportunity just because it's not full time or permanent. Sometimes contracts are repeatedly extended, and if a permanent position comes up, you'll have the inside track.

Networking is a critical skill, so it's a good idea to get out and meet people, attend career fairs and gain some insight into the local job market. The Work Futures website (www.workfutures.bc.ca) provides comprehensive labour market information for all of BC. Check the site to identify which markets best suit your skills, and preferably adapt those skills to those industries that are in demand. It is a good idea to contact some recruitment agencies. They're in tune with the job market and have built long-term relationships with many large companies.

Tourism is also a burgeoning sector in Vancouver, and related retailers, tour operators and guides often look for seasonal staff. Go2 (www.go2hr.ca) is dedicated to all facets of BC's tourism sector and it has a great job board. Speaking a second language (especially Japanese, Korean, Cantonese or Mandarin) will help your employment prospects. Companies organising outdoor recreation on Grouse Mountain, Cypress Mountain and Mount Seymour regularly hire temporary seasonal staff during winter. Sometimes they'll host job fairs at the beginning of the season, or post jobs online.

## Recruitment Agencies

| | | |
|---|---|---|
| Adecco | 604 669 1203 | www.adecco.ca |
| Accountemps | 604 685 4253 | www.accountemps.com |
| Angus One | 604 682 8367 | www.angusone.com |
| David Aplin Recruiting | 604 648 2799 | www.aplin.com |
| Goldbeck Recruiting | 604 684 1428 | www.goldbeck.com |
| Hays Specialist Recruitment Canada | 604 648 4297 | www.hays.ca |
| Holloway Schulz & Partners | 604 688 9595 | www.recruiters.com |
| Hunt Personnel Temporarily Yours | 604 688 2555 | www.hunt.ca |
| Medi-Office Services | 604 924 1137 | www.medi-office.com |
| Miles Employment Group | 604 694 2500 | www.miles.ca |
| The Personnel Department | 604 685 3530 | www.goodstaff.com |
| Pinton Forrest & Madden | 604 689 9970 | www.pfmsearch.com |
| Robert Half Finance & Accounting | 604 688 7572 | www.roberthalffinance.com |
| ZSA Recruitment | 604 681 0706 | www.zsa.ca |

*Recruitment Agencies*
Vancouver has plenty of recruitment agencies that can do the networking and legwork for you. While a number of these still provide temporary and permanent administrative opportunities within large companies, there are many that specialise in recruiting accountants, IT specialists, executives, engineers, and hospitality industry workers, such as chefs. The best recruiters don't simply wait for job seekers to walk in the door – they actively pursue skilled professionals who may already be in the job market. There's no harm in signing up with a recruitment agency that might help you find your dream job while you're toiling away at a lacklustre nine-to-five job.

## Voluntary & Charity Work

If you want to expand your skills, pursue a hobby or support your community, there are numerous opportunities. Volunteer Vancouver has an extensive online database (www. govolunteer.ca) of available positions so you can find whatever suits your interests, skills and availability. Most positions simply require a time commitment and positive attitude; special skills aren't necessarily needed, but they can help if you're trying to secure a coveted role.

Volunteers at the Vancouver Art Gallery (604 662 4700, www.vanartgallery.bc.ca) undergo a six-month training programme and need to make a two-year obligation in order to be considered. If you're interested in the arts, and less of an obligation, consider volunteering at the three-week long annual Vancouver International Film Festival (604 683 3456, www.viff.org), the International Jazz Festival or Winterruption Festival (both are organised by the Coastal Jazz and Blues Society; 604 872 5200, www. coastaljazz.ca), or the Vancouver Folk Music Festival (www.thefestival.bc.ca). They are all popular events so make sure to get your application in early.

Volunteering with children and young people in daycare or recreational programmes, for example, can be an enriching experience for everyone involved. You will, however, need to submit to a criminal record check and provide some references. There are many local organisations that need volunteers to provide support to adult or youth offenders in a correctional setting. You can participate in sports programmes, lead cooking or craft classes, or simply play cards, hang out and talk. The Elizabeth Fry Society of Greater Vancouver (www.elizabethfry.com) takes on about 300 volunteers each year. Hospitals and rehabilitation centres are also in need of adult volunteers to help take patients to occupational therapy programmes, provide one-on-one visits and lead recreational programmes. Contact Vancouver Coastal Health (604 875 5277, www.vch.ca/volunteers) to find out about local opportunities.

*Play For Pay*

*Vancouver is said to have the highest concentration of gaming companies in the world; Action Pants, Propaganda, Rockstar, and Electronic Arts are just some of the 100 or so game development studios in the city. The industry is known for hiring expats to fill temporary and permanent positions. If you're looking for a career in software development, digital animation, video game or web development, check out New Media BC's online job board at www.newmediabc.com.*

## Working As A Freelancer Or Contractor

Vancouver's buzzing workplaces are often in need of temporary staff to help out with large, time-sensitive projects. In some industries, such as construction, companies are given bonuses or incentives to complete projects ahead of time, so delays due to lack of staff aren't tolerated. Since tradespeople are in high demand, you can pretty much show up at a site to see if they'll take you on. Some companies are purported to offer on-the-job training, but if you're here temporarily you'll still need a work permit.

If your heart is set on writing, working in the arts or for a non-profit company, freelance assignments and contracts can be found. It may be difficult to get your foot in the door, but once you do the assignments will start to trickle in. Networking helps; Vancouver is a small city and in these industries, everybody often knows everyone else. Gaulin Media (www.jeffgaulin.com) is one of the best sources for writing, editing and art director jobs, and Media Kitty (www.mediakitty.com) is great for travel writers. Magazines Canada (www.magazinescanada.ca) and the BC Association of Magazine Publishers (www.bcmags.com) have online job postings. Charity Village (www.charityvillage.com) has a website full of employment opportunities in the non-profit sector.

## Employment Contracts

When you've landed that dream job, you'll probably have to fill out a couple of forms, but you generally won't be provided with an employment contract. Your new employer will most likely give you a 'welcome' letter that outlines the position you've been offered, along with the annual rate of pay. Sometimes new recruits are subject to a three to six-month probationary period. While it might seem odd not to be given a contract, BC's robust labour laws and protections make it unnecessary, unless you have a temporary work permit or you're working on contract. All employers have to abide by certain legislative rules and regulations, or risk being sanctioned by the BC government's Employment Standards Branch, which is the first line of defence for employees when it comes to disputes.

## Labour Law

Working in Canada can open up a whole host of opportunities to expats, but there is a web of labour rules and regulations that can be confusing. Although BC has clearly defined employment standards, it doesn't hurt to become informed of your rights as a worker. There are employers who will try to ignore the rules, and speaking up can be intimidating when you're new. BC's Employment Standards Branch falls under the responsibility of the BC Ministry of Labour and Citizens' Services (www.labour. gov.bc.ca/esb). Its role is to adjudicate disputes between employers and employees under the authority of the Employment Standards Act.

### *Wages*

Whether you're waiting tables, picking fruit or building houses, regulations are in place to ensure that all workers are paid the correct rate and in a timely manner. In

BC the minimum wage is $8 per hour, but there can be lots of overtime in booming industries. Once you have worked more than 40 hours a week, you must be paid time and a half. There are variations among industries, however, so ensure you're being treated fairly. Not all employers play by the rules.

## Pension Plans

If you work for a good company that contributes to a pension plan on behalf of its employees, you'll be lucky enough to have a tidy nest egg to rely on when retirement comes. BC has more than 800 pension plans that are registered and regulated under the Pension Benefits Standards Act. Employers are also required to contribute to the Canada Pension Plan (CPP), which is the country's national scheme. On your behalf they deduct the appropriate amount from your pay cheque. You can access CPP benefits once you reach 60. At 65, if you have lived in Canada for at least 10 years, you may qualify for the federal Old Age Security (OAS) pension. You should apply for these benefits at least six months before you turn 65.

## Health Plans

**No Permit Required**

*If you're travelling to Canada on business or for a specific reason (as an athlete, for example) you don't need a work permit since you're not actually entering Canada's labour market. However, you may need a temporary residence visa if your home country isn't on Canada's visa waiver list. This also applies to military personnel, foreign representatives and their families, and business visitors whose main source of income and business is outside of Canada. There are always exceptions, so do your homework before you arrive.*

The majority of employers offer full-time employees some sort of health plan that generally covers basic medical and dental benefits. Nominal deductions will be taken from your pay, but you can opt out of the plan if you choose, especially if you already have coverage on your spouse or common-law partner's plan. A good benefits package can be worth an additional 20% on top of your annual salary. Not all plans offer the same cover, however. Some companies cover massage therapy, acupuncture and so forth on their plans, but others just pay for the basics.

## Maternity Leave

The number of people having babies in Canada is falling despite the country's generous pregnancy and parental leave benefits. You can't be fired for being pregnant and when you return from your pregnancy leave (or parental leave if the father or co-parent chooses to use some of the time), you can't be demoted to a position that pays less. The time you will be given off and the pay varies from province to province, but new parents nationwide enjoy a maximum of 52 weeks of unpaid leave. In BC, mothers are entitled to 17 weeks' maternity leave, plus 35 weeks' parental leave (the parental leave can be shared with the father). If eligible, they'll get Employment Insurance (EI) benefits for part or all of that time, depending on the number of hours they have worked in the past. Employment Insurance benefit will only cover a percentage of the employment typically earned and it is capped at $421 a week. Some employers (the government for example) will provide supplementary payments to 'top up' or increase the employees' income to 100% of their gross salary. In the end, it's not uncommon for most parents to enjoy many weeks of paid leave with their new bundle of joy (see Maternity, p.154).

### Contractor Or Employee?

Sometimes the distinction between employees and contractors is slim, but it's critical to know the difference. If you make a mistake, you could find yourself in hot water with the Canada Revenue Agency, which is responsible for collecting income tax. If you're a contractor, you're considered to be self-employed and you're not protected under the Employment Standards Act. On the other hand, if you're expected to show up for work at an office every day, using the company's equipment and so forth, you might be an employee. If that's the case, you're entitled to benefits and wages, plus a paid lunch break, and you'll need to pay for employment insurance and Canada Pension Plan benefits.

*Holiday Time*

By law, companies are only required to give new recruits a paltry two weeks' paid vacation once they have worked a minimum of 12 months for the company. In the interim, employers must pay employees 4% vacation pay on top of their wages. Luckily, most employers are more generous and tend to give new staff three weeks off for their first year. Holiday time only goes up to three weeks after five years, so try to negotiate some extra vacation when offered a new job.

If you leave your job before you have taken all your holidays, you'll be paid your share of outstanding vacation days, usually in your final pay cheque.

*Unemployment Benefits*

Once affectionately dubbed 'UI', the old unemployment insurance system has been replaced with what's now called Employment Insurance (EI). Along with this name change came stricter regulations for qualifying for benefits, in the event that you need them when you leave your job. A percentage of your income gets deducted from each pay cheque by your employer and remitted to the federal government. You can't be fired from your job or simply quit and collect EI, but if you're laid off, or made redundant, you might qualify if you have worked a minimum number of hours. If you do decide to apply for EI, make sure to get a record of employment (ROE) from your former employer.

## Employment Lawyers

| | | |
|---|---|---|
| Blake, Cassels & Graydon | 604 631 3300 | www.blakes.com |
| Fasken Martineau | 604 631 3131 | www.fasken.com |
| Hamilton Howell Barristers & Solicitors | 604 696 0556 | www.hamiltonhowell.ca |
| Kornfeld Mackoff Silber | 604 331 8300 | www.kmslawyers.com |
| Lawson Lundell | 604 685 3456 | www.lawsonlundell.com |
| Own Bird Law Corporation | 604 688 0401 | www.owenbird.com |
| Rose A Keith | 604 669 2126 | www.rosekeith.bc.ca |
| Singleton Urquhart | 604 682 7474 | www.singleton.com |
| Shapiro Hankinson & Knutson Law Corporation | 604 684 0727 | www.shk.ca |
| TevlinGleadle Employment Law Strategies | 604 648 2966 | www.tevlingleadle.com |

*Equal Employment*

Canada has a whole host of legislation designed to ensure that all workers are treated fairly in the workplace. You can't be discriminated against because of your race, religion, sexual orientation, disability, gender, or if you are a visible minority. Though it's not technically called 'affirmative action,' on some job applications (usually those for government positions), you can identify yourself as a visible minority, person with a disability or a First Nations person for special consideration for the position. While some people view this process as unfair, others feel that it's a good way to ensure the workforce is representative of BC's diverse population. If you want to file a complaint on the grounds of discrimination you can contact the BC Human Rights Tribunal, which is a quasi-judicial agency that is designated to deal with human rights complaints as outlined by the BC Human Rights Code. You can call 604 775 2000 or visit the Downtown office (1170-605 Robson Street). For more information, check the website (www.bchrt.bc.ca).

*Unions*

BC is considered to be a particularly pro-union province and most labour-based industries have their own. Though they can be quite powerful, unions still need to follow provincial and federal regulations and employees can choose to be exempt without repercussions. If you belong to a union, the chances are that you have a high salary and a good benefits package, along with more flexible working hours and increased job security. In recent years, the provincial government has taken a great deal of power away from unions by passing emergency legislation to force striking workers back on the job, or risk heavy penalties, including fines or jail time.

## Changing Jobs

Although you may have just settled into a job, if a more lucrative offer comes along, you're really under no obligation to your current employer. However, it is a good idea to give a minimum of two weeks' notice before you pack your proverbial box and head off to greener pastures. If you're working as a consultant to a contractor, make sure you have fulfilled the terms of your contract or you could be sued. Besides, keeping good relationships is critical, especially if you plan to use your previous employer as a reference. If you're a permanent resident you don't need a work permit, but if you have a temporary work permit you'll need to get a new one for a new job.

If you're working in a highly competitive industry, you might have been asked to agree to or sign a non-compete or non-disclosure agreement, or you might be asked to sign one when you resign. If it's a legally binding contract (you may need to consult a lawyer for advice), you may have to refrain from starting up a competing business or working for a competitor for a period of about six months.

## Company Closure

If your sponsor company files for bankruptcy and subsequently closes, your employer isn't exempt from paying you outstanding wages, vacation pay and possibly some severance pay. It is important, however, to move quickly and contact the bankruptcy trustee right away. A trustee is usually an administrator appointed under the federal Office of the Superintendent of Bankruptcy to make sure money is disbursed fairly among all creditors. Doing this doesn't guarantee you'll get anything, but it's worth a try. If you don't know who the trustee is, contact the local Office of the Superintendent of Bankruptcy (www.osb-bsf.gc.ca) to find out. It is located Downtown at 300 West Georgia Street, or phone 604 666 5007. It is best to have a list of what you're owed, along with pay slips and any other proof you may have. If the company simply closes down without warning, or if you think the company is starting up under a different name, contact the Ministry of Labour and Citizens' Services Employment Standards branch (604 660 4946) and file a complaint.

*Railway workers*

# Bank Accounts

After decades of discussion on whether Canada needed a central bank, the Bank of Canada Act was finally drafted and ratified in 1934. Though the Bank of Canada opened its doors the following year, it wasn't until 1938 that Canada's central bank was officially publicly owned. Since then, the institution has been charged with the task of setting policy to regulate inflation, issuing and distributing bank notes and managing public funds.

*Banking Rights*

*Even if you don't have a job, or if you have been declared bankrupt, under Canadian law you still have the right to open a bank account. You don't need to put money in the account right away, either. If you have a criminal record, or if the bank thinks you may use the account to commit a crime, it can refuse to open an account for you.*

Canada's 22 domestic banks, which have hundreds of branches scattered throughout the nation (and internationally), are probably the most visible financial institutions in Vancouver. Each offers an extensive range of personal and commercial banking services, from cheque and savings accounts to mortgages, mutual funds and Registered Retirement Savings Plans.

More than ever, banks are competing against one another by 'one-upping' services and undercutting fees. When one bank virtually eliminates ATM user fees, others soon follow suit with a similar offer. Some banks have no-fee accounts for children and seniors, others are open evenings and weekends. And when a few of one financial institution's branches were difficult to visit because of the Canada Line rapid transit line construction, it offered to make 'house calls' to clients who couldn't make it to another branch.

But despite these grand gestures, the majority of financial institutions still charge a dizzying array of user fees, which range from 50 cents to $1.50 per transaction, to a monthly flat fee of $25. There is a complex matrix of fees for using an ATM or debit card, and for overdraft protection. These fees will be waived, however, if you keep a minimum balance in your account, which can range from $1,000 to $4,000 depending on the financial institution and type of account. Banking online is a good method of keeping fees to a minimum. If you do need to visit a local branch to conduct a transaction, most are open from 09:00 to 17:00 Monday to Friday, and various branches open evenings and weekends.

To open an account, bring your social insurance card and another piece of identification (such as your passport, permanent resident card, or driving licence) to a branch. You don't need to have a permanent address, but if you're a non-resident, you must provide a bank reference letter from your current financial institution. Staff can help you decide which account will suit your needs best. You'll be given an ATM card, which you'll need to bring with you whether you conduct in-bank transactions or use an ATM. You'll find ATMs, which are accessible all day, every day, located throughout the city. Some occupy corners inside petrol stations, supermarkets and convenience stores. And on a rainy winter day, a drive-through ATM comes in handy.

Many international banks maintain a presence in Canada; there are six foreign bank lending branches and 24 foreign bank subsidiaries. The Bank of East Asia and State Bank of India, for example, each operate subsidiary branches in Vancouver. Almost all offer online and telephone banking; some of the main ones are listed below.

## Major Banks

| | | |
|---|---|---|
| Bank Of Montreal | 1 877 225 5266 | www4.bmo.com |
| Canadian Western Bank | 604 688 8711 | www.cwbank.com |
| CIBC | 604 665 1645 | www.cibc.com |
| HSBC | 604 525 4722 | www.hsbc.ca |
| Royal Bank Of Canada | 1 800 769 2511 | www.rbcroyalbank.com |
| Scotiabank | 604 668 2094 | www.scotiabank.com |
| TD Canada Trust | 604 654 3665 | www.tdcanadatrust.com |
| Vancity | 604 877 7000 | www.vancity.com |

## Financial Planning

It can take some ingenuity, sacrifice and tenacity to save money in Vancouver – particularly when you're constantly dazzled by the lure of shiny new cars, high-end shopping, and shimmering glass condominiums that promise the ultimate urban lifestyle. Many people have jumped into the hot real estate market with both feet, hoping to make a bundle on their investment. The sector has been booming in recent years, with as many analysts believing the market will continue to stay strong as those who say the bubble is about to burst.

It's not an uncommon sight over the last few years to see people camping out overnight to gain a spot in line for 'pre-sale' homes that will be built a couple of years down the line. They're routinely snapped up by investors who might resell the condo at a profit before ground is even broken.

On the flipside, many homeowners have difficulty trying to pay an impenetrable mortgage. Couple that with the allure of pricey sporting opportunities, such as golf, snowboarding and sailing, as well as season tickets to watch the Canucks, and it's easy to understand how money disappears as quickly as it's earned.

Some manage to make a good chunk of change by buying real estate and quickly reselling it at a higher price to make a profit on their pint-sized pied-a-terre, while others move to the suburbs to find a more affordable place to live. If you work close to home, this is ideal. Those who don't find themselves spending hours of their day commuting to work (and a fortune on fuel, thanks to Vancouver's dubious distinction of having the nation's highest petrol prices).

Although people like to gripe about the factors that challenge Vancouver's appeal, they put it down to the price you have to pay to live in one of world's most beautiful cities. Many overseas and US citizens own property in Vancouver (you don't need to be a resident or a citizen to do so), which has proven to be a lucrative investment. There can be tax implications, though, so it's wise to consult an agent who understands the international market. If you're a resident of Canada you may qualify for a mortgage to finance part of your investment (65% to 75%), but you'll need to provide information, including credit references, job history and immigration documents.

### Financial Advisors

If you want your money to stretch as far as a half-million dollar condo, or you intend to squirrel away a tidy sum for retirement, it's a good idea to employ the services of a financial planner. If you plan to purchase mutual funds, your advisor must be licensed under the Mutual Funds Dealers Association of Canada (www.mfda.ca) Licensed members of the Investment Dealers Association of Canada (www.ida.ca) can sell stocks, bonds and mutual funds. Bear in mind that both are self-regulated organisations.

If you have a good understanding of the investment laws and practices in Canada you can certainly take an active role in your own financial planning. There are many online resources that provide current information on this rapidly changing industry. Be aware that insufficient knowledge can be dangerous; it is best to hire a licensed professional who will put your interests first.

---

**Canada's Colourful Banking History**
Canada's oldest charted bank is the Bank of Montreal, which was officially opened in 1817. Prior to the creation of Canada's central bank in 1935, which is the sole issuer of bank notes, individual banks were free to issue their own notes. Historically, however, animal pelts, shells and glass beads were all traded as legal tender. Today, the future of Canada's penny is in question as the Royal Canadian Mint explores the idea of removing it as a unit of currency.

---

### Canadian Deposit Insurance Corporation

When choosing a bank to safeguard your hard-earned cash, make sure it's a member of the Canadian Deposit Insurance Corporation (www.cdic.ca). The CDIC is a Crown corporation that insures member financial institutions in case they go bankrupt or 'fail.' That means that up to $100,000 of your savings will be covered, but there are some exceptions. Mutual funds, stocks and bonds, travellers' cheques and foreign currency deposits are not covered.

*Offshore Saving Accounts*

Keeping a savings account open in your home country is a good idea if you plan to maintain regular ties, especially if you have investments or need to pay property taxes. If your home country isn't politically stable or if you find that you're constantly paying currency conversion fees, it might be better to open up a Canadian bank account, at least to take care of your day-to-day finances. In some cases, you might require proof of a Canadian bank account to get a permanent resident card or work permit, or vice versa.

Many Canadian banks also have international branches in Caribbean island nations considered to be tax havens. Though it's not illegal to have an offshore account, Canadian residents who fail to report income and capital gains generated by them are violating their obligation to report their 'world income' under Canada's Income Tax Act. Canada has tax treaties with 86 countries. In an effort to protect its tax base, the Canada Revenue Agency co-founded the Joint International Tax Shelter Information Centre (JITSIC), along with Australia, the US and the UK (Japan has recently joined) and has made it a priority to aggressively pursue tax dodgers and punish them severely.

*Pensions*

Most private companies offer pension plans to employees, but some publicly traded companies offer profit sharing or stock options instead. If you're lucky, you'll get all three. If you're a teacher, nurse or other type of public-sector worker, or you belong to a union, you could get a generous pension benefit package. Even if you leave your job for a few years and then return, you have the option of 'buying back' time. Everyone who works in Canada, including self-employed people and foreigners, must make annual contributions to the Canada Pension Plan. Employers deduct contributions from pay cheques and contribute the equivalent amount to the Canada Revenue Agency. If you're employed for a short period of time, or for example you're here on a SWAP programme, you may be able to get a refund on some of the taxes you paid once you leave the country. You'll need to fill out a tax return form and submit it to the Canada Revenue Agency. For more information, download Canada Revenue Agency's guide, Non-Residents and Income Tax (www.cra-arc.gc.ca).

## Taxation

If you own property in Vancouver, you'll have to pay annual property taxes, which fund schools, roads, policing and other city services.

Each year, the BC Assessment Authority, which is run by the provincial government, determines the 'fair market value' of your property and uses that 'assessment' amount to determine what you should pay. In Vancouver, calculations on property taxes are based on the assessed value of the property, which is divided by 1,000 and then multiplied by the mill rate (per $1,000 taxable value), which changes from year to year. To find out the annual mill rate, go to the City of Vancouver website (www.vancouver.ca) and search for 'property tax'. You can also call or email the property tax office (604 873 7633, propertytax@vancouver.ca).

| Financial Advisers | |
|---|---|
| Advisor.ca | www.advisor.ca |
| Advocis | www.advocis.ca |
| Benefits & Pensions Monitor | www.bpmmagazine.com |
| Customplan Financial Advisors | www.customplanfinancial.com |
| Financial Consumer Agency Of Canada | www.fcac-acfc.gc.ca |
| Financial Post | www.financialpost.com |
| Invest British Columbia | www.investbc.com |
| Investment Executive | www.investmentexecutive.com |
| The Investment Funds Institute Of Canada | www.ific.ca |
| Morningstar Canada | www.morningstar.ca |
| Report On Business | www.reportonbusiness.com |

## Cost Of Living

| | |
|---|---|
| Bananas (per kg) | $1.25 |
| Bottle of house wine (restaurant) | $20-$35 |
| Bottle of wine (off licence) | $10-$100 |
| Burger (takeaway) | $5-$8 |
| Bus (10km journey) | $2.50-$3.75 |
| Camera film (36 exposure) | $7.75 |
| Tin of dog food | $1.50 |
| Can of soft drink | $1 |
| Cappuccino | $3.50 |
| Car rental (small car, per day) | $35-$45 |
| Carrots (per kg) | $2 |
| CD album | $17 |
| Chocolate bar | $1.10 |
| Cigarettes (pack of 20) | $8-$10 |
| Cinema ticket | $9-$12 |
| Eggs (dozen) | $2.50-$4.75 |
| Film developing (colour, 36 exposure) | $15-$18 |
| Fresh beef (per kg) | $5-$35 |
| Fresh chicken (per kg) | $5-$16 |
| Fresh fish (per kg) | $6-$35 |
| Golf (18 holes) | $22-$100 |
| House wine (glass) | $7 |
| Large takeaway pizza | $18 |
| Loaf of bread | $1-$5.50 |
| Local postage stamp | $0.52 |
| Milk (1 litro) | $1.60-$3 |
| Mobile-to-mobile call (local, per minute) | $0.05-$0.30 |
| DVD (new release) | $39 |
| Newspaper (international) | $3-$10 |
| Newspaper (local) | $.75-$1.50 |
| Orange juice (1 litre) | $3 |
| Pack of 24 aspirin | $4-$5.50 |
| Petrol (1 litre) | $1.07-$1.20 |
| Pint of beer | $5 |
| Postcard | $0.75-$2 |
| Potatoes (per kg) | $1.50-$2 |
| Rice (1kg) | $2.50-$5.69 |
| Salon haircut (female) | $30-$150 |
| Salon haircut (male) | $15-$90 |
| Six-pack of beer (off licence) | $7-$10 |
| Strawberries (per punnet) | $2.50-$4.99 |
| Sugar (2kg) | $3.69 |
| Taxi (10km journey) | $17 |
| Text message (local) | $0.10-$0.25 |
| Tube of toothpaste | $1-$4.98 |
| Water 1.5 litres (restaurant) | $3.50 |
| Water 1.5 litres (supermarket) | $1.75 |

Rates vary depending on where you live. So even if you got a deal on that fixer-upper, you'll pay more for it if you live in West Vancouver than you would if it was in Vancouver, which are two different municipalities. City taxes are due each July.

### Income Tax

When income tax time rolls around each spring, everyone (including permanent residents) gets into a frenzy. Rest assured, tax preparation specialists set up shop all over the city to assist with the last-minute rush to meet the 30 April deadline (30 June if you're self-employed) and avoid late penalties. When the federal government has finished its calculations as to whether you've underpaid (or overpaid), you'll soon know whether you'll get a refund, or if you'll have to pay up and send more of your hard-earned dollars to the Canada Revenue Agency (CRA).

Unless you're self-employed, your employer will deduct a range of taxable benefits (including Canada Pension Plan, employment insurance and federal tax) from each pay cheque. If your employer is deducting enough, you probably won't have to pay much income tax at the end of the year, especially if you contribute to a Registered Retirement Savings Plan (RRSP) or other type of tax-shelter plan. If you're self-employed and have not been paying instalment taxes to the Canada Revenue Agency, you'll get a big bill at the end of the year.

Most people file electronically and the whole procedure is simple and user-friendly, speeding up the process immensely. Although everyone has to pay both federal and provincial income taxes, BC residents benefit from one of the nation's lowest provincial rates. Regardless, the more money you make, the more taxes you'll pay, depending on what bracket you fall into. There are many deductions you can claim as well, which can help reduce the amount you have to pay. To get the maximum deductions and exploit every benefit or loophole to full effect, consult an accountant to wade through the legalese for you.

If you disagree with your official tax assessment from Canada Revenue Agency, you can request redress under the federal Taxpayer Bill of Rights. There are also taxpayer relief provisions for people who have special hardships that prevent them from being able to pay their taxes. Regardless of your situation, you must file taxes each year or you could face serious penalties, possibly even jail time. If you owe taxes and don't make an attempt to arrange for a monthly payment schedule, don't be surprised if the CRA deducts from your wages or bank account. Even if you don't have income to report, you should still file a return; you may be entitled to benefits or credits.

### Other Taxes

Provincial sales tax (PST) and a federal goods and services tax (GST) are levied on most things you purchase, including petrol (the price you pay at the pump alone is estimated to be 35% tax) and food. PST (7%) and GST (5%) are not included in retail price tags, but you'll see them itemised on the receipt for anything you buy. There's also a tax on alcohol, which is much more expensive here than across the border in the US. In an effort to cut smoking, federal and provincial taxes on cigarettes have rocketed over the years. The provincial government is toying with the idea of creating a carbon tax, which may be tagged on to the price of petrol, in an effort to curb greenhouse gas emissions.

*Free Legal Info*
*The BC branch of the Canadian Bar Association has a great free service called Dial-A-Law (604 687 4680, www.dialalaw.org), where you can listen to scripts on a variety of subjects (in English, Punjabi and Chinese). You can also read the information online (in English only).*

## Legal Issues

Like many Commonwealth countries, Canada's laws are based on the English Common Law system, with the exception of Quebec, which derives its laws from the French civil system. Canada has a Charter of Rights and Freedoms that guarantees all persons equal protection and benefit under the law without discrimination due to race, ethnic origin, physical ability or religion. The charter also prevents any level of government (federal, provincial, municipal) from creating laws (statutes) that contravene it.

The Supreme Court of Canada is the highest court in the land and has the ultimate say when it comes to interpreting laws. There are also civil (traffic court, divorce court) and criminal provincial courts, courts of appeal and speciality courts (such as youth courts).

Canada is a democracy, and anyone accused of committing a crime is considered to be innocent until proven guilty as determined during a trial. Some trials involve only a judge, while more serious offences will involve a judge and jury. If you go to court, you'll find out that prosecutors are referred to as 'Crown counsel'. In BC they work on behalf of the attorney general. Contrary to other countries where lawyers are barristers or solicitors, Canadian lawyers are both.

Judges are not elected, they're appointed by the federal or provincial government. The judicial system is politically independent. Judges rely heavily on precedents – similar cases that have been decided previously – as guidelines for interpreting statutes and their corresponding regulations. Few serious crimes other than murder carry mandatory minimum sentences. Because of this, the general public often expresses outrage at seemingly light sentences given to convicted criminals. In Canada, most criminals are punished under one of three federal statues: Criminal Code, the Controlled Drug and Substances Act and the Youth Criminal Justice Act (which only applies to youths between the ages of 12 and 17). If you're convicted of a crime in Canada and you are a temporary or permanent resident, you could be deported. Jail sentences act as punishments for crimes and can be served in a provincial (sentences of less than two years) or a federal (sentence of two years or more) correctional centre.

Canadians for the most part don't tend to have a 'lock them up and throw away the key' attitude to crime. But offences such as robbery, sexual assault and murder are treated very seriously. Though capital punishment was repealed in Canada in 1976, there are 'dangerous offender' provisions that allow the most serious offenders to be kept in prison for an indeterminate length of time. While in jail, prisoners are encouraged to engage in treatment and rehabilitative programmes that will prepare them for their eventual return to society.

## Divorce

Before you decide to get a divorce, it's important to have a good understanding of the law, especially if you have children or property. The laws in your home country might give you a more favourable outcome. In Canada, divorce falls under federal jurisdiction and is administered under the Divorce Act. You don't need to be a Canadian citizen or married in Canada to get a divorce, but you must have lived in the country for at least a year. You'll also have to 'prove fault' or show that your marriage has broken down and there's no chance of reconciliation. If you and your spouse have lived apart for at least a year, or if your spouse has been adulterous or physically or mentally cruel to you, you have grounds for divorce. Your divorce can be either uncontested (if you both agree on the terms of the divorce), or contested (if you don't agree on things such as custody of children and division of property). If you can't work out an agreement on your own, you may have to go to court, and if there's a trial it can be lengthy and costly for both parties.

> ### Do-It-Yourself Divorce
>
> While it might seem crass to some, it's entirely possible to complete your own divorce and make it quick, cheap and virtually painless. You just need to gather the proper forms, follow the directions and avoid using a lawyer altogether. Self-Counsel Press (www.self-counsel.com) publishes a range of legal do-it-yourself guides, including one for divorce. You can pick one up at a local bookstore and you'll be well on your way to unwedded bliss.

## Support For Children & Spouses

When parents can't agree on child custody or support, the courts will step in. A judge will take all factors into consideration and decide what's best for the child. If the child is old enough, the judge may ask their opinion too.

In Canada, the individual provinces and territories are responsible for enforcing child custody, access and support payments, but the actual amount of support to be paid

Strike action

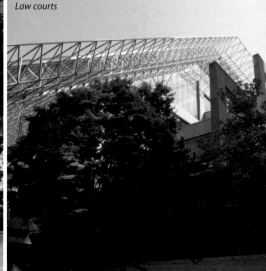
Law courts

is determined by the federal Child Support Guidelines. These guidelines take the number of children and both parents' incomes into consideration, and they were created to help make the process fair and to avoid lengthy and costly court processes.

Similarly, if couples can't agree on the provision of spousal support, the court will get involved and ultimately try to ensure each person has a comparable standard of living after the marriage has ended.

### Family Assets

When the time comes to divide up family assets, BC's Family Relations Act stipulates a 50/50 split among spouses. Assets might be property, pensions, or a family business. Generally speaking, if the asset was acquired during the marriage it may be considered a family asset.

A judge will issue 'court-ordered support payments' for children and spouses, which are enforceable under BC's strict Family Maintenance Enforcement Act. For example, a parent who doesn't pay support on time may be subject to sanctions, including having their driving licence or passport suspended. If you are divorced and have legal guardianship of your children, you still need permission from the other parent to move out of the country with the children. You may need additional court visits to determine the non-custodial parent's access to the children. The judge will make a decision that weighs up many factors, but ultimately puts the child's best interests first.

*Vancouver, Not Amsterdam*

*Though the pungent smell of marijuana can be detected pretty much everywhere in Vancouver, especially at beaches, nightclubs and festivals, the drug is not legal. If a police officer catches you smoking a joint, you'll probably be let off with a warning, but it could easily go the other way. If you have enough drugs in your possession to give police reason to think you might be supplying, you could find yourself facing substantial jail time.*

## Making A Will

The idea of planning for your eventual death is hardly pleasant, but it's especially important if you have children or assets. Similar to divorce, you can get do-it-yourself will kits, but it's a good idea to consult an estate lawyer if your holdings are complex. When you make a will in BC, you (the testator) must have your will witnessed by two people, both of whom need to be present when you sign the document. The witnesses must know you and cannot be beneficiaries. When it's their turn to sign the will, you must be present. A handwritten will is legal, as long as it's witnessed as explained above.

You can register a Wills Notice with the BC Vital Statistics Agency, which provides details on when the will was made and its location. This way someone can trace it easily. Contract the Vital Statistics Agency (250 952 2681, www.vs.gov.bc.ca/wills) or go to the office Downtown at 605 Robson Street to apply for a Wills Notice (there is a fee of $17).

Although you're not required to appoint an executor to administer your will, it's a good idea to choose a trusted friend or family member to take on this task. Wills don't necessarily need to be probated, but if they are, certain fees apply if the estate exceeds $10,000. Canada does not have an inheritance tax, but someone will need to file final income taxes on behalf of the deceased person.

## Adoption

Adopting a child either from within the province or from another country is a common practice in Canada. It is, however, a time-consuming, expensive and complicated process that involves many laws. Many people persist and manage to adopt successfully. Recent changes to federal laws have made the Canadian immigration process, within the international adoption process, slightly easier (see Citizenship of Adopted Children, p.69.)

Custom adoption is an organisation that ensures children are placed with First Nations families in order to maintain their cultural heritage. For further information, visit www.cf.gov.bc.ca.

# Housing

Vancouver is consistently rated as one of the world's most liveable cities, and an increasing number of people want to move to the city. With a forecast of more than 30,000 new residents per year, the Greater Vancouver region is expected to grow from 2.2 million people in 2007 to three million people by 2031, according to Metro Vancouver (www.gvrd.bc.ca). Growth is also driven by the fact that Vancouver will host the 2010 Winter Olympics. As a result, housing in general is increasingly expensive. A two-bedroom condo (a term commonly used for apartment) can cost anything from $1,600 to $3,000 a month to rent in the Downtown area, while a suburban three-bedroom house located in Surrey will start at about $1,000 a month. It can take some work to find somewhere suitable, but fortunately there is still a variety of housing options in different neighbourhoods that will accommodate all budgets.

## Renting In Vancouver

*Sorry Pet*
*Finding a home for you and your pet can be a challenge. Landlords may prohibit pets entirely, restrict their size, type or the number of pets you can have. They can also create rules regarding pets and charge a one-off pet deposit of up to half a month's rent if a pet is allowed. The landlord can evict your tenancy if you acquire a pet and they are prohibited in your tenancy agreement.*

First-time visitors are always amazed at the natural beauty of Downtown Vancouver, with its slender, green glass residential towers, surrounded by snow-capped mountains and ocean views. For many Vancouverites, getting a room with a view is a critical factor when choosing a place to live. It is still possible to find a place to rent with a beautiful vista of the mountain or the Pacific without having to spend thousands of dollars, but be prepared to pay a premium.

If you want to be close to the beaches or Stanley Park, the West End and Kitsilano areas are your best choices. A two-bedroom apartment in those areas will cost anywhere from $1,300 to $2,500 a month to rent. The downside is that the housing stock in these communities tends to be older and without all the amenities that some of the newer Downtown condos offer. If you want to be at the heart of the alternative art scene and experience a true community feel, Commercial Drive and Main Street might be more suitable. A two-bedroom apartment in this area will cost between $1,000 and $1,600 a month to rent. If you are looking for a combination of child-friendly amenities, high-end restaurants and access to modern housing developments, Yaletown is a prime choice. A two-bedroom apartment here costs from $1,600 to $3,500 a month to rent.

Rental contracts are usually made on an annual basis and cover the amount payable, when it is due, the lease terms and duration. A contract should also stipulate any services and facilities included in the rent, the amount of security deposit required and other details related to the rental unit. Rent is paid monthly and tenants usually provide the landlord with a set of post-dated cheques. Vancouver features the lowest vacancy rates and some of the highest rents in Canada. Rent continues to increase in the city, but you can always try to negotiate.

Whichever neighbourhood you pick, you are likely to find a wide range of community centres, shops, restaurants, schools and parks within walking or cycling distance. There is a commitment to creating a high-density city where people can live, play and work without having to drive their cars.

One important factor to consider if you choose to live outside central Vancouver is access to public transportation. The SkyTrain is a fast way to get to places such as Burnaby

## Housing Disputes

Tenants are protected by the Residential Tenancy Act. You can use the act to deal with problems you have with your landlord, like asking for repairs or disputing an eviction notice. Dispute resolution hearings are held at the Residential Tenancy Branch. The Tenants' Rights Action Coalition can advise you in this process and you can also view its Tenant Survival Guide on its website (www.tenants.ca).

or New Westminster, but some of the suburban communities such as Surrey are highly car dependent and not well served by buses. Traffic at rush hour is a real issue in the region.

## Amenities

Hot water and heating are generally included in your rent, but electricity is not. Other amenities such as cable television, high-speed internet connection and parking may also be included. Be sure to ask what your rent covers. Most modern condos have laundry facilities, but older rental buildings mainly offer coin-operated washers and dryers in the basement. Newer condos, like the ones located in Downtown or Yaletown, provide additional amenities for residents, such as swimming pools, gyms, billiard rooms or meeting rooms. Ask to view these facilities when you are shopping for a place as they can make a difference to your decision.

Do not forget to ask about storage and bike lockers. Some apartment buildings offer a storage locker separate from the suite for no extra fee. Others simply have built-in storage, which usually amounts to a small room within the apartment itself. If access to a balcony is important to you, do not let yourself be fooled by the 'enclosed balcony' feature that many new condos advertise. The term refers to a small additional room in the unit that might be suitable as a play area for children or an office space, but has no access to the outdoors.

Your landlord is responsible for the maintenance of the property, such as replacing defective appliances or fixing leaks. Your building manager might also be able to provide such services.

## Finding A Home

Most people look for places on their own when they get to Vancouver. Initially, you may want to rent furnished accommodation on a short-term basis in order to give yourself sufficient time to find a permanent home. You can look for a place to rent by searching specialised websites, including www.renthome.ca and www.rentbc.com). Craigslist is also an excellent resource (vancouver.craigslist.ca). You can browse the local newspapers such as *The Vancouver Sun* and *The Province*. An excellent way to find a place to rent is to walk around a neighbourhood that you like and look for 'rent' or 'vacancy' signs. Alternatively, local relocation companies might be able to assist you in your home search.

## Shared Accommodation

Housing in Vancouver can be expensive, and as a result many people find it cheaper to have housemates to share costs. It is important to choose who you live with carefully and check that all parties understand their rights and responsibilities. Conflicts are difficult to resolve legally since the BC Residential Tenancy Act does not cover the rights and responsibilities between housemates. To find a housemate, Craigslist is a good resource. You may also want to check ads posted on community centre bulletin boards located in the neighbourhoods where you want to live.

## Subsidised Housing

Public housing and buildings operated by non-profit societies and housing cooperatives are included in subsidised housing managed by BC Housing. This is a Crown agency that also delivers the provincial government's social housing programme. Housing cooperatives (co-ops) are jointly owned and managed by residents, who become cooperative members. Members participate in decision-making, share the responsibilities of running the co-op, and select new members. The BC Housing website (www.bchousing.org) provides information on how to apply.

Vancouver homes, from plot to penthouse

CAFE

## Real Estate Agents

Realtors, also known as real estate agents, generally do not deal with rental properties in Vancouver. Buyers may choose to hire a realtor to assist them in purchasing or selling a home. The best way to choose a realtor is through recommendations from friends and relatives. Interview several realtors, ask for references from past clients and evaluate how well they know the local market. Realtors not only specialise in specific geographical areas, they also specialise in various types of housing. Make sure they have the expertise you need. Visiting 'open houses' is also a good way to meet realtors. Real estate agents must pass an examination to obtain a provincial licence, and they also have legal obligations and have agreed to maintain ethical standards. Check out the Canadian Real Estate Association's website to know more about a real estate agent's ethical obligations (www.crea.ca).

Those selling property pay a commission to the sales agent, who then shares it with the buyer's agent. Real estate commissions are negotiable and there are no standard rates. There are thousands of real estate agents in Greater Vancouver. The table below should help you get started on your search.

| Real Estate Agents | | |
| --- | --- | --- |
| Century 21 In Town Realty | 604 685 5951 | www.century21.ca/intownrealty |
| Real Estate Board Of Greater Vancouver | 604 303 7000 | www.realtylink.org |
| Real Estate Council Of BC | 604 683 9664 | www.remax-selectvanbc.com |
| Re/Max | 604 737 8865 | www.remax.ca |
| Rennie Marketing Systems | 604 682 2088 | www.rennie.com |
| Royal Pacific Realty | 604 266 8989 | www.royalpacific.ca |
| Sutton Group Realty Services | 604 691 1620 | www.sutton.com |

## The Lease

Required by law, the most important document required when starting your tenancy is the residential tenancy agreement. It is signed and dated by both the landlord and yourself, and it includes information such as the amount of rent payable and when it is due, lease terms and duration, services included in the rent, and the amount of security or pet damage deposit required. Tenants are usually asked to pay a security deposit to cover potential unpaid rent, cleaning or any damage. The deposit amount cannot exceed half of the first month's rent and is returned when the tenants move out. Rent is paid on a monthly basis, and you will be expected to provide a set of post-dated cheques to your landlord.

Initial lease duration is typically for one year and is then renewed on a month-by-month basis, but other arrangements can be made. A fixed-term tenancy will finish automatically on the end date that is specified in your lease and no notice by the tenant is necessary. If you are in a month-to-month tenancy, you are required to give the landlord one full month's notice. If you break the lease early you may be legally responsible for making rental payments until the landlord finds another tenant.

Rent is always negotiable and it does not hurt to ask for a reduction if you feel the accommodation is overpriced. Some owners will offer a discount from the first month's rent for newly renovated buildings as an incentive to get tenants in quickly.

The Canada Housing and Mortgage Corporation offers excellent resources on all you need to know about renting in BC (www.cmhc-schl.gc.ca).

## Main Accommodation Options

Vancouver offers a variety of accommodation to buy or rent. Larger housing (three bedrooms or more) can be particularly difficult to find in the city. It can also be expensive, and will rent for $3,000 per month or more. People who cannot afford to

## Housing Abbreviations

| | |
|---|---|
| appl | Appliances |
| bdrm or br | Bedroom |
| bsmt or bst | Basement |
| gar | Garage |
| hdw | Hardwood floors |
| hi ceils | High ceilings |
| inc util | Utilities included |
| n/p | No pets |
| n/s | No smoking |
| prkg | Parking |
| refs | References |
| t/h | Townhouse |
| w/d | Washer and dryer |
| w/w | Wall-to-wall carpeting |
| n/s | No smoking |

rent or buy a house in the city have the option of moving out to the suburbs where prices are more affordable.

### Condominiums & Rental Apartment Buildings

One-bedroom apartments or one-bedroom and den units will typically range from 600 to 1,000 square feet, and will cost between $1,000 and $1,500 per month in rent. Two-bedroom units are usually between 800 and 1,200 square feet. Expect to pay between $1,500 and $3,000 per month in rent, depending on the location.

High-rise rental apartment buildings are taller than five storeys and are made of concrete. Low-rise rental apartment buildings have a wooden structure and are up to five storeys high. Most of the rental apartment buildings are owned and operated by a company that may have several other rental properties in the area. The company usually employs a resident building manager who is responsible for showing, renting and maintaining apartments, as well as collecting rent. Condominiums in high-rise, low-rise or townhouse buildings are owned by individuals who will often rent out their apartments if the building strata committee allows it. Condos are usually more expensive and contain a full set of appliances and fancy amenities such as a fitness room or sauna.

### Townhouses

Townhouses are very popular as they give the owners, or those renting, some private outdoor space on the ground level, and offer two to three storeys of living space. The inclusion of townhouses at the base of apartment towers has become a signature of Downtown Vancouver. Townhouses are particularly suitable for families with children, and others who want to live close to the ground. Rental costs for townhouses vary depending on the size of the accommodation and its location. Prices can start at $1,000 a month for a townhouse in one of the suburbs of Greater Vancouver, and rise to $3,000 or more in Downtown Vancouver.

### Houses

Single, detached houses for rent in Vancouver are a rarity and can be quite difficult to find. They will also tend to be very expensive. You will be more likely to find a house for rent outside Vancouver, but be prepared for extra scrutiny from the landlord. Tenants using properties for marijuana growing operations have been a problem in BC and it can lead to immense property damage.

If you do want to live in a house and do not want to move out of Vancouver, you have the option of renting an apartment in a house. Many older, large houses have been divided by their owners into two or more apartments. The units frequently include a kitchen and a separate bathroom, but sometimes they have to be shared. A communal laundry facility is common. Basement suites, usually with a separate entrance, are particularly popular because they are more affordable than independent apartments. The main advantage of this option is that it is relatively affordable (you can live in one of Vancouver's great neighbourhoods, such as Kitsilano) and the houses often have a small garden and a unique character. The downside is that you may have to abide by the rules of shared living, which isn't for everybody.

Rental costs for houses vary depending on the size of the property and the location. Prices can start at $1,000 a month for a house in one of the suburbs of Greater Vancouver, rising to $5,000 and more for a house in the city or in elite communities such as West Vancouver.

## Other Rental Costs

While some costs such as hot water and heating may be included in your rent, you will probably have to pay for additional services such as cable television, telephone and an internet connection. Parking may be included in your rent or you may have to pay an extra monthly fee for an underground space in the building. A parking spot can cost anywhere from $45 to $100 a month. Landlords may also charge you a deposit for access devices such as keys and automatic garage door controls.

*Leaky Condos*

*Any prospective buyer in Vancouver should be aware of leaky condos. 'Leaky condo syndrome,' where water enters the building envelope and can result in rot and other forms of decay, has affected condominiums, detached homes, schools and hospitals. The majority of problem buildings were built between the early 1980s and the late 1990s. More recent developments have improved the construction and design of this type of housing.*

## Buying Property

Buying a home is one of the largest financial investments you will make in your life. Although price increases have slowed down recently, Vancouver's real estate market remains very strong. The Downtown area is the most expensive housing market in Canada. In December 2007, the Real Estate Board of Greater Vancouver reported that the sale price for a typical detached house in Greater Vancouver was about $730,400, which represents an increase of 95% over the last five years. The sales price of a typical townhouse was about $457,000, an increase of more than 100% since December 2002. A typical Greater Vancouver apartment sold for about $377,580 in December 2007, an increase of 112% over the previous five years. Forecasters who had expected Lower Mainland real estate markets to moderate during 2007 instead saw sales rebound and price increases continue at rates that have doubled values in many markets over five years. Fuelling the high-end market are foreign buyers and the growth associated with the upcoming 2010 Winter Olympics.

Before you start looking for a home, you need to determine what you can afford, which neighbourhood you want to live in, and the type of property you need. If owning a house is what matters to you, your most affordable option might be to move outside of the city to the suburbs. If a Downtown location is your priority and you are ready to compromise on square footage, you could consider a condo. Several residential towers are currently being built in the area, including the 62 storey Living Shangri-La (www.livingshangri-la.com), which will be Vancouver's tallest building when it is completed. There are no restrictions on buying property in Vancouver or building a new house on land, as long as you comply with the zoning regulations in place for the area.

*Real estate*

## Non-Citizen Restrictions

You can buy a property in Canada even if you are not a citizen, and you may also apply for mortgages from Canadian banks if you possess a minimum of 25% of the cost of the property as a cash deposit for a downpayment. Non-citizen buyers will be required to pay annual property taxes and capital gains tax when they sell property.

## The Process

Once you've found the perfect home and are ready to make an offer, you'll need to fill out a Contract of Purchase and Sale form. If the seller accepts your offer, you have to carry out a number of steps before the sale is completed, which include conducting a property inspection (if you have made the sale subject to a certified inspection), and finalising your mortgage. You also have to put down a deposit when you make an offer.

## Buying To Let

It is common practice to buy a property in order to rent it out. In 2004 the City of Vancouver approved a change to the zoning bylaw, permitting homeowners to have a secondary suite in any detached single family home. A secondary suite refers to an additional, separate dwelling unit in a home that would normally accommodate only one dwelling unit. The secondary suite usually has its own entrance, kitchen, bathroom and living area. Homeowners frequently rent out secondary suites in their primary residence to help them repay their mortgage.

## Selling Property

When preparing your home for the market, you need to look at your house in a new way. Think of it as a product and how it might be competing with brand new housing already on sale; it needs to be well presented, which means clutter free and well kept.

You can sell your home yourself by advertising in newspapers or on the internet, or you can engage a real estate agent to market your property and represent you through the offer, negotiation and acceptance process.

When someone offers to buy your home they will prepare a written offer or a contract of purchase and sale. Once you have completed the sale, there are some costs you need to be prepared to pay. These include the realtor's commission (if you have engaged an agent), legal fees, any penalties for paying off your mortgage early, goods and services tax (GST) on the real estate commission and on your legal fees, and your share of the property taxes for the year.

The website for the Canada Mortgage and Housing Corporation has excellent resources and tips for home buyers and tenants, and offers a step-by-step guide to buying and selling (www.cmhc-schl.gc.ca).

## Mortgages

Many banks and financial institutions offer mortgages, so it is usually best to shop around as most lenders will reduce their posted interest rate if you negotiate. You can contact banks and credit unions directly or work with a mortgage broker. A broker will help you find a lender and the best mortgage package. Obtaining prior approval for your mortgage, even before you start home hunting, will save you time because you will know how much you can borrow. You won't have to worry about rising interest rates while shopping for a home; the mortgage broker will usually guarantee the rate for 60 to 90 days and you will save time when you are ready to make an offer.

Lenders use two rules to determine how much you can afford. The first rule is that your monthly housing costs should not exceed 32% of your gross monthly household income. Housing costs include monthly mortgage payments, taxes and heating expenses. If applicable, this sum should also include half of the monthly condominium fees (a form

---

**Home Inspections**
*You should consider having any home you are thinking of buying examined by a certified inspector. Their role is to inform you about the property's condition. He or she will tell you if something is not functioning properly, needs to be changed, or is unsafe. You will also be informed of repairs that need to be done. Inspection fees are generally $200 or more, depending on the size and condition of the home. A good home inspector generally belongs to a provincial or industry association such as the Canadian Association of Home and Property Inspectors (www.cahi.ca).*

of building maintenance). Secondly, your entire monthly debt load should not be any more than 40% of your gross monthly income. This includes housing costs and other debts such as car payments, personal loans, and credit card payments.

An open mortgage gives you the most flexibility in making extra payments towards your mortgage principal and even lets you pay off your mortgage entirely whenever you wish to. If your mortgage is not fully open, you may be charged a penalty if you decide to pay off all or part of your mortgage before the end of the fixed term. A prepayment penalty is charged to the borrower if they choose to pay their mortgage early, and is usually attached to a loan in exchange for a slightly lower rate, which is more attractive to borrowers.

*Downpayments*

For a conventional mortgage, you must pay at least 20% of the purchase price as a downpayment. However, you can find mortgages that require as little as a 5% or 0% downpayment. If you are a non-citizen, you will have to pay 25%-35%.

## Mortgage Providers

Most banks and credit unions provide mortgage services. You can also approach a mortgage broker. You can search for qualified mortgage brokers, located throughout the province, on the Mortgage Brokers Association of British Columbia website (www.findabettermortgage.ca).

| Mortgage Providers | | |
|---|---|---|
| BMO Financial Group | 1 877 225 5266 | www4.bmo.com |
| Canadian Bankers Association | 1 800 263 0231 | www.cba.ca |
| HSBC | 604 525 4722 | www.hsbc.ca |
| Mortgage Brokers Association of British Columbia | 604 408 9989 | www.findabettermortgage.ca |
| Royal Bank of Canada | 1 800 769 2511 | www.rbcroyalbank.com |
| Scotiabank | 604 668 2094 | www.scotiabank.com |
| TD Canada Trust | 604 654 3665 | www.tdcanadatrust.com |
| Vancity | 604 877 7000 | www.vancity.com |

## Other Purchasing Costs

There are additional costs when you buy a home. These include mortgage insurance, taxes, legal fees, house insurance, inspection reports, appraisal and survey fees. For example, if you obtain a mortgage where you put less than 20% as a downpayment, you will have to buy mortgage loan insurance. The mortgage loan insurance is based on the size of your loan and will cost anywhere between 1% and 4% of the loan value. The property transfer tax is paid to the BC government by the purchaser of any piece of real estate in the province. The tax is usually 1% on the first $200,000 of the purchase price, plus 2% on the remainder. If you are a first-time buyer, you may be exempt from this tax. If you buy a newly constructed home, you must pay the 5% goods and services tax.

## Real Estate Law

There are three main real estate laws in BC that you should be aware of. The Land and Equity Act sets out most of the rules that govern foreclosures and redemption; the Land Title Act administers BC's land title system; and the Property Law Act requires that a vendor of land delivers a title that can be registered under the Land Title Act. The Property Law Act also covers the transfer of the responsibilities under an existing mortgage from the seller to a buyer. In most situations, the seller will use the proceeds

**Living The Olympic Dream**
*One of the hot areas to live in Vancouver in the near future will be the south-east False Creek site. Built on industrial lands to house the Olympic Village for the 2010 Winter Olympics, the development will then be converted into luxury waterfront condominiums and townhouses. South-east False Creek is envisaged as a model sustainable community, featuring green buildings and other energy-efficient design features (www.city.vancouver.bc.ca/commsvcs/southeast).*

to pay off the mortgage, and so give the title to the purchaser free of any mortgage. The purchaser will then allow his or her own mortgage to be registered against the property. The act is for those situations where the seller's mortgage survives the sale. The Property Law Act also makes it clear that Canadian citizenship is not required to buy or sell land in British Columbia.

**Rental Assistance**
*If you are having difficulty meeting monthly rent payments you may qualify for assistance from the Rental Assistance Program. Visit www. bchousing.org for further information on eligibility and advice.*

## The Offer To Purchase

When you are ready to buy a home, you have to go through the process of putting in an offer to purchase it. The offer is a legally binding document and if for some reason you back out of the deal without having covered yourself, your deposit may not be refundable. The deposit is part of your downpayment and must be paid when you make an offer to purchase. The cost varies depending on the area, but it may be up to 5% of the purchase price. If you only wish to make a downpayment of 5% and you give a deposit of 5%, then your downpayment is considered to be made. An offer to purchase can be made conditionally. That means that the sale will be final if you can get financing, and there is a satisfactory professional home inspection. You may want to talk with your lawyer before making an offer to purchase.

## Types Of Properties

If you buy a condo, your property will be overseen by a strata corporation that manages the building via a strata council. The strata corporation has the responsibility for the overall management of the condominium and is owned by all the owners of the strata units. It has the responsibility to insure the building, keep the common areas in good repair, establish a contingency fund for emergencies, and generally manage the building. It also prepares the annual budget for the building.

The rules are fairly standard but the strata council may amend them, for example, to exclude pets or rentals. Before you buy a condo, make sure you can live with these rules. Also check the minutes of the strata council meetings. This will give you insights into any hidden problems with the building and will help you determine how well the building is managed.

A freehold title gives the holder ownership of land and buildings for an indefinite period of time. A leasehold title gives the holder a right to use and occupy land and buildings for a defined period of time. In a leasehold arrangement, actual ownership of the land, sometimes along with the buildings, remains with the landlord, and the lease fee is payable on top of mortgage and property taxes, as well as condo fees. Lenders also usually require higher downpayments for leaseholds.

The south False Creek community is a good case study of the pros and cons of leasehold. It was built 30 years ago on former industrial lands, and homeowners who bought condos there entered into a lease agreement with the city. As leasehold purchases are cheaper than freehold, this made buying a property in such a popular area as False Creek an attractive proposition. However, in 2006 the City of Vancouver significantly increased lease rates with no warning to residents, meaning leaseholders who may have got a good deal when buying the property suddenly were obliged to pay higher rates.

## Getting A Lawyer

Having a lawyer or a notary to oversee your home purchase will give you peace of mind. Your lawyer will help you with tasks such as searching the property title to see if there are any outstanding work orders, checking the offer to purchase, ensuring property taxes are up to date, preparing all the documents to transfer ownership to you, and making sure that the seller's mortgage is discharged. Fees for closing the sale vary according to the complexity of the deal, but they will probably be at least $400.

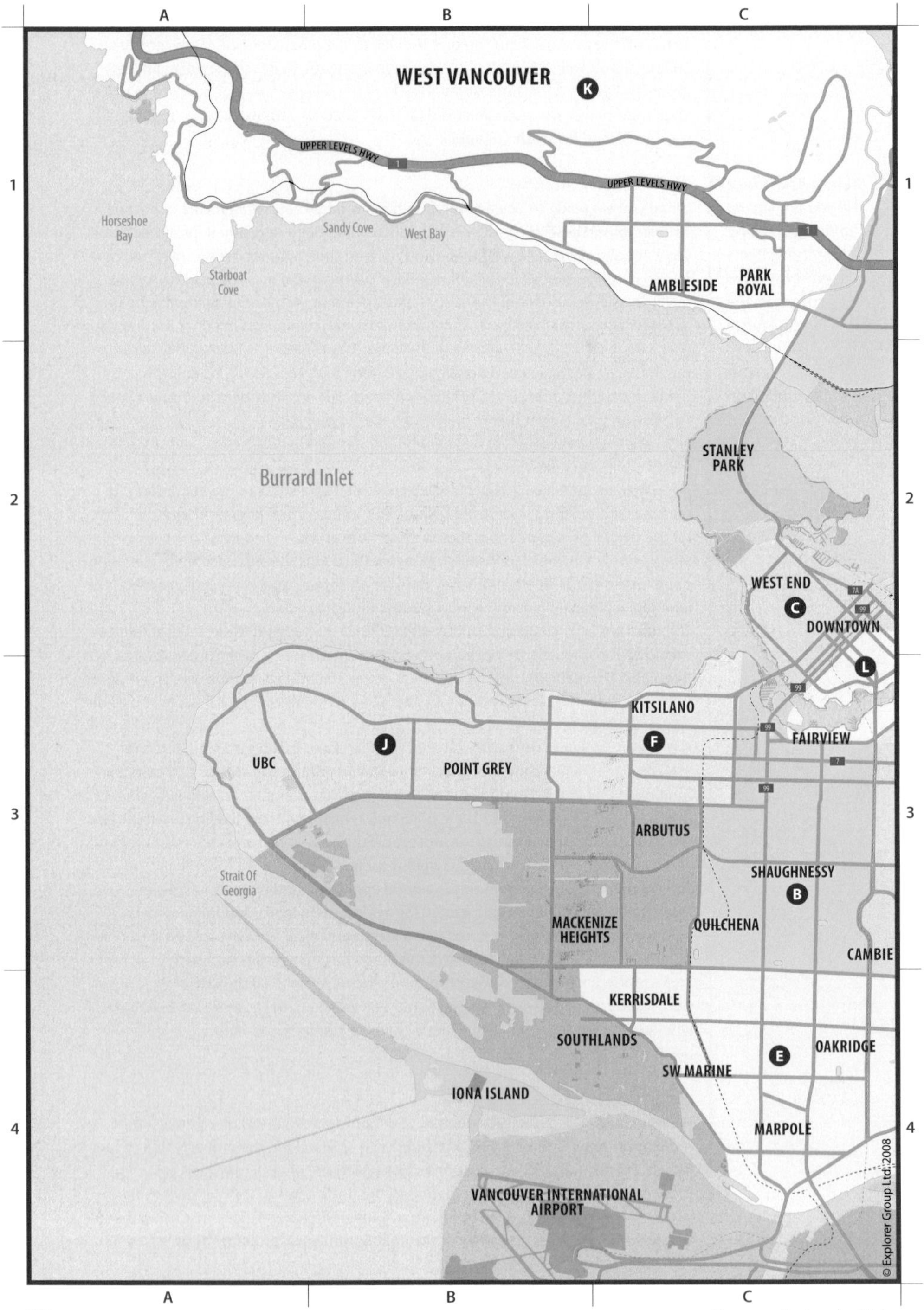
A
B
C
1
2
3
4
WEST VANCOUVER
K
UPPER LEVELS HWY
1
UPPER LEVELS HWY
Horseshoe Bay
Sandy Cove
West Bay
Starboat Cove
AMBLESIDE
PARK ROYAL
STANLEY PARK
Burrard Inlet
WEST END
C
DOWNTOWN
7A
99
L
KITSILANO
F
FAIRVIEW
J
UBC
POINT GREY
7
ARBUTUS
SHAUGHNESSY
B
Strait Of Georgia
MACKENIZE HEIGHTS
QUILCHENA
CAMBIE
KERRISDALE
SOUTHLANDS
OAKRIDGE
E
SW MARINE
IONA ISLAND
MARPOLE
VANCOUVER INTERNATIONAL AIRPORT
© Explorer Group Ltd. 2008

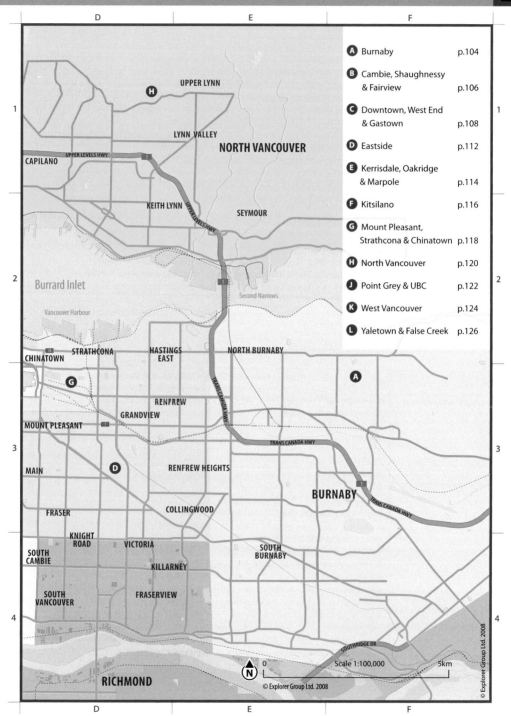

D      E      F

**A** Burnaby    p.104

**B** Cambie, Shaughnessy & Fairview    p.106

**C** Downtown, West End & Gastown    p.108

**D** Eastside    p.112

**E** Kerrisdale, Oakridge & Marpole    p.114

**F** Kitsilano    p.116

**G** Mount Pleasant, Strathcona & Chinatown    p.118

**H** North Vancouver    p.120

**J** Point Grey & UBC    p.122

**K** West Vancouver    p.124

**L** Yaletown & False Creek    p.126

UPPER LYNN

LYNN VALLEY

**NORTH VANCOUVER**

CAPILANO

UPPER LEVELS HWY

KEITH LYNN

SEYMOUR

Burrard Inlet

Vancouver Harbour

Second Narrows

CHINATOWN

STRATHCONA

HASTINGS EAST

NORTH BURNABY

**A**

**G**

RENFREW

GRANDVIEW

MOUNT PLEASANT

TRANS CANADA HWY

TRANS CANADA HWY

MAIN

**D**

RENFREW HEIGHTS

**BURNABY**

TRANS CANADA HWY

FRASER

COLLINGWOOD

KNIGHT ROAD

VICTORIA

SOUTH BURNABY

SOUTH CAMBIE

KILLARNEY

SOUTH VANCOUVER

FRASERVIEW

RICHMOND

SOUTHRIDGE DR

Scale 1:100,000

0      5km

N

© Explorer Group Ltd. 2008

© Explorer Group Ltd. 2008

*Area* **A** *p.103*
*See also Map 6*

# Burnaby

Burnaby is the third largest city in British Columbia, behind Vancouver and Surrey. It is located on the Burrard peninsula between Vancouver to the west and New Westminster and Coquitlam to the east. Because of its proximity to Vancouver and its good transportation options, Burnaby is an attractive community to many, and a good compromise for people who cannot quite afford to live in the city but do not want to be too far from central Vancouver. Its convenient geographical location has also attracted many businesses and offices.

Burnaby is divided into three sections: North Burnaby, South Burnaby, and Central Burnaby, each with its own characteristics and demographics. North Burnaby is home to the Simon Fraser University campus, located on Burnaby Mountain. South Burnaby has the majority of the suburb's commercial and retail businesses, as well as Metrotown mall, a large retail and entertainment complex. Central Burnaby contains Deer Lake Park, Burnaby's cultural centre. It is also the economic and industrial hub, with many large companies having offices and facilities in the area (including Electronic Arts, Kodak, and United Way).

*Best Points*
Burnaby is close to Vancouver and well served by the SkyTrain, making it a cheaper option to live here and work Downtown. Many large companies have offices in Burnaby, so it's also possible, and convenient, to live and work there.

## Accommodation

Burnaby provides a full range of housing, from single-family homes to high-rise apartment buildings. The Metrotown area is home to most of the high-rise modern condos and apartment complexes. Two-bedroom apartments cost between $1,000 and $1,500 a month to rent. Newer apartment units usually have in-suite washer and dryer, and may have access to common amenities such as a pool and an exercise room.

*Worst Points*
While some areas are well connected and are only a SkyTrain ride from Downtown Vancouver, other sprawling neighbourhoods are less accessible. If you don't have a car, you'll spend a lot of time waiting for buses.

## Shopping & Amenities

There are several retail and commercial centres of interest. The huge Metrotown mall (p.415) has hundreds of stores, services and cinemas, and is connected to the Metrotown station on the SkyTrain system. The Heights in North Burnaby is a multicultural commercial neighbourhood, with many Italian, Chinese and Portuguese restaurants, delis and shops. Lougheed Town Centre Mall (www.lougheedmall.com) serves the needs of the residents of East Burnaby, while Brentwood Mall (www.brentwoodmall.com) caters for residents of the north-west area. For grocery shopping, there's a large Choices Market (6855 Station Hill Drive, 604 522 6441) and a MarketPlace IGA (1601 Burnwood Drive, 604 421 1574). Recommended restaurants in Burnaby include Pear Tree, which features imaginative west coast cuisine (4120 East Hastings Street, 604 299 2772), and Horizons Restaurant (100 Centennial Way, 604 299 1155), which is situated on top of Burnaby Mountain Park.

## Entertainment & Leisure

Burnaby is home to several beautiful parks. The Burnaby Lake Regional Nature Park offers a variety of trails through a forest and open marshland, while Burnaby Lake is a good spot for observing waterfowl. Deer Lake Park takes visitors through grassy meadows, woods and lakeside vistas, and is a good spot for birdwatching, as well as a great place to enjoy outdoor concerts in the summer. The cultural hubs of the Shadbold Centre for the Arts (604 291 6864) and the Burnaby Art Gallery (604 205 7332) are both found minutes from Metrotown, and has an urban forest with walking trails, an outdoor pool, and a pitch and putt golf course. There are several cinemas in Burnaby, plus a wide variety of restaurants and bars. Leisure facilities include Bonsor Recreation Complex (6550 Bonsor Avenue, 604 439 1860), CG Brown Memorial Pool (3702

Kensington Avenue, 604 299 9374) and Eileen Dailly Leisure Pool & Fitness Centre (240 Willingdon Avenue, 604 298 7946).

### Healthcare
There is a full range of health facilities in the city, including Burnaby Hospital (3935 Kincaid Street, 604 434 4211), which has 267 beds and provides a range of health services for individuals requiring care, and the Station Square Medical Clinic (6200 McKay Avenue, 6004 498 8288).

### Education
Two major post-secondary institutions are here. The British Columbia Institute of Technology, one of the leading technology and trade colleges in the province, is in Central Burnaby (3700 Willingdon Avenue, 604 434 5734), while Simon Fraser University (8888 University Drive, 778 782 3111) has more than 25,000 students, and its original Burnaby campus has now extended to other locations in Vancouver and Surrey. Burnaby School District lists full details of all of Burnaby's elementary and secondary schools (604 664 8441, www.sd41.bc.ca).

### Transport
With several SkyTrain stations, a good road system, and a public bus network that includes express and rapid buses, Burnaby has excellent connections within the city and to other parts of the region. The SkyTrain rapid transit system crosses Burnaby from east to west in two places: in the south along the Expo Line, and in the middle along the Millennium Line. The SkyTrain has encouraged dense transit-oriented urban development around Lougheed Town Centre, Brentwood Centre, and, most notably, Metrotown. It takes about 25 minutes by car from Burnaby to Downtown Vancouver during morning and evening peak hours, and about 18 minutes by SkyTrain.

### Safety & Annoyances
The major annoyance about living in Burnaby is that, like any other of the sprawling suburbs of the Greater Vancouver region, you will need to rely on a car to get to places. Despite the close proximity of Burnaby to Vancouver, be prepared to embrace a suburban lifestyle.

*Burnaby Heights*

Area **B** p.102
See also Map 5

# Cambie, Shaughnessy & Fairview

Cambie sits between Cambie Street and Oak Street, and 16th Avenue and 41st Avenue. It is mainly a residential community, but is also well known for its top medical facilities.

The last few decades have seen Fairview transformed from an industrial area fronting False Creek to a family-oriented neighbourhood offering waterfront living in the heart of the city. Fairview stretches from Burrard Street to Cambie Street, and from 16th Avenue to False Creek, and includes the neighbourhoods of False Creek, Fairview Slopes, Burrard Slopes and Fairview Heights, as well as the area of Granville Street known as South Granville, or the South Granville Strip.

Shaughnessy centres on Granville Street, which is a major thoroughfare linking Vancouver with the southern suburbs and the airport. This exclusive, elite community is situated between 16th Avenue and 41st Avenue and between West Boulevard and Oak Street, and features large, well-maintained expensive homes along curving tree-lined streets.

**Best Points**
*A one-time busy industrial area filled with shipyards and sawmills, Fairview has been transformed into one of Vancouver's premier neighbourhoods, complete with parks, schools, shops, and a seawall used for walking, jogging, biking and rollerblading. Residents are just steps away from two of Vancouver's most popular shopping destinations: South Granville and Granville Island.*

## Accommodation

Family homes and low-rise apartment buildings dominate the landscape in South Cambie and Shaughnessy, and a number of heritage homes can be found in these neighbourhoods. Shaughnessy in particular is an expensive neighbourhood, with large townhouses going for a monthly rent of between $2,500 and $5,000. Housing in Fairview consists of apartments, condos, duplexes and cooperatives, some of which are rent controlled, allowing young families to live in this area. Some of these places feature great views of the city and False Creek. In Fairview, small townhouses and two-bedroom apartments are available to rent for between $1,600 and $2,500 a month.

## Shopping & Amenities

**Worst Points**
*There are few disadvantages to living in this area, save one: price. Shaughnessy is a very exclusive and expensive neighbourhood, and Fairview's housing prices, once reasonable, are climbing.*

South Granville Street and 10th Avenue have excellent shopping. Residents of Fairview are just a short walk from both Granville Island and South Granville Street, an upmarket area filled with boutique shopping, independent art galleries and coffee shops. For the latest in designer fashion, there are several high-end clothing stores, including Boboli (2776 Granville Street, 604 257 2317). Restoration Hardware (2555 Granville Street, 604 731 3918) carries distinctive home furniture, while great dining options include Vij's (p.434), for a divine Indian fusion cuisine experience. For grocery shopping, Capers Community Market (3277 Cambie Street, 604 909 2988) is a great destination for organic produce and speciality items, and there's a large Choices Market at 3493 Cambie Street (604 875 0099).

## Entertainment & Leisure

Situated on Little Mountain, the highest point in the city, Queen Elizabeth Park (p.244) features beautiful gardens and a tropical plant conservatory. VanDusen Botanical Garden (p.246) offers diverse plant collections, gardening courses, family and children programmes, and stages the popular Festival of Lights (p.59). For evening entertainment there's a decent Park Theatre cinema at 3440 Cambie Street (604 709 3456), and for live theatre the Stanley Industrial Alliance Stage (2750 Granville Street, 604 687 1644), part of the Arts Club Theatre Company, is a popular venue. Kino Cafe (3456 Cambie Street, 604 875 1998) is a great place to see flamenco shows.

## Healthcare

South Cambie is home to many of BC's top medical facilities. BC Women's Hospital & Health Centre (p.152), on Oak Street, is the only facility in BC devoted primarily to the health of women, newborns, and families. Neighbouring BC Children's Hospital (p.152) provides expert care for seriously ill or injured children from across the province, including newborns and adolescents. Vancouver General Hospital on West 12th Avenue (p.153) offers specialised and tertiary services to city and province residents; it is also a teaching hospital, affiliated with the University of British Columbia, and home to one of the largest research institutes in Canada. Main pharmacy options include City Square Pharmacy (West 12th Avenue, 604 872 4322) and Pharmasave (4054 Cambie Street, 604 873 9277).

### Education

These residential communities each have access to several schools, including the Point Grey Secondary School (5350 East Boulevard, 604 713 220), the Shaughnessy Elementary School (4250 Marguerite Street, 604 713 5500), and the Edith Cavell Elementary School (500 West 20th Avenue, 604 713 4932). Fairview is served by Kitsilano Secondary School (2550 West 10th Avenue, 604 713 8961), Eric Hamber Secondary School (5025 Willow Street, 604 713 8927) and L'École Bilingue (1166 West 14th Avenue, 604 713 4585), which is Vancouver's largest French immersion centre. The Emily Carr Elementary School (4070 Oak Street, 604 7134941), False Creek Elementary School (900 School Green, 604 713 4959), Henry Hudson Elementary School (1551 Cypress Street, 604 713 5441), and Trafalgar Elementary School (4170 Trafalgar Street, 604 713 5475) are all accessible. Private schools

*Granville Street*

Madrona School (101-910 West 6th Avenue, 604 732 9965) and Blessed Sacrament School (3020 Heather Street, 604 876 721) are also based in the neighbourhood.

### Transport

The area is well served by the public bus system, including the number 9, 15 and 99 routes, which offer a frequent service. The number 15 services Cambie at 64th Avenue to Downtown via Cambie Street, and the 99 runs from Granville Street to Alma Street via Broadway. In 2009, the new SkyTrain Canada Line will run from Waterfront Station Downtown to Richmond via Cambie Street. The Aquabus allows the communities surrounding False Creek to get around on water. A regular service is offered between Granville Island and locations including Fairview Slopes (www.theaquabus.com).

### Safety & Annoyances

These residential areas are generally very safe and do not present any major annoyances. However, Cambie Street has recently been affected by the construction of the Canada Line rapid transit system, which will traverse the whole of Cambie Street through the South Cambie neighbourhood. Some businesses closed when construction began in 2005.

Area **C** p.102
See also Map 7

# Downtown, West End & Gastown

Downtown Vancouver is the triangular promontory of land nestled between Burrard Inlet and False Creek. The area is a patchwork of distinct communities, including the business district, the West End, Coal Harbour and Gastown.

**Best Points**

The proximity to the beach and Stanley Park makes Downtown one of the best places to live in Vancouver. Wherever you are, you always stumble on a view of the ocean or the mountains. The West End is the most diverse community in the city. It has a relaxing and welcoming feel, is gay friendly and many immigrants and students live here.

The densely populated Downtown has been described as a model for urban living in North America. You can live, work and play in the Downtown peninsula without ever having to get into your car. The community is a beautiful blend of high-rise buildings, quiet tree-lined streets, and older low-rise apartment buildings.

The West End, running from Burrard Street to Denman Street, in between Robson Street and Beach Avenue, has some of the city's most beautiful views of the ocean. It is close to English Bay beach and Stanley Park.

Overlooking Stanley Park and the North Shore Mountains, Coal Harbour stretches from Canada Place to Cardero Street, along the Burrard Inlet shore, and is a new upmarket high-rise condo district. A harbourside waterfront walkway and bicycle route along Coal Harbour connects with the Stanley Park Seawall.

The oldest part of Vancouver, Gastown's charm shines through the souvenir shops and panhandlers. The community retains the feel of an old Victorian town, and in the last few years it has become a trendy place to live and play. Because commercial rents in Gastown have stayed low, it is still the area to look for new art galleries, young fashion designers, or a piece of beautiful, hand-carved First Nations art in one of the galleries along Water Street and Hastings.

## Accommodation

**Worst Points**

The West End is mostly a transient community. Most of the housing stock is made up of older rental apartments, and people usually only stay for a few years before moving on. With its upmarket waterfront condominiums, Coal Harbour is often described as a resort community for those with second homes, and lacks the community feel found elsewhere.

The Downtown and West End areas are primarily made up of apartments and townhouse developments, although you can also find interesting artists' lofts in Gastown. The price range varies tremendously according to the age of the building, its amenities, the view, and the square footage. Expect to pay anywhere between $1,500 and $3,500 a month to rent a two-bedroom unit ranging in size from 800 to 1,400 square feet. Downtown apartments tend to be newer, with building amenities such as a pool, gym, and meeting facilities. The units usually have in-suite storage and washer and dryer facilities. On the downside, the apartments are small and often have enclosed balconies rather than real outdoor space. Older West End apartments are usually larger in size and often have large outdoor balconies, but lack the modern amenities that the Downtown apartment complexes provide. A two-bedroom apartment typically costs less to rent in Gastown because the area is undergoing redevelopment, and is considered less desirable because of its proximity to Downtown Eastside. You can find beautiful large spaces and high ceilings in heritage buildings, and many artists have established their studios here. Expect to pay between $950 and $2,200 for rent per month for a two-bedroom Gastown apartment.

## Shopping & Amenities

Shopping highlights revolve around Robson Street, with its designer fashion stores, and Gastown, which is full of small boutiques and gift shops. Major department stores such as The Bay and Holt Renfrew are located at the intersection of Georgia and Granville streets. Capers Community Market is a great place to shop for organic food (1675 Robson Street, 604 687 5288), and Urban Fare (305 Bute Street, 604 669 5831) and MarketPlace IGA (909 Burrard Street, 604 605 0612) are also useful outlets for groceries. If you are craving high-quality, local meat, a visit to So.Cial butcher's shop in the heart of Gastown will not disappoint (332 Water Street, 604 669 4488). You can buy bread, pastries, and other gourmet food at nearby Brioche (401 West Cordova Street, 604 682 4037).

*Downtown and Gastown*

### Entertainment & Leisure

The West End holds an eclectic mix of ethnic restaurants, coffee houses, and nightclubs. Denman is a great place to grab an icecream and head down to English Bay to watch the sunset on the beach, while the city's premier outdoor space, Stanley Park (see p.244), is right on your doorstep. Davie Street is the gay centre of Vancouver, and home to one of the most popular nightclubs in the city, Celebrities (see p.468). There are plenty of entertainment options, including GM Place, where you can watch hockey games (p.337), the Queen Elizabeth Theatre (649 Cambie Street, 604 665 3050), the Orpheum (884 Granville Street, 604 665 3050), and the Commodore Ballroom (868 Granville Street, 604 739 7469). Gastown is home to many new restaurants, including the unique Salt Tasting Room (p.440), while nearby Chambar (p.440), close to GM Place, is an excellent Belgian eatery.

### Healthcare

St Paul's Hospital is an acute care, teaching and research hospital located on Burrard Street (see p.153). It runs many medical and surgical programmes, including cardiac services, and HIV/Aids and kidney care. There are walk-in medical clinics and health centres serving the three areas, including the Downtown Community Health Centre (569 Powell Street, 604 255 3151), the Pender Community Health Centre (59 West Pender Street, 604 669 9181), and the Three Bridges Community Health Centre (1292 Hornby Street, 604 633 4219).

### Education

The two main schools in the West End and Downtown areas are the Lord Roberts Elementary School (1100 Bidwell Street, 604 713 5055) and the King George Secondary School (1755 Barclay Street, 604 713 8999). Downtown schools tend to be at capacity, so children often have to take the bus to go to schools in other parts of the city. Vancouver School District has proposed an additional elementary school on the Downtown International Village site that would accommodate up to 500 students from kindergarten to grade 7 (www.vansd.org).

### Transport

There are four major bridges connecting Downtown Vancouver to other areas in the Lower Mainland: the Lions Gate Bridge, joining the city to the North Shore municipalities and the Trans-Canada Highway, and the Burrard, Cambie and Granville bridges, providing access to the commercial and residential areas south of False Creek. The historic Waterfront Station is a major transit hub for the Downtown core. Most north-south Vancouver bus routes serve the area, in addition to suburban routes from the North Shore, Burnaby, Coquitlam, Port Coquitlam, Port Moody, Richmond, Delta, and South Surrey. Several subway SkyTrain stations (Waterfront, Burrard, and Granville) connect Downtown Vancouver to the rest of the region through the Expo and Millennium lines. The SeaBus ferry provides passenger services to the North Shore, the West Coast Express commuter rail system travels to the eastern suburbs, and there are terminals for seaplane and helicopter services along Burrard Inlet. A new rapid transit line, the Canada Line, is under construction, and will originate at the Waterfront Station, linking Downtown to Richmond and Vancouver International Airport.

### Safety & Annoyances

Granville Street is a club and bar district, and you are likely to meet rowdy revellers most nights. Gastown is close to Downtown Eastside, one of the poorest neighbourhoods in Canada, with rampant homelessness and drug abuse problems. Traffic congestion can be an issue at peak times.

# Not big, but very clever…

Perfectly proportioned to fit in your pocket, this marvellous mini guidebook makes sure you don't just get the holiday you paid for but rather the one that you dreamed of.

### Los Angeles Mini Visitors' Guide
Maximising your holiday, minimising your hand luggage

*Area* ❹ *p.103*
See also Map 6

**Best Points**

*Housing prices on the Eastside are lower than in adjacent west neighbourhoods, making the area popular with young professionals who want to be close to Downtown but cannot afford the higher prices. It is also a great place to connect with environmentalists and community activists.*

**Worst Points**

*The vibrant alternative, radical culture that makes The Drive such a creative place is in jeopardy from gentrification.*

# Eastside

The Eastside presents residents with a variety of accommodation options. Grandview, between Burrard Inlet and Broadway, and Clark Drive and Nanaimo Street, is one of the most culturally diverse neighbourhoods in Vancouver. The area was traditionally made up of working class communities, but there has been an influx of young professionals in recent years, especially in the trendy Commercial Drive and Main Street areas.

Commercial Drive, more commonly known as 'The Drive' to Vancouverites, has a counterculture feel. This is where Greenpeace is located, and many radical movements are born here. In addition to being the rallying point of Vancouver's activists, The Drive is also one of the best places in the city for good food. Many Italian and Portuguese immigrants arrived in the area after the second world war, and today the Latin influence is still present, with pizzerias, cafes, bakeries, and delis dotting the street. Main Street has in recent years become one of the city's coolest neighbourhoods, and has a great assortment of second-hand clothing stores, antique shops, and funky restaurants and coffee shops.

## Accommodation

Rows of older cottage-style houses mixed with a few larger, elaborate houses line the Eastside streets. There are very few apartment buildings in the area. New houses are starting to replace older, single family homes, and both residential and commercial development is increasing, especially around the area's SkyTrain stations. A two-bedroom unit in a large, older house or a low-rise apartment building costs between $1,000 and $1,500 a month to rent. Because the housing stock is older, do not expect any fancy amenities; washer and dryer facilities are often shared. If you're lucky, you may be able to find a cosy small two or three-bedroom cottage house with a backyard to rent for about $1,500 a month.

## Shopping & Amenities

The Drive is the heart and soul of Grandview. It has some of Vancouver's best ethnic restaurants, from Havana (p.427), which features Latino cuisine and also has a vibrant art gallery where local artists display their work, to Cafe Carthage (851 Commercial Drive, 604 215 066), which has some of the best couscous in the city. There are plenty of Italian delis and organic food stores along The Drive too. You can buy organic produce and other grocery items at Drive Organics (1046 Commercial Drive, 604 678 9665), and the usual range of groceries at Safeway (1780 East Broadway, 604 873 0225). Santa Barbara Market (1322 Commercial Drive, 604 253 6326) is a good place to purchase fruit, vegetables, and deli meats and cheeses. La Grotta Del Formaggio is the place for a great selection of cheeses, Italian meats, olive oil and pasta (1791 Commercial Drive, 604 255 3911).

Away from The Drive, Main is the other shopping hub. Antique Row, between 14th and 33rd avenues, features antiques and country furniture shops, plus a wide variety of ethnic restaurants, coffee shops and cafes. There are a number of funky clothing stores, as well as a collection of good coffee shops and restaurants, including Liberty Bakery at 3699 Main Street (604 709 9999), Habit Lounge at 2610 (p.449), and Aurora Bistro at 2420 (p.446).

## Entertainment & Leisure

Trout Lake Park is where most residents go for a stroll. In the summer and the autumn, the popular East Vancouver Farmers' Market is hosted in Trout Lake Park Community Centre's parking lot (3350 Victoria Drive, 604 257 6955). There are numerous events and festivals held in and around Commercial Drive and Trout Lake Park, including the

Alice in Wonderland Festival in July and the Parade of the Lost Souls in October (p.59). For movies, Van East Cinema (2290 Commercial Drive, 604 251 1313) is a good option, while the Vancouver East Cultural Centre (1895 Venables Street, 604 254 9578) is an excellent arts venue. The Eastside has a vibrant arts community, and every year the area's artists open up their studios during the Eastside Culture Crawl, an annual three-day visual arts festival (p.220). For active leisure pursuits, the Britannia Community Services Centre (1661 Napier Street, 604 718 5800) has an indoor swimming pool, skating rink, fitness centre, seniors, youth and adult learning centres, or for some 10 pin action there's the Grandview Bowling Lanes (2195 Commercial Drive, 604 253 2747).

### Healthcare
There are several medical clinics located on The Drive, including Commercial Health Centre (2703 Commercial Drive, 604 874 3445), Broadway Station Medical Clinic (2516 Commercial Drive, 604 872 5377), and FirstCare Medical Centre (2590 Commercial Drive, 604 871 1535). The closest major hospital is St Paul's (1081 Burrard Street) which is Downtown, about 15 minutes away by car. Pharmacy options include East End Pharmacy (2021 Commercial Drive, 604 255 9890), Fred's (1517 Commercial Drive, 604 255 0434) and Shoppers Drug Mart (1755 East Broadway East, 604 872 8451).

### Education
The King Edward campus of the Vancouver Community College (VCC) is located in the heart of East Vancouver (1155 East Broadway, 604 871 7000). The college educates 26,000 students a year in a variety of disciplines. Also in the area are the Britannia Elementary Community School (1110 Cotton Drive , 604 713 4497), the Britannia Secondary School (1001 Cotton Drive, 604 713 8266), and Lord Nelson Elementary School (235 Kitchener Street, 604 713 4595).

### Transport
The Eastside area has excellent transport links; it is served by many different bus routes, as well as the SkyTrain's Expo and Millennium lines, at the Broadway and Commercial Drive stations, respectively. The 9 and 20 bus lines run to Downtown from East Vancouver on a regular basis.

*Eastside homes*

### Safety & Annoyances
There is a charming bohemian feel to Commercial Drive, but along with this comes a certain grittiness to the neighbourhood. While the area is generally safe, property theft, especially house break-ins, seem to be a little more frequent than in other areas. The major annoyance compared with most other Vancouver neighbourhoods is that it does not have easy access to the city's beaches – if you need your daily dose of sea air, it's not the best place to be.

Area **ⓔ** p.102 ◀
See also Map 5

# Kerrisdale, Oakridge & Marpole

Kerrisdale is a quiet, affluent neighbourhood in Vancouver's West Side, situated between Granville Street and Blenheim Street, and 41st Avenue and South West Marine Drive. It has long been an upmarket community, containing many of Vancouver's exclusive golf courses and riding clubs, and is inhabited mainly by professionals, doctors, business people, and professors from the nearby UBC.

**Best Points** ◀
Kerrisdale is home to numerous top-notch schools, upscale shops, and has various parks to enjoy the outdoors, making it an ideal neighbourhood to raise a family – if you can afford it.

Oakridge, which lies between 41st Avenue and 57th Avenue, and Granville Street and Main Street, was a heavily forested area until the late 1950s, when Oakridge Mall was built and became the focal point for the residential boom in the area. Today it's a mature neighbourhood, with mainly single-family bungalow houses.

Marpole is a residential community on the southern tip of Vancouver. It rests between the Fraser River and 57th Avenue, and Angus Drive and Ontario Street. Because it's a high-volume traffic area, house prices are lower than in other parts of the city, and tend to attract students and seniors.

## Accommodation

In Kerrisdale, accommodation largely consists of single-family homes mixed with a few low and high-rise apartments, and many of the homes exist in their original forms. Expect to pay about $1,500 a month for a 1,000 square foot two-bedroom suite. Oakridge is dominated by bungalow homes constructed in the 1950s and 1960s, though more multi-family residences are being built. A two-bedroom unit in a house in Oakridge or Marpole starts at about $1,000 a month.

**Worst Points** ◀
These communities are mostly quiet, residential, and mature neighbourhoods, meaning they don't score highly in terms of innovative restaurants, clubs, bars, and entertainment.

## Shopping & Amenities

It is shopping that many people think of when they hear the name Oakridge. Since it opened in 1959, at the corner of 41st Avenue and Cambie Street, Oakridge Centre (p.415) has drawn customers from throughout the Lower Mainland.

The main Kerrisdale shopping area centres around 41st Avenue and West Boulevard. For groceries there's a large Choices Market (1888 57th Avenue West, 604 263 4600) and a MarketPlace IGA (3535 West 41st Avenue, 604 261 2423). There are many small shops and restaurants in the area. If you like seafood, make sure you visit Finest at Sea (4675 Arbutus Street, 604 266 1904), a shop and bistro that supplies some of the best seafood restaurants in the city and offers sustainable, local fare. There are a number of places for eating and drinking, including Caffe Artigiano (2154 West 41st Avenue, 604 267 1008) for good lattes, and Senova (1864 West 57th Avenue, 604 266 8643) for authentic Portuguese and Spanish classics.

## Entertainment & Leisure

Vancouver's oldest community centre, the Marpole Oakridge Community Centre (990 West 59th Avenue, 604 257 8180), offers a full recreational facility for residents, gym and sports programmes, and a sports court for street hockey, soccer, and basketball. The Jewish Community Centre is located in Oakridge (950 West 41st Avenue, 604 257 5111); facilities include a theatre and a pool. The Kerrisdale Community Centre has outdoor and indoor swimming pools (5851 West Boulevard, 604 257 8100), and there's a skating rink at 5670 East Boulevard (604 257 8121). Several golf courses occupy the land to the south of Kerrisdale (see Activities, p.299).

## Healthcare

The Pacific Spirit Community Health Centre (2110 West 43rd Avenue, 604 261 6366) serves residents of these communities. The George Pearson Centre (700 West 57th Avenue, 604 321 3231), located in Marpole, is a home for adults with severe disabilities. The nearest hospital is Vancouver General (855 West 12th Avenue, 604

875 4111), and the closest 24 hour pharmacy is Shoppers Drug Mart at 885 West Broadway (604 708 1135).

### Education

Langara College (100 West 49th Avenue, 604 323 5511) provides programmes and courses to 23,000 students annually in a variety of subjects. Kerrisdale is home to many excellent schools, including Crofton House School (3200 West 41st Avenue, 604 263 3255) which is a private school for girls, Kerrisdale Elementary School (5555 Carnarvon Street, 604 713 5446), Prince of Wales Secondary School (2250 Eddington Drive, 604 713 8974), and Point Grey Secondary School (5350 East Boulevard, 604 713 8220). Elementary schools in Marpole include David Lloyd George Elementary School (8370 Cartier Street, 604 713 4895) and Sir Winston Churchill Secondary (7055 Heather Street, 604 713 8189).

### Transport

Because of the Oak and Arthur Laing Bridges, traffic jams are common in the Marpole region, especially during peak hours. However, the area is well served by public transport – almost all the buses going to the southern suburbs pass through Marpole. In 2009 the Canada Line will replace most of the suburban routes and the 98 B-Line that goes from Downtown to Vancouver International Airport. The SkyTrain route will run along Cambie Street, and will have stations at Marine Drive, Langara (49th Avenue), and Oakridge (41st Avenue). The number 17 bus line goes all the way from Downtown to UBC, passing through Oakridge.

### Safety & Annoyances

As this is mostly a residential community, there are not many restaurants or cafes open in the evening, giving the neighbourhood a rather sleepy feel. Although the extensive network of public transport is good for accessibility, the high volume of buses in Marpole creates a lot of traffic.

*Kerrisdale condos*

*Family home in Kerrisdale*

Area ❻ p.102
See also Map 5, 8

# Kitsilano

Kitsilano, or 'Kits' as the locals call this neighbourhood, stretches from the English Bay waterfront south to 16th Avenue, and from Burrard Street westwards to Alma Street. With its long beaches, beautiful views of the mountains, proximity to Downtown, a unique collection of individual shops, niche boutiques, sports outlets and restaurants, this trendy community is one of the most desirable areas to live in the city. The heart of Kits is West 4th Avenue, which has many restaurants and shops. Broadway is the other main shopping street, and has a good mix of retail, coffee shops and restaurants.

### Best Points

*Kits is an energetic and active community in which to live. As well as boasting the wonderful Kits Beach, the neighbourhood also has great upmarket, independent shops and restaurants.*

## Accommodation

The majority of the housing in Kitsilano consists of low-rise apartment buildings and duplexes, as well as older character houses. Renting a two-bedroom basement suite in a house will start at about $1,200. A two-bedroom condo will cost from $1,600 to $2,000 a month. Most of the newer low-rise apartment buildings have in-suite washers and dryers, gas fire places, and access to sun decks with great views of the water and the mountains. The downside is that they usually do not have the communal facilities (such as gyms or meeting rooms) that the modern Downtown high-rise condos offer.

### Worst Points

*Kitsilano is a mature neighbourhood, and some of the housing stock shows its age, but the buying and rental prices remain some of the city's highest.*

## Shopping & Amenities

At the heart of Kitsilano, 4th Avenue is a trendy shopping spot where you can browse through the expensive boutiques, bookshops, organic grocery shops, trendy furniture outlets and snowboard shops, or grab a bite to eat at one of the many restaurants and cafes. This is also the place to shop for baby-related items, as several baby shops are located along this stretch of road, including Crocodile at 2156 (604 742 2762) and Hip Baby at 2110 (604 737 0603). Supermarkets in the area include Safeway (2315 West 4th Avenue West, 604 737 9803), Choices Market (2627 West 16th Avenue, 604 736 0009) and Capers (2285 West 4th Avenue, 604 739 6676). Kits is also home to some great eating options, including two of the most well-known fine dining establishments in the city, both on Broadway: Lumière (p.431) and Bishop's (p.447). For health-conscious residents, of which there are many in this neighbourhood, there are also plenty of spas, such as Spa Ethos (2200 West 4th Avenue, 604 733 5007). Kits is home to probably the best video shop in town, Videomatica, at 1855 West 4th Avenue (604 734 0411) – it's the place to go if you are looking for foreign films.

If cheese is your thing, you'll be well catered for in Les Amis du Fromage at 1752 West 2nd Avenue (604 732 4218). Next door is Barbara-Jo's Books to Cooks (604 688 6755), which offers classes as well as something to read.

*Kits character*

*Modern renovations*

### Entertainment & Leisure

The popular Kitsilano Beach (p.238) is a highlight of this neighbourhood. In the summer, it's the perfect spot for a picnic or a leisurely stroll. Kits Beach also has a fabulous outdoor heated saltwater swimming pool that kids love. Alongside Kits Beach and the equally popular Jericho Beach (p.238), there are also many parks in the area. Vanier Park (p.244) is the most well known. Housing the Vancouver Maritime Museum and the HR MacMillan Space Centre, the park is also home to annual events such as the Children's Festival and Bard on the Beach Shakespeare festival (p.56). The Kitsilano Community Centre (2690 Larch Street, 604 257 6976) offers good local recreational facilities, and moviegoers have the Fifth Avenue Cinemas (2110 Burrard Street, 604 734 7469) to keep them entertained.

### Education

Kitsilano has a number of schools, including Bayview (2251 Collingwood Street, 604 713 5433), Henry Hudson (1551 Cypress Street, 604 713 5441), and Lord Tennyson (1936 West 10th Avenue, 604 713 5426) elementary schools, and Kitsilano Secondary School (2550 West 10th Avenue, 604 713 8961).

### Healthcare

The Pine Community Health Clinic is located at 1985 West 4th Avenue (604 736 2391), and neighbourhood residents are close to St Paul's Hospital, located Downtown at 1081 Burrard Street (604 682 2344). St Paul's is an acute care, teaching and research hospital. There's a Maple Medical Clinic (2025 West Broadway, 604 730 9769) in the area, as well as a 24 hour Shoppers Drug Mart (2302 West 4th Avenue, 604 738 3138).

### Transport

Kitsilano is well served by Vancouver's bus system. It takes 10 minutes to drive from Kits to Downtown, and the main bus routes that take you into the city centre are the 4, 7 and 44. The 22 line will take you to most places in Kits, or you can catch the Aquabus from the dock at the Maritime Museum on Kits Point to a number of locations on the Downtown side of False Creek.

### Safety & Annoyances

Kitsilano is a very safe area, and it is unlikely that you will have any problems walking around, even late at night. Because of their proximity to both the beach and Downtown, Kits properties tend to be expensive.

### Easy As A-B-Tree

Many of the streets in Kits are named after trees, such as Elm, Birch and Cypress. Local legend has it that they were intended to be arranged in alphabetical order for ease of navigation but the draftsman who drew up the original street map neglected to order the list he was given alphabetically.

Area **G** p.103

See also Map 6, 10

# Mount Pleasant, Strathcona & Chinatown

Mount Pleasant is a centrally located community between 2nd Avenue and 16th Avenue, and Cambie Street and Clark Drive. Once considered a working class community, the area is now one of Vancouver's emerging neighbourhoods. Because of its lower housing costs, many first-time homeowners and young professionals have moved into Mount Pleasant, turning it into an energetic, vibrant community. Adding to the diversity of the area is an eclectic mix of new and old homes, apartments, and artists' studios.

**Best Points**

*Strathcona contains a unique mix of people, history, land use and architecture. It has a lot of charm and character. People have a very strong sense of loyalty to their community.*

Over the past few years, Strathcona, to the north of Mount Pleasant, has been revitalised, with many of the old homes restored, and gardens overflowing with flowers and herbs.

To Strathcona's west is Chinatown. Although much of Vancouver's huge Asian population has moved out to Richmond, this area retains a lively community. The low-rise buildings are painted in bright colours, and street markets abound.

The neighbouring Downtown Eastside, tagged 'Canada's poorest postal code', is well known for its high concentration of drug users and is not considered a desirable location by any stretch of the imagination. However, there are rumblings that it is about to undergo a critical transformation. The big red 'W' that looms over the intersection of Abbott and Hastings streets used to mark the abandoned site of Woodward's department store in the heart of Downtown Eastside, but it's currently being converted to high-end residential condos.

**Worst Points**

*Speculation and gentrification are driving lower-income residents out of the neighbourhood and the housing prices are going up.*

## Accommodation

These areas contain a mix of single-family homes, apartment buildings, rooming houses, and social housing developments. Older-style houses can also be found throughout this part of town. A two-bedroom suite in a house rents for between $1,000 and $1,500 a month, while a house is likely to go for $2,000 to $2,300.

## Shopping & Amenities

Chinatown is a great place to shop and eat. Wild Rice (117 West Pender Street, 604 642 2882) is a popular contemporary restaurant serving modern Chinese cuisine, while for everyday grocery shopping the T&T Supermarket (179 Keefer Place, 604 899 8836) provides everything you need, with a focus on Chinese products. Also close at hand are the shopping hot spots of Main Street and Commercial Drive.

## Entertainment & Leisure

The Dr Sun Yat Sen Classical Chinese Garden in Chinatown (p.246) provides a feeling of tranquillity in the middle of the city and is a great place to meditate. Strathcona Community Garden is one of the oldest and largest of its kind in Vancouver, featuring 115 plots and approximately 100 gardeners from various ethnic backgrounds and regions of the world.

Tinseltown Mall (88 West Pender Street) has small restaurants, retail outlets, and a cinema, and is the area's main draw. The bars and restaurants of Gastown are nearby for evening entertainment.

## Healthcare

Strathcona and Downtown Eastside are served by the Downtown Community Health Centre (569 Powell Street, 604 255 3151) and the Pender Community Health Centre (59 West Pender Street, 604 669 9181). The Bridge Community Health Clinic (2450 Ontario Street, 604 709 6400) offers services in English and other languages. Mount Saint Joseph Hospital (3080 Prince Edward Street, 604 874 1141) is a community hospital in Vancouver that has a multicultural approach to service delivery and clinical programmes. Drug stores in the area include Vancouver Pharmacy (50 East Hastings Street, 604 669 5990) and the Downtown Pharmacy (348 Powell Street, 604 669 0446).

### Education
Admiral Seymour (1130 Keefer Street, 604 713 4641) and Lord Strathcona (592 East Pender Street, 604 713 4630), both elementaries, are the two main schools in Strathcona. There are several schools in Mount Pleasant, including the Mount Pleasant Elementary School (2300 Guelph Street, 604 713 4617) and the Simon Fraser Elementary School (100 West 15th Avenue, 604 713 4946). The nearest secondary schools are located in the adjacent Grandview/Woodland neighbourhood, and include the Britannia Secondary School (1001 Cotton Drive, 604 713 8266) and Templeton Secondary School (727 Templeton Drive, 604 713 8984).

### Transport
The area is well served by several bus routes, and the Stadium SkyTrain station next to Tinseltown easily connects this community to Downtown and other cities in the Lower Mainland. Pacific Central and Main Street-Science World SkyTrain stations sit between Mount Pleasant and Strathcona/Chinatown.

### Safety & Annoyances
Strathcona and Chinatown are not unsafe areas in themselves, but they are close to Downtown Eastside, one of North America's most highly impoverished places. Drug addiction, crime and prostitution have become so prevalent in this neighbourhood that most Vancouverites avoid it.

Chinatown

Area **ⓗ** p.103 ◀
See also Map 4

# North Vancouver

*Upper Lonsdale*

**Best Points**

*North Vancouver is perfect for nature lovers. The abundance of parkland allows residents to choose from a wide range of outdoor activities. Even if you are not a skier, you can hike and cycle on miles of trails. This is also a family-oriented community, and many parents with young children choose to live here.*

Surrounded by the stunning North Shore Mountains, the City and District of North Vancouver are located on the North Shore of the Burrard Inlet, stretching east from Lions Gate Bridge to Seymour Arm. North Vancouver's location makes it very attractive for anyone who loves the outdoors. You can ski and hike on the Grouse and Seymour mountains, kayak in Deep Cove, or give out-of-town visitors a thrill by taking them to the popular Capilano Suspension Bridge – all right on your doorstep.

## Accommodation

The majority of North Vancouver's residents live in single-family houses, although there are high-rise apartments and condos scattered throughout the area, mainly in Central and Lower Lonsdale. Housing prices are cheaper than in neighbouring West Vancouver, but higher than most other suburbs in Greater Vancouver. Two bedroom units cost between $1,100 and $2,000 a month to rent. Because there is a high concentration of single-family detached houses in the area, units available for rent are often suites that are part of a house where you have to share facilities such as laundry. Basement suites are less expensive than units on higher floors of the houses. Some of the apartment buildings may provide amenities such as an indoor swimming pool and a sauna.

**Worst Points**

*For all its recreational opportunities, North Vancouver is still a suburb, and if you're a city person, living here can feel a little isolated.*

## Shopping & Amenities

North Vancouver has several shopping districts that offer a wide range of services, restaurants, and retail outlets. The historic heart of North Vancouver is Lower Lonsdale. With the addition of the SeaBus, the area has enjoyed a revival. Lonsdale Quay is a pleasant area with an open food market and plenty of art galleries and speciality boutiques to discover (p.408). Capilano Mall (www.capilanomall.com) on Marine Drive, Edgemont Village (www.edgemontvillage.ca), the Lynn Valley Centre (www.lynnvalleycentre.ca) and the Deep Cove area also have a variety of shops and services. There's a MarketPlace IGA at 130-150 West Esplanade (604 985 4431).

## Entertainment & Leisure

North Vancouver is home to a broad range of hiking and mountain bike trails, making for a great escape from city life. The North Shore Mountains nearby provide a whole host of activities – an outdoor attraction that's hard to beat not just in Vancouver, but anywhere in the world. On the water, one of the highlights is the quiet little village of Deep Cove, on the east side of North Vancouver, a departure point for kayakers paddling up Indian Arm (p.258). The Capilano River Regional Park also offers several attractions (p.241). For more urban entertainment, there are several cinemas, including Empire Esplanade 6 Cinemas (200 West Esplanade, 604 983 2762) and Park & Tilford Cinemas (200-333 Brooksbank Avenue, 604 985 3911), as well as a live venue, the Centennial Theatre Centre (2300 Lonsdale Avenue, 604 984 4484), which stages an interesting range of productions.

### Healthcare

North Vancouver is well served by a range of health facilities. The Lions Gate Hospital (p.152) provides a full range of general and many specialised acute care services, and there is also the Central Community Health Centre (132 West Esplanade, 604 983 6700) and the Parkgate Community Health Centre (3625 Banff Court, 604 904 6450). There are several pharmacies in North Vancouver, including London Drugs (2032 Lonsdale Avenue, 604 980 3661), Pharmasave (3160 Edgemont Boulevard, (604 988 6396), Safeway Pharmacy (1300 Lonsdale, 604 985 0450), and various Shoppers Drug Mart branches, but they are not open 24 hours.

### Education

The area is home to 28 elementary and seven secondary schools that serve different attendance areas; for full details about the options available contact the North Vancouver School District (604 903 3444, www.nvsd44.bc.ca). North Vancouver is home to the Ecole Francaise Internationale de Vancouver (4343 Starlight Way, 604 924 2457) and Capilano College (2055 Purcell Way, 604 986 1911), which offers a range of post-secondary programmes.

### Transport

North Vancouver is connected to Vancouver by two bridges (Lions Gate and Second Narrows), and also by a passenger ferry, the SeaBus, which links Lonsdale Quay to Downtown through a 12 minute ride. There is a well-developed public bus system, with a hub in Lonsdale Quay. Travelling to and from Downtown can be particularly frustrating during peak times, with the bridges becoming bottlenecks.

### Safety & Annoyances

North Vancouver is a family-friendly place with no major safety issues, save for the occasional hungry black bear coming down from the mountains in search of food. However, if you work in Vancouver and commute by car, expect morning and evening delays on the bridges during rush hour.

Waterfront

View homes

*Area* ❶ *p.102*
See also Map 3

**Best Points**
*West Point Grey
retains most of its
original properties
and features some
wonderful older
mansions by
the beach.*

**Worst Points**
*This is a conservative
residential community,
so if you're looking
for some action,
alternative stores,
and good nightlife,
it's probably not for
you. The houses here
are among the most
expensive in the city.*

## Point Grey & UBC

Point Grey is an affluent community located in the north-west corner of Vancouver. It is bounded by English Bay to the north and 16th Avenue to the south, by the University Endowment Lands to the west, and Alma Street to the east. It is a mostly residential area, containing some of Vancouver's most expensive waterfront properties, and offers beachfront living, a strong sense of community and great views of the city and the North Shore Mountains. The University of British Columbia (UBC), the province's largest university, neighbours Point Grey, as does the huge Pacific Spirit Regional Park. If you are after a good place to shop, try 10th Avenue, and the cluster of antique and collectible shops at the bottom of the 10th Avenue hill at Alma Street.

### Accommodation

Accommodation in this neighbourhood is primarily made up of upmarket single-family homes, some with great views of the water, the city's skyline and the North Shore Mountains. Two-bedroom suites in older 'character' buildings cost between $1,500 and $3,000 to rent per month. If you are after a large house on the waterfront, West Point Grey is the place to look – but it won't come cheap. For a monthly rent of between $3,000 and $10,000, you will get a living space of up to 3,700 square feet, possible water views, and a private back garden.

### Shopping & Amenities

There is a small shopping district along 10th Avenue and Alma Street, complete with grocery shops, retail shops, restaurants, and a small pocket of antique and collectibles stores. For everyday grocery shopping, West Point Grey residents can rely on the Safeway supermarket (4575 West 10th Avenue, 604 228 1511). For more specialist foods, Pane e Formaggio is an artisan bread and speciality cheese store that offers a complete selection of gourmet foods, balsamic and extra-virgin olive oils (4532 West 10th Avenue, 604 224 1623). The Patisserie Bordeaux is famous in the city for its almond croissants (3675 West 10th Avenue, 604 731 6551).

*Point Grey*

*English Bay*

*Point Grey*

### Entertainment & Leisure

Two of Vancouver's most beautiful and popular beaches, Spanish Banks and Locarno Beach (p.239), are in Point Grey. With endless sand, and logs to rest up against, these beaches are a haven for sun worshippers, beach volleyball players and surfers. The area attracts a younger crowd creating a good dose of energy and adding a fun vibe to the neighbourhood. Also found in Point Grey is the Pacific Spirit Regional Park, an extensive forested park which offers plenty of opportunities for hiking.

Sporting facilities include Jericho Tennis Club (3837 Point Grey Road, 604 224 2348), Locarno Sailing Club (1300 Discovery Street , 604 224 6117) and Royal Vancouver Yacht Club (3811 Point Grey Road, 604 224 1344), while various activities are run by the West Point Grey Community Centre (4397 West 2nd Avenue, 604 257 8140).

UBC boasts one of the city's best cultural facilities, the Chan Centre for the Performing Arts, which features first-class classical music performances (3265 Crescent Road, 604 822 9197), while the Museum of Anthropology (p.231) lies on the edge of the campus and possesses one of the finest displays of west coast First Nations art.

### Healthcare

Pacific Spirit Community Health Centre, a primary care clinic, is located at 2110 West 43rd Avenue (604 261 6366). UBC Hospital, situated on the campus (2211 Westbrook Mall, 604 822 7121), is one of two acute care facilities that are part of Vancouver Hospital and Health Sciences Centre. Speciality areas include acute medicine, general surgery, psychiatry, and gerontology. The main pharmacy is Point Grey Pharmacy (4520 West 10th Avenue, 604 224 1377), and the closest 24 hour pharmacy is Shoppers Drug Mart (885 West Broadway, 604 708 1135).

### Education

In addition to UBC, the province's largest university (p.171), the area has a variety of excellent schools for all ages, including Lord Byng Secondary School (3939 West 16th Avenue, 604 713 8171), Queen Mary Elementary School (2000 Trimble Street, 604 713 5464), Queen Elizabeth Elementary School (4102 West 16th Avenue, 604 713 5408), and Jules Quesnel Elementary (3050 Crown Street, 604 713 4557).

### Transport

UBC and Point Grey areas are well served by bus lines, with numbers 44, 22, and 17 running all the way to Downtown. Travelling by car to central Vancouver takes about 30 minutes.

### Safety & Annoyances

Point Grey is a very safe and quiet area. The main issue is the high price of property, which makes this community out of reach for most.

*Area* **K** *p.102*
See also Map 3

# West Vancouver

Bordered on two sides by water, and to the north by mountains, the district of West Vancouver is surrounded by natural beauty. It sits on the North Shore, across the Burrard Inlet from the main city, and stretches along 28 kilometres of coast and up the lower slopes of Hollyburn Mountain, between the Capilano River valley and Horseshoe Bay. This neighbourhood is the richest in Canada, and it's not difficult to believe when you drive past the beautiful waterfront homes on Marine Drive. The Lions Gate Bridge connects West Vancouver to Downtown.

The Ambleside area on Marine Drive serves as a commercial district for West Vancouver residents, and is home to many restaurants, banks, grocery stores, gourmet food shops, and other amenities. West Vancouver also features the Park Royal Shopping Centre (p.416), which was Canada's first mall.

At the north-west edge of the district, Horseshoe Bay is a major terminus for the provincial ferry system. It services Nanaimo on Vancouver Island, Bowen Island, and the nearby Sunshine Coast.

**Best Points**
*If you can afford it, West Van has amazing skiing and hiking opportunities, a beautiful scenic park with great views of the city and the ocean at Lighthouse Park, and great restaurants and shops along Marine Drive.*

## Accommodation

West Vancouver is a residential area, and most of the accommodation stock consists of single-family homes, a choice of old summer cottages, modest houses and multimillion-dollar waterfront estates. If you're looking for a property of outstanding architectural quality with breathtaking views, this is the place. According to the Real Estate Board of Greater Vancouver, the benchmark sales price for a detached house in West Vancouver in 2007 was about $1.3 million. A four to six bedroom house will cost between $3,000 and $8,000 a month to rent. Multi-family developments are relatively scarce, but there are a few high-rise apartment buildings located along the eastern beachfront. Rental prices for these start at $1,500 per month for a two-bedroom unit, but can go up significantly based on the location, the view, and the amenities.

**Worst Points**
*Price and traffic. West Van is as expensive as it gets in Canada, and crossing Lions Gate Bridge to get to Vancouver can be torturous.*

## Shopping & Amenities

Park Royal (p.416), just to the west of Lions Gate Bridge, is one of the largest malls in the region, and offers the full range of shops, from clothes to food and home entertainment. Ambleside and nearby Dundarave are the liveliest retail areas of

*British Properties*

West Vancouver. Located a block from the waterfront, these two centres feature many shops, galleries, organic grocery shops and good restaurants. Savary Island Pie Company Bakery & Café (1533 Marine Drive, 604 926 4021) is a favourite with locals, while La Régalade (2232 Marine Drive, 604 921 2228) is a great French bistro. There are several Whole Foods outlets in West Vancouver, including the 925 Main Street branch (604 678 0500). Horseshoe Bay's commercial centre abounds with restaurants and other tourist and traveller-related amenities.

## Entertainment & Leisure

Cypress Provincial Park offers day and night downhill skiing, snowboarding, tobogganing, hiking and cross-country skiing, along with fabulous views of Vancouver – and the rest of the North Shore

*Downtown views*

Mountains are right on hand. Lighthouse Park (p.243) is a popular waterfront stretch for hiking and picnic lunches in the summer. With its rugged shoreline and cobble beach, Whytecliff Marine Park, in Horseshoe Bay, is very popular with beach lovers and is also an attraction for local divers. The West Vancouver Aquatic Centre (2121 Marine Drive, 604 925 7210) is a state-of-the-art fitness facility for residents, while the Kay Meek Centre (1700 Mathers Avenue, 604 913 3634) stages a variety of live productions.

### Healthcare

Lions Gate Hospital (p.152) in North Vancouver also serves West Vancouver, the Village of Lions Bay, and Bowen Island Municipality. The West Community Health Centre (990 22nd Street, 604 904 6200) provides a full range of services to residents, as well as offering care for the elderly, immunisation clinics, mental health services, and educational programmes. There are several pharmacies in the area, including the Hollyburn Pharmacy (1695 Marine Drive, 604 922 4174) and London Drugs (875 Park Royal North, 604 926 9616).

### Education

West Vancouver has 14 primary and elementary schools, and three secondary schools. These include Cypress Park Primary (4355 Marine Drive, 604 981 1330) and Rockridge Secondary (350 Headland Drive, 604 981 1300). Contact the West Vancouver School District for full listings information (604 981 1000, www.sd45.bc.ca).

### Transport

West Vancouver is proud of its Blue Bus, which connects various parts of the district to other municipalities. It was the first public transport system in Canada to become totally wheelchair accessible. Park Royal is a terminal for both the Blue Bus and North Vancouver TransLink buses. Lions Gate Bridge separates the North Shore from Vancouver and is the main commuting route for residents who work in the city. You can drive, walk, or bike across the bridge to Downtown – but congestion can be a real issue at peak times. The other options for crossing the water into town are the SeaBus (p.44) and the Second Narrows Ironworkers Memorial Bridge, both of which are located in neighbouring North Vancouver. Access to West Vancouver from the north is through the Sea to Sky Highway, which connects the Lower Mainland to Squamish and Whistler. Additionally, BC Ferries operates routes departing from Horseshoe Bay in West Vancouver to Nanaimo, Bowen Island, and the Sunshine Coast.

### Safety & Annoyances

West Vancouver is a very safe area and has a low crime rate; residents are strongly committed to maintaining the quality of life of their community, as well as a high standard of municipal services. The major bind can be trying to access Downtown across Lions Gate Bridge in heavy traffic. There is the risk of occasional landslides and mudslides in West and North Vancouver – residents have been forced to evacuate their homes in the past due to the threat. Heavy snowfall can also be an issue and can disrupt transportation routes for a short period of time each year.

*Area* ❶ *p.102*
See also Map 7

# Yaletown & False Creek

Once Vancouver's warehouse district, Yaletown has been one of the most successful revitalisation projects in the city, and is now a trendy place to live, work and play. The area has been converted into a residential community, complete with high-end restaurants, furniture shops, art galleries, designer boutiques and high-tech offices. Over the past 10 years, many glass-fronted residential towers have risen on Pacific Boulevard along the north edge of False Creek, making the neighbourhood a model of high-density living (and the development still continues).

This community combines a unique urban feel with family-friendly amenities. Yaletown is particularly attractive to families with young children who enjoy the convenience of the Seawall (p.211), the David Lam Park (p.242), and the Roundhouse Community Centre (p.340), which offers a range of activities for people of all ages.

Just a short boat ride away, Granville Island is well known for its colourful and popular public market. The area also features artists' studios, theatres, pubs, restaurants, and craft shops.

**Best Points**

*Ideal for families with young children who will find everything they need within walking distance: the lively Seawall, an urban park with plenty of sports activities, several grocery stores, and one of the most active community centres in the city.*

**Worst Points**

*Due to its popularity, Yaletown and False Creek have become very expensive. Living space is an issue, and families keen on this urban experience will often have to settle for small apartments.*

## Accommodation

The area is mostly made up of modern glass-fronted residential towers, and townhouses at the base of high-rise buildings, many with beautiful water views of False Creek. Some of the former industrial buildings and warehouses in Yaletown have also been transformed into designer loft-style residences. Most buildings provide common amenities such as a gym, sauna, meeting space, pool, and even play areas for children. Apartments typically include in-suite laundry facilities and storage, two bathrooms, and modern kitchens with granite counter tops. On the downside, units tend to be smaller and more expensive than in the West End and often lack balconies. Small two-bedroom apartments (700 to 800 square feet) can go for as much as $1,800 a month, with larger two-bedroom units or townhouses costing up to $4,000 a month. Prices are higher for fully furnished units, or those offering views of the creek. Townhouses are very popular as an alternative to high-rise urban living in the middle of Downtown, and are generally spacious and suitable for parents with children.

## Shopping & Amenities

Downtown shopping is a short walk away from these areas. Even closer, virtually right on the doorstep, Mainland and Hamilton streets feature some interesting cafes, clothing shops, hairdressers and high-end spas, as well as some of the trendiest restaurants in the city, such as Cioppino's (p.434) and the Blue Water Café (p.441). Urban Fare (177 Davie Street, 604 975 7550) provides convenient grocery shopping opportunities for neighbourhood residents, while Choices Market (1202 Richards Street, 604 633 2392) offers a range of fresh, organic produce and other grocery items. Next to Urban Fare, Provence Marinaside (p.432) is a popular brunch spot located on the Seawall.

## Entertainment & Leisure

The Roundhouse Community Centre (181 Roundhouse Mews, 604 713 1800) is a spectacular facility that was built over and named after the turning point for trains in the area. Today the Roundhouse is a focal point for the local community and offers an incredible range of activities for adults, the elderly and children. For outdoor-oriented residents, the Seawall along False Creek can take you from Yaletown to Kits Beach, and to Stanley Park in the other direction. It is very popular and used by walkers, runners, cyclists and rollerbladers, rain or shine. Granville Island is a great family destination, and kids will spend countless hours playing at Kids Market (1496 Cartwright Street, www.kidsmarket.ca). The Vancouver Aquatic Centre (1050 Beach Avenue, 604 665 3424) offers good swimming facilities.

### Healthcare

The Yaletown Medical Clinic (1296 Pacific Boulevard, 604 6323 2474) is a family practice and urgent care facility that provides comprehensive primary care to community residents. The clinic also offers sports medicine, travel vaccines, immunisations and wellness programmes. The Khatsahlano Medical Clinic (920 Seymour Street, 604 731 9187) also offers primary medical care. The nearest hospital is St Paul's (1081 Burrard Street, 604 631 5245), and the closest 24 hour pharmacy is the Shoppers Drug Mart at 1125 Davie Street (604 669 2424).

### Education

When the Elsie Roy Elementary School (150 Drake Street, 604 713 5890) opened in 2004 next to the David Lam Park, Yaletown really took off as a family-friendly community. Unfortunately the school tends to be at capacity, and it is not uncommon for parents to line up overnight to reserve a spot for their children on the first day of registration each year. The Emily Carr University of Art and Design (1399 Johnston Street, 604 844 3800) on Granville Island is one of BC's oldest post-secondary institutions and offers continuing studies courses in art-related disciplines such as painting, sculpture and photography. Other options nearby include Lord Strathcona Elementary School (592 East Pender Street), and the Mole Hill Montessori (1155 Thurlow Street, 604 687 6701).

### Transport

Water is a popular way to get around for False Creek residents. The Aquabus offers a service year round between Granville Island and locations including Hornby Street, Fairview Slopes and Yaletown. Two community shuttles, the C21 Yaletown-Beach-Burrard station and the C23 Yaletown-Davie, run every 10 minutes during peak times, while Downtown's bus and rail networks are nearby.

### Safety & Annoyances

For a city centre suburb, Yaletown can be considered a relatively safe, family-oriented area. The biggest problem is that some of the community amenities are so popular it can be hard to register for them. Its central location means it can be very difficult to find parking too, especially at weekends.

Yaletown

False Creek

See Map 2 ◀

# Greater Vancouver

If you want to look beyond the city limits, there are many communities in Greater Vancouver to choose from. Richmond, Surrey, New Westminster, Delta, Langley, Coquitlam, and Port Moody all surround Vancouver, and each of these suburban municipalities has its own characteristics, flavour, and pros and cons. You'll have to consider several factors before you pick the one that suits your needs the best, but the following descriptions will give you a brief idea of what to expect.

**Richmond** lies on a series of islands at the estuary of the Fraser River, immediately south of Vancouver. It is a fast-growing suburb and has a huge Chinese community. It is also home to Vancouver International Airport. Accommodation in Richmond is mainly single-family houses, with some high-density multi-family developments concentrated around the city centre. A two-bedroom unit starts at about $1,000 per month to rent. The new SkyTrain Canada Line, currently under construction, will connect Richmond to Downtown Vancouver, and will have four stations in the area. It takes an average of 35 to 45 minutes to commute by car from Richmond to Downtown Vancouver during peak times. A Richmond highlight is Steveston, a quaint historic fishing village that features waterfront fish and chip eateries and art galleries, and is also a departure point for whale watching expeditions in the summer.

Below Richmond is **Delta**, surrounded by water on three sides and Surrey to the east. It includes three distinct communities: North Delta, Ladner, and Tsawwassen. A major attraction of the area is Ladner Village, which has historic buildings, open-air cafes and a relaxed atmosphere. Tsawwassen is home to some of the most luxurious waterfront homes in the region. It is best known for its ferry terminal, which is the main hub for transportation to Vancouver Island, the Gulf Islands, and Washington state in the US. On average it takes between 50 minutes and an hour to commute by car to Downtown Vancouver from Tsawwassen ferry terminal during morning and evening peak times.

To the east of Richmond, **Surrey** is one of Canada's fastest-growing urban areas. With a population of approximately 400,000, it is the second-largest city in British Columbia and attracts significant numbers of immigrants looking for affordable housing. Surrey is mostly made up of single-family houses, but the city centre in Surrey's north-west features high-density residential housing around a retail and business centre, connected to Vancouver by rapid transit. A two-bedroom suite in a house starts at $600 a month to rent. It takes at least an hour to travel to Surrey from Downtown Vancouver.

To the south of Surrey is **White Rock**, a quiet seaside community with a beautiful stretch of beach and a waterfront promenade full of fish and chip restaurants and shops. Many retirees choose to live in this area. A house in White Rock can be rented for a monthly price ranging from $1,800 to $3,000. It takes an hour or more to reach White Rock from Downtown Vancouver by car, and up to two hours by bus.

North-east of White Rock, **Langley** is predominantly an agricultural community with plenty of pastures and farmland, and housing developments sprinkled throughout. The historic village of Fort Langley is a highlight, and the Fort Langley National Historic Site is a popular attraction. A two-bedroom suite for rent here starts at $850 and can go up to $1,200 a month. On average it takes from 50 minutes to more than an hour to commute to Vancouver.

Between Surrey and Burnaby, south-east of Vancouver on a hillside along the north banks of Fraser River, is **New Westminster**. It features beautiful heritage buildings, sloping streets and views of the water. The area offers a variety of housing, from large heritage homes to new condominiums along the banks of the river. A two-bedroom unit costs between $950 and $1,800 a month to rent, depending on the location, the age of the building, and the view. New Westminster is served by the SkyTrain, which takes about 30 minutes to reach Downtown Vancouver. Doing the same journey by car will take an average of 30 to 45 minutes at morning and evening peak times.

**Best Points** ◀

*These areas are more affordable. Housing prices are generally lower, and there's a chance to live somewhere with more space and a garden.*

**Worst Points** ◀

*Some of these suburbs are far from Vancouver, so be prepared for long commutes. It can be difficult to get around if you don't have a car. Surrey, in particular, is not a pedestrian-friendly community.*

# Residential Areas

To the north, **Port Moody** is a relatively small community that sits on the shore of the Burrard Inlet and is surrounded by mountains, water and forested hillsides. This area has been steadily growing in the past few years due to the lower house prices and the beauty of the natural surroundings. A car ride from Port Moody to Downtown Vancouver takes between 30 and 40 minutes.

East is **Coquitlam**, which along with **Port Coquitlam** and Port Moody, is known as one of the 'Tri-Cities'. It is mainly a residential municipality, with many single-family homes and recently developed townhouses. Its relative affordability has made Coquitlam an attractive choice for new families and young couples. A two-bedroom suite costs about $1,000 a month to rent, and Downtown Vancouver is 35 minutes away.

Greater Vancouver municipalities each have their own healthcare facilities, including the Richmond Hospital, Delta Hospital, Langley Memorial Hospital, Belvedere Care Centre in Coquitlam, Eagle Ridge Hospital and Health Care Centre in Port Moody, and Surrey Memorial Hospital. Shopping amenities, entertainment facilities and schools and colleges are scattered throughout the suburbs.

*Richmond*

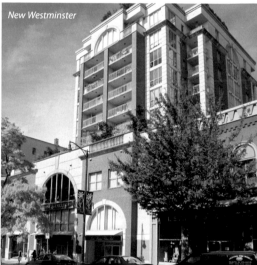
*New Westminster*

*White Rock*

*Surrey*

# Setting Up Home

Now that you've successfully navigated your way through the Vancouver housing scene and acquired a home, you're ready to move on to the fun job of furnishing your house and finding a butcher, baker, and aromatherapy maker. Moving costs can vary widely depending on how much you intend to ship and how long you plan to live in Vancouver. Local labour is not cheap and shipping costs can be prohibitive, so buying furnishings and household goods locally is often a more cost-effective option.

## Moving Services

*Smooth Moves*
*Before you start contacting moving companies for quotes, take some time to purge. Go through every inch of your home, decide what you can get rid of, then have a huge garden sale. Anything you do not sell can be donated to charity or thrown out. This will save you packing time and lower your moving costs.*

Removal companies can provide packing, shifting and storage services for local moves. Most charge an hourly rate of between $69 and $100, with additional fees for packing services, supplies and insurance. Hourly rates are usually higher between the 25th and 4th of each month. The cost of moving a typical one-bedroom apartment within the Greater Vancouver area starts at around $300. If you have the muscles and time to move yourself, a local U-Haul truck (www.uhaul.com) can be rented for about $40 per day. Hiring a person with a truck is also possible and usually costs about $20 to $30 hourly. You can find someone easily by browsing the classified section of any local paper. You don't, however, have any guarantee that your possessions will survive the experience, so you may want to splurge on a moving company. For international moves, feel free to ship as little as possible. Although most Vancouver rental properties are unfurnished, household and furniture items tend to be easily available at every price range. Fully furnished rentals usually include everything except a complimentary toothbrush, but they are normally let on a short term or seasonal basis and are often booked long in advance by film companies for cast and crew on location. They also tend to be considerably more expensive than unfurnished rentals.

Vancouver has several relocation experts, but be wary of real estate agents who offer 'relocation services' – this is usually just a fancy term for showing you their listed properties. Proper relocation experts will offer you pre and post-arrival services on everything from work opportunities, insurance, driving licence and schools through to pet regulations and orientation tours of the city. Rates range from $400 to $4,000, depending on how much help you need.

### Arrive Unarmed

If you want to bring any type of firearm into the country, be aware that Canada has highly restrictive laws about guns. Firearms are listed as prohibited, and this includes replica firearms, which are not allowed under any circumstances. Restricted firearms may be allowed, but only for a specific purpose, such as target practice or if part of a collection and never for personal protection. The Canadian Firearms Centre website (www.cfc-cafc.gc.ca) has full details.

## Relocation Companies

| | | |
|---|---|---|
| AMJ Campbell International | 604 940 8410 | www.amj-international.com |
| Astra International Moving & Shipping | 604 422 8001 | www.astrainternational.com |
| Brytor International Moving | 604 273 0100 | www.brytor.ca |
| Coastal Relocation | 604 351 4796 | www.coastalrelocation.com |
| Coming To Vancouver Relocation Services | 604 264 1269 | www.comingtovancouver.ca |
| Friendly Planet Consulting | 604 985 4304 | www.friendly-planet.ca |
| Highland-Worldwide Group | 604 581 2300 | www.highland-worldwide.com |
| The MI Group | 604 273 2012 | www.themigroup.com |
| Williams Moving International | 604 941 9411 | www.williamsmoving.com |

## Removal Companies

| | | |
|---|---|---|
| AJK Moving | 604 875 9072 | www.ajkmoving.com |
| ABC Moving | 604 633 9577 | www.abcmovingcompany.com |
| Angel's Moving | 604 642 6683 | www.angelsmoving.ca |
| Edgemont Moving & Storage | 604 984 9101 | www.moversedge.com |
| Great Canadian Van Lines | 604 540 6683 | www.greatcanadianvanlines.com |
| LaPorte Moving & Storage Systems | 1 800 267 2088 | www.laportemoving.com |
| MiniMove | 778 327 5659 | www.minimove.ca |
| Salmon's Transfer | 604 273 2921 | www.salmonstransfer.com |
| Two Small Men With Big Hearts | 604 986 2222 | www.twosmallmen.com |

## Furnishing Your Home

Other options **Home Furnishings & Accessories** p.386

Vancouver real estate for sale is generally unfurnished, with about 20% of all rentals furnished to varying degrees. Major appliances such as refrigerators, ovens, dishwashers, washing machines and clothes dryers are not normally included in the sale of a home. All rentals come with a minimum of a fridge and cooker. Most apartment buildings have communal coin-operated washers and dryers on the premises, while higher-end rentals will have built-in (and coin-free) versions. Dishwashers are fairly common, but older buildings and houses often don't have them. Many people buy cheap, portable dishwashers that hook up to the kitchen sink. Fully furnished rentals will include electronics, appliances, dishware, cooking utensils and linens, but this can vary depending on the quality of accommodation. Semi-furnished rentals usually include a bed, a table, some chairs, lamps, and, if you're lucky, a sofa. Those catering to students will usually have a desk and some shelving.

If your employer offers a healthy moving allowance, it makes sense to ship your own furniture, otherwise buy local. For lower priced items, there is always IKEA (www.ikea.ca), but if you don't want to transport and assemble everything yourself, the cost can rise quite steeply. Other budget stops are United Furniture Warehouse (www.ufw.com) or The Brick (www.thebrick.com), franchises which offer monthly payment options on furniture, mattresses, appliances and electronics, and also have various locations across Vancouver. For more eclectic tastes, there are a range of furniture shops on West Broadway and West 4th Avenue, as well as along Marine Drive in North Vancouver. Italian leather furnishings are available on Commercial Drive, and higher-end shops are clustered in the Yaletown and False Creek areas. Most furniture shops have in-store customisation, so if you really can't live without a tan micro suede over-stuffed sofa with bamboo legs and matching draperies, chances are you'll find it for a reasonable price. For soft furnishings, branches of Pier 1 (www.pier1.com) and Urban Barn (www.urbanbarn.com) have a good selection of linens, accessories, glassware and small furnishings, while discount stores including The Kitchen Corner (1955 West 4th Avenue, 604 734 4244) and Gourmet Warehouse (1340 East Hastings Street, 604 253 3022) offer excellent prices on everything you could need for your kitchen and bathroom. Supermarkets such as Real Canadian Superstore (www.superstore.ca) offer great deals on most household items and appliances.

### Second-Hand Items

There is a thriving second-hand market in Vancouver. Newspaper classified listings and community websites such as Craigslist (vancouver.craigslist.org), Kijiji (www.kijiji.ca), Buy and Sell (www.buysell.com) and Used Vancouver (www.usedvancouver.com) all list thousands of household items for sale, of every possible make and variety. Yard sales are also popular and are listed in *The Vancouver Sun* and *The Province*, as well as on the above websites. Finally, there is the Vancouver Flea Market (703 Terminal Avenue, 604 685 0666), a large indoor jumble sale that opens at weekends and during holidays year round, selling everything from antiques to books and appliances.

## Tailors

Other options **Tailoring** p.402

Most furniture companies have in-store tailoring and custom services, and there are several speciality tailoring companies. Any private tailor can make up customised curtains and other soft furnishings for you (although this is a rarely used option), but you can usually find the best prices at a furniture or drapery shop, where labour and customisation costs are often included with your fabric or furniture purchase. For tailormade clothing and fabrics, see Tailoring on p.402 and Textiles on p.403.

| Tailors | | | |
| --- | --- | --- | --- |
| Arlene's Interiors | 751 Terminal Av | Main | 604 608 1177 |
| Canada Upholstery | 2153 Kingsway | Victoria | 604 437 5402 |
| Chintz & Company | 950 Homer St | Downtown | 604 689 2022 |
| The Natural Textile Company | 2571 West Broadway | Kitsilano | 604 736 2101 |
| Oscar Grann's Furniture | 237 East 1st St | North Vancouver | 604 987 9833 |

## Household Insurance

While often touted as one of the safest cities in the world, Vancouver does have one of the highest property crime rates in North America. Add to this the rising levels of property damage caused by heavy rains over the past few years and household insurance becomes highly recommended, whether you own or rent. There are three types of household insurance: detached home, condo, and tenant (for rentals). Since the landlord's insurance hardly ever covers the tenant's personal effects, it's advisable to have your own insurance even if you rent. Costs start as low as $25 a month, depending on how much you own, and the same insurance also covers any property lost or damaged while in your vehicle, or when you are on vacation. In addition, if you're the victim of a fire, the insurance can cover temporary hotel accommodation and out-of-pocket expenses for renters and owners.

Because of the heightened risk of flooding over the past few years, it's also a good idea to have additional water damage protection to cover leaking due to heavy rainfall or the occasional mudslide. Standard policies don't often provide full coverage against flood-related damage. Insurance can be customised to cover just about anything, from home-based businesses and high-value items to protection against identity theft.

| Household Insurance | | |
| --- | --- | --- |
| Alexander Park & Associates | 604 222 3544 | www.alexanderparkinsurance.com |
| BCAA | 604 268 5600 | www.bcaa.com |
| Gold Key Insurance Services | 604 325 1241 | www.goldkeyinsurance.ca |
| Kitsilano Insurance | 604 731 6331 | www.kitsilanoinsurance.com |
| Park Georgia Insurance | 604 261 7302 | www.pgins.com |
| Park Insurance | 604 659 4800 | www.parkinsurance.ca |
| Pat Anderson Insurance Group | 604 323 8100 | www.patand.com |
| Reliance Insurance Agencies | 604 255 4616 | www.reliance.bc.ca |
| Westland Insurance | 604 682 6115 | www.westland-insurance.com |
| Yaletown Insurance Services | 604 899 0511 | www.insurebc.ca |

## Laundry Services

Most rentals include both washers and dryers, either communal or one set per suite. For those that don't, there is always a coin-operated launderette within walking distance. These offer self-service machines, as well as special cleaning for large items such as duvets and curtains. Some also offer dry cleaning and alteration services. Speciality dry cleaners can be found in any neighbourhood (almost on every block), and some can pick up and deliver to your home. Most are reliable and rarely lose or damage items. If the worst should happen, a reputable cleaner will reimburse you. Dry cleaning prices vary, but expect to pay $4 to $6 per item for shirts, trousers and skirts, and slightly more for dresses and jackets. Washing and ironing services are also charged per item, but most places will give a discount for a regular contract.

## Domestic Help

While Vancouver is a relatively inexpensive place to live compared with places such as New York, it's still not cheap. The cost of living has been going up dramatically in recent years due to the city's rising popularity.

Most people don't have maids, although it is becoming more common to have a weekly cleaning service. The very wealthy often have full-time domestic help, but it's extremely rare for anyone to have live-in help. The exception is busy families who might employ a live-in nanny or au pair.

| Domestic Help Agencies | | |
|---|---|---|
| Absolutely Clean | 604 628 4517 | www.absolutelyclean.ca |
| The Maids | 604 278 6243 | www.maids.com |
| Merry Maids | 604 321 0400 | www.merrymaids.com |
| Molly Maid | 604 734 7260 | www.mollymaid.ca |
| Summit Maid Services | 604 291 1001 | www.summitmaids.com |
| UMaids | 778 284 1205 | www.umaids.com |
| Vancouver Maid Service | 778 785 0995 | www.vancouvermaids.ca |

There are numerous agencies that offer domestic help on a part-time basis, but their rates tend to be higher than simply hiring a person who is available to clean. They do, however, conduct background and criminal checks on all of their employees. Agency rates start at $60 to $80 per hour for one or two people to do a thorough clean. Rates go up depending on the size of your home and how many cleaners are required. There are also cleaning agencies that provide 'green' cleaning options for their clients, where they use environmentally friendly and biodegradable products. You can find independent cleaners in the classified listings of any local paper, but it's safer to get someone through referral. You can also find a cleaner through community websites such as Craigslist (vancouver.craigslist.org). You'll normally pay $15 to $25 per hour to an individual, with some cleaners expecting you to provide the cleaning supplies.

## Babysitting & Childcare

Childcare in Vancouver has been at a premium in the last few years, with supply not quite meeting demand. Babysitters and nannies are becoming more popular as a result, and there are a variety of options available. Most hotels offer babysitting services on request, either through their own staff or an agency. Vancouver has several agencies that offer highly qualified nannies and babysitters for full-time, part-time and occasional needs. Agencies conduct criminal and background checks and they generally hire nannies with a minimum of two to five years' experience. Many have Early Childhood Education (ECE) training and certification. Hourly rates through an agency are between $15 and $19, in addition to the agency fee. Private nannies (usually with less qualifications or experience) tend not to charge as much and advertise their services on community websites and in local papers, but even teenagers

doing after- school and evening care charge $10 per hour. Always ask for several references and preferably find someone through a personal referral.
Mothers' groups are normally informal gatherings that are set up either between friends or through listings at community centres or on local websites, and are more geared towards providing play opportunities rather than babysitting.

### Daycare Categories

The Ministry of Children and Family Development sets and oversees requirements for daycare facilities, which are divided into two categories: licensed and licence-not-required (LNR). Licensed group childcare centres can have a maximum of 25 children between the ages of 30 months and 6 years. Alternatively, they can have up to 12 children less than 36 months old. Licensed family childcare means childcare is offered in the caregiver's own home. These serve children from birth to 12 years and can have up to seven children. Licence requirements for both are the same and cover areas such as staff qualifications, criminal and medical record checks, staff-child ratios, space, equipment, nutrition and emergency procedures. LNR providers are always based out of their own home and are able to register with Westcoast Child Care Resource Centre (www.westcoast.org), which keeps a list of both licensed and registered facilities. Registered LNRs must provide a criminal record check for anyone over 12 living in the home, submit to an inspection of their home, and undergo a medical assessment to gauge their physical and emotional capacity to deal with children. They must go through first aid and childcare courses and they are also eligible for group liability insurance, which unregistered providers are not. Registering is not mandatory, however, so if you end up using unregistered care, always ask for several references. LNRs can provide care for up to two children, in addition to their own children. LNRs are usually stay-at-home mums and represent a growing percentage of childcare providers.

### Babysitting & Childcare

| | | |
|---|---|---|
| ABC Nannies Canada | 604 581 1018 | www.abcnannies.org |
| Clara's Caregiver Services | 604 255 3440 | www.claras.ca |
| Happy Kidz Agency | 604 880 3656 | www.happykidz.ca |
| International Nannies & Homecare | 1 800 820 8308 | www.internationalnannies.com |
| Nannies On Call | 604 734 1776 | www.nanniesoncall.com |
| Paragon Personnel | 604 298 6633 | www.paragon-personnel.com |

### Facilities For Children

Vancouver's restaurants and shopping malls offer the basics when it comes to outings with children. Most include bathrooms with changing tables, while shopping malls have strollers for rent and high chairs or booster seats in the foodcourts. Most restaurants will have high chairs, but some frown on crying babies. Park Royal Shopping Centre (p.416) in West Vancouver is a particularly good option for those with children. It features a supervised play area where you can drop off your kids for up to two hours while you shop. The Oakridge Centre (p.415) also has a parent-supervised play area. A great find for those looking for a particularly family-friendly restaurant is Little Nest (1716 Charles Street, 604 251 9994) off Commercial Drive, which is specifically geared towards parents and young children. There is a large play area, and the menu (which features separate kids' options) offers local, seasonal and organic produce. Most gyms, community and recreation centres offer childminding while you use their facilities. A small hourly fee is normally charged, anywhere from $2 to $5.

### Sponsoring A Live-In Caregiver

With the current labour shortage in British Columbia, more people are turning to foreign workers, despite the long and complicated application process. Foreign domestics are normally only sponsored as caregivers. The Canadian government

*Golf for kids*

defines a caregiver as someone who provides care in your home (and possibly does some light housework) for children, seniors, or a person with disabilities. After working two years in this role, they can apply for permanent residency. You must first register as an employer with Service Canada (www.servicecanada. gc.ca), then complete a form for a 'labour market opinion', requesting permission to hire a foreign worker. Service Canada assesses what impact hiring a foreign worker would have on jobs in your region. Once your application is approved (which can take up to two months) you can then prepare and sign an employment contract and send it to your potential employee, along with the confirmation letter from Service Canada. The caregiver can then apply to Citizenship and Immigration Canada (CIC, www.cic.gc.ca) for a work permit, including copies of the Service Canada letter and your employment contract. CIC makes the final decision as to whether they are granted a work permit.

There are strict guidelines; employers must provide a fully furnished private room, abide to minimum wage restrictions (there's a limit on how much can be taken off for room and board) and employ the person on a full-time basis in their home. The minimum hourly wage is $8 in BC and the maximum working week is 40 hours. The maximum that can be deducted for room and board is $325 per month. Due to the high demand for caregivers, most employers pay between $9 and $10 per hour, deduct less for room and board and also cover Medical Services Plan fees (p.149). Some also offer two or three weeks of paid vacation and dental benefits, as well as higher rates, anywhere up to $12 per hour. There are several agencies that can assist in the paperwork involved in hiring a foreign worker, as well as conducting background checks and interviews. These normally charge a flat fee, anywhere from $600 to $800. Databases such as www.caregiverlistings.com and www.caregivers.ca provide listings of pre-screened foreign workers free of charge or for a small fee.

## Domestic Services

If you are renting, your landlord is responsible for all major repairs and regular maintenance that may need to be done. This includes any pest control issues (such as mice, cockroaches and fleas) that may arise, as well as any mould occurrences (unless, of course, you caused it yourself). If you feel you have a pest problem and your landlord isn't taking care of it, you can call Vancouver City Hall (453 West 12th Avenue, 604 873 7011) to ask an inspector to visit. The city can then issue a letter forcing the landlord to take care of the problem. For homeowners, the best way to find someone is to consult a property management office or get a referral from a friend. *The Vancouver Courier*, the *Westender* and *The Vancouver Sun*, as well as local websites such as vancouver.kijiji.ca, have hundreds of listings for carpenters, electricians, plumbers and general handymen. Most are competent and fairly reliable. It is a good idea to make sure that whoever you hire has Workers' Compensation Board (WCB) and liability insurance, as these are only available to licensed and ticketed professionals. Rates for general odd jobs start at $35 per hour, while a skilled journeyman plumber or electrician usually

| Domestic Services | |
|---|---|
| Abell Pest Control | 604 853 9218 |
| Canadian Pest Control | 604 873 2813 |
| Mantis Pest Control | 604 722 3002 |
| North Shore Pest Detective | 604 685 3377 |

starts at $60 per hour and can go as high as $100. For emergency evening or weekend calls, the price is usually doubled. There are numerous pest control companies that homeowners can turn to. Rates start at $100 to $200 for a small one-bedroom apartment, and increase depending on the size of your home.

## DVD & Video Rental

While online DVD rental is slowly gaining in popularity, the majority of people still head out to browse the shelves, and there are plenty of stores. The best way of finding one is simply to walk down the street. Several also offer VHS versions of older movies. Most stores operate on a membership system and registration is usually free, as long as you can put a credit card number on file. If you don't have a credit card, you'll normally have to put down the retail value of whatever you rent as a deposit. Larger chains allow longer rentals of up to a week or two on certain films, while smaller outlets usually give you one or two days. New releases usually rent for $4 to $6, while older movies can be taken for $2 to $4. The larger stores offer discounts to members who rent with more frequency or in higher volume.

| DVD & Video Rental | | | |
|---|---|---|---|
| Black Dog Video | 3451 Cambie St | Cambie | 604 873 6958 |
| Blockbuster | Various Locations | www.blockbuster.ca | 604 682 5657 |
| Happy Bats Cinema | 198 East 15th Av | Main | 604 877 0666 |
| Limelight Video | 2505 Alma St | Point Grey | 604 228 1478 |
| Rogers Video | Various Locations | www.rogersplus.ca | 604 687 8000 |
| Videomatica | 1855 West 4th Av | Kitsilano | 604 734 0411 |

Certain shops specialise in particular genres, such as Videomatica (www.videomatica.bc.ca) with its complete Woody Allen collection and extensive range of foreign films. Limelight Video (www.limelightvideo.ca) has classic and independent films, and Happy Bats Cinema (www.happybatscinema.com) offers special collections of British TV shows, documentaries and movies from the 1980s. If you want to order online, websites www.videomatica.ca, www.dvdflix.ca and www.rogersvideodirect.ca offer various monthly subscription packages that mail DVDs directly to your home with pre-paid postage envelopes to return them in. Subscriptions range from $10 to $25 per month, depending on how much you watch.

## Pets

If there is one sight that is more typical of Vancouver than a young, hip parent out pushing their urban buggy stroller, it's someone walking their dog. More than half of BC's residents own a pet, and Vancouver is generally considered an extremely pet-friendly city. Dogs and cats are most common, but birds, fish and hamsters are kept as well. Many hotels allow pets, and the miles of trails and parks that surround the city are ideal for exercising animals. There are several annual pet shows, and for purebred owners the Canadian Kennel Club (www.ckc.ca) sponsors breed-specific shows throughout the year. The CKC also has a national registration service for purebreds, as well as offering ID chip programmes.

Health certificates are normally only required if you are selling your pet or bringing one into the country (and can be issued by any veterinarian), but it is common to give your pet regular vaccinations. If you want to leave your pet at a kennel or with a groomer, they will require proof of vaccinations and health. If you want to buy a pet, the cheapest and most popular options are to buy privately or adopt from an animal shelter. Local newspapers abound with listings of pets for sale, and the animal shelters have an enormous variety of pure and mixed breeds of everything from dogs to llamas. The BC Society for the Prevention of Cruelty to Animals (SPCA) is the largest animal rescue society in the province and is also responsible for enforcing animal cruelty laws. Its website (www.spca.bc.ca) has an enormous amount of information on adopting and maintaining pets.

## Pet-Friendly Rentals

A word of caution to those with pets: there is a difficulty when it comes to rental accommodation. Unlike other cities where landlords can't discriminate against pet owners, Vancouver favours the rights of landlords and allows them to ban all pets from their properties if they wish. Currently only about 5% of rentals allow dogs and 9% allow cats. You may also be required to put down a pet damage deposit of up to half a month's rent (even if you only have goldfish), in addition to the standard half month's security deposit. The pet damage deposit is only paid once, regardless of how many pets you have. Make sure your rental agreement clearly spells out which pets, if any, you are allowed. A great place to find a home for you and your furry friend is www.pa.petsandapartments.com, which lists pet-friendly rentals.

| Pet Boarding & Sitting | | |
|---|---|---|
| Coast Canines | 604 715 6684 | Walking |
| Cozy Mountain Pet Resort | 604 894 1561 | Boarding |
| Dogcity | 604 733 0012 | Boarding |
| Hazelmere Kennels | 604 535 3649 | Boarding, cattery |
| Hounds Around Town | 604 618 5918 | Walking, sitting, boarding |
| Mountainview Kennels | 604 944 4087 | Boarding, cattery |
| Pets In The City | 604 642 6455 | Sitting, walking |

## Bringing Your Pet Into Canada

All pet imports are regulated by the Canadian Food Inspection Agency (don't worry pets are not considered edible items in Canada; it's just the government's way of streamlining services). There is no quarantine in place for most pets and the process of entry is determined by which country you come from. Canada divides all countries into two groups: rabies-free and everyone else. If you are from a country listed as rabies-free, then the process is relatively straightforward. Cats under three months of age can enter the country without vaccinations or a health certificate. Cats over three months will usually need a certificate signed by a government or licensed veterinarian from the country of origin, stating that the animal has either been vaccinated for rabies or comes from a country where there haven't been any cases of rabies for the previous six months. The same type of certificate is generally required for all dogs of any age. If you are coming from a country that Canada has not listed as rabies free, there will be additional forms and possibly extra vaccinations. Full import information on all kinds of animals is available on the CFIA's website (www.inspection.gc.ca).

To take your pet back home, you'll need a Canadian international health certificate (available on the CFIA website), signed by a licensed veterinarian and also by an official Canadian government veterinarian, but it's a good idea to check with your destination country as to specific requirements. Be aware that Air Canada, one of Canada's largest domestic and international carriers, no longer allows pets in the passenger areas of planes, with the exception of guide dogs, so your pet would have to fly in a special cargo area. Other airlines are more tolerant, but it's advisable to check before you book if you don't want your beloved stuck below deck.

## Cats & Dogs

Cats and dogs are the most common types of pet in Vancouver. Dogs over the age of three months require licences, and must wear an ID tag or have a tattoo. Licences can be purchased in person at City Hall (453 West 12th Avenue, 604 873 7011) or Vancouver Animal Shelter (1280 Raymur Avenue, 604 871 6888) or by phoning the shelter. You can also apply online at www.city.vancouver.bc.ca through the community services page. Licence fees are $35 for spayed or neutered dogs and $65 for all other dogs. Dog owners are required to clean up after their animals at all times, unless the owner is a disabled person or the dog is being used as a guide dog. If you don't, you could get hit with a hefty fine, so always keep some bags handy. Dogs must be kept on a leash at all times when out in public, except in off-leash areas. There are more than 30 off-leash parks in Vancouver. You can find a detailed listing with maps and directions on the Vancouver Parks Board's website (www.city.vancouver.bc.ca/parks). In addition, most Vancouver parks have off-leash times between 06:00 and 10:00, and again between 17:00 and 22:00. A great online resource for dog owners is www.petsmo.com, where you can find listings for vets, trainers, groomers, dog food bakeries, walkers and more. Vancouver is such a dog-friendly city that most cafes and supermarkets, including Urban Fare, Choices and Capers, keep bowls filled with water just outside their premises. The most dog-friendly neighbourhoods are Kitsilano, the West End and Yaletown, where it often seems like the ratio of dogs to humans is 1:1.

## Birds & Fish

Most pet shops sell birds and fish, as well as supplies. There are dozens of stores such as Big Al's (4501 North Road, 604 444 3474) and Aquariums West (1262 Burrard Street, 604 669 9249) that specialise in aquatic pets, of which goldfish, koi and small sea turtles tend to be the most common. The most popular birds are parrots, parakeets and various smaller breeds.

## Pet Shops

With as many pet and pet-supply shops as there are in Vancouver, it's surprising that more people don't buy their animals from a store, but the preferred methods are definitely adopting from an animal shelter or buying privately. Where pet stores really shine is in their services and products. They have everything from doggie haute couture, designer pet beds and organic pet bakeries to grooming services that rival the fanciest human spa. Care to give your dog a seaweed botanical facial followed by a

## Pets Grooming/Training

| | | | |
|---|---|---|---|
| Absolute K9 | 604 435 5505 | www.absolutek9.ca | Training, grooming, daycare |
| Alpha Dog Training Company | 604 802 8251 | www.alpha-dogtraining.ca | Training |
| Big Dog Little Dog Bakery | 604 299 3644 | www.bigdoglittledog.com | Bakery |
| Bow Wow Haus | 604 682 1899 | www.bowwowhaus.ca | Bakery, boutique |
| Camelot Dog Daycare & Spa | 604 984 0611 | www.camelotdogs.com | Grooming, daycare |
| The Dog & Hydrant | 604 633 3845 | www.thedogandhydrant.com | Bakery, boutique, photography |
| Dog Stars | 604 878 7827 | www.dogstars.ca | Training, talent agency |
| Fetch – A Dog's Dog Store | 604 879 3647 | www.fetchstore.ca | Boutique, grooming |
| Hot Diggity Dogs Services | 604 202 2010 | www.hotdiggitydogs.ca | Training, walking |
| Luv My Dog | 604 687 6238 | www.luvmydog.ca | Boutique |
| Momo Food | 604 288 5663 | www.momofood.com | Bakery |
| Paw Prints Grooming Salon | 604 733 1144 | www.pawprintsgrooming.com | Grooming |
| Pawsh Dog Spa | 604 685 6088 | www.pawshdogspa.com | Grooming, daycare |
| Pets Beautiful | 604 261 5310 | www.petsbeautiful.com | Grooming |
| Three Dog Bakery | 604 737 3647 | www.threedog.com | Bakery |

## Canine Companions

If you have guests arriving in Vancouver who have had to leave their much-loved canine friends behind, you could always suggest they stay at the Fairmont Vancouver hotel. In keeping with Vancouver's pet-loving culture, the hotel's two resident dogs are part of its guest services and can be booked in advance by hotel guests to make those long walks across Stanley Park even more worthwhile.

eucalyptus breath treatment? No problem. There are also several large warehouse-style shops for pets, such as Petcetera (various locations, www.petcetera.ca) that sell everything from toys and food to books on depression in animals.

### Grooming & Training

Grooming services abound in Vancouver, and the only difficulty is deciding how chic you want your pet to be. While there are plenty of basic 'wash and brush' establishments, there are a growing number of more refined services for your dog or cat, with places available in every neighbourhood. Rates vary with the service, but an average nail clipping costs $15, while a basic wash for a medium-sized dog starts at $25. There are numerous private training schools, as well as courses offered through community and recreation centres. You'll pay anywhere from $100 to $200 for a six-week basic obedience course, and up to $300 for advanced training. Pet food bakeries are also on the rise, as owners are becoming more concerned about nutrition and the effects of additives and preservatives. There are also many stores dedicated to pet accessories, toys and fashions – having a Gucci-clad Yorkie is not out of the realm of possibility.

### Vets & Kennels

All veterinarians in BC must be licensed through the British Columbia Veterinary Medical Association (www.bcvma.org), which keeps a complete list of clinics online. There are almost 50 clinics in the city of Vancouver alone, with an additional 30 on the North Shore. Several only serve a feline clientele and there is even a bird-only hospital. All offer a full range of services, but expect to pay between $70 and $90 for an annual check up at the vet, including basic vaccinations. Costs go up depending on what your pet needs, but emergency surgery can be well over $1,000, so keep that chicken bone away from Rover.

Many pet hospitals and clinics also offer boarding services for smaller animals. Petsitting is widely available, both through individuals and licensed kennels. The best ones are insured and have K9 first-aid certification. Any reputable business will have its business licence and first-aid and insurance certificates prominently displayed, or will be able to produce them on request. Many are located in the districts surrounding Vancouver due to space requirements, but most of these offer pick-up and drop-off services. Several kennels are more like resorts and feature water parks, private trails and gourmet food. Rates can vary anywhere from $15 to $75 per day, depending on the quality of the establishment. Walking and sitting services start at around $15 per hour for a group walk and can go up to $35 per hour for taking your pet to and from appointments or for in-home sitting.

## Veterinary Clinics

| | | | |
|---|---|---|---|
| Arbutus West Animal Clinic | 2809 West 16th Av | Arbutus | 604 736 6701 |
| Cats Only Clinic | 2578 Burrard St | Fairview | 604 734 2287 |
| Cypress Street Animal Hospital | 1893 Cornwall Av | Kitsilano | 604 734 2500 |
| Granville Island Veterinary Hospital | 1635 West 4th Av | Fairview | 604 734 7744 |
| Kerrisdale Veterinary Hospital | 5999 West Blvd | Kerrisdale | 604 266 4171 |
| Night Owl Bird Hospital | 1956 West Broadway | Kitsilano | 604 734 5100 |
| Vancouver Animal Emergency Clinic | 1590 West 4th Av | Fairview | 604 734 5104 |
| Vancouver Feline Hospital | 2299 Burrard St | Fairview | 604 738 5100 |
| Yaletown Pet Hospital | 79 Smithe St | Downtown | 604 682 7389 |

## Utilities & Services

Vancouver is blessed with an abundance of natural resources, especially when it comes to water. Rivers, lakes, creeks and high annual rainfall provide a plentiful water supply, and shortages are rare. Residents are mainly affected between 1 June and 30 September, when lawn sprinkler regulations come into effect as a way to balance the higher demand for drinking water. Your lawn might suffer a little, but that's about it.

The various city governments working in partnership oversee all water, sewerage, rubbish disposal and recycling services in Greater Vancouver. There are no separate bills for these; instead, flat fees are included in the annual property taxes paid for by homeowners. If you own a condo or townhouse, there is usually a strata fee that partially covers these costs. A strata fee is a monthly surcharge by the owner of the development to cover the cost of maintenance, cleaning and repair funds for all common areas. Strata fees sometimes include gas costs as well (see Buying Property, p.98). Those who rent do not pay property taxes.

Electricity and gas are provided through separate utilities, for which you will receive monthly bills. If you are renting an apartment or a separate suite within a house, gas heating and hot water are often included in the price, but this varies widely so it's always a good idea to be sure of what is and isn't included before you sign a rental agreement. If you are renting a house, you are always responsible for the electricity and gas, in addition to the monthly rent. Most houses in Vancouver do not have air conditioning, but many of the newer high-rise apartment towers have this built in. Because it runs off electricity, expect a higher bill in the summer. If you are the owner of a newly built home then you will need to apply for city services to the City of Vancouver Engineering Department, which can be done online at www.city.vancouver.bc.ca. Otherwise, the service is automatically transferred from the previous owner's name to yours when you purchase the property. Renters do not have to deal with this at all, as it is the landlord's responsibility to ensure that all city services are in place by the time you move in.

## Electricity

*Fire Enough*

Vancouver has banned construction of wood-burning fireplaces. If you live in a home with one, you can continue to use it, but if major repairs need to be made you will need to receive permission from City Hall, which can insist that you install a gas fireplace instead.

When it comes to electricity, the government holds a virtual monopoly through its Crown corporation, BC Hydro (604 224 9376, www.bchydro.com), which is the largest electric utility in BC. It serves more than 90% of the population, so unless you're planning to relocate to the remote north and have your own generator in the backyard, this is where your bill will come from every two months. You can set up your account online or by phone through the 24 hour automated system, and you can pay your bill online, by phone, through your bank, by mail or in person at various Pharmasave locations (www.pharmasave.com).

Electricity is measured in kilowatt hours (kWh). The current cost in BC for 1,000kWh is about $66. Average monthly costs vary depending on the size of your home, but in a one-bedroom apartment where the heat is gas based, you can pay as little as $25 per month ($50 per bill). In detached homes, or where the heating is powered by electricity, expect to pay between $120 and $600 every two months. Costs are generally higher in the winter months due to the increased use of lights and heating systems.

Most plugs are the standard three-pin variety operating on 110 volts at 60 hertz. In older homes you can sometimes find two-pin outlets, but these operate on the same voltage, minus an earth wire. If you have two-pin outlets in your home, you can have them easily changed to three-pin versions by BC Hydro. No appliances and electronics sold locally need adaptors, although surge protectors are recommended for computers and high-powered televisions or sound systems.

## Water

Vancouver is a very environmentally conscious city. The government has numerous conservation schemes in place to help reduce the use of water and prevent shortages. These are entirely optional, but most people try to do what they can. The rain barrel subsidy programme (www.city.vancouver.bc.ca) provides residents with barrels at a 50% discount, to provide water for garden use. Indoor water-saver kits help to make dishwashers, toilets, sink faucets and showerheads more efficient, and outdoor versions regulate sprinklers and garden hoses.

Vancouver tap water is completely safe to drink and cook with, and most of the population uses it with no extra precautions. For those who prefer to make doubly sure, there are numerous water filtration companies that can install filters and special drinking faucets in your kitchen. Alternatively, there are several bottled-water suppliers who will deliver bottled water to your home. These companies can provide you with a water dispenser for an additional monthly fee, or you can buy your own for $100 to $200 at home hardware outlets such as Canadian Tire (see Shopping, p.384). You can also buy your own filtration systems, but you will have to install them yourself.

| Water Suppliers | |
| --- | --- |
| Aquapure Systems | 604 681 5996 |
| Cascade Water Corporation | 604 877 0061 |
| Clear Water Solutions | 604 910 0306 |
| Microclear | 604 609 2837 |
| Premium Springs | 604 881 2211 |
| White Springs Water Company | 604 576 9339 |

### Drinking In The Rain

Heavy winter rains can occasionally cause sediment run off from the mountainous terrain surrounding the region's reservoirs. This can sometimes make your tap water cloudy. Before dashing out and spending a fortune on bottled water, try running your tap for a few minutes, as this can often clear up any sediment in the system. If that doesn't work and there is a water advisory update, then boiling water or using bottled water are your best options.

## Gas

Nearly all residential gas is supplied through Terasen Gas (250 979 4900, www. terasengas.com), a private company that took over the provincial gas utility several decades ago and is regulated by the British Columbia Utilities Commission (www. bcuc.com). You can choose to have your gas supplied by another supplier, but you will still be charged through Terasen for midstream rates (a fee for managing the storage and transportation of gas) and delivery rates, and will simply see your gas marketer's commodity fees in a separate table on your bill. A gas marketer acts like a mortgage broker, offering a fixed rate that will not fluctuate with the market, for a set period. With the constant instability in the market, there's no guarantee that you will end up paying less through a gas marketer. You can find a list of gas marketers through the BCUC website, and you can set up an account online or over the phone.

If you don't have a credit rating within North America, then expect to pay a security deposit equivalent to two months of gas supply. Credit reference letters from former credit card companies or utilities companies you have had business with can also be used, and it's probably easier to get these before you leave your previous home. The average home in BC pays about $100 every month for gas, but this varies widely depending on the size of your home and how many gas appliances you have. Most homes have electric cookers, but gas cookers are growing in popularity, and many now have gas fireplaces due to the restrictions on wood-burning fireplaces within Greater Vancouver (see Fire Enough, opposite). Most apartments and homes use hot water or radiant heat, which is often included in monthly rent payments, but a growing number of new homes and condominiums use gas heating systems.

## Sewerage

Vancouver's sewerage system is extremely reliable and is continuously being upgraded. Separate sewers for stormwater and sanitary drainage are now the norm, with a few combined-purpose sewers still waiting to be converted. All sanitary sewage, and some stormwater sewage, is sent to treatment plants to be sanitised and then released back into the surrounding waters. Costs for sewerage are included in annual property owner taxes, with no extra cost for renters.

## Rubbish Disposal & Recycling

Vancouver has weekly rubbish removal services that are operated by the city. For detached homes, the city provides homeowners with separate containers for garbage, grass and hedge trimmings, and recyclable items. The cost for these is included in your property taxes. The Blue Box Recycling Program supplies each household with a blue box for setting out metal, foils, plastic and glass containers, a reusable yellow bag for paper and cardboard products, and a reusable blue bag for newsprint. If you have extra non-recyclable waste that doesn't fit into your garbage container, you will have to buy refuse stickers and attach them to any extra bags. Stickers cost $2 each (you need one per bag) and can be purchased at City Hall, any Safeway supermarket (www.safeway.ca) or at most local community centres. There are separate pick-up schedules for household waste and recycling, which are available on the city's website. In addition, there is unlimited leaf collection all year-round, as long as you put them out in clear plastic bags. For apartment or townhouse dwellers, each complex will have large bins where the residents can drop their rubbish and recyclable items at any time, and which are cleared weekly. All refuse collected is taken first to the Vancouver South Transfer Station (which is also the recycling and yard trimmings depot) and then to the Vancouver Landfill in Delta. Certain larger apartment and townhouse complexes have their recycling picked up by the city's contractor, International Paper Industries. It operates on a separate schedule. All refuse and recycling schedules are available online at the city's website. You can also choose to drop off garbage and recyclable items yourself at the transfer station, which is located at 377 West Kent Avenue North, although there is no discount for this.

## Telephone

As with most utilities, Vancouver's landline phone service operates under an almost complete monopoly. Telus (604 310 2255, www.telus.com) is a private company that is the major provider of landline phone services in the region. Primus (1 800 806 3273, www.primustel.ca) also offers a landline phone service, but with less calling features, and is the same or higher in price. Despite frequent complaints about poor customer service, Telus does provide a reliable and efficient phone service for the most part, with few interruptions and an excellent international network. There is a flat fee for the basic service of around $25 per month. This includes all local calls and free installation.

If you want additional features, including voicemail, caller identification, call waiting or call forwarding, you can add a bundled package giving you several calling features for an additional $20 or so. For just one feature, such as voicemail, it's normally between $4 and $7. Most people pay around $50 per month for a landline phone service, which can include unlimited long-distance calls within Canada and the US. If you have a fax machine there is no additional charge for using it, unless you want to pay for a dedicated line. You can set up a Telus account online or by phone. You will need to provide proof of address and a credit card or security deposit. Monthly bills can be paid online through your bank, or by cheque.

### Online Communities

There are numerous expat-focused websites offering advice and advertising services especially for expatriates. See p.52 for a list. And check out www.explorerpublishing.com, where you can join an online community for your city, share tips, get updates, ask questions and make friends.

**Hold All Calls**

*Most phone companies offer security services to protect you from harassing calls, telemarketers or stalkers. Your number can be listed as private, and will not show up on someone's call display. There is also a flagging service where you can ask your phone company to track harassing calls and submit the information directly to the police. You can block specific numbers from calling you, or numbers that call using automatic dialling systems (like telemarketers). Call your phone provider to find out about rates and procedures.*

## Digital & Internet Phone

If you prefer a digital or internet option, there are several providers that offer comparable services to Telus. Currently, the only local provider of digital phone services is Shaw (604 629 8888, www.shaw.ca). Service plans include multiple-calling features and variable amounts of long-distance minutes within North America. The digital phone service comes through a broadband connection, but you don't need to have the internet to access it, or any special equipment. Expect to pay around $30 or $55 per month. The higher rate includes unlimited long distance calls in Canada and the US, as well as 1,000 minutes per month for overseas calls to most countries.

For internet phone lines, you will first need to get a high-speed broadband internet account through an internet service provider before you sign up for the phone service. The two main providers of internet phone services are Primus and Vonage (1 888 898 8647, www.vonage.ca). Both companies offer similar rates and services, and any equipment needed is often provided for free. Expect to pay anywhere from $15 to $40, depending on the service plan you choose.

## Cheap Long Distance & Overseas Calls

If you don't want to go with a long-distance plan from your main phone provider, there are other options available. Internet calls through your computer are practically free if you use programmes such as Google Talk (www.google.com/talk), Yahoo! Voice (voice.yahoo.com) or Skype (www.skype.com). The problem is that calling quality from a PC depends on a range of things; how much traffic there is, your connection speed and the connection speed of the person you're talking to if they are on a PC. You can often end up having garbled, repetitive conversations. Calling cards are the cheapest way of ringing overseas and provide the clearest connections. There are dozens of cards available at any local tobacconist or newsagent, as well as pharmacies and supermarkets. You can normally buy them in $5, $10, $20 or $50 denominations. Always ask about hidden connection costs, as some companies charge a per minute or per-call connection fee, on top of the call rate. One of the best cards for calling in Canada and the USA is Beyond Canada, with rates starting at one cent per minute, but there are many comparable cards available. Be aware that there are additional charges for calling from or to a mobile phone or toll-free number.

## Local Area Codes

The Greater Vancouver region currently has two area codes: 604 and 778. The 778 code was added several years ago as an overlay due to the area almost running out of available phone numbers. For all local calls 10 digit dialling is mandatory. There is no differentiation between landline and mobile phones. Both use each of the area codes, so don't assume that a 778 number is a mobile phone. The rest of coastal BC uses 604, while the interior and Vancouver Island use 250. All calls outside of the Lower Mainland, regardless of area code, are considered long distance and are normally not included in the basic landline service. Toll-free numbers start with 800, 888, 877 or 866 and you must dial 1 in front of the number, whether it's a local or long-distance call.

## Phone Boxes

Public phone boxes (or payphones, as they are referred to locally) are widely available throughout the city. They have become less popular with the increase in mobile phone use, but are still well maintained and easy to use. Local calls from payphones cost 25 cents per call. Long-distance calls vary depending on where you're calling and for how long. You can also 'call collect' (meaning the person you're calling can agree to accept the charges) from any phone. Most phones accept coins and credit cards. Emergency 911 calls (to reach the police, fire or ambulance services) are free.

*Mobile Phones*

Mobile (sometimes called wireless or cell) phones are extremely popular in Vancouver. More than two-thirds of the population uses one and the number is growing rapidly. Some companies now offer unlimited local talk time and include long-distance minutes as well, so some people have switched from their landline to just using a cell phone. There are several service providers and rates vary according to the plan you choose, but expect to pay between $30 and $50 per month. You can sign up for a monthly contract or buy a prepaid phone for which you buy minutes in blocks. The disadvantage of the pay-as-you-go option is that if your minutes run out in the middle of a call, you're cut off, and then you have to go and buy another block of time. If you're a day or two late paying your monthly bill, however, the chances are the phone company won't shut off your service (unless you start making it a habit). If your phone is lost or stolen, call your phone company right away; it will block service to your number to prevent unauthorised calls. It can also arrange a replacement phone (with the same number) if you need one.

| Mobile Service Providers | | |
|---|---|---|
| Bell Canada | 1 800 667 0123 | www.bell.ca |
| Fido | 1 888 945 3436 | www.fido.ca |
| Rogers | 1 877 764 3772 | www.rogers.com |
| Telus Mobility | 604 291 2355 | www.telusmobility.com |

To sign up with a provider on a monthly contract you'll need two pieces of ID: a credit card and a local mailing address (these don't need to be Canadian). You can sign up over the phone, online or in person at any wireless store.

## Internet
Other options **Websites** p.52

Almost every home in BC has access to internet service, and most are high-speed broadband or DSL connections, with download speeds of three to six mbps (megabytes per second), rather than dial-up, which is usually no faster than 256kbps (kilobytes per second). Rates are normally charged as a flat fee, rather than being based on usage. Expect to pay $30 to $40 per month for a high-speed service, and around $20 for dial up or slower download speeds. 'Dial and surf' options are not common, as the rates tend to be equal or higher than the usual monthly rates.

Bills can be paid online, through your bank, and by a pre-authorised payment plan. Most companies don't charge connection fees for new customers and will provide you with a free modem or gateway. They will also provide you with at least one email account (usually up to three) for which you can choose your own alias, as well as offer free basic web hosting for a personal webpage through their site. Emails are usually POP/IMAP types and can be operated through any email software. You will also be able to access your email through webmail if you are away from home. There is no legal censorship of the internet in Canada, however local laws regarding child pornography and hate material apply to any of the web-hosting companies located in Canada, as well as to Canadian residents. In 2006, all of the major Canadian internet service providers started an anti-child pornography project called Project Cleanfeed Canada, which blocks access to hundreds of such sites.

*Internet Cafes*

There are hundreds of internet cafes in Vancouver, with the highest concentration Downtown, but they're easy to find in any shopping district or

| Internet Service Providers | | |
|---|---|---|
| Bell Canada | www.bell.ca | 1 800 667 0123 |
| Primus | www.primustel.ca | 1 877 704 4269 |
| Shaw | www.shaw.ca | 604 629 8888 |
| Telus | www.telus.com | 604 310 2255 |

**Broadly Speaking**
*Telus (www.telus. com), Rogers (www. rogers.com) and Shaw (www.shaw.ca) offer discounts to customers who sign up for multiple services, such as phone, internet, television and wireless. You can usually save 10% to 20% on your total bill.*

mall. Rates range from $2 to $4 per hour and many charge per minute or per half hour. In addition, there are numerous coffee shops, restaurants, malls and public libraries that offer free wireless internet access for your laptop or mobile device. These normally run on an 802.11b/g system. A great resource is Wifi Mug (vancouver.wifimug.org), an online directory that lists more than 100 free wireless spots across the city.

## Postal Services

Canada Post (www. canadapost.ca) is the national government postal system.

*Mailbox*

A home delivery system is the norm, but more remote or rural areas often use PO boxes. You can also choose to use one if you don't want mail to come to your home. There are hundreds of PO box centres in Vancouver that can provide a box for a low monthly rate. The postal service is extremely efficient and cheap. There are hundreds of post offices in Greater Vancouver, and there are postal counters in pharmacies, supermarkets, stationery shops and cornershops. Postal services are available between 08:00 and 17:30, Monday to Friday.

You can buy stamps and mailing supplies at any post office, or order them online through the Canada Post website. Red postal drop-off boxes can be found every few blocks, whether in a residential or commercial area, either on a street corner or in a mall or retail outlets. To post a standard letter costs 52 cents within Canada, 93 cents if you are sending it to the US, and $1.55 overseas. It normally takes one to two business days for post mailed locally to arrive within the city, three to four days to reach another Canadian city or province, about a week to any destination in the US and up to two weeks to reach Europe, Asia and Australia. Rates are based on weight, destination and which service speed you choose, but a parcel sent by basic registered mail to the US starts at $11 for 0.5kg and can go up to almost $100 for a 30kg parcel. Insurance for up to $100 is included in the cost of postage when you send post within Canada or to the US via registered mail, and up to $60 when sending overseas. Additional coverage is only available for Canadian destinations for an extra fee. When sending parcels to the US or overseas, always ensure you include the full name and address of both sender and addressee on the parcel, as well as relevant customs details, or it could be denied entry at the border.

| Courier Services | | |
|---|---|---|
| Atlas Courier | 604 875 1111 | www.atlascourier.com |
| Corporate Couriers Logistics | 604 685 5900 | www.corporatecouriers.net |
| DHL Express Canada | 604 665 4881 | www.dhl.ca |
| FedEx Canada | 1 800 463 3339 | www.fedex.ca |
| Phantom Couriers | 604 899 5447 | www.phantomcouriers.com |
| Purolator | 1 888 744 7123 | www.purolator.com |
| Swift Dispatch Service | 604 873 5422 | www.swiftdispatch.com |

*Courier Services*

There are numerous courier companies in the city offering local and international services. Most use bonded and insured personnel (meaning criminal record and background checked) and offer guaranteed deliveries. Rates depend on what service speed you choose and the destination, but expect to pay at least $10 to ship a large envelope within Canada by the next day and $30 to reach the US within two business days.

## Radio

No matter what your taste, Vancouver probably has a radio station to suit. If you want to learn more about what it means to be Canadian, then CBC Radio is the ticket. It is the only national government-sponsored network, and has three stations. CBC Radio One (690AM) provides news and pop culture programmes, and focuses on life in British Columbia. CBC Radio Two (105.7FM) offers classical, opera, jazz and world music, arts programmes, and serves up world news every hour. Radio Canada International offers Canadian content in nine languages through shortwave and satellite radio. There are also several local multicultural stations (check out FM 90.1, 93.1, 96.1 and 97.7), as well as dozens of local and national news, chat, pop, rock, jazz and country stations. Satellite radio is very popular. Like mobile phones it can be accessed by signing up to a monthly or yearly plan, and you need to buy a satellite radio. Costs start as low as $12 per month. The two local satellite radio providers are Sirius (www.sirius.com) and XM (www.xmradio.ca).

## Television

Cable television is a standard service in BC, offering about 50 channels, as well as multiple movie, sports and speciality channels. Cable service providers are divided by region, with the entire Lower Mainland serviced by Shaw Cable (www.shaw.ca). You can choose a digital or satellite TV service through various providers, which normally offer more than 100 channels and a pay-per-view service. All channels must comply with regulations set by the Canadian Radio-television and Telecommunications Commission (www.crtc.gc.ca) and have restrictions on things such as full nudity, coarse language and extreme violence. TV programmes must have parental ratings indicating which shows are suitable for which age group. Most channels are in English, but there are several

| Satellite & Cable Providers | | |
|---|---|---|
| Bell Canada | 1 800 667 0123 | www.bell.ca |
| Shaw | 604 629 8888 | www.shaw.ca |
| Telus TV | 604 310 2255 | www.telus.com |

French-language channels and a few multicultural stations that broadcast in various languages. Content is largely Canadian, but there are several American stations that provide the latest sitcoms, dramas and reality TV shows. CBC TV, CTV, Channel M, Chan, Omni and CKVU are channels that broadcast mainly Canadian and multicultural content. KSTW, KIRO, KING, KCPQ and KOMO are the most popular American channels. W Network is a female-focused channel, and Slice offers everything from home improvement and fashion makeover shows to travel programmes.

Sports channels include TSN and ESPN, both of which have broad international coverage. CBC also airs regular hockey and soccer games. For performing arts, classic movies and music videos, there are channels including Bravo, Arts & Entertainment Network, Showcase and Encore. There are also several public television stations (such as PBS and Knowledge Network) that offer arts, education and cultural programmes. To connect to cable, you simply need to open an account and connect your television to the cable wall outlet. For digital you will also need a digital terminal, which you can buy from your service provider. For satellite, you will have buy a satellite dish, but if you are in rental accommodation you will need to get your landlord's permission. Monthly rates for cable and digital are $40 to $50. Digital terminals cost between $60 and $600, but you can opt to pay in monthly instalments. New customers can often benefit from promotions offering free or low-cost satellite dishes, receivers and installation.

# Is getting lost your usual excuse?

Whether you're a map person or not, this pocket-sized marvel will help you get to know the city like the back of your hand – so you won't feel the back of someone else's.

**Vancouver Mini Map**
Fit the city in your pocket

# General Medical Care

Vancouver is comparable to any large international city in terms of health facilities, with specialists available in every field and a high standard of care in hospitals and clinics. Canada has a publicly funded healthcare system that in BC operates under the provincial ministry for health (www.health.gov.bc.ca). Medical coverage is offered through the Medical Services Plan (MSP) and is mandatory for all BC residents. MSP (or Health Insurance BC as it is now called) covers medically required services by physicians and hospitals, maternity care by a physician or midwife, diagnostic services, oral and dental surgery when performed in a hospital, and regular eye exams for children under 19 and seniors over 64.

Unlike some provinces, BC charges a monthly premium for MSP services, amounting to $54 per month for an individual, $96 for a family of two, and $108 for a family of three (additional family members are included at this rate). Premium assistance, which offers discounts anywhere from 10% to 100%, is available for those who cannot afford to pay. Regardless of whether you have paid your premiums, you won't be refused medically necessary care. Your financial file, however, will be transferred to Revenue BC, the government branch that handles collections. Revenue BC will send you warning letters and if you don't pay or make some kind of arrangement, it will proceed to legal action, which can include getting a claim for funds from your salary or bank account.

Prescription drug and medical supply subsidies are offered through PharmaCare (www.health.gov.bc.ca/pharme), the government drug-subsidy programme. Anyone eligible for MSP is able to register for PharmaCare as well; the subsidy level depends on your level of income and family size. The Healthy Kids programme provides subsidised dental care and automatically registers any children under 19 from families who receive premium assistance. Most employers and unions offer their employees or members extended health coverage through private insurers, as well as covering MSP premiums. Extended health insurance covers areas such as ambulance services, routine dental and vision care, alternative health services such as physiotherapy, massage therapy and homeopathy, as well as extended sick leave and wage compensation. If your employer doesn't offer medical benefits, you can purchase extended health insurance directly, although many people make do with just the MSP services. Further information on both MSP and PharmaCare services can be found on the ministry's website.

*Get Insured*

*For more information on health insurance, how to enrol and who is eligible, visit the Ministry of Health website at www.health.govbc.ca/insurance.*

## Public Healthcare

Despite frequent complaints about bed shortages and long waiting times, most BC residents receive prompt and efficient treatment. A pressing problem is the shortage of primary care physicians. A general practitioner, also known as a family doctor, handles primary care, but finding a primary care physician can be problematic and often involves a waiting list – you may have to make do with walk-in clinics until a spot opens up. The only difference in care between walk-in clinics and having a regular family doctor is that there is no guarantee you will see the same doctor each time you visit, but you can also choose to use your local walk-in clinic as your primary care provider.

Vancouver has many walk-in clinics (staffed by a team of rotating GPs) that offer non-emergency services on a first-come, first-served basis. Many of these also let you book an appointment. Some clinics include GPs who focus their practice on women, maternity or infant care. Specialists are normally only available after referral from a GP. Almost all hospitals have 24 hour emergency departments. Wait times at emergency departments can sometimes be lengthy, but the highest tend to be for surgery which involves hip or knee replacements, vision, the heart and cancer, as well as for diagnostic imaging services such as an MRI or ultrasound. If you are not covered by MSP or another insurer, you will still go through the same clinics or hospitals (and deal with the same wait times) in virtually all cases. If you have MSP, you will need to show your CareCard at any clinic or hospital to get treatment. If you are covered by a private insurer, you will have to show proof of coverage (most insurance companies provide a card you can keep in your wallet). If you have no insurance, you will need to provide identification such as your Social Insurance Number, driver's licence or passport, along with a mailing address and contact information. If you cannot pay up front, you will be sent a bill by mail.

## Private Healthcare

There has always been controversy surrounding Canada's two-tier system of basic public care and extended private care, and the legislation covering private healthcare is complex. The main thing to know is that it is illegal for any private facility to charge you for a medically necessary service that is covered by MSP at a public hospital or clinic, such as setting a broken bone, having necessary x-rays, or undergoing emergency or medically necessary surgery.

A couple of private hospitals and clinics have opened up in recent years and offer services such as MRI, ultrasound and various surgical procedures on a fee paying basis. The advantage to patients who can afford this option is the dramatically reduced waiting times compared with public facilities. For the most part, however, all medical care is administered through public-access hospitals and clinics, regardless of whether or not you have insurance.

## MSP & PharmaCare

**BC Nurseline**

*If you need advice on general health issues you can speak to a trained nurse 24 hours a day through the BC Nurseline (604 215 4700). You do not need to provide information from your CareCard to use this service – although the nurse may request it.*

Health Insurance BC is the administrative body that runs the MSP and PharmaCare programmes. To qualify for MSP, you must be a Canadian citizen, a permanent resident, or hold a study or work permit issued under the Canada Immigration and Refugee Protection Act (see Residence Visa, p.68).

You should apply for coverage as soon as you arrive in the province. There is a waiting period of up to three months before your benefits begin, so you should make sure that your previous health insurance continues to provide coverage for your first few months in BC. The waiting period is waived for Canadian military personnel and their families who are moving to BC for the first time. When you are approved for MSP, you will receive a CareCard with a personal health number. This number will allow any clinic or hospital to access your information through an online database. It's a good idea to keep your CareCard in your wallet in case of emergency. Regardless of whether or not you qualify for MSP, make sure that you have coverage during your stay in BC, as medical care can be expensive without it.

## Medical Coverage Outside BC

If you need emergency treatment while travelling in other Canadian provinces, the hospital will bill its own provincial health plan if you can show a valid BC CareCard. In Quebec and outside Canada you will be asked to pay up front and then be reimbursed by MSP. Non-emergency medically necessary treatment, whether in Canada or abroad, is only covered when provided by a physician (so no massage or physiotherapy appointments), and only up to the dollar amount that would be spent in BC. Costs for most services can be higher in other provinces, and are definitely much more in the US, so it's a good idea to get travel insurance, even if you're only leaving BC for a few days, as ambulance services, prescription drugs and hospital stays are not covered by MSP or private medical insurance.

## Emergency Services

If you have an emergency, dial 911 for police, ambulance or fire services, and an operator will connect you to the appropriate department. Whoever you speak with will ask you for your street address, but you don't need to provide a cross street or directions. You may also be asked questions about the situation and anyone who is hurt or in distress. All information is relayed to the personnel en route to your location. If you need to go to a hospital emergency room, the ambulance staff will usually decide which hospital to take you to, based on which is the least busy at that particular time. You can also request a specific hospital if you are in labour or if you would prefer one that is closer to your home, but this is also dependent on where beds are available. All BC hospitals provide similar levels of care, but certain ERs have much higher waiting times. St Paul's in the West End and Vancouver General in the City Hall area have two of the busiest ERs in the province, although the level of care at both is also among the highest in BC.

Ambulance response times tend to be extremely quick, and quite often both fire and ambulance personnel arrive for medical calls. Most callers wait less than 10 minutes (and often less than five) for someone to arrive. All emergency services except for ambulance rides are covered by MSP and by most private insurers. If you do not have any coverage, you will be billed for services after your stay (at present, this is a flat fee of $80 for an ambulance ride, although it is free with MSP Premium Assistance), but you cannot be refused necessary emergency treatment at any time.

### Pharmacies

Pharmacists in BC cannot prescribe medication or provide prescription drugs without a doctor's prescription. Doctors will normally only issue a prescription during a patient's appointment, but if you need your medication renewed, your doctor can indicate on the prescription form how many renewals are approved. Pharmacists can suggest over-the-counter or off-the-shelf remedies for common ailments, but there are strict laws regarding the distribution of prescription drugs, which includes most forms of antibiotics and painkillers that have narcotic ingredients. Most pharmacies are open seven days a week, usually between 09:00 and 18:00. Pharmasave (www.pharmasave.com), Shoppers Drug Mart (www. shoppersdrugmart.ca) and London Drugs (www.londondrugs.com) all have multiple locations with varying hours. All London Drugs locations are open until at least 22:00 on weekdays and 20:00 at weekends. Shoppers Drug Mart has three 24 hour locations: 885 West Broadway, 1125 Davie Street and 2302 West 4th Avenue. All Safeway, Overwaitea Foods, Save On Foods and Real Canadian Superstore locations have in-store pharmacies that usually operate between 08:00 and midnight.

### Health Check-Ups

You can get a check up at any general or walk-in clinic or through any GP. Most clinics also provide well-woman programmes that coordinate such things as Pap tests, mammograms, birth control, pre-screening for diabetes and high blood pressure, as well as regular testing for sexually transmitted diseases.

A new patient at any clinic is entitled to a complete head-to-toe physical with all necessary tests. Further check-ups are done on a need basis. If you are not covered by health insurance, expect to pay $100 to $200 for a complete physical. MSP will only cover a new patient's first complete physical, unless you have a medical condition that requires regular check ups.

## Health Insurance

While it is not mandatory for resident expats to have health insurance, it is highly recommended. BC employers are not legally obliged to offer medical benefits, but most companies do for their full-time staff, and a growing number are offering benefits to part-time employees as well. Employer benefits can range from simply covering your

MSP premiums to offering extended vision, dental and alternative therapy coverage. Most private health insurance companies group their benefits packages into three main categories: core extended health, dental and drugs. You can choose which options you prefer, or all of them. Many people choose one option to supplement a spouse's extended coverage or to cover dental costs for children. Core extended health packages cover things such as eye exams, prescription glasses or contact lenses, ambulance costs, private or semi-private hospital rooms, in-home nursing care, extended disability and critical illness costs. If you are buying private health insurance to supplement your MSP coverage, expect to pay anywhere from $120 to $1,500 per year depending on how many options you choose and how many people are in your family. If you need full coverage, expect to pay between $1,000 and $2,000 a year for one person and $2,000 to $3,000 for a family of three. Most companies offer monthly, biannual and annual payment options, as well as discounts for family plans. Plans can be purchased for any length of time between 10 days and one year.

## Health Insurance Companies

| | | |
|---|---|---|
| Aetna | 1 800 694 3258 | www.aetna.com |
| BCAA | 1 877 325 8888 | www.bcaa.com |
| Bridges International Insurance Services | 604 408 8695 | www.biis.ca |
| The Co-operators | 1 800 869 6747 | www.cooperators.ca |
| Health Care International | 00 44 207 590 8800 | www.healthcareinternational.com |
| International Health Insurance | 00 457 023 2313 | global.ihi.com |
| Industrial Alliance Pacific Life Insurance Company | 604 734 1667 | www.iaplife.com |
| Norfolk Mobility Benefits | 403 232 8545 | www.norfolkmobility.com |
| Pacific Blue Cross | 604 419 2200 | www.pbchbs.com |
| RBC Insurance | 1 800 565 3129 | www.rbcinsurance.com |
| TFG Global Insurance Solutions | 604 351 5278 | www.tfgglobal.com |

## Donor Cards

The British Columbia Transplant Society (555 West 12th Avenue, 604 877 2240) runs the provincial organ donor registry. You can download the online form at www.transplant. bc.ca or pick up a brochure at any doctor's office, ICBC centre, Motor Vehicle Branch, London Drugs location or Save On Food or Overwaitea pharmacy. Once your signed form is received, your information is entered into the online database and can be accessed by hospital personnel using your personal health number. You can choose which organs or tissue you wish to donate, but you won't receive a donor card or any confirmation – a hospital will only access the database in the event of a death.

## Giving Blood

Canadian Blood Services handles all blood donations. In Vancouver, the main office is at 4750 Oak Street, next to Vancouver Women's Hospital. It also maintains the national bone marrow registry. Annual blood drives are quite popular and all blood types are welcome. You can find locations to donate blood online at www.bloodservices.ca or by calling 604 739 2300.

## Giving Up Smoking

With British Colombia's recent blanket ban on smoking in all indoor public spaces and work places, as well as most outdoor spaces, more and more people seem to be trying to quit smoking.

Most hospitals have free clinics available for smokers trying to give up, and any GP can give you a prescription to ease your addiction. There are also many over-the-counter remedies available at any pharmacy. Alternative healing practitioners (p.159) such as massage therapists and acupuncturists often have specific programmes for those trying to quit, and counselling and support groups (p.164) are widely available.

## Hospitals

There are more than a dozen hospitals in the Lower Mainland, with a large concentration in Vancouver and on the North Shore. Most have emergency departments, and several are teaching hospitals in conjunction with the UBC medical programme. Standard amenities at most hospitals include cafeterias and gift shops, as well as learning and information resources, interpreter services and specialised clinics.

### BC Children's Hospital

*4480 Oak St*
*Shaughnessy*
*Map 5 F2* **1**

*604 875 2345* | *www.bcchildrens.ca*
This is the only children's hospital in BC. It offers numerous specialised programmes not available anywhere else, and serves children from newborns to adolescents. The emergency room is open 24 hours. It is famous for its Children's Heart Centre, as well as its cancer, genetics and mental health programmes. BC Children's also offers regular clinical and family services, as well as support services and child safety schemes focusing on car seats and home safety.

### BC Women's Hospital & Health Centre

*4500 Oak St*
*Shaughnessy*
*Map 5 F2* **2**

*604 875 2424* | *www.bcwomens.ca*
This is the only facility in British Columbia devoted to the care of women, newborns and their families. It is primarily a maternity hospital, and is the largest in the country. It also offers programmes in reproductive health, breast assessment and diagnosis, and osteoporosis, as well as sexual assault services, abuse and violence programmes, clinics for women and children with HIV/Aids and women with disabilities, and clinical programmes for various ethnic groups. It works in partnership with BC Children's Hospital on many of its initiatives, and the two hospitals are joined to one another.

### Burnaby General Hospital

*3935 Kincaid St*
*Burnaby*
*Map 6 D2* **3**

*604 434 4211* | *www.fraserhealth.ca*
Burnaby is one of the largest hospitals outside the City of Vancouver. It offers a full range of facilities including a 24 hour emergency department, neurology, oncology and maternity services, and specialised units such as the Children's Urgent Care Clinic and the speech and language pathology programme. The hospital also offers health and nutritional counselling, as well as physiotherapy and mental health programmes.

### Lions Gate Hospital

*231 East 15th St*
*North Vancouver*
*Map 4 B2* **4**

*604 988 3131* | *www.nscg.ca*
A major trauma and neurosurgery centre, Lions Gate serves the North and West Vancouver communities and is one of the busiest hospitals in the province. Specialised services include orthopaedics, paediatrics, chemotherapy and coronary care. The emergency department is open 24 hours.

| Dermatologists | | | |
|---|---|---|---|
| Dr Alastair McLeod | 1160 Burrard St | West End | 604 688 1388 |
| Dr James Bergman | 1803-805 West Broadway | Fairview | 604 876 4433 |
| Dr Joanna Day | 103-2419 Bellevue Av | North Vancouver | 604 628 1125 |
| The Face & Skin Clinic | 888 West 8th Av | False Creek | 604 731 5353 |
| The Skin Care Centre | 835 West 10th Av | Fairview | 604 875 5151 |

## Mount Saint Joseph Hospital

**3080 Prince Edward St**
Mount Pleasant
Map 6 A1 **5**

*604 874 1141* | *www.providencehealthcare.ca*

This is a smaller hospital that focuses on the multicultural community. Information is available in more than five languages. The hospital specialises in extended and elderly care, with a geriatric day hospital and outpatient clinics, as well as excellent geriatric dentistry and psychiatry departments. Most surgeries are on an outpatient or day basis. Mount Saint Joseph is the leading provider of cataract and corneal transplant surgeries in BC, and also specialises in plastic surgery and urology. The small emergency department is open from 08:00 to 20:30 daily.

## St Paul's Hospital

**1081 Burrard St**
West End
Map 6 C4 **6**

*604 682 2344* | *www.providencehealthcare.ca*

This is an acute care and teaching hospital. St Paul's is the designated heart centre for the province and its research focuses on cardiovascular and pulmonary care. It also has a designated HIV/Aids ward, as well as specialised programmes for those with eating disorders, chronic pain and diabetes. It has the second-largest maternity care department in Vancouver. The emergency department is one of the largest and busiest in the city, and is open 24 hours.

## UBC Hospital Urgent Care Centre

**2211 Westbrook Mall**
UBC
Map 5 B1 **7**

*604 822 7121* | *www.vanhosp.bc.ca*

Primarily a teaching and research institute, this hospital is located on the University of British Columbia campus. The Urgent Care Centre offers treatment of non-life threatening emergencies such as sprains or broken bones, minor burns, fevers and injuries that need stitches or similar attention. Emergency services are available between 08:00 and 22:00 every day. The hospital is well known for its general and juvenile psychiatry departments, as well as its reconstructive orthopaedic surgery specialists.

## Vancouver General Hospital

**855 West 12th Av**
Cambie
Map 5 F1 **8**

*604 875 4111* | *www.vanhosp.bc.ca*

Vancouver General is one of the largest hospitals in the province. In addition to providing acute care, VGH is a teaching hospital and houses one of the largest research institutes in Canada. It offers specialised services for a variety of degenerative illnesses, as well as oncology, sports medicine and spinal cord injury. The burns unit is one of the best in the city. The emergency department is open 24 hours a day.

### Private Health Centres & Clinics

| | | | |
|---|---|---|---|
| Ambulatory Surgical Centre Vancouver | 1200 Burrard St | West End | 604 669 6181 |
| Cambie Surgery Centre | 2836 Ash St | Cambie | 604 874 1349 |
| Continuum Medical Care | 202-520 17th St | West Vancouver | 604 913 8183 |
| Copeman Healthcare Centre | 1128 Hornby St | West End | 604 707 2273 |
| False Creek Surgical Centre | 555 West 8th Av | Fairview | 604 739 9695 |

## Health Centres & Clinics

Health centres (usually called family clinics) are where people go for any non-emergency medical treatment. This can be anything from getting sutures for a minor cut and flu vaccines to treatments for general ailments and referrals to specialists. A family clinic is staffed by a group of GPs, and many are open six or seven days a week.

## Health Centres & Clinics

| | | | |
|---|---|---|---|
| Aquarius Medical Clinic | 202-179 Davie St | Yaletown | 604 669 7772 |
| Care Point Medical Centre | 5619 Victoria Dr | Victoria | 604 656 2090 |
| | 5138 Joyce St | Renfrew Heights | 604 436 0800 |
| | 1175 Denman St | West End | 604 681 5338 |
| | 1623 Commercial Dr | Grandview | 604 254 5554 |
| Khatsahlano Medical Clinics | 2689 West Broadway | Kitsilano | 604 731 9187 |
| Mid-Main Community Health Centre | 3998 Main St | Main | 604 873 3666 |
| Pacific Medical Clinic | 6176 Fraser St | Fraser | 604 301 9955 |
| QE Park Medical Clinic | 4060 Cambie St | Cambie | 604 874 4060 |
| Stein Medical Clinic | 180-550 Burrard St | Downtown | 604 688 5924 |
| Tiddlycove Medical Clinic | 4915 Marine Dr | West Vancouver | 604 922 8216 |
| University Village Clinic | 228-2155 Allison Rd | UBC | 604 222 2273 |

## Maternity

Other options **Maternity Items** p.391

If you are on MSP, then your maternity care is fully subsidised and covers all antenatal and postnatal care up to six weeks after delivery by either a physician or a registered midwife. This also includes your hospital stay and the pain relief of your choice, usually an epidural or gas and air, although other options are also available. Extended health insurance often covers optional costs like having a private room and any ambulance expenses, as well as paternity leave for your partner or spouse.

If you are moving to BC from another province, make sure your previous provincial coverage lasts until your MSP becomes effective. If you are relying on travel insurance from your home country, it's a good idea to check whether maternity costs are covered or buy additional insurance for this before you arrive in Canada, as the maternity costs can be prohibitive. Water births can be done at home or in the hospital. You can also choose to have a caesarean instead of a natural birth, and can book the hospital date in advance. Caesareans are covered by MSP and most private health policies.

### Maternity Care Providers

In BC, obstetricians, family physicians and registered midwives are all licensed to offer maternity care. You can find a registered midwife through the College of Midwives of British Columbia (604 742 2230, www.cmbc.bc.ca). It's your choice as to what type of health professional you use and whether you would like to deliver at home or in the hospital. Registered midwives have hospital privileges, meaning they can order tests, refer you to specialists as needed, and deliver your baby. Most women use a family physician for their maternity care. Obstetricians are normally only consulted in the case of complicated pregnancies, if the mother is over 40, or for multiple births (twins, triplets and so on).

For Vancouver residents, there is also the option of using BC Women's Hospital Family Practice Maternity Service (FPMS) (604 875 3436, www.birthdocs.ca), which is a group of family physicians whose sole focus is maternity care. An FPMS would care for you and your baby until six weeks after the birth, at which point you would transfer back to your regular family doctor.

In addition to your maternity care provider, you can have an assistant (a doula) to help during the labour, although this is not covered by MSP. Doulas cannot deliver your child but can provide emotional and physical support before, during and after the delivery. You can find a qualified doula through the Doula Services

Association BC (604 515 5588, www.bcdoulas.org). After your baby is born, you will need to fill out the birth certificate, social insurance and MSP forms, all of which are available at the hospital or from your doctor. For more information, see the Birth Certificate & Registration section on p.74.

## Maternity Care In Hospitals

Although any major hospital can deliver your baby, the majority of women in Vancouver deliver either at BC Women's Hospital or at St Paul's Hospital (see p.153). BC Women's is the only dedicated maternity hospital in the province, and St Paul's general hospital has a large and well-staffed maternity department. Regardless of which hospital you choose, you can make a birthing plan to inform hospital staff about any personal preferences or religious customs. Women normally give birth in a private birthing room and are then transferred with their child to a private or semi-private room for the duration of the hospital stay. If you would like to guarantee a private room, the cost is $100 daily. However, you could be put into private rooms without requesting it, space permitting, and you don't have to pay in that case.

You can bring music, pillows or anything you like that will make you more comfortable. You can also choose to have more than one person in the delivery room with you, such as your spouse, a parent or an older child, or a doula. Hospitals recommend no more than two additional people in the delivery room. Most women stay in the hospital for one to three days following a normal birth, and for up to five days following a caesarean.

## Going Back To Your Home Country

If you decide to go back to your home country to give birth, make sure to check on any airline restrictions. In general, Canadian airline companies allow pregnant women to travel up to their 35th week and allow newborn travel seven days after birth. If your pregnancy is visible, you will need a note from your doctor saying you are fit to travel. You should take any records of antenatal care with you when you leave, and bring all postnatal records if you return with your newborn. When crossing international borders, all children must have their own passport. If you are travelling without your spouse or partner, you may also need to show birth and custody documents at the border.

## Antenatal Care

During your pregnancy, you will see your physician or midwife for a maternity check-up once each month until you reach five months, after which you will have a check-up once every two weeks. When you're in the last month of your pregnancy you may have to come in weekly.

Ultrasounds are part of standard care, as is foetal heart rate monitoring and blood tests. Your doctor or midwife will refer you to an obstetrician if you need additional specialised care. There are numerous pregnancy support groups run by each hospital as well as various classes covering Lamaze and other breathing techniques, birthing options and additional advice. If you want to deliver at a specific hospital, you need to make sure that your doctor or midwife has privileges there, as most Vancouver doctors and midwives deliver at either St Paul's or BC Women's, but rarely both. Each hospital keeps a list on file of attending doctors, or your regular family doctor can refer you.

### Postnatal Depression

In a recent Canadian study, more than 30% of new mothers were found to suffer from some degree of postnatal depression. In BC, the Pacific Post Partum Support Society (604 255 7999, www.postpartum.org) offers a free telephone helpline and numerous support groups throughout Greater Vancouver.

*Postnatal Care*

When your child is born in the hospital, a paediatrician will examine it immediately. A community health worker, usually a nurse, will visit you in your home about a week later. You would normally go for a check up at your doctor's around week two and then again after one month. Breastfeeding is highly encouraged by local health professionals, and each hospital has lactation consultants on call who are available to help with any difficulties or questions. Hospitals will provide milk formula if you request it or if it becomes necessary. Each hospital also has various free workshops on breastfeeding techniques and options like getting breast milk from a milk bank. It is completely acceptable in Canada to breastfeed in public. Many women use a cover cloth while breastfeeding for personal privacy, but this is not a legal requirement.

*Maternity Leave*

Anyone who works in BC qualifies for 18 weeks of unpaid maternity leave as soon as they begin a job. Maternity leave can be taken if you are pregnant or if you decide to adopt. An employer cannot fire you or lay you off for this, and must hold the job for you until your return. If you have worked more than 600 hours in the 52 weeks before you take your leave, then you qualify for paid maternity and parental benefits through Service Canada's Employment Insurance scheme (www1.servicecanada.gc.ca). Benefits are paid out for up to 50 weeks at a rate of 55% of your earnings, up to a maximum of $435 per week. If your employer offers extended health benefits, this can also include a top-up of up to 90% of your salary for the first 15 to 19 weeks. You can start your maternity leave through Employment Insurance up to eight weeks before your due date, but be aware that you are legally required to continue your leave until at least six weeks after you deliver. Partners can also apply for parental benefits, but the combined limit for both parents is 35 weeks on top of the 15 weeks of maternity leave paid to the birth mother or primary care parent in the case of adoption. If you decide not to return to work after your leave ends, you do not have to pay back Employment Insurance or your employer, as the amount paid out to you is based on your past work hours.

# Gynaecology & Obstetrics

Your GP can provide routine care such as Pap tests or contraceptives. If you need more specialised care, the best way of finding a gynaecologist is by asking your family doctor for a referral. Female gynaecologists are in higher demand than their male counterparts, so if you're comfortable seeing a male doctor, this can often be a quicker option.

*Contraception & Sexual Health*

There is a wide range of contraception options available in BC. Birth control is not covered by MSP, but some extended and private insurance plans do subsidise it. Choices include daily birth control pills, weekly skin patches, Depo Provera injections (good for 12 weeks), Norplant (up to five years), intra-uterine devices (up to five years), condoms, diaphragms and spermicide. Tubal ligation or vasectomies are also available for those seeking more permanent options. You will need to get a prescription from a GP for birth control pills, and injections and IUD insertions can be done in a doctor's office. An emergency contraceptive, also known as the morning-after pill, is available over the counter at any pharmacy without a doctor's prescription and can be taken up to 72 hours following unprotected sex.

*Fertility Treatments*

Fertility treatments are available in BC, but most are not covered by MSP or private insurance. MSP does cover the following services: gynaecological exams and diagnostic tests to determine the cause of female or male infertility, tests to measure hormone

*Breast Cancer & Mammograms*

In BC, breast cancer screening is conducted through the BC Cancer Agency's Screening Mammography Program (604 660 3639, www.bccancer. bc.ca). Mammograms are available free at least once every two years to women aged between 40 and 79, without a doctor's referral. If you are under 40, you can have a free mammogram if your doctor requests it. There are several mammography locations in Vancouver, including one at BC Women's Hospital. A full listing is available on the BC Cancer Agency's website.

levels related to ovulation, and intra-uterine artificial insemination (when performed in a doctor's office). Costs for other treatments can range from $150 to upwards of $5,000, depending on the service. Options include in-vitro fertilisation (IVF), embryo freezing, intra-cytoplasmic sperm injection (ICSI), donor insemination, ovulation induction and sperm banks.

Greater Vancouver has the following fertility clinics: UBC Centre for Reproductive Health, BC Women's Health Centre (604 875 3060, www.ubcfertility.com); Genesis Fertility Centre (604 879 3032, www.genesis-fertility.com); and Pacific Centre for Reproductive Medicine (604 422 7276, www.pacificfertility.ca).

## Abortions

Abortions are a legal publicly funded service in BC, and you do not need a doctor's referral in order to get one. Clinics offering abortions also provide free counselling on pregnancy, sexual health, contraceptives and other alternatives. Most abortions are performed in the first 12 weeks of pregnancy, and no later than 20 weeks unless there are serious health risks to the mother or severe abnormalities in the foetus. If you are not covered by MSP or private health insurance, an abortion can cost between $400 and $600, but some clinics have funding for those without resources, or offer payment plans. For a complete list of clinics that offer abortions, as well as free telephone helplines, contact the Pro-Choice Action Network (604 736 2800, www.prochoiceactionnetwork-canada.org) for more information.

**Children & Disabilities**
*There are various services for children with developmental, physical and learning disabilities. BC Children's Hospital has comprehensive programmes for infants, children and young people with ADHD, autism spectrum disorder, mood and anxiety disorders, eating disorders, substance abuse problems and various other physical and mental disabilities. Vancouver Coastal Health (604 736 2033, www.vch. ca), the regional health authority, also provides programmes for children and young people with early psychosis and mental health problems.*

# Paediatrics

General infant and child care in BC is handled through a GP. If your child has a specific condition or illness, your doctor will refer you to the appropriate paediatrician. All referred specialist visits are covered under MSP and private health insurance. Currently, there is a high demand for paediatricians in BC, so regardless of whether you have MSP or private insurance, waiting times can stretch several months for non-urgent conditions. Babies are not assigned a paediatrician when they're born, and are instead seen by whichever doctor happens to be on call. Who you see after that depends on who your doctor refers you to.

## Vaccinations & Immunisations

All vaccinations and immunisations for children are covered by MSP and normally start when the baby is two months old. Standard vaccinations at two, four, six and 12 months are hepatitis B, Pentacel (covers diphtheria, haemophilus B, pertussis, polio and tetanus), Prevnar (conjugated pneumococcal vaccine) and Neisvac-C (common forms of meningitis). At one year infants are also given the MMR (measles, mumps, rubella) and Varivax (chickenpox) jabs. The MMR vaccine is only available in Canada in its combined form, so if you want your child to receive three separate shots, you will have to find a clinic in the US or your home country. Between 4 and 6 years of age, children are also given Quadracel, which gives further protection against tetanus, diphtheria, whooping cough and polio. While your doctor may strongly recommend all vaccinations, it is entirely up to the parents which shots they want administered and in which order. Elementary schools do require, however, that all entering children have up-to-date vaccinations, so by the age of 6, your child should have had all of the above shots.

# Dentists & Orthodontists

There is a full range of dental and orthodontic services in Vancouver, but MSP only covers specific emergency dental services and surgeries. If you receive MSP Premium Assistance, your children automatically have access to free basic dental care until age 19 at participating clinics through the BC Healthy Kids Program (up to $700 worth of services per year). The British Columbia Dental Association (604 736 7202, www. bcdental.org) lists participating dentists online, as well as other general and paediatric clinics. It's recommended that children start seeing a dentist every six months from age 1, or six months after the first tooth appears. If you have extended health coverage through your employer, or private insurance, most of your costs can be covered, depending on your plan. A typical visit to the dentist for x-rays, inspection, cleaning and fillings ranges from $160 to $300. Crowns, bridgework and caps start at $500, while braces, retainers and other orthodontic treatments can run into the thousands. Laser dental treatments have become very popular and are used for cleaning, whitening and breath-freshening treatments.

## Dentists & Orthodontists

| | | | |
|---|---|---|---|
| Alma Dental Centre | 265-2083 Alma St | Point Grey | 604 222 8430 |
| Arbutus Point Dental Centre | 2696 Arbutus St | Kitsilano | 604 224 8000 |
| Atlantis Dental Centre | 1278 Pacific Blvd | Yaletown | 604 899 0775 |
| Broadway Station Dental Centre | 12-2495 Commercial Dr | Grandview | 604 874 6322 |
| Coal Harbour Dental Centre | 45-200 Granville St | Downtown | 604 696 9299 |
| Davie Dental Clinic | 1236 Davie St | West End | 604 681 1720 |
| Metrotown Centre Dental | 264-4820 Kingsway Av | Burnaby | 604 439 0999 |
| Scident Family Dental Clinic | 120 East 15th St | North Vancouver | 604 985 7032 |
| Vancouver Downtown Dental | 1328 Alberni St | Downtown | 604 669 1111 |
| Willow Dental Care | 807-805 West Broadway | Fairview | 604 873 9794 |

## Opticians & Ophthalmologists

MSP covers eye exams for children under 19 and seniors over 64. The BC Healthy Kids Program also covers annual prescription glasses (lenses and basic frames) for qualifying children under 19, and MSP is valid too for visits to an ophthalmologist if referred by a GP for a medical condition. Extended health plans often include adult vision care and annual amounts for glasses or contact lenses.

Most opticians are located in malls or commercial areas, while ophthalmologists normally have regular doctor's offices. Any optician can conduct an eye exam and prescribe glasses, prescription sunglasses or contact lenses. Expect to pay about $50 to $100 for an eye exam. Some opticians offer free eye exams with your purchase of glasses or contact lenses, but you can have them made at any optical shops. Contact lenses can be purchased directly from your optician or from an optical shop, while contact lens solution can be bought from your local pharmacy or supermarket.

Laser eye surgery has become quite popular in Canada, and there are several clinics that offer both Lasik and PRK laser treatments. Costs range from $300 to $1,000 per eye, depending on the level of myopia or farsightedness. Recovery times tend to be very fast; it's often less than a few hours before you can see normally, and a few days

## Opticians & Ophthalmologists

| | | | |
|---|---|---|---|
| English Bay Eye Care | 1112 Denman St | West End | 604 685 7001 |
| Granville Eyeland Opticians & Framemakers | 15-1666 Johnston St | Granville Island | 604 488 0909 |
| Granville Mall Optical | 807 Granville St | Downtown | 604 683 6419 |
| Image Optometry | 2529 East Hastings St | Hastings East | 604 251 3937 |
| | 716 West Broadway | Fairview | 604 874 3937 |
| Iris Optometry | 908 Park Royal South | West Vancouver | 604 925 3470 |
| Kerrisdale Optical | 2428 West 41st Av | Kerrisdale | 604 267 1618 |
| Kitsilano Optometry | 1813 West 1st Av | Kitsilano | 604 732 5487 |
| West 10th Optometry Clinic | 4320 West 10th Av | Point Grey | 604 224 2322 |
| Your Choice Optical | 6248 Fraser St | Fraser | 604 327 1110 |

before your eyes completely heal. If you are worried about your child's vision, your GP can refer you to a paediatric ophthalmologist.

For driver's licences, the Motor Vehicle Branch conducts its own eye exam, and the cost is included in your application.

## Cosmetic Treatment & Surgery

Cosmetic treatments and surgeries are widely available in Vancouver through doctors, nurses and licensed aestheticians. Both medical clinics and day spas offer these services. Hospitals mainly deal with facial reconstruction or cosmetic surgery for facial deformities. Plastic surgery is fairly common, but the most popular procedures are the less invasive variety, such as Botox and other fillers, masks, laser skin and hair removal treatments, tattoo removal, cellulite removal and chemical peels. Services can be pricey, so be prepared. Some clinics have payment programmes or offer discounts on multiple services.

### Latest Therapies

Some clinics now offer combined cosmetic/medical programmes designed to improve your body inside and out. Services include hormone replacement therapy, diet and exercise plans, early disease detection and prevention programmes, acupuncture, plus a variety of cosmetic procedures.

### Cosmetic Treatment & Surgery

| | | | |
|---|---|---|---|
| Afterglow Skin & Laser Centre | 104-2609 Westview Dr | North Vancouver | 604 980 3993 |
| Anti-Aging Medical & Laser Clinic | 2482 West 41 Av | Kerrisdale | 604 261 9121 |
| Arbutus Laser Centre | 106-2025 West Broadway | Kitsilano | 604 731 5512 |
| Carruthers Dermatology Centre | 740-943 West Broadway | Fairview | 604 730 6133 |
| Dermal Laser Centre | 803 Davie St | Yaletown | 604 638 7546 |
| Dr Andrew Denton | 202-943 West Broadway | Fairview | 604 879 3223 |
| Oakridge Laser & Skin Care Clinic | 1015 West King Edward Av | Oakridge | 604 267 7757 |
| Pacific Dermaesthetics | 1790-1111 West Georgia St | Yaletown | 604 682 7546 |
| Skinworks | 3568 & 3578 West 41st Av | Dunbar | 604 737 7100 |
| Vancouver Laser & Skin Care Centre | 309-750 West Broadway | Fairview | 604 708 9891 |
| Younger Facial Surgery Centre | 105-2025 West Broadway | Main | 604 738 3223 |

## Alternative Therapies

Virtually every type of alternative treatment is available in Vancouver. There are thousands of practitioners in every discipline, from massage therapy to acupuncture and aura cleansing. If you receive MSP Premium Assistance, you are eligible for a $23 subsidy per visit, for up to 10 visits per year, to a physiotherapist, acupuncturist, massage therapist or chiropractor. Extended health plans often cover a limited number of these types of services as well. Rates can range from $60 for a 45 minute massage to $150 for an aromatherapy session, and upwards.

### Naturopathy & Homeopathy

A naturopathic doctor is a licensed physician of alternative health practices. Doctors in this field in BC are regulated by the British Columbia Naturopathic Association (604 736 6646, www.bcna.ca). Naturopaths receive similar education to GPs in that they must have at least three years of premedical university training, then successfully complete a four-year programme at an accredited naturopathic college. Homeopaths are not licensed or regulated in BC, and are only permitted to prescribe homeopathic medicines and treatments. Families who can afford it often use naturopathic doctors as an alternative primary care provider.

### Traditional Chinese Medicine & Acupuncture

The College of Traditional Chinese Medicine Practitioners and Acupuncturists of British Columbia (604 738 7100, www.ctcma.bc.ca) regulates these disciplines and is the provincial licensing authority. Qualifications include doctorates in traditional Chinese medicine (TCM), and becoming a registered TCM practitioner, herbalist or acupuncturist. The CTCMA keeps a public online database of all registrants. Chinese medicine is extremely popular in Vancouver, and many people buy health remedies and supplements from one of the numerous Chinese herbalists in the city.

### Massage Therapy & Reflexology

Massage is probably the most accepted and standardised alternative therapy in BC. Many people use massage or reflexology services for stress relief as well as physical healing. The government considers massage therapy a viable alternative to physiotherapy, and coverage is standard under MSP Premium Assistance and virtually all extended health plans. The Massage Therapists' Association of British Columbia (604 873 4467, www. massagetherapy.bc.ca) is the province's professional body – most massage therapists belong to this association, although it's not a legal requirement. All therapists must be registered with the College of Massage Therapists of BC (604 736 3404, www.cmtbc. bc.ca), which also keeps a list of registrants. A masseur or masseuse refers to a general unregistered personal care service, or someone who offers more exotic forms of massage. There are also numerous providers of various speciality services such as shiatsu, Swedish and aural massage.

Reflexologists are also widely available, but their services are not usually covered under any health plans. The Reflexology Association of BC (604 435 8325, www.reflexologybc. com) keeps a list of registered members online; this is not an official regulatory body, but its members meet standard criteria and commit to a code of ethics.

The British Columbia Acupressure Therapists' Association (250 704 2888, www. acupressurebc.org) is the professional body for this field, and maintains an online listing of registered members.

### Aromatherapy

Aromatherapy has become more popular in recent years, although it is still an unregulated profession in BC. The British Columbia Alliance of Aromatherapy (604 515 2226, www.bcaoa.org) is a professional body whose members meet certain educational and ethical requirements. Most aromatherapists are registered through the organisation, and often combine their services with massage, reflexology or acupressure.

### Music & Art Therapy

Both the music and art therapy professions are regulated and licensed by the Music Therapy Association of BC (604 924 0046, www.mtabc.com) and the British Columbia Art Therapy Association (604 878 6393, www.bcarttherapy.com). These types of therapies are often used for children with disabilities or those who are recovering from traumatic

## Alternative Therapies

| | | | |
|---|---|---|---|
| Acubalance Wellness Centre | Fairview | 604 678 8600 | TCM for infertility |
| Acupuncture & Chinese Medicine Clinic of Vancouver | Kitsilano | 604 568 1712 | TCM/acupuncture |
| Agape Natural Wellness Centre | Kitsilano | 604 737 2273 | Naturopathic clinic |
| Ambiantz Aromatherapy & Massage | Cambie | 604 873 1518 | Aromatherapy/massage |
| Kitsilano Massage Therapy Clinic | Kitsilano | 604 732 7272 | Massage therapy/craniosacral |
| Massage & Therapy Centre | Mount Pleasant | 604 873 4150 | TCM/acupuncture/massage therapy |
| Mewsic Moves (mobile service) | Various Locations | 778 888 0077 | Music therapy |
| Northview Acupuncture & Herbal Clinic | North Vancouver | 604 986 3771 | TCM/acupuncture |
| Sage Clinic | Yaletown | 604 697 0397 | Naturopathic clinic |
| Westside Naturopathic Clinic | Kerrisdale | 604 263 6338 | Naturopathic clinic |

experiences. Music and art therapy are also used to complement group and family counselling and psychotherapy, or as standalone treatments.

## Physiotherapy

Physiotherapy, sports medicine and other physical rehabilitation programmes are available through hospitals and in private clinics. Extended health plans will often cover a certain number of physio visits per year, if you are referred by your doctor. Rates range from $60 to $80 for a 30 minute session. Hospital services are mainly for those who are recovering from surgery or a traumatic injury or illness. Many physiotherapy clinics also offer massage therapy, exercise therapy, personal training and acupuncture services. The Physiotherapy Association of British Columbia (604 736 5130, www.bcphysio.org) regulates all licensed physiotherapists in the province.

### Physiotherapy

| | | | |
|---|---|---|---|
| Allan McGavin Sports Medicine Centre | D101, 770 Pacific Blvd | Yaletown | 604 642 6761 |
| Chinatown Physiotherapy Clinic | 230-181 Keefer Place | Chinatown | 604 681 6630 |
| City Sports & Physiotherapy Clinic | 420-890 West Pender St | Downtown | 604 606 1420 |
| Main Yan Physiotherapy Centre | 3139 Main St | Main | 604 874 8668 |
| Marpole Physiotherapy & Rehabilitation Clinic | 8301 Granville St | Marpole | 604 263 4414 |
| Seva Physiotherapy | 101-3429 West Broadway | Point Grey | 604 874 7382 |
| South Centre Physiotherapy | 5854 Victoria Dr | Victoria | 604 324 1222 |
| West 4th Physiotherapy Clinic | 216-2211 West 4th Av | Kitsilano | 604 730 9478 |
| West End Physiotherapy Clinic | 440-1550 Alberni St | West End | 604 684 0047 |
| Westside Physiotherapy & Hand Clinic | 303-2150 West Broadway | Kitsilano | 604 731 6225 |

## Back Treatment

In addition to the physiotherapy and massage therapy services, Vancouver has a thriving chiropractic community. The British Columbia College of Chiropractors (604 270 1332, www.bcchiro.com) is the provincial regulatory authority. Many chiropractic clinics also offer massage therapy, craniosacral therapy and acupuncture as part of their services. Rates are usually slightly higher than those charged by registered massage therapists and physiotherapists. Osteopaths are not as popular, but are also available and can be found through the Society for the Promotion of Manual Practice Osteopathy (604 730 5350, www.osteopathybc.ca).

### Back Treatment

| | | | |
|---|---|---|---|
| Aquarius Chiropractic | 210-179 Davie St | Yaletown | 604 605 5800 |
| The CARE Clinic | MO2-1750 East 10th Av | Grandview | 604 876 4988 |
| Coal Harbour Natural Health Clinic | 1177 West Hastings St | Downtown | 604 688 0029 |
| Denman Place Chiropractic Clinic | 103-1030 Denman St | West End | 604 646 4645 |
| Foran Chiropractic Clinic | 8041 Granville St | Marpole | 604 266 1461 |
| Harbourview Chiropractic & Massage | P1-999 West Hastings St | Downtown | 604 669 3298 |
| Peak Performance Chiropractic Health Center | 4526 West 10 Av | Point Grey | 604 224 7325 |
| Thrive Chiropractic Wellness Centre | 1546 West 2nd Av | False Creek | 604 730 0111 |
| Vancouver Spinal Decompression Center | 206-168 East 13th St | North Vancouver | 604 984 4601 |
| Vancouver West Chiropractic | 300-2245 West Broadway | Kitsilano | 604 732 0664 |

## Nutritionists & Slimming

There are numerous nutritionists in Vancouver, with wildly varying qualifications, so it's always a good idea to check the credentials and experience of whoever you plan to use. A Registered Holistic Nutritionist (RHN) will have completed the Canadian

## Nutritionists & Slimming

| | | | |
|---|---|---|---|
| Bella Vita Holistic Health & Nutrition | Yaletown | 7-1238 Homer St | 604 728 5378 |
| Dr Bernstein Diet & Health Clinic | Downtown | 1038 West Georgia St | 1 888 372 3438 |
| Eating for Energy | Fairview | 720-999 West Broadway | 604 739 3290 |
| Elements Wellness Centre & Studio | Kitsilano | 207-2678 West Broadway | 604 732 9355 |
| Herbal Magic Weight Loss & Nutrition Centre | South Cambie | 593 West 57 Av | 604 325 0053 |
| Hollywood North Weight Loss Clinics | Kitsilano | 2423 Burrard St | 604 731 1311 |
| Jenny Craig Weight Loss Centres | Kitsilano | 2160 West Broadway | 604 733 3077 |
| LA Weight Loss | Point Grey | 215-2083 Alma St | 604 224 1924 |
| Power Play | Various Locations | Mobile service | 604 818 8348 |
| Weight Watchers | Various Locations | www.weightwatchers.ca | 1 800 651 6000 |

School of Natural Nutrition's accredited programme. A qualified nutritionist can also have a diploma or an undergraduate degree in human nutrition from an accredited institution. Dietitians are regulated by the College of Dietitians of BC (604 736 2016, www.collegeofdietitiansbc.org) and must be registered in order to use this title. There are also numerous weight loss clubs and programmes that offer weekly membership meetings, medical supervision, customised eating plans and personal training. Hospitals also have nutritionists and registered dietitians for patients with digestive or weight disorders. These services are covered by MSP. Costs for private services range from the low hundreds to the high thousands, depending on the practitioner and the type of programme that you sign up for.

**Culture Shock**

*Moving to a new country can be overwhelming, and many new emigrants experience culture shock or depression. Any GP can prescribe antidepressants, but meeting with other expats could also help. A great resource is www.meetup. com, which provides information on organised meetings in Vancouver.*

## Counselling & Therapy

There are hundreds of registered clinical counsellors, psychologists, therapists and social workers in Vancouver. Many specialise in one or more of the following areas: depression, anxiety, marital and family counselling, children and young people, eating disorders, addictions, and mental illness. A great resource for finding a qualified and registered professional in your area of need is Counselling BC (604 729 6059, www. counsellingbc.com), an online directory that lists counsellors, psychologists, social workers and therapists, along with the fees they charge. An average fee for a counsellor or psychologist starts at $100 per hour for individual or couples' sessions. BC Mental Health and Addictions Services (604 524 7000, www.bcmhas.ca) is an agency run by the Provincial Health Services Authority, and provides programmes in several areas, including the following: adult and geriatric psychiatry and neuropsychiatry services for adults with severe mental illnesses, at Riverview Hospital; children and youths mental health services at BC Children's Hospital; and a specialised eating disorders programme for children and youth at BC Children's Hospital, and for adults at St Paul's Hospital. Both BC Children's and UBC Hospital have extended mental health observation units for young people experiencing psychosis. Vancouver General Hospital and St Paul's have temporary psychiatric observation wards and facilities for adults. All of the major

## Counsellors & Psychologists

| | | | |
|---|---|---|---|
| Alpine Anxiety & Stress Relief Clinic | Point Grey | 604 732 3930 | Counselling, therapy |
| Arbutus Counselling Services | Kitsilano | 604 266 2303 | Multiple areas |
| BC Schizophrenia Society | Richmond | 604 270 7841 | Schizophrenia, family support |
| Cindy Trevitt Counselling | Various Locations | 604 518 1394 | Multiple areas |
| CoreQuest Counselling & Consulting | North Vancouver | 604 980 2673 | Marriage, couples |
| Jericho Professional Counselling Services | Fairview | 604 434 5727 | Individual, couples, family |
| Neurofeedback Center | Downtown | 604 697 0475 | Multiple areas |
| Westcoast Stress & Trauma Clinic | Burnaby | 604 937 0348 | Anxiety, trauma, depression |
| Woman's Solace Counselling | Yaletown | 604 986 5152 | Women's issues |

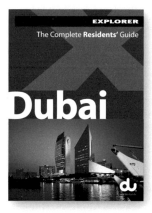
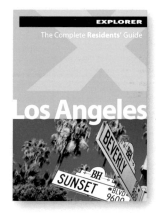
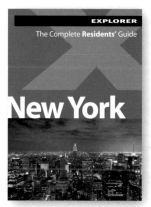

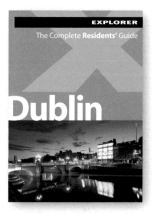

# Turn to the team page and ask yourself…
## …would you like to see your face?

Explorer has grown from a one-man operation a decade ago to a 60+ team today and our expansion isn't slowing down. We are always looking for creative bods, from PR pro's and master marketers to daring designers and excellent editors, as well as super sales and support staff.

So what are you waiting for? Apply online at www.explorerpublishing.com

hospitals also have various departments and clinics for treating a variety of mental and behavioural conditions. Your family doctor can refer you to the appropriate clinic. For people with mental illnesses who need long-term housing and assistance, there are several options available. These range from licensed community residences with 24 hour supervision to group homes, supported apartments, and emergency accommodations. More details are available through the BC Partners for Mental Health and Addictions Information (604 669 7600, www.heretohelp.bc.ca), which is a group of seven provincial non-profit agencies funded by the PHSA.

## Addiction Counselling & Rehabilitation

Vancouver Coastal Health (604 736 2033, www.vch.ca), the regional health authority, runs several addiction programmes. This includes hospital, community health centre and free clinic alcohol and drug rehabilitation programmes. Various non-profit organisations, as well as several private centres, run residential and outpatient addiction recovery and rehabilitation courses. Non-profit organisations usually require a referral from a doctor or social worker and often have free or low-cost programmes, depending on your finances. Youth programmes are mainly free and available on a drop-in basis. One of the largest non-profit agencies in Vancouver is Family Services of Greater Vancouver (604 731 4951, www.fsgv.ca), which offers education, counselling and treatment to children, youth, families and adults in areas including addiction, abuse, specialised youth services, special needs support, and adoption services. Private treatment centres may not need a referral and can charge $5,000 to $15,000 for a 10 or 14 day outpatient programme and over $20,000 for residential programmes that last up to 60 days. For those who suffer from addictions that are not substance-based, there are numerous counselling services and support groups available. The British Columbia Partnership for Responsible Gambling (1 888 795 6111, www.bcresponsiblegambling. ca) has various resources, as well as specialised programmes for youth, women, seniors and ethnic groups affected by gambling. For a list of counselling services, see p.162.

### Addiction Counselling & Rehabilitation

| | | |
|---|---|---|
| ACARA Addiction Counselling & Resources | 604 926 3642 | www.acara-counselling.com |
| Agora Regeneration Clinic | 604 688 6848 | www.agoraforlife.net |
| City Centre Care Society | 604 681 9111 | www.cccares.org |
| Family Services Of Greater Vancouver | 604 731 4951 | www.fsgv.ca |
| From Grief To Action | 604 454 1484 | www.fromgrieftoaction.org |
| The Orchard Recovery & Treatment Center | 604 947 0420 | www.orchardrecovery.com |
| Pacific Community Resources Society | 604 412 7950 | www.pcrs.ca |
| Pacifica Treatment Centre | 604 872 5517 | www.pacificatreatment.ca |
| Sunshine Coast Health Centre | 604 487 9010 | www.sunshinecoasthealthcentre.ca |
| Vancouver Area Network Of Drug Users | 604 683 6061 | www.vandu.org |

## Support Groups

Vancouver has branches of all the major support group associations, including Alcoholics Anonymous, Narcotics Anonymous, Gamblers Anonymous, Overeaters Anonymous and Sex Addicts Anonymous. You can also find help through community centres, websites and health centres. There are support groups for single parents, people going through divorce, dieting, mental health, illness, grief, sexuality and sexual orientation, new immigrants and expats, youth, and those suffering from abuse. Hospitals and clinics can also refer you to a specific support group for your illness or addiction.

### Support Groups

| | |
|---|---|
| Alcoholics Anonymous | 604 494 3933 |
| Battered Women's Support Services | 604 687 1867 |
| Gamblers Anonymous | 604 878 6535 |
| Narcotics Anonymous | 604 873 1018 |
| Overeaters Anonymous | 604 878 4575 |
| Sex Addicts Anonymous | 604 290 9544 |

# Education

Canada has a free public education system that is open to all residents between the ages of 4 and 18, whether they are citizens, new immigrants or resident foreigners. The BC Ministry of Education oversees all public and private education in the province. City school boards manage public schools in their area. Private schools report directly to the ministry. Education is mandatory for all children from the age of six, but parents can choose to home school their children or enrol them in distance education, which offers print and online courses. The ministry doesn't regulate home schooling other than to stipulate that all children register with a school or distance education centre, so that they have free access to materials and resources.

If you are coming from outside of Canada with your child and want to enrol them in a public school, you will need their birth certificate and all transcripts and report cards from their previous schools. If you arrive in the middle of the school year (which runs from September to June) or don't have your child's school records, the school board will assess your child and place them in the most appropriate grade level for their age and education level. If your child does not speak English, they will receive additional second-language support.

Schools operate on a catchment basis and are required to accept all students living within the relevant boundaries. Students can also enrol in any school outside of their catchment area, space permitting. Public education begins at the kindergarten grade level (normally around age 5) and continues through grades 1 to 12. Students graduating from grade 12 (around age 17 or 18) receive a high school graduation certificate and can enrol in a college or university. Elementary schools teach from kindergarten through to grade 7, and secondary schools (or high schools) handle grades eight and up. High school students take provincial exams in grades 10 to 12. Class sizes in public schools vary widely depending on the area, but the average number per class is 20 to 25. The Ministry of Education sets the standard curriculum, but many public and private schools offer approved alternative programmes to meet a wide variety of needs and cultural backgrounds – check with the school directly.

*Tennis Anyone?*
*It may not be a ripe training ground for tennis stars such as Maria Sharapova or Roger Federer, but Vancouver is home to 177 free tennis courts that are located in parks across the city – meaning any kids with a keen eye for an ace have plenty of opportunities to sharpen their skills (see Tennis, p.330).*

# Nurseries & Pre-Schools

Pre-schools in Vancouver offer a wide range of programmes. Children between the ages of 3 and 5 can attend, but this is optional, and many only start school at kindergarten level. Pre-schools are not part of the public education system and fees average between $100 and $600 per month. Many community centres and religious organisations also offer pre-school programmes, while some pre-schools also have their own private kindergarten classes. Most schools offer either morning or afternoon sessions; those that offer full days tend to be more like childcare centres, with less structure. Many schools also run part-week schedules, where your child attends for two, three or four full or half days per week. PPPs (Parent Participation Preschools), which involve the parents directly in the running of the school and its programmes, are becoming quite common as well.

Most pre-schools follow the school year from September to June, but some operate all year round. Entry dates are September and January for most schools, and drop-off facilities are practically non-existent. It's also a good idea to register as far in advance as possible, as many schools have waiting lists of up to a year. Each pre-school has its own programme, hours and rates, so it's a good idea to visit several before deciding. There are many Francophone schools, as well as Montessori and Waldorf centres. All pre-school teachers are licensed and have Early Childhood Education (ECE) certification, and have normally also completed an undergraduate diploma in an education-related field. The establishments listed overleaf represent a selection of the diversity of pre-schools in Vancouver.

## Happy Corner

**3434 Falaise Av**
*Renfrew Heights*
*Map 6 C2* **9**

*604 433 7923* | *www.happycorner.ca*
This is a parent-participant pre-school, where parents must attend monthly council meetings and each family must help at the school one full morning each month. Programmes are offered to 3 and 4 year olds, during mornings only. Three year olds attend on Tuesday and Thursday, and 4 year olds attend Monday, Wednesday and Friday. The focus is on emotional and social development and play-based learning.

## Little Ark Preschool

**4509 West 11th Av**
*Point Grey*
*Map 5 C1* **10**

*604 222 1318* | *www.littlearkpreschool.com*
A non-profit school that uses the Reggio Emilia learning method, Little Ark offers a morning programme for 3 year olds (three days a week) and an afternoon programme for 4 year olds (four days a week). It also has a once-weekly programme for two-and-a-half year olds that runs from January to June. The pre-school is located in the lower level of West Point Grey Baptist Church and has a private outdoor playground.

## Little Rae Kids' Club

**1155 Thurlow St**
*West End*
*Map 7 C4* **11**

*604 687 2233* | *www.littlerae.com*
This licensed childcare facility offers a play-based, unstructured pre-school programme for 3 to 5 year olds, as well as English as a second language (ESL) for 5 to 8 year olds. There's also out-of-school care and summer camps for children up to 8 years of age. The school operates out of a large facility in the Central Presbyterian Church in the West End. There are no private outdoor play areas, but Little Rae is located near several large public parks and playgrounds.

## Montessori World

**75 East 43rd Av**
*Fraser*
*Map 6 A3* **12**

*604 325 3301* | *www.montessoriworld.ca*
A popular school franchise located in the Fraser area, Montessori accepts children from two and a half to 6 years of age (children do not need to be toilet trained). All teachers are AMI (Association Montessori Internationale) and ECE certified, and the school offers pre-school and kindergarten programmes. Morning and afternoon sessions are three hours, five days a week. Full-day programmes are also offered. French and Mandarin language instruction is available, in addition to academic and fine arts subjects.

## Pomme d'Api Preschool

**2551 East 49th Av**
*Killarney*
*Map 6 B3* **13**

*604 877 1122* | *www.pommedapi.org*
This is a non-profit school run by parents as a PPP. It features two French language programmes, both of which last two years. The French immersion programme is for children new to the language. Children who are 3 years old attend two mornings a week and 4 year olds attend three mornings a week. The school offers a programme available only to French-speaking children, or those who have a Francophone parent, where 3 year olds attend three mornings a week and 4 year olds four mornings a week. Both programmes emphasise learning through play, with a heavy focus on language skills.

## Vancouver Bilingual Preschool

**949 West 49th Av**
*Oakridge*
*Map 5 F3* **14**

*604 261 1221* | *www.vancouverbilingual.com*
One of the oldest pre-schools in the city, Vancouver Bilingual is located in the Oakridge area. It is a moderate-sized facility with large classrooms and private indoor and outdoor play areas. The school offers bilingual instruction in maths, reading, science, art and music, as well as teaching languages. Children can attend a morning or afternoon programme, two and a half hours a day, five days a week.

## Primary & Secondary Schools

The public school system in BC maintains a high standard of programmes and facilities. All schools in the province are currently going through a process of seismic upgrades as needed, and most are equipped with computer labs, extensive sports facilities and outdoor playing fields. School boards try to keep teacher-to-class ratios low (usually less than 1:25) and encourage parental involvement. Parent advisory councils are standard, as are additional support services such as counsellors, educational psychologists, speech-pathologists, ESL (English as a second language) specialists and special needs educators.

There is a huge variety of programmes available for public students of all ages, including traditional, multi-age, First Nations, international baccalaureate, Francophone and French immersion (as well as other languages), special needs, fine arts, sports, trades, and self-directed learning (Montessori and Waldorf methods). There are also many 'gifted student' programmes available at both the elementary and secondary level.

Many schools offer before and after-school care schemes for a monthly fee. All schools offer extra-curricular sports, clubs and arts groups for interested students. Most schools run five full days a week, Monday to Friday, from 08:30 to 15:30, but some offer half-day or four-day programmes for students who are heavily involved in various arts disciplines.

Public school registrations are handled through the Vancouver School Board (www.vsb.bc.ca), and the VSB can help you find a school that is in your area or that follows a specified structure. If you choose to enrol your child in a private school, expect to pay between $8,000 and $25,000 in tuition fees per year, as well as the cost of uniforms and supplies. Public school fees are normally limited to paying for individual supplies and equipment such as notebooks and pencils, as well as for any special activities or class outings.

A range of elementary and secondary schools are detailed in this section, and some of the well known private and independent options in the area are featured in the table below. For a full list, see the Federation of Independent Schools Association website (www.fisabc.ca).

### Private Schools

| | | | | |
|---|---|---|---|---|
| Bodwell Acadamy | 955 Harbourside Dr | North Vancouver | 604 924 5056 | www.bodwell.edu |
| Brentwood College School | 2735 Mount Baker Rd | Victoria | 250 743 5521 | www.brentwood.bc.ca |
| Crofton House School | 3200 West 41st Av | Southlands | 604 263 3255 | www.croftonhouse. |
| Notre Dame Secondary | 2855 Parker St | Hastings East | 604 255 5454 | www.ndrs.org |
| St George's School | 4175 West 29th Av | Dunbar | 604 224 1304 | www.stgeorges.bc.ca |
| St Michaels University School | 3400 Richmond Rd | Victoria | 250 592 2411 | www.smus.bc.ca |
| Vancouver College | 5400 Cartier St | Quilchena | 604 261 4285 | vc.bc.ca |
| West Point Grey Academy | 4125 West 8th Av | Point Grey | 604.224.1332 | www.wpga.ca |
| York House School | 4176 Alexandra St | Shaugnessy | 604 736 6551 | www.yorkhouse.ca |

**3351 Glen Drive** ◀
*Grandview*
*Map 12 E4* **15**

## Charles Dickens Elementary

*604 713 4978* | *dickens.vsb.bc.ca*

Considered one of the top 40 elementary schools in Canada, Charles Dickens Elementary offers an alternative schooling programme with multi-age classes, each led by two teachers working together. Students stay with the same teacher group for up to three years. The school integrates special needs and ESL students into each class, and has a mentorship scheme with two universities.

**4710 Slocan St**
Collingwood
Map 6 C2 **16**

## John Norquay Elementary

*604 713 4666 | norquay.vsb.bc.ca*

John Norquay is a community school with a strong multicultural focus and emphasis on fine arts, technology and sports. It offers resources for special needs and ESL students, as well as tutoring programmes. Music courses focus on composition and choir, as well as joint projects with the Vancouver Symphony Orchestra, and there is a leaning towards developing strong reading skills at an early age.

**3939 West 16th Av**
Point Grey
Map 5 D1 **17**

## Lord Byng Secondary

*604 713 8171 | byng.vsb.bc.ca*

This school runs a standard ministry curriculum with an extremely strong arts department, offering practical elements such as film production. There are numerous student clubs and sports groups, and a mini-school that offers intensive arts programmes in music, visual arts and theatre. Its theatre company puts on at least two full-scale productions a year, and the student symphony orchestra offers a subscription concert series. Entrance is by application and audition only.

**4055 Blenheim St**
Dunbar
Map 5 D2 **18**

## Lord Kitchener Elementary

*604 713 5454 | kitchener.vsb.bc.ca*

This elementary school operates the standard ministry curriculum, plus an extensive extra-curricular programme. Lord Kitchener is well-known for its strings music programme, as well as a strong sports set up. Parental participation is highly encouraged and each class has an assigned parent to assist the teacher. There is also a before and after-school care scheme, run jointly with a local community centre.

**6360 Maple St**
Fairview
Map 5 E3 **19**

## Magee Secondary

*604 713 8200 | mageelions.ca*

Magee Secondary offers a standard ministry curriculum as well as multiple programmes for gifted learners, First Nations, alternative studies and French immersion. It runs numerous fine and performing arts courses, as well as applied skills programmes covering everything from hairdressing and fashion design to tourism and hospitality training. Magee has one of the strongest applied-technology schemes in the province, with courses in woodwork, metalwork, jewellery design, drafting, electronics, carpentry and business technology skills.

**7055 Heather St**
South Cambie
Map 5 F3 **20**

## Sir Winston Churchill Secondary

*604 713 8189 | churchill.vsb.bc.ca*

One of the most popular secondary schools in BC, Winston Churchill Secondary offers French immersion and international baccalaureate programmes in addition to the ministry curriculum. It also features a 'middle years' programme in grades 8 and 9 to help students make the transition from elementary to secondary school. A strong technology department includes robotics and graphics programmes, and the school runs one of the largest ESL courses in the city.

**5351 Camosun St**
Southlands
Map 5 D2 **21**

## Southlands Elementary

*604 713 5414 | southlands.vsb.bc.ca*

Southlands Elementary School runs special programmes including gardening initiatives, and large-scale art projects such as school murals. Extra-curricular programmes include First Nations education, and cooperative ventures with the local community centre. Its location next to UBC Endowment Lands allows for extensive nature field trips.

**2600 East Broadway** ◄
*Grandview*
*Map 12 E3* **22**

## Vancouver Technical Secondary
*604 713 8215* | *vantech.vsb.bc.ca*

Lessons here are based on the standard ministry curriculum, with a big emphasis on performing arts and political involvement. There is a leadership programme for above-average students, which stresses social responsibility, community service and cultural awareness. Numerous extra-curricular language, environmental, political and debating clubs are open to students, and there are active music, choral and strings groups, as well as a popular theatre company.

# University & Higher Education

Higher education in British Columbia operates under the Ministry of Advanced Education and divides along three main lines:

- The province's six universities offer undergraduate and postgraduate degree programmes in various subjects like humanities, science, social science, artistic and business subjects, as well as diploma and certificate programmes for various professional fields.
- Institutes offer practical undergraduate and graduate degree and diploma programmes in trade, technical and vocational fields.
- Colleges, of which there are over a dozen, offer mainly trade, vocational and technical certificate and diploma programmes, as well as undergraduate liberal arts and science courses that are transferable to any university. Several colleges also offer undergraduate and graduate degree programmes in various disciplines.

The major universities and institutes routinely attract international students. Admission standards can be high at these top institutes, especially at the University of British Columbia and Simon Fraser University. As well as the establishments listed on the next page, Capilano College (www.capcollege.bc.ca) has campuses in North Vancouver, Squamish and the Sunshine Coast. The college's broad range of courses is offered to students throughout Vancouver and internationally.

Many BC students pay for their education with provincial and federal student loans, which are interest free during your study period and which you do not start to pay back until after you leave. If you are a Canadian citizen or permanent resident, expect to pay $4,000 to $6,000 annually for tuition at a university or institute. Tuition fees are standard across the provinces, so many BC students study outside their hometown. International students pay from $18,000 to $30,000 a year and must apply for a student visa, once they have been accepted into a specific programme. Colleges generally have lower tuition fees, but this varies, so check the website of the school you're interested in.

### Student Life

International and out-of-town undergraduates make up a large part of the city's student population. The local universities have limited housing options, so sharing a house or suite off campus with fellow students is quite common. Vancouver rents are rather high, but there are many places to look for affordable options. The website www.homes4students.ca is a great place to start, as well as the shared accommodation listings (broken down by area) in the classified sections of *The Vancouver Sun* and *The Province*. In addition, each university and college often has its own online bulletin board system, where landlords list available suites or rooms. For shared accommodation, expect to pay between $400 and $700 in rent per month.

Vancouver has many cheap cafes and restaurants that mainly cater to a student clientele. Many coffee shops have frequent buyer cards, so always ask, and a large selection of retail and service shops offer discounts on everything from books to air tickets, so always keep your student card handy. In addition, all of the cultural and arts organisations offer student discounts, such as the Vancouver Symphony Orchestra's

Access Pass (www.vancouversymphony.ca), which allows a full-time student to buy any ticket for $10. The Vancouver Playhouse (www.vancouverplayhouse.com), Vancouver Opera (www.vancouveropera.ca) and Vancouver Recital Society (www.vanrecital.com) also offer student discounts on season passes and individual tickets. Certain pubs, such as The Yale (1300 Granville Street, 604 681 9253) and The Railway Club (579 Dunsmuir Street, 604 681 1625), are popular student hangouts and routinely offer students special offers on drinks and food (just make sure you're over the legal drinking age – 19 in BC). Cinemas The Hollywood (3123 West Broadway, 604 738 3211) and The Ridge (3131 Arbutus Street, 604 738 6311) offer student discounts on movie tickets (and real butter on their popcorn). Calhoun's bakery (3035 West Broadway, 604 731 7062) is a popular student hangout and is open 24 hours. Another popular late-night option is The Naam (2724 West 4th Avenue, 604 738 7151), with its cheap and hearty vegetarian food – try one of the dragon bowls.

### Further Education

Every university, college and institute in BC offers continuing education programmes geared towards adults who want to complete their secondary school requirements, upgrade their professional skills, train for a new career or simply explore a hobby. Langara College and Kwantlen University College (604 599 2100, www.kwantlen.ca) both have the most comprehensive continuing education programmes in BC, covering graphic design, publishing, business, photography, computer programming and much more. All colleges list their continuing education courses and fees online. There are also numerous online education options. You can view a complete listing of available courses at all post-secondary institutions at www.bccampus.ca.

**3700 Willingdon Av**
*Burnaby*
*Map 6 D2* 23

## British Columbia Institute of Technology
*604 434 5734 | www.bcit.ca*
The British Columbia Institute of Technology (BCIT) is the largest polytechnic institute in the province, with more than 16,000 full-time and 32,000 part-time students. It offers certificates, diplomas and applied bachelor degrees in areas such as business, construction, aerospace and aviation, health sciences, transportation, computer and applied sciences, as well as various trades and apprenticeship programmes.

**1399 Johnston St**
*Granville Island*
*Map 9 C2* 24

## Emily Carr University of Art and Design
*604 844 3800 | www.eciad.ca*
The Emily Carr University of Art and Design (upgraded from an 'Institute' in 2008) is wholly focused on arts, design and media programmes, and offers undergraduate and postgraduate degrees in related subjects, as well as continuing and part-time studies. Despite its relatively small student population (just over 1,600 full-time), it is considered one of the best arts establishments in Canada.

**100 West 49 Av**
*Oakridge*
*Map 6 A3* 25

## Langara College
*604 323 5511 | www.langara.bc.ca*
One of the largest colleges in the Greater Vancouver region, Langara has more than 23,000 students. Courses are in three main streams: university studies, career studies and continuing adult education. It offers numerous degrees, diplomas and certificates and is famous for its professional acting programme, known as Studio 58. It's also well known for its criminal justice, business, journalism and graphic design courses, and has one of the largest arts and science university transfer programmes in BC.

**8888 University Drive** ◀
*Burnaby*
**Map 2 C2**

## Simon Fraser University

*778 782 3111 | www.sfu.ca*

The Simon Fraser University (SFU) started out as an alternative university in the 1960s, and now has 25,000 students spread across three campuses (Burnaby, Vancouver and Surrey). It has earned a reputation for its innovative teachers and excellent cooperative programmes. In addition to the standard liberal arts and sciences, SFU offers courses in criminology, corporate governance, business administration, policy research, ecology and marine sciences, among others.

**2329 West Mall** ◀
*UBC*
**Map 5 B1 27**

## University Of British Columbia

*604 822 2211 | www.ubc.ca*

This is the largest post-secondary institution in BC, and is considered to be one of the top universities in the world. It has more than 45,000 students and runs a wide range of courses. UBC's main campus is located on the extensive University Endowment Lands, west of Point Grey and the Pacific Spirit Regional Park. The Vancouver campus is located Downtown at Robson Square, and UBC has also recently opened a third campus in the Okanagan.

## Special Needs Education

In British Columbia, special needs children include those with physical, learning and intellectual disabilities, those who are emotionally or behaviourally challenged, those with special gifts or abilities, or those with any combination of the above. Advanced placement and remedial courses are common and all public schools have dedicated special needs programmes. There are additional programmes for those children who are unable to attend school. At present, there are no public segregated special needs schools, although the ministry is considering opening a test school in the next few years.

*Emily Carr University of Art and Design*

# Transportation

Other options **Getting Around** p.41

Vancouver's public transportation system is a model of energy efficiency and environmental consciousness. It is also rather limited (albeit very inexpensive). There are constant improvements being made, however, so the next few years should show some dramatic changes. The SkyTrain, which is an electric-powered light rail system, currently has only two lines, both of which begin at Waterfront Station on the edge of Downtown and Gastown and overlap each other for more than half of their routes. Both the Expo and Millennium lines connect Vancouver to Burnaby, New Westminster and Surrey. There is also a new Canada Line being built along the Cambie corridor, which will connect Downtown to Richmond and the international airport. It is scheduled to be completed in 2009, ahead of the 2010 Winter Olympics. The SeaBus is a passenger ferry that travels between Waterfront Station and Lonsdale Quay in North Vancouver every 15 minutes. The bus system covers more ground, providing frequent stops along most major roads. On any Downtown route, there's a bus every five minutes or so. The further away you get from Downtown, however, the stops are less frequent, which is why so many Vancouver residents own cars. Unless you live within walking distance of work, most people drive. In fact, there were almost 1.4 million cars registered in Greater Vancouver in 2007. Parking, both on the street and in garages, is plentiful, although it can be expensive in the Downtown area. Taxis are not normally used for commuting purposes, but are easy to hail on the street or order by phone. See the TransLink transit maps on the inside front and back covers for detailed routes.

## Driving In Vancouver

*Traffic Updates*

*AM 730 is a local all-traffic news station that continually gives updates round the clock relating to roads, ferries, mountain conditions, and school closures in winter. News 1130 Radio (1130 AM) also has local traffic updates every 10 minutes.*

Driving is a moderately expensive business in Vancouver, especially with recent hikes in petrol prices. Unleaded petrol is the only form of fuel allowed in BC for passenger vehicles, although trailers or recreational vehicles can use diesel. There are not many diesel stations in the region, but Husky petrol stations tend to be the main provider. Relying on cabs doesn't tend to be a cheaper alternative to driving, and you have to deal with waiting times during busy periods. Car-sharing is an option that is usually informally arranged, and a great place to find other people looking to share rides is www.rideshare.com, where you can find hundreds of offers and requests.

### Vancouver Roads

Vancouver's city planners have consistently designed pedestrian-friendly communities, so most people don't need to drive the short distance from their homes to get to various amenities. For drivers though, this means frequent traffic lights, numerous roundabouts in residential areas and an almost complete absence of left-turning lanes and signals. In addition, several of the major Downtown streets (mainly those on a north-south line) are one-way only. Most are parallel to one another and alternate direction each block, so that you can always circle around if needed.

As far as hazards go, a common problem is parked vehicles on three-lane roads. Vancouver allows parking on most major routes between 09:30 and 15:00 and from 18:30 to 06:00 on weekdays (24 hours on weekends), but does not restrict driving in those lanes – so watch out for parked cars that suddenly appear in front of you.

The bridges leading to North and West Vancouver were built to accommodate half the traffic they service, so weekday congestion early in the morning and again between 15:00 and 18:00 is normal. Most destinations, no matter where you are in the city, are no more than 20 minutes' drive away. From Downtown to Kitsilano it takes 5-10 minutes, and to the airport from the centre normally takes 30 minutes. At peak traffic times add up to 10 minutes to your journey time.

## Driving Habits

Vancouver drivers are generally a pleasant and courteous group. Most people signal before changing lanes, allow other cars to merge in front of them, and are fairly restrained with their horns. There are annoying drivers, as in any city, but they tend to be few in number. The biggest nuisance to watch out for are SUV drivers, who can act as if the road belongs to them. Cutting off other cars and speeding through changing lights are two of the most common issues. There are about 50,000 reported accidents each year, most causing minor to moderate damage, and a small percentage causing injury or death. Distractions from mobile phones, eating, drinking or putting on makeup while driving are some of the leading causes of collisions.

**Drinking & Driving**
*The legal driving limit in BC is 80mg per 100ml of blood (0.08 for short). This is normally equivalent to a glass or two of wine, or one beer. If you are stopped by police you can be asked to blow into an ASD (a roadside screening device) or a breathalyser. If it registers between 0.05 and 1.0, you can be arrested. Refusing to take the test is also grounds for arrest. About a third of all accidents in BC are caused by drivers under the influence of alcohol or drugs, so tough fines and penalties are in place. During the winter festivities, Operation Red Nose volunteers will drive you home in your car (www.operation nezrouge.com).*

## Non-Drivers

Unlike most other cities, pedestrians always have the right of way on Vancouver roads. It doesn't matter if someone has jumped off the pavement into oncoming traffic or is crossing against the light – if you hit someone, you are responsible. Pedestrians are mainly sensible and cautious, and pavements are large and well kept, but if you're Downtown don't expect pedestrians to stop crossing the street just because the 'do not walk' signal (normally a red hand) is flashing. Pedestrians, like in any city, will cross until the last possible moment, so always take extra care when turning right or left, even if you have the right of way. If you are a pedestrian, watch out for cars turning right in front of you as you cross the road. Drivers can turn right on a red light, unless there is a sign specifically prohibiting it, so always have a quick glance to your left before you cross. Most drivers wait until the do not walk sign appears, but it's best to be sure. Cyclists are considered part of traffic, and most employ hand signals and have reflectors on themselves and their bikes, but they also have right of way before cars, so extra caution is needed. Vancouver's roads are not especially bike friendly. Most do not have cycle lanes, and lanes are usually too narrow for both a cyclist and a car, meaning a car has to move partially into the next lane to pass a bicycle.

## Traffic Rules & Regulations

All Vancouver city streets have a speed limit of 50kph. School zones have a limit of 30kph that is in effect from Monday to Friday during the school year. Playgrounds and parks usually have a speed limit of 30kph every day from dawn to dusk. Police issue all speeding fines on the spot. If you run a red light and a traffic camera catches you, you will receive a violation notice in the post. Be aware that at four-way stop intersections, the car to your right has the right of way if you both arrive at the intersection at the same time. Slower traffic is supposed to keep right on highways and major roads, but many Vancouver drivers ignore this, so don't be surprised if you get stuck in the left lane on the highway behind a little old lady driving 20kph under the speed limit. Passing on the right is prohibited as well, but with all the left-lane layabouts, drivers in Vancouver often take matters into their own hands and pass as safely as possible (just watch out for police cars). If you rent a car, you are responsible for any fines incurred. The rental car company will normally send you a bill or automatically take the money from your credit card.

## Parking

Parking in Vancouver has become more of an issue in recent years, but is still easily found, both on the street and in private carparks (called parking lots). All street parking is managed by the city. Street parking in commercial and shopping districts is paid for through coin-operated meters that charge varying amounts, depending on which part of town you are in. Most have two or three-hour time limits that are regularly enforced. The financial and waterfront district of Downtown, by Coal Harbour, has some of the most expensive meters, where 10 cents will buy you two-and-a-half minutes or 25 cents will get seven and a half minutes. In comparison, some meters on Commercial Drive still charge 25 cents for 15 minutes. Most residential areas have free two-hour parking or parking for residents of the street. Many residential streets in Kitsilano and the West End, as well as certain high-traffic areas around hospitals, require a permit from the city, which can only be purchased by residents, and costs anywhere between $30 and $60 per year, depending on the area. If you park in these areas without a permit, expect to be towed. Most carparks offer hourly, daily and monthly parking rates, which vary depending on the area. Monthly parking Downtown can cost up to $200, while daily parking throughout the city ranges from $6 to $22.

*Driving Dangers*
*Vancouverites tend not to come to a halt fully at stop signs, but rather just roll slowly through. This is especially common in residential areas where traffic is lighter. Even if you have the right of way, look both ways as you cross, and slowing down as you approach the intersection isn't a bad idea either.*

*Petrol Stations*

Petrol (gas) stations are present in every neighbourhood, and most major intersections have at least one, if not two, on the corner. The main petrol providers are Petro-Canada, Shell, Chevron, Esso and Husky. All provide unleaded petrol at octane levels of 87, 89, 91 and 93. Husky is the most popular provider of diesel. Most stations offer both self-serve and full-serve options. You have to pay more per litre for full-serve, but they will check and fill your oil, wash your windows, and check your tyre pressure, as well as fill up your car. A few stations also offer repair services, but these are rare. The current price for gasoline ranges between $1.04 and $1.11 per litre, depending on the octane level you choose and the area you are in. The outskirts of the city tend to be slightly cheaper but, overall, prices are fairly similar throughout the region.

# Vehicle Leasing

Leasing a car is normally done on a three to five-year contract, and you don't need to have a residence visa to lease (or buy) one. A lease is usually best for people who like to change cars every couple of years, as at the end of the lease you are free to walk away from the car, exchange it for a newer make or model, or buy it outright. Leasing is also often a more cost-effective option than buying a car through monthly payments; the terms of a lease are often identical to a car loan as far as interest rate, rate of repayment and downpayment amounts are concerned, but buyers will have much higher monthly payments, often almost double that of a lease.

The main requirement for undertaking a lease is a good credit history. If you don't have a credit history within North America, try to get references from your previous utilities provider or credit card company. Even if you have bad credit, the car dealer can refer you to a company that specialises in financing for people who have gone through bankruptcies or have a poor rating.

Leasing is very common in BC, and most new and used car dealers offer lease and buyout financing options. The process is similar to buying a car. You go to a dealer, pick the new or used car you like (and can afford) and then sign a lease agreement committing to a certain amount over a set number of years. You may or may not have to give a downpayment. You can lease virtually any make or model; the

## Luxury Cars & Limousines

If you've got a wedding, anniversary, graduation or other special day coming up, you can rent a luxury car or even a stretched SUV limousine to give the day extra polish. Companies such as Star Limousine (www.starlimousine.com) and 604 Motorsports (www.604motorsports.com) offer high end short-term rentals at hourly, daily and weekly rates.

most common are North American and Japanese cars such as Ford, Chrysler, Chevrolet, Honda, Toyota and Mazda. Certain European makes such as BMW, Volkswagen and Audi are also widely available. More expensive makes such as Porsche and Mercedes-Benz are considerably more expensive, and rarely available for lease.

An average monthly lease payment ranges from $200 to $600, depending on the car and interest rate. Current interest rates are usually between 3% and 6%. Insurance, maintenance and petrol are not included in the lease amount. Your insurance rate is exactly the same whether your buy, lease or rent a car, as it is based on your driving record and the type of car you're driving. In addition, most leases specify a maximum number of kilometres per year, usually around 20,000. If you drive over this you will pay an additional fee based on the mileage.

## Car Sharing

Another alternative to buying or leasing a car is to join an auto-cooperative or car-sharing service, which basically allows you to jointly own a car with other members. A car co-op will have several locations where vehicles are stored. When you need a car, you reserve one by phone or online, and then pick it up at the location closest to you. You may have to pay an initial registration fee of up to $500 (which is usually refundable). After that, you pay based on your usage. There are no extra costs for insurance, petrol or maintenance. Currently, there are two companies in Vancouver offering this service, the Co-operative Auto Network (www.cooperativeauto.net) and Zipcar (www.zipcar.com).

### Vehicle Leasing Agents

| | | |
|---|---|---|
| Avis Car Rental | 1 800 879 2847 | www.avis.com |
| Budget Car & Truck Rental | 604 668 7144 | www.bc.budget.com |
| Discount Car & Truck Rentals | 604 207 8180 | www.discountcar.com |
| Enterprise Rent-A-Car | 1 800 261 7331 | www.enterpriserentacar.ca |
| Hertz | 1 800 654 3131 | www.hertz.com |
| National Car Rental | 1 800 227 7368 | www.nationalcar.ca |
| Renta Wreck | 604 688 0001 | www.rentawreck.ca |
| Thrifty Car Rental | 604 606 1666 | www.thrifty.com |

## Hiring A Car

For getting out and seeing the sights, or just for a busy day of shopping, a hired car is a great option. There are numerous car rental companies that offer hourly, daily and weekly rates. Some also offer monthly rates. Expect to pay around $30 per day for an economy or compact car. Insurance is not included, and can be purchased directly from the car rental company or through any broker. During the summer expect the prices to go up, and definitely book at least a week or two ahead. The rest of the year you can usually rent a car by walking up to a counter, but if you want a specific make or model, then it's good to call a few days in advance.

Most companies also offer discounted weekend or midweek packages from as low as $15 per day (not including insurance). Cars range from compact economy models like the Ford Focus to SUVs such as Jeep Cherokees (these can cost up to $100 per day). For luxury and exotic car rentals, expect to pay at least $200 to $600 per day, plus a hefty deposit, usually around $1,000. You can get a discount if you rent for six days or longer, but this varies from company to company.

## Company Cars

If you need a car for your work, your company will normally either lease one in your name or finance you to lease your own. Most companies also give a petrol and maintenance allowance, as well as subsidising part of the insurance. If you already own a car, your company may cover part of the monthly payments and give you a gas and maintenance budget.

## Buying A Vehicle

While the allure of buying a brand new car speaks for itself, many people in BC buy used to save on depreciation costs. A new car can depreciate by over 20% in its first year, so buying a car that is two or three years old can save you a lot of money. The upside to a new car is that you will always get a complete 'bumper-to-bumper' warranty on it, usually lasting for five to seven years. All car warranties are transferable, so if you buy a two-year-old car that came with a seven-year warranty, you'll still have a five-year guarantee. When you buy a used car through a dealer, the firm may also include additional dealer insurance of up to three years in the sale.

Practically all car dealers in the Greater Vancouver region sell both new and used cars on the same lot. Individual dealerships normally sell only one make of car, like Honda or Ford, so if you're interested in looking at several different makes, then an auto mall is a good option. These are monster lots shared by several different dealerships of both domestic and import cars. Most auto malls are on the outskirts of Vancouver and in the neighbouring districts (due to space requirements), and the biggest ones are in Richmond and Surrey.

The highest percentage of cars are US brands, like Ford or Chevrolet, or Japanese makes like Honda and Toyota. The Honda Civic is currently one of the most popular cars on the market, followed by the Mini and the Smart Car. Vancouver car buyers tend to be an eco-conscious bunch, so gas-guzzling tanks are usually frowned upon. That said, Vancouver has its fair share of SUV, minivan and pickup truck drivers. Hummers have become extremely popular, especially in the Downtown core.

There are no restrictions or prerequisites for BC non-residents who want to buy a car. If you have the money or can be approved for financing, it's an open field. Car prices

*Mini Yaletown*

are slightly more expensive than in the US. A typical new Honda Civic or Ford Focus starts at around $20,000 and a Chrysler PT Cruiser or VW Beetle starts at around $25,000. Used cars range in price depending on make, model, year, general condition and, most importantly, what the seller or dealer is willing to settle on.

### Private Sales

If you want to buy a car through a private sale, just look through any newspaper's classified section (*The Vancouver Sun* and *The Province* are the largest) or a community website such as Craigslist or Kijiji to read thousands of listings. There are also trade newspapers such as *Auto Trader* and *Buy and Sell* that list private and dealer offers. Just make sure to always have the car checked out by a certified mechanic before you sign anything or hand over cash, and be wary of a seller who won't let you take the car to a mechanic of your choosing. It's also a good idea to check out the car's history through a website such as CarProof (www.carproof. com) or CARFAX (www.carfax.com). You can find out if it has had any major accidents or damage, or if there are any outstanding debts, as well as odometer readings. All you need is the car's VIN number, which is usually located on the top of the dashboard on the driver's side of the car.

## Importing Or Exporting A Vehicle

Importing a car into Canada, and especially into BC, is a time-consuming, paper-laden, bureaucratic nightmare that only the brave of heart should attempt. The exception is if you bring your vehicle into the country for touring purposes only, for up to a maximum of six months. All vehicle imports to Canada are controlled by the national Registrar of Imported Vehicles (1 888 848 8240, www.riv.ca), a branch of the federal government. Full details on the process for importing a vehicle are available on the RIV website. Vehicles that have been manufactured outside of Canada or the US cannot be imported under any circumstances, unless the vehicle is more than 15 years old.

## New Car Dealers

| | | | |
|---|---|---|---|
| Acura | Burrard Acura | 604 736 8890 | www.burrard-acura.com |
| Audi | OpenRoad Audi | 604 293 2834 | www.openroadaudi.com |
| BMW | Brian Jessel BMW | 604 222 7788 | http://brianjessel.bmw.ca |
| Chevrolet | Wolfe Chevrolet | 604 293 1311 | www.wolfechev.com |
| Chrysler, Dodge, Jeep | Vancouver Chrysler Dodge Jeep | 604 687 5337 | www.vancouverchrysler.com |
| Ferrari, Maserati | Ferrari Maserati Of Vancouver | 604 215 8778 | www.ferrarimaseratiofvancouver.com |
| Ford, Lincoln | Brown Bros. Ford Lincoln | 1 888 518 9784 | www.brownbrosford.com |
| Honda | Carter Honda | 604 736 2821 | www.carterhonda.com |
| Jaguar, Land Rover | MCL Motor Cars | 1 877 872 8707 | www.mclmotorcars.com |
| Kia | Kia Vancouver | 604 326 6868 | www.kiavancouver.com |
| Lexus | Regency Lexus | 604 739 1212 | www.regencylexus.com |
| Mazda | Morrey Mazda Of Vancouver | 604 253 4221 | www.mazda.ca |
| Mercedes-Benz | Mercedes-Benz Vancouver | 604 637 0132 | www.mbvancouver.com |
| Mini | Mini Yaletown | 604 899 6464 | www.yaletown.mini.ca |
| Nissan | Southside Nissan | 604 324 4644 | www.southsidenissan.ca |
| Smart Car | Smart Centre Vancouver | 604 736 7411 | www.vancouver.thesmart.ca |
| Subaru | Don Docksteader Motors | 604 325 1000 | www.dondocksteader.subarudealer.ca |
| Toyota | Jim Pattison Toyota Downtown | 604 682 8881 | www.jptoyota-downtown.com |
| Various makes | North Shore Auto Mall | 604 696 2886 | www.northshoreautomall.com |
| Various makes | Richmond Auto Mall | 604 270 2886 | www.richmondautomall.com |
| Volkswagen | Clarkdale Volkswagen | 604 872 5431 | www.clarkdale.com |
| Volvo | Volvo Of North Vancouver | 604 986 9889 | www.volvoofnorthvancouver.com |

To import a vehicle from the US or any other country, there are numerous steps you need to follow. These include checking the make of your car against Transport Canada's (www.tc.gc.ca) list of admissible vehicles and making sure that required modifications can be made. Modifications can include installing daytime running lights, metric speedometer and odometer labels, high-impact bumpers, child-restraint anchoring hardware, French labels for airbags that need periodic maintenance, and electronic immobiliser systems for 2007 or newer models. You will also need a statement of compliance from the country of origin and a recall clearance letter from the original manufacturer (which can be obtained through an authorised dealer), stating that no parts in the car have been recalled, or that all such parts have been replaced. You will need title documents, vehicle registration and sales receipts. You are required to schedule an appointment with US Customs (if your car is coming through or from the US) at the border, and will need to provide copies of all documents. It's also a good idea to check with Canada Border Services Agency (1 800 461 9999, www.cbsa-asfc. gc.ca) as to what kind of duties and taxes you may have to pay at the border, as these can vary wildly depending on your citizenship, residency status, length of stay in Canada, how long ago you purchased your car, and what make of car you have. Each province also has additional requirements on top of those listed above. In BC, this means meeting various mechanical, structural and emission standards within 45 days of importing the car. After you pay your RIV fee (about $200), duties and taxes, make all modifications to your car and register and insure it in BC, you can easily have spent between $3,000 and $5,000 to bring the vehicle to Canada. This doesn't include the actual shipping costs if your car is coming from overseas. Shipping costs depend on the distance between origin and destination, as well as fuel surcharges, but expect to pay at least $2,500 to ship your car from anywhere in Europe to BC. In addition, you are not permitted to sell your car for at least one year after importing it.

To export your car from British Columbia, you need to check the vehicle regulations of your destination country. If you just want to export a car from BC to another province within Canada, all you will need is to switch your insurance, registration and driving licence to your destination province's government insurance provider within six months of exporting. For fees, check the insurance website of the province you will be moving to.

*When Good Cars Die*

*If your car does not pass AirCare or has reached the end of its life, you have the option of turning it into a scrapping programme that will give you up to $1,000 of incentives in return. The Scrap-It Program (1 888 655 1000, www.scrapit.ca) takes cars made before 1993 and in return offers money towards items like a new hybrid vehicle, an electric bike, membership of a car co-op, or up to 18 months of public transport passes. If your car doesn't qualify for this programme and you need to get rid of it, try a service such as Junk My Car (1 877 586 5692, www.junkmycar.com) that will tow away for free.*

## Vehicle Finance

Car loans and leases are normally handled directly through the dealer you buy from, whether for a new or used car. Because they deal with a high volume of vehicles, dealers can offer extremely low interest rates and extended terms on cars for sale or lease. You can often find no-down-payment options, as well as interest rates between 1% and 5%. In the rare case where a dealership does not have its own in-store finance department, it will direct you to a finance company with which it has arranged special rates for clients. Banks never give car financing to individuals without going through a recognised dealer. Private sales are usually on a cash-only basis.

## Vehicle Insurance

Basic insurance and registration is mandatory in Canada for all cars. In addition, all cars must pass AirCare vehicle emission standards (604 930 5633, www.aircare.ca). All basic insurance and registration in BC is handled by the government through the Insurance Corporation of British Columbia (604 661 2800, www.icbc.com). Registration (which is only done once, costs $18 and is kept on permanent file at ICBC) is done on the same form as the insurance.

Basic insurance, known as AutoPlan, covers third-party liability up to $200,000, basic accident benefits, and protection against hit-and-runs and underinsured motorists. It does not cover things like collision repairs or replacement of your vehicle if it cannot be repaired, or damage from things like fire, theft, vandalism and natural disasters. If you want to have coverage for all of these, you will need to get collision and comprehensive insurance, either from ICBC or a private insurance provider. The latter is optional, but most people at least get the collision insurance, if not both.

The average monthly rate for basic insurance will vary according to the make, model and year of your car, as well as your driving record, but most drivers pay anywhere from $80 to $200.

When you buy a new or used car, either privately or through a dealer, both you and the seller need to go to an insurance broker to have the registration transferred into your name and to purchase insurance. All dealers will have an insurance broker on site. For private sales, go to your closest insurance broker. You need to provide proof of the sale and your driver's licence, and, if the car is used, the seller needs to sign a transfer form, meaning they agree to transfer ownership of the car to you. The seller will also provide their registration and insurance papers, as well as the licence plates on the car, so that their insurance on that particular car will be cancelled, the licence plates can be destroyed by ICBC and the registration information (including the car's VIN number) can be recorded under your name. If you're buying a new car from a dealer, then you will be the first registered owner and insurer of the car, and will only need to provide proof of sale, the car's VIN number and your driving licence. For more information on registering and insuring your vehicle, contact ICBC.

Once you have registered your vehicle and paid for the insurance, you will receive a single-page form that has both your registration and proof of insurance on it – you should always keep this in the car. You will also receive new licence plates and a licence sticker indicating when your insurance expires. Insurance is valid for up to 12 months, but you can also purchase insurance for shorter periods of time. If you are involved in an accident and found at fault, your insurance will not go up until it is time for it to be renewed. You will normally have the option of paying back ICBC a flat amount to cover the accident payout to the other party (if you don't want your rates to go up). ICBC awards good drivers with progressive annual discounts for each year of accident-free driving. You can receive up to 40% off the annual cost of your insurance in this way. There are no premiums for driving your car across the border into the US.

## Traffic Fines & Offences

BC's Motor Vehicle Act contains fines and penalties for every possible type of offence. The most common infractions are speeding, drunk driving and failing to signal properly. Most traffic fines range from $109 to $167, but certain offences can cost upwards of $500. There is no law against using your mobile phone while driving, but it's recommended that you use a hands-free device. Wearing a seatbelt is required at all times by all occupants of the car. Areas around schools and parks generate higher fines. In addition to the fine, you will receive driver penalty points, usually two or three per offence. These affect your insurance rates in the form of an additional annual bill. Rack up too many points and not only will your insurance go through the roof, but you can lose your licence for up to three years, or even permanently. If you receive three points or less during a 12 month period, you will not be charged any premiums. If you have more than three points you will be charged for the total number of points, so if you have five points, you would have to pay about $200. There is also a driver risk premium for drivers who have committed criminal driving offences, have roadside suspensions or numerous motor convictions. This premium costs around $500 per year, in addition to the higher insurance rate. The multiple crash premium penalises drivers with three or more crashes within a three year period. The fine is $1,000 annually, plus an extra $500 annually for each additional crash. This is all on top of the hike in your annual insurance rates. Depending on the total cost of the crash, your insurance rates can go up anywhere from 5% to 100%. All fines must be paid before you can renew your licence (usually once every five years), and, in most cases, before you can renew your insurance. Parking illegally or parking and not paying a meter do not count as traffic fines, but rather as city bylaw infractions, and you do not receive any penalty points, just a fine of $30 to $60. You may also be towed if you are blocking traffic, and will have to pay for the towing costs (around $70 to $100).

Speeding tickets are graduated depending on how much above the speed limit you were going and where you were at the time, and range from $138 to $438. Failing to yield to a pedestrian, or passing a car that is yielding to a pedestrian, will cost you $167 and three penalty points. If you're caught driving while uninsured, you'll get a fine of almost $600 and may lose your licence for up to a year. Most other fines range from $109 to $169 for offences such as making a U-turn, failing to give way to a merging car, passing a stopped school bus or disobeying construction signs. All fines can be paid by mail, in person at City Hall, or over the phone with a credit card.

*Child Safety*
*You can get a 'baby on board' sign in any drugstore or shop selling household goods. BC recently upgraded its child safety laws, which apply to all passenger vehicles, including taxis. Infants and children under 9 are not allowed in the front seat, and children under 12 are not allowed in the front seat of a car with airbags. Infants less than 12 months old (or weighing under 9kg) must be secured in a rear-facing infant car seat.*

## Breakdowns

If your car breaks down while you are driving, try to get it off to the side of the road, if it is safe to do so. If not, stop the car and turn on the emergency lights, and prop open the hood if you're blocking traffic, so that passing drivers know that your vehicle has broken down. It's worth joining the BC Automobile Association (604 293 2222, www.bcaa.com), which costs around $80 per year for basic membership. This includes towing services and roadside assistance for things like flat tyres or a dead battery. Most BC drivers use this service, as the savings compared with using a private towing company are considerable. Some new car warranties offer free 24 hour roadside assistance, which includes towing. If you don't have this or BCAA membership, expect to pay well over $100 for a local tow. It's a good idea to always have a mobile phone with you in case you get stuck in a remote area or on a highway, as emergency phones are few and far between. A bottle of water and a first aid kit are also handy if you have to wait for a while. If you need a tow, the average wait time is 20 to 40 minutes. The two main private towing companies are Drake Towing (604 251 3344, www.draketowing.com) and Busters Towing (604 685 8181, www.busterstowing.com), both of which offer a 24 hour service.

## Traffic Accidents

Other options **Vehicle Insurance** p.178

Statistics say there is almost one car crash every two minutes and one injury every seven minutes around the province. Certain parts of Vancouver certainly seem more prone to accidents than others. Knight Street between East 26th Avenue and Marine Drive is a constant source of traffic news, with several fatalities over the past few years. This is due in part to the increase in illegal late-night teenage street races in Vancouver, which have resulted in pedestrian casualties. The police are coming down hard on these types of offences though, and new drivers are not allowed to drive between midnight and 05:00.

*Downtown intersection*

If you are involved in a traffic accident, you must stop and exchange information with the other driver. You will need to give (and receive) a driving licence number, your full name and address as printed on your driver's licence card, the vehicle colour, make, model and year, as well as licence plate number. If one or both of you is injured or the car has sustained serious damage, you will need to call 911 and wait for the police and ambulance to arrive.

Leaving the scene of an accident is a

serious offence. The police will probably take both of your statements before you go to hospital. Each driver is responsible for reporting the accident to ICBC (Insurance Corporation of British Columbia). ICBC makes the final decision as to who was at fault and will pay out any repair or medical costs directly. If you are at fault, your insurance rates will go up when it is time to renew.

It may be stating the obvious, but you should never get into an argument or fight with the other driver. Road rage is rare and it's quite common for people in accidents to calmly exchange insurance information and leave with a wave and a (small) smile. Make sure that your insurance and registration form is in the car at all times. Most people keep theirs in the glove compartment, along with a notepad and pencil.

## Vehicle Repairs

If your vehicle breaks down or you want to take it in for maintenance work, all you will need is to show proof of ownership, which is on your insurance and registration form. If you need to get repairs on damage caused by an accident, and these repairs are covered by your insurance, then you'll need a claim form from ICBC, estimating the cost of repairs and authorising a licensed mechanic to make them. You can take your car to any mechanic you wish, as long as he or she is licensed (meaning they have passed a provincial mechanic's exam). You can get a list of licensed shops from ICBC, and mechanics display their licence prominently in their business area. BCAA also keeps a list of approved repair shops for its members and conducts individual inspections of each shop before granting an approval certificate, which the mechanic can display in the shop.

If you have a deductible on your insurance, you will need to pay this directly to the mechanic. It's up to you if you want to have a deductible on your insurance or not – no deductible means paying more per year. Deductible amounts usually range from $100 to $500. If your car is under warranty, you can take it to the dealership repair centre for no additional cost. If you want to take your car for regular maintenance and repairs to your dealer, then be aware that it will normally cost more than an independent repair shop.

**Tint The Done Thing**

*If you want to spruce up your car with upgrades, check with a licensed garage first as to whether it's legal. Tinting, for instance, is no longer allowed on front windscreens or front side windows. You can get your rear windscreen and rear-side windows tinted, but it's not recommended if you have children, as your child's car seat and 'baby (or child) on board' sign (highly recommended for all cars carrying children) will not be as visible.*

## Vehicle Repairs

| | | |
|---|---|---|
| ABC Main Auto Centre | Main | 604 872 7804 |
| Allied Complete Auto Repair | North Vancouver | 604 985 7646 |
| Axle Alley Auto Repair | Mount Pleasant | 604 875 9988 |
| BMC Motorworks | Mount Pleasant | 604 875 9911 |
| Boyd Autobody & Glass | Fairview | 604 873 2693 |
| Broco Auto Glass | Downtown | 604 682 5311 |
| Budget Brake & Muffler | South Cambie | 604 321 7288 |
| Craftsman Collision | Gastown | 604 255 7600 |
| Discount Auto Repair | Strathcona | 604 251 2600 |
| The Garage | Kitsilano | 604 733 1312 |
| Kal Tire Vancouver | South Vancouver | 604 322 4060 |
| Mackenzie Heights Service & Tire Sales | Mackenzie Heights | 604 263 2704 |
| Magic Touch Auto | West Vancouver | 604 922 6005 |
| Main Street Automotive | Main | 604 879 5595 |
| OK Tires Store | Fairview | 604 879 1457 |
| Save On Mechanics Auto Repair | North Vancouver | 604 984 3038 |
| Showcase Automotive Detailing | Mount Pleasant | 604 732 1113 |
| SRA Glass & Auto Repair | North Vancouver | 604 990 4449 |
| Swedish Autosport | Knight Road | 604 253 3119 |
| Tremblay Motors | Granville Island | 604 682 0044 |

GREATER SPENDING POWER.

RESERVED FOR CARDMEMBERS.

## JOIN US.

With the American Express® Gold Card there's no Pre-set Spending Limit. You're free to spend as much as you've shown us you can afford. You can also enjoy extensive travel benefits such as complimentary access to airport lounges across the Middle East. What's more, you earn Membership Rewards® points on every purchase with your Gold Card, which you can redeem for free flights, holidays and much more. To know about these and other enhanced privileges, call 800 4931 or visit www.americanexpress.co.ae

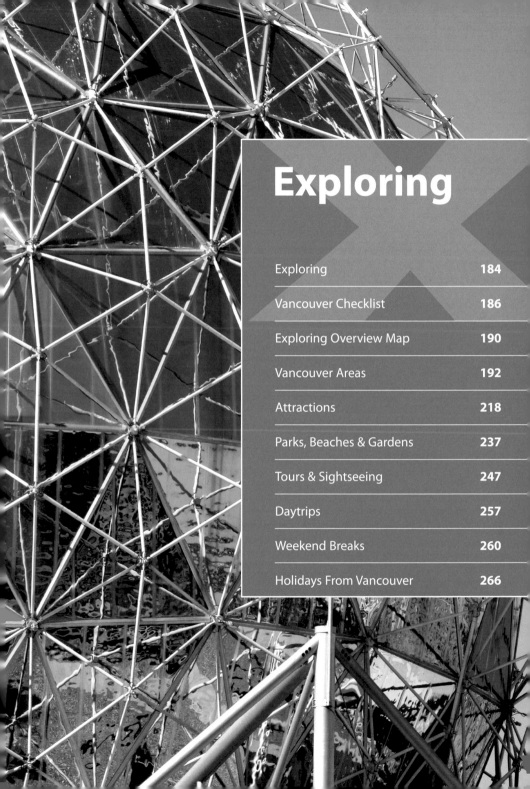

# Exploring

# Exploring

## Exploring

It's postmodernity's Babylon. East meets west and hyper-contemporary collides with geeky-granola in the streets. Rain, snow, sleet or shine, Vancouver remains a place for all seasons during all seasons. It has been this way since First Nations people first fished its creeks and settled its rain-kissed shores. The site's natural charms have attracted people throughout the centuries; from the arrival of George Vancouver in 1792, the Fraser Valley Gold Rush of 1858, and the introduction of the first transcontinental locomotive in 1887, Vancouver has always been a city of immigrants. Expo 86 and the return of Hong Kong to China in 1997 were two recent catalysts for its population boom.

Today, as in the past, many are drawn by the promise of spectacular natural beauty; wide-open vistas of rugged, snow-peaked mountains meet the wild, west coast, while its heartland, a tightly woven peninsula of climbing sky scrapers peering in all directions, satisfies. The city's passion for Pacific seaside walks and disdain for freeways appeal to those in search of that rare combination of natural beauty and tranquillity entrenched in a cosmopolitan setting.

But the pulse of Vancouver goes beyond its spectacular backdrop. From the agricultural hamlets dotted along the Fraser Valley, through bustling Burnaby, past Robson Square and all the way to the exclusive Point Grey waterfront real estate, its macro-scaled microcosms and cultural networks transform what at first glance seems like a disjointed combination of mismatched villages into a thriving metropolis.

The bright lights and electric speed of Downtown's 'City of Glass' move the modernists and house the wealthy. Meanwhile, the cobblestone roads and still-flickering neon signs along the Hastings corridor hark back to the time when Vancouver housed the greatest arts scene west of Chicago. Pender and Water streets still serve up vestiges of the city's industrial past, including the 17 storey Sun Tower, once the highest building in the British Empire, along with some world class art deco architecture, in particular the green and gold gilded Marine Building on Burrard Street.

While history is one reason to explore, many revel in the glorious present. The hipped-out flock here for Vancouver's essential lack of fanfare and cultural location on the 'left coast'. Those looking for arts and international entertainment on a human scale fuel their passion with cups of coffee and live music along the Commercial Drive and Main Street axes, while the nude find their peace on the sand-laden shores of Wreck Beach, one of the largest clothing-optional venues on the planet. The burgeoning Chinese population tends towards Richmond and the busy streets of Chinatown, and the unable-to-age-without-a-fight to Kits Point. The Japanese and Korean middle class students who study English and have the time of their lives while their parents foot the bill fill the innumerable language schools, while the city's handful of post-secondary schools and microbreweries provide hospice to the crowds of undergraduates in search of higher education. Just streets away, legions of Canada's homeless and hapless find community throughout the East End's alleys.

## Seawall-To-Wall

Vancouver has a reputation for having the most active, outdoors population in Canada, and one way people manage to keep themselves off the couch is by walking the various seawalls. West Vancouver's seawall starts at Dundarave Pier and continues for 5km along to Ambleside Park, but the daddy of seawalls is of course the one around Stanley Park – this one took over 50 years to complete. Once work on the new Convention Centre is finished, it will be possible to walk continuously along the seashore from Canada Place, around Coal Harbour and Stanley Park, past English Bay, all the way around False Creek, past Kits beach and ending just past Kits Pool: 19km featuring an unbeatable combination of urban and natural landscapes.

The city's markets continue to bring its people and produce together. Granville remains the hub for meeting and greeting tourists and locals over organics, fresh fish and dazzling, hand-crafted products made by local artisan-run cooperatives. The summer-long Richmond Night Market offers flavours of the east, while the permanent Punjabi Market transports a mosaic of Indian scents, smells and languages to the city's streets as its many visitors meet over curries, samosas, incense and chai.

A city of green space, Vancouver offers its residents hundreds of natural areas to wander in. The spectacular Stanley Park is the crowning achievement. Burnaby's Mountain Conservation Area and Deer Lake are havens for walking and picnicking, with forests of fresh air and public cultural areas to boot. Green thumbs can follow their noses to any of the city's fabulous plots, including the expansive UBC Botanical Garden, along with the quarries at Queen Elizabeth Park and VanDusen Garden. Those looking for a taste of the tropics can get their fix at the plant-filled Bloedel Floral Conservatory. Beyond the city's bountiful offerings, innumerable homeowners put their pride to pot in aromatic house-front gardens throughout the residential districts.

Vancouver can also seem a city in waiting. It houses a fanatical hub of hikers, skiers and outdoor enthusiasts, trapped in its economic offerings, waiting to explore the North Shore, English Bay, Indian Arm and beyond. It's easy to tell who these are: they wear their hearts on their sleeves – GORE-TEX and Polar Fleece are their codes. They seize every opportunity to take advantage of Vancouver's second-to-none infrastructure of sailing and boating clubs, hiking trails and ski areas.

The sum of the city is more than its districts combined. Its myriad of opportunities and possibilities seduces its guests, and newcomers don't, or can't, leave. Instead, they spiral in like crazed houseflies towards a honey trap. Be forewarned: once visited, forever stuck. Exploring Vancouver is not a means to an end, but rather the beginning of a never-ending adventure.

*Downtown*

### Bike Or Blade The Seawall p.211

The 8.9km promenade around Stanley Park is ideal for an afternoon ride. Pack a picnic and sprawl on one of its several beaches and many benches overlooking Burrard Inlet. Start out at Coal Harbour as the Seawall path winds anti-clockwise around the park's periphery. Expect traffic at weekends – cyclists and inline skaters of all shapes, sizes and abilities share the unidirectional trail.

### Life's A Beach p.237

Vancouverites take their coast seriously. Squeeze into your slinkiest swimsuit and catch more than the sun's rays at Kits Point, or avoid tan lines altogether at Wreck Beach – the city's clothing-free option. And while English Bay Beach draws in hordes of families and romantics, you can steer clear of the crowds at the south end of Sasamat Lake in Belcarra Park. Dog-friendly Hadden Park and Spanish Banks are prime places for your pet to get wet.

### Kayak Deep Cove p.284

Deep Cove offers some of the best wilderness kayaking, right within the urban world. Located at the mouth of Indian Arm, a pristine tree-lined fjord, you can easily hop in a kayak and within minutes be winding through an archipelago filled with million-dollar mansions. Those with a bit more time should pack their sleeping bags and paddle north to the Granite Falls campsite, a spectacular and remote four hour trip north-east.

### Pose At The Gallery p.224

At the epicentre of Downtown, the steps leading to Vancouver Art Gallery are the perfect place from which to watch the world go by. As the city's most accessible public building, this is a starting point for most of Vancouver's political events and the transient home for local hoola hoopers, Marxists, Maoists and the odd wannabe. The steps also offer a prime spot for viewing the summer-long dancing that takes place below at Robson Square.

### Caffeine On Commercial p.202

Unsurprisingly, Vancouver's 'little Italy' serves up the city's best coffee. If you would like to sip cappuccino surrounded by naked Romans (statues, that is), then try Calabria. Want to take in the city's biggest selection of international soccer matches? Try Expresso up at Abruzzo. And for an uber-bohemian experience, try JJ Bean. As for who serves the best brew… there are dozens more and you'll just have to see for yourself.

### Hockey Night In Vancouver p.301

The thrill of this game is all about the speed, and there is no better place to share in the fun than at the Pacific Coliseum. The semi-professional Vancouver Giants rattle their Western Hockey League opponents with bone-crunching body checks, nose-breaking punches and high-speed skating. The Vancouver Canucks regularly do battle with their National Hockey League opponents at GM Place.

### Do The Grind p.242

Join the post-work surge as hundreds flock to the flanks of Grouse Mountain to test their will against the 2.9km suburban to sub-alpine stair master. Take anywhere from 26 minutes to an hour to climb up the 853m, thigh-burning vertical. Grouse Mountain also offers ice skating and skiing through to the evening in the winter. While most take the tram down, if you're not up for the hike, you can take it up too.

## Window Shop On Granville Island p.204

There are few better places to while away the hours than on Granville Island. The tiny False Creek hub boasts an impressive mix of artists' cooperatives and ateliers, a wonderful market, a pair of microbreweries, galleries, restaurants and theatres. It also features a renowned art school, an active cement factory, numerous buskers and a yachting centre. It is best to peruse at the weekend.

## Surf & Turf p.272

With snow-topped peaks up high and temperate forests down below, in Vancouver it's possible to do both summer and winter sports in the same day, from autumn through to spring. Ride the wind in English Bay or tee off at a local golf club, then head to the mountains to do some night riding for the ultimate experience in cross-training.

## The Totem Trail p.231

To check out the towering First Nations' totems, make a stop in at the Coal Harbour side of Stanley Park, or drop by the Granville Island longhouse where they still chop up cedar. You'll run into a few more along False Creek and in Vanier Park. While the Vancouver International Airport greets visitors with a world-class collection of poles and masks, UBC's Museum of Anthropology holds the mother lode.

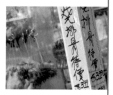

## Get Lost In Translation p.209

Boasting the city's largest Chinese population, Richmond has grown from a blueberry patch into a suburban shopping mall practically overnight. Look for some of the city's best Asian eats here, but you may have to point at the menu when ordering. With more than 57% of the population foreign born at the last census, English is at best a second language in Canada's most multicultural suburb.

## Get Artsy p.112

Vancouver's bohemian Eastside is renowned for its cutting-edge art scene. From installation and woodwork to painting and ceramics, these artists do it all. For a one-stop shop, call at the labyrinthine 1000 Parker Street artist-run facility. The annual three-day Eastside Culture Crawl, known as 'The Crawl', which takes place in November, offers the best way to get acquainted with the local scene. (Photo – Valerie Arntzen.)

## Picnic At Lighthouse Park p.243

Perched on a rocky outcrop in Burrard Inlet (pictured), the 75 hectare park offers a tranquil spot to view the city while lying on a blanket with a hamper. Its towering douglas firs are some of the largest in all of Vancouver. This area is the last remnant of a once-abundant old-growth rainforest that covered the entire lower mainland.

## Contemplate A Temple p.233

Looking for a little spiritual rejuvenation? The city plays host to numerous religious denominations. Try the International Buddhist Society Temple in Richmond, or for the Confucian who wants to avoid confusion, drop by Chinatown's peaceful Dr Sun Yat Sen Classical Chinese Garden. Surrey's ornate Masjid at-Taqwa mosque suits the Sunni, while Downtown boasts the grand-daddy of Vancouver's religious centres – the century old Christ Church Anglican Cathedral.

## Watch The Salmon Run p.297

Just upriver from the famous suspension bridge, Capilano River Regional Park is the perfect place to stretch your legs and observe the salmon. The free installations offer a multitude of easy hiking trails through ancient forest, with bridges, steps and banisters to get you over all obstacles. Stop in at the hatchery where you can watch the salmon scale the waterfall with monumental leaps. (*Photo courtesy Capilano Salmon Hatchery.*)

## To Be Or Not To Be p.56

There is no question that the beauty of English Bay and the North Shore mountains is the best backdrop for Vancouver's favourite theatre troupe. Join the tens of thousands of annual guests that flock to Bard on the Beach, Shakespearian productions that take place on two separate stages in Vanier Park from May to September every year. (*Photo – David Blue, courtesy Bard on the Beach.*)

## Walk The Bridges p.241

Take a leisurely stroll across Lions Gate, Cambie and Granville bridges for spectacular views of the city. Or escape to the Capilano and Lynn Canyon suspension bridges to get up close with the exuberant nature of the North Shore ravines, perhaps most spectacularly in the former where eagles regularly glide beneath the hanging crossing in search of spawning salmon.

## Cruise Georgia Straight p.44

Hop aboard BC's fabulous year-round ferry system to any one of the 47 ports of call throughout the British Columbian coast. Bring your binoculars as whales, orcas and dolphins ply the waters. For those who want to see more, the ferries navigate as far north as the Queen Charlotte Islands, or you can arrange an Alaska cruise, with weekly Downtown departures from spring to autumn.

## See The Silver Screens p.475

Check out the city's impressive screening rooms, which include one of the largest dome theatres on the planet, OMNIMAX, an IMAX at Canada Place, as well as rooftop showings at the world-class HR MacMillan Space Centre. The city hosts over a dozen film festivals, including ones focused on Latin America, Asia, mountains, and documentaries, plus the main event, the Vancouver International Film Festival.

## Fishin' 'n Chippin' p.210

Located in south-western Richmond, Steveston was once one of the busiest fishing ports in the world. Over the past century it has slowly morphed into a tourist hub and suburb where locals can stroll along the boardwalks and haggle with fishermen for the catch of the day. Drop by any one of the many pierside restaurants for some battered fish and chips, the local speciality.

## Flower Power p.244

With plenty of precipitation and the mildest temperatures in the country, Vancouver sports numerous important garden centres, including VanDusen and UBC botanical gardens, Dr Sun Yat Sen Classical Chinese Garden, and Nitobe Memorial. Expect a colour and allergy explosion during spring time with the city's cherry blossoms and rhododendrons in full bloom. And don't despair during winter; you can still find flowers at the Bloedel Conservatory for tropical plants.

*British Columbia beauty*

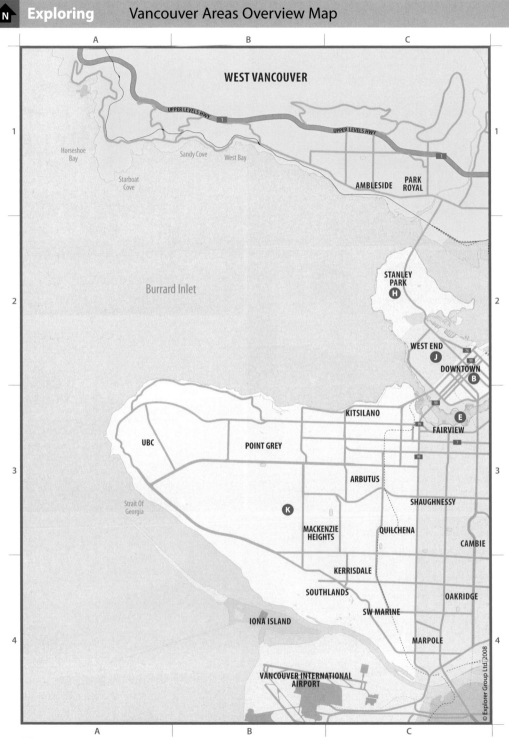

WEST VANCOUVER

UPPER LEVELS HWY

Horseshoe
Bay

Sandy Cove

West Bay

Starboat
Cove

UPPER LEVELS HWY

AMBLESIDE

PARK
ROYAL

Burrard Inlet

STANLEY
PARK
H

WEST END
J

DOWNTOWN
B

KITSILANO

UBC

POINT GREY

FAIRVIEW
E

Strait Of
Georgia

ARBUTUS

SHAUGHNESSY

K

MACKENZIE
HEIGHTS

QUILCHENA

CAMBIE

KERRISDALE

OAKRIDGE

SOUTHLANDS

SW MARINE

IONA ISLAND

MARPOLE

VANCOUVER INTERNATIONAL
AIRPORT

© Explorer Group Ltd.,2008

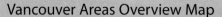
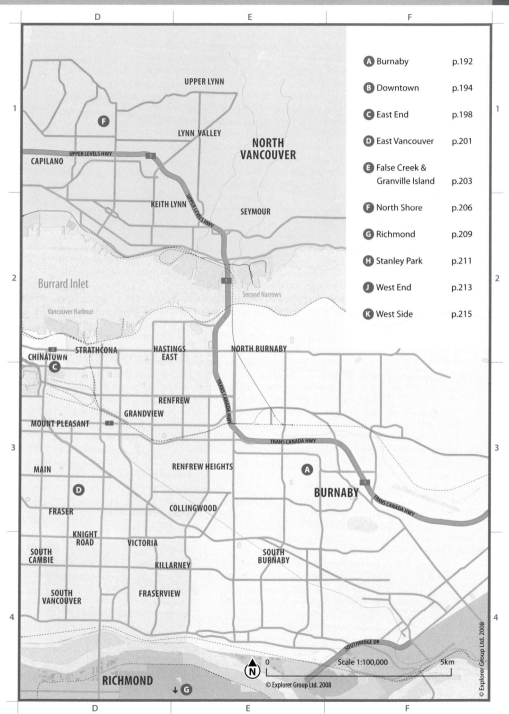

| A | Burnaby | p.192 |
| B | Downtown | p.194 |
| C | East End | p.198 |
| D | East Vancouver | p.201 |
| E | False Creek & Granville Island | p.203 |
| F | North Shore | p.206 |
| G | Richmond | p.209 |
| H | Stanley Park | p.211 |
| J | West End | p.213 |
| K | West Side | p.215 |

Scale 1:100,000          0        5km

© Explorer Group Ltd. 2008

© Explorer Group Ltd. 2008

Area **A** p.191
See also Map 6

# Burnaby

Vancouver's eastern neighbour, the booming municipality of Burnaby (population 202,000), is home to stunning parks, fascinating cultural offerings, and the province's second-largest university. Most know it for its enormous Metropolis at Metrotown super mall (p.415), which includes a two-tower office complex, some 470 stores covering everything from Sears to label outlets such as Banana Republic, Bowring and the Sony Store, and the largest food court in western Canada.

**Lowdown**
*The municipality of Burnaby is home to British Columbia's second most populated urban area and offers stunning parks, vibrant city and cultural life, and terrific shopping.*

There's much more to Burnaby than shopping though. The residential area around Metrotown is the province's largest urban region outside of central Vancouver. Here you'll find the wonderful Bob Prittie Metrotown Library (6100 Willingdon Avenue, 604 436 5410). You can pick up just about any book or video you please in this large, modern space (it's open seven days a week, and until 21:00 on weekdays if you fancy some late-evening reading), and its expansive outside gardens are perfect for strolling. If you want to give your body as well as your brain some exercise, the well-equipped Bonsor Recreation Complex is worth frequenting (6550 Bonsor Avenue, 604 439 1860).

**The Good**
*Excellent parks, particularly Burnaby Mountain and the cultural hot pot overlooking Deer Lake.*

The city's largest public recreation centre contains a 37m swimming pool, leisure pool, sauna, whirlpool, racquetball and squash courts, a pair of gyms, weights room, plus fine arts and dance studios. For those who prefer to be outside, Central Park, just west of the mall, offers several walking trails through its forest and is home to the city's top soccer venue, Swangard Stadium (Kingsway and Boundary Road, 604 435 7121), the stadium where the Vancouver Whitecaps play (p.338).

On the other side of Metrotown from Central Park is Deer Lake Park, where Burnaby's cultural core sits on the tranquil, north-eastern shores of Deer Lake. One of the main attractions is the Shadbolt Centre for the Arts (6450 Deer Lake Avenue, 604 291 6864), which boasts first-rate studios for dance, visual arts, and ceramics. Music lovers can catch shows at either of its two indoor theatres, or at the natural 10,000 seat amphitheatre which hosts numerous big name artists throughout the summer season, including the Burnaby Blues+ Roots Festival every August (www.burnabybluesfestival.com). Bring your lawn chair and tune into some of the big names who drop by.

**The Bad**
*Avoid the rainy day weekend shopping madness at Metropolis – it's people overload.*

The Burnaby Art Gallery (p.221), which features an eclectic blend of artists on two floors, is located next to the Shadbolt Centre. Across the street you can time-warp back to the 1920s at the interactive Burnaby Village Museum (p.230), open from May to September and featuring a walk-through town with costumed staff. In this corner of the park you'll also see the impressive Tudor manor that now contains the Hart House Restaurant (p.228). For peace and quiet, walk the 300m boardwalk to Deer Lake beach area. The park concession (604 839 3949, www.paddlevancouver.com) rents canoes, kayaks and other watercraft from Easter to Thanksgiving, from $10 an hour.

**The Must-Dos**
*Don't miss the day-long, mid-August Burnaby Blues+Roots Festival at the amphitheatre at Deer Lake Park; catch a soccer match at Swangard Stadium; contemplate life and eternity at Burnaby Mountain's 'Playground of the Gods'.*

Overlooking much of the area, plus Indian Arm, from atop Burnaby Mountain is the main attraction of Simon Fraser University (p.171). Master architects Arthur Erickson and Geoffrey Massey created a spectacle of low-rise buildings on stilts, surrounded by open fields and forest. It's visually stunning from the outside, but inside is a nearly impenetrable labyrinth of Orwellian corridors and staircases. Surrounding the school is the Burnaby Mountain Conservation Area, with its aromatic rose gardens, protected forest, totems and public artwork. The park also features 23km of multi-use trails and is a favourite for biking and hiking, while its open fields are perfect for Frisbee and football, or simply a picnic.

## Totem Recall

Burnaby Mountain Conservation Area contains a collection of man-made sculptures – tens of totems carved by Japanese artist Nuburi Toko and his son Shushei. Called Kamui Mintara (Playground of the Gods), it depicts a Japanese-First Nations creation legend, and is an impressive piece of work.

Dry Cleaners p.74
Divorce Lawyers p.108

Written by residents, the Hong Kong
Explorer is packed with insider info, from
arriving in the city to making it your home
and everything in between.

**Hong Kong Explorer Residents' Guide**
We Know Where You Live

*Area* **B** *p.190*
*See also Maps 7 & 9*

# Downtown

Vancouver's centre has steadily evolved westward from its early incarnation in today's East End. At present it occupies an area of some 10 by 10 city blocks between False Creek and Burrard Inlet, and offers a striking contrast between the glass and concrete sky rises and busy avenues of the central business district and the turn-of-the-century Victorian constructions along the narrow streets of Gastown.

**The Lowdown**
*The heart of the city where past and present mix.*

Downtown's first-rate accessibility by public transport together with its numerous landmarks within walking distance make it the perfect place to visit on foot. A good place to begin exploring the area is at the Canadian Pacific Railway's (CPR) former terminus, now known as Waterfront Station (p.110). It's the hub for all three of the SkyTrain lines, the SeaBus, and the West Coast Express (the commuter rail that services various Fraser Valley towns all the way to Mission). Recently renovated, this impressive construction was the third and last of the CPR's stations. It was slated for destruction in the 1960s by authorities that sought to blaze a highway through East Vancouver until grassroots organisations halted the project. You can, however, still see evidence of the destructive nature of the plan at the west end of the CPR building. Thinking that the terminal was terminal, the neighbouring car park was built butted against the edifice, shutting off the north exit completely. During the later renovation, architects had to build a staircase over the construction, exiting where the second storey window used to be.

**The Good**
*The high energy of the city centre; classic architecture at the Marine Building; the art and political scene at Vancouver Art Gallery.*

**The Bad**
*Inner city poverty and overdevelopment.*

Just across West Cordova Street from the station stands Vancouver's tallest building (if you count its antennae), the Harbour Centre. It is home to Simon Fraser University's Downtown campus (www.sfu.ca), a small shopping mall and an ample food court at its lower level, as well as the city's highest viewpoint in its upper floors. On a clear day (or night), Vancouver Lookout (p.232) offers spectacular 360 degree vistas of the city, mountains and water. You can also enjoy the view over a steak and bottle of syrah at the Top of Vancouver revolving restaurant (604 669 2220, www.topofvancouver.com). Back at street level, some of the notable architecture worth seeing includes the neoclassical building at 698 West Hastings Street, which once housed the headquarters of the Canadian Imperial Bank of Commerce and is now home to one of the city's pre-eminent jewellery stores, Birks. The green-and-gold-edged Marine Building at 355 Burrard Street was opened at the beginning of the 1930s in a no-holds-barred art deco style. The attention to detail goes far beyond the maritime designs embossed on its facade – take a peek inside to see the intricate trim work of the lobby and elevators.

**The Must-Dos**
*Visit the Marine Building for a dose of art deco; go dancing under the streets at Robson Square; hit the Lookout for a prime view of the city.*

Modern architecture is also alive and well in the Downtown core. The best place to get an idea of how Vancouver combines old and new is at Robson Square. Designed by Arthur Erickson (see p.192), the area sits partially below street level between the Law Courts and Vancouver Art Gallery, and acts as a public meeting place. Part of the space, below Robson Street, is used as a dance floor that hosts salsa lessons in the summer (www.sundayafternoonsalsa.com) and ice skating in the winter. Its unique wheelchair accessible staircase – a ramp actually zig-zags down through the steps – has become an icon for local photographers.

Erickson also designed the Law Courts, with the concept of 'transparent justice' as the major theme, and the courts are accessible to the public – both to watch the law in action, and take in the impressive glass roof.

The Vancouver Art Gallery (p.224) on the north of the square is not to be missed. An institution that *Time* magazine described as moving 'at the same speed as the cyclotron that is Vancouver's art scene', it is the city's most accessible building with a welcoming set of street level stairs, and has become one of the top meeting places in the city, as well as the scene for public protests. Its upstairs patio bistro is a favourite place to go for a bottle of wine. Behind the gallery, Vancouver's Olympic clock ticks down towards 2010 like a time bomb.

# Vancouver Areas

*Views of Downtown*

An avenue to the east, past the giant, multi-block Pacific Centre shopping mall (p.416), Granville Street remains the city's party centre with a barrage of bars, clubs and late night restaurants lining the streets, particularly between Robson and Nelson – although the future of Granville's northern-most quarter is presently under wraps as SkyTrain workers dig out the new Canada Line (p.47). On the south side of Granville, trendy Yaletown is also undergoing changes. Most of the once grungy railway depot warehouses have been speedily remodelled into high-end urban lofts housing shops, restaurants and cutting-edge businesses. It's a pleasant place for an afternoon of shopping and eating, and the Yaletown Brew Pub on Mainland Street (p.466) serves up its selection of beers in a vibrant atmosphere, and is a good place to soak up the feel of the area.

Not all of the warehouses were renovated though – some were demolished to make way for the new wave of concrete and glass apartments that are becoming the modern face of Vancouver, and have earned it the moniker City of Glass. A forest of glazed concrete buildings now covers much of the Downtown core, and front both False Creek and Coal Harbour.

**Eagle Eyes**
*Bring a pair of binoculars for your Downtown stroll. Some of the buildings have impressive details on their facades, not visible to the naked eye.*

Some of the best examples of this 21st century see-through architecture can be seen along the Burrard Street corridor, including the 150m, 48 storey, elliptical One Wall Centre tower, which was featured in the movie *X-Men: The Last Stand*. Home of the Sheraton Hotel, its two-tone windows (the lower are darker than the upper floors) are the result of a compromise between government officials and developers. Half-way through construction, the former insisted the developers install lighter-coloured windows so that the building would blend into the sky, as opposed to dominating the landscape. Rather than remove those windows already in place, construction continued with the new shade on the top floors. The government's strict code has had its way with most developers though, and the lightly coloured 'Yaletown green' windows can be seen throughout the Downtown core.

## Gastown

East of the Downtown core, between Waterfront Station and Chinatown, is the pretty area of Gastown. The area sits on the site of the city of Vancouver's birthplace, where, in 1867, John Deighton (known as 'Gassy Jack' to his friends, as a result of his talkative tendencies

*Gastown*

rather than anything less savoury) inaugurated his first saloon. Before long, the area became the cultural hub of town due to the constant influx of Hastings Mill workers. Despite an official decree naming the town Granville after the British colonial secretary, locals stuck to calling it Gastown, in reference to the man that made their after-work hours merrier. The Great Fire of 1886 destroyed all of Gastown's wooden structures, but stone and brick buildings replaced it and the area boomed after the 1887 completion of the Canadian Pacific Railway's western terminus, just a few blocks away. At the turn of the century, Gastown started a slow and steady decline, and was almost demolished as part of the failed 1960s plan to construct a highway, but

*Canada Place*

since then the area has seen a flourish of restoration, and today its buildings stand as some of the finest examples of Victorian and Edwardian architecture in the city. Gastown's accessibility by public transport and its pleasant and narrow cobblestone streets make it the perfect place for a walking tour. Start at the corner of Richards and Water streets, just outside Waterfront Station, where you'll find two beautifully renovated former warehouses. The Landing (375 Water Street) was built in 1905 and is now home to offices, eateries and one of the finest breweries in town, Steamworks (p.465). On the same street, at 321, is Hudson House, erected in 1895 by the Hudson's Bay Company and presently host to a souvenir and antique shop. Further along Water Street are several First Nations art galleries, which are interesting to visit, while on the corner of Cambie Street stands the neighbourhood icon, the photogenic Gastown Steam Clock (p.225). Built in 1977, but based on an 1875 design, it whistles to the tune of the Westminster Chimes every 15 minutes, and attracts the crowds. Once motored by an ingenious steam system, it now works with the aid of an electrical circuit board, but the bells and whistles remain the same.

At Water's intersection with Carrall Street, the two-storey Italianate Byrnes Block is one of the oldest brick buildings in the city, and is where Gassy Jack's second saloon used to be. Around the back is the cobbled Gaolers Mews, the site of Vancouver's first jail, customs house, telegraph office and fire station, and this little area, which also incorporates the darkly named Blood Alley, is now home to a couple of good watering and eating holes, including Irish Heather (p.462) and Salt Tasting Room (p.440). Yards away, in Maple Tree Square, the city's first public plaza, is the lovely Hotel Europe. Built in 1908, this triangular, flatiron-style building was the first reinforced concrete structure in the country and the earliest fireproof hotel in western Canada. And in the middle of the square, Gassy Jack is immortalised, standing (some may say staggering) in front of his former red brick saloon.

## *Canada Place*

To the west of Waterfront Station, sitting at the prime crossroads between historic Vancouver, its financial district, the Coal Harbour condominiums and Burrard Inlet, the Canada Place promontory (www.canadaplace.ca) has positioned itself as a world class multi-use facility. The futuristic complex, with its distinctive peaked fabric roof, is home to the city's IMAX theatre (p.476), the five-star Pan Pacific Hotel (p.36), the Vancouver Port Authority, the World Trade Centre office complex, and the expanding Vancouver Convention and Exhibition Centre (www.vcec.ca). To add to its offerings, it is also one of the city's two cruise ship terminals. With well appointed restaurants and plenty of public places to sit and admire the scenery, it makes for an ideal spot to stroll around and shoot the breeze, as well as offering great views across Burrard Inlet towards North Vancouver and the peaks beyond.

Area **C** *p.191*
See also Map 10

# East End

Once the site of the important 19th century Hastings Mill, from which the town site of Granville (which would later become the city of Vancouver) was built (see p.4), over the past hundred or so years, the action has slowly morphed seaward from Vancouver's East End. Nonetheless, the East End's numerous districts and historic architecture – including some of the most interesting turn-of-the-century buildings in the city – tell the ongoing story of life in these parts. Immigration has always played a large role here, and the result is visible throughout the multicultural streets of Chinatown and Japantown. On the other hand, rampant poverty, homelessness and a serious drug problem have befallen the infamous Hastings corridor of the Downtown Eastside, and the avenue remains a shock to most.

*Lowdown*
*Downtown Eastside is the heart of old Vancouver, and home to a vibrant Chinatown and Japantown as well as the city's homeless along Hastings.*

## *Chinatown*

*The Good*
*Chinatown's vibrant street life with its busy shops and restaurants and dazzling smells and sounds.*

Chinese Canadians in British Columbia have not had the easiest of times. The community, first exploited as a cheap and tough-as-nails labour force, has been the engine of much of the economic prosperity of the province; they did the grunt work on the Canadian Pacific Railway, prospected for gold, and were instrumental in farming throughout the late 19th and early 20th centuries. Then, in the 1960s, Chinatown was slated to be razed to make way for the proposed town freeway, until protests shot down the plans.

But times have changed; since 1997, when China resumed sovereignty over Hong Kong and many citizens moved to Vancouver, the city has again seen a massive influx of Chinese speakers, many of who are wealthier than a lot of locals. Despite the alteration in social strata, some things never change: today, as much as ever, the Chinese population remains an integral part of the province's social fabric and economy. One of the best ways to partake in the Chinese cultural offerings is by strolling through vibrant Chinatown. Considered the largest in North America after San Francisco and New York, it offers a real slice of Asian market life and is brimming with colours, scents and styles straight out of the Middle Kingdom.

*The Bad*
*Beyond boasting a rampant drug problem, the Downtown Eastside harbours a hepatitis dilemma of epidemic proportions.*

Chinatown stretches as far south as East Georgia Street and butts against the residential district of Strathcona on Gore Avenue at its eastern terminus. Its roadways are packed with numerous stores selling just about everything imaginable, including dried bats, juicy guavas and barbecue duck. While many of today's Chinese immigrants are moving to Richmond (see p.209), Chinatown is experiencing a kind of gentrification of late. Many of the city's long-standing elderly Chinese are opting to move back here to live out their days.

*The Must-Dos*
*Walk the Silk Road; meditate in the Dr Sun Yat Sen Classical Chinese Garden; eat noodles; load up on ancient Chinese remedies during the cold season.*

At the western entrance to Chinatown, south of Gastown, is its magnificently ornamented 15m high Millennium Gate. Inaugurated by prime minister Jean Chretien in 2002, its colourful beams and elaborate roof span the girth of Pender Street. The relationship between residents and government officials wasn't always this sweet though. In 1912, local authorities seeking to widen the street expropriated all but a 1.8m slice of a nine metre wide plot of land owned by the prosperous Sam Kee Company on the corner of Pender and Carrall streets. Rather than selling the remaining fragment though, the company commissioned a defiant, two storey building, complete with protruding bay windows. Today, it is said to be the world's narrowest office building.

The functional-looking Chinese Cultural Centre (50 East Pender Street, 604 658 8883) is located just down the street. The giant complex, which takes up the better part of the entire city block, offers various classes such as traditional dance, painting and lessons in Mandarin and Cantonese, as well as a pleasant second floor gallery which hosts art exhibits. On Fridays at 10:30, you can also check out free screenings of films in Mandarin. Those looking for in-depth explorations of the area can sign up for the centre's guided tours which are offered on an appointment basis for groups of more than three (tours cost $10, reserve by calling 604 658 8883). Many pass through the centre's courtyard to enter the peaceful one hectare Dr Sun Yat Sen Classical Chinese Garden (p.246). This tranquil oasis is the first full-scale Chinese garden built outside China and was meticulously constructed in the mid 1980s by 52 master craftsman from Suzhou using techniques and principles of the original Ming dynasty gardeners. No nails, screws or glue were used. Through the garden you can access a succinct, three room museum (p.230), which presents elements of Chinese culture and arts, including some fine calligraphy, and the history of Chinese people in Vancouver.

## Japantown

Initially known as Little Tokyo, the diminutive size of Vancouver's Japantown is in many ways directly related to a Canadian wartime policy that saw its Japanese citizens as 'enemy aliens'. After the attack on Pearl Harbour Japanese Canadians were rounded up for resettlement in distant labour camps and their homes and possessions confiscated. Although the Japanese were finally given their freedom of movement and resettlement in 1949, the once-busy commercial area that surrounded the vicinity of Powell and Alexander streets never recovered. Still, a walk down its alleys harks back to the old

Chinatown

days and offers a few vestiges of its past, including the not-for-profit Vancouver Japanese Language School & Japanese Hall (475 Alexander Street, 604 254 2551). The rectangular building was constructed in 1928 and features triple arched windows with ornate column separators crowned by black-and-gold-tile mosaics. However, the architecture takes second place to its sombre historical significance; this is the sole property returned to the Japanese Canadian community after the war. A few dilapidated, once-Japanese wooden shop fronts remain along Powell Street across from Oppenheimer Park (named after David, Vancouver's second mayor, not Robert, the brains behind the Manhattan Project). Also on Powell Street, on the corner of Dunlevy Avenue, is the area's most impressive structure, the ornate Tamura Building, which features Corinthian columns, sheet metal ornamentation and granite block foundation stones. The building once housed the well-to-do New World Hotel; today it has been converted into low-cost accommodation. Despite its downbeat appearance, Japantown comes alive every first weekend of August, during the Powell Street Festival (p.57), which celebrates the arts and culture of Japanese and Asian Canadians. Expect a two-day sampling of contemporary dance, music, film and video, visual arts and martial arts demonstrations, along with an amateur sumo tournament and delicious Japanese snacks.

**The Beat Goes On**

*An educational way of taking in the sites of the Downtown Eastside is by embarking on the Vancouver Centennial Police Museum's 'Walking the Beat' tour through old Vancouver. The two-hour guided Eastside stroll explores the criminal influences – from prohibition to today's drug problem – that have impacted the area.*

## Downtown Eastside

East Hastings Street was the site of the city's original 'skid road', a path of timber greased with fish oil so that, in the 19th century, lumbermen could 'skid' their logs by ox cart to the mill. In the same century, the Canadian Pacific Railway claimed the banks of the Burrard Inlet here for its western terminus, and the transcontinental trains that rolled in brought with them an economic boom which transformed the sleepy timber town of Granville into the metropolis of Vancouver. The area became the city's locus of immigration and action, and, within years, it transformed into the cultural centre of western Canada, housing the foremost theatres, hotels and restaurants west of Chicago. Today, the skid row tag is applicable for different reasons – it is now Vancouver's most dilapidated quarter, and the poorest urban area in the whole country, with homelessness and substance abuse rampant – but the remnants of more prosperous times can be seen in the dusty facades and peeling paint of the old brick and mortar buildings of the Downtown Eastside.

Of the important structures worth seeing, don't miss the 1912 Sun Tower at 100 West Pender Street, which held the claim to fame of being the highest building of the British Empire in the early 1900s. The 17 storey, 82 metre high building comes with an ornate beaux art-styled, faux-copper roof along with some impressive detailing on the facade. Also worth visiting is the Vancouver Police Centennial Museum (p.231), which offers visitors a morbid chance to get up close with the city's most famous criminals, and the squads that caught them. The museum is housed in the 1932 coroner's court, which served as the city's original courtroom, forensics laboratory, autopsy room and morgue. Just next door, the Firehall Theatre Society (p.478) is one of the city's busiest performing and visual arts venues, with some 300 shows per year staged in the renovated 1906 fire station.

### Follow The Yellow Silk Road

Follow the yellow banners of the 'Silk Road' connecting the city and Chinatown. The excellent self-guided walking loop is approximately 3km in length. It begins at Vancouver Public Library and crosses all of Chinatown's key attractions and cultural highlights along Keefer and Pender streets, including the Millennium Chinatown Gate, the Dr Sun Yat Sen Classical Chinese Garden and the Chinese Cultural Centre.

The grandeur of the Eastside's potential invariably falls in the shadow of the rampant drug and homelessness problem, and its disenfranchised population find hospice in poorly done conversions that have taken over many of the old hotels. Yet with all of the cultural capital locked up in the area's turn-of-the-century buildings, a municipal agenda for beautification and gentrification threatens to displace its residents once again, turning the area into a hotbed of political and social activism.

Area D p.191
See also Map 6

# East Vancouver

East Vancouver is bordered by Burrard Inlet to the north, the Fraser River to the south and Burnaby to the east. This residential area, also known as East Van or the Eastside (not to be confused with the Downtown Eastside, p.200, or the East End, p.198), has had a vibrant history of immigration since the 1887 completion of the Canadian Pacific Railway. Today its tranquil streets retain their international flair and diversity, and the area also plays host to the finest artist-run ateliers in the country, along with some of the city's most international bars, restaurants and music.

## The Main Street Corridor

One of the main streets in East Vancouver is, aptly, Main Street, and its many personalities come with a touch of everything Vancouver. Near its southern terminus, the five-block Punjabi Market around 49th Avenue embodies the thoroughfare's continuous appeal to immigrants. Here you will find stores and pavements reminiscent of India, chock-a-block with trinkets, colours and odours of the subcontinent. Searching for a stylish saree? Nosing for a spicy home-made curry or samosa? Step through the clouds of incense and redemption will be yours. Moving northward towards town, take a short dogleg west on 33rd Avenue to Queen Elizabeth Gardens (p.244). At 167m above sea level, this is the highest point in Vancouver and boasts the postcard vista of the city's glass towers sandwiched between False Creek and the North Shore peaks. The flower-filled park began as a construction quarry for homes in the affluent suburb of Shaughnessy. The municipality then transformed the gaping holes with lovely sunken gardens and topped the hill with the impressive Bloedel Floral Conservatory (p.245), a geodesic dome brimming with tropical plants and birds. The place is a real oasis, particularly during Vancouver's dreary grey season. You can also try out your swing at the pitch-and-putt golf course or go lawn bowling. With all of these attractions the park has metamorphosed into a romantic paradise; on any given weekend expect numerous brides, their paparazzi, and young lovers picnicking about the lawns. While there is some debate about building a viewing tower in the park, at present the best vista is served up at any of the three windowed dining rooms at the on-site Seasons in the Park restaurant (604 874 8008, www.vancouverdine.com). Specialising in west coast dishes, the exclusive eatery has served the likes of Yeltsin and Clinton.

Back on Main Street, north of 30th, the avenue slowly busies with action, building to its high point between the Starbucks and JJ Bean cafes on the east side of 14th Avenue, across from St Patrick's parish building. This is the city's newest urban-chic hotspot. Gritty cafes in industrial buildings appear on every corner, interspersed with quirky antique and furniture stores, just about every kind of yoga studio imaginable and a smattering of low-priced restaurants. Architecturally speaking, the 1916 beaux arts-styled Heritage Hall (3102 Main Street, 604 879 4816) remains the area's landmark. The giant brownstone, with its red-roofed clock tower, is one of the city's oldest municipal buildings and has functioned over much of the past century as a post office and police station. Its atrium has been renovated to resemble a ballroom from a French chateau, and rents out for receptions. Downstairs, the Stage Door troop (604 872 1252, www.stagedoor.bc.ca) presents theatre productions by people with developmental and other challenges. The heated outdoor patio of the gritty Five Point pub next door is as good a place as any to while away the hours watching people walk by. North of Terminal Avenue, Main's old brick buildings offer a glimpse of the richness of the area's past, while the Georgia viaduct, an ungainly elevated highway span to the city centre is a reminder of what could have been – this is the most visible remnant of the proposed 1970s highway that threatened to destroy much of the Eastside. The area remains serviced by rail; the monumental Pacific Central Station, where you can catch the Amtrack south or any of the Via Rail coaches across Canada, sits diagonally opposite the always-busy Main Street/

**Lowdown**
East Vancouver is the city's most bohemian urban area and home to some of the oldest residential architecture, the best cafes and the finest artists.

**The Good**
Commercial Drive offers an oasis of laidback services and international restaurants. Its selection of imported meats, cheeses and produce are some of the most varied in the city – and its coffees some of the most potent around.

**The Bad**
With housing prices growing by leaps and bounds, East Vancouver has become more and more inaccessible to the city's newest immigrants, artists, seniors, and young families.

**The Must-Dos**
Browse the dozens of artist-owned workshops in the labyrinthine 1000 Parker Street warehouse conversion; sip coffees on any of the Commercial Drive patios; pick up samosas at the Punjabi market; enjoy the view of the city from Queen Elizabeth Park.

Science World SkyTrain station. Expect more century-old architecture further north until you reach the Main and Hastings intersection site of the stately Carnegie Centre (401 Main Street, 604 665 2220). Built in 1908, it was once the city's main library. Today it is described as the Downtown Eastside's living room. Converted into a community centre, it houses a seniors' centre, art gallery, auditorium, learning centre, gym, and several art studios. Its kitchen doles out well-prepared, low-cost meals three times a day.

*Main, Strain And Automobiles*
*As Main Street stretches for over 50 blocks, exploring this corridor is best done with the aid of public transport – bus number 3 – or a car. It's a little busy for bikes.*

### Strathcona

Vancouver's first residential district takes its name from the president of the Canadian Pacific Railway and reaches from Main eastward to Clark Drive. Due to the traditional influx of passengers and commerce from the railway line, the area has always been an international hub – its school was nicknamed the 'League of Nations' in the 1930s and considered to be the most multicultural in the world at the time. Today the neighbourhood retains its international flair and affords visitors views of some of the older wooden Arts and Crafts residential architecture in the area, with some particularly nice examples along Hawks and Princess Streets. With its eclectic mix of people and structures, many of the city's artists' workshops dot the landscape. Drop by the numerous ateliers at the retro-fitted warehouse at 1000 Parker Street for the area's largest conglomeration of independent artists. You can also get a fantastic introduction to the art scene in mid-November during the annual three day Eastside Culture Crawl (see p.220).

### Commercial Drive

Home to the city's hippest and most community oriented, owner-operated sales and service district, Commercial Drive, just east of Strathcona, is one of the city's favourite places to sip on cappuccinos and watch the world whirl by. Offering old-time shopping and dining at a decisively human scale – you won't find any big-box franchises here – expect a smorgasbord of sales and service outlets from all corners of the planet selling all kinds of wares and foods, with live music emanating from every other doorway. From the eclectic mix of delicious home-baked organic muffins with live Cuban music on weekend nights at the End Cafe (2360 Commercial Drive, 604 215 3888) to the wide selection of world music at Highlife Records (1317 Commercial Drive, 604 251 6964), and the pre-eminent hemp and bong emporium at Grass Roots (2048 Commercial

*Commercial Drive*

Drive, 604 253 4146), you're sure to find everything you ever wanted on this road. Commercial Drive was once known as Little Italy, and it retains some of that flavour – the top place to watch international soccer matches is at the low-key Abruzzo Cafe (1321 Commercial Drive, 604 254 2641). The place packs to standing room only when big games are on, particularly during the Italian, Mexican and South American league finals. The area is also unofficially prime real estate for the lesbian crowd. With its strong and inclusive community base, every summer it hosts a pair of not-to-be-missed car-free festivals (www.commercialdrivefestival.org) in the heart of the district between 1st Avenue and Venables Street. The Drive packs with live entertainment, buskers, bands and, inevitably, the free-lovin' gang which doles out bear hugs to passersby. The annual Halloween 'Parade of the Lost Souls' is another animated event (see p.59).

*Area* **E** *p.190*
See also Map 9

# False Creek & Granville Island

Named by Captain George Richards during an 1859 survey, False Creek remains a dead end waterway that borders Downtown to the south. Its popularity as a residential area began when locals moved here to escape the smouldering ashes of the city's 'Great Fire' of 1886 (see p.204). Today it's as in-demand as ever, and is the fashionable place to live for condo-lovers – Yaletown's glass towers garner some of the top prices in the country. The trend to populate this inlet continues apace as the 300,000 sq m Olympic Village rises in its south-eastern corner. Set to host 2,800 athletes and officials during the winter games in 2010, it will be the first of several phases of development that will transform this once industrial area into a showcase of sustainable development which seeks to construct 5,000 low-rise residential units, a full-size community centre, a non-motorised boating facility, and a handful of childcare facilities, along with an elementary school, an interfaith spiritual centre, and 10 hectares of parkland. Other unique features of the area include a new island with bridge, boardwalk, and seaside greenway and bikeway that will connect with the False Creek walkway. By 2020, Southeast False Creek will be home to 16,000 people. While the project sounds fascinating, combine the massive construction with the installation of the SkyTrain's Canada Line, and you've got a daily, peak hour traffic nightmare until its 2009 completion, particularly at the Cambie Street and Broadway intersection.

**Lowdown**

*Peaceful False Creek is home to the bustling Granville Island Public Market along with dozens of artist-run ateliers and pleasant restaurants. Those looking to stretch their legs can enjoy the spectacular waterfront walkway loop throughout. Expect great views of the city from every turn.*

**The Good**

*Some of British Columbia's freshest produce and best artisans at Granville Island, wonderful walking, and the future home of the Olympic Village.*

**The Bad**

*Parking is near impossible on Granville Island, and Cambie Bridge traffic is nearly unbearable with the construction of the Canada Line and Olympic Village.*

**The Must-Dos**

*Drink beer, listen to the buskers, and chomp on the freshest produce and prepared foods on Granville Island; walk, jog or bike along the seaside promenade; charter a yacht at Cooper Boating on Granville Island, fill the fridge with local brew and sail into the sunset.*

## False Creek

The greatest icon of False Creek, the geodesic-domed Telus World of Science (p.233), is located at the inlet's eastern terminus. The structure has done double duty since it was built. It began as home to the international media during the 1986 World Expo and has since operated an engaging interactive museum dedicated to science. Movie goers will appreciate the rooftop 'golf ball' as it houses one of the world's largest OMNIMAX screens. Outside you'll find a pleasant waterfront park with open lawns, a children's play area and a dock. On most weekday evenings between Valentine's Day and Thanksgiving, the waterfront bustles with numerous dragon boat teams readying for practice. North False Creek continues to peel away its industrial past. In place of the railways and warehouses that once lined the shore is the Plaza of Nations (750 Pacific Boulevard, 604 682 0777), a multi-use entertainment and shopping area that was the heart of Expo 86. It is now home to the giant Edgewater Casino (604 687 3343), a small shopping and services centre and an outdoor concert venue which is presently undergoing reparations. Vancouver's 'City of Glass' – the crowded skyline of modern, opaque towers – begins around Cambie Bridge and goes on past Burrard Street. The waterfront walkway continues uninterrupted through to the Stanley Park Seawall (see p.211) and is ideal for biking, walking and people watching. Of course, boating is still a big part of life here. Beyond being the favourite training spot for leagues of dragon boaters on after-work paddling forays, it is also popular for kayakers and the yachting crowd which moors in the bay or uses the docks at the several local marinas. If you want to add a slice of leisurely water transport to your exploring, hop on a

### City Of Glass Or Grass?

Taking advantage of the spectacular natural scenery in all directions, Vancouver's architects have glassed up their high-rises allowing for plenty of natural light with a minimum of walls. The result is a futuristic metropolis with a forest of towering see-though constructions – good news for local voyeurs who can get an eyeful when the lights go on. Local author and visionary Douglas Coupland picked up on this and entitled his 2000 book on Vancouver *City of Glass*. However, with the growing number and popularity of illegal marijuana plantations along with lax consumption laws, some suggest 'City of Grass' as a more appropriate moniker.

False Creek ferry (p.44), a passenger service that runs throughout the day and stops at seven locations along the creek, from Telus World of Science to Vanier Park's Maritime Museum (p.232). Fares cost from $2.50 per adult.

## Granville Island

Granville Island (www.granvilleisland.bc.ca) is the hub of south False Creek action and rates as the most visited attraction in the city after Stanley Park. The artificial land mass was created in 1915 by the dumping of vast quantities of mud, dredged off the False Creek floor as part of the works to create Vancouver's harbour. A manufacturing core quickly set up corrugated tin factories and used the island as a combined sea and railway port to support the booming mining and forestry industries. After the second world war, the Canadian Pacific moved north and industry slowed, making the area a prime location for a bohemian transformation.

The centrepiece of the island's new persona, Granville Island Public Market (p.413), opened in 1979. The once-industrial corrugated shacks now shine in brightly painted colours and house dozens of different artisans and cooperatives from around the province, with a focus on local produce. Yet evidence of Granville Island's past still exists: old railway lines poke through the asphalt and the Ocean Construction Supplies cement factory operates between the province's high-profile Emily Carr University of Art and Design (1399 Johnston Street, 604 844 3800), one of Canada's top fine-arts institutions, which houses the Charles H Scott Gallery (p.222), and the 450 seat stage of the Arts Club Theatre (1585 Johnston Street, 604 687 1644), whose productions range from musicals and classics to contemporary comedies. With the recent construction boom taking place just around the corner, an eclectic blend of oversized concrete trucks, easel-toting arts students and theatre goers melds together seamlessly in this area.

The market (www.granvilleisland.com), a colourful pierside edifice made up of a handful of interconnected buildings, is still the big draw. Open 09:00 to 19:00 daily, on any given day you'll find it full of gregarious vendors. With all the spare change rattling around, the market hasn't gone unnoticed by the city's skilled buskers, who please the ear at every passageway, in particular the areas surrounding the popular food court and the waterfront pier. The island also hosts numerous shops and restaurants, including two of the city's finest microbrews. Granville Island Brewery (1441 Cartwright Street, 604 687 2739) and Dockside Brewing Company (1253 Johnston Street, 604 685 7070) both offer samplers of their creations at a charge, and are good places to soak up the vibe of the island, as well as the beer. Rice wine fans will enjoy Osake's (1339 Railspur Alley, 604 685 7253) three styles of home made sake, while children love Kids Market (1496 Cartwright Street, 604 689 8447). Housed in a 100 year old factory and an adjacent train caboose, the fun facility offers shops and activities for youngsters and their families. Wood lovers can check out the country's top showcase for quality handcrafted design at the Wood Co-op (1592 Johnston Street, 604 408 2553), which displays the work of some of British Columbia's most talented woodworkers.

---

**At The Creek Without A Paddle?**

The best way to explore False Creek is via its waterfront walkway. Crossing the water to make a circuit is as simple as hiking over any of the bridges. Of the three, Granville and Cambie are better for pedestrians. If you want to paddle across try Granville Island's Ecomarine Ocean Kayak Centre (1668 Duranleau Street, 604 689 7575), or Cooper Boating (1620 Duranleau Street, 604 687 4110) offers a selection of power boats and yachts.

**Hoppy Times**

Brewing is big on the little island. Both Granville Island Brewery and the Dockside Brewing Company provide wonderful samples. The former is a dedicated brewery and no-frills tap room, offering half a dozen hand-crafted draft beers plus a seasonal speciality; the latter serves up its eight brews in a great setting, including its scenic east-facing patio.

---

### The Great Fire Of 1886

On 13 June, 1886, a Canadian Pacific Railway clearing blaze between Granville and Hamilton streets burst out of control. Fuelled by a sudden squall from the west, it razed the entire settlement of Vancouver in a matter of minutes (one eyewitness claimed that 'Vancouver didn't burn, it exploded'). Only months old, the wooden city saw most of its 1,000 buildings burn to the ground in less than 45 minutes. At least eight people died in the blaze. The city's building code was quickly amended and called for fireproof stone and mortar constructions – thus began the erection of some of the century-old buildings that remain today in Downtown and the Eastside.

# Vancouver Areas

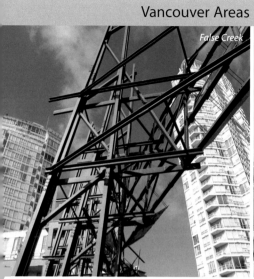
*False Creek*

*Burrard Bridge*

*Boats in front of BC Place*

*Granville Island Public Market*

*Granville Island*

*Area* **F** *p.191*
*See also Maps 3 & 4*

**Lowdown**
*Vancouver's mountain playground comes complete with spectacular alpine scenery, verdant forests and lively rivers, along with a pair of postcard bays at either end.*

**The Good**
*A world of adventure less than 30 minutes from the city centre.*

**The Bad**
*The rain and clouds – but then again, this is a rainforest.*

**The Must-Dos**
*Do the Grind; picnic at Lighthouse Park; kayak out of Deep Cove; ride all three ski areas; hike to Seymour's first peak; gaze out over the spectacular canyon beneath Capilano Suspension Bridge.*

# North Shore

The North Shore lies in the narrow gap of land sandwiched between the snowy peaks of the Coastal Mountains and the placid Burrard Inlet waterfront. Access is limited to two bridges from the city's western and eastern-most extremes, along with a passenger ferry from Downtown. With the lack of direct contact between the two areas, the mountainous landscape lends itself to a more natural, easy going sensibility than its big city counterpart across the bay.

As well as being Vancouver's postcard-perfect backdrop, this is the gateway to some of the most accessible big mountain terrain of any urban area on earth. With a range of difficulty from simple to suicide, just about anyone can bring their boots, backpack, and sense of adventure into its impressive hiking paths, alpine terrain, and salmon-filled rivers. Add to that a pair of spectacular seaside harbours and you've got the makings of Vancouver's ultimate backyard playground.

The Lions Gate Bridge is the most famous gateway to the North Shore – it's a Vancouver icon, loved by all that see its elegant lines, and hated by most that drive it. The three-lane suspended causeway opened in 1938, crossing the First Narrows of Burrard Inlet and marking the entrance to Vancouver's harbour. It took the combined effort of the brains of a local businessman, the beer money of Ireland's Guinness family, a city wide referendum and the low-as-you-can-go Depression-era labour costs to make it happen. The plan: to encourage residential development on the mountain slopes of West Vancouver. Today, anyone looking at the thousands of homes and condominiums carved up along the flanks of these shores can attest that they were exceedingly successful.

## West Vancouver

To the west of Lions Gate Bridge lies the well-heeled neighbourhood of West Vancouver (not to be confused with West End or the West Side, p.213 and p.215). Here you will find some of the city's most treasured real estate, with unbeatable views over the city, but pity the rich: the North Shore peaks sure know how to attract clouds and rain. The region gets over 170cm of that 'liquid sunshine' every year. Although primarily residential, West Van has several attractions worth visiting. Its top draw is the Cypress Mountain ski area (Cypress Bowl Road, 604 926 5612), in the sizeable Cypress Provincial Park. Only 30 minutes from Downtown, it offers the most vertical drop, most terrain and most lifts on the highest skiing and riding peak of the North Shore. It also hosts 19km of cross-country skiing trails, a snowtubing park with surface lift, and phenomenal snowshoeing. With the Olympics coming to town, it has something else to boast about: Cypress is the official freestyle skiing and snowboard venue for the games. Cypress Bowl Road also has several wonderful pull-offs with spectacular views and educational interpretative panels.

Back at water level, don't miss visiting Lighthouse Park (p.243), which protects one of the last vestiges of old growth forest remaining in all of the Lower Mainland. There's more to it than huge trees though, as the 75 hectare green space offers wonderful vistas of the sea as well as some short hikes. Its precipitous setting ensures that you'll be breathing hard wherever you choose to hike, and its location, just 8km west of Lions Gate Bridge, makes it an ideal destination for a day bike trip. The coastline along West Van's shore is largely rugged, but there are several coves and beaches worth investigating, including the community beach parks at Ambleside (p.237) and nearby Dundarave. Both have beach facilities and places to eat, and are connected for a large part of the 3km between them by the West Vancouver Centennial Seawalk.

Further west, the picturesque inlet at Horseshoe Bay has become a transportation hub, as BC Ferries operates its Sunshine Coast and Nanaimo runs from here (p.44).

Arrive early for your ferry and enjoy the pierside attractions, which include several restaurants and delis, a supermarket, a pub and a bakery.

## North Vancouver

**Bridge The Cost**
The cheapest (in fact, free) way of getting that suspension bridge feeling is by going to Lynn Canyon. While only half as long as the Capilano Suspension Bridge, it is actually higher. The Lynn bridge hangs some 20 storeys above the canyon floor.

The busy district of North Vancouver, or North Van as it's known to residents, lies east of West Vancouver and continues all the way to scenic Deep Cove, and hosts some of the most popular tourist areas of the North Shore. Access is relatively easy as both of the bridges, the Lions Gate Bridge and the steel-trussed Ironworkers Memorial Second Narrows Crossing, known locally as the Second Narrows Bridge, connect the North Shore to the city. The SeaBus has its terminal at the foot of the area's main commercial district, Lonsdale Quay, too. Beyond being a hub for the public transport system (it also hosts a busy bus terminal), Lonsdale Quay (p.408) is an animated indoor market serving up some of the area's freshest produce and coffees. Its lively restaurants and open seating make it an ideal place to meet before setting off to the local attractions. Capilano Suspension Bridge (p.241) is by far the busiest tourist magnet in the area, and one of the oldest in Vancouver. In operation since 1889, its claim to fame is a spectacular 137m long wood-and-wire pedestrian suspension bridge spanning the canyon 70m above the Capilano River. The bridge is surrounded by the Capilano River Regional Park (www.gvrd.bc.ca/parks/capilanoriver), where you can expect to see a vibrant forest and a splendid canyon populated by raptors, particularly during the autumn-time salmon run. The tourist mecca also presents several small historical displays, a small collection of totems, an impressive treetop adventure trail and a cliff side walk, all for the same pricey admission ($27). Access to the bridge is just a short drive from Lonsdale Quay.

The park extends north to the Cleveland Dam, the city's most important supply of drinking water. Its 26km of trails wander through the forest and access the Capilano Salmon Hatchery. This self-guided facility offers educational displays on the life cycle of the west coast's most important fish species. It's open year round, and from March to November you can watch the salmon live through glass windows as they struggle up the fish ladder to fulfil their legacy of returning to the river they were born in to spawn. Three species ply the waters; you can witness the steelheads climbing the ladder in March and April, the cohos from June to November, and the chinook in October and November. If you prefer to see your salmon end up on a dinner plate, you can join the riverside anglers.

**Car Strangled Spanner**
Commuters don't call the Lions Gate Bridge the 'car-strangled spanner' for nothing. Lose-the-will-to-live traffic is notorious on this three-lane bridge. Avoid crossing during peak hours if at all possible, particularly before holiday weekends when the whole city escapes north.

Capilano Road continues up to the alpine base of the 1,250m high Grouse Mountain (www.grousemountain.com). Here you can partake in one of the rites of Vancouver life – the Grouse Grind, Vancouver's most popular hike. Designed as a training ground for a Canadian Everest expedition, this thigh-breaking natural Stairmaster takes you up 1km of elevation along a wooded staircase that is less than 3km long.

Those wanting to get up without breaking a sweat can hop aboard Grouse Mountain's Skyride ($33 round trip), North America's largest aerial tramway. Operating year round, expect breathtaking views and a pinch of vertigo during the eight-minute ride up. Both the Grouse Grind and the Skyride take you to the base of operations for the four season resort. In winter you can ski and snowboard on its peaks, or skate on a pond. The summertime offerings consist of plenty of hiking, along with several wildlife sanctuaries – including one accommodating the popular grizzly bears. The Altitudes Bistro and upscale Observatory Restaurant (604 980 9311) are both located on site and offer great views, if you can find a window seat.

One of the lesser-known natural attractions worth a visit is the Lynn Canyon Park, 7km east of the Capilano River. Here you can hike the mild-to-moderate trails and cross its 20 storey high suspension bridge for free. Those interested in furthering their environmental knowledge can ask the friendly folk at the Lynn Canyon Ecology

Centre (3663 Park Road, 604 981 3103). The facility is also a good place to get up-to-the minute information on longer and more difficult hikes through the neighbouring Lynn Headwaters Regional Park (www.gvrd.bc.ca/parks).

At the eastern end of the north shore, Mount Seymour Provincial Park (www.env. gov.bc.ca/bcparks) protects a forest of western hemlock, cedar and giant douglas fir. Its ski area (1700 Mount Seymour Road, 604 986 2261) offers good terrain for riding and snowshoeing during the winter as well as terrific hiking on its 14 trails during the snow-free months. You can also get unbelievable views of Mount Baker from its summit.

Back at sea level lies the picturesque town of Deep Cove. Situated on the western shore of peaceful Indian Arm (see p.258), its waterfront parks are a picnic paradise and its docks are the prime jumping off spot for exploring the spectacular Indian Arm fjord. Kayak rentals and instruction are available during all seasons from the Deep Cove Canoe and Kayak Centre (see p.284).

Lions Gate Bridge

Horseshoe Bay

Lonsdale Quay Market

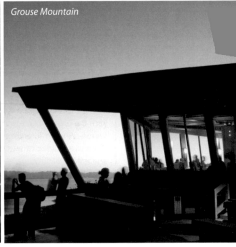
Grouse Mountain

Area **G** p.191
See also Map 2

# Richmond

With 57% of its 185,000 residents foreign born, Richmond (www.richmond.ca) is Canada's most multicultural city. The huge suburb spans a flat-as-a-pancake archipelago made up of the sizeable Lulu and Sea islands, and 15 smaller islets that are held between the north and south arms of the Fraser River.

**Lowdown**
*Canada's most ethnically diverse community and home to its largest fishing fleet.*

Its welcoming nature derives from its history as a transportation hub. Virtually all international visitors to Vancouver pass through the suburb as both Vancouver International Airport (p.42) and US-bound Highway 99 reside here.

Once the heart of Vancouver's agricultural district, Lulu Island has shed its potato fields and transformed its landscape with high rises and condominiums as part of BC's recent immigration boom. Today Richmond is known for shopping along Number 3 Road; religious diversity along Number 5 Road; the fishing town of Steveston; its 90 plus protected parks; and the Vegas-like River Rock Casino.

**The Good**
*Fresh fish and good seafood restaurants in Steveston, cultural and religious diversity along Number 5 Road and the spectacular International Buddhist Temple.*

Running parallel to Highway 99, Richmond's Number 5 Road is home to numerous impressive temples hosting a wide variety of denominations including the monolithic Shia Az-Zahraa Islamic Centre (8580 Number 5 Road, 604 274 7869), complete with its pair of towering minarets, and the equally massive India Cultural Centre of Canada next door (604 274 7479). Open 06:00 to 20:00 daily, it features a large, aromatic open kitchen buzzing with volunteers all weekend long to provide free food to people that need it. Buddhists have two beautiful facilities and denominations to choose from: the lovely Lingyen Mountain Temple (10060 Number 5 Road, 604 271 0009), which is a working monastery for female monks (visits by lay male and female practitioners are welcome), open daily from 08:00 to 22:00 with free sit-down lunches; and the nearby International Buddhist Temple (9160 Steveston Highway, 604 274 2822), which is modelled on Beijing's Forbidden City and widely regarded as the best example of traditional Chinese architecture in Canada. All the temples are open to the public for meditation, and vegetarian meals and tea are available at these last three locales for free or a small donation (call in advance for times and days).

**The Bad**
*Strip malls and MSG.*

Just west of its 'Highway to Heaven', Richmond's Number 3 Road has evolved into a strip mall hell. The ultimate one-stop shop is Richmond Centre, between Granville Avenue and Westminster Avenue (www.richmondcentre.com), which houses some 240 shops and services including the big box Bay and Sears emporiums at either end, along with brand-based stores such as Gap, Guess, and Nike. Down the street, the bountiful food court at Yaohan Mall (3700 Number 3 Road) is a local favourite for cheap and tasty lunches powdered with MSG and flash-fried in oil. With all the sales tax accumulating in their busy tills, it's no surprise that the government is pitching in with increased access – the new Canada Line SkyTrain corridor (see p.47) will connect Number 3 Road with the airport and Downtown Vancouver by 2009. For a more cultural shopping experience, the summertime Richmond Night Market (12631 Vulcan Way, 604 244 8448), which features more than 400 stalls selling all kinds of goods, plus entertainment and activities, is a popular weekend draw between May and October.

**The Must-Dos**
*Walk along the West Dyke Trail; eat fish and chips on the docks of Steveston; meditate in a different temple every day of the week.*

There's another way to get rid of the money burning a hole in your pocket besides shopping. For a taste of Vegas, BC style, head to the River Rock Casino Resort (8811 River Road, 604 247 8900). The city's superlative gaming and entertainment venue features over 1,000 slot machines and western Canada's largest poker room. If you're not a gambler, it also houses nine restaurants, lounges and bars, a 220 room all-suite hotel, a health and fitness centre and a marina, while the 950 seat River Rock Show Theatre has put on shows from the likes of Air Supply, Trailer Park Boys, The B52s, and Diana Ross.

Once you're ready to come out blinking into the light, Minoru Park, which lies north of Granville Avenue between Minoru Boulevard and Gilbert Road, is a wonderful green space to visit. With its various ponds and flower-filled gardens, the park is a favourite breeding ground for ducks and rabbits, not to mention couples of all ages. Its diminutive chapel (6540 Gilbert Road, 604 687 7068) is a hot spot for weddings. The chapel sits opposite the wonderful Richmond Cultural Centre (7700 Minoru Gate, 604 247 8300), a one-stop cultural shop that features public areas for painting, fabric arts, pottery, print-making, dance, and lapidary arts. It also houses the City of Richmond Archives, the Richmond Art Gallery, which focuses on contemporary art, the informative Richmond Museum, and the main branch of Richmond Public Library.

### Steveston

At the western edge of Richmond, 15 minutes south of the airport, the picturesque fishing village of Steveston remains a popular weekend destination. In the 1880s it was the world's largest fishing port and had 50 plus canneries. Today, the docks still house Canada's largest fishing fleet and continue to be the best place around Vancouver to purchase seafood (the fresh-off-the-boat sushi-grade shrimp from the vessels at Fisherman's Wharf are particularly tasty). You can also get the catch of the day cooked on the spot – try Pajo's (corner of Bayview and 3rd Avenue, 604 272 1588) for the ultimate fish and chips experience right on the wharf.

The other key fishing attraction is the Gulf of Georgia Cannery and National Historic Site (12138 4th Avenue, 604 664 9009), which commemorates Steveston's vibrant fishing past and present through a range of exhibitions and artifacts. Entrance is $7. If you want to stretch your legs and see the birds, the West Dyke Trail is a leisurely 5.5km gravel walk or bike ride that stretches north from Steveston to cover the entire western end of Lulu Island, with unobstructed views over the strait.

_Steveston_

_Richmond_

Area **H** p.190
See also Map 3

# Stanley Park

Stanley Park has remained both an icon of and anomaly to the burgeoning metropolis over the years. Just minutes from Downtown, its bounty of natural and man-made attractions have rightfully made it the best and most convenient place to escape the urban madness. Within it lie a fabulous waterfront walkway, a centuries-old forest, dazzling gardens, a pair of beaches and ponds, a world-class aquarium, petting zoo, public pool, tennis courts, pitch and putt golf, kids' play areas, numerous restaurants and wild animals at every turn. The 405 hectares of parkland have been a hotly contested piece of real estate ever since the European arrival in the late 18th century. Interest groups fought to turn it into a railroad depot, a lumber mill, a military base, a cemetery and a place of quarantine, until it was finally dedicated as a park by governor general Lord Stanley in 1889. As recently as 1958, the area known as Hallelujah Bay housed a small population of runaway sailors and First Nations peoples. Today it is all park and can be visited through several means – the paved Seawall promenade around the perimeter, wooded paths through the interior, Park Drive for motorists, and, to a lesser extent, the Causeway which links Downtown and Lions Gate Bridge. Public transport also accesses Stanley Park; the terminal of the 19 Metrotown bus is located at the Stanley Park Loop, at the heart of the park, near the Rose Garden between the pavilion and the miniature railway.

## The Lowdown
*The nation's most beautiful urban green space, right on the doorstep of the city of Vancouver.*

## The Good
*Excellent walking and biking routes around the Seawall and through the interior, great family attractions, and wonderful scenery.*

## The Bad
*Sorry, no evil lurks here, unless you bring your car and try to park.*

## The Must-Dos
*Bike the Seawall; picnic on Stanley Park's Third Beach; check out the marine life at the aquarium.*

### The Seawall

The lion's share of the park's estimated eight million annual visitors stroll at least a segment of the 8.8km long Seawall walkway (you can add another 3.5km by starting on the Downtown waterfront and continuing past English Bay to Burrard Bridge). This paved (and thus wheelchair, bike, scooter, and in-line skate friendly) seaside promenade offers unsurpassed vistas from every twist and turn. Cyclists and skaters ride from Coal Harbour anti-clockwise around the park (pedestrians, on the other hand, can head in either direction). Several shops rent bikes and blades at the corners of Denman and Georgia Streets, including Bayshore Bike Rentals (745 Denman Street, 604 688 2453 – bicycles cost from $5.60 per hour, blades from $5 per hour). The full tour takes roughly two and a half hours to walk, and considerably less to pedal or skate.

Beginning at the north end of Denman Street, expect spectacular views of the Downtown core through the masts of the million-dollar boats docked at the Royal Vancouver Yacht Club. After The Vancouver Rowing Club and Deadman's Island, now the scarcely used HMCS Discovery naval base, lies Hallelujah Point. This is the first stop of most tour bus visits as the small promontory offers ample space for parking and photographing the city. Across Stanley Park Drive are eight intricate totems from around the Pacific north-west, carved from the giant trunks of western red cedar, and a much-snapped icon of the city. Informative interpretive signage explains how these artistic renderings represent either a mythical or real event in the lives of the First Nations peoples. A souvenir stand, bathrooms and information centre are situated just across from the poles.

Inland is Brockton Oval, a manicured rugby pitch, along with a pair of cricket fields which are busy during the summer. Returning to the Seawall is the 9 O'Clock Gun, a working cannon with its sights seemingly set on the Pan Pacific Hotel (no need to worry, the cannon doesn't fire projectiles). Installed in 1894, it blasts a nightly 21:00 sounding for the area's mariners, a necessity for staying in tune with the region's hull-breaking tides.

Heading north-west along the Seawall, you pass Brockton Point Lighthouse, the greening Girl in Wetsuit statue, and the replica of the figurehead of the Empress of Japan, a turn-of-the-century commercial

## Wild Days Are Calling

Stanley Park is a refuge for more than 200 bird species, including double crested cormorants, Canadian geese, wood ducks, greater scaup, mute swans, great blue herons, rufous hummingbirds, and bald eagles. Pileated woodpeckers and saw-whet owls are also found here. Several species of mammals call the park home too. Look for eastern grey and douglas squirrels, coyotes, striped skunks, river otters, mink and raccoons. These are wild animals though, so no feeding. Contact the Stanley Park Ecology Society for more information (604 257 6908, www.stanleyparkecology.ca).

vessel. You'll have to drop by the Maritime Museum (p.232) in Vanier Park if you want to see the real one. At this point, it's worth deviating from the Seawall and climbing the switch-backed Avison Trail under the bridge to Prospect Point, the highest location in the park. The licensed Prospect Point Cafe (604 669 2737) and a souvenir shop crown the hill, from where you'll get great views of the Lions Gate Bridge and the North Shore peaks. Back on the Seawall, a sizeable colony of pelagic cormorants nestles into the cracks and crevices of the basalt outcrop. Continuing south, Siwash Rock, the 15.2m pinnacle located just offshore, is perhaps the most famous icon of the Seawall, conjuring up images of a remote South China Sea island. Around the corner, Third Beach is the park's best place to bake in the sun. A couple of food and beverage concessions also take advantage of the idyllic location. Beyond this, Ferguson Point marks the Seawall's western-most edge. From here you begin veering south-east, with views over English Bay and its iconic trans-Pacific tankers anchored idly off-shore. The towers of UBC to the south-west and Burrard Bridge to the south-east frame Vancouver's West Side (p.215) across the bay. As you continue eastward, the Seawall bustles as you pass the oval-shaped public pool, Second Beach, and the picnic and play area nearing English Bay Beach (see p.238).

## Inside The Park

The Causeway, which leads a line of grumbling, stop-and-go traffic to and from Lions Gate Bridge, roughly splits the park into eastern and western halves. The southern end of the eastern section is populated by man-made attractions, including the Children's Farmyard and Miniature Railway (see p.233). Just across the street you can stroll through the Rose Garden and catch a Theatre Under the Stars presentation from mid-July to mid-August at the outdoor concert shell at Malkin Bowl (www.tuts.ca, tickets start from $28). Also in this area is the world-famous Vancouver Aquarium (p.219), where you can get up close and personal (not to mention a little wet) with beluga whales. Further north is a web of trails stretching for kilometres through the forest, including the pleasant self-guiding interpretative trail around Beaver Lake (which is actually more of a large pond, certainly by Canadian standards). Take in the scene at Stanley's Park Bar & Grill (610 Pipeline Road, 604 602 3088), serving lunch year round, and evening meals in the summer. In the same spot is the classic Stanley Park Pavilion (www.stanleyparkpavilion.com), one of Vancouver's premier wedding reception venues. On the western side of the Causeway, you'll find wooded paths through the park's half-million trees with emotive names such as Lovers Walk and Cathedral Trail. Bring a camera for the park's photographic hotspots: the Hollow Tree, which is actually a giant stump with a hole big enough to ride a motorbike through, and the duck and swan-filled Lost Lagoon. Just west of the wetland are the park's 17 tennis courts (use is free, on a first-come first-serve basis), a noisy and rather smelly heron rookery, the Rhododendron Gardens, an 18 hole par three pitch and putt golf course ($12 green fees, open 07:30 to dusk in summers, and from 09:00 in winter) and several food concessions, most notably the pleasant Fish House restaurant (8901 Stanley Park Drive, 604 681 7275) – a great place to dine on mussels once you've finished flexing muscles.

*Stanley Park*

Area ❶ p.190
See also Map 7

**Lowdown**

*Some of the city's most vibrant shopping, eating and strolling along Robson Street and the Davie Street Gay Village.*

**The Good**

*Terrific views from Coal Harbour and English Bay, excellent restaurants and wonderful window shopping on Robson, Denman and Davie.*

**The Bad**

*Traffic is stop and go and parking is next to impossible on weekends.*

**The Must-Dos**

*Dig in at the Asian restaurants on Robson.*

# West End

Vancouver's West End comprises the entire area of the city seaward of Burrard Street. With its prime location connecting the metropolis, Burrard Inlet, English Bay and Stanley Park, the highlights are many. Here you can window shop the bustling Robson-Denman-Davie commercial corridor, stroll along its quiet suburban streets with beautifully restored turn of the century homes and all the while catch terrific views

*Robson Street*

of the coast. Beyond its commercial attractions, Davie Street and its surroundings are home to the city's renowned Gay Village.

## Robson, Denman & Davie

Those looking for the season's most fashionable finds will feel right at home along the Robson promenade between the city and its intersection with Denman Street. As well as the range of trendy shops, you'll also encounter some of the hippest and busiest restaurants in town on this celebrated strip. Of note are the ever busy Japanese izakayas (tapas bars), in particular Hapa (1479 Robson Street, 604 689 4272) and one of several incarnations of Guu at 1698 (see p.437). If you prefer to do your own cooking and are searching for some fresh ingredients, check out Robson Public Market at 1610 (604 682 2733), open from 09:00 to 21:00 every day.

Turn south on Denman Street and the pace lessens. At the centre of this laidback commercial axis you'll find the West End Community Centre (870 Denman Street, 604 257 8333), part of which is the small but well-frequented Joe Fortes Library. You'll also find numerous worthwhile eating and watering holes – and not just for humans; doggy bags are the speciality rather than the leftovers at Doggy Style Deli at 985 (604 488 0388). For doggy styling of a different sort, check out the Rubber Rainbow Condom Factory (604 683 3423) a little further along the street at 953.

Denman meets the waterfront at either end, and the two beaches are both city highlights. At its northern end it spills on to upscale Coal Harbour, while at its southern terminus it intersects with Beach Avenue. Here it fills with the brunt of the city's beach-going traffic heading for English Bay and Sunset Beach Park. Turn left before you reach the beach and you'll hit Davie Street, home to more shops, restaurants, cafes and bars, catering to (but not exclusively for) the gay crowd. It's chock-a-block with shops and services that cater to every possible whim, from cheap Asian eats at Davie Mongolian BBQ (1161 Davie Street, 604 669 4545), to the Calla Lily florists (1688 Davie Street, 604 633 0503), Little Sister's Book & Art Emporium, the city's leading lesbian and gay bookstore and purveyor of adult and Pride merchandise (1238 Davie Street, 604 669 1753), to gay friendly bars such as The Pumpjack Pub at 1167 (see p.471). The Davie Street vendors and consumers are a proud bunch. Rainbow coloured flags flank the shop front windows and city bus stops are painted pink throughout. Expect lots of leather and lace as many of the locals follow the old adage: 'Don't come out of the closet unless you have something fabulous to wear.' During sunny weekends the streets are at their best as the entire city – gay and straight – converges here to enjoy the park, the beaches, the views, the restaurants and the upbeat vibe of the area.

## Coal Harbour

The dense Stanley Park forest blends into the urban jungle at the northern end of Denman Street. Here you can still avoid the chaos of traffic and concrete by staying on the parallel wheel and walker trails known as the Coal Harbour Seawalk. The sometimes paved pathway skirts the fine line between the Coal Harbour marinas and Vancouver's most sought after high-rises. Like the Seawall that surrounds Stanley Park (see p.211), you can expect plenty of people-watching action, although with many more drinking and dining options, like the stylish Cardero's Restaurant (see p.447). At present the Coal Harbour walk ends at the Floatplane Terminal, from where you can catch a flight with West Coast Airlines or Harbour Air Seaplanes (see p.252) to just about any local destination. The monster-sized Vancouver Convention & Exhibition Centre (VCEC) expansion project next door is set for completion in early 2009, and will triple its former capacity to cover more than four city blocks on the waterfront. With a short dogleg past the construction site you'll reach Canada Place (p.197), and the original VCEC with its iconic sail-like roof. It shares the promontory with the bustling cruise ship terminal which sees some half a million tourists sailing off to Alaska each year. Even if you're not boarding, the pier makes for a nice stroll and offers great views across to the North Shore.

## English Bay

At the other end of Denman Street from Coal Harbour, Sunset Beach Park (p.239) is a finger of shoreline which stretches between Stanley Park and Burrard Bridge. The Seawall promenade continues for another kilometre or so through the area and leads by English Bay Beach, Vancouver's most populated sandy spot and first pick among locals for watching the sunset. It's also the place to catch the Celebration of Light fireworks festival, which happens over two consecutive Wednesday and Saturday nights in the middle of summer (see p.57). The city's giant Inukshuk – an Innuit statue made from piled rocks in the form of a human, which traditionally acts as a compass or way-marker, and now also doubles as the official emblem of the 2010 Winter Olympics – along with several small beaches, an Aids memorial and the Vancouver Aquatic Centre (p.219) can be found near the park's southern terminus.

English Bay

Coal Harbour

# West Side

Area **K** p.190
See also Maps 5, 8 & 9

Located across English Bay from the city, the West Side (not to be confused with the West End, p.213, or West Vancouver, p.206) holds on tightly to its isolation. Made up of the primarily residential municipalities of Kitsilano, Point Grey and the new village around the University of British Columbia (UBC), it spans the entire area from Burrard Bridge west. With its sprawling beachfront, numerous parks and cafe-going culture, this is the place to be for those that want to slow down and style up. Local fashion remains standard for certain members of the community, whether they're 15 or 65: tight-fitting lululemon yoga pants with an oversized purse and exercise mat for the women, designer jeans with muscle-bearing shirts for the men. Sunglasses with attitude are mandatory.

**Lowdown**
*Home to the sun-loving, outdoor crowd along with a burgeoning student population and skyrocketing real estate prices, life's a beach along the West Side's endless shorefront.*

## Kitsilano & Point Grey

Kitsilano, also known as Kits, is the easternmost of the West Side districts, and is named after Khahtsahlanough, a chief of the Squamish Nation. It shares its north-eastern boundary with the expansive Vanier Park (p.244), once the site of the Kitsilano First Nations Reserve. Beginning at the Burrard Bridge, the park (1000 Chestnut Street) stretches over the waterfront and is the cultural hub of the region. It is home to the Vancouver Maritime Museum (p.232), the HR MacMillan Space Centre (p.233), the Vancouver Museum (p.232), and a wonderful totem that is occasionally crowned by eagles. During the summer, the Shakespearian Bard on the Beach festival (p.56) takes over the carnival tents near the bridge.

**The Good**
*West is best. Find great watersports possibilities at Jericho Beach, a fantastic collection of First Nations art at UBC's Museum of Anthropology, and unbeatable road biking throughout. The Arts and Crafts styled homes along with their exuberant gardens are also a real treat to the eye.*

The oasis of cool at Kits Beach lies just west (p.238). Volleyball, tennis, people watching and dog walking are the favourite pastimes in this breezy green space. Swimming is also popular in the oceanside heated outdoor pool and along its beach (lifeguards are on duty from Victoria Day to Labour Day). If you get the munchies, there are plenty of great restaurants and cafes along the nearby Cornwall Street commercial corridor, as well as the park's own upscale concession, Watermark (see p.452). This west-facing restaurant comes complete with an extensive wine list and excellent appetisers, while its fabulous deck makes it the perfect place to take in the scene at any time of day.

The West Side's commercial activity is concentrated on just about every fifth east-to-west-going avenue. Cornwall near the beach comes first, then 4th Avenue, then Broadway (which is actually 9th), and so on. On each of these commercial corridors expect block after block of pleasant window-front restaurants and charming boutiques – each street is worth a wander. As the area is one of the city's more affluent, these eateries and shops tend to do a booming business, despite their high prices.

**The Bad**
*Growth at all costs? UBC's recent surge in development is replacing stands of lush forest with ski chalet-styled condominiums.*

Those not in a rush tend to cruise in their cars or on bikes along Cornwall Street, which winds its way along the waterfront until it connects with Point Grey Road, home of one of the city's most exclusive neighbourhoods. Its splashy residences occupy most of the spectacular waterfront. The seaside drive ends around Alma Street where you can stop in at the quaint Old Hastings Mill Store Museum (p.227), located in the only building to survive the Great Fire of 1886 (it was brought here on a barge in 1930). You can also check out the upscale Royal Vancouver Yacht Club (3811 Point Grey Road, 604 224 1344) nearby. Alma then doglegs back to West 4th Avenue, the southern perimeter of Jericho Beach Park (p.238), one of the area's premier green spaces.

**The Must-Dos**
*Get naked at Wreck Beach; hang out in the quiet oasis at Locarno; go for a swim or sail at Jericho; see the gardens and totems at UBC; bike or walk along the coast.*

## Jericho, Locarno & Spanish Banks

The beachfront made up of Jericho and Locarno beaches, along with Spanish Banks just north-east of UBC's perimeter, is one of the best places to enjoy Vancouver's world-class views. The three beach areas connect via a sandy waterfront path, popular during all seasons with the jogging and cycling crowd.

Jericho was an active 1860s logging camp run by a fellow named Jeremiah Rogers. Its name comes from the vernacular abbreviation of Jerry's Cove. Throughout its 54 hectares are a handful of open playing fields, stands of forest brimming with blackberries in the autumn, and a fantastic life-guarded beach. It is also home to the popular Jericho Sailing Centre Association (p.334). Here you can pick up sailing, windsurfing and kayaking lessons and gear for a small price – one of the best watersports deals in town. Its wharf is a favourite for romantics, local fishermen and crabbers. Check out the club's no-frills Galley Patio & Grill (604 222 1331, www.thegalley.ca) for good pub grub with great views. Just inland are half a dozen public tennis courts, a baseball diamond and a rugby pitch. Across the street, Hostelling International runs its Jericho Beach summertime facility (1515 Discovery Street, 604 224 3208) out of a refurbished 1930s military barracks. While always busy, the park explodes with life every July during the hugely popular Vancouver Folk Music Festival weekend (www.thefestival.bc.ca).

Just west of the sailing club you'll find peaceful Locarno Beach (p.239). Backed by stands of tall evergreens, it offers a tranquil respite to all beach goers. Its designation as a quiet area means no loud music and plenty of calm to make sandcastles, and watch the boats and eagles sail by. Its waterfront is extremely shallow, perfect for small kids and wading. Just west of here, Locarno Beach becomes Spanish Banks (p.239), a popular destination for the beach volleyball crowd. Cyclists can be seen careening down (and huffing and puffing their way up) the relatively steep hillside back towards West 4th Avenue at all hours of the day.

## UBC & Pacific Spirit

The impressive University of British Columbia, the public 18 hole University Golf Club (see p.300), and the Pacific Spirit Regional Park (p.243) take up the end of the peninsula that juts out into the Strait of Georgia. The university, already one of the country's largest and most prestigious, is growing rapidly and is presently in the middle of a massive building phase. Aside from its numerous ski resort-like condominiums, work is also under way on the $50 million UBC Thunderbird Olympic Arena, which will stage some of the ice hockey events for the 2010 games, as well as matches for UBC's sports teams.

While construction is going on everywhere, those with green thumbs still have lots to look at: UBC Botanical Garden and Centre for Plant Research (p.246) will take you on a trip around the world within its ample gardens. Don't miss the Nitobe Memorial Garden (p.246), considered to be one of the top five traditional gardens outside Japan.

The Rose Garden is a favourite for brides and is located just outside the Chan Centre for the Performing Arts (6265 Crescent Road, 604 822 9197), one of the city's premier arts venues. Perhaps the most outstanding of UBC's attractions is the world famous Museum of Anthropology (p.231) with its spectacular collection of Native American totems and art – it's a not-to-be missed highlight of any campus tour, or even Vancouver visit.

The 763 hectare Pacific Spirit Regional Park (p.243) rings the campus and offers a tremendous array of 33 trails to hike, plus more beaches through the heavily forested coastline. And don't worry if you forget your shorts or bikini – at the nearly 6.5km stretch of Wreck Beach (p.240) clothing is optional – most wear nothing more than their birthday suits. The sandiest part can be found at the base of Trail 6's long wooden staircase, under clouds of marijuana smoke.

### Time & Space

Head to the HR MacMillan Space Centre Observatory (p.233) on Friday and Saturday nights all year round as volunteers from the Astronomic Society let you get up close to the skies with their heavy-duty portable telescopes. Access is free. Showings start from darkness to as late as 23:00, weather permitting. Call in advance (604 738 7827), especially when cloudy.

# Vancouver Areas

Chan Centre

Point Grey

Museum of Anthropology

HR MacMillan Space Centre

Nitobe Garden

## Attractions

At just over 120 years of age, the incorporated city of Vancouver is a babe in the woods, and has often been maligned by Montrealers and Torontonians as a city without culture. While there may be a lack of giant museums or galleries with blockbuster shows, no mystical ancient ruins and few historical heroes, Vancouver has something else to give. The varied ethnic and cultural composition has made creating a homogeneous society virtually impossible, and, consensus has it among Vancouverites, undesirable. Indeed the beauty and dynamism of the city lies in its diversity. It is a fermenting work in progress, continuously drawing vitality from a host of ideas and attitudes, and constantly changing and reinventing itself. The results appear in some rather unique if modest examples of architecture, culture and other artistic endeavours. These gems reside in the cracks of this modern city, and require a modicum of effort to discover.

## Amusement Centres

With so many outdoor opportunities such as mountain biking, skiing, snowboarding, canoeing, kayaking and sailing so close at hand, Vancouver doesn't have as many indoor amusement centres as cities in less spectacular surroundings. There are, however, an interesting few to choose from, and they can be a welcome relief for those who don't want to risk getting wet when the winter rains hit. From amusement parks to paintball and go-karting, there is an adrenaline rush for every age.

**670 Industrial Av**
*Main*
*Map 11 D1* **1**

### Cliffhanger Indoor Rock Climbing Centre
*604 874 2400* | *www.cliffhangerclimbing.com*
At 15,000 square feet, and with beginner to advanced level climbs, this facility is touted as the best in Canada. Features include 53 top ropes, lead climbing, crack climbing and a separate level with boulder climbing. Once you scale the 40 foot walls, you're rewarded with views north of the local mountains. The centre opens weekdays from 12:00 to 22:30 (closing an hour earlier on Fridays), and offers summer camps and birthday parties. This is a healthy and challenging way to spend a couple of hours on a cold, rainy winter's day. Introductory courses cover basic knots, belaying and climbing techniques. Rates range from $18 for a day pass to $549 annually.

**7391 Elmbridge Way**
*Richmond*
*Map 2 B3*

### Planet Lazer
*604 448 9999* | *www.planetlazer.net*
This is tag with a laser gun (a gentle alternative to paint ball) in a three-level high-tech arena filled with ramps, catwalks, a maze, graphics, theatrical smoke, freaky lighting and futuristic music. Computers track movements and score your hits in this surreal environment. For groups of up to 40, this facility is often used by corporations for team building, and by friends and acquaintances for good clean fun. Prices range from a minimum $8 per individual per game (approximately 25 minutes) to assorted discounted group rates that include pizza and soft drinks. Open daily from 10:30 to 22:30, this is an unusual rainy day alternative for all ages. Group reservations required.

**Hastings &**
**Renfrew St**
*Hastings East*
*Map 4 C4* **3**

### Playland
*604 253 2311* | *www.pne.bc.ca/playland*
With extreme rides, a traditional roller coaster and Ferris wheel, a maze, haunted house, climbing wall, mid-way games, petting zoo and a vast assortment of greasy fast food, Playland has everything you would expect from a large scale amusement park. It's no Disneyland, but with about 30 rides ranging from terrifying to soothing, it's good for a half to a full day of fun for the young and the young at heart. The park is open from late April to late September with varying days and hours of operation, depending on the month and weather. Day passes are a maximum of $30, with lower rates depending on age and ride choices.

**6631 Sidaway Rd**
*Richmond*
*Map 2 B3*

## Richmond Go-Kart Track

*604 278 6184* | *www.richmondgokarts.com*

For the Schumacher in all of us, this half-mile track complete with straights, S-turns and a hairpin, is open from March through until October, seven days a week, noon to dusk. Children must be a minimum of 10 years old and at least 148cm tall. Young ones under 10 can ride with an adult in a two-seater. The site also has a concession stand, picnic area and video game arcade. Located near the airport in Richmond, rates are $10 for a 10 minute ride.

**100B Lower**
**Capilano Rd**
*North Vancouver*
*Map 3 F2* **5**

## Vancouver Paintball

*778 896 7529* | *www.nspaintball.ca*

If an adrenaline rush is in order, this paintball facility delivers. Located in a forested field and equipped with nets, stacks of tyres and log barriers to hide behind, the object is to capture your opponents' flag without getting hit. Players are equipped with air guns that fire paint pellets, protective goggles or masks and overalls when available. Located 15 minutes from Downtown in the suburb of North Vancouver, this is a popular activity for birthday parties and corporate events. Participants aged 17 and up must sign a waiver; 12 year olds must have their waiver signed by a parent or guardian. It costs $10 for 100 rounds, with discounted rates for larger amounts. Rain or shine, games start every 10 minutes, with seasonal hours.

## Aquariums & Marine Centres

**845 Avison Way**
*Stanley Park*
*Map 3 F3* **6**

## Vancouver Aquarium

*604 659 3474* | *www.vanaqua.org*

One of Vancouver's prime attractions located in its best park, this facility is divided into climatic and geographic zones, from the tropics to the poles, with each environment inhabited by the corresponding sea life. Pavilions also contain native plants and birds, and in the Amazon rainforest exhibit, an occasional cloudburst keeps the humidity at an appropriate level. This is a very child friendly aquarium with lots to excite and inspire children such as shark feedings, scary insects, and beluga whale and dolphin shows.

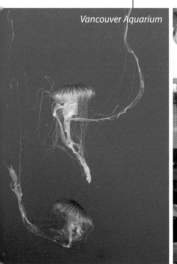

*Vancouver Aquarium*

There are also tidal pools where the little ones can handle slimy creatures. Among the 60,000 inhabitants are seals, sea lions, otters, sharks, alligators, snakes, barracudas and, of course, salmon. In recent years, more attention is being paid to local species and ecosystems. A gift shop provides books and souvenirs from the kitsch to the scholarly. From the park entrance, follow the road for a few hundred metres and look for a sign indicating a left turn to the aquarium parking lot. Admission is $20 for adults and $12 for children aged 4 to 12.

## Archaeological Sites

First Nations people had lived on the Pacific coast for as long as 10,000 years when Captain Cook visited what is now Vancouver in 1791. With the subsequent colonisation and settlement, many of the former native village sites were abandoned, taken, destroyed and eventually covered with asphalt and concrete. Their houses, clothes, tools and utensils were mostly fashioned from wood and other degradable material, and this combined with exposure to a wet climate caused them to decompose in a relatively short time. In many cases all that remained were middens, or refuse piles of bones, shells, weapons, tools and other artefacts that indicated human habitation, scattered throughout the Vancouver area. When road construction by European settlers began, the tonnes of material found in middens were even used to pave roads. Since little evidence of native history remains in Vancouver, a trip to the Museum of Anthropology (p.231) at UBC provides the best testimony to a once-thriving civilisation.

*1410 West 72nd*
*Av & Cartier St*
*Marpole*
*Map 5 F4* **7**

## Marpole Midden

Marpole Midden in south Vancouver was discovered in 1889 during the road extension of Granville Street. Archaeologists believe that the site dates back to as early as 3500BC. Among the artefacts were two remarkable finds. The first was a two metre high pyramid shaped rock cairn topped with a 20kg stone statue which contained human bone fragments packed with orange sand. Its square base was aligned perfectly with the points of the compass. The second was a male skeleton encased in sheets of beaten copper, with a copper crown on its head. The remains of two women with shattered skulls were part of this elaborate grave, but today all that remains is a plaque and rock cairn in Marpole Park to remind us of what was once one of the largest villages in North America.

## Art Galleries

Other options **Art & Craft Supplies** p.366, **Art** p.365

Vancouver only discovered modern art after the second world war and was until then considered a backwater by European standards. An anomaly named Emily Carr and her few disciples and admirers helped to drag the city kicking and screaming into the 20th century. These followers taught the next generation, and since the 1960s, Vancouver has caught up in many ways with major art centres. It now boasts some international superstars of its own, mostly in the conceptual and photo-text realm. The approximately 100 galleries in the city

### Eastside Culture Crawl

Hundreds of East Vancouver studios' doors open to the public every late November for three days in this growing visual arts festival, known as The Crawl. Artists and artisans exhibit, selling everything from trinkets, crafts and jewellery to colossal oil paintings and cast iron sculptures – with prices to match. The Crawl originated with artists who either couldn't or didn't want to show in the more traditional gallery settings. There really is something for everyone and every budget, and the entire extravaganza attracts thousands. Check out www.eastsideculturecrawl.com or call 604 817 9130 for further information.

and the dozens in the suburbs generally fall into four categories: public, private, alternative and indigenous. The public galleries function in three ways: to stretch the public's perception of what art can be, to placate the sceptical with grand shows of blue chip modernists from Europe and the US, and to introduce the public to old and new trends in native art. The private galleries range from the blatantly commercial to the more edgy, and the alternative galleries feature work that is either too avant garde, subversive, offensive, ill-conceived or poorly executed to be shown at any of the mainstream galleries.

The bulk of the high-end commercial galleries lies on what locals call Gallery Row, on Granville Street between 6th and 16th Avenues. A few notable alternative galleries where your preconceptions of art may be stretched are Access Artist Run Centre (206 Carrall Street, 604 689 2907), Artspeak (233 Carrall Street, 604 688 0051), Grunt Gallery (116-350 East 2nd Avenue, 604 875 9516) and Or Gallery (103-480 Smithe Street, 604 683 7395). *Preview* (www.preview-art.com), the most comprehensive art listings magazine in the province, is available free in most galleries.

**108-808 Nelson St**
*Downtown*
*Map 7 D4* 8

## Art Beatus Vancouver
*604 688 2633* | *www.artbeatus.com*
A cultural island in an otherwise residential, commercial and office district, Art Beatus was the first and still the most important gallery of its kind in Vancouver. The gallery showcases contemporary Chinese, Chinese-Canadian, and Chinese expat painters, sculptors, photographers, printmakers and mixed media artists generally working in modernist or post-modernist styles, albeit with a Chinese sensibility. An important stop on a gallery tour in order to appreciate the profound impact Chinese culture has had on Vancouver and the profound effect the west has had on the Chinese. Admission is free and the gallery opens Monday to Friday from 10:00 to 18:00. The owners run two additional galleries in Hong Kong.

**3045 Granville St**
*Fairview*
*Map 5 F1* 9

## Bau-Xi Gallery
*604 733 7011* | *www.bau-xi.com*
One of the old guard in Vancouver, this gallery was instrumental in developing the reputations of such local legends as Jack Shadbolt, Gordon Smith and Gathie Falk. This came at a time when Vancouver had few places for these trailblazers to show their work – although their abstract west coast themes seem tame by today's standards. This large gallery focuses on the old guard, mid-career and emerging Canadian painters and printmakers, and often runs two shows simultaneously, one downstairs and a smaller one upstairs. Admission is free, and the gallery opens Monday to Saturday from 10:00 to 17:30 and Sunday from 11:00 to 17:30.

**6344 Deer Lake Av**
*Burnaby*
*Map 6 E2* 10

## Burnaby Art Gallery
*604 205 7332* | *www.burnabyartgallery.ca*
This large 19th century mansion houses a permanent collection of paintings, prints and sculptures, as well as touring national and international exhibits. Its mandate is typical of public suburban galleries, the progressive alternating with the more traditional, but its location in a lovely park on Deer Lake make it a must-visit destination. It's also adjacent to another mansion-cum-fine-dining restaurant, Hart House (p.228), the Burnaby Village Museum (p.230), and the Shadbolt Centre for the Arts (p.192). Most Vancouverites don't make the effort, but it's well worth a 40 minute bus ride from Downtown, especially in the summer. Take the Expo Line SkyTrain from any Downtown station to Metrotown and transfer to bus 144 SFU. The gallery opens Tuesday to Friday 10:00 to 16:30, and 12:00 to 17:00 at weekends. Admission is by donation.

## Buschlen Mowatt Gallery

*1445 West Georgia St*
*Downtown*
*Map 7 C2* **11**

*604 682 1234* | *www.buschlenmowatt.ca*

Robert Indiana's renowned 1960s 'Love' sculpture marks the entrance to this spacious and airy Downtown gallery, with its views of Stanley Park and the North Shore mountains. The gallery opens from 10:00 to 18:00 Monday to Friday and 12:00 to 17:00 on Sundays, and tends to show big name Canadian and international artists whose paintings, prints and sculptures command prices up to the hundreds of thousands of dollars. The museum-calibre shows range from established American modernists such as Sam Francis, Helen Frankenthaler, Jules Olitski and Frank Stella to significant emerging talent. The owner has a sister gallery in Palm Springs, California. Free admission.

## Catriona Jeffries Gallery

*274 East 1st Av*
*Main*
*Map 11 C1* **12**

*604 736 1554* | *www.catrionajeffries.com*

One of the more avant-garde commercial galleries in the city, Catriona's post-modern taste was something of an anomaly on the South Granville Strip's uptown gallery row. She then moved from a modest sized site to an enormous warehouse-type location in the grittier and perhaps more appropriate Main Street area. Her artists tend to be conceptual in nature, and exhibitions are often photo based or feature installations. This is an interesting find that attempts to challenge those seeking more traditional paintings and sculptures. Open Tuesday to Saturday, 11:00 to 17:00, with free admission.

## Charles H Scott Gallery

*1399 Johnston St*
*Granville Island*
*Map 9 C2* **13**

*604 844 3809* | *http://chscott.eciad.ca*

Located in the Emily Carr University of Art and Design, this gallery exhibits works produced by students, alumni, faculty and nationally and internationally renowned artists, in all media, ranging from solo shows to thematic group exhibitions. The shows reflect the kinds of projects and activities students are engaged in during their enrolment at the institute. The gallery's mandate is to educate, foster in-depth analysis and critical awareness, and stimulate dialogue surrounding the creation of art and the role and function of artists in contemporary society. Admission is free, open Monday to Friday from 12:00 to 17:00, Saturday and Sunday 10:00 to 17:00, and there is also an adjacent store with a comprehensive selection of art related books.

## Contemporary Art Gallery

*555 Nelson St*
*Downtown*
*Map 7 E4* **14**

*604 681 2700* | *www.contemporaryartgallery.ca*

In spacious modern premises with large glass windows and high ceilings, this Downtown public gallery's mandate is to show both established and emerging local, national and international artists. It tends to be more progressive than the Vancouver Art Gallery, showing artists who work in less traditional media and who push people's perceptions of art. Don't expect still lifes or landscapes here, except in perhaps an ironic context. Here you can see everything from video, to laser, to bags of sand. If you don't get it, come to its regular artist and curator talks. Admission is by donation, and the gallery is open Wednesday to Sunday from 12:00 until 18:00.

## Douglas Reynolds Gallery

*2335 Granville St*
*Fairview*
*Map 9 B4* **15**

*604 731 9292* | *www.douglasreynoldsgallery.com*

An airy and bright space with lovely wooden accents, this gallery is noted for presenting quality contemporary and historic Pacific north-west coast native art to gallery goers on the South Granville Strip. Exhibits include exquisite prints, carvings, totems and jewellery by such notables as Bill Reid, whose giant *Spirit of Haida Gwai* sits in front of the Canadian Embassy in Washington DC. Other notables include Robert Davidson and

Beau Dick. It is open throughout the week, from 10:00 to 18:00 Monday to Saturday and 12:00 to 17:00 on Sunday, with free admission. This gallery is a must see for anyone interested in what the best native artists are producing in the 21st century.

**1558 West 6th Av**
*Fairview*
*Map 9 B3* **16**

## Douglas Udell Gallery

***604 736 8900*** | *www.douglasudellgallery.com*

Small, with a garage-like entrance and half a block from gallery row on Granville Street, this space is one of the top commercial galleries in Vancouver. The gallery boasts museum-quality shows by well-known Canadian and international painters, photographers, sculptors, and printmakers. In addition to his Vancouver location, the owner has galleries in Edmonton and Calgary, which explains the large number of important prairie artists on show. Also exhibited are historical works by the likes of Picasso, Matisse and Riopelle. The gallery opens Tuesday to Saturday, 10:00 to 18:00, with free admission.

**2321 Granville St**
*Fairview*
*Map 9 B4* **17**

## Equinox Gallery

***604 736 2405*** | *www.equinoxgallery.com*

This is the premier gallery in Vancouver for nationally and internationally renowned Canadian painters, printmakers, photographers and sculptors. Although not exceptionally controversial or edgy, some of the artists are progressive in the conception and execution of their works, which range from abstract expressionism to high realism. The high-ceiling on the ground floor gallery is well suited for large works and smaller works and prints can be viewed in the upstairs gallery. The rule of thumb here is quality. Open 10:00 to 17:00, Tuesday to Saturday. Free admission.

**206 Cambie St**
*Gastown*
*Map 10 A1* **18**

## Inuit Gallery

***604 688 7323*** | *www.inuit.com*

Occupying a historic brick building in Gastown, the gallery exhibits original Inuit sculpture and prints, as well as north-west coast native masks, totem poles, panels, bentwood boxes, rattles, paddles, drums, an assortment of gold and silver jewellery, and custom designed furniture. The eclectic mix of works feature commercial trinkets alongside finely crafted art. The gallery opens Monday to Saturday from 10:00 to 18:00 and 10:00 to 17:00 on Sundays (opening an hour later during the winter). It is often overlooked by locals due to its touristy Gastown location, but it's a good place to start for those interested in art produced in northern Canada. Admission is free.

**308 Water St**
*Gastown*
*Map 10 A1* **19**

## Marion Scott Gallery

***604 685 1934*** | *www.marionscottgallery.com*

Founded in 1975 by the late Marion Scott, whose vision is carried on by her daughter, this is a serious gallery promoting the works of contemporary and historical artists from Canada's north, from both home and abroad. The gallery curates two major exhibitions a year, and in the months between these, it maintains a display of high quality Inuit prints, sculpture, drawings and wall hangings.

### Bill Reid

Half Haida Indian and half Scot, Bill Reid (1920-1998) is synonymous with the rebirth of silver and gold smithing and wood carving among the north-west coast native peoples. Schooled in Haida carving techniques and European art traditions, Reid drew from both in an attempt to bridge the gap. Maligned by purists and adored by iconoclasts, his place in west coast art is still being argued and evaluated. His giant, stylized sculptures of humans and animals can be seen in Vancouver International Airport, the Museum of Anthropology at UBC (p.231), in front of the Vancouver Aquarium in Stanley Park (p.244), and in numerous public and private spaces, galleries and museums worldwide.

The gallery also handles some southern Canadian artists, and publishes high quality books and catalogues. Its new location is directly across from the Steam Clock in Gastown. Open Monday to Friday from 10:00 to 18:00, Saturday 10:30 to 17:30 and Sunday 11:00 to 17:00, with free admission.

*2339 Granville St*
*Fairview*
*Map 9 B4* **20**

## Monte Clark Gallery

*604 730 5000* | *www.monteclarkgallery.com*

This small gallery has built its reputation on showing serious work by post-modern Canadian and American photographers and painters whose themes range from the sublimely beautiful to the less than attractive side of the city: urban decay and renewal. Clark has attracted a who's who of contemporary local and international artists, including the likes of Roy Arden and Douglas Coupland. Shows are generally small, up to 10 works, but the quality is often exceptional, and Mr Clark has a loyal local and foreign clientele. He also has a gallery in Toronto. Open Tuesday to Saturday, 10:00 to 18:00, admission is free.

*2235 Granville St*
*Fairview*
*Map 9 B3* **21**

## Petley Jones Gallery

*604 732 5353* | *www.petleyjones.com*

With stairs leading down from street level, this small gem could easily be missed. Once inside though, it's one of the less pretentious galleries in the city and looks more like a sunken living room with a den – homely and inviting. The owner, an artist, has generally specialised in 19th and 20th century Canadian, American and European paintings, sculptures and prints. In recent years he has added more local and national contemporary work, the sum of which is a feeling of eclecticism. His policy ranges from abstract expressionism to traditional nautical paintings, and if you want it and he doesn't have it, he will try his best to get it. There is a framing shop attached which also restores historical pieces. Admission is free, open Monday to Saturday 10:00 to 18:00.

*750 Hornby St*
*Downtown*
*Map 7 E3* **22**

## Vancouver Art Gallery

*604 662 4719* | *www.vanartgallery.bc.ca*

A former courthouse, this neoclassical 1911 brick and stone building with a revamped interior exhibits everything from the ancient to the avant garde. The exhibitions include major thematic shows, presentations of solo artists and smaller, more focused shows. The main floor is reserved for touring shows with mass appeal that will bring in the dollars, the second floor is often quirky and progressive, and the third and fourth floors generally exhibit local heroes and their Canadian contemporaries. There is also a lovely patio cafe, art rental, a library and a variety of education and outreach programmes. This is a great place to go for a sense of the traditions and evolution of art in Vancouver. It is open daily 10:00 to 17:00, and until 21:00 on Tuesdays and Thursday. Admission is $16 for adults, $7 for children, and by donation on Tuesday nights from 17:30 to 21:00.

*Vancouver Art Gallery*

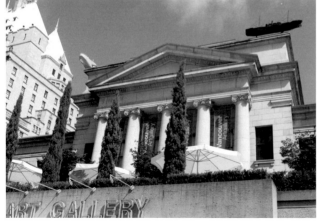

# Heritage Sites

With the arrival of the first Europeans on the west coast of Canada came an upheaval that would have a lasting effect on the country's indigenous traditions and heritage. The government, then business and pioneers, focused on monetary advancements, taking full advantage of the land, often to the detriment of native tribes in the area. First Nations people with their finely crafted, colourful longhouses, canoes and totems, often inhabited prime beachfront real estate, and were soon moved, assimilated, or killed by European diseases. As the white settlements grew, the more the legacy of the native people was buried – with each successive generation tearing down and rebuilding communities and neighbourhoods. Remnants of this eagerness for rejuvenation remain today; there is a somewhat temporary feel to the city, the lifespan of buildings being measured in decades. The results of this raze and rebuild aspect to Vancouver is that so few heritage sites or buildings have survived. Unfortunately museums do not have the much-needed support or money to do the history of this vital city justice. In many cases the only surviving evidence of the country's past is in the form of journals, illustrations and photographs, or the commemorative plaques on buildings. In spite of this, a few gems have survived and, in order to get a real sense of how the city looked and felt in past years, they should be included on an informal walking tour, or in some cases, a short excursion to a suburb.

## Fort Langley National Historic Site

*23433 Mavis Av*
*Langley*

**604 513 4777** | *www.pc.gc.ca*

Built in 1827, about 48 kilometres up the Fraser River from Vancouver, the Hudson's Bay Company fur trading post provided protection for its employees and their families. It also established a British presence in territories that were coveted by rival Americans and Russians. The original wooden fort was dismantled and moved in 1839 and subsequently burnt down. It was then rebuilt in 1840, eventually falling into disuse by 1886. In 1923 it was declared a historic site of national importance but it took until the 50s before it was restored. The fort now serves as a glimpse of south-western BC's pioneer past. Admission is $7 for adults and $3.50 for youths, with group and family discounts available. The fort is open from 10:00 to 17:00 in winter, and 09:00 to 18:00 in the summer. Visiting the neighbouring town of Fort Langley, with its cafes and funky arts and craft shops, makes this an interesting day trip.

## Gaolers Mews

*Off Carrall St*
*Behind 2 Water St*
*Gastown*
*Map 10 B1* 24

Off Carrall Street and behind the Byrnes Block building (2 Water Street) is a cobblestone alley which was the site of Vancouver's first jail. The 1850s log cabin is long gone but the name survives. The story goes that Gastown's first chief of police, Jonathan Miller, chained prisoners by the ankle and they were then guarded by a one-armed drunkard named John Clough. The narrow back street has almost a storybook look to it. It is narrow, adorned with Victorian signage, and leads to another quaint passage with the unfortunate name Blood Alley – apparently so called because of the drunken brawls that occurred here after the bars closed.

## Gastown Steam Clock

*Cnr Water &*
*Cambie St*
*Gastown*
*Map 10 A1* 25

Hordes of summer tourists gather round this quirky clock located in Gastown, near the corner of Water Street and Cambie Street, in anticipation of a blast from its steam whistle. Based on an 1875 British design, the clock was built by horologist Raymond Saunders, whose Gastown Steam Clock Company sits opposite the clock. Powered by an underground system of pipes that provide steam to some of the nearby buildings, it was until recent years the only steam clock in the world. Ironically, the clock hands were powered by electricity for years because of mechanical problems, but local money has restored it to its former glory. This is no Big Ben, but it is an unusual landmark and the archetypal Gastown photo opportunity.

**Vanier Park**
*Kitsilano*
*Map 7 A4* **26**

## Heritage Harbour

Surrounded by and beholden to the sea for its very existence, it's only fitting that the city should have a harbour where wooden boats and ships are moored. This dock, located on Kits Point near Vancouver Maritime Museum, framed by spectacular views of the sea and mountains, is small and unassuming but worth a stroll to check out the boats that are tied up. Permanent residents include Black Duck, an RCAF rescue vessel, and in the summer months the Viking longboat replica Munin and a working steam tug called Master. An Australian-built replica of the HMS Bounty and other tall ships are occasionally sighted in the area as well. Not a trip unto itself, but an interesting part of a Kitsilano Beach stroll.

*Gastown Steam Clock*

**Water & Carrall St**
*Gastown*
*Map 10 B1* **27**

## Maple Tree Square

The decision to change the name of a fledgling mill town from Granville to Vancouver was made in 1886 under a maple tree that once grew on this site. 'Gassy' Jack Deighton, so named for his propensity to talk a lot about nothing, was the area's first white citizen, first bar owner and self-appointed mayor, and is deified here in the form of a statue. The square is lined with Victorian buildings, each with restaurants, cafes, and gift shops occupying the ground floors. The restaurants and cafes have outdoor seating in the warmer months, and it's a fine place to sit and sip a beverage while the world walks and drives by. If you're lucky, you'll catch a free outdoor concert in the summer. It's on the eastern edge of Gastown, where Alexander, Powell, Carrall and Water Streets converge. The neighbourhood quickly deteriorates a block further east, so visitors should be careful walking alone at night.

**355 Burrard St**
*Downtown*
*Map 7 F2* **28**

## Marine Building

Inspired by New York's Chrysler Building and opened in 1930, this classic 25 storey art deco structure was one of the first modern skyscrapers in Vancouver and the tallest building in the British Commonwealth until 1939. The building materials include brick, concrete, marble, copper, hardwood, brass and tile, and the interior and exterior walls are adorned with a variety of bas-relief marine motifs, from scallops and seaweed to depictions of trains and Captain Vancouver's ship. Inside, the main lobby employs a ship's prow as lighting. The building fell into disrepair until restorations, beginning in the 1980s, brought it to its current state of splendour. Originally on the waterfront, it has since 'moved' inland due to land reclamation projects. As an office tower, the splendid lobby with its temple-like atmosphere and brass elevators can be entered by the public during business hours, and it's included in one of the summertime architectural walking tours offered by the Architectural Institute of British Columbia (604 683 8588).

**1575 Alma St**
*Kitsilano*
*Map 5 D1* **29**

## Old Hastings Mill Store Museum
*604 734 1212*

Built in 1867 at the foot of Dunlevy Street in the Downtown area, the structure is thought to be the oldest intact building in Vancouver. It once served as a store for Hastings Mill employees, supplying them with food, utensils, tools and clothing, and was the economic centre of the growing logging towns of Granville and Hastings. The only building to survive the great fire of 1886, it served as a hospital and morgue in the tragic aftermath. The store finally closed in the 1920s, and was towed by barge in 1930 to the foot of Alma Street, where it now serves as a museum in the summer months. Inside you will find an array of artefacts from the early days of Vancouver, including children's toys, burnt and twisted knifes, forks and spoons found after the 1886 fire, a Hansom cab, native artifacts, and relics of the SS Beaver, the first steam ship on the Pacific coast. In the winter the store opens Saturday and Sunday only, from 13:00 to 16:00, during the summer it opens Tuesday to Sunday, 11:00 to 16:00. Admission is by donation.

**8 West Pender St**
*Chinatown*
*Map 10 B2* **30**

## Sam Kee Building

Constructed in 1913 as a result of a land dispute between the owner, his neighbour and the city, this Chinatown landmark, 1.5 metres at the base and 1.8 metres at the second floor level, is entered in the *Guinness Book of Records* as the narrowest commercial building in the world, although the claim is perennially in dispute due to the structure's irregular dimensions. Part of the basement extends under the pavement and originally housed public baths and shops, while the ground floor and second floor were used for retail and living quarters. Local lore has it that a tunnel beneath the building was used as an escape route from raids on opium dens situated on neighbouring Shanghai Alley, but the tunnel has never been found. The building is also fronted by the only remaining glass pavement in Chinatown, built to allow sunlight into the shops below. Renovation of the building was completed in 1986, and today it serves as an insurance office, with not much to see inside.

*Marine Building*

**601 West Cordova St**
*Gastown*
*Map 7 F3* **31**

## Waterfront Station

This 1915 neoclassical station was originally the western terminus of the Canadian Pacific Railway's transcontinental line, but now serves as the terminus for both the commuter SkyTrain, which links the eastern suburbs with Downtown, and passenger ferry SeaBus, which sails to and from North Vancouver's Lonsdale Quay. The interior is airy and ornate, with a domed ceiling and romantic scenes of the Canadian Rockies adorning the walls. At eye level however, it's all ticket machines and retail shops, one of which has the often maligned distinction of being Vancouver's first Starbucks. It's definitely worth a visit en route to Gastown.

# Historic Houses

Vancouver's lost lot of late 19th and early 20th century Queen Ann, Edwardian and Victorian homes is a classic case of a city that didn't know what it had until it was gone. Most of the city's treasures were bulldozed in the 1950s, 60s and 70s, until hippies and heritage societies eventually put enough pressure on the city to rethink its development and zoning strategies. The result is a few pockets and solitary examples of older homes lying among encroaching newer developments. There are still beautiful older homes in neighbourhoods such as Shaughnessy, Kerrisdale, Kitsilano and in the adjacent municipality of New Westminster, but in the Downtown core they have all but disappeared. Vancouver still has some of the laxest heritage laws in the western world, and developers and speculators are tearing down the world-class modernist buildings of the 1940s and 50s, which will be sorely missed in the years to come.

Nevertheless, a few fine examples have survived adding charm to what some call an architecturally sterile city. Some headway is being made though, and there is increasingly more restoration going on in the city in accordance with stricter zoning and building laws and regulations.

**Address On Request** ◀ ## Arthur Erickson House

*604 738 4195 | www.ericksongarden.org*

More garden than house, this humble but elegant abode is the home of the renowned Canadian architect Arthur Erickson, who razed the original structure, converted the garage into a cottage, and designed and built a Japanese style garden where the original home once stood. The garden centres around a pond with a marble moon viewing platform and is surrounded by cultivated rhododendrons and bamboos. Erickson is more famous as the designer of the Museum of Anthropology, Simon Fraser University, Robson Square, the courthouse, the Vancouver Art Gallery and numerous buildings and urban renewal projects all over the world. The garden is now managed by the Arthur Erickson House and Garden Foundation, through which visits should be booked. The foundation can arrange appropriate visiting times and information on the location of the house so as not to invade the architect's privacy. Guided tours are $10 per person, and private viewings for groups of four or more can be made by appointment.

**6664 Deer Lake Av** ◀
*Burnaby*
*Map 6 E2* 33 ## Hart House Restaurant

*604 298 4278 | www.harthouserestaurant.com*

Built in 1910 by New Westminster businessman Frederick Hart, this spectacular Tudor manor is characterised by a flat-roofed central square tower, steep gables and leaded glass windows. The property changed hands a number of times until the city of Burnaby purchased it in 1979. For eight years it was occasionally used as a film set, until it was sold again to private investors, restored, and opened as a fine yet casual restaurant in 1988. Currently, lunches and dinners run between $15 and $30. Additional to the restaurant's architecture and fine dining, the surrounding estate is now a lakeside oasis complete with rose gardens, walking trails, an art gallery and an arts centre. The restaurant opens throughout the week, except Monday. Lunch is 11:30 to 14:30 and dinner from 17:30 during the week. There is a brunch on Sunday that runs from 11:00 to 14:00.

**302 Royal Av** ◀
*New Westminster*
*Map 2 C3* ## Irving House

*560 427 4640 | www.nwpr.bc.ca*

Built in 1865 by Scottish sea captain William Irving, this gothic revival style home was reported to have been the handsomest of its day in the province. Irving himself pioneered the steamboat trade industry on the lower Fraser River in the late 19th century, and it was within a few hundred metres of the river that he built his home. The interior of the house features the original wallpaper, as well as period furniture and mementoes of the Irving pioneer family. Designated a heritage home in 1981, it now serves as a museum and archive for the city of New Westminster. Hours are seasonal: May to September, Wednesday to Sunday 12:00 to 17:00; October to April, Wednesday to Sunday 12:00 to 16:00. Admission is by donation.

**1169 Pendrell St** ◀
*West End*
*Map 7 C4* **35**

## Mole Hill
*604 687 1145* | *www.mole-hill.ca*

Near the corner of Comox and Bute streets is an enclave of 11 Edwardian and Victorian houses that was saved from the wrecking ball due to the efforts of locals insistent on preserving some of Vancouver's architectural past. In the 1970s the houses were bought by the city, which planned to rent them out temporarily before knocking them down to make way for a park. With demolition looming, residents formed a preservation society and convinced the city that the dilapidated homes were worth saving. They have since been restored and are representative of Vancouver in the 1920s. Combined with the community food gardens in the lane, they provide welcome housing and respite from the surrounding concrete and glass. Entry is not permitted, but a walk around the block is a walk back in time.

**1415 Barclay St** ◀
*West End*
*Map 7 C2* **36**

## Roedde House Museum
*604 684 7040* | *www.roeddehouse.org*

Built in 1893 for local bookbinder Gustav Roedde, this house was restored for use as a museum to its period finery inside and out. One of the surviving nine turn-of-the-century homes occupying a block in Vancouver's high-density West End, the house and its neighbours were saved from the bulldozer and designated it a heritage building. The Queen Anne revival style home, with its large porches and bay windows, was designed by Francis Rattenbury, who also left his mark in Victoria in the form of the parliament buildings and the Empress Hotel. Admission from Tuesday to Friday is $5.00, and Sunday is $6.00, which includes tea and cookies.

## Museums

In comparison with other cities around the world, Vancouver's offering to museum enthusiasts is not on a grand scale. Many Vancouverites seem more enthused by skiing, rollerblading, restaurants, golf and tennis than they are by history or culture, so supply meets with demand. However, Vancouver still has some interesting options, and although most of the larger museums are reserved for federal and provincial capitals, the city's smaller offerings are a quirky loot for those looking for their fix.

There is a collection of thematic museums that play a combined role in providing a view of the region's history. The largest of the batch, and a good choice for those interested in native history and art, is UBC's Museum of Anthropology, in its splendid Arthur Erickson building fronted by totem poles and longhouses. To view natural, human and cultural history, the Vancouver Museum can supply a comprehensive overview.

The smaller museums in the city tend to be more eccentric choices, housing collections as varied as fly fishing paraphernalia and preserved body parts. As always, the great outdoors is never too far away, and the majority of visits can be combined with a leisurely stroll. Most facilities in the city are generally situated away from the Downtown skyscrapers, in parks or near the beach.

## BC Sports Hall Of Fame & Museum

*BC Place Stadium*
*777 Pacific Blvd South*
*Downtown*
*Map 9 F1* **37**

*604 687 5520 | www.bcsportshalloffame.com*

Sports enthusiasts will be sure to enjoy this one, with each of its 20 galleries devoted to a decade, starting with aboriginal sports and games in 1800. All the local football, ice hockey, soccer, track and field, and lacrosse heroes are commemorated here in uniquely designed and state of the art technology displays. Kids (and adults) will enjoy the participation gallery, with its hands on activities to measure strength and speed. It's located in the giant mushroom shaped dome, home of the Canadian Football League's BC Lions. It's a good fun place to visit for an hour's enjoyment. The 60,000 seat stadium's address is on Pacific Boulevard, but the museum is near the well-marked Gate A and best entered from Expo Boulevard. Open daily, 10:00 to 17:00; admission is $10 for adults and $8 for students.

## Burnaby Village Museum

*6501 Deer Lake Av*
*Burnaby*
*Map 6 E2* **38**

*604 293 6500 | www.burnabyvillagemuseum.ca*

Thirty buildings on a 3.5 hectare site recreate an early 20th century village, complete with period homes, a dentist's office, an electric tram stop, blacksmith's shop, school, church, ice cream parlour serving light meals and, the star of the show, a working restored carousel. Staff and volunteers are clothed in period garb, and give demonstrations of the kinds of jobs and responsibilities that were common at the time. In summer the village is a fine place to spend a morning or afternoon. There are picnic tables and the village is next to a lovely lakeside park with an art gallery and flower garden. In winter there are Christmas theme displays and activities. It really does feel as if you've stepped back to a simpler time. Admission is $11 for adults and $6 for children.

## Chinese Cultural Centre Museum

*555 Columbia St*
*Chinatown*
*Map 10 B2* **39**

*604 658 8881 | www.cccvan.com*

This oasis of a complex, which houses a museum, research room, a presentation room and a gallery for art displays, was designed in the classical Suzhou garden style, which was popular during the Ming Dynasty (1368 to 1644AD). The museum runs both temporary and permanent displays of artefacts and photos that show the history and lives of Chinese Canadians in British Columbia, from the gold rush and the building of the railway, to the settlement of Vancouver's Chinatown. The museum complex is linked to the Chinese Cultural Centre and is adjacent to the Dr Sun Yat Sen Classical Chinese Garden (see p.246). Admission is free, and a half hour to an hour would be enough to kindle an interest in a walk through the streets of Chinatown.

## Granville Island Museums

*1502 Duranleau St*
*Granville Island*
*Map 9 B2* **40**

*604 683 1939 | www.granvilleislandmuseums.com*

In the labyrinth of aisles and passageways in the Maritime Market building in the heart of Granville Island are three museums in one that go unnoticed by many: the Model Ship Museum, Sport Fishing Museum, and Model Train Museum, which is purportedly the largest private museum of its kind in the world. Inside are displays of sailing ships, submarines, warships and other model vessels built in BC, all the fishing paraphernalia you can imagine, and pictures, display cases and dioramas with working steam trains. The owner had operated the market, marina and boat yard for 20 years before opening two of the museums in 1997. Admission is $7.50 for adults and $6 for students and seniors. The museums are located almost under the bridge, but the Island's layout can be confusing so it's best to go to the tourist information centre at 1398 Cartwright Street first for directions and maps. After the museums there is a whole day of activities and sights on the island (p.204).

### Samson V Museum

**105-1005**
**Columbia St**
*New Westminster*
*Map 2 C3*

*604 522 6894*

Before the construction of good roads and railways, 300 steam-powered paddle wheelers provided the safest and fastest means of transport on the lakes and rivers of the province. The last one in operation was the Samson V, a snagpuller that kept the river clear of floating debris. Built in 1937 for the federal government, it was finally retired in 1980 and turned into a floating museum. The galley, mess and cabins have remained virtually unchanged, but a number of photographic exhibits describing life on the river have been added. Admission is by donation. The paddlewheeler's location in the suburb of New Westminster makes it a 25 minute SkyTrain trip from Downtown, but also in the area are the New Westminster Quay Market (810 Quayside, 604 520 3881) with its shops, restaurants and riverside boardwalk, the Irving House museum (302 Royal Avenue, 604 527 4640) and the New Westminster Police Museum (555 Columbia Street, 604 525 5411).

### UBC Museum Of Anthropology

**6393 North West**
**Marine Drive**
*UBC*
*Map 5 A1* **42**

*604 822 5087* | *www.moa.ubc.ca*

Modest in size, but located on a cliff top overlooking the sea in what many believe to be one of Arthur Erickson's finest buildings, this collection is a must-see for anyone interested in the native peoples of the Pacific coast. Totems, sculptures, jewellery, funeral boxes, masks, artworks, tools and clothing, as well as 19th century photos of villages, give a sense of how this culturally rich society lived before and after contact with Europeans. There are also displays from Asia, Africa, South America and Oceania, but the focus is on local native history. The museum provides a variety of lectures, tours and even musical performances in one of Vancouver's favourite spaces. It opens daily during the summer from 10:00 to 17:00, but is closed on Mondays during winter and opens at 11:00. There is a late opening until 21:00 on Tuesdays. At least an hour would be needed to take it all in. Adults pay $9, students $7, children under 6 gain free entry.

### Vancouver Centennial Police Museum

**240 East Cordova St**
*Gastown*
*Map 10 C1* **43**

*604 665 3346* | *www.vancouverpolicemuseum.ca*

Opened in 1986 to celebrate the 100 year anniversary of the Vancouver Police Department, this morbidly fascinating museum is housed in what was previously the

*UBC Museum Of Anthropology*

morgue and coroner's court. Errol Flynn's body was brought here after his death in October 1959, and the museum describes the scandalous days following. The autopsy room is adorned with mangled body parts rife with bullet and stab wounds, and there are graphic displays of methods for determining how long a corpse has been decomposing: first come the blowflies after 15 days, then cheese skippers after 40, and so on. Other rooms include a radio room, a forensic lab, a cell and a gift shop, and there are displays of crime scenes, gruesome weapons, drugs, counterfeit money and gambling. Open Monday to Saturday, 09:00 to 17:00, this is not for the weak of stomach. Admission is $7 for adults and $5 for students.

*1905 Ogden Av*
*Kitsilano*
*Map 8 F1* **44**

## Vancouver Maritime Museum

*604 257 8300* | *www.vancouvermaritimemuseum.com*

This small and somewhat understated museum in Vanier Park will be of interest to maritime enthusiasts, but could be a bit disappointing for someone looking to be awed by this major North American port's maritime past. There are some interesting displays, original charts and maps of Captain George Vancouver, and assorted photos and illustrations of great tall ships at anchor, which conjure up images of a romantic past. The centrepiece of the museum is a 1928 RCMP schooner called the Saint Roch, the first ship to navigate the Northwest Passage in a single season. Unfortunately, however, the museum is simple and unimaginative in its conception and presentation. The location is lovely though, near the beach and close to the Vancouver Museum and Space Centre. Admission is $10 for adults and $7.50 for students and seniors.

*1100 Chestnut St*
*Kitsilano*
*Map 9 A1* **45**

## Vancouver Museum

*604 736 4431* | *www.vanmuseum.bc.ca*

Canada's largest civic museum isn't as fulsome as you might expect, despite its unmistakable native hat design and impressive stainless steel crab sculpture and fountain in front. It opens Tuesday to Sunday from 10:00 to 17:00, and includes some small but interesting exhibits of the natural, human and cultural histories of the area and abroad. The museum also provides a variety of events, lectures and touring thematic exhibits, but the real draw is its location in the lovely seaside Vanier Park on Kits point. A planetarium, an observatory and a space centre are all attached to it and the Vancouver Maritime Museum and Heritage Harbour are a stone's throw away. It's also on the Vancouver Trolley Company bus route, so take a tour, jump off at Vanier Park, and spend an afternoon seeing the museums or walking on the beach. Admission is $10 for adults, $7 for kids aged 5 and up, while under 5s are free. Family passes are also available.

## Other Attractions

*555 West*
*Hastings St*
*Downtown*
*Map 7 F3* **46**

## Harbour Centre Tower

*604 689 0421* | *www.vancouverlookout.com*

Appearing in almost every picture, funky illustration or advertisement for Vancouver is this distinctive box with a flying saucer on top, the design of which seems more suited to an airport than the edge of the oldest part of the city. The 40 storey, one minute ride up to the observation deck (Vancouver Lookout) is nothing short of exhilarating, and the 360 degree views from the observation level of the mountains, Burrard Inlet, Downtown and points further afield are magnificent, day or night. The Top of Vancouver revolving restaurant (604 669 2220) is no elaborate affair, but if you choose to go for a meal, the $11 fee is waived. Tours pointing out all the landmarks are free every hour on the hour.

**1100 Chestnut St**
*Kitsilano*
*Map 9 A1* **47**

## HR MacMillan Space Centre

*604 738 7827* | *www.hrmacmillanspacecentre.com*

A planetarium, spaceship simulator, museum, theatre, games arcade and observatory all in one. Located in the beautiful Vanier Park near Kitsilano beach, this leading edge technology centre will appeal to all ages. Open Tuesday to Sunday, 10:00 to 17:00, you can view the night sky, both in the planetarium or from the adjacent observatory. You can watch multimedia presentations on space-related themes and laser productions set to music by bands such as Pink Floyd (sometimes with the subtle aroma of marijuana wafting around you), fly on a dramatic mission in a 30 seat spacecraft simulator, play video games or even touch a piece of rock from the moon. A very hands-on facility that brings astronomy to life. Admission is $15 for adults and $11 for children.

**Nr Pavillion**
*Stanley Park*
*Map 3 F3* **48**

## Stanley Park Children's Farmyard

*604 257 8530* | *www.city.vancouver.bc.ca/parks*

Within easy walking distance of the aquarium, this half-hectare petting zoo is home to over 200 animals representing 50 domestic and wild species. Children will delight in familiar barnyard characters: sheep, goats, pigs, ducks, geese, rabbits, cows, donkeys, and Shetland ponies, but the zoo is also home to peacocks and a number of snakes and lizards. The park is an active participant in celebrations for seasonal themes such as Easter, Halloween and Christmas, and organises activities and displays like Easter egg hunts, ghoulish decorations and Santa and the elves. Open daily, 11:00 to 16:00, from Easter to late September, weekends only in winter. Admission is $5 for adults, $2.50 for children under 12.

**Nr Pavillion**
*Stanley Park*
*Map 3 F3* **49**

## Stanley Park Miniature Train

*604 257 8531* | *www.city.vancouver.bc.ca/parks*

Located near the aquarium and beside the petting zoo, this little steam train has become one of Vancouver's most popular attractions, carrying more than 200,000 passengers per year. The original 2km track was laid down on the spot where a 1964 typhoon stripped the park of a huge grove of trees, and the train now winds past babbling brooks and ponds, through a picturesque cathedral forest, over wooden trestles and through pitch black tunnels. One of the engines is a miniature replica of the first transcontinental passenger train that steamed into Vancouver in the late 1880s. The facility also has additional seasonal displays such as the Halloween Ghost Train ride and the dazzling Bright Nights Christmas lights display. Admission is $5 for adults and $2.50 for children.

**1455 Quebec St**
*Main*
*Map 10 B4* **50**

## Telus World Of Science

*604 443 7443* | *www.telusworldofscience.com*

Housed in an unmistakable geodesic dome, this fun and educational centre has been delighting kids since its inception during Expo 86. The dome is actually an OMNIMAX theatre with a concave screen showing nature and science films that make you feel like you're walking, swimming or floating in jungles, oceans and space. The centre's large exhibition space features interactive displays, hands-on experiments and live demonstrations and exhibits with subject matter as varied as the human body, cyclones, cameras, electrically charged exploding zucchinis, synthesisers, and laser shows – all great fun for toddlers to teens. The centre also organises science competitions with prizes. Open daily from 10:00 to 17:00, and until 18:00 on weekends. Admission for adults is $21 all inclusive, with lower rates for restricted gallery viewing.

## Religious Sites

The pious and the devout may be mystified by the small collection of places of worship in the city – it has been called the most secular city in North America. However, what the city lacks in volume, it makes up for in diversity, which is a reflection of the range of ethnic and religious communities in the city. From Christian and Jewish, to Buddhist, Islamic, Hindu and Sikh, there are some elegant structures to behold, many of which are open to the public for a peek or a prayer. Most also provide lectures and concerts, as well as the expected religious services.

**690 Burrard St** ◄
*Downtown*
*Map 7 E3* **51**

## Christ Church Cathedral

*604 682 3848 | www.cathedral.vancouver.bc.ca*

Constructed with sandstone and douglas fir timbers and fitted with stunning stained glass windows, this gothic revival style Anglican church is the oldest in Vancouver, having been completed in 1895. It has a storied past, complete with a plot to raze it for a large payoff, but after much debate and protest the cathedral was finally saved as a heritage building in 1976. It was originally in a residential area, but now sits anomalously in a high-rise business district and is considered by most to be a welcome break from the concrete and glass, providing glimpses of the sky above. The cathedral also hosts a number of musical performances. Open Monday to Friday 10:00 to 16:00. Admission is free but donations are appreciated.

**646 Richards St** ◄
*Downtown*
*Map 7 F4* **52**

## Holy Rosary Cathedral

*604 682 6774 | http://hrc.rcav.org*

When completed in 1900, this asymmetrical building with its twin pointed towers was considered the finest example of its kind west of Toronto and north of San Francisco. Built on a foundation of granite, the walls are of sandstone from nearby Gabriola Island, and its pointed arch, vaulted ceiling, clerestory windows, buttresses, large stained-glass windows and exterior carvings all reflect a neo-gothic style. Eight bells hang in the 66m east tower. The cathedral also hosts a variety of concerts, from gospel choirs to First Nations and jazz. Admission is free but donations are accepted.

**8000 Ross St** ◄
*South Vancouver*
*Map 6 A4* **53**

## Khalsa Diwan Gurdwara Temple

*604 324 2010*

With the increase of the Sikh population in Vancouver and the subsequent rise in donations to the Khalsa Diwan Society, it was determined that a larger facility was needed, and in 1970 the society moved from its modest 1908 structure on 2nd Avenue to this prize-winning and exquisite Arthur Erickson-designed temple. Moving from the ground upwards, the building is essentially a stack of progressively smaller white rectangular levels topped with a metal framed open pointed dome, which can only be described as the meeting of western modernism and eastern tradition. Colourful late morning Sikh wedding ceremonies frequently take place at the temple and visitors are welcome to observe a ceremony if they call for permission in advance.

**9160 Steveston** ◄
**Highway**
*Richmond*
*Map 2 B3*

## Kuan Yin Buddhist Temple

*604 274 2822 | www.buddhisttemple.ca*

Driving along Steveston Highway through Richmond, you cannot miss the most exquisite example of Chinese architecture in Canada. With its golden roof, flared eaves, murals, calligraphy, dragons, lotus ponds, classical Chinese gardens and courtyards and statues of Buddha and bodhisattvas, this is one of the great structures of the entire region. Conceived in 1981 by two Chinese immigrants committed to sharing Buddhism with the world, the temple has become an international centre for the religion. It is open to all interested in learning more, from 09:30 to 17:30. Free admission but donations gratefully accepted.

## Water Parks

With dozens of beaches, outdoor swimming pools and lakes nearby, there doesn't seem to be much of a market for large-scale water parks within the city limits. Most of what's available is small scale and for younger kids. What does exist is generally located in

# Attractions

*Burrard Bridge*

*Vancouver Public Library*

*Telus World Of Science*

*Granville Island*

neighbourhood parks providing tots with water cannons, small slides and geysers that spray without warning. The water parks are free and generally surrounded by comfortable benches and perhaps a concession, so parents can sip a coffee and watch the children frolic. There is one exception, 40 kilometres south of Vancouver – a colossal complex called Splashdown, with every terrifying slide you can imagine.

## Granville Island Water Park

*1318 Cartwright St*
*Granville Island*
*Map 9 C3* **55**

**604 666 5784** | www.granvilleisland.com

Bring towels and trunks to Granville Island for when the children get tired of being dragged around the shops and galleries. This free water park is an ideal spot for a cooling break. The supervised area has two waterslides (one large), a water play area with geysers and cannons and a playground. It also provides free summer activities such as face painting and art. You can even rent a battery-operated car for your children. Open May to September, 10:00 to 18:00.

## Splashdown Park

*4799 Nulelum Way*
*Tsawwassen*
*Map 2 B4*

**604 943 2251** | www.splashdownpark.ca

About 40km south of Vancouver and near the Tsawwassen ferry terminal for Victoria is a 13 acre mammoth water park good for a whole day of fun. With 13 slides sporting names such as Black Death, Corkscrew and Whippersnapper, this park has rides from the terrifying to the tranquil. There is also an inner tube slide, baby slides, hot tub, basketball court, video arcade, mini-golf, concession facilities and picnic tables, although an umbrella might be a good idea since shade can be at a premium on a hot summer day. There is also a water play area for toddlers. Admission is $15 for youths and adults, with free parking. Take Highway 99 south, exit on Highway 17, drive towards the ferry terminal, and look for the huge and clearly marked signs.

## Stanley Park Spray Park

*North end of*
*Georgia St*
*Stanley Park*
*Map 3 F3* **57**

**604 257 8400** | www.city.vancouver.bc.ca/parks

Located in Stanley Park, with dramatic views of the North Shore Mountains and Burrard Inlet, this area is ideal for an afternoon of family fun. The park was originally one of Vancouver's draw-and-fill saltwater swimming pools, but the site was filled in and turned into a water park, equipped with assorted water cannons and geysers that thrill the tots with unpredicted blasts. There is a small slide as well, but nothing too hairy. Nearby is a large grass field with picnic tables, a small beach, and concession and washroom facilities. Since there is no lifeguard on duty, numerous benches have been provided for parents to sit and enjoy the sights and sounds of delighted kids. Free and open May to September, 10:00 to 18:00, but subject to weather restrictions.

## Zoos

## Greater Vancouver Zoo

*5048 264th St*
*Langley*

**604 856 6825** | www.gvzoo.com

Vancouver's offering to those wanting to admire wildlife is a game farm, located an hour from the city, that has changed its focus to conservation and education over the past 10 years. It has a variety of animal enclosures, with lions, tigers, cougars, rhinos, elephants, camels, mountain sheep, hippos, giraffes, and assorted exotic birds and reptiles. A safari bus ride takes you through an area where black bears and wolves co-exist, and then into another habitat for elk, mule deer and bison. There are also miniature train rides, a picnic park with covered gazebos and barbecues, interpretive and educational programmes and activities. Open year round with seasonal hours, admission is $18 for adults and $14 for children 4 to 14, and there are reduced rates for families and groups.

## Parks, Beaches & Gardens

The future appeared bleak in the 1950s, 60s and 70s when the population was burgeoning and developers were given almost free reign to pave paradise. Thanks to a handful of enlightened hippies, environmentalists, citizens groups, planners and politicians, lands were rescued from the bulldozer and Vancouver now boasts hundreds of designated green spaces. The waterfront consists of a series of public beaches and parks linked by a seaside path which, when unobstructed by maintenance and improvement projects, spans over 40 kilometres. Inland communities are now connected by networks of paths for walking and cycling called greenways, some of which are cultivated by nearby apartment dwellers in the city's urban garden programme. The end result is that outside of the Downtown core, Vancouver is one of the greenest cities in the country, with a trail, park, beach or garden never more than a few minutes' walk away.

## Beaches

Other options **Swimming** p.328, **Parks** p.241

Vancouver's location at 49 degrees north should make beaches and ocean swimming an activity for only the bravest or feeble of mind. But the Japan Current makes its way across the Pacific and keeps the water temperatures bearable. With over 40 kilometres of coastline (Vancouver is essentially a peninsula) and a city government that has by and large protected the waterfront for public use, there is a summertime beach culture comparable with destinations much further south. Most Vancouverites will tell you that between June and September there is no place they'd rather be. The beaches also reflect the city's eclectic demographic, inundated in summer with families, windsurfers, skim-boarders, Rastafarians, body builders, blonde bombshells, volleyballers and even nudists.

There are occasional stretches where access to the shoreline is impeded, but the law states that all waterfront areas between high and low tides are for the public. This means that virtually the entire shore, where nature allows, is navigable on foot. At low tide it is conceivable to walk from the Fraser River in south Vancouver, around Point Grey, along Spanish Banks to Kitsilano and Granville Island, along False Creek to Telus World of Science, back on the north side of False Creek to Stanley Park, and around the park, a distance of well over 30km, during which time you will barely have to leave the coast. The water, although sometimes murky due to algae and river silt, is relatively clean and safe for swimming.

All of the 12 public beaches in Vancouver fall under the jurisdiction of the Vancouver Parks Board (www.city.vancouver.bc.ca), and consequently provide services that you would expect at any public park. So you can expect an adjacent grassy park with washrooms and changing rooms, cold showers, concession stands of varying sizes and menus, lifeguards and first aid facilities. There are always free or pay parking facilities, volleyball posts and sometimes even outdoor swimming pools, water parks, basketball and tennis courts and skateboard parks. All city beaches are free, have cordoned-off swimming areas, and lifeguards from late May to early September between the hours of 11:30 and 19:00, and all are on or near the Seawall path system, which makes them accessible by bicycle.

### Ambleside Beach & Park

*Marine Drive &*
*13th Av*
*West Vancouver*
*Map 3 E2* 59

Across the Lions Gate Bridge from Stanley Park, in the municipality of West Vancouver, is the community of Ambleside, with its seaside park and beach on the edge of a residential and commercial area. The drive across the bridge is an event in itself, providing spectacular views west as far as the Gulf Islands and Vancouver Island. The long narrow strip is a favourite for strollers, and provides tennis courts, a basketball court, volleyball posts, a skateboard park, grass fields, a pitch and putt course and an area where dogs can roam leash free. The ambience is much like a resort town for locals, since most tourists don't venture across the bridge. The views are south to Kitsilano, Point Grey, Stanley Park and the Downtown core, and the mountains tower above to the north. Locals like to refer to the area as an attitude as much as a beach, and it can be a little slower paced than the urban beaches.

## English Bay Beach & Park

*Beach Av*
*Btn Gilford &*
*Bidwell St*
*West End*
*Map 7 A2* 60

You'd think you were in the tropics as you stroll past the palm trees that line Beach Avenue along English Bay. Located at the gateway to Stanley Park and bordering the most densely populated area in the country, this beach is the most urban of the bunch, bounded by busy streets, high rises, hotels, shops and restaurants. It attracts an eclectic group, from families to singles to alternative lifestyle folk, with a significant gay presence. It is an ideal sunset viewing location, and hosts the HSBC Festival of Light (p.59), an international fireworks competition spanning four nights in the summer. It has all the required and expected amenities, including two sand volleyball courts and kayak rentals, but parking can be a problem. Most people leave their cars in the pay parking lot in the nearby Stanley Park, or further east towards Sunset Beach.

## Jericho Beach & Park

*Btn Wallace &*
*Discovery St*
*Kitsilano*
*Map 5 D1* 61

First a native village, then a logging camp, then Vancouver's first golf course, then a military base and finally a public property, this naturally sandy beach and accompanying spacious tree-filled park with full concession and washroom facilities, pond and walking trails provides a family with a great all-day outing. It's a fantastic place to learn to sail or windsurf, under the tutelage of the nearby Jericho Sailing Club (p.334), which provides aquatic sports lessons for reasonable membership fees. There are also tennis courts, a youth hostel and large grass fields for picnicking and barbecues. In July, the renowned Vancouver International Folk Festival (p.56) turns the area into a squeaky clean and healthy version of Woodstock.

## Kitsilano Beach & Park

*Cornwall St*
*Btn Arbutus & Yew St*
*Kitsilano*
*Map 8 E2* 62

The most crowded and happening of the West Side beaches, this is a mecca for the young, the young at heart, the fit and the beautiful. It has every amenity, either at the beach, in the adjacent park or in the nearby neighbourhood, that you could possibly need or imagine. There is a 137m-long salt water seaside swimming pool (the longest in Canada), volleyball net posts, tennis courts, a basketball court, a playground, concession, washrooms, a fine dining restaurant, seaside path and shops and restaurants across the street. Large chestnut, oak and willow trees provide shade

*English Bay Beach & Park*

on hotter days. Noisy and packed at weekends, this is not a place to get away from it all – rather it's a place to people watch.

## Locarno Beach & Park

**North West Marine Dr**
*Btn Trimble & Tolmie St*
*Point Grey*
*Map 5 C1* **63**

An eastern extension of Spanish Banks, this lovely sand beach is a family favourite, with free parking, a pier to fish from or drop a crab trap off (you need a licence), and full concession and washroom facilities. Tall stands of fir and pines provide shade on the hotter days, and the grassy fields are dotted with picnic tables. It has been designated a quiet beach, with no amplified music allowed. The views of the mountains, English Bay and the Downtown skyline, like from all the West Side beaches, are stellar.

## Second Beach & Park

**Stanley Park & North Lagoon Dr**
*Stanley Park*
*Map 3 E4* **64**

A little further west from English Bay will bring you to the first of two Stanley Park beaches. A favourite among families, the beach itself is not the best the city has to offer, but it is part of a park with a playground, large grass field and a huge heated outdoor pool. It has a full concession, washrooms, showers, a picnic shelter, antique fire engine, and pedal cars for the kids to learn traffic safety in the summer. Its proximity to Stanley Park means you are minutes away from dozens of kilometres of trails and seawall, as well as numerous sights, attractions and recreational opportunities. Pay parking available.

## Spanish Banks Beach & Park

**North West Marine Dr**
*West of Tolmie St*
*Point Grey*
*Map 5 C1* **65**

Named by Spanish explorers in the late 1700s, this three kilometre sandy shelf towards UBC is actually three beaches in one: Spanish Banks East, Spanish Banks West and Spanish Banks Extension, which makes it the longest beach in the city. The strong afternoon winds attract windsurfers and paraboarders, the shallow pools at low tide are ideal for skim-boarding, and its large attached park area is perfect for Frisbee, soccer and volleyball. In the evenings it is barbecue central as folks watch the sun set over Bowen Island, with alternative views of the Downtown skyline and the North Shore Mountains. In the warmer months the long car park is a venue for antique and classic car owners to show off their machines.

## Sunset Beach & Park

**Beach Av**
*Btn Thurlow & Bute St*
*West End*
*Map 7 B4* **66**

An extension of English Bay, this is a series of sandy jetties that jut out into the mouth of False Creek (actually a salt water inlet), with views across to the Maritime Museum, Space Centre and the community of Kitsilano. This beach is less frequented than most of the others and has been designated a quiet zone, so no amplified music is permitted. Nearby is a skateboard park, an Olympic-sized indoor pool, a large grass field, and kilometres of Seawall for walking, jogging, rollerblading and cycling. Concession and washroom facilities are available, as is an off-leash area for well-behaved dogs. There is pay parking, and since it's near an Aquabus pier, a short jaunt across the inlet to Granville Island can add to the experience.

## Third Beach & Park

**Stanley Park Dr & Ferguson Point**
*Stanley Park*
*Map 3 E3* **67**

Walking north-west along the Seawall from Second Beach, you will reach a relatively secluded sandy beach at the foot of the forested bluffs of Stanley Park, with impressive views of the North Shore mountains, the Gulf Islands and Point Grey. This is arguably the best-situated beach in the city in terms of its views and the fact that the Downtown core is out of earshot, out of sight and out of mind. Because this beach is on the west side of Stanley Park and somewhat off the beaten track, it doesn't get as busy as many of the other beaches. The atmosphere is laid back and attracts a comfortable mix of people for swimming and sunset picnic dinners. The stairs lead up to the top of the bluff where there's a grassy field and all the basic amenities, including showers, changing rooms, washrooms, a concession and pay parking lot.

*University Blvd* ◀
*South West Marine Dr*
*Point Grey*
*Map 5 A1* **68**

## Wreck Beach

*604 946 7545 | www.wreckbeach.org*

With its beginnings in the rebelliousness of the 1960s, this clothing-optional beach is a survivor of an idealistic time when students at the nearby UBC shed their clothes, rolled joints and frolicked in the surf and sun. Today, the nudity and the pot smoking have survived, but the rebels are all but gone, save for a few older veterans. Due to the beach's location at the bottom of a long and steep path (Trails 3, 5 or 6 off South West Marine Drive), the city has generally turned a blind eye to the activities of the nude sun worshippers, but in recent years the police have become more of a presence. There is constant and heated debate on how much development should be allowed, the extremes being from none at all to full-on exploitation with paved access roads, condos, parking lots and fast food outlets. As it's not officially a city beach, there is no lifeguard on duty, and it lacks flush toilets, fresh water and concession facilities, so bring all the food and beverage you need – or you may choose to get a sandwich, a drink, a massage or illicit treat from one of the many vendors who ply the beach.

## Nature Reserves

Since Vancouver is essentially an enormous clearing in the wilderness, there aren't the designated nature reserves you would find in cities situated in more domesticated environments. There are sanctuaries in some of the suburbs, the most notable being the 890 acre Reifel Bird Sanctuary in Ladner (www.reifelbirdsanctuary.com), a 30 minute drive south from Downtown on Highway 99. The distinction between a park and a nature reserve is blurred, with larger parks like Stanley, Queen Elizabeth and Jericho featuring ponds with frogs, turtles, geese, swans, forested areas for birds, and meadows for rabbits and burrowing rodents. Only 100m along the coast from a public beach you are likely to see a great blue heron fishing for smelt, or a cormorant, otter or seal. Canada geese have all but taken over the parks and are considered pests due to their refusal to migrate south in the winter. Some of the streams previously covered over for development are now being excavated and reclaimed for salmon and trout spawning. Raccoons and skunks are found in most green areas and in the adjacent residential areas where they scavenge for rubbish. Coyote sightings are common in and around the larger parks such as Pacific Spirit, Stanley and Jericho, and warning signs were put up a few years ago when dogs and cats were disappearing at an alarming rate. There are also eagles, hawks and ospreys along the coast and pairs tending their nests and young can often be seen on the tops of trees and even atop totem poles. Small dogs should be kept close at hand; there have been cases of eagles swooping down and grabbing them. Seymour and Cypress provincial wilderness parks are 30 minutes drive from Downtown in the North Shore Mountains. The mountain peaks and vast forests of hemlock, cedar and fir found here

*Wreck Beach*

are the perfect habitat for black bears, deer, cougars, lynx and bobcats. Used by mountain bikers, hikers and backpackers in summer, these transform into skiing and snowshoeing meccas in winter. If bears are foraging in a given area, it may be closed until the rangers can remove them. They are more frequent in spring and autumn, when they are either preparing for or coming out of hibernation.

## Parks

Other options **Beaches** p.237

What Vancouver lacks in history, museums, galleries and high culture it easily makes up for with its abundant number of parks. There are 200 parks ranging in size from one hectare to over 750 within the city. Visitors from even the greenest of cities in Europe, South America and Asia are always amazed by the amount of land designated as green space. So, although the Downtown core is mostly concrete, steel and glass, there is always a park within walking distance, and the beauty is that most of the larger ones are by the sea and are connected by seaside paths that allow people to walk, jog, cycle or rollerblade between them, away from the traffic. All small parks contain washroom facilities, playgrounds and playing fields, and the larger ones usually include tennis and basketball courts, recreation centres and walking paths as well. All the city parks are free to enter (Capilano and Grouse Mountain, which are listed in this section, charge for admission) and have either pay or free parking. The car parks have posted hours and rates, which vary in their fees and closing times (watch out for gates that may trap you inside overnight). In the neighbouring municipalities and districts there are regional and provincial parks, which tend to be much larger and wilder, and provide a perfect setting for skiing, hiking, backpacking, camping, boating and even scuba diving in the marine parks. The beauty about Vancouver is that residents can get off work at 17:00 on a Friday afternoon, and be climbing a mountain in the wilderness an hour later.

*Expo Blvd*
*Cnr Carrall St*
*Chinatown*
*Map 10 B2* **69**

### Andy Livingstone Park

*604 257 8400 | www.city.vancouver.bc.ca/parks*

In an otherwise urban no-man's land, this park is noticeable for its large expanse of artificial turf fields, which are used all year round for men and women's soccer, field hockey and softball leagues. There is also a basketball and tennis court, playgrounds and a skateboard park. On the fringes are streams, a pond, and gardens of ferns, salal and dogwood. Though it is not the most beautiful of Vancouver's parks, its creation is a definite upgrade for a site that used to be an eyesore.

*3735 Capilano Rd*
*North Vancouver*
*Map 3 F1* **70**

### Capilano River Regional Park

*604 985 7474 | www.capbridge.com*

A perilous 70m above the Capilano River is Capilano Suspension Bridge, one of Vancouver's biggest tourist draws. Those who love wildlife (and are unperturbed by heights) can enjoy the area's spectacular landscape and rainforest fauna, just a short journey from Downtown in Capilano Park. The bridge was once made with hemp ropes and cedar planks, but today's visitors amble over sturdier stuff – the 137m long bridge, made of reinforced steel, provides a safe vantage point. The park itself offers ample amusement for children too, with information about the forest vegetation, trees and insects, and a Kids' Rainforest Explorer programme that takes them 30 metres above the trees in the park's newest attraction, 'Treetops Adventure'. Visit the Totem Park to see First Nations story totem poles and the First Nations Cultural Centre to witness traditional carving and weaving. Entry to the park costs around $27, but rates fluctuate with the seasons.

**Pacific Blvd & Drake St**
False Creek
Map 9 D2 **71**

## David Lam Park

*604 257 8400 | www.city.vancouver.bc.ca/parks*

Part of the huge redevelopment project on the former Expo 86 site, this seaside park provides locals and visiting strollers with open space and respite from the huge high-rise complexes surrounding it. Set around a large central grass field and with views of False Creek, the park contains basketball and tennis courts, a soccer field, a playground and huge modernist sculptures, and it borders the False Creek Seawall, with its endless walking, rollerblading and cycling opportunities. In the summer months, the Vancouver Jazz Festival (p.56) and other outdoor concerts and events utilise the open space, which comfortably seats thousands. A great place to get a coffee, sit down and read a book.

**801 West 22nd Av**
Cambie
Map 5 F2 **72**

## Douglas Park

*604 257 8130 | www.city.vancouver.bc.ca/parks*

A former logging camp in the 1870s and later an elk grazing site, this 5.3 hectare park now serves a large residential area with grass playing fields, a basketball court, a community centre with numerous classes, teams and activities, two cricket pitches, jogging trails, playgrounds, soccer and softball fields, and, in summer, a wading pool for the kids. It's well used, but far away from the hustle and bustle of Downtown.

**6400 Nancy Greene Way**
North Vancouver
Map 2 B1

## Grouse Mountain

*604 984 0661 | www.grousemountain.com*

Grouse Mountain is more a 'great outdoors' wilderness area than park, but either way it remains one of Vancouver's most famous outdoor leisure spots. A lovely 20 minute drive through Stanley Park and over Lions Gate Bridge will bring you to the Grouse Mountain gondola, a huge and fast rig that whisks you up to the observation level at 1,138 metres above sea level. Of course there's skiing in winter, but from May to October you can hike or take a chairlift to the peak at 1,249m, from where the views of the adjacent mountains, the city and the distant islands are as good as it gets. Like the hill, admission is steep at more than $30, but the vistas take the sting out. At the top are restaurants with outdoor decks and the Grouse Mountain Refuge for Endangered Wildlife, which includes a pair of orphaned grizzlies, wolves and a raptor show. In

*Lynn Canyon Suspension Bridge*

*Grouse Mountain*

summer there's an entertaining lumberjack performance as well, complete with axe throwing, log burling and pole climbing. It is possible to hike up from the car park below from late spring to autumn on the notorious Grouse Grind, a very steep and difficult 90 minute hike, but hikers are rewarded with a $5 gondola ride down.

**3350 Victoria Dr**
*Grandview*
*Map 12 C3* **74**

## John Hendry Park
*604 257 6955* | *www.city.vancouver.bc.ca/parks*
One of the most complete parks in the city in terms of the range of facilities and services offered, this lovely 27 hectare tree-filled park with a small lake and beach is an institution among eastsiders. The park provides pitches for all field sports, a community centre with a variety of indoor facilities and activities, jogging trails, picnic sites, playgrounds, a roller-hockey rink, and tennis and basketball courts. There is a farmers' market from May to October, as well as an amazing lantern festival in early summer, when people set lights adrift on the waters of the glistening lake.

**Beacon Ln at**
**Marine Dr**
*West Vancouver*
*Map 3 A2* **75**

## Lighthouse Park
*604 925 7200* | *www.westvancouver.ca*
This rugged 74 hectare coastal park crisscrossed by trails through towering old growth douglas fir, hemlock and red cedar is just eight kilometres west of the north end of the Lions Gate Bridge in the city of West Vancouver. Trails lead from the Marine Drive car park down to Point Atkinson, a 10 minute walk, where the tall white and red lighthouse stands, a landmark for Vancouver sailors since 1912. The smooth granite outcrops and beach are favourite spots among locals for picnics and views of Stanley Park and the Vancouver skyline to the south, and the Gulf Islands to the west. Wear good walking shoes for some of the steep trails down to the pebble beach. Bus 250 from Downtown takes you on a lovely trip along the coastal Marine Drive and will drop you off near the park entrance at the end of Beacon Lane. Service is infrequent in the evenings, so check the transit schedule. As with all public parks in the area, admission is free.

**3663 Park Rd**
*North Vancouver*
*Map 4 D2* **76**

## Lynn Canyon Park
*604 981 3103* | *www.dnv.org/ecology*
The dense forest of Lynn Canyon Park features a wide variety of wildlife, including wild birds, black bears, raccoons, and the banana slug, one of the world's largest. The steep walkways, unmarked tracks and varying terrain of some areas in the park will suit those looking for a more strenuous adventure, and the 30 Foot Pool tempts intrepid challengers with highly dangerous cliff diving. Those who wish to do serious hiking can also connect the walks through Lynn Headwaters Park or Crowne Mountain. The popular Lynn Canyon Suspension Bridge offers elevated forest views along its swaying (but sturdy) steel walkway 50m above the river (free, and a less crowded option than the Capilano Suspension Bridge). The park also features an ecology centre, gift shop, cafe, and designated picnic area that can be accessed by wheelchair. Admission is free, and the Ecology Centre is by donation.

**West 16th Av**
*Point Grey*
*Map 5 C2* **77**

## Pacific Spirit Regional Park
*604 224 5739* | *www.pacificspiritparksociety.org*
At 767 hectares of dense forest, meadows and foreshore, this is the largest and most pristine of all Vancouver's parks. And with a labyrinth of trails connecting all the perimeter routes, it is favoured by hikers, mountain bikers and equestrian enthusiasts. The trails are all clearly marked, with restrictions posted. Many paths are multi-use, necessitating right-of-way rules. Free maps are available at the major entry points, which are necessary if you don't want to walk in circles in this wild forest. The park lies on Point

Grey, the westernmost part of the city, on land given to UBC. It is surrounded by sea and beaches to the north and west, and by the Fraser River to the south. Washroom and other facilities are few and far between, so be prepared for a wilderness hiking experience, carrying with you food and water. This is the most tranquil experience available in the city, and eagle and coyote sightings are common.

## Queen Elizabeth Park

*Cambie St at West 33rd Av*
*Cambie*
*Map 5 F2* **78**

*604 257 8584* | *www.city.vancouver.bc.ca/parks*
A former quarry, this bountiful and beautifully maintained 52 hectare park is, at 167m in elevation, the highest point in Vancouver, allowing 360 degree views of the surrounding city, mountains and sea. It features an arboretum containing many indigenous north-west coast and exotic tree species, a botanical garden, pitch and putt golf course, a conservatory in a geodesic dome, a pavilion that can be booked for wedding receptions and meetings, a fine dining restaurant with an outdoor patio, tennis courts, walking paths and a sculpture by renowned British artist Henry Moore. Because of the lovely gardens, this park is a favourite for wedding parties and their accompanying photo sessions.

## Stanley Park

*North end of Georgia St*
*Map 3 E3* **79**

*604 257 8400* | *www.city.vancouver.bc.ca/parks*
Dedicated by Lord Stanley in 1889, the park that bears his name deserves its own section in any guide, so diverse are its features and history (see p.4). Attached to the Downtown core by a narrow isthmus and 400 hectares in area, Stanley Park ranks with the best in the world. It boasts three beaches, dozens of kilometres of walking and cycling paths, an aquarium, a par three golf course, restaurants, tennis courts, rose and rhododendron gardens, two lakes, a petting zoo, a miniature railway, an outdoor concert bowl, totem poles, sculptures, art exhibitions, street entertainers, resident wildlife and a host of other attractions too numerous to list here. Yet, despite its eight million annual visitors and because of its sheer size, visitors are never more than a few hundred metres away from a quiet bench in a relative wilderness. Near hurricane force winds blew down over 1,000 trees along the north-west part of the park in 2006, but the fallen giants are slowly returning to the ground that bore them. Bicycles and rollerblades are a great way to get around the 9km Seawall. A full day is only enough to glimpse the park, and locals are still discovering enclaves after years and dozens of visits.

## Vanier Park

*1100 Chestnut St*
*Kitsilano*
*Map 9 A1* **80**

*604 257 8400* | *www.city.vancouver.bc.ca/parkfinder_wa*
With nearly 17 hectares of fields, gardens, ponds, and a seaside pathway, all located near the HR MacMillan Space Centre (p.233), Kitsilano Beach, the Maritime Museum, a public boat ramp, a marina, and the shops of Kitsilano and Granville Island, this is an area that deserves a whole day. Summertime brings entertainment to the area, including the Vancouver Children's Festival (p.55) and Bard on the Beach (p.56), the local Shakespeare festival performed in enormous tents. It's also the best park for kite flying, attracting enthusiasts from near and far.

## Gardens

Vancouver has some lovely botanical gardens due in many cases to the foresight of private citizens and institutions determined to save some prime areas from the developer and the excavator. Assisting the variety of species contained in the gardens is the city's moderate climate which with appropriate care and attention can maintain even polar and tropical species. There are also many Asian accents, representing the city's history of multiculturalism and its proximity to the Pacific Rim. Among the best are VanDusen, UBC, Bloedel, Nitobe and Dr Sun Yat Sen, all good locations for vivid aesthetic experiences, and in the case of the latter two, places for tranquil contemplation and meditation. All have fees and seasonal hours.

**Cambie St at West 33rd Av**
Cambie
Map 5 F2 **81**

## Bloedel Floral Conservatory

*604 257 8584 | www.city.vancouver.bc.ca/parks*

Situated on top of Little Mountain in Queen Elizabeth Park and overlooking the city stands this spectacular plexiglass triodetic dome. The inside is climate controlled and filled with lavish displays of 500 different desert and tropical flowers, plants and trees. The paths wind past streams and ponds filled with colourful Japanese koi fish, and overhead 50 bird species from parrots to quail fly freely from perch to perch. The sum of the parts is a more southern atmosphere, a great one hour antidote to the dark and wet days of December and January. Open daily, 10:00 to 17:00, the dome can also be booked for weddings, photo sessions and other events. Adults pay $4.50, youths aged 13 to 18 pay $3.40, and children aged 6 to 12 pay $2.25. Family and group rates are also available.

*Queen Elizabeth Park*

*Vanier Park*

*UBC Botanical Garden*

*Dr Sun Yat Sen Classical Chinese Garden*

## Dr Sun Yat Sen Classical Chinese Garden

*578 Carrall St*
Chinatown
Map 10 B2 **82**

*604 662 3207* | *www.vancouverchinesegarden.com*

The only full-sized one of its kind outside China, this garden typifies a style common during the Ming Dynasty, between 1368 and 1644 AD. Walking inside to view the lush green floral arrangements and ponds framed by wooden walkways and accented with Chinese architectural elements instantly gives the viewer relief from the hustle and bustle outside. The Chinese designers have essentially condensed and simplified nature, and laid out this garden to reflect natural harmonies, balance and rhythms, with each plant, rock and architectural piece possessing a meaning or creating a mood. In ancient China, these gardens were sanctuaries for scholars and their colleagues, friends and families, but this one is an oasis for any urbanite needing a break. To appreciate this garden fully, take a 45 minute tour, complete with tea and explanation of the Taoist Chinese aesthetic. Entry is $9 for adults, students $7, children under 5 gain free entry.

## Nitobe Memorial Garden

*1895 Lower Mall*
UBC
Map 5 B1 **83**

*604 822 9666* | *www.nitobe.org*

On the UBC campus and minutes from the Museum of Anthropology and Botanical Gardens (see p.231 and p.246), this authentic one-hectare traditional Japanese garden is divided into two: the tea garden, designed to inspire serene contemplation of life and nature, and the stroll garden, which is laid out to represent the passage of time from birth to old age. Among the meticulously designed and cultivated pools, streams, waterfalls, rocks, plants and trees are also lanterns and a ceremonial teahouse. This garden is noted for its authenticity of concept and design combined with its use of indigenous west coast flora. Entry is $5 for adults and audio guide rental is $2. Tours are recommended to help understand the Japanese aesthetic and sensibility regarding the harmonious relationships among natural elements.

## UBC Botanical Garden

*6804 South
West Marine Dr*
UBC
Map 5 B2 **84**

*604 822 9666* | *www.ubcbotanicalgarden.org*

Surrounded by a forest of towering fir, hemlock and cedar, this 44.5 hectare garden is Canada's oldest, and home to more than 10,000 species of plants, shrubs, flowers and trees. The garden is divided into eight smaller sections with varying themes, such as alpine, edible, Asian and British Columbian. Uncompromising botanical purists claim it's superior to rival VanDusen due to its better organisation. Although summer is the best time for alpine displays, April and May are best for spectacular floral shows of magnolias, rhododendrons and spring ephemerals. September and October are best for viewing autumn colours and harvestable fruits and vegetables in the food garden. Adults pay $7 to enter, and audio guide rental is $2; a double entry ticket to Nitobe Memorial Garden and UBC Botanical Garden is $10.

## VanDusen Botanical Garden

*5251 Oak St*
Oakridge
Map 5 F2 **85**

*604 878 9274* | *www.vandusengarden.org*

Earmarked to become a housing development in the 70s, this parcel of 55 acres was saved by a group of concerned citizens supported by first private and then municipal money. The spot has blossomed into a garden of international repute, with 7,500 kinds of plants, flowers, shrubs and trees from six continents. Amid streams, ponds, waterfalls, a Buddhist temple, a restaurant and meandering paths, the gardens are arranged in thematic landscape displays according to species, climatic or geographic origins. Good for flower gazing at any time of year, there are also seasonal displays and events, such as the fantastic Festival of Lights (p.59) at Christmas, as well as concerts and talks. Rates are seasonal, approximately $8 to $10 for adults and about $4 for kids. Family and group rates are also available.

# Tours & Sightseeing

With its abundance of shops, bars, restaurants, galleries, extensive seaside paths and proximity to Stanley Park, Downtown Vancouver is a great area to explore. But so many tourists and new residents fall into the trap of rarely, if ever, crossing a bridge or, in some cases, a psychological barrier. The nearby municipalities and communities of North and West Vancouver, Kitsilano, south Main Street, Commercial Drive and a host of others all have their own unique ambiance and charm, and beg to be explored. Hop on one of the many trolley buses to get the lay of the Downtown and Kitsilano areas, and then perhaps a Landsea bus tour (p.250) for some of the nearby mountains and wild provincial parks. SkyTrain also connects some of the areas with frequent service. For a cheap and fun marine perspective of the city, board one of the False Creek Ferries vessels that putt from marina to marina all the way from Kitsilano to Main Street. And with so many paths crisscrossing the city and connecting the beaches and parks, renting a bike may be the answer to all your sightseeing needs. A good resource for touring information, from city buses to Alaska cruises, is bcpassport.com, with an abundance of options, contact information and online booking capabilities from reputable companies.

## Activity Tours

**1695 West 4th Av**
*Kitsilano*
*Map 9 A3* 86

### BC Dive & Kayak Adventures

*604 732 1344 | www.bcdive.com*

Search for octopus and wolf eels on two-tank dives from a custom dive vessel, or kayak in the waters of Howe Sound. This one-stop marine centre offers rentals of all diving and kayaking equipment, as well as guided tours and charters. Dive charters cost $85 per person, dive gear is $60 per day, guided dives are $100 a day, and kayak rentals $30 daily. All safety equipment and car racks are included. Available year round, every day from 10:00 to 18:00.

**2745 West 4th Av**
*Kitsilano*
*Map 8 C3* 87

### Diving Locker

*604 736 2681 | www.vancouverdivinglocker.com*

A Kitsilano institution since 1967, this shop opens every day and has all your scuba and snorkelling needs. It also organises Sunday diving safaris to assorted destinations near Vancouver, such as the Sunshine Coast, Vancouver Island and the Gulf Islands, each for $50. An additional $50 is charged for equipment rental, $30 for personal gear including mask, snorkel, fins and boots, and $25 for an optional DVD. Certified PADI instructors will guide all levels of divers on these two-tank dives.

**Various Locations**

### Natural Trekking

*604 836 2321 | www.naturaltrekking.com*

You can organise anything from a private leisurely walk to more strenuous hikes and snowshoeing trips through the myriad of trails on the North Shore Mountains of Vancouver. Two hour to full day tours are offered ranging from $79 to $139 per person for a group of three, with pick-up and drop-off included.

**6409 Bay St**
*West Vancouver*
*Map 2 A1*

### Sewell's Marina

*604 921 3474 | www.sewellsmarina.com*

Located in the lovely ferry terminal town of Horseshoe Bay, about a 30 minute drive from Downtown, this company offers high-speed boat trips along the beaches, cliffs and sea caves of Howe Sound. Seals, eagles and sea birds frequent the coastal waters to a backdrop of jagged peaks and some of the highest priced beach front homes in the city. A bouncy and sometimes cold ride, but the views are well worth it. Fares are $67 for adults, and $37 for children. Bookings available from April 1 to October 31, each leaving at 10:00, 13:00 or 16:00.

## Bicycle Tours

Cycling has become a way of life for Vancouverites. Both the cause and the consequence is a network of cycling paths throughout the city, from the urban core to the forested parks and sandy beaches. At the gateway to each large park or community there is usually a bike shop with rentals. All you really need is a map, which many provide, and a little curiosity. But if a tour is to your liking for orientation or insider information, some of the shops can be of service.

*1040 West 7th Av*
*Fairview*
*Map 9 D4* **90**

### City By Cycle

*604 730 1032 | www.citybycycle.com*

Guided tours are on offer here for participants of all levels. Take one of the trips along the Downtown Seawall, through the forest trails of Pacific Spirit Regional Park, the mountain trails of the Seymour Demonstration Forest and through Steveston, a fishing village 30 minutes south of Vancouver. The Downtown route takes you on the Seawall through Stanley Park, English Bay, over to Granville Island by water taxi, then on to Yaletown, Chinatown, Gastown and back to where you started. You get an hour on your own (if you choose) at Granville Island Market to have a snack and explore. The cost is $69 for adults and $49 for kids aged 8 to 16, which includes bicycle, helmet, guide and water taxi fare. Pick-up from a Downtown location is available, and the tours are packed with information about Vancouver's history and points of interest. Groups of four or more can register by phone or online.

*1798 West*
*Georgia St*
*West End*
*Map 7 C1* **91**

### Spokes Bicycle Rentals & Tours

*604 688 5141 | www.spokesbicyclerentals.com*

One of Vancouver's oldest, this store has a wide selection of bikes for rent and is conveniently located near the Seawall cycle route at the Georgia Street entrance to Stanley Park. Store hours are Monday to Sunday, 09:00 to 16:30, and tours run from mid-May to mid-September. The choices are the 09:00 90 minute tour of Stanley Park for $30, or the 11:00 three hour tour of Granville Island for $60. Rollerblades are also available to rent year round.

## Boat Charters

Walk on to any dock in Vancouver and you will see a multitude of signs directing you to boat charters offering everything from an hour in a rowing boat, to a couple of days on a small sailing boat, to weeks on a luxury power cruiser. The companies range from one rustic looking vessel with a salty sea dog as owner, skipper and bottle washer, to fleets of state of the art vessels with full galleys, chefs, skippers in dapper uniforms, and professional crews of eight. The vast majority of companies are above board, but the rule of thumb is that if it looks suspect, it might be. Ask to see a business licence from smaller companies and qualifications if you hire a skipper.

*1620 Duranleau St*
*Granville Island*
*Map 9 B2* **92**

### Cooper Boating

*604 687 4110 | www.cooperboating.com*

This is the largest charter company in Canada, with a variety of new and state of the art fully equipped sailing and power vessels. Charters can be planned and booked online. Other than a driving licence, no formal certification is required, but lessons and orientation are available if needed. Charters range from 24 hours to as many days or weeks as required. Summer charters cost from $600 to $900 for five days for a 40 foot vessel, with discounts in the shoulder and off seasons. Skippers can be hired for $325 to $500 per day, depending on the vessel. Additional costs such as changes of linen and food provisions are not included.

## Boat Tours

Vancouver is surrounded by the sea to the north and west and by the mouth of the 1,300km Fraser River to the south, so it's no surprise that boating and cruising are popular among locals and tourists alike. There is a myriad of rentals and charters at the ubiquitous marinas, so a walk down to any of these will uncover a tour or charter of some kind, from small sailing boats to luxury cruise vessels. The larger marinas are at Coal Harbour near Stanley Park, Canada Place, Plaza of Nations, near George Weinburn Park and at Granville Island.

**100-1676**
***Duranleau St***
*Granville Island*
*Map 9 B2* **93**

## Accent Cruises

*604 688 6625 | www.dinnercruises.com*

Open 362 days a year and centrally located at one of the beautiful marinas at Granville Island, Accent offers regular dinner cruises (open to all), or seasonal theme parties such as Christmas and Valentines Day for $60. Private tours are available for groups of 10 to 400, for business functions, conferences, banquets, weddings, anniversaries, stags and even burials at sea. There are several package menus to choose from, or you can have one of the onboard chefs customise one to suit specific needs.

**1804 Boatlift Lane**
*Granville Island*
*Map 9 C2* **94**

## False Creek Ferries

*604 684 7781 | www.granvilleislandferries.bc.ca*

The cheapest way to see Vancouver from the water is from one of the two fleets of water taxis that scoot around the bays, inlets and harbours, the captain serving as tour guide. False Creek Ferries and Aquabus (604 689 5858, www.theaquabus.com) serve commuters and sightseers every day from 07:00 to 21:00 every five to 30 minutes, depending on the dock, the time of year, and the time of day. The ferries operate along False Creek, and they connect the popular living, entertainment and business districts of the West End, Kitsilano, Granville Island, Yaletown and Main Street. The 20-seater boats are brightly coloured and resemble the putt-putt tugboats of children's stories. Fares range from $2.50 to $5 a leg, with discounted fares for frequent riders, children and seniors.

**Harbour Cruises**
***Marina***
*Denman St*
*West End*
*Map 7 C1* **95**

## Harbour Cruises

*604 688 7246 | www.boatcruises.com*

This company offers a variety of cruises ranging from 75 minute harbour rides at $25 for adults, to two-and-a-half hour brunch cruises for $45, and evening dinner and live music cruises for $65, from May to October. Cruises provide stunning views of the Downtown skyline, Stanley Park, Lions Gate Bridge, and the North Shore Mountains and Indian Arm, among others. Also available for private and corporate charters.

## Brewery & Vineyard Tours

Sampling BC's beers and wines is as easy as ducking in to any neighbourhood bar or restaurant and asking for local products. There are a few brew pubs, such as Steamworks (p.465) in Gastown, and the Yaletown Brewing Company (p.466) and Dix (p.426) in Yaletown, that brew their tasty beers and ales on site, and Dix does offer samplers, but not an actual tour. Wine is everywhere, and although most of the wineries are in the famed Okanagan Valley (p.261, 400 kilometres to the east, there are a few west coast nooks and crannies where wine grapes flourish. In recent years the product has improved significantly, especially among the white wines.

**1441 Cartwright St**
*Granville Island*
*Map 9 B2* **96**

## Granville Island Brewery

*604 687 2739 | www.gib.ca*

Although Canada is not famous for its beer, there are an increasing number of microbreweries that are moving beyond the bland factory brews. This small company on Granville Island serves exceptional beer which can be sampled on its daily tours at 12:00, 14:00 and 16:00. The brews range from lagers and pilsners to stouts, bocks and porters. Tours are limited to 12 people and are booked on a first-come, first-serve basis in the retail store. You can sample four different styles of beer for $10, including the latest limited release.

*Vancouver Trolley Company*

**7330 6th St**
*Burnaby*
*Map 6 F3* **97**

## Stay & Tour

*604 524 8687* | *www.stayandtour.ca*

Fraser Valley wineries are gaining some ground on the larger and more illustrious Okanagan Valley in terms of quality and awards. This five hour tour picks you up from Downtown or points elsewhere, visits five wineries, stops for dinner (price not included) at the Bedford House restaurant in historic Fort Langley, and drops you off back where you started. Pick up time and location confirmed upon reservation. The cost is $87 per person.

## Bus Tours

A quick and efficient way to get the lay of the land and check out some of the sites and neighbourhoods is to join one of the many bus tours. The buses are large, comfortable and safe, and the tours narrated with interesting titbits and anecdotes that many locals don't know. They leave from convenient points Downtown, and some have a hop on, hop off policy that allows you to spend more time in a particular area.

**Various Locations**

## Landsea Tours

*604 662 7591* | *www.vancouvertours.com*

Landsea offers a range of tours in and around Vancouver in comfortable buses. The half day Vancouver tour takes you through Downtown, Gastown, Chinatown, Granville Island, Queen Elizabeth Park and other places of interest for a $59 adult fare, running twice daily at 09:00 and 14:00. It also offers daily North Shore Mountain tours that take approximately five hours for $114, as well as 10 hour seasonal Whistler tours for $199 and 13 hour bus and ferry tours to Victoria for $169.

**Various Locations**

## Vancouver Trolley Company

*604 801 5515* | *www.vancouvertrolley.com*

Probably the only tour you'll need if Downtown and environs are what you're interested in. Starting in Gastown, but on a continuous loop and seemingly ubiquitous, these San Francisco style trolley buses have a hop-on hop-off policy, with 23 stops in Downtown, Stanley Park, Chinatown, Granville Island, Kitsilano and more. The trip is narrated with historical and cultural facts and anecdotes. From mid-April through to the end of September, you can also use your ticket on any Gray Line or Vancouver double decker. Trolleys and double deckers alternate every 15 minutes. A total tour takes two hours if you stay on, and costs $35 for adults, $18.50 for children.

## Culinary Tours

Vancouver has become one of the top cities on the continent for the number, variety and quality of its restaurants. From French to Italian, to Chinese, Japanese and Indian, to a west coast fusion, there is more than likely something to fit the taste and budget of most people. Some of the restaurants offer tastings and tapas style menus for diners to try a bit of everything before deciding on a main dish.

**Unit 565**
**1689 Johnston St**
*Granville Island*
*Map 9 B2* **100**

### Edible British Columbia

**604 662 3606** | www.edible-britishcolumbia.com
A very cool concept: a store that sells high quality local food products, lets you try them at a tasting bar, and at weekends and on special occasions will teach you what exciting dishes you can prepare with the in-store products. It also offers chef-guided market tours, cooking classes and unique gourmet kayaking trips. A novel idea worth checking out.

## Dolphin & Whale Watching

A variety of sea mammals, ranging from porpoises, dolphins and sea lions to orca, humpback and grey whales, occupy the waters of the Georgia Strait, the Strait of Juan de Fuca and the open Pacific on the west coast of Vancouver Island. Some species such as the humpback and greys are migratory and are best seen on the west coast of Vancouver Island in the spring, but there are also pods of orcas that show up for the salmon runs, and others that hang around all year. The whale tour companies can give you good odds of seeing one, and if you don't, they offer free return trips until you do. The boats leave from Steveston, a suburb 25 minutes south of Downtown, but shuttle buses are available for folks living in the city. The companies are licensed and have high standards for safety and equipment.

**12551 No 1 Rd**
*Richmond*
*Map 2 B3*

### Steveston Seabreeze Adventures

**604 272 7200** | www.seabreezeadventures.ca
From April until the end of October this company claims to have a 95% sighting success rate. You may be lucky enough to spot orcas, humpback or minke whales, dolphins, porpoises, seals, sea lions, eagles and seabirds. And if you don't see one, you get a rain check to go again at a later date. Tours for groups of 12 to 23 passengers on 40 foot covered vessels are a minimum of three to five hours. Boats carry a certified naturalist/interpreter on board and hydrophones to hear the whales' vocals. Inquire about the shuttle service from Downtown Vancouver and onboard lunch which are both available at an additional cost. Tours are $105 for adults and $69 for kids.

**12240 2nd Av**
*Richmond*
*Map 2 A3*

### Vancouver Whale Watch

**604 274 9565** | www.vancouverwhalewatch.com
Catch a shuttle from Downtown to Steveston, a fishing village 25 minutes south, board a hydrophone equipped semi-enclosed zodiac, and head for the lovely Gulf Islands. Vancouver Whale Watch runs two departures daily, either at 10:00 or 11:00, with trips lasting a total of three to five hours depending on availability and number of sightings, which are guaranteed. If you don't see a whale, you can return for free until you do. Guided by a professional naturalist, you should spot orca (killer) whales, porpoises, sea lions, bald eagles, seals and other wildlife. Tours run from April to October, rates are $109 for adults and $75 for children.

**1806 Mast Tower Rd**
*Granville Island*
*Map 9 B2* **103**

### Wild Whales Vancouver

**604 699 2011** | www.whalesvancouver.com
This tour company is based on Granville Island, providing easy access for those who don't want to travel to Richmond. Tours run from mid-April to the end of October, and

spotters can choose between a fully enclosed boat, or, for those who want to brave the elements, and open-decked vessel.

## Helicopter & Plane Charters

A flight over Vancouver and environs or across the Georgia Strait and over the Gulf Islands en route to Victoria is about as good as it gets. The size of the province and the extent of the endless range of mountains and forest is nothing short of awe-inspiring. The main point of departure is from Coal Harbour between Canada Place and Stanley Park, where a number of companies are based.

### Harbour Air Seaplanes

*1075 West Waterfront Rd*
*Downtown*
*Map 7 E2* **104**

*604 274 1277* | *www.harbourair.com*

North America's first carbon neutral airline, this company offers a good number of options. There is a 20 minute Vancouver panorama flight featuring aerial views of the city and surrounding mountains, and a fly-and-dine tour on a seaplane flight to Bowen Island, followed by a three course dinner at Doc Morgan's Inn, and a return ferry and limousine ride back to Downtown. Prices range from $99 for the Vancouver Panorama, to $189 for the fly and dine, to $289 for a Victoria overnighter. It also offers fishing and whale watching flights. Harbour Air operates year round, but check for seasonal availability of certain flights.

### Helijet

*5911 Airport Road South*
*Richmond*
*Map 2 B3*

*604 270 1484* | *www.helijet.com*

A daily service between Vancouver and Victoria in Sikorsky S76 or S61 helicopters. Terminals are located at the downtown Whistler Heliport, Vancouver Harbour Heliport, Vancouver International Airport and Victoria Harbour Heliport. Vancouver Harbour to Victoria Harbour one-way economy class flights are $229 for adults and $186 for children.

### West Coast Air

*1075 West Waterfront Rd*
*Downtown*
*Map 7 E2* **106**

*604 606 6800* | *www.westcoastair.com*

Operating out of Coal Harbour and Richmond, this expansive fleet of floatplanes – Twin Otters to those who carry a small notepad in their top pocket – runs regular scheduled services to Victoria and other Vancouver Island destinations, as well to other popular locations such as Whistler. It also runs sightseeing tours over Downtown and beyond, and planes are available for charter too.

## Heritage Tours

### Takaya Tours

*2156 Banbury Rd*
*North Vancouver*
*Map 4 F2* **107**

*604 929 2268* | *www.takayatours.com*

This First Nations company offers guided interpretive paddles in either ocean-going canoes, sea kayaks or zodiacs. Guests paddle or motor in the protected waters of Burrard Inlet and Indian Arm, while guides from the local tribes sing songs, tell legends and point out ancient village sites. A visit to the anthropology museum beforehand is useful for a historical context, but this tour brings it alive. Two hour canoe trips are $54 and motorised five hour eco-cultural tours are $140. Tours operate from May to October, for all ages and fitness levels, and passenger minimums apply.

## Island Resorts

Between the Vancouver area and Vancouver Island lies an archipelago known collectively as the Gulf Islands. This area is divided into the north, reachable from the ferry terminal in Horseshoe Bay, and the south, reachable from the terminal at Tsawwassen. Some are well-populated and have plentiful services, amenities and roads, and others are wild, lacking in amenities and reachable only by private boat. The main ones have ferry docks and are on the BC ferries routes, making it easy to island hop. A day or even a week trip by car, bicycle or on foot is a tranquil escape to a world unaffected by the bustle of Vancouver. See also Weekend Breaks, p.260.

## Gulf Escape Vacations

*295 West 8th Av*
*Main*
*Map 11 A2* **108**

*1 866 407 7811* | *www.gulfescapes.com*

This company gives advice, organises itineraries and makes accommodation, ferry and some meal reservations for self-driving tours to the Gulf Islands and Vancouver Island, off the coast of southern British Columbia. Ferries hop from island to island taking travellers to a world of walking trails, empty beaches, funky villages, artist studios, cosy cottages, and bed and breakfasts with fire places and excellent west coast cuisine. Tours can also include whale and grizzly bear watching. Prices start at about $500 for three days including ferries, accommodation, some meals, a travel kit with maps and a few other extras, while you provide the car.

## Union Steamship Company Marine Resort

*Snug Cove*
*Bowen Island*
*Map 2 A1*

*604 947 0707* | *www.ussc.ca*

Drive (avoid rush hour because everything bottlenecks at Lions Gate Bridge) or take the bus from Downtown to West Vancouver's Horseshoe Bay, hop on a ferry and in 20 minutes you're on an island that seems light years away from the hustle and bustle of the city. Situated on the aptly named Snug Cove, this village resort offers rental cottages with views of the towering peaks to the west across Howe Sound, the marina and the tiny village, with its boardwalks, restaurants and pubs, and quaint shops surrounded by 600 acres of park. Room rates are $130 to $250, with additional beds priced at $10 each.

## Other Tours

## Early Motion Tours

*1-1380 Thurlow St*
*West End*
*Map 7 C4* **110**

*604 687 5088*

Offers personalised sightseeing tours around Vancouver in the comfort of a restored 1930 Model A Ford convertible big enough for four passengers. If the sun is shining, there's nothing better, and the looks and smiles of onlookers are in themselves worth the fee and a picture. Reservations are required for the $100 hourly ride, and when divided by four this makes quite a good deal. All rides begin at Canada Place. Longer tours to more distant locations are available by special arrangement and at a reduced hourly rate.

## Stanley Park Horse-Drawn Tours

*Coal Harbour*
*Car Park*
*Stanley Park*
*Map 3 F4* **111**

*604 681 5115* | *www.stanleypark.com*

These old-fashioned horse-drawn carriages meander through the natural beauty of Stanley Park. A professional guide narrates this tour highlighting Deadman's Island, the harbour, Lions Gate Bridge, a coastal red cedar forest, and it includes stops at the totem poles, the 'Girl in Wetsuit' sculpture, the SS Empress of Japan figurehead, and the Rose Garden. The carriages depart daily a few hundred metres into the park from the Georgia Street entrance on Park Drive, from 09:30 to 17:30 in the summer, with shortened hours in winter. The one hour trip is $25 for adults and $15 for kids up to age 12.

## Pub Crawl Tours

Vancouver is a bit of an oddity when it comes to pubs, clubs and restaurants. Each has a distinct licence, which governs when it can open and close, what it can serve, and how loud it can be, since many of them are in combined commercial and residential areas. Compared with large European, Asian or American cities, Vancouver is relatively quiet when it comes to nightlife. Nevertheless, with a bit of scouting, there is something for most drinkers in the main pub, club and restaurant areas of Gastown, Yaletown, Robson Street, or the entertainment district on Granville Street. Granville has become somewhat notorious for its late night antics when the bars close at 03:00.

*Various Locations* ◄ 

### Bust Loose

***604 682 6044*** | *www.bustloose.com*

Beginning at Ceili's Irish Pub (670 Smithe Street, Downtown), these 40 seat buses, equipped with sound systems, reconfigured seating, dance poles and lighting, escort merrymakers to some of Vancouver's hottest pubs and nightclubs. Reservations are recommended for seasonal and event parties, or you can just show up and take your chances. The $35 fee includes all nightclub cover charges, queue jump, interactive ice breaker games, munchies, prizes, taxes and guides. Private bus bookings for stags or corporate escapades are also available, starting at $800 per night. No trainers or T-shirts are allowed, and a dress code applies for club crawls.

## Shopping Tours

The main shopping areas in the city conveniently cater for many tastes. Robson Street is filled with boutiques and shoe shops while Gastown is a great place to pick up something kitsch. Chinatown offers Asian treats and Yaletown is great for houseware and designer furniture, while SoMa (south Main Street) can provide funky items and antiques. Granville Island is great for arts and crafts, and 4th Avenue or the conservative Kerrisdale and South Granville Strip are all equally good shopping locales. And if a mall is in order, there is always Downtown's Pacific Centre or Burnaby's colossal Metrotown. See Shopping, p.360, for more information.

*Various Locations* ◄ 

### Shopabout Tours

***604 739 4048*** | *www.shopabout.ca*

This company provides set itinerary or custom shopping tours on foot through the key shopping areas. You can take their pick as you wander through trendy Yaletown and the chic shops along Robson Street. Tours can also feature the funky shops along Main Street, the arts and crafts of Granville Island, the night market in Chinatown, or the more classic South Granville Strip. Guides will orient you, give fashion tips, and steer you towards the best items for the fairest prices. Shoppers will also receive discount cards valid for three days. Reservations are required.

## Walking Tours

There are relatively small distances between major attractions in Vancouver making this, in combination with the plenitude of designated pedestrian areas, a great walking city. There are beachside seawalls, park paths and neighbourhood greenways on or along virtually every street. Just step outside and head for any of the lovely districts, beaches or parks and you'll discover new and alternate routes. Most areas are safe 24 hours a day, although there have been some problems in Stanley Park after dark. Let common sense dictate your walks by avoiding isolated areas after dark.

*Various Locations*

## Walkabout Historic Vancouver
**604 720 0006** | www.walkabouthistoricvancouver.com
Two hour walking tours of Downtown, Gastown, Chinatown and Granville Island are on offer here, including a lively narrative on the history, scoundrels, scandals, culture and architecture of the areas. Daily tours are $25 per person, rain or shine at 10:00 and 14:00, with customised times available. All starting points are within walking distance or a short bus ride from Downtown, and the sites are wheelchair accessible. Phone or email for reservations.

*Various Locations*

## Walking Tours Of Vancouver With John Atkin
www.johnatkin.com
Offering a unique perspective of the city's development, architecture and history, John Atkin is both a historian and an author with a deep interest in the quirks and eccentricities of this city. Heritage walks, Chinatown's architecture and a Cherry Blossom tour through Vancouver's tree lined streets are themes offered throughout the year. A two hour tour can be taken by individuals or larger groups of up to 35 for $10 per head with a minimum of $75 for smaller groups of five.

## Tours Outside Vancouver
Vancouver is conveniently located near a myriad of natural wonders, resorts, towns and cities. But to citizens of the second largest country in the world, 'near' could mean hours in a car, bus or ferry or any combination thereof. The good news is that the journey often equals or surpasses the destination in terms of natural beauty. Visit Whistler Mountain, with its alpine adventures, shops, bars and restaurants, and Victoria, with its history, culture and gardens. Tofino's pristine coastline, beaches, surf and whales and Harrison's lakeside shops and hot springs are also popular options. Also not to be missed is Seattle, Vancouver's American cousin, the Okanagan Valley with its sun, lakes, skiing, vineyards and wineries, or the Rocky Mountains and Alaska by cruise ship past coastal mountains and glaciers. There are so many companies offering tours that the whole thing can be a little overwhelming. A good starting point is bcpassport.com, which provides lists of tours and online booking, as well as comprehensive information and services. See also Daytrips, p.257.

*Pacific Central Stn*
*1150 Station St*
*Strathcona*
*Map 10 C4* **116**

## Amtrak
**1 800 872 7245** | www.amtrak.com
Book a trip with Amtrak, an American rail company, for a day, overnight or extended trip to Seattle. There you'll find a variety of attractions including the towering Space Needle, the bustling Pike Place Market, the Boeing factory, the Flight Museum, the historic Pioneer Square, a great art museum, and even underground tours of the city. Beforehand or once there, check out Seattle Tours (www.seattletours.us, 1 800 305 9617) for bus tours in and around the city. Comfortable trains with full facilities and services leave every day and cost $90 return. Don't forget your passport.

*Various Locations*

## BC Passport
**604 990 9299** | www.bcpassport.com
Probably the best one-stop shopping website for booking tours and general information about Vancouver and other points of interest in BC. This company provides every tour imaginable, from 20 minute float plane rides over Vancouver harbour, to coach, rail and boat cruises to such destinations as Victoria, Whistler, the Rocky Mountains and Alaska. As well as tour booking services, the website also contains a wealth of information about schools, businesses, jobs, entertainment, accommodation, activities, medical services, real estate and other useful facts and advice for new arrivals.

*909 West Cordova St*
*Gastown*
*Map 7 F2* **118**

## Key West Travel & Tours

*1 888 632 3757* | *www.keywesttravelandtours.com*

This company offers a variety of coach, rail or combination tours from Vancouver to the Okanagan Valley, for sun, beaches and wineries, and to the Rocky Mountains for spectacular views of alpine lakes, mountains and glaciers. Trips include activities such as short hikes and wine tasting. Prices start at $600 for five-day coach tours, which include motels, activities and some meals. Most tours are from May to October.

*Various Locations*

## Landsea Tours

*604 662 7591* | *www.vancouvertours.com*

Landsea offers daily North Shore Mountain bus tours for approximately five hours, and includes a gondola ride to the top of Grouse Mountain for spectacular views of the city. It includes a walk across the stunning Capilano Suspension Bridge with the Capilano River deep in a canyon hundreds of feet below. The cost is $114 for adults and $75 for children. It also offers a seasonal 10 hour Whistler tour of the mountain resort, which will host the 2010 Winter Olympics. Costs for this tour are from $199 for adults. Additionally, for $169 there is a 13 hour bus and ferry trip to Victoria, with its historical neighbourhoods, parliament buildings, lush gardens, and the inner harbour, featuring street artists, performers and buskers. High tea at the Empress Hotel is a favourite.

*101-369*
*Terminal Av*
*Strathcona*
*Map 10 C4* **120**

## Rocky Mountaineer Vacations

*604 606 7200* | *www.rockymountaineer.com*

The most complete rail tour company in the country, this firm offers a multitude of rail, rail and drive, rail and cruise, and rail and wilderness trips to Whistler, the Rocky Mountains, the Prairies or all the way across Canada to the Atlantic provinces. The trains are older, but well maintained with comfortable reclining seats, elegant dining and glass domed observation cars. You have a choice of packages, with a range of seat and hotel prices, starting at $1,200 for a basic four day train tour and going as high as $17,000 for the ultimate 17 day Alaskan cruise.

## Tour Operators

Whether to use an operator to book a trip requiring multiple forms of transport and accommodation or to organise it yourself is a question that plagues travellers. You can definitely do it cheaper on your own, but a great amount of energy and effort is required to make it all work seamlessly, and in many cases the tour operator can do a better job. Obviously Vancouver tour operators charge fees, but since the volume is high and the industry is so competitive, commissions tend to be low, and service is generally good and reliable, each company adhering to local laws and industry standards. The larger Vancouver tour operators provide extensive tours to all parts of the province and beyond. Prices are generally not negotiable, but companies often offer sales at certain times of year. The rule of thumb is to shop around.

| Tour Operators | | |
| --- | --- | --- |
| Early Motion Tours | 604 687 5088 | na |
| Landsea Tours | 604 662 7591 | www.vancouvertours.com |
| Maxima Travel | 604 454 9944 | www.maximatours.com |
| Shopabout Tours | 604 739 4048 | www.shopabout.ca |
| Stanley Park Horse-Drawn Tours | 604 681 5115 | www.stanleypark.com |
| Tourism BC | 1 800 435 5622 | www.hellobc.com |
| Vancouver Coast & Mountains | 604 739 9011 | www.vcmbc.com |
| Vancouver Tours | 1 888 321 3635 | www.vancouvertours.net |
| Vancouver Trolley Company | 604 801 5515 | www.vancouvertrolley.com |

# Daytrips

There are plenty of exciting day trips to embark on throughout the area. Hop aboard a ferry to beautiful Bowen Island, shop in the States, or soak up the area's best mineral hot springs. Looking for a wet and wild experience? Board a whale watching excursion leaving Granville Island or Steveston, or go windsurfing or kite boarding in Squamish. Fort Langley offers an ideal setting for getting steeped into local history, folklore and fruit wines. And of course hiking is always an option – your biggest dilemma is deciding on which of the hundreds of kilometres of local trails to take.

## Bowen Island

Bowen is the closest of the Gulf Islands to Vancouver. Ferries leave on an almost hourly basis to and from Horseshoe Bay. It's a small place, and just about all of its highlights can be reached on foot. For the best views and the island's most invigorating hike, climb the 11km to the Mount Gardner summit. At nearly 700m it is the island's highest peak. Trailhead access is 3km from the ferry terminal on Mount Gardner Road. Picnickers will enjoy the 323 hectare Crippen Regional Park (www.gvrd.bc.ca/parks). This lovely protected green space offers easy hiking including the Dorman Point Trail, which winds to a prime view over Howe Sound, and the trail around Killarney Lake, perfect for freshwater angling. BMX and mountain bikers can try the challenging Bowen Island Mountain Bike and Skills Park (open dawn to dusk, helmets are mandatory) near the southern end of Killarney Lake, a 20 minute pedal from the ferry landing. For a walk back in time, take in the gift store and ice cream shop of the Union Steam Ship Marina Chandlery (604 947 0707, www.ussc.ca), located in one of the few remaining buildings of a 1920s resort on the southern side of the ferry landing. Next door you can enjoy a cold pint and good food at Doc Morgan's Restaurant and Marine Pub (604 947 0808).

## Fort Langley

Located in a rural setting on the south bank of the Fraser River, Fort Langley has several cultural and historical offerings in a natural setting. Access is either via an hour's drive east along the Trans-Canada Highway, or via public transport (SkyTrain to Surrey Central station, then bus 320 to Langley Centre and transfer on to the C62 to Fort Langley). The major attraction is the restored Fort Langley National Historic Site, which details the lives of the 19th century fur traders who founded the outpost for the Hudson's Bay Company (604 513 4777, www.pc.gc.ca/fortlangley), while those interested in First Nations people and pioneers, as well as top-notch art exhibits, should check out the Langley Centennial Museum (604 888 3922, www.langleymuseum.org). If you're thirsty you can taste and purchase locally made fruit wines in the old-fashioned saloon bar at the Fort Wine Company (604 888 3922, www.thefortwineco.com). Farming buffs can visit the BC Farm Machinery and Agricultural Museum (604 888 2273, www.bcfma.com), while animal lovers should check out the Mountain View Conservation & Breeding Centre (604 882 9313, www.mtnviewfarms.com), which breeds species at risk and reintroduces them into their natural habitat. Equestrian enthusiasts can see some of the top riders in North America compete at the Thunderbird Show Park's five major hunter and jumper show tournaments, which take place between May and October, or sign up for private lessons (604 888 4585, www.thunderbirdshowpark. com). There is good paddling and fishing on Fraser River, which winds through the area, and you can go running, cycling and hiking on the area's well-kept trails.

## Harrison Hot Springs

A great place to soak it up is the southern shores of Harrison Lake. The spa town of Harrison Hot Springs is accessible via a 125km drive out of the city east on the Trans-Canada to Agassiz and north on Highway 9. Here you can enjoy the luxurious lakeside Harrison Hot Springs Resort & Spa (604 796 2244, www.harrisonresort.com), and if you stay there you can soak in the five indoor and outdoor hot mineral pools. The hotel also operates the Harrison Public Pool for day visitors. The indoor facility is not as upscale as the hotel, but the thermal waters and their effects are the same. Beyond the warm mineral pools, there are other natural offerings to explore. Backed by snow-capped peaks, Harrison Lake offers good trout fishing, canoeing, windsurfing and swimming during summer (you can rent equipment at the hotel's dock). Bring your binoculars when hiking and camping in the nearby Sasquatch Provincial Park, to the east of the lake – this is the home of BC's mythical mountain beast of the same name, and although sightings are rare, you never know. The town's biggest parties take place in May and September when the lakefront turns into an art garden with master sand sculptors competing for prize money (604 796 3425, www.harrisand.org). You can still come afterwards to enjoy the work; as long as the elements don't destroy them, the sculptures remain in place until mid October.

### Hell's Gate

There are few better places than this rocky gorge on the Fraser Canyon to get a grasp of the fury and power of BC's glacier-fed rivers. It's a two-and-a-half-hour drive east of Vancouver on the Trans-Canada Highway, and once there you can hop aboard the Hell's Gate Airtram (604 867 9277, www.hellsgateairtram.com, $16) from April to October for a two minute crossing of the raging 35m wide river. Once on the other side of the thundering, perilous ravine, you can enjoy the tourist displays of the area's natural history, picnic on one of the benches, pan for gold with the kids, pick up some home-made fudge or dig in at the Salmon House Restaurant. Your tram ticket also gives you access to the area's suspension bridge. This is the best spot to pause and take in the spectacular views of the foaming Fraser River. Bring warm clothes; while hell is often thought to be hot, when the wind and rain picks up here, it can be cold as hell too.

### Indian Arm

**Ride The Tides**

*Indian Arm is protected from the rough sea surf, but it isn't immune from tides. Check the charts (www.waterlevels.gc.ca) and plan ahead; it's easier to kayak into the fjord on a rising tide. Mornings are the best time to return south as northerly winds pick up in the afternoon. When camping, store boats above the tide line.*

The spectacular Indian Arm Provincial Park protects an 18km long fjord just minutes away from the city centre. Most access it through the picturesque town of Deep Cove, just a short drive or ride on buses 211, 212, 290 and C15 east of the Second Narrows Bridge. Here you can get all the services of a small tourist town set around the lovely waterfront Panorama and Deep Cove Parks. For those who want to get right into the inlet, rent a canoe or kayak (Deep Cove Canoe and Kayak, 604 929 2268). Another option is to drive past Port Moody to the Belcarra Regional Park, where you'll find beaches, a lake, kilometres of hiking, cycling and horse riding trails, playing fields, picnic shelters and a wharf with a great view of Indian Arm. A favourite overnight trip is to leave from either Belcarra (if you have your own boat) or Deep Cove (if you are renting), and paddle to the northern terminus of the inlet. Less experienced paddlers can pit stop or stay overnight at the North Twin Island campsite (an hour's paddle north), while those with more time and strength can go further to find a full throttle wilderness experience with abundant forest reaching from sea to sky. Many drop by Silver Falls, a high, thin cascade partially hidden in the folds of the mountainside. The falls are located on the western banks about two-thirds of the way up the fjord. Harbour seals are often seen swimming or sunning themselves on the rocks nearby. Further on still is Granite Falls campsite, roughly a four hour paddle from Deep Cove. The base of the rushing, 50m high cascade makes a wonderful place to soak. Like all campsites in Indian Arm Provincial Park, there is no cost to overnighting here, although fires are not permitted. Check www.env.gov.bc.ca/bcparks for up-to-the-minute details or warnings before you embark on your adventuring.

### Squamish

The Coastal Salish named this breezy area Squamish, or 'Mother of the Wind'. An hour north of Vancouver on Highway 99, the town can seem like nothing more than a good pit stop

*Squamish*

for gas, a double shot of espresso or a burger on the way to Whistler, but Squamish has numerous natural and man-made attractions that make it a worthwhile destination on its own. With its prime location at the head of Howe Sound, its heavy winds have made it a magnet for the region's top windsurfers and kite-boarders, and it's one of the top sites in the country for rock climbing. Most come to scale the nearly 1,000 free and aided routes up the 762m Stawamus Chief, whose profile is etched in the cliff face. The granite monolith is the second largest on earth and provides good nesting habitat for the peregrine falcon. For climbing guides, instructors and information, contact Squamish Rock Guides (604 815 1750). Experienced climbers can visit www.squamishclimbing.com, a community-based website which offers plenty of advice and free, downloadable climbing maps. If you want to appreciate the view without testing your wits on the cliff, you can also hike around the back in about two hours. The well marked trail splits at the top where you can choose between three different peaks. Each offers a wonderful view over the region. Be prepared though; the hikes are challenging and require a fair bit of dexterity to get to the top. There is also a rustic provincial park camping ground (www.env.gov.bc.ca/bcparks) complete with pit toilets and bear boxes to store your food at the entrance to the hike.

Several nice provincial parks line the road to Whistler, including Alice Lake, which is good for swimming holes and fishing, and Brandywine Falls. Garibaldi Provincial Park is the gem of them all. A dozen kilometres north of Squamish, this is a true wilderness play land and offers plenty of opportunities to get lost for hours or days. You can access its five most important trailheads by following signs along Highway 99 between Squamish and Pemberton. There are 160 walk-in wilderness camp sites ($5 per person per night, no reservations). In winter Garibaldi is popular for cross-country and back-country skiing. Man-made attractions around Squamish include the West Coast Railway Heritage Park (604 898 9336, www.wcra.org), the small Squamish Valley Museum (250 898 3273), and the BC Museum of Mining (604 896 2233, www.bcmuseumofmining.org). The latter offers gold panning to visitors during the summer, and you can keep what you find.

## Shopping South Of The Border

With the huge comparative drop of the US dollar to the 'loonie' (see p.49) over the past few years, southbound cross-border shopping has never been so popular. Birch Bay Square (formerly Peace Arch Outlet), at barely 10km from the border on the west side of Interstate 5, is the closest place to find a bargain (360 366 3128, www.birchbaysquare.com). Most shoppers head to the Seattle Premium Outlets (360 654 3000, www.premiumoutlets. com), two hours south of Vancouver off Exit 202, Interstate 5. The bustling mall offers 110 designer outlets including brand names such as Adidas, Nike, Calvin Klein, Guess and Burberry. Of course, since you are purchasing outside of Canada, residents are legally obliged to declare all purchased items at customs. In terms of duty free items, you are officially allowed to return with $50 after being away 24 hours, $200 after 48 hours and a maximum of $750 if you have been gone for more than a week. If you don't have a car, you can still make the trip to the Seattle Premium Outlets with Quick Shuttle for US$24 each way (604 940 4428, www.quickcoach.com). Just make sure to bring your passport.

### The Bald & The Beautiful

*Every winter as many as 3,000 bald eagles converge near the Cheakamus and Mamquam tributaries of the Squamish River to feed on the remains of a late run of chum salmon. The best views are generally between Tenderfoot Creek Fish hatchery in the Cheakamus Valley down to the Squamish Estuary. For the latest eagle updates, check the Visitor Information Centre in Squamish (604 892 9244).*

**On The Buses**

*If you want to do some out of town exploring, but don't have a car, taking the Greyhound bus is often the cheapest way of getting around mainland British Columbia. Buses leave the Pacific Central Station (1150 Station Street) and cost around $10 per hour of transport (weekend travel is slightly more expensive). You can usually buy tickets just before you travel, but for optimal pricing, reserve at least a week in advance. Check www.greyhound.ca or call 1 800 661 8747 for more information.*

# Weekend Breaks

With its unique natural setting on the edge of the Pacific Rim, Vancouver offers a plethora of exciting weekend getaways. Expect islands to the west, mountains to the north, the bucolic Fraser Valley to the east and some spectacular shopping and cities to the south. Best of all, getting there is half of the fun. The metropolis offers an extensive variety of transportation, including the world's largest ferry system, a sizeable fleet of seaplanes, as well as good rail and bus services. Due to its location just north of the Washington state border, you'll need your passport for all trips south.

## Gulf Islands

Scattered throughout the Strait of Georgia, the Gulf Islands are made accessible by BC Ferries (see p.44). With their penchant for the alternative, ancient VW buses, beautiful bed and breakfasts, plentiful book shops and cosy bakeries, the islands are the chosen home for many of the province's most accomplished artists and a weekend haven for Vancouver's back-to-the-land crowd. Of the southern Gulf Islands, Salt Spring is the most populated with 10,000 residents. It also offers great diversity – from the spectacular coastal Ruckle Provincial Park to the heights of Bruce Peak, and the burgeoning service town of Ganges.

Long and thin, Galiano Island's highlight is Montague Harbour, a small, sheltered beach renowned for ocean kayaking. Accessible only by boat, the remote Dionisio Point Provincial Park has 30 camping sites near the beach (www.env.gov.bc.ca/bcparks). Those visiting the Pender islands should not miss seeing the Beaumont Marine Park, which boasts arguably the region's best views, from the top of Mount Norman. At water level, Bedwell Harbour offers idyllic sites for walk-in camping and swimming (www. pc.gc.ca/gulf). The Penders also have a couple of high-end resorts, including Poet's Cove (1 888 512 7638, www.poetscove.com), and wine lovers will enjoy the pleasant Morning Bay Winery (250 629 8351, www.morningbay.ca).

Mayne Island offers terrific kayaking, particularly around Horton and Bennett bays. Try Mayne Island Eco Camping (250 539 2667, www.mayneisle.com) for one of the islands' best campsites, complete with waterfront hot tub. With a population of only 326, sleepy Saturna offers excellent beach access and quiet roads perfect for cycling. Most stop to wine and dine at the wonderful Saturna Island Family Estate Winery (250 539 5139, www.saturnavineyards.com).

*Gulf Islands*

The northern Gulf Islands are slightly more remote and therefore even more laidback than their southern counterparts. Texada, the largest of them all, remains an important mining and forestry town and a favourite for birdwatchers. Access is via Powell River. Quadra and Cortes islands are known for their legendary sports fishing, first-rate scuba diving and vibrant First Nations culture. Gabriola Island is the site of the Malaspina Galleries (www.env.gov.bc.ca/bcparks), an impressive series of sandstone formations sculpted by surf and tides into dramatic caves and caverns. Access is via a 20 minute ferry from Nanaimo.

# Weekend Breaks

## Manning Provincial Park

With more than 70,000 hectares of mountain, forest, stream and lakes, Manning Provincial Park is one of the best places around Vancouver to get deep into nature. Access is via curvy Highway 3, which bends through the park as it climbs from the valley into the Cascade Range, three hours from Vancouver. The best way of experiencing Manning is by getting out and hiking its huge network of trails, swimming, canoeing or trout fishing in its lakes, camping in one of over 400 sites, and observing the plentiful wildlife. If you'd rather not rough it, stay at the Manning Park Resort (1 800 330 3321, www.manningpark.com). Double room rates begin at $165. During winter you can also go downhill skiing at the Manning Park Resort ski area, as well as snow tubing, Nordic skiing and skating.

## Okanagan Valley

The Okanagan's dry, tumbleweed BC interior hills juxtapose with long and narrow crystal blue lakes, creating an oasis for cottage life, outdoor sports and a booming wine industry. With excellent food options, mountain resorts, and an abundance of hotels, B&Bs and camping spots, the valley is a popular year-round destination. The growing number of services and amenities in the northern valley town of Kelowna (population 165,000), including its international airport and growing satellite campus of UBC, have seen it become the centre of economic activity for the region. Its location on the eastern banks of Okanagan Lake also make it a great vacation destination, particularly for those who enjoy golf, watersports and camping. Popular nearby adventures include riding at Silver Star Mountain Resort (1 800 663 4431, www.skisilverstar.com), Big White Resort (250 765 3101, www.bigwhite.com) and Sun Peaks Resort (250 578 5474, www.sunpeaksresort.com). You can play golf at any of Kelowna's several championship courses and, of course, partake in the region's favourite pastime – visiting the local wineries. Of the numerous annual events, the highly competitive Kelowna Dragon Boat Festival on Lake Okanagan in mid-September (www.kelownadragonboatfestival.com) makes quite a splash.

Further south, Penticton straddles the space between lakes Skaha and Okanagan. It's a smaller, decidedly more laidback town, with all the action focused on it short but sweet Main Street. Penticton is home to a booming wine industry which has been recently dubbed 'Napa North'. The Burrowing Owl Estate Winery (1 877 498 0620, www.bovwine.ca), half an hour south of town, has a particularly delightful dining room, lovely guest rooms and renowned wines. Rock climbers, if they can peel themselves away from the free wine samples, won't want to miss the multi-pitch climbs just east of Penticton at the Skaha Bluffs (check www.skaha.org for information). During winter, the Apex Resort offers advanced ski terrain for downhill enthusiasts (1 877 777 2739, www.apexresort.com). If you are there in August, don't miss Penticton's five-day Peach Festival (www.peachfest.com). The waterfront community in Osoyoos at the southern end of the Okanagan was once the region's top attraction. However, the complex of big box hotels plonked on the southern end of the lake with the same name hasn't aged gracefully. If anything it's a reminder of how far along tourism has come further north in the Okanagan Valley.

Vehicle access from Vancouver to the region takes as little as four hours via the straight-shot Highway 5 (Coquihalla) toll road ($10 per car). This direct route ends near Kamloops, and accesses Kelowna via the 97C Okanagan Connector. The other option is the southern Hope to Princeton scenic route on Highway 3 which winds through Manning Park (see p.261). You can also catch a scheduled flight to the Okanagan airports of Kamloops, Kelowna and Penticton from Vancouver on Air Canada, West Jet and Pacific Coastal Airlines. Flight times are just under an hour and costs start from $100.

**Many Wine Houses**
The Okanagan hosts four wine festivals, one for each season. The Spring Festival is held throughout the valley in early May; Silver Star Mountain Resort near Vernon hosts the Summer Wine Festival in August; October ushers in Harvest Festival with more than 165 events throughout the region; and mid January is reserved for the Sun Peaks Icewine Festival. Contact the Okanagan Wine Festivals Society (250 861 6654, www.owfs.com) for full details.

Seattle

## Seattle

Home of the emblematic Bill Gates and Microsoft, *Frasier*, Boeing and Starbucks, as well the birthplace of grunge music, Jimi Hendrix, and the World Trade Organisation riots, the 'Emerald City' (population 3.2 million) is a land of stark contrasts. Access from Vancouver is primarily limited to driving through the Peace Arch Border Crossing, or with Amtrak (1 800 872 7245, www.amtrak.com), which services downtown Seattle with four bus trips and one train every day (US$28 by bus or US$37 by train). Aside from the cheaper prices on consumer goods and flights, Seattle also offers numerous attractions such as the panoramic view from the 158m Space Needle (206 905 2100, www.spaceneedle.com). Closer to earth is the action around Pike Place Market, which nestles between First Avenue and Western from Pike to Virginia streets (www.pikeplacemarket.org). This century old tradition now has more than 200 businesses operating year-round, with craftspeople, farmers' booths and a wonderful brewpub, The Pike (206 622 6044, www.pikebrewing.com), to boot. Make sure to catch the famous flying fish action at the Pike Place Fish Market. Other attractions include strolling along Seattle Waterfront (Piers 52 to 70 on Alaskan Way), where you can shop or hop aboard a cruise or ferry. Baseball fans can check out the Mariners (www.mariners.com) and football fans can catch the Seahawks (www.seahawks.com), Seattle's pro teams. Families will enjoy Woodland Park Zoo (206 684 4800, www.zoo.org), where you can get up close to its collection of 1,000 animals situated in naturalistic exhibits. Travel time from Vancouver to Seattle generally ranges between three and five hours depending on your mode of transport, although on holiday weekends the border crossing can be a nightmare.

### Spend Less In Seattle

*Things are cheaper in the US. To take advantage of the savings, many use the Quick Shuttle (604 940 4428, www.quickcoach.com) with stop offs in the Bellingham outlets and airport (US$24), Seattle city centre (US$36), and the Seattle-Tacoma (Sea-Tac) International Airport (US$49).*

## Sunshine Coast

This strip of land between peak and ocean north-west of Vancouver harbours plenty of forest and mountain, several pristine lakes, a couple of wonderful retreats, and a few service towns. There's no direct road connection from Vancouver, so getting there involves taking the 40 minute Langdale ferry from Horseshoe Bay. Most explorers begin in the pleasant hillside town of Gibsons, a 10 minute drive west of the ferry terminal. Known as the 'Gateway to the Sunshine Coast', it welcomes visitors with its perennial arts and outdoors focus and prime location at the mouth of Howe Sound. Some of the favourite stop offs include window shopping along Gibsons Landing and Gawer Point Road and strolling the night-lit Seawalk at the harbour. Offshore fishing, sailing and kayaking are also popular activities. The town swells with music aficionados during the mid-June jazz festival (www.coastjazz.com). Highway 101 weaves north-west through the small service town of Sechelt. Expect several good bakeries, art studios, a pleasant beachside promenade and numerous parks. Porpoise Bay, just outside of town, is arguably the nicest with views of the inlet and places to picnic and camp. For a taste of local First Nations' culture, check out Sechelt's impressive House of Hewhiwus (604 885 8991) and the adjacent Raven's Cry Theatre (604 885 4597, www.ravenscrytheatre.com). On summer Saturdays there's a bustling farmers' market in the car park.

For an exclusive getaway, try Rockwater Secret Cove Resort (1 877 296 4593, www.rockwatersecretcoveresort.com) just north of Sechelt. This exclusive getaway offers 13 tenthouse suites scattered along an elevated cliff-side boardwalk overlooking Halfmoon Bay. Further on, Garden Bay and Pender Harbour have plenty of holiday options with their complexes of marinas, cottages, scenic restaurants, pubs and convenience stores.

Highway 101 ends at Egmont, where experienced kayakers can ride the tide at the world famous Sechelt Rapids in the Skookumchuck Narrows. To continue to the Upper Sunshine Coast, take the Earls Cove to Saltery Bay ferry across Jervis Inlet. The town of Powell River is surrounded by water and is considered the Dive Capital of Canada. Its incredible wintertime visibility and large number of sites led Jacques Cousteau to hail the locale the best place to scuba dive after the Red Sea. Fishing, hiking, kayaking, canoeing and mountain biking are also favourite pastimes. BC Ferries connects Powell River to Texada Island and to Comox on Vancouver Island.

**Let It Rain**

*Tofino's three metres of annual precipitation result in not just a rich rainforest, but a fertile sea. Because of the abundance of nutrients that percolate through the forest floor, the waters of Clayoquot Sound host a huge variety and quantity of marine life – half a dozen species of whales, a recovering sea otter population, two species of seals, and some of the mightiest salmon and herring runs in the world.*

## Tofino

Sandwiched between the mighty Pacific and one of the greatest old-growth forests left on the planet, Tofino, on Vancouver Island, has quickly become the top west coast destination to get that nature fix. It is located at the centre of the enormous Clayoquot Sound Unesco Biosphere Reserve, which covers some 340,000 hectares of land including the Pacific Rim National Park Reserve, 16 provincial parks, two ecological reserves and spans significant expanses of ancient temperate rainforest, lakes, rivers, alpine peaks and rocky and sandy shores. To get to this remote destination, most catch the two hour ferry to Nanaimo, then make the scenic three hour, 208km drive across the island. The direct, one hour Orca Airways flight (1 888 359 6722, www.flyorcaair.com) offers a quicker alternative – prices start at $159. Tofino sits at the northern terminus of the Pacific Rim National Park (250 726 7721, www.pc.gc.ca). Here you can surf throughout its numerous bays, kayak along its coastline, go salmon and halibut fishing, and hike over 12km of national park trails. Those looking for more relaxing pleasures can simply make sandcastles in the 22km expanse of Long Beach. You can also pitch a tent at the Green Point Campground in the national park from mid-March to mid-October (1 877 737 3783, www.pccamping.ca). Whatever you decide to do, it's worthwhile packing a pair of binoculars. An abundant population of black bears roams the forest, hundreds of species of birds, including a thriving population of bald eagles, rule the sky, and you can hop aboard a Remote Passages zodiac (1 800 666 9833, www.remotepassages.com) to watch the thousands of migrating and resident whales at various times throughout the year.

Don't think going green means a lack of luxury though. Despite its claim as a wilderness outpost, Tofino offers a wide selection of services, including the top-rated Wickaninnish Inn resort (250 725 3100, www.wickinn.com), the lovely three storey units at the Pacific Sands Beach Resort (1 800 565 2322, www.pacificsands.com), plus excellent laidback restaurants such as SoBo (250 725 2341, www.sobo.ca) and the cosy Common Loaf Bakeshop (250 725 3915). Tofino and Long Beach fill to capacity during the dry summer months and on long weekends, so book ahead. Expect rain if you are travelling during the shoulder season.

**Whistler Mountaineer**

*During the warm season (from mid April to mid October) you can hop aboard the Whistler Mountaineer (604 606 8460, www. whistlermountaineer. com) for some old-fashioned rail travel. The train travels at 'Kodak speed', giving passengers a chance to snap some of the impressive scenery along the corridor (total time on board is approximately three hours). Attendants provide hot breakfasts on the 08:30 departure northbound and the famous Fairmont High Tea service on the 15:00 afternoon departure to the city. Standard fares are $110 one way and $200 return. You'll pay a little more to be in the Glacier Dome, a glassed-in carriage with panoramic views.*

Whistler

## Victoria

Victoria – the capital of British Columbia – ranks as Vancouver's number one weekend getaway for good reason. It's easy to get to, has plenty to see, offers good museums and sites to visit, and has wonderful food and drink options. The city is completely walkable (so bring comfortable shoes), with most of the activity taking place around the Inner Harbour, fronted by the wonderful, turn-of-the-century Fairmont Empress Hotel (see table, p.265). Aside from being widely regarded as the top hotel in the city, the Empress is where you can indulge in Victoria's age-old tradition of enjoying afternoon tea (from $50 per person, smart dress and reservations essential).

The Royal British Columbia Museum (1 888 447 7977, www.royalbcmuseum.bc.ca) across the street from the Empress is one of the most visited in Canada. Its natural and modern history galleries display true-to-life, multi-sensory exhibits; you can also descend into the depths via the ocean station exhibit, which replicates the experience of a Victorian-era submarine, or learn more about Canada's indigenous people in the First People's Gallery. Lovers of oversized films can catch an IMAX presentation for an extra charge. Back outside, the neighbouring Thunderbird Park on the corner of Belleville and Douglas streets showcases a wonderful collection of totems. Those interested in history, architecture and politics should visit the early 20th century Provincial Legislative Buildings (www.leg.bc.ca). The best place to rest your feet is at the public seating at the Inner Harbour. Here you can while away the hours looking at the boats or watching the buskers perform. The Tourism Victoria centre at the northern end of the harbour (www.tourismvictoria.com) is an excellent place to find out more about local events. Just north of here, the lively, cobble-stoned streets of Old Town are filled with souvenir shops, some lovely restaurants and several excellent pubs like the Canoe Brewpub (250 361 1940, www.canoebrewpub.com). You can also wander around historic Chinatown. Outside the city centre, drive through the historic neighbourhood of Oak Bay and don't miss the magnificent Butchart Gardens (1 866 652 4422, www.butchartgardens.com). If you are interested in coastal flora, a half hour drive west takes you to beautiful Botanical Beach. Here you are guaranteed to see the island's best tidepools and sealife. Of course with its idyllic coastal location, Victoria offers numerous whale watching tours and fishing charters which leave from the harbour. To get to Victoria, Harbour Air flies across in less than an hour (1 800 665 0212, www.harbour-air.com), while BC Ferries offers almost hourly departures for its 90 minute crossings of Georgia Strait (see p.44).

## Whistler

Vancouver's ultimate weekend getaway is just a 115km, two hour drive north. Home of the signature alpine events of the forthcoming 2010 Olympic and Paralympic Winter Games, the bustling four-season resort at Whistler hosts some of the best mountain terrain on the continent. Adrenaline junkies have two huge interconnected mountains to ski and snowboard on in the winter (the season lasts from late November to early June), and hike and bike during the summer. Of the two peaks, Whistler

*Sold only to Canadian and Washington State residents online (www.whistlerblackcomb. com), the Edge Card gives discounts on lift tickets and services all season long (buy online before mid November for the best deal: lift tickets from $57 plus taxes). You can also purchase discount passes from the 7-Eleven stores outside Whistler ($69 plus taxes).*

is the more family friendly, while the edgier Blackcomb has harder runs and includes glacier skiing. Combined, the two offer a total of 3,307 hectares, 1,609 vertical metres, 38 lifts and more than 200 trails. You can access both mountains with the same lift pass ($77-$83 plus taxes) on separate gondolas leaving from the centre of the resort town. For those looking for more relaxed adventures, stroll through the pedestrian village. Here you'll find plenty of boutiques, souvenir and convenience shops, restaurants, pubs, and a liquor shop. You can also swing a round of 18 holes at the four championship golf courses. Those looking for an inspiring walk or bike ride can get out on the 30km long Whistler Valley Trail which connects the village to the region's main attractions. Cross-country skiers can also get a leg up along 28 kilometres of track-set trails that take skiers through scenic Lost Lake Park, the Chateau Whistler Golf Course, and Nicklaus North Golf Course. Nordic trail maps and rental equipment are available in sports shops throughout the village. Whistler also satisfies those who prefer extravagance over exercise. The mountain town hosts more than 100 hotels, including several luxury resorts (see table, p.265), and more than 20 spas that you can access through the central reservation system (1 888 403 4727). With Whistler's world class set up and reputation, you can expect all the amenities along with a high price tag. If possible, avoid the holiday season line-ups and price surges during the Christmas and Easter breaks. You'll find the best deals during late spring and autumn, and can hire ski and boarding equipment from outlets in the village.

### Twin Peaks

Whistler is a place of superlatives. Not surprising then that it will soon be the site of the world's longest gondola. The Peak to Peak is a 4,400m-long tramway which will connect the Blackcomb and Whistler summits by December 2008. Riders with vertigo beware; the gondola is also the world's highest, hovering 415m above the forest floor at some points.

## Weekend Break Hotels

| | | | |
|---|---|---|---|
| Gulf Islands | Harbour House Hotel | 250 537 5571 | www.saltspringharbourhouse.com |
| | Poet's Cove | 1 888 512 7638 | www.poetscove.com |
| | Seal Beach Cottage At Mayne Island Eco Camping | 250 539 2667 | www.mayneisle.com |
| Manning Park | Manning Park Resort | 1 800 330 3321 | www.manningpark.com |
| Okanagan | Burrowing Owl Estate Winery | 250 498 0620 | www.bovwine.ca |
| | Coast Capri Hotel | 250 860 6060 | www.coasthotels.com |
| Seattle | Best Western Loyal Inn | 206 682 0200 | www.bestwestern.com |
| | The Edgewater | 206 269 4565 | www.edgewaterhotel.com |
| | Sheraton Seattle | 206 621 9000 | www.sheraton.com/seattle |
| Sunshine Coast | Absolute Heaven Bed & Breakfast | 604 885 3241 | www.absoluteheavenbb.com |
| | Rockwater Secret Cove Resort | 1 877 296 4593 | www.rockwatersecretcoveresort.com |
| Tofino | Pacific Sands Beach Resort | 1 800 565 2322 | www.pacificsands.com |
| | Wickaninnish Inn Resort | 250 725 3100 | www.wickinn.com |
| Victoria | Fairmont Empress | 250 384 8111 | www.fairmont.com |
| | Hotel Grand Pacific | 250 386 0450 | www.hotelgrandpacific.com |
| | Traveller's Inn | 1 888 877 9444 | www.travellersinn.com |
| Whistler | Fairmont Chateau Whistler | 604 938 8000 | www.fairmont.com/whistler |
| | First Tracks Lodge | 1 866 385 0614 | www.firsttrackslodge.com |
| | Four Seasons Resort Whistler | 1 888 935 2560 | www.fourseasons.com/whistler |
| | Hilton Whistler Resort & Spa | 1 800 515 4050 | www.hiltonwhistler.com |
| | Holiday Inn Sunspree Resort | 1 800 229 3188 | www.whistlerhi.com |
| | Pan Pacific Village Centre | 1 877 324 4856 | www.panpacific.com |
| | Pan Pacific Whistler Mountainside | 1 877 324 4856 | www.panpacific.com |
| | The Westin Whistler Resort & Spa | 1 888 634 5577 | www.westinwhistler.com |

# Holidays From Vancouver

## Alaska

**Flight time**
2.5 hours to Anchorage
(most fly out of Seattle)

Alaska lives in the collective imagination as the capital of cold, for obvious reasons. It's home to more glaciers than the rest of the inhabited world combined and sits next to the North Pole. But because of its northern latitude, summer days are warm and longer than just about anywhere else. You can follow the footsteps of turn-of-the-century gold rush miners, explore historic villages such as Skagway and Juneau, hike the numerous peaks and kayak the lakes and fjords. Wherever you go, Alaska's mountains and forests come alive with abundant wildlife including a thriving population of mammals such as black and grizzly bears, wild rams and moose. Off-shore, you're also likely to see several species of whales, orcas and dolphins. Take binoculars. Remember too that Alaska is a US state, so border regulations apply. Alaska is also a popular cruise destination from Vancouver, with stops at the Hubbard Glacier, Skagway and Juneau.

**Best time to visit:** The long days of summer are wonderful and the autumn colours are dazzling. Northbound cruises leave Vancouver from May to October.

## California

**Flight time**
2.5 hours to San
Francisco, 3 hours to Los
Angeles and San Diego

California offers a taste of just about everything. Its coastal highways wind south of stunning San Francisco through the towering redwoods of the Big Sur coast, past the designer labels of Beverly Hills' Rodeo Drive and end near the elegant La Jolla district in San Diego. Head inland to the heart of North America's wine growing industry in the Napa and Sonoma valleys, or go for a hike, climb or ski in the towering peaks of the Sierra Nevada. And with one of the continent's most productive farmlands coupled with the country's top chefs, expect excellent, fresh cuisine during all seasons.

**Best time to visit:** Is there ever a bad time to visit California?

## Canadian Rockies

**Flight time**
2.5 hours to Calgary
plus a two hour drive
to Banff

Canada's Rocky Mountains are a land of stark peaks, abundant forests and giant glaciers protected by a series of adjacent national parks. The area hosts some of the best hiking and skiing in the continent, with jaw dropping views at every turn. The postcard pretty service towns of Banff, Lake Louise and Jasper offer first-rate accommodation and food options, as well as a plethora of tours for getting around. However, if you are on a budget, remember Banff as an acronym: Be Aware Nothing For Free.

**Best time to visit:** Summer is beautiful but busy; autumn is spectacular and quiet; winter is long and cold; spring is winter.

## East Asia

**Flight time**
from 11 hours

With its prime location on the shores of the north Pacific, Vancouver has become an excellent base from which to access the far east (which is actually to the west). Join the ranks of the city's 'astronauts' – businesspeople who work in Asia and commute from their west coast homes. Whether it is walking the Great Wall of China, shopping in Seoul's busy electronics markets to meditating in the Zen temples of Japan and negotiating million dollar deals in Hong Kong's skyscrapers, you can do it all from here. There are daily departures to all points east.

**Best time to visit:** With the wide range of attractions available in east Asia, any time is a good time to plan a trip.

## Hawaii

**Flight time**
6 hours

Surf and turf never knew a better location than Hawaii's half dozen islands. Most begin at the world famous Waikiki Beach on Oahu. Nearby you can play golf, fish, surf or snorkel along its busy coast. Those looking for more solitude can escape to Kauai, the exclusive resorts of Lanai or the rural paradise at Molokai, while the more active can choose between the windsurfing paradise at Maui and the adventure tourism mecca on the Big Island of Hawaii.

**Best time to visit:** Hawaii's popularity soars during Vancouver's cool winters, but is cheaper during its dry season (April to October).

*Flight time*
*3 hours*

## Las Vegas, Grand Canyon & Monument Valley

Home to gambling, great food and unbeatable entertainment, Las Vegas is the ultimate getaway for the hedonist. Here you can let loose and hit the slots or spa, catch a top-rated show or just pig out on the free cocktails and buffets open all hours of the day. But don't think 'Sin City' is just for adults; it hosts dozens of family and child-friendly amusement parks and attractions, including the wild and crazy Adventuredome, America's largest indoor theme park. And if you need a break from the madness, find some serenity at the southern edge of the spectacular Grand Canyon or spin your wheels through the other-worldly sites of Monument Valley in neighbouring Arizona and Utah.

**Best time to visit:** Gambling knows no seasons (thanks to air-conditioning). If you're going outdoors, though, stay clear of summers when the desert heat burns.

*Flight time*
*4 to 8 hours depending*
*on the destination*

## Latin America

The many natural and cultural wonders of Latin America rest just a short-to-medium flight south of Vancouver. Most head to Mexico's world class beach resorts dotted throughout its Caribbean and Pacific shoreline, most notably Los Cabos, Puerto Vallarta and Cancun. Its colonial and pre-Hispanic heritage and enticing cuisine can also be appreciated in amazing highland cities such as Oaxaca, Guanajuato and Mexico City. Cuba's Havana and Varadero and the Dominican Republic's Puerto Plata and Punta Cana remain popular winter destinations for those seeking the Caribbean sun. Although there are no direct flights, Costa Rica has positioned itself as a naturalist's and adventurer's haven, with dozens of protected areas and superlative beach access on its Pacific coast.

**Best time to visit:** At Christmas and spring break southbound charters are packed with tourists of all shapes and sizes. Better deals can be found from January to March. The Caribbean hurricane season (June to November) can be treacherous.

*Flight time*
*5 hours*

## Montreal, Toronto & Niagara Falls

The streets of Montreal (population 3.6 million) are always a party. Join the city's joie de vivre at its Festival International de Jazz and L'International des Feux fireworks festival in June, or the Just for Laughs and FrancoFolies celebrations in July. The fun continues even in the winter when you can catch the frosty Fête des Neiges. Toronto (population five million), Canada's largest metropolis, hosts a multicultural scene like no other, along with the important Toronto International Film Festival every September. Both cities are home to important National Hockey League teams, and baseball fans can also get their fix at the modern Rogers Centre (formerly known as the Sky Dome), located just below the 553m high CN Tower in downtown Toronto. Don't miss visiting Niagara Falls. Just two hours from the burgeoning metropolis, the most powerful cascade in North America drains up to 168,000 cubic metres of water every minute from the Great Lakes.

**Best time to visit:** Fiery tempered Montreal is a true four seasons town with hot, humid summers and cold-as-hell winters. Toronto is more mild mannered in both its weather and character. The autumn colours in October are glorious throughout the region.

**Flight time**
*1.25 hours to Portland*

*Oregon*

Sandwiched between the US states of Washington and California and famed for its laidback, grass-roots style, Oregon offers a spectacular 580km long coastline, some of the world's best windsurfing along the Columbia River Gorge, and superb skiing and hiking around the dormant volcanic cone at Mount Hood. Expect a booming fruit industry through the Willamette Valley and a thriving urban vibe in the wonderful city of Portland, which is surrounded by pinot noir producing vineyards. Shopaholics beware: the state is completely tax free, and its outlet stores offer the best prices on consumer goods of all of the coastal states.
**Best time to visit:** Summer; winter can be rainy.

**Flight time**
*Varies, depending on
how far south you go*

*Western US National Parks*

They don't call it the wild west for nothing. From Montana to the New Mexico border and all points west, you will come across some of the most beautiful and remote national parks and recreation areas in all of continental America. Some not-to-be-missed gems include California's Yosemite for its giant sequoias and spectacular waterfalls and Death Valley for its rugged extremes. Closer to home, Utah's enigmatic Glen Canyon and Zion stand out as miracles of nature, while Yellowstone, the country's first national park, protects the habitat of wild bison, wolves and grizzly bears along with a series of active geysers. Just across the border from BC, Washington's giant Olympic National Park offers wonderful water access at Rialto Beach as well as terrific rainforest to alpine meadow hikes throughout Hurricane Ridge.
**Best time to visit:** The autumn and spring shoulder seasons offer less tourist traffic and heat than the popular summer. Winter can be touch and go in some of the parks due to inclement weather.

**Flight time**
*2.5 hours*

*Yukon*

Bordering Alaska, British Columbia, the Northwest Territories and the frozen Beaufort Sea, Canada's north-westernmost territory is a land of giant proportions. It hosts numerous parks protecting thousands of kilometres of mountain, forest and coast, including the 5,959m high Mount Logan, Canada's highest peak. History and literature buffs won't want to miss a trip to Dawson (population 1,200), which is the Yukon's second-largest community and home to the late Klondike poet Robert Service. The northern territory plays host to one of the key celebrations of the Canadian winter, the world famous 1,600km Yukon Quest dog sled race which leaves the capital of Whitehorse (population 24,000) every February.
**Best time to visit:** Summer and autumn have the best weather. Spring can be mucky. Winter is ideal for seeing the northern lights.

## Travel Agencies

| | | |
|---|---|---|
| BC Passport Bookings | 604 990 9299 | www.bcpassport.com |
| CheapTickets.Canada.com | 1 877 922 6359 | www.cheapticketscanada.com |
| Cruise Ship Centres | 604 687 4545 | www.cruiseshipcenters.ca/yaletown |
| ExitNow.ca | 1 866 561 3948 | www.exittravel.com |
| Forbes Travel International | 604 689 0461 | www.forbes-travel.com |
| Marlin Travel | 1 877 894 4333 | www.marlintravel.ca |
| North South Travel & Tours | 604 736 7447 | www.northsouthtravel.com |
| Paramount Travel | 604 575 6200 | www.wegothere.ca |
| Quest Travel | 604 875 9125 | www.questtravel.ca |
| Senior Tours Canada | 604 647 0100 | www.seniortours.ca |
| Travel Cuts | 1 888 359 2887 | www.travelcuts.ca |
| Travel Dimensions | 604 685 8636 | www.tditravel.com |

# Holidays From Vancouver

*San Francisco*

*Lake Louise*

*Mexico City*

*Tokyo*

*Beijing*

# Activities

## Sports & Activities

The opportunities afforded to active Vancouverites by the spectacular natural environment are a big part of why the city is regarded as one of the best places in the world to live. There are snow-topped mountains to the north, water and beaches to the west, and a mild enough climate for the sporty to be active all year round. Couple this with a multicultural, health-oriented population and you've got an incredible variety of sports and activities for a mix of ages and interest groups. There are also social leagues and clubs galore to help you find a niche in the city, with teams for common sports such as tennis, soccer and baseball, sports brought from abroad such as netball, and those that are particularly popular in Vancouver, such as ultimate Frisbee and dodgeball.

Ice hockey is a huge part of Vancouver's culture, thanks largely to the local National Hockey League team, the Canucks, and Canada's propensity for cold sports; the area is also well known for its skiing and snowboarding. Internationally renowned Whistler Blackcomb (where the 2010 Winter Olympics will be based) is just a few hours' drive away, and there are three other developed mountains right on the North Shore. Off-season, you can make daytrips to nearby campsites or white water rafting companies to get away from the city.

A sport that prospers within the city is beach volleyball. Head down to one of the beaches lining the Point Grey shore during the summer and you're guaranteed to see people playing recreationally or competitively. Vancouver also has a number of indoor facilities, both public and private, for sports such as squash and badminton. As the focus on holistic well-being among residents grows, along with an increasing awareness of their relationship with the environment, more and more

## Activity Finder

fitness facilities are beginning to offer yoga, Pilates and other strengthening and relaxation classes.

If you're searching for a way to get into Vancouver's social athletics community, try Urban Rec (604 879 9800, www.urbanrec.ca), an organisation with teams for indoor volleyball, beach volleyball, ultimate, slo-pitch, dodgeball, basketball, floor hockey, indoor and outdoor soccer, curling and flag football. A general starting point for amateur sports is Sport BC (604 737 3000, www.sport.bc.ca), or check out the city's website (604 257 8400, www.city.vancouver.bc.ca/parks/rec) for a listing of public fitness centres, ice rinks, swimming pools, ball fields, golf courses, skateboard parks, youth and senior activities and children's day camps. If you move to the city with limited means, you can apply for a discount for the city's parks and recreation programmes (a Leisure Access card) through the Parks Board. For arts and entertainment, pick up the free independent newspaper *The Georgia Straight* for a weekly look at what's going on in the city.

## Aerobics & Fitness Classes

Vancouver has a broad range of fitness options; whether you want to incorporate some exercise into your life, lose weight and increase your strength and flexibility, or train for a sports team or big event, there's a programme for you. The Parks Board runs 13 fitness centres (with weights rooms and fitness classes) in the various community centres (see p.341). You don't need to be a member to work out in a public community centre. Prices vary, but if you buy punch cards or monthly passes you'll get a better deal. A Flexipass provides unlimited access to Parks Board recreation facilities; an adult annual pass costs $325. Typical classes include step, yoga and dance.

There's also a plethora of private gyms in Vancouver which require membership. Generally, private gyms have newer weight and cardio equipment, give you more personal attention, and run classes you won't find at the community centre, but it comes at a higher price. Most member gyms do not have swimming pools (although YWCA Health & Fitness does), but some offer tanning and steam rooms.

*Deep Cove*

Vancouver is also home to a number of personal training studios, where you hire your own coach to lead your workouts. Boot camps are another option for those looking for an intense, all-encompassing workout. These are four-week programmes, with zealous instructors who knock you into shape by incorporating everything from weights to cardio training, yoga to Pilates, and stretching.

## Aerobics & Fitness Classes

| | | | |
|---|---|---|---|
| Body & Soul | 604 224 2639 | Point Grey | Various types of Pilates and yoga, ski fit, stretch and qigong (breathing and relaxation) |
| Denman Fitness | 604 688 2484 | West End | Kick boxing, step, abs, ball fit, muscle classes, squash courts, yoga and Pilates |
| Figure It Out Fitness | 604 980 2710 | North Vancouver | Circuit training for women |
| Fitness World | 604 581 4447 | Various Locations | Varies at each location. Usually includes body sculpt, step, power yoga and body ball |
| Gold's Gym | 604 224 4653 | Various Locations | Cardio dance, cardio kickboxing, cycling, Pilates, stretch, total body and step and sculpt |
| Innovative Fitness | 604 714 1661 | Various Locations | Personalised exercise programmes |
| Just Ladies Fitness | 604 904 4451 | Various Locations | Step and strength, cardio ball, spinning, yoga, Pilates, dance fit |
| Kitsilano Workout West | 604 734 3481 | Kitsilano | Aerobic step classes, dance, yoga, core stability training and spinning courses |
| Level 10 Fitness | 604 985 8910 | North Vancouver | Spinning, boxing, boot camp |
| Mixx Co-Fitness Studio | 604 682 6499 | Downtown | Yoga, Pilates, body ball, nutritional coaching, injury rehabilitation |
| My Adventure Bootcamp | 604 329 7867 | Various Locations | Bootcamp for women |
| Ron Zalko Fitness Club | 604 737 4355 | Kitsilano | Stroller strides for mum and baby |
| Survivor Bootcamp | 604 518 1374 | Various Locations | Bootcamp |
| Sweat Co Studios | 604 683 7938 | Downtown | Step and sculpt, spinning, Pilates, stretch, power core, yogalates |
| Tantra Fitness | 604 738 7653 | Kitsilano | Female-only classes offering pole dancing, ball fit, cardio striptease |
| YWCA Health & Fitness | 604 895 5777 | Downtown | Cardio, strengthening and aquatics programmes; members get free workshops on health and nutrition |

## Art Classes

Other options **Art & Craft Supplies** p.366, **Art Galleries** p.220

Vancouver has a vibrant art scene that's slowly gaining recognition internationally. For aspiring professional artists, there are reputable schools such as the Emily Carr University of Art and Design (1399 Johnston Street, 604 844 3800), and other fine arts programmes at universities and colleges. For those who can do little more than draw a stick figure, community centres often have art programmes that are less intimidating, inexpensive and welcome beginners. Families should check the schedule of community programmes offered by local institutions such as Burnaby Art Gallery (p.221) or Richmond Art Gallery (7700 Minoru Gate, 604 247 8300). Vancouver Art Gallery (p.224) becomes a hub of child-friendly art projects on the third Sunday of each month.

## Federation Of Canadian Artists

*1241 Cartwright St*
*Granville Island*
*Map 9 C3* **1**

*604 681 2744 | www.artists.ca*

Purchase a membership to the FCA if you're an artist of any skill level interested in workshops, lecture series and other art-related educational programmes. The federation has a number of affiliated groups, but is primarily based in Vancouver, which means easy access to the gallery and its courses. Educational workshops are held at the Centre for Peace (1825 West 16th Avenue) for beginners through to advanced artists, covering everything from acrylics and oils to life drawing, charcoal and inks. These courses can cost from $250 to $425 for two to four day workshops, depending on the subject. At the gallery on Granville Island, keep an eye out for the professional development lecture series and the occasional Monday night artist-in-action demonstration for $10 (free if you're taking part in a workshop).

## Langara College Continuing Studies

*100 West 49th Av*
*Fraser*
*Map 6 A3* **2**

*604 323 5322 | www.langara.bc.ca/cs*

If you don't want to be a full-time student, but still want to take professionally taught advanced art classes, try Langara College's visual and applied arts programme. Subject areas include art history, drawing (charcoal, figure drawing and illustrating children's books), and painting (acrylic, egg tempura, mixed media, oil and watercolours). The classes are popular so register early. Fees vary, but are affordable.

## Roundhouse Community Arts & Recreation Centre

*181 Roundhouse*
*Mews*
*Yaletown*
*Map 9 E2* **3**

*604 713 1800 | www.roundhouse.ca*

This Vancouver community centre has an ongoing mission to promote the arts, from acting and dancing to visual arts. Housed in the building which used to service Canadian Pacific Railway trains, its range of programmes includes an arts drop-in for at-risk youth, 'Petit Picassos' for toddlers, and pottery and woodworking workshops for beginners to advanced participants. Petit Picassos classes cost $50, once a week for six weeks, whereas a two month, one day a week introductory pottery course costs $145.

## Badminton

Racquet sports are incredibly popular in east Asian countries and, thanks to the steady influx of immigrants from that region, badminton has emerged as one of the preferred sports in Vancouver, and in particular Richmond, over the past decade. For many, badminton is much more than whacking a few shuttles back and forth in your garden – a top player can smash a badminton shuttle close to 200mph. For the casual player, community centres generally have badminton court rentals or drop-in times (see p.341 for your nearest one), or you can join a club and take lessons.

## ClearTwo Badminton Centre

*100-4351 No 3 Rd*
*Richmond*
*Map 2 B3*

*604 278 0221 | www.cleartwobadminton.com*

You can rent a court for $18 an hour or drop-in at designated times for $3 a session at ClearOne. You can also take group or private lessons, enter a tournament, or sign up for a summer camp. There is also a ClearOne Badminton Centre on the same road (at 4551, unit 138, 604 231 8281), with slightly different rates for court rentals and drop-in sessions, but it does not offer lessons.

## Richmond Badminton Club

*9460 Alberta Rd*
*Richmond*
*Map 2 B3*

*604 323 8131 | www.richmondbadmintonclub.com*

On Tuesday, Thursday and Sunday evenings, the gym at Henry Anderson Elementary School is home to this non-profit badminton club. It also holds a skills development programme aimed at ages 9 to 17 at another local school, and hosts social events for club members. Membership for a season depends on how many evenings you want to play, or you can pay a drop-in fee of $8 a session.

## RichmondPro Badminton Centre

**130-5800**
**Minoru Blvd**
*Richmond*
*Map 2 B3*

*604 231 0999* | *www.richmondprobadminton.com*
This is Richmond's newest badminton centre, and it also claims to be the largest such facility in all of North America. RichmondPro has 15 courts and is open seven days a week from 09:00 to 23:00. It costs $16 to rent a court for an hour, or there are drop-in times when fees range from $4.50 to $6 for three hours, based on the time and day of the week. For continuous competitive play, join the men's or junior ladder. There are also lessons, summer camps and the occasional tournament on offer.

## Vancouver Racquets Club

**4867 Ontario St**
*Fraser*
*Map 6 A2* **7**

*604 874 0242* | *www.vrc.bc.ca*
The VRC has facilities for badminton, squash and weight training (as well as access to personal trainers). Eager badminton players can conveniently gain 24 hour access to courts if they become a member. The club has also developed competitive doubles, mixed doubles and junior ladders, social nights for doubles games and a training programme for under 19s. For an adult, membership is $710 a year plus a $99 initiation fee.

# Ballet Classes

Other options **Dance Classes** p.290

There are plenty of opportunities to dance in Vancouver, but if it's the grace, strength, flexibility and overall style of ballet that draws you in, you're in luck. You can watch a Ballet BC performance at the Queen Elizabeth Theatre, introduce your toddler to ballet at one of the many kids' programmes, or audition for pre-professional courses to further your chances of making the discipline into a career.

## Ballet BC

**677 Davie St**
*Downtown*
*Map 9 D1* **8**

*604 732 5003* | *www.balletbc.com*
Ballet BC stages classic shows year round, but the company also offers development opportunities for young dancers. Its kids club provides children with Sunday morning workshops (three one-hour workshops for $25) where they learn how to tell stories through dance, and steps that are inspired by different eras. For older, serious dancers, Ballet BC has an intensive programme in August, a pre-professional training programme that must be auditioned for. For those who enjoy watching ballet but object to the ticket prices, Ballet BC holds cheaper matinees, where you can enjoy tea and cookies in the lobby before taking in a Saturday afternoon show. There's also the chance for students to grab a $10 ticket an hour prior to the start of a performance, but these are limited.

## Classical Ballet Conservatory Of Vancouver

**200-8713 Cambie St**
*Marpole*
*Map 5 F4* **9**

*604 321 7678* | *www.classicalballetvancouver.com*
The CBCV has ballet programmes for toddlers right through to inexperienced and professional adults. To encourage boys to take ballet, it offers a free term for budding Billy Elliotts up to age 12, and a 25% discount after that. Adults can take beginner classes on Thursday evenings for $12.50 a class or $150 for a 12 week term. Dancers who want to try something different can also take tap. Level one is $8.50 a class, or $102 for a 12 week term. For ballerinas who want to develop a career in the field, the CBCV has a pre-professional programme to help prepare for auditions for professional schools.

**2345 Main St**
*Main*
Map 11 B2 **10**

## Goh Ballet Academy

*604 872 4014 | www.gohballet.com*

This well-known ballet school enables serious dancers to continue with their high school studies while taking the full-day or half-day professional programme. Dancers must audition for any of the professional divisions, although there is a children's introductory programme in the summer with ballet, jazz, hip-hop and Chinese dance for kids aged 6 to 13. Adults can take drop-in classes from level one (absolute beginners) to level three, at a cost of $15 a class or 10 classes for $135.

## Baseball

Baseball has a rich history in Vancouver. The game broke down racial barriers between Japanese and Canadians when the Japanese Asahi ball team was created in 1914. At a time when Asians were not allowed to vote, the Vancouver baseball team was a symbol of strength and pride, until the players were split up when Japanese-Canadians were sent to internment camps after the bombings at Pearl Harbour during the second world war. Today, the city is home to the Vancouver Canadians Baseball Club (604 872 5232, www.canadiansbaseball.com), a Single A farm team for Major League Baseball's Oakland Athletics. For adults who would rather play than sit on the sidelines, there are a couple of baseball leagues (usually for males) and softball leagues (generally for females). Softball is played with a larger ball and is pitched underhand, windmill-style. Most ball leagues are for youngsters, so there are plenty of baseball and softball opportunities for those under 19.

**200-1367 West**
**Broadway**
*Fairview*
Map 9 B4 **11**

## Baseball BC

*604 737 3031 | www.baseball.bc.ca*

Baseball BC is an organisation that promotes amateur ball in the province. You can find a list of ball leagues and contact information, including a handful of little leagues for boys and girls from ages 4 up to 18. Boys can also check out Vancouver Community Baseball (www.vancouverbaseball.com). For baseball camps and other teams, visit the affiliated BC Minor Baseball Association (www.bcminorbaseball.org).

**Various Locations**

## Lower Mainland Baseball Association

*www.ballcharts.com/lmba*

For men aged 18 and older, this website features divisions with teams from Burnaby, Richmond, Delta, White Rock, Surrey and beyond, including the Vancouver Abbies. The season runs from April to early September. Adult male ball players in North Vancouver can try the North Shore Men's Baseball Association (www.ballcharts.com/nsmba).

**Various Locations**

## Vancouver Westside Minor Softball Association

*604 224 5161 | www.vwmsa.ca*

This organisation runs a softball league for girls aged 5 to 19. Registration starts in January and costs $60-$120, depending on age and how early you register. The association also puts together Vancouver's premier softball team for girls, the Vancouver Wildcats A and B teams. The Wildcats play at a competitive level against softball teams in other districts of Metro Vancouver. For players living in Richmond, check out the Richmond Girls Softball Association (www.rgsa.ca). If you're female, over 19 and yearn for a softball team, visit Softball BC (www.softball.bc.ca) for information on teams in your area.

## Basketball

Vancouver hasn't hosted a professional basketball team since The Grizzlies left in 2001 for warmer pastures in Memphis, Tennessee. But basketball is still immensely popular (it was invented by a Canadian after all – see Doctor Hoop on p.278), especially in elementary and secondary schools, and many continue to play casually or competitively in their adult life. Courts and baskets exist on practically every school ground, begging for a weekend game of pick-up, and most community centres offer drop-in gym times. Alternatively you can watch some high-quality university ball for $10 at the War Memorial Gym during the UBC Thunderbirds basketball season (www.gothunderbirds.ca).

## Basketball BC

*310-7155 Kingsway*
*Burnaby*
*Map 6 F3* **14**

*604 241 4667 | www.basketball.bc.ca*
Basketball BC is a one-stop shop for information about leagues, teams and camps for all ages and skill levels in the province. It also provides various forms of support for the advancement of basketball in the area. Its website offers information about local athletes, how to become a coach or official, what high school teams are up to and who's in the BC Hall of Fame. It also has links to youth and adult leagues such as Steve Nash Youth Basketball (see below) or the BC Elite Development Programme.

## BC Wheelchair Basketball Society

*3820 Cessna Drive*
*Richmond*
*Map 2 B3*

*604 333 3530 | www.bcwbs.ca*
BC Wheelchair Basketball Society offers programmes for players with disabilities of all ages, from recreational regional leagues to club teams and competitive tournaments, as well as an integrated junior league for ages 8 to 20. Through BCWBS, Richmond and North Vancouver both offer Thursday evening recreational leagues. You must be a member to register for the BC-CWBL provincial league, made up of juniors and adults, both mixed. Adult annual membership costs $35, or $20 for under 19s. The society also has an equipment loan programme for those unable to afford wheelchairs designed for sports.

## Kerrisdale Basketball League

*Various Locations*

*604 738 2333 | www.kerrisdalebasketballleague.ca*
There are a number of basketball leagues associated with Basketball BC, and this one is based in Vancouver and caters for both girls and boys. The spring league runs from March to June with registration beginning in February, at a cost of $450 per team. Autumn league begins in October and runs until January. There are two divisions of play and games take place in either the Kerrisdale or Kitsilano community centres.

## Kings Basketball League

*1755 Barclay St*
*West End*
*Map 7 B2* **17**

*604 719 6783 | www.kingsbasketballleague.com*
This adult men's basketball league plays games at King George Secondary School (1755 Barclay Street) in the West End. The league runs from January until playoffs in May and games are played on Sundays between 10:00 and 19:00. It costs $1,500 per team. Kings is also affiliated with Basketball BC.

## Steve Nash Youth Basketball

*Various Locations*

*604 718 7773 | http://snyb.ca*
The purpose of this organisation is to teach the fundamentals to kids and teens in a positive environment. It's named after Steve Nash, the BC-born point guard for the Phoenix Suns, twice voted the most valuable player in the National Basketball Association and all-round nice guy. There are now Steve Nash leagues throughout the

### Doctor Hoop

Basketball was created by a Canadian, Dr James Naismith. Born in Ontario, he became a physical education teacher at the YMCA Training School in Springfield, Massachusetts. There, he was asked to create an indoor sport to entertain his students during the cold winter months – and so basketball was born. In its early form, players dribbled a soccer ball and shot it into peach baskets 10 feet above ground at each end of the gym. It wasn't for another decade that someone decided to remove the bottom of the baskets so the ball could be easily returned to players.

province, including the Vancouver Eagles (604 738 2377, www.cplc.ca), the Mount Seymour League in North Vancouver (604 833 9488, www.seymourbasketball.com), Victory Sports Camps in Burnaby (604 636 3356, www.balloholic.com), and the Richmond Youth Basketball League (604 276 4300, www.rybl.net). Registration fees vary; to practise twice a week with the Vancouver Eagles for a season (autumn, winter, spring or summer) is $190 and once a week is $120. To play a season in the Richmond Youth Basketball League is $139, but includes the $30 Steve Nash Youth Basketball membership that comes with a Steve Nash jersey (in some leagues this cost is separate).

## Birdwatching

Other options **Environmental Groups** p.295

In short, Vancouver is a bird watcher's paradise. It is on the flight path of millions of winged warriors that stop to rest and refuel, making it one of the top places in Canada to see hundreds of species of birds. In Canada's annual 'Christmas bird count', Vancouver's main competitor when it comes to the number of species spotted is Ladner, a village just south of the city. If you want to stay within Vancouver to do your bird watching, there are plenty of options. Stanley Park, Pacific Spirit Park and Queen Elizabeth Park are just a few birding locations (see Parks, p.244). Vancouver is most well-known for its waterfowl, such as the tens of thousands of lesser snow geese that fly in from northern Russia in the autumn and the fuzzy mallard ducklings born in the spring. It is also known for its birds of prey, including hawks, owls and eagles.

*Various Locations*

## Birding In British Columbia

*www.birding.bc.ca*

Visit this online magazine for links to various birding locations in Vancouver, Fraser Valley, Vancouver Island and Okanagan Valley. Keen birders also discuss sightings in the forum, and rare bird alerts are posted regularly. In addition to the Vancouver parks (see Exploring, p.244), Birding BC also recommends Iona Island by Vancouver International Airport, where you can spot everything from loons to cormorants and wigeons.

*Westham Island*
*Ladner*
*Map 2 A3*

## George C Reifel Migratory Bird Sanctuary

*604 946 6980 | www.reifelbirdsanctuary.com*

Located in Ladner, about 30 minutes south of Vancouver and past Richmond, is a wildlife habitat within the Fraser River estuary that is recognised globally as an important bird area. It's a wetland with trails and dykes, where an arm of the Fraser River meets the ocean and where hundreds of bird species come to nest, take a break and eat. Sanctuary staff have recorded over 280 species here, everything from snowy owls and golden eagles in winter to mute swans and ospreys in summer. Annual adult membership is $20 and single entry is $4, a small price to pay for anyone remotely interested in Lower Mainland wildlife.

## Bowling

Both 10 pin and 5 pin bowling are popular recreational activities for Vancouverites. In the city, there are bowling alleys for all ages, from children celebrating birthdays to adults looking for active entertainment with the option of enjoying a drink or two. Some bowling alleys even offer cosmic bowling in the evening, where you can bowl balls that glow under black light – a great option for special events. One game should cost between $4 and $10. Bowling shoes can be rented onsite for a couple ot bucks, but bring your own socks. Most alleys have leagues for serious players, kids, seniors and beginners who simply want to up their game. Many facilities feature pool halls in an adjacent room.

## Bowling

| | | | |
|---|---|---|---|
| Commodore Lanes & Billiards | 838 Granville St | Downtown | 604 681 1531 |
| Grandview Bowling Lanes | 2195 Commercial Dr | Grandview | 604 253 2747 |
| North Shore Bowl | 141 West 3rd St | North Vancouver | 604 985 1212 |
| Town & Country Bowl & Billiards | 745 SE Marine Dr | South Vancouver | 604 325 2695 |
| Varsity Ridge Bowling Centre | 2120 West 15th Av | Arbutus | 604 738 5412 |
| The Zone Bowling | 150-14200 Entertainment Blvd | Richmond | 604 271 2695 |

## Boxing

As a fitness option, boxing has become increasingly popular with both men and women in Vancouver. Today, many gyms offer kickboxing or boxercise classes, and most boxing clubs also provide recreational workout classes and circuit training if you'd rather punch air or a bag instead of a person. If you are interested in the sweet science of sparring, competitive boxing has carved out a niche in BC. The Boxing BC Association (604 291 7921, www.boxing.bc.ca) has a directory of clubs in the province, including a few of the ones listed below. While kids can start boxing aged 11, they cannot legally compete internationally until they are 17. Competitive boxers over the age of 34 must have a physical examination.

*101 Bowser Av*
*North Vancouver*
*Map 3 F3* **21**

### 30 Minute Hit
*604 904 9654 | www.30minutehit.com*
Trainers at this women-only fitness centre have put together a half-hour workout circuit of boxing, kickboxing, self-defence and core stability training. The intense, condensed sessions are intended to accommodate 'the busy lives of modern day women.' Annual membership at this North Vancouver gym is $39 a month with a one-time fee of $89, which includes a pair of boxing gloves.

*1055 Dunsmuir St*
*Downtown*
*Map 7 E3* **22**

### Contenders Boxing Training
*604 661 5059 | www.contenders.ca*
Contenders offers training in boxing, as well as upper and lower body and core training camps. For $99 a month you'll get unlimited access to all classes, but you must also pay a start-up fee that will include equipment if you don't already own gloves and hand wraps. A personal trainer can be booked for $75 an hour.

*125 West 1st St*
*North Vancouver*
*Map 4 B3* **23**

### Griffins Boxing & Fitness
*604 980 1900 | www.griffinsboxing.com*
Griffins offers training for sports teams, personal and circuit training and high cardio boxing classes, in addition to classes that teach the sport's fundamentals and techniques. The club employs a 'glove system' where, similar to karate, different coloured gloves indicate increasing levels of skill. Most classes are non-contact, but members can spar once they've reached the third level and received their green gloves. Griffins' youth programme is for ages 6 to 16, aiming to teach self defence while increasing confidence, sportsmanship and strength. The gym also has women-only cardio boxing sessions. Membership is $100, which includes a T-shirt and set of gloves. After that, high cardio boxing is $50 a month for once a week, $99 a month for three times a week and $119 for unlimited access (less if you pre-pay). If you choose to train through the glove system the cost is $69, $109 or $129 a month, depending on how often you want to attend each week.

# Fashion Boutiques p.123
# Financial Advisors p.95

Written by residents, the Dubai Explorer is packed with insider info, from arriving in the city to making it your home and everything in between.

## Dubai Explorer Residents' Guide
We Know Where You Live

*250 Willingdon Av*
*Burnaby*
*Map 4 D4* **24**

## North Burnaby Boxing Club
*604 377 2607 | www.bcboxers.com*

If you want to focus solely on your competitive boxing skills, this no-frills club is for you. For adults, $35 a month will get you full contact boxing classes. Youths aged 10 to 16 are charged $15 a month. To join, you must also be a member of the BC Amateur Boxing Association (yearly membership is $27.50).

*Level 10 Fitness*
*110 Harbourside Dr*
*North Vancouver*
*Map 4 A3* **25**

## ProBox Fitness
*604 802 2488 | www.proboxfitness.com*

Located on the North Shore, ProBox Fitness offers both personal training for more serious boxers and BoxFit classes for those looking to learn boxing techniques while getting a good workout. The trainers have also created opportunities for coaches of sports teams who want an intense conditioning programme for their athletes. For boxers at any level, ProBox offers a Saturday morning (10:00) drop-in for $25.

## Camping
Other options **Outdoor Goods** p.394, **Daytrips** p.257

Within the confines of Metro Vancouver, you can find a few moderately quiet spots to sit down with friends or loved ones for a peaceful night away from the hustle of the city. But if you are looking for a more intimate relationship with nature, then you may want to visit one of the many provincial parks in close proximity to Vancouver. The summer yields generally good weather, but camping in the autumn (or winter if your campsite allows it) can bring a lot of rain and moisture, so wear synthetic fibres rather than cotton and bring tarps and rain jackets – all of which can be purchased at any good camping store (see Shopping on p.359). Just beware: while the Lower Mainland rarely freezes at night, you will often find yourself waking up not quite as dry as you had hoped.

Before you head out, ensure you have enough cash to pay for camping fees and firewood, as that is the only acceptable form of payment in the wilderness. Fees vary between sites, but expect to pay about $14 to $22 a night, plus $5 per bundle of wood. Due to park regulations, you are not allowed to use any wood from the park for making fires, even if it has already fallen. Opposite are a few of the larger campsites – check out the BC Parks website at www.env. gov.bc.ca/bcparks for more information and a complete listing of all the provincial camping locations in British Columbia – it features driving directions and information about amenities. In the busy summer season you might want to make reservations, particularly if planning a trip on a long holiday weekend.

*Backcountry camping*

**North of Squamish**

## Alice Lake Provincial Park
*604 986 9371*

Follow Highway 99 for just over an hour to reach Alice Lake. This popular park has great hiking trails as well as four freshwater lakes, attracting many families from Squamish and Vancouver. It is hard to get a spot in the summer, so it's best to plan ahead and reserve a spot early in the year.

*Alice Lake*

**Cultus Lake**

## Cultus Lake Provincial Park
*604 824 2306*

This smaller camping ground is situated right on the shores of the warm and welcoming Cultus Lake, just an hour's drive east of Vancouver along Highway 1. You may not get a lot of privacy at this site as there are residents nearby, but you will probably want to spend all your time on the lake anyway, waterskiing or fishing. And don't worry if you can't catch your dinner because there's a catch-and-release policy, so take a trip into town for some fish and chips instead.

**North of Maple Ridge**

## Golden Ears Provincial Park
*604 824 2306*

Just north of Maple Ridge is one of the largest provincial parks in BC. Within it is the Golden Ears campsite, broken up into three camping areas along Alouette Lake. The draw of full facilities, plus a boat launch and hiking and cycling trails, may entice you to stay in the developed areas; however, you can opt to spend all day trekking to the peak of Golden Ears Mountain for the real backpacking experience. Just make sure you dress warmly, it gets cold at the 1,706m apex. For the keenest campers, this site is also open in winter.

**Harrison Hot Springs**

## Sasquatch Provincial Park
*604 824 2306*

Make your way to Harrison Hot Springs and then continue north to find Sasquatch Provincial Park, surrounding two warm lakes. There is a short hiking trail around the perimeter of Hicks Lake, while Deer Lake has trails on either side that don't connect. Enjoy walking and cycling, or spend time on the water canoeing and sport fishing. Avoid swimmer's itch by making sure you towel off immediately after leaving the water.

## Canoeing
Other options **Outdoor Goods** p.394, **Daytrips** p.257

Canoeing and kayaking are tremendously popular activities in and around Vancouver, with endless inlets, coves and bays to explore. A number of paddle sport clubs and businesses have developed to meet the demand. Some are more for recreational paddlers who want to rent a canoe for a few hours or take a sea tour, while other clubs are geared toward competitive canoers who want to fiercely zip across the water. False Creek, Burrard Inlet and Indian Arm are all generally calm locations, ideal for learning. For a list of clubs visit CanoeKayak Canada (www.canoekayak.ca).

*2156 Banbury Rd*
*North Vancouver*
*Map 4 F2* **30**

## Deep Cove Canoe & Kayak Centre
*604 929 2268 | www.deepcovekayak.com*
In addition to boat rentals and lessons, this group offers guided natural history tours, exploring marine life in the Indian Arm, and $4 power paddling. A single canoe or kayak costs $32 for two hours at the weekend or during holidays, up to $110 for two days. The rate for renting a double kayak during prime times is $44 for two hours, up to $154 for two days. Lessons range from an introduction to kayaking, capsize recovery and trip preparation to more advanced courses in coastal navigation and rescues.

### Clayoquot Sound
If you're interested in weekend or week-long kayaking adventures, consider a guided tour of Clayoquot Sound off Vancouver Island, where you'll visit practically empty island beaches facing nothing but the crashing waves of the vast Pacific Ocean to the west. Contact one of the countless companies in Tofino, such as Rainforest Kayak Adventures (250 726 2868, www.rainforestkayak.com) or Tofino Sea Kayaking (250 725 4222, www.tofino-kayaking.com) for lessons, a daytrip or overnight experience. As you'll be ocean kayaking, be prepared for rough waters at times.

*Various Locations*

## Dogwood Canoe & Kayak Club
*604 590 5321 | www.dogwoodcanoe.com*
This longstanding and popular club offers multiple member benefits, including scheduled trips, training sessions, a lending library, forums and an active social calendar. Annual rates are $40 for joint membership (for up to two adults), $30 single and $20 for associate membership. Weekly daytrips take place on both flat and fast-flowing waters. Sign up online for more information.

*1668 Duranleau St*
*Granville Island*
*Map 9 B2* **31**

## EcoMarine Ocean Kayak Centre
*604 689 7575 | www.ecomarine.com*
This kayak centre has locations at Granville Island (all year), and Jericho Sailing Centre and English Bay (seasonal). All levels of ocean kayak lessons are offered but if you just want to paddle about for the day, register for a local tour around Granville Island, English Bay or Jericho Beach. Rentals are also available: single kayak hire starts at $34 for two hours, while double kayaks cost $46. A one-day beginner recreational course at Jericho Beach or English Bay costs $69.

*Kayaking*

**1318 Cartwright St**
*Granville Island*
*Map 9 C3* **32**

## False Creek Racing Canoe Club

*604 684 7223 | www.fcrcc.com*

Targeting those who are eager to learn outrigger canoeing, flatwater kayaking and dragon boat racing, this False Creek club offers adult membership for $240 a year, or $125 for paddlers under 19. Members have a better deal on training programmes, such as stroke improvement clinics (10 sessions) for outrigger canoeing and flatwater kayaking, which costs $40 for members and $80 for non-members.

**Jericho Sailing Ctr**
*1300 Discovery St*
*Point Grey*
*Map 5 C1* **33**

## Jericho Outrigger Canoe Club

*www.jerichooutrigger.com*

Based out of the Jericho Sailing Centre, this club concentrates solely on outrigger paddling. It holds practise sessions throughout the year for everyone (men's, women's and mixed teams). There are also year-round events, including a local January race at Jericho, a spring race in Victoria, and a summer trip to destinations in the interior or even Hawaii. To participate, members must also join the Jericho Sailing Centre Association (which costs $76.65 for an adult and involves signing a liability waiver) and the Canadian Outrigger Racing Association (the $20 annual fee gives you access to sanctioned events).

## Chess

Capture your opponent's king at a number of chess clubs in the city. The BC Chess Federation (www.chess.bc.ca) lists clubs in Vancouver, North Vancouver, Burnaby, Richmond and other municipalities for both adults and children. A Canada Federation of Chess and BCCF membership costs $48 for ages 17 and up and a junior membership totals $27 – this gets you access to sanctioned tournaments and discounts on books and equipment. Or, sharpen your strategic skills at The Vancouver Chess Centre (201-1050 Kingsway, www.vanchess.com), which regularly hosts leagues and tournaments.

## Climbing

When it comes to finding ways to strengthen your fingers, sending out hundreds of emails a day is no match for climbing in the great outdoors. Possessing both wiry power and flexibility, climbers are often regarded as some of the most athletic, fittest people around. Whether you want to reach that mountain summit or just fancy a bit of wall time, there are quite a few options in and around Vancouver. There are a few indoor climbing centres where you can practise your technique, each offering day passes or yearly memberships. You can either rent or supply your own gear. Adventurous types who want the true outdoor experience have lots of options to the north, in Squamish and beyond. Mount Waddington, the tallest peak in the Coast Mountains, sits at 4,016m. If you're up to the challenge, consider joining one of the clubs that attempts to climb this giant.

**Various Locations**

## British Columbia Mountaineering Club

*604 268 9502 | www.bcmc.ca*

Members of this club are passionate about mountaineering and back-country skiing as well as conserving the wilderness they explore. In addition to organising trips, there is also the occasional summer camp or wilderness first aid workshop. Trips are graded based on technical difficulty and how many hours you'll hike in a given day. Membership costs $45 to $68 depending on whether you're an associate or active member. Being part of this club gets you discounts on passes at the local climbing centres The Edge, Cliffhanger and The Hang Out, as well as discounts on instructional programmes at Canada West Mountain School.

*47 West Broadway*
*Mount Pleasant*
*Map 11 A2* **35**

## Canada West Mountain School

*604 878 7007 | www.themountainschool.com*

Canada West claims to be one of the premier mountaineering and avalanche safety centres in Canada, which is quite a reputation to live up to. It offers courses in mountaineering, hiking, ski touring, winter camping, winter climbing and more, plus guided mountaineering and skiing trips. A rock climbing adventure might take you north of Vancouver to Squamish, or you could choose a mountaineering experience on Mount Waddington, the tallest in BC. Costs can vary, covering the guides, instruction and safety equipment. An introduction to rock climbing at Squamish can cost $225, while a guided two day climb up Garibaldi Mountain costs $795 for two climbers.

*670 Industrial Av*
*Strathcona*
*Map 11 D1* **36**

## Cliffhanger Indoor Rock Climbing Centre

*604 874 2400 | www.cliffhangerclimbing.com*

Adults, teens and kids are welcome to this climbing centre, where you can scramble over 15,000 sq ft of climbing walls. Membership is $549 for an annual pass, or you can purchase a day pass for $18 (there are also options like monthly passes and family plans). You can bring your own equipment or rent what you need, such as climbing shoes and harnesses. Adults can take courses such as an introduction to climbing and learning to lead, while kids and teens can sign up for drop-in, the junior climbing programme or summer climbing camps. The gym is open from noon to 23:00 Monday to Thursday, and noon to 21:30 Friday to Sunday.

*2-1485 Welch St*
*North Vancouver*
*Map 3 F3* **37**

## The Edge Climbing Centre

*604 984 9080 | www.edgeclimbing.com*

If you step inside this North Shore climbing centre during peak season (1 October to 30 June) you can buy a day pass for $17, or if you're a passionate climber you can pay $499 for a year-long pass (youths pay $428 for the season or $12 for the day). The cost off-season (1 July to 30 September) is $13 for a day pass. In addition to the introductory courses, The Edge offers different levels of tuition for those interested in the techniques of climbing, teaching skills such as route finding and heel and toe holding. Hours are 13:00 to 23:00 Monday to Friday and noon to 21:00 at weekends.

*520-3771 Jacombs Rd*
*Richmond*
*Map 2 B3*

## The Hang Out Indoor Climbing Centre

*604 276 0012 | www.hangoutclimbing.com*

A day pass at this indoor climbing centre costs $14 for an adult, or you can purchase passes for the year ($385) or multiple months. The Hang Out offers a basic introduction to climbing course as well as private technique and lead climbing instruction. The centre also hosts events such as kids' birthday parties and corporate get-togethers. The centre is open on Mondays and Tuesdays from 15:30 to 23:00, Wednesdays to Fridays from 14:00 to 23:00, and between 11:00 and 20:00 at weekends.

*The Stawamus Chief, Squamish*

## Cookery Classes

Dining out in Vancouver can be an exciting and delectable experience. There are restaurant menus featuring foods from nearly every ethnicity in the city and at both ends of the price spectrum (see Going Out, p.420). But what if you want to design scrumptious meals for yourself and your loved ones, or entice diners to buy your own edible creations? Whether you're an ambitious would-be chef, a foodie who loves to cook at home, or someone who can barely boil an egg, there are schools and workshops for you.

### Cookshop & Cookschool

*3-555 West 12th Av*
*Fairview*
*Map 5 F1* 39

*604 873 5683* | *www.cookshop.ca*
Anyone can sign up for one-time cooking classes at this combination shop and cooking school ($49 and up, depending on the type of class and ingredients used). Click on the online calendar to see what's on the menu. One day a chef might teach a class on how to make sushi and the next the focus could be on classic French sauces, Spanish cuisine, or knife-cutting techniques. You and your friends or colleagues can also opt to take private cooking classes as a group and create delicious west coast tapas or Thai barbecue.

### Northwest Culinary Academy

*2725 Main St*
*Main*
*Map 11 B3* 40

*604 876 7653* | *www.nwcav.com*
This professional cooking school offers a culinary course and a pastry and bread making programme (both 15 weeks) for aspiring chefs and pastry chefs. The school is owned by its food-loving instructors, who claim to teach the way they'd want to be taught if they were students. You must apply for admission if you want to take either programme – check the website for requirements and deadlines. The application fee is $50 for Canadian residents and tuition is $6,950 (or $13,500 for one year, including both programmes). Tuition fees increase for international students. If cooking is a passionate hobby of yours but you don't want to make it a career, check out the academy's serious foodie courses, where you can learn culinary basics such as making breads and sweet dough, or how to prepare and cook a duck. One class a week for eight weeks costs $695. The instructors also organise classes and camps for children and teens. Kids can bake holiday goods or take a camp to learn a number of recipes and techniques.

### Pacific Institute Of Culinary Arts

*1505 West 2nd Av*
*Fairview*
*Map 9 B3* 41

*604 734 4488* | *www.picachef.com*
If your goal is to make delicious meals and get paid for it, look into the professional programmes at the Pacific Institute of Culinary Arts. Programmes include culinary arts, baking and pastry arts, and online courses on restaurant management. You can also enrol in weekend or evening classes on topics such as cake decorating, artisan bread making and wine making. Teens thinking about pursuing culinary arts should look into the institute's spring break camp and other courses. And if you'd rather eat than cook, visit the restaurant, where students cook under the guidance of their instructors – and you can enjoy a three-course dinner or seafood buffet for only $36.

### Vancouver Community College

*250 West Pender St*
*Downtown*
*Map 10 A2* 42

*604 443 8453* | *www.vcc.ca*
Vancouver Community College's hospitality department features a full-time student programme with courses ranging from pastry and Asian culinary arts to cooking combined with English as a second language. If you'd rather take a course to improve your cooking at home, or are a seasoned professional who wants to enhance your

repertoire, VCC's continuing studies programme has part-time courses on baking and pastry arts, as well as a sommelier certificate. For an idea of prices, the sugar craft and display course in the continuing studies programme is $195 for one evening a week for about a month.

## Cricket

Cricket has been in BC since the late 1800s, but has grown slowly in Vancouver. While baseball is truly a North American pastime, there are options for south Asian and British expats who like their wickets, bowlers and oval fields. The largest organisation is the BC Mainland Cricket League (www.bcmcl.org), with more than 25 teams in Metro Vancouver and an over-40s league. If you're interested in observing rather than playing, check the BCMCL schedule then settle down for a picnic in Stanley Park at the Brockton Oval cricket ground.

## Curling

Canada is known for its cold winters and frozen lakes, so it's no wonder curling is a favourite traditional pastime. The sport spread across the country to the west with the advent of the Canadian Pacific Railway, and even though Vancouver was one of the last cities to get it, curling has become a favourite for local residents. There are lots of clubs in and around the city and new members are always welcome. Hourly rentals for casual curlers are available at around $40, or if you want to get in on league action, there are usually spots open in a variety of leagues, including men's, women's, juniors, seniors and wheelchair leagues. Contact your local club for specific schedules and member rates.

### Curling

| | | | | |
|---|---|---|---|---|
| Marpole Curling Club | 8730 Heather St | Marpole | 604 327 3400 | www.marpolecurling.com |
| North Shore Winter Club | 1325 East Keith Rd | North Vancouver | 604 985 4135 | www.nswc.ca |
| Richmond Curling Club | 5540 Hollybridge Way | Richmond | 604 278 1722 | www.richmondcurling.com |
| Vancouver Curling Club | 4460 Dinmont Av | South Cambie | 604 874 0122 | www.vancouvercurlingclub.com |

## Cycling

Other options **Mountain Biking** p.312, **Sports Goods** p.401, **Bicycle** p.368

The temperate climate and abundance of bike shops makes Vancouver a great city for cyclists of all varieties. Commuters, athletes and socialites alike can enjoy year-round pedalling on the many roads dedicated to cycling. And, in an attempt to promote an environmentally friendly consciousness, the month of June is dedicated 'bike month' in Vancouver. Check out TransLink (www.translink. bc.ca/maps) or the city's transportation website (www.city.vancouver.bc.ca) for route information and maps. There are a number of clubs that cater to everyone, from those keen on doing some serious training to those who just want to have a relaxing bike ride with some new friends. See Cycling BC (www.cycling.bc.ca) for a comprehensive list.

If you don't own a bike but want to cycle Stanley Park and the Seawall, Spokes Bicycle Rentals (1798 West Georgia Street, 604 688 5141) lets you rent by the hour, half day or full day. Prices per hour start at $5.71 for a one-speed to $9.52 for a mountain bike. If you're looking to buy a bike, Sports Junkies (102 West Broadway, 604 879 6000) is an excellent place to get reliable on and off-road bikes, both new and used. Start shopping early, as you won't be the only one looking to pick up some wheels in the spring. Whatever bike you ride, make sure you wear a helmet – it's the law, as well as common sense.

**Various Locations**

## Central Vancouver Cycling Club

*www.cvcracing.com*

This newer club has been around for about four years and targets those who take cycling seriously. Organised club rides are held on Sundays, when members cycle 60km to 120km in various parts of Metro Vancouver and Fraser Valley. In the warmer months of spring and summer, test your limits with the higher tempo group on Saturdays. The club meets at a coffee shop on Main Street prior to taking off. Keeping fit and pushing your boundaries with this enthusiastic group requires a $50 yearly membership fee. No guest riders are allowed and you need your own equipment.

**100-400 Brooksbank Av**
*North Vancouver*
*Map 4 C3* **44**

## John Henry Bikes Cycling Club

**604 986 5534** | *www.johnhenrybikes.com*

Residents of North Vancouver can buy a bike and sign up for group rides in one stop at John Henry Bikes. For a one-time club fee of $45, you can become a member of its Pedals and Pints Road Club (yes, pints as in beer). The group meets on Sunday mornings in front of the store and rides the North Shore. Youngsters (aged 10 to 18) can get involved in riding through the Alien Adventures programme. This group starts up in late spring and runs until early autumn, offering Sunday rides which emphasise community and fun.

**Various Locations**

## Vancouver Bicycle Club

**604 733 3964** | *www.vbc.bc.ca*

This volunteer-run, non-profit organisation has been functioning since 1976. The Vancouver Bicycle Club holds weekly rides for all levels of adult cyclists on Wednesday evenings and Saturdays. Wednesday cyclists meet on the west side of Canada Place (at the north end of Howe Street) at 17:30, while Saturday rides start at 10:00 from a coffee shop on Arbutus and 6th Avenue. Longer rides (averaging 60km) are held on most Sundays and starting points and destinations vary. Check the website for specific ride times and difficulty levels. In July and August, you can join a group that tours not only in Metro Vancouver but the Fraser Valley, Vancouver Island, the Sunshine Coast, the BC interior and even Washington state in the US. If you are interested, you can try out a few guest rides for free. To become a member there is a $30 annual fee.

*Cycling*

## Dance Classes

Other options **Ballet** p.276, **Music Lessons** p.314

Multicultural Vancouver is home to every style of dance imaginable. If you're a beginner it'll be difficult to choose one to start, but many organisations offer drop-in classes in a fun learning environment. If you're a professional dancer, there are a number of high quality programmes in the city.

Dance Sport BC's (www.dancesportbc.com) main mission is to promote ballroom dancing in the province, but the organisation's directory provides a list of other dance studios, schools and clubs that offer both ballroom and other forms. Many dance centres in Vancouver offer a wide variety of styles in one location; a small selection of the ones available are listed below. In North Vancouver, for instance, Vanleena's Dance Academy (1174 Welch Street, 604 983 2623) features ballet, tap, jazz, lyrical, hip-hop and musical theatre. There are also programmes that specialise in particular styles, such as swing at Jungle Swing (West 7th Avenue, 604 420 0087) and flamenco at Al Mozaico Flamenco Dance Academy (828 East Hastings Street, 604 671 9182).

**677 Davie St**
*Downtown*
*Map 9 D1* 8

### The Dance Centre

*604 263 9555* | *www.thedancecentre.ca*

The Dance Centre is a comprehensive organisation aimed at serious dancers. Membership costs either $50 or $75, depending on what benefits you wish to receive. Perks include access to the centre's directory of organisations, discounts for events and workshops, and eligibility for awards and programmes, such as Global Dance Connections, which aims to connect local dancers with other artists from around the world.

**154-4255 Arbutus St**
*Arbutus*
*Map 5 E2* 47

### Dance Co

*604 736 3394* | *www.danceco.com*

This professional dance company offers programmes for toddlers through to adults at recreational, competitive and company levels. Most classes run for nine months, from September to May – students are expected to commit for the entire season and participate in a year-end performance. Dance Co offers programmes in styles such as breakdance, hip-hop, jazz and tap, which are practised along with classical ballet. For adult classes, a January to end-of-May session is $288 for one hour a week, up to $420 for 90 minutes a week.

**927 Granville St**
*Downtown*
*Map 7 E4* 48

### Harbour Dance Centre

*604 684 9542* | *www.harbourdance.com*

The Harbour Dance Centre caters to everyone from absolute beginners to professionals. The centre offers ballet, jazz, modern dance, hip-hop, tap, power yoga, Pilates, house dance and a style of Japanese dance called butoh zen jazz. Participants can come by for drop-in classes or sign up for workshops, with discounts for members. A one year membership costs $30, and drop-in 90 minute sessions cost $15 for members and $17 for non-members. Buy a punch card for 20 sessions and save $1 a class.

**339 West Hastings St**
*Gastown*
*Map 10 A1* 49

### Kokoro Dance Theatre Society

*604 662 7441* | *www.kokoro.ca*

Kokoro combines western modern dance styles with traditional Japanese butoh. The society has been around for two decades but has recently come into the spotlight when it was chosen among the top three dance companies by readers of *The Georgia Straight* for 2007 (along with Ballet BC and Goh Ballet Academy). Its dancers are trained at the Harbour Dance Centre on Granville Street and take both styles of dance. It costs $12 a class, but works out cheaper if you buy in bulk or become a member. An annual membership to Kokoro is $25. In addition to workshops and stage shows, every summer Kokoro butoh dancers head to Wreck Beach to present a few nude performances.

## Urban Beat Dance Co

*202-8168 Granville St*
*Marpole*
*Map 5 E4* **50**

*604 299 2199* | *www.urbanbeatdanceco.com*
The organisers at Urban Beat Dance Co know how to have fun with dance. If you're unsure whether a dance style is for you, instructors will let you watch a class with no pressure to pay for lessons. Urban Beat offers salsa, hip-hop and different styles of swing at various skill levels. It also hosts $3 Sunday swing dances and $2 Wednesday salsa mixers.

## Vancouver Academy Of Dance

*118-12838 Clarke Place*
*Richmond*
*Map 2 B3*

*604 231 8293* | *www.vancouverdance.com*
The Vancouver Academy of Dance has its headquarters in Richmond, and has studios in both Richmond and Vancouver. Professional dancers perform through the academy's TranscenDance Co, but the centre offers courses for various ages and skill levels in ballet, jazz, tap, breakdancing and styles of Chinese dance. New on the programme is a series of hip-hop dance classes. The one hour Sunday courses on street dances cost $260 to join.

## Disc Golf

Other options **Frisbee** p.299

Disc golf is a hybrid of golf and Frisbee. It's a casual game that can be played at courses set up in local parks. Participants aim to throw a disc in a target – a standing metal basket – in the least amount of tosses. A course will have a number of baskets spread out among the trees and will have a posted par, the number of throws expected to complete each hole. The activity is cheap and easy to pick up as most courses are free to access; all you need is your own disc. The game is also known as 'frolf', and while most people play casually, there is a growing community of frolfers who enter tournaments. Vancouver has a couple of permanent disc golf courses, including at Queen Elizabeth Park (p.244) and at the Jericho Hill Community Centre (p.341). More information on disc golfing in the region can be found at the British Columbia Disc Sports Society (www.bcdss.bc.ca).

## Diving

Vancouver may not have the coral reefs of Australia, but it's surrounded by some pretty interesting marine life. While watching orcas from a boat can be exciting, you won't get the same thrill as a dive to the depths of the waters of Indian Arm and Howe Sound. There are plenty of good diving spots in these areas, such as Whytecliff Park and Porteau Cove in Howe Sound, or you can search for a sunken US Navy vessel-turned-fish packer and explore around islands in Indian Arm. Depending on where you dive, you can see hermit crabs, mussels, sea urchins, starfish, sea cucumbers, octopuses, anemones, eels, fish and maybe even seals. Visit your local dive shop – Kitsilano is a great place to start – and ask the experts about marine life, lessons, guided trips, hazards and other safety tips for Vancouver's waters. In addition to offering beginner programmes, all three companies listed below offer more advanced PADI courses for serious divers looking to improve their technical skills.

**1695 West 4th Av**
Kitsilano
Map 9 A3 52

## BC Dive & Kayak Adventures
*604 732 1344 | www.bcdive.com*

If your nerves are jangled at the thought of breathing underwater, don't worry. BC Dive & Kayak Adventures provides one-off introductory scuba courses, where for $35 you get use of the necessary equipment and are instructed in a swimming pool. Like other diving companies, it offers both recreational and professional scuba diving lessons, plus day and multi-day trips.

**2572 Arbutus St**
Kitsilano
Map 8 E4 53

## International Diving Center
*604 736 2541 | www.diveidc.com*

Speak Japanese? No problem, you can take Japanese-language diving courses at the International Diving Center (lessons are offered in English too). In addition to your basic intro to diving and advanced diving courses, the company features trips to places such as Nanaimo as well as day and evening dives to local destinations such as Howe Sound.

**2745 West 4th Av**
Kitsilano
Map 8 C3 54

## Vancouver Diving Locker
*604 736 2681 | www.vancouverdivinglocker.com*

Don fins and snorkels for the first time to test the waters or become a certified professional through a company that has trained divers in Kits for over 40 years. Once you've become comfortable with underwater sightseeing, you can sign up for a scuba holiday with the Diving Locker. You can take a day-long Sunday safari to Porteau Cove on the North Shore, or travel to Vancouver Island for a weekend trip.

## Dodgeball

Dodgeball is a sport most Vancouverites play in elementary and secondary school gym class. Many people don't consider it a sport – but that's because they haven't played in an adult league. A few keen residents felt the city was ready for a league or two and now hundreds of people gather weekly to pelt each other with foam balls. Dodgeball appeals to active people, and the constant dodging is great exercise. No equipment besides a pair of running shoes (and a strong arm) is needed.

**Various Locations**

## Vancouver Dodgeball League
*www.vdldodgeball.ca*

The VDL has recently completed five seasons, plays four nights a week (Monday, Tuesday, Wednesday and Thursday), and has grown to 128 teams. Co-ed sides of six face-off in the VDL's autumn and spring seasons and try to pelt each other with balls while those under fire jump, duck and dodge – the first team with every player eliminated loses. It's a fast paced, fierce game that the staff keep fun and spirited.

## Dragon Boat Racing

Dragon boat racing is a water sport with a team of up to 20 paddlers in a 40 foot boat, and a drummer at one end pounding a beat to keep them in time. One of the biggest water-related events in Vancouver is the Alcan Dragon Boat Festival (see p.55) held in June. Tens of thousands of people are drawn to the festival to watch nearly 200 teams compete. Dragon boat racing has its roots in China, and the Vancouver festival was actually created 19 years ago in part to foster relationships between the various ethnicities and cultures in the city. There is a large and growing dragon boat community in the city, promoted and connected by a number of groups that offer boat rentals, programmes and practise times on the water. For more information on dragon boating in Canada, visit Dragon Boat Canada (www.dragonboatcanada.org), which lists festivals in various regions of the country and links to paddling organisations (in addition to the ones mentioned below).

**Burrard Civic Marina**
*Whyte Av*
*Kitsilano*
*Map 9 A1* **56**

## Chinese Cultural Centre Dragon Boat Association

*604 644 8384 | www.dragonboatassociation.ca*

Run by volunteers, the CCC Dragon Boat Association caters to both new and skilled paddlers – anyone is allowed to join. It also rent boats to teams on single visit rates for $90, or for the season. You can also get involved by volunteering to help put on the races. The association also hosts the yearly Taiwanese dragon boat races at False Creek.

**Various Locations**

## Dragon Boat West

*www.dragonboatwest.net*

Dragon Boat West is a key information source for dragon boat paddlers in the province looking for news, information on where the next tournament is, or for paddlers to connect with each other via the forum. The group also links visitors to race organisations in their region and to dragon boat festivals in BC.

**7277 River Rd**
*Richmond*
*Map 2 B3*

## John MS Lecky UBC Boathouse

*604 247 2627 | www.ubcboathouse.com*

The UBC Boathouse was established as a home for the University of British Columbia's varsity rowing teams and as a facility to run dragon boating and rowing programmes for the community through the city of Richmond. The UBC Boathouse offers adult and junior dragon boating courses for newcomers and experienced paddlers, and lunch hour drop-in paddling from 12:00 to 14:00 ($100 for 20 sessions). See p.319 for further opportunities at the Richmond boathouse.

**Barnet Marine Park**
*Burnaby*
*Map 4 F4* **59**

## Lotus Sports Club

*www.lotussports.com*

Members of the Lotus Sports Club take dragon boats and outrigger canoes out on Burrard Inlet, by Barnet Marine Park in Burnaby, all year round. An adult dragon boat membership is $135, but the club offers $5 drop-in opportunities to those who are not sure if it takes their fancy. Lotus Sports also has a youth junior paddling programme for those between the ages of 14 and 20.

**Burrard Civic Marina**
*Whyte Av*
*Kitsilano*
*Map 9 A1* **56**

## Vancouver Ocean Sports

*604 685 5955 | www.poguesports.com*

Vancouver Ocean Sports, which used to be called the Pogue Sports Canoe Club, paddles out of the Burrard Civic Marina by the end of Burrard Bridge. The club owns dragon boats for teams to use during practise sessions ($1,200 for once-a-week use from 1 February to 30 November) and it has also developed an outrigger canoe programme. A year-long outrigger paddling membership costs $310 and includes use of equipment and coaching, or just an introduction to outrigger canoeing (four weeks, twice a week) is $85.

*Dragon boating*

## Drama Groups

For those who thrive in the spotlight but are not yet experienced enough for centre stage, there are a few amateur and community-based theatre organisations that put on a range of performances. Most hold auditions, so if you're completely green, see if they offer acting workshops. Alternatively you might be able to volunteer your time helping out behind the scenes to get experience with the lights, cameras and action.

**The Metro Ctr**
*1370 South West*
*Marine Dr*
*Marpole*
*Map 5 F4* **61**

### The Metropolitan Cooperative Theatre Society

*604 266 7191 | www.metrotheatre.org*
This society bills itself as a regional training centre for actors, technicians and directors of all types. It's all about giving and learning here, since it is a non-profit theatre society run by volunteers on stage and off. Metro Cooperative has volunteer positions for lighting, sound, stage management, costumes, makeup and publicity, and will welcome you even if you have no experience – as long as you're passionate about theatre. Open audition dates where you conduct cold readings (no practising) are posted on the website. If you just want to watch a show, tickets for adults cost $16 to $18.

**The Hendry Hall**
*815 East 11th St*
*North Vancouver*
*Map 4 C3* **62**

### North Vancouver Community Players

*www.northvanplayers.ca*
A North Shore theatre organisation, the Community Players put on a number of shows each season of a wide variety, including comedies, dramas, satires and performances for children, as well as the occasional workshop. Open auditions are held for casting, with dates posted online. Auditions are cold readings and preference is given to members of the organisation – membership can be purchased for $20. The group performs at the Hendry Hall in North Vancouver and show tickets cost $16 for an adult, although if you catch a preview it's $8.

**Various Locations**

### Theatre BC

*250 714 0203 | www.theatrebc.org*
Theatre BC promotes grassroots theatre in the province, holds workshops on screenwriting and acting, hosts an annual playwriting competition and organises regional community theatre festivals featuring its member clubs. The organisation is based in Nanaimo, on Vancouver Island, but it also has theatre groups in the Vancouver area such as the Leaping Thespians (www.leapingthespians.ca) and Vagabond Players (www.vagabondplayers.ca). Members on the North Shore include the Deep Cove Stage Society (www.deepcovestage.com), Theatre West Van (www.theatrewestvan.com) and the SMP Dramatic Society (www.smpdramatics.com).

**4397 West 2nd Av**
*Point Grey*
*Map 5 C1* **64**

### Theatre Terrific

*604 222 4020 | www.theatreterrific.ca*
Actors with disabilities develop professional productions performed locally, including at Granville Island's annual Fringe Festival, and participate in workshops such as 'character creation' at this organisation. They also participate in events such as the free day of theatre classes. The mailing address is as listed, but its programmes are held at various locations in Vancouver including the Jericho Arts Centre (1675 Discovery Street) and Vancouver Japanese United Church (4010 Victoria Drive). Theatre Terrific is a non-profit society and you can support by donation or becoming a member for $10.

**1601 Johnston St**
*Granville Island*
*Map 9 B2* **65**

### Vancouver Theatre Sports League

*604 738 7013 | www.vtsl.com/workshops*
The Vancouver Theatre Sports League has Vancouverites in stitches four nights of the week at the New Revue stage on Granville Island. If making people giggle is your

forte, you can hone your improvisation skills at one of the workshops. Players on the improvisation team teach open drop-in workshops every Saturday for $11, but you can also register for courses (beginner to advanced) or sign up for Monday night workouts (five sessions for $90). Intrigued teens can stretch their creative minds with a two week summer improvisation camp for $330.

## Environmental Groups

Other options **Voluntary & Charity Work** p.81

Canada has a mixed record when it comes to environmental advocacy. On one hand, Vancouver is the birthplace of scientist and author David Suzuki, a renowned environmental guru who has inspired thousands to make their daily lives greener, while Metro Vancouver has spearheaded a zero waste campaign, challenging residents to reduce their waste and limiting what is disposable by requiring more items be recycled. On the other hand, the country is up there with the USA in terms of $CO_2$ emissions per capita and received 'fossil awards' at the 2007 United Nations climate change summit in Bali for obstructing talks. Luckily, at the grassroots level, many Vancouverites are concerned about their environmental footprint. If you're interested in learning more about what you can do to reduce emissions, save wildlife habitats and support local farmers, try one of the environmental groups that have sprouted in the city.

**219-2211 West 4th Av**
*Kitsilano*
*Map 8 E3* 66

### The David Suzuki Foundation

*604 732 4228* | *www.davidsuzuki.org*

The environmentalist David Suzuki has something of a cult following in Canada. He's so well respected that he was voted among the 10 greatest living Canadians in a CBC contest in 2004. Canadian women also voted him the person they'd most want to be marooned with on a desert island, and *The Vancouver Sun* decided it would be a smart move to make him their first guest editor in 2007. Visit his website for his ideas on how to solve global warming and build a sustainable economy, or, along with 381,000 other people, you can sign up for his Nature Challenge for tips on how you can live green. There are also ready-made letters to send to the premier and minister of the environment about issues such as enacting strong endangered species legislation and protecting coastal areas. Suzuki gives talks throughout North America; check the online schedule for the next one in Vancouver.

**1726 Commercial Dr**
*Grandview*
*Map 12 B1* 67

### Greenpeace Canada

*604 253 7701* | *www.greenpeace.org/canada*

Greenpeace is well known as an activist group worldwide, but its historical roots are firmly planted in Vancouver (see General Information, p.20). Current campaigns are focused on saving BC's Great Bear Rainforest, stopping climate change and halting the genetic engineering of crops. Those who want to become a Greenpeace activist must sign up for 'basic action training,' a three-day session on subjects such as handling the media, legal briefing and non-violent activism.

### The 100 Mile Diet

In 2005 two Vancouver writers decided to only eat and drink products that were produced within 100 miles of their home. They learned that ingredients in a typical meal usually travel 1,500 miles and dubbed that an 'SUV diet.' They wrote a book about their experience and what they learned about community gardening, organic produce from the other side of the world and vegetarianism. They also started a website (www.100milediet.org) where people eager to limit their impact can find tips on how they can eat locally in their community. People across North America have made the 100 mile diet their own, creating locally grown Thanksgiving feasts or limiting their range to as little as 10 miles.

**341 Water St**
*Gastown*
*Map 10 A1* **68**

## The Wilderness Committee

*604 683 8220 | www.wildernesscommittee.org*

Members of The Wilderness Committee, formed in 1980, are passionate about protecting wilderness areas and educating the public about threatened environments and wildlife. Current campaigns focus on preventing the commercialisation of BC parks, saving the spotted owl and protecting wild salmon. Becoming a member costs $35 a year ($52 for a family, $50 for people outside of Canada), or if you're feeling more generous you can arrange to donate monthly. You can also adopt a tree in the Canadian rainforest for a minimum of $30 or apply to be a volunteer.

## Fencing

En garde! Fancy drawing your sword and challenging your friends to duels? At first consideration, fencing might seem a bit silly or medieval. However, it's a sport that requires dedication, skill, speed and strength, not to mention use of your mental muscle for what's been called 'physical chess.' The sport has a rich history too – it's one of four events to have been in every modern-day Olympics. Thrust, parry, lunge and leap with the best of Vancouver's fencers, or learn to 'foil' your opponent for the first time with fellow beginners at one of the organisations below.

**302-1367 West**
**Broadway**
*Fairview*
*Map 9 B4* **69**

## BC Fencing Association

*604 737 3044 | www.fencing.bc.ca*

This is the official organisation for fencing in BC. Members can take part in the BCFA and Canadian Fencing Federation sanctioned tournaments listed on the site. There are a range of membership options that are available; an individual membership for a year costs $80, or $25 for those who are interested in joining for recreational purposes only (a $10 CFF fee is also charged).

**3122-12811 Rowan Pl**
*Richmond*
*Map 2 B3*

## Dynamo Fencing

*778 862 8467 | www.dynamofencing.com*

The Richmond fencing club coaches both children and adults at the introductory and intermediate levels. Equipment is provided for beginners and can be rented for the intermediate courses. Members of the club get perks like free admittance to open fencing nights, discounts on equipment and camps and the ability to compete on the team. An annual adult membership is $865, private lessons are charged separately. Drop-in fencing is $15.

**1839 Commercial Dr**
*Grandview*
*Map 12 B1* **71**

## LaSalle Fencing Club

*604 253 2513 | www.lasallestudio.com/fencing*

New fencing recruits can take classes here, where they'll learn fancy footwork and the fundamentals of scoring, offence and defence, whether they're children, teens or adults. For those who've got the basics, club members meet five times a week to train as a group then fence with others. Newcomers are welcome to watch a session and see if it's a sport they're interested in. LaSalle also hosts the Vancouver open tournament in January.

**6138 Student**
**Union Blvd**
*UBC*
*Map 5 B1* **72**

## UBC Fencing Club

*www.ubcfencing.blogspot.com*

The UBC Fencing Club promises you'll get to live the life of a musketeer without losing blood, yet still experience the clash of steel in the heat of battle. Members of this association tend to be university students, but anyone can join. The casual, fun atmosphere means the action is not intimidating for beginners, yet at the same time tournaments for more competitive fencers are staged, and there is a Canadian Fencing

Federation coach to teach all levels. And because the organisation is a students' club, it's one of the cheapest fencing organisations around. To join is $15 for non-students ($10 for UBC students) and training classes start at $140 for two terms, twice a week, rising to as little as $60 for one term, once a week. As a member you get to use the club's equipment.

## Fishing

Other options **Boat Charters** p.248

BC is a dream for the recreational angler. Commercial fishing is a huge industry in the province, but sport fishing attracts its share of anglers, tourists and revenue to the lakes, rivers and tributaries. The Lower Mainland is best known for the salmon-rich Fraser River, where the five species of Pacific salmon (chinook, coho, sockeye, pink and chum) swim, as well as types of trout, steelhead and sturgeon.

Overfishing, habitat destruction and other factors mean it's important to protect declining fish populations. To help the recovery, the federal Department of Fisheries and Oceans regulates when species can be caught. Check the DFO website for details (www.pac.dfo-mpo.gc.ca) or call the 24 hour line at 1 866 431 3474. Many anglers practise catch-and-release fishing, even if you are allowed to keep them.

For three days of the year, you don't need a licence. BC's Family Fishing Weekend in June celebrates the sport in BC by organising fishing events in various communities, which are great to attend if you're just starting out. Another option for beginners is the guided tours offered by many companies in the Fraser Valley and in and around Vancouver. More experienced anglers can buy equipment, licences and check out fishing reports at local tackle shops. Some also offer courses and fishing trips for beginners. Berry's Bait & Tackle, for instance, offers full-day learn-to-fly-fish courses, while Michael & Young offers beginners' fly tying and fly casting and on-the-water fly fishing and rod building. If you want to join a sport fishing club, Vancouver Angling and Game membership is $35 per person or $38 for a couple (email avents@shaw.ca). If you decide you'd rather watch the fish than catch them, visit the Capilano Salmon Hatchery in North Vancouver (4500 Capilano Park Road, 604 666 1790), free of charge.

### Licences & Regulations

If you are 16 or older, you need to buy a licence for both freshwater and saltwater recreational fishing and carry it with you in case a conservation officer, fishery officer, or police officer asks to inspect it. An annual angling licence costs BC residents $36 (more for non-residents), and you can also get one day or eight day licences. You can purchase a licence through the Ministry of Environment website as well as at a number of sporting goods and tackle stores. Before you head out to the water, ensure that you also have the appropriate conservation stamps if you want to keep certain fish, including rainbow trout and salmon (it's illegal to hook salmon during spawning season). These can cost you from $10 to $25. To find out more about licences, regulations and fishing locations check out the BC Ministry of Environment, Fish and Wildlife (250 387 9771, www.env.gov.bc.ca/fw).

**Various Locations**

### Fishing With Rod

*www.fishingwithrod.com*

This reliable BC-focused online angling magazine features fishing reports, articles, news and a library of fish profiles. The site contains information on everything from fish recipes and biology to conservation efforts and fishing locations in the province. Here you'll also find links to tackle stores, clubs in BC, plus fishing guides such as Ultimate Sportfishing in Langley (604 230 9757, www.ultimatesportfishing.ca), Bites On Salmon

Charters in Downtown Vancouver (604 688 2483, www.bites on.com) and STS Guiding Service in Mission (604 671 3474, www.guidebc.com).

**3336 Ocean Blvd**
*Victoria*
*Map 1 A1*

## Sport Fishing BC
*250 721 1173 | www.sportfishingbc.com*

This organisation and website is a great resource if you're new to BC and enjoy recreational fishing. At Sport Fishing BC you'll find information about saltwater and freshwater fishing in the province, places to go (and lodges to stay in), maps on how to get there, tackle tips and articles on topics such as chub fishing for kids. If you know what you're talking about, you can even submit your own article on your favourite fishing hot spot.

### Fishing

| | | | | |
|---|---|---|---|---|
| Berry's Bait & Tackle | 14651 Westminster Hwy | Richmond | 604 273 5901 | www.berrysbait.com |
| Highwater Tackle | 113 Lonsdale Av | North Vancouver | 604 986 3239 | na |
| Michael & Young Fly Shop | 105-1245 West Broadway | Fairview | 604 639 2278 | www.myflyshop.com |
| Nikka Fishing & Marine | 3551 Moncton St | Richmond | 604 271 6332 | www.nikka.ca |
| Pacific Net & Twine | 3731 Moncton St | Richmond | 604 274 7238 | www.pacificnetandtwine.com |

## Flower Arranging
Other options **Flowers** p.381, **Gardens** p.383

Whether you have a casual interest in flower arranging, want to make a career as a florist or desire the chance to express yourself creatively, there are workshops and courses available in Metro Vancouver which feature floral design. For a national floriculture association that holds information on education and news about related events in each region, try Flowers Canada (www.flowerscanada.org). To jumpstart a career in floriculture (a successful industry in BC), Kwantlen University College (www.kwantlen.ca) has campuses across Greater Vancouver and offers a commercial floristry certificate programme that teaches the design and business aspects of the field. Another training school for florists is the Academy of Floral Design in New Westminster (335 East Columbia Street, www.learn-flower-design.com).

### Ikebana
Thanks to Vancouver's multicultural population and residents' fascination with many things Japanese (such as sushi and martial arts), courses in ikebana (the Japanese art of flower arranging) are readily available for those who want to learn floral design with some Asian flair. For listings of ikebana schools and classes, check out www.vancouver-ikebana.ca or look for workshops and demonstrations by Hitomi Gilliam (www.hitomi-art.com). She lives in the Fraser Valley, but is internationally renowned in the world of floral design and every so often comes to Burnaby and Vancouver to impart her knowledge of inspirational floral art.

## Football
Not to be confused with soccer, the North American version of football has little to do with fancy footwork, and you'd be a fool not to use your hands. While football doesn't enjoy the popularity in BC that soccer does, those who do play are passionate about it. Still, with all the equipment required, football can be an expensive sport, so it tends to take a back seat to some of the other field sports in BC. If you'd rather not get tackled, you can always play touch or flag football, or cheer on the Lions at one of the reasonably priced Canadian Football League games at BC Place (see p.337).

*Various Locations*

## Touch Football BC

*778 840 9030* | *www.touchfootball.bc.ca*

For those seeking new ways to run around and have some fun, touch football is a non-contact sport, and this league offers recreational to competitive divisions for adults. There are male and female flag football teams (ladies should email womens-rep@touchfootball.bc.ca), boasting a total of 800 players. Entry costs are $800 per team, and there are two seasons of play: April to June, and September to November.

*185-9040 Blundell Rd*
*Richmond*
*Map 2 B3*

## Vancouver Mainland Football League

*604 313 1701* | *www.vmfl.ca*

The VMFL is a league for youngsters aged 6 to 18. Within the association are teams from across the Lower Mainland, such as the Richmond Raiders and Vancouver Trojans. Teams are divided into age groups, starting with flag football for ages 6 to 9 (it's a non-contact sport, so no equipment is required). Atom (which involves tackling) is for ages 8 and 9. The price increases with age up to the 'midget division' for ages 16 to 18. All kids playing tackle football need their own boots. Equipment can be rented through the league for a refundable deposit of $300.

## Frisbee

Other options **Disc Golf** p.291

Vancouver is one of the prime places in North America to become immersed in the Frisbee scene, better known as 'ultimate'. The sport, in which the two teams toss a disc in an attempt to catch it in their end zone, has been growing steadily over the decades. Once considered an activity for hippies, now high schools and even elementary schools boast teams. New players are welcomed with open arms because the sport is constantly growing in popularity. Many people are drawn to ultimate's use of speed and skill, and also to the fact that it's so cheap (all you need is a disc and studded shoes). While the seven-on-seven game is usually unisex, Vancouver is home to one of the best men's ultimate teams in the world: Furious George (www.furiousultimate.com).

*345 West Broadway*
*Mount Pleasant*
*Map 9 F4* **77**

## Vancouver Ultimate League

*604 878 6403* | *www.vul.bc.ca*

This unisex ultimate league runs year-round on fields scattered throughout the city. In the summer, the league operates four evenings a week, with more than 230 teams ranging from beginner to advanced. Register with a team, or as an individual on the website's matchmaker page and you'll be placed with an existing team that is at your skill level and requires a player of your gender.

## Golf

BC is a golfing mecca for many people, known in particular for its courses in the interior, Vancouver Island and Whistler. However, Vancouver, Richmond and the North Shore have made themselves into something of a golfing destination with an assortment of public courses and private clubs. For an idea of fees, the city's public courses (Fraserview, Langara and McCleery) cost from $51.50 to $59 for 18 holes at the weekend. At Mayfair Lakes in Richmond, which is a public course with a private

### Pitch & Putt

The city's Parks Board has three pitch and putt, par three courses for beginners looking for an inexpensive way to spend a day outdoors. Queen Elizabeth, Rupert and Stanley parks each have 18 short holes (from 40 to 120 yards at the most) and are inexpensive at about $12 for an adult, or you can purchase an annual pass or punch cards. You can also pay $3.50 to practise on a putting green. See www.city.vancouver.bc.ca/parks/golf or call the board at 604 257 8400.

*Golf challenge*

members club, a round costs $89 at weekends in the summer ($79 during the week, less in other seasons). If you want an unlimited membership, you need to pay a $15,000 licence fee and $258.50 in monthly dues. At the Seymour Golf and Country Club on the North Shore, a full membership costs the entrance fee of $39,000 plus monthly dues. At public courses, while you could show up and play, you may want to book your tee time in the busier summer months. If you're looking to learn or improve your game, a few courses boast golfing academies. The McCleery Golf Academy features summer camps, lessons for adults and kids and an after school golf programme for ages 9 to 17. The Musqueam Golf and Learning Academy also offers camps, group and private lessons and has multilingual instructors for those who speak English as a second language. Mayfair Lakes is another place with a golf school and the public 18 hole University Golf Club has instructors ready to impart their knowledge year-round (green fees start at $45). Many golf clubs also have driving ranges (often heated in the winter months), including Fraserview, University, Musqueam, McCleery, Seymour and Mayfair Lakes. Golf clubs can be rented at most facilities. Visit the websites below for a comprehensive look at what each private and public course has to offer.

## Golf

| | | | |
|---|---|---|---|
| Burnaby Mountain Golf Course | Burnaby | 604 280 7355 | www.burnaby.ca/visitors/golf |
| Capilano Golf and Country Club | West Vancouver | 604 922 9331 | www.capilanogolf.com |
| Fraserview Golf Course | Fraserview | 604 257 6923 | www.vancouver.bc.ca/parks/golf |
| Langara Golf Course | Oakridge | 604 713 1816 | www.vancouver.bc.ca/parks/golf |
| Mayfair Lakes Golf & Country Club | Richmond | 604 232 2650 | www.golfbc.com/courses/mayfair_lakes |
| McCleery Golf Course | Southlands | 604 257 8191 | www.vancouver.bc.ca/parks/golf |
| Musqueam Golf Course | Southlands | 604 266 2334 | www.musqueamgolf.com |
| Northlands Golf Course | North Vancouver | 604 924 2950 | www.golfnorthlands.com |
| Point Grey Golf and Country Club | Point Grey | 604 266 7171 | www.pointgreygolf.com |
| Quilchena Golf & Country Club | Richmond | 604 277 1101 | www.quilchenagolf.com |
| Richmond Country Club | Richmond | 604 277 3141 | www.igolfsoftware.com/richmond |
| Seymour Golf & Country Club | North Vancouver | 604 929 5491 | www.seymourgolf.com |
| Shaughnessy Golf & Country Club | Shaughnessy | 604 266 4141 | www.shaughnessy.org |
| University Golf Course | UBC | 604 224 1818 | www.universitygolf.com |

## Hiking

Other options **Outdoor Goods** p.394, **Daytrips** p.257

Hiking enthusiasts will never get bored with the high-altitude destinations the Vancouver area has to offer. Only a 30 minute drive north from Downtown Vancouver is the legendary Grouse Grind, where a 2.9km gruelling hike takes you up 853m for a breathtaking view of the city. Go a little bit further east to Mount Seymour or Lynn Canyon Regional Park in North Vancouver for daytrips on developed trails. For one of the most impressive hikes around, the Stawamus Chief just south of Squamish has three peaks to explore, each with their own beauty. Check out BC Adventure (www. bcadventure.com) for a complete list of the major hikes available and Mountain Equipment Co-op noticeboards (www.mec.ca) for groups. Students, staff and club alumni of the University of British Columbia can join the Varsity Outdoor Club (www.ubc-voc. com) to get in on the action. No matter where you go, make sure you take appropriate gear, as the weather can change quickly (lightweight rain gear is recommended).

## The Alpine Club Of Canada

*130 West Broadway*
*Mount Pleasant*
*Map 11 A2* **78**

*604 878 5272* | *www.accvancouver.ca*

For those who see hiking as a way of life, the Alpine Club of Canada is a countrywide group with affiliations in all the major cities, including Vancouver. More or less every weekend it plans a hiking expedition, which occasionally incorporates climbing to get over those mountain peaks. You'll need to take your own gear, and car pooling is the best way to go as you may find yourself travelling to Squamish or Lillooet from time to time. A no-frills membership with this respected club will cost $61 yearly, but it can go up to about $87 with extra perks. No climbing experience is required, but it is recommended that members have good physical fitness levels. The main office is based in Canmore, Alberta (403 678 3200), but monthly meetings are held at the VanDusen Botanical Garden (5251 Oak Street). Call or email for further info.

## Club Tread

*Various Locations*

*www.clubtread.com*

This recently formed online community consists of people of all levels who are friendly and enthusiastic about the great outdoors. Membership is free and well worth your time. It not only functions as a portal to other groups and further contacts, but it comes with lots of perks such as discounts and updates on the hiking scene. Visit Club Tread's 'trail wiki', where users post information about hikes in BC and other areas.

## Greater Vancouver Orienteering Club

*Various Locations*

*www.orienteeringbc.ca/gvoc*

This orienteering group takes hiking a step further. Using a compass and map in popular Metro Vancouver areas, such as Stanley Park and Queen Elizabeth Park, plot your way through checkpoints for the ultimate orienteering experience on scheduled Sundays. Every Wednesday there is an evening training hike that goes to many popular Vancouver sites. Yearly membership is $5 per person. Adults participating in the Why Just Run? series pay $10 for the season, while under 19s pay $5. All levels are welcome, just take your running boots and the club will supply the rest.

## Hockey

Other options **Ice Hockey** p.303

There are many variants of this sport, although ice hockey is definitely the most popular in Vancouver. For those who would rather run around than power skate on ice, there's ball hockey (played with a little orange ball). Considered by many as a fringe sport, it's a great way to get some exercise, meet new people and enhance those skills. The BC Ball Hockey Association (604 606 6050, based in Delta), oversees leagues in the province, including adult men and women, mixed teams and minors. For male players in the Lower Mainland, visit the Western Ball Hockey League (www.wbhl.ca), which has varying divisions for different skill levels and starts in mid-April with playoffs in July.

Field hockey has similar rules to ice hockey and, contrary to its name, can also be played indoors. Field Hockey BC's list of clubs shows just how established the sport is in the province (604 737 3046, www.fieldhockeybc.com). Although it's most popular among young females, there are a number of teams for men, women and boys in the Lower Mainland who are interested in the 11-a-side game using sticks with rounded heads. Field Hockey BC's affiliated clubs include the Vancouver Hawks (604 261 1243, www.vancouverhawks.com), Richmond (www.rfhc.ca), West Vancouver (www.wvfhc.com) and Burnaby Lake (604 468 0469, www.burnabyfieldhockey.com). For female teams, check out the Vancouver Women's Field Hockey Association (604 299 9712, www.vwfha.org). Field Hockey BC also provides coaching and umpiring certification opportunities, coach education workshops and developmental programmes. Players must register with Field Hockey BC and Field Hockey Canada to play in associated leagues.

## Horse Riding

Commercial zoning and congested roads have pushed simple endeavours such as horse riding out of town, but a bit of the country still remains in the city. The Southlands area, a unique semi-rural agricultural land reserve, is a quiet equestrian community that lies just south of highly developed Dunbar. Here you can find stables and riding clubs that make use of the many horse trails of Pacific Spirit Regional Park near UBC. Richmond also has a number of stables where you can take lessons, either privately or in groups. Residents on the North Shore will find the mountains are covered in good trails, with quite a few riding organisations close by. Those who just want to hop on a horse and go will have to be patient – most stables offer private or group lessons and summer camps, but few pander to the casual riding crowd. The commitment is worth it though and getting horse-friendly is more than just emission-free fun, it can be good for your well-being and is a fun way to exercise. The Richmond Therapeutic Equestrian Society (604 241 7837, www.rtesrichmond.com) uses horse riding as therapy for those with disabilities.

**1301 Lillooet Rd**
*North Vancouver*
*Map 4 D3 81*

### North Shore Equestrian Society
*604 988 5131 | www.wecreateriders.com*
Conveniently located near the Lower Seymour Conservation Reserve, this business has a lot to offer horse lovers: lessons, livery, summer camps, horse leasing and sales. The instructors can tailor lessons to suit your needs, no matter what level you are. Riding is possible all year round in the nearby trails for those taking lessons. Classes lasts for 45 minutes and costs $44 per person for groups or $55 for individuals.

**12551 Gilbert Rd**
*Richmond*
*Map 2 B3*

### Richmond Stables
*604 275 1830 | www.richmondstables.com*
This stables offers young horse enthusiasts the chance to ride ponies in their tailored preschool programme. Introductory packages for kids and adults are available for $200, with the aim of getting new riders comfortable with horses in just six lessons. Private and group lessons are available year round for all skill levels. There are also half and full-day camps in July and August, which teach horsemanship, grooming, handling and riding skills.

**7025 MacDonald St**
*Southlands*
*Map 5 E3 83*

### Southlands Riding Club
*604 263 4817 | www.southlandsridingclub.com*
This organisation, found in Vancouver's well-hidden Southlands area, acts as the hub for many of the horse riding businesses around. It offers facilities such as an indoor arena, a cross-country course, jumping rings and a half-mile track. While public lessons

are not done directly through the club, many of its qualified instructors offer private lessons on their own horses. There are many membership options for those interested in joining the club, depending on age and privileges. Riders over 21 can get a year's membership for $1,300 (plus an initiation fee for new members), kids under 12 pay $714. There is even the option of social membership for those who love horses, but just aren't keen on riding one.

**13671 No 3 Rd**
*Richmond*
*Map 2 B3*

## Twin Oaks
*604 277 7722* | *www.twinoaks.ca*

Equestrian fanatics should watch out for the annual Twin Oaks Derby Show every August. About 300 different horses are showcased over an entire week in speed and jumping competitions at the Twin Oaks fields. Another feature of the club is its partnership with Richmond Therapeutic Equestrian Society. Since Twin Oaks donated the space in 2002, people with disabilities have been introduced to horse riding here to aid in their social, physical and psychological development.

## Ice Hockey
Other options **Ice Skating** p.304, **Hockey** p.301

Ice hockey defines popular culture in Vancouver. 'Canucks' is slang for Canadians, and the saying 'we are all Canucks' has a double meaning: we are all Canadians, we are all hockey fans. When the Vancouver Canucks went to the Stanley Cup finals in 1994 with hockey legend Pavel Bure, it inspired athletes across the country to join the national winter sport. The level of participatory interest has sustained over the years, just as hardcore fans have stayed by their team's side in good times and bad (as high ticket prices show). At a local level, there are various options for playing ice hockey, for kids who've never handled a stick up to elite players aspiring to be the next Bure.

**1325 East Keith Rd**
*North Vancouver*
*Map 4 C3* 85

## North Shore Winter Club
*604 985 4135* | *www.nswc.ca*

The NSWC Winterhawks team caters to both boys and girls, with teams playing in the Pacific International Junior Hockey League. The club also offers a variety of development programmes. Girls from as young as 3 up to age 10 can join the female skills programme, where they learn to skate, pass, control the puck and shoot in nine sessions. It costs $90 if you're a member (club membership is a one-time fee of $7,500 plus monthly dues, while non-members can participate but pay more ($130 for female skills). Girls aged 10 to 19 can continue developing skills for another $90. Boys age 3 to 6 have a chance to learn the basics through cookie monsters for $160. Ultimate power skating ($220) is unisex and can be taken once a week for eight weeks. Other programmes include defence skills and goalie school. Adults can come out for some three on three action at the club's Christmas tournament (at $250 a team for members) or men can join the senior men's hockey league (ages 25 and up).

**114-3993 Henning Dr**
*Burnaby*
*Map 6 D1* 86

## Pacific Coast Amateur Hockey Association
*604 205 9016* | *www.pcaha.bc.ca*

Male and female hockey players from ages 5 to 20 can find a team affiliated with this association. There are a number of tiers within each age group to accommodate a variety of skill levels. Associated leagues are located throughout Metro Vancouver for both genders, including in Burnaby, New Westminster, Richmond, North Vancouver, West Vancouver and the city. To play in the Vancouver Minor Hockey League costs $325 for the youngest division (born in 2002) up to $650 for the juvenile division. For 'atom level' and up, skating skills are required. For the Vancouver Girls Ice Hockey league, players in the novice division (ages 5 to 8) pay $350, while the midget level (ages 15 to 17) pay $600 a player. A jersey deposit is also required.

**Various Locations** ◄

## Pacific International Junior Hockey League
*604 942 6500 | www.pijhl.com*

If your skills surpass recreational hockey, Junior B clubs feature elite male hockey players from ages 16 to 21. The Grandview Steelers (www.grandviewsteelers.com) and Richmond Sockeyes (www.richmondsockeyes.com) are the local Vancouver and Richmond squads, and account for two of the eight teams in the PIJHL. These are also great games for spectators to watch if you don't want to pay Canucks prices – tickets are $10 for adults, $5 for students and seniors and $2 for kids. Check the teams' websites for upcoming games. The season runs from August to the end of February.

**Various Locations** ◄

## Vancouver Adult Co-Ed Hockey League
*604 718 5836 | www.vachl.com*

This recreational unisex ice hockey league competes from September to March at two arenas in Vancouver. Beginners can join the league, which encourages players to be safe and have fun. Players' skills are evaluated at the beginning of the season. For more information, contact the league or call one of the programmers at the Britannia (1661 Napier Street, 604 718 5836) or Kerrisdale (5851 West Boulevard, 604 257 8122) arenas. Fees to join are $400 per player, $75 per goalie.

## Ice Skating
Other options **Ice Hockey** p.303

There's something magical and innocent about gliding across a frozen rink. Ice skating is perfect for inexpensive, active family outings (it costs less than $5 a person), or a charming first date. Adult skating times are available for groups who don't want little ones zooming by. A list of the city's community ice rinks and skate times can be found at www.city.vancouver.bc.ca/parks/rec/rinks, or call the Parks Board at 604 257 8400. Two of the eight rinks are currently closed for construction in preparation for the 2010 Winter Olympics, but others can be found in the communities of Britannia, Kerrisdale, Kitsilano, Riley Park, Sunset and the West End. All offer lessons for children and adults,

*Ice hockey*

and some even have lessons in power skating (to improve ice hockey and ringette skating skills) and figure skating. Wheelchairs are welcome during public skating sessions.

If you want to ice skate safely outdoors, you'll have to wait a while – water doesn't freeze enough to bear weight in the mild climate, and the outdoor rink Downtown at Robson Square has been closed since 2000 – it's anticipated to re-open in time for the Olympics. However, the top of Grouse Mountain on the

North Shore is another story. Up there, you can skate on an 8,000 sq ft pond for the cost of admission to the mountain ($11.95 for a child, $32.95 for an adult, which includes the gondola ride).

The coming Winter Olympics have boosted the profile of a number of winter sports, and you may want to check out other athletic options on ice such as speed skating (Richmond will host the Olympic speed skating event and is constructing a speed skating oval).

*Various Locations*

## BC Speed Skating Association
*604 557 4020* | *www.speed-skating.bc.ca*

If you have a need for speed, check with this BC association for speed skating clubs in your area. Groups include Burnaby Haida, Richmond Rockets, and Vancouver Velocity, which practises at the Kitsilano Community Centre ice arena. As an example of costs, Richmond Rockets charges $230 a season for once-a-week sessions or $380 for twice a week, plus $100 to rent skates for the season (and a $500 refundable deposit). While skates can be rented, clubs ask that you purchase protective gear such as helmets, knee pads, gloves and shin guards. The season runs from September to March, and is for all ages and skill levels.

*Various Locations*

## Burnaby Figure Skating Club
*604 836 6556* | *www.burnabyfigureskatingclub.com*

Children from as young as 3 can start ice skating with this club. Classes are held for first-time skaters, those who want an introduction to figure skating, and for the serious figure skater. It's $20 for BFSC membership, and after that kids can register for the 'learn to skate programme' for $32.15, providing they can go on the ice without adult accompaniment (although parents must be present at the arena). Registering for the junior academy (intro to figure skating) and private skater programme costs the same. There are also ice fees and coaching fees, which can range from $9 to $15 for a 15 minute lesson. Programmes are held at three Burnaby locations: Kensington Park Arena (6159 Curtis Street), Burnaby Lake Sports Complex and Bill Copeland Sports Centre (both at 3676 Kensington Avenue).

*1325 East Keith Rd*
*North Vancouver*
*Map 4 C3 85*

## North Shore Winter Club
*604 985 4135* | *www.nswc.ca*

Not only does the North Shore Winter Club have learn to skate programmes, adult training and off-ice training, it has also developed an academy for figure skaters and ice hockey players. Preschool and school-age classes for 10 weeks of learning to skate costs $100 for Winter Club members ($175 for non-members). To register for the figure skating programme costs $595 for members. Membership of the club is a one-time fee of $7,500, plus monthly dues.

*Various Locations*

## Vancouver Skating Club
*604 924 1134* | *www.vancouverskatingclub.ca*

This club has been teaching ice skating since 1934, and today offers beginners' lessons, a Jumpstart Academy for passionate young skaters, off-ice conditioning and a competitive programme for both youngsters and adults. The club makes use of two facilities in North Vancouver (Ice Sports North Shore, 2411 Mount Seymour Parkway, and the Karen Magnussen Recreation Centre, 2300 Kirkstone Road) and one in Vancouver (Pacific National Exhibition Agrodome, 2901 East Hastings Street). A junior skate package costs $762 for three days a week, or $1,270 for five days a week, and includes dance coaching fees to learn techniques, style and turns. Participation in the high performance programme costs $1,471.

## Kids' Activities

You won't fall short of interesting things to offer children in a city that boasts snow tubing and skiing on local mountains, numerous sports teams, family book clubs at the library, or the chance to take swimming, ice skating or dance lessons. For outings, you can head to attractions such as Telus World of Science, the Vancouver Aquarium and the HR MacMillan Space Centre (see Exploring, p.183), or somewhere as simple as the beach or park. You can also visit

*Kids' golf*

your nearest community centre to find out about its summer day camps and other kids programmes. Most of the sports and activities listed in this guide provide options for children, but here are a few more kid-specific organisations.

### Arts Umbrella

**1286 Cartwright St**
*Granville Island*
*Map 9 C3* **93**

*604 681 5268* | *www.artsumbrella.org*

Arts Umbrella provides visual arts, dance and theatre classes to kids and teens ages 2 to 19. Here, a child as young as 6 can take animation and cartooning while pre-teens audition for professional dance programmes. The centre holds more than 260 classes a week on a spectrum of activities such as dress-up drama for toddlers, the fundamentals of architecture for kids, improvisation workshops and the art of film making for teens.

### West Side Music Together

**102-2285 West 6th Av**
*Kitsilano*
*Map 8 E3* **94**

*604 730 8622* | *www.westsidemusictogether.ca*

Get into the groove with your kids. Parents are encouraged to bring their infant, toddler or preschooler to 45 minute sessions of singing, playing instruments and interacting with each other. The programme is based on research that shows a child's early development benefits from a music programme that involves their parents and other children. Classes take place at various community centres in Vancouver (including the Roundhouse, Kerrisdale, False Creek, Gleneagles and St James Community Square).

## Lacrosse

Before any other modern sport in Canada, there was lacrosse. Created by First Nations people, who called it 'baggataway', the game was played between natives and settlers when Europeans first arrived. Lacrosse was one of the few aspects of First Nations culture that was accepted instead of suppressed by the new arrivals. The game fascinated Canadians so much that it was named as the national sport in the late 1800s, and is still the country's national summer sport (ice hockey being the national winter sport). Lacrosse changed over the years with the addition of more structure and rules, and now there are

### Family Fun

The Vancouver Parks Board (www.vancouver.ca/parks) recommends plenty of outdoor kid-friendly activities available in the city, including the Children's Farmyard (with more than 200 creatures) and Miniature Train at Stanley Park (see p.233). You can also find the locations of playgrounds, wading pools and water parks on the website.

three variations: field, box and inter-lacrosse. Box is played in an indoor arena with six players per side. Men's field lacrosse, on a grass or artificial field, has 10 players per team, and women's (non-contact) has 12. Inter-lacrosse is a unisex form of the game, often played in schools, that uses a softer ball and plastic sticks. To play, you'll need a lacrosse stick, gloves, padding and other protective equipment that can be picked up at a sporting goods store. Give the game that's been dubbed 'the fastest sport on two feet' a try.

**4041B Remi Place**
*Burnaby*
*Map 6 F2* **95**

## BC Lacrosse Association

*604 421 9755 | www.bclacrosse.com*

Visit this website for information on lacrosse camps, box and field lacrosse leagues for adults and young players, and general information about the sport. The site includes details on equipment, a community announcements page and a fan forum. Various forms for coaches, officials and team members can also be found here, as well as links to other associations in BC.

**186-8120 No 2 Rd**
*Richmond*
*Map 2 B3*

## Richmond Lacrosse Association

*604 303 7529 | www.richmondlacrosse.com*

Run by volunteers, this Richmond association offers both box and field lacrosse for boys and girls in various age divisions. Alongside information on upcoming events, photos and general administration, the site also includes parent feedback forms, information on equipment and even offers tips for excited parents during and after the game.

**Various Locations**

## Vancouver-Killarney Lacrosse Association

*www.vancouverlacrosse.org*

If you're interested in local lacrosse at various levels of skill, this is the association to turn to. The minor lacrosse association governs teams of ages 5 to 16, and the senior association is responsible for intermediate (under 18), junior (under 21) and senior (no age cap) divisions. Registration closes at the end of February for box lacrosse and at the end of August for field. The cost depends on age group and type of lacrosse, and can range from $100 to nearly $300.

**4041B Remi Place**
*Burnaby*
*Map 6 F2* **95**

## Western Lacrosse Association

*604 421 9755 | www.theboxrocks.com*

The Western Lacrosse Association is the next best thing for elite players to the National Lacrosse Association (www.nll.com), which doesn't have a team in Vancouver (the short-lived Vancouver Ravens folded in 2004). Highly skilled competitive teams in the WLA exist in Burnaby, Langley, Maple Ridge, Nanaimo, New Westminster, Victoria and Coquitlam.

# Language Schools

If English is your second or third language, you're not alone in this city. Statistics Canada's 2006 census report shows only 56.7% of Metro Vancouver's residents claim English as their mother tongue. Because of Vancouver's multicultural makeup, copious English as a second language (ESL) schools have popped up in the city. Universities and colleges all offer English programmes for non-native speakers, such as UBC's English Language Institute (www.eli.ubc.ca), Langara College (www.langara.bc.ca/international/esl/leap), Vancouver Community College (www.study.vcc.ca) and North Vancouver's Capilano College (www.capcollege.bc.ca). Otherwise, look for programmes accredited by the Canada Language Council (www.c-l-c.ca), such as the ones listed below. You can visit the CLC for French programmes as well, or post-secondary institutions for even more languages.

## Canadian College Of English Language

*1477 West Pender St*
*West End*
*Map 7 C2* 99

*604 688 9366* | *www.canada-english.com*

This college offers morning or afternoon courses towards a certificate or diploma in English. It also offers intensive English programmes in preparation for exam courses or for those interested in taking their language skills to the next level. University preparation and business English courses are also offered, where you can focus on public speaking, writing and presentations. Prices vary; a certificate course in English costs about $3,600 for 12 weeks, while rates for other courses depend on how many weeks you register for. English courses for executives can be anywhere from $300 a week to $850 a week, depending on your time commitment.

## Global Village English Centres

*Yaletown Campus*
*888 Cambie St*
*Downtown*
*Map 9 F1* 100

*604 684 2112* | *www.gvenglish.com*

Global Village caters to people around the world who want to study English in Canada or the US. In Vancouver, English courses include business English, exam preparation programmes, private tutoring and paid work experience in entry-level customer service jobs. A general English course with 20 lessons a week of interactive communication for four to eight weeks costs $270 (morning lessons) per week. Signing up for 13 to 24 weeks costs $255 a week. International students can find accommodation through Global Village, and there is even an option to live with an English-speaking family. There is another campus in Gastown, on Cambie Street (604 684 2354).

## Immigrant Services Society Of BC

*501-333 Terminal Av*
*Main*
*Map 10 C4* 101

*604 684 2561* | *www.issbc.org*

This organisation provides a number of services to immigrants in BC, including its language college. It offers general English courses, exam preparation, conversational or business English, writing skills and special ESL courses where you can learn English through use of the media. The language school also has basic and intermediate computer courses. Lessons are more affordable for immigrants, citizens and refugees – a part-time general English course costs $195 for people who fall into these categories, and $330 for those on a work, student or visit visa; a course on pronunciation is either $75 or $110.

## International House Vancouver

*200-1215 West*
*Broadway*
*Fairview*
*Map 9 C4* 102

*604 739 9836* | *www.ihvancouver.com*

International House features the standard general English and business English courses for adults. What makes it unique is its young learner programmes. The children's and junior adventure programmes focus on kids ages 5 to 17, teaching English through field trips and activities in the classroom. Adventure programme fees are about $325 for one week, plus registration costs.

## Language Studies Canada

*200-570 Dunsmuir St*
*Downtown*
*Map 7 F3* 103

*604 683 1199* | *www.lsc-canada.com*

At LSC students can take courses in both of Canada's official languages, English and French (although the French programmes are based at LSC Montreal). In Vancouver, general and business English courses are offered as well as exam preparation; 20 lessons cost anywhere between $220 and $280 per week, depending on how many weeks you register for. LSC also offers one-to-one private lessons, and international students have the option to rent accommodation organised by LSC, such as a home stay or private residence.

**8888 University Dr**
*Burnaby*
*Map 2 C2*

## Simon Fraser University

*778 782 5100 | www.sfu.ca/cstudies*

One of the goals of the English language and culture programme at SFU is teaching students English in tandem with understanding how language is used in Canadian culture. Those interested can choose from full-time, evening or business programmes. For people interested in other languages, the continuing studies programme also offers French, German, Japanese, Korean, Cantonese and Mandarin. The cost for these courses is $384 for weekly sessions. While SFU's main campus is in Burnaby, continuing studies courses are also offered on the university's Downtown and Surrey campuses.

**Ponderosa Annex C**
*2021 West Mall*
*UBC*
*Map 5 B1* **105**

## University Of British Columbia

*604 822 0800 | www.languages.ubc.ca*

Adults wishing to learn another language can choose from 16 offered in the continuing studies programme: French, Spanish, Japanese, Italian, Mandarin, Arabic, German, Hindi, Korean, Danish, Dutch, Greek, Punjabi, Russian, Thai and Latin. All are part-time conversational courses, but some languages are offered in a range of levels. Most courses are $295 for two-hour sessions, once a week for about two months. You can take all languages at the main campus in Point Grey, but a number are offered at the Robson Square campus too.

## Libraries

Other options **Second-Hand Items** p.398, **Books** p.370

Libraries in Metro Vancouver offer free borrowing services to residents. To use resources you simply need a library card, which you can get with proof of residency. Most public library branches develop programmes for their community, such as book clubs and family storytimes. For a list of public libraries in Vancouver visit www.vpl.ca/branches, or find out more about the central branch, the Vancouver Public Library, below. If you want to try a book by a local author, you're in luck: a wealth of talented writers hail from Vancouver. One to look for is Douglas Coupland, a novelist, artist and playwright who explores mass culture and is famous for popularising the term 'Generation X'. Another is non-fiction writer Maggie de Vries, best known for her recent story about her sister Sarah, a missing woman from Vancouver's Downtown Eastside. The city also hosts a multi-day International Writers' Festival (www.writersfest.bc.ca) each autumn featuring authors from around the world.

**515 West Hastings St**
*Downtown*
*Map 7 F3* **106**

## Simon Fraser University Library

*778 782 7411 | www.lib.sfu.ca*

Simon Fraser University has three libraries: the Samuel and Frances Belzberg Library in Vancouver, the Surrey Library (250-13450 102nd Avenue), and the Bennett Library at the top of Burnaby Mountain (8888 University Drive). Students and faculty can borrow from the library free of charge; members of the public can purchase a 12 month card for $100 or per semester (four months) for $35.

**UBC Campus**
*1961 East Mall*
*UBC*
*Map 5 B1* **105**

## University of British Columbia Library

*604 822 6375 | www.library.ubc.ca*

For those in need of speciality or academic resources, UBC has over two dozen branches, including ones specialising in education, First Nations, mathematics, music, law, biomedicine and Asian focus. Students, faculty, staff and alumni borrow for free and have remote access to journals and articles from home. If you don't fall into one of those categories, you can purchase a community borrower card for $120 a year ($40 for seniors) or $40 for a four-month term.

*350 West Georgia St*
*Downtown*
*Map 7 F4* **108**

## Vancouver Public Library

*604 331 3603 | www.vpl.ca*

Vancouver Public Library is housed in a striking nine-storey building that stocks more than 1.3 million books, periodicals, videos and other resource materials. The building has been used in a number of movies, including the Arnold Schwarzenegger film *The 6th Day*. Membership is free as long as you offer proof that you're a resident of Vancouver or live in what the library calls the 'interLINK area', which extends to member libraries as far away as Whistler and the Fraser Valley. Community programmes include book clubs for adults and teens and story times for children. The library opens at 10:00 every day and closes at 21:00 Monday to Thursday, 18:00 Friday and Saturday, and 17:00 on Sundays. While this is the city's main public library, there are 22 local branches throughout Vancouver; visit the website for the opening times and locations.

### Other Libraries

| | | | | |
|---|---|---|---|---|
| Burnaby Public Library | 6100 Willingdon Av | Burnaby | 604 436 5427 | www.bpl.bc.ca |
| North Vancouver District Public Library | 1277 Lynn Valley Rd | North Vancouver | 604 984 0286 | www.nvdpl.ca |
| Richmond Public Library | 100-7700 Minoru Gate | Richmond | 604 231 6405 | www.yourlibrary.ca |

## Martial Arts

Martial arts have become very popular as both competitive sports and fitness options in Vancouver, so you've got lots of choices. A number of dojos, dojangs and fitness centres have been established to offer Japanese martial arts such as karate (traditional styles like shito-ryo, goju-ryu and shotokan), jujutsu, aikido and kendo (the way of the sword), taekwondo from Korea, Brazilian jujutsu and axe capoeira. If you want to learn self-defence techniques, build strength both physically and mentally, exercise and eventually compete in tournaments, training in a martial art is for you. One city community centre that offers karate is the Roundhouse (see p.275), out of which the Yaletown Wado Karate Academy operates. For other options, see the companies below or call a federation to find an affiliated member club in your area.

*703 West 70th Av*
*Marpole*
*Map 5 F4* **109**

## Canada Shoseikan

*604 377 2833 | www.shoseikan.com*

Affiliated with Karate BC, this Vancouver club teaches goju-ryu karate to both kids and adults. An annual club membership is $40 for those under 15 and $50 for those aged 16 and up. You can pay for lessons by the month, or in three or six month packages. Youngsters pay $210 for six months while adults pay $270. Canada Shoseikan also run their programmes out of Richmond, at the Richmond Chinese Community Society (208-8171 Park Road) and the River Club (11111 Horseshoe Way).

*341 East Broadway*
*Mount Pleasant*
*Map 11 C2* **110**

## Capoeira Ache Brasil Academy

*604 876 2422 | www.achebrasil.com*

Ache Brasil is both a performance group and martial arts academy. You can watch members perform at events and festivals, combining martial arts with acrobatics, dance and music, and it often puts on shows for local elementary schools (see the website for a schedule). You can register for its academy and learn the rhythmic Brazilian art that incorporates acrobatic dance with self-defence. The academy offers kids' and adults' introductory courses, right up to intermediate and advanced level. The intro to capoeira is $10 per class (the first class is free) and you must take at least seven classes before moving up to level one. At level one, drop-in is $15, or one class per week for a month is $43 (two per week is $75, unlimited is $105). It has been voted Vancouver's best martial arts academy by readers of *The Georgia Straight*.

**West Point Grey**
**Community Ctr**
4196 West 4th Av
Point Grey
*Map 5 C1* **111**

## Vancouver West Aikikai
*604 874 7707 | www.aikido.bc.ca*

There's no sparring at this martial art facility – instructors teach aikido students self-defence, but alongside a philosophy of harmony, non-conflict, self-discipline and spiritual growth. Drop-in (not for beginners) is $7 for members of this or other BC Aikido Federation dojos, and $10 for non-members. Vancouver West Aikikai classes are held on Mondays, Wednesdays and weekends. Children aged 6 to 13 pay $135 a semester (January to March or April to June), and adult beginners pay $65 a month, or $165 a semester. Both children and adults are charged $220 from September to December.

## Martial Arts

| | | | |
|---|---|---|---|
| Axe Capoeira | 150 West Hastings St | Downtown | 604 537 8943 |
| BC Taekwondo Federation | Various Locations | www.taekwondobc.com | 604 469 9206 |
| BC Aikido Federation | Various Locations | www.aikido.bc.ca | 604 432 6770 |
| British Columbia Kendo Federation | Various Locations | www.bckf.org | na |
| Champions Martial Arts Academy | 125 East 1st St | North Vancouver | 604 983 3799 |
| Cocoon Athletics | 244 East Broadway | Mount Pleasant | 604 916 9441 |
| Karate BC | Various Locations | www.karatebc.org | 604 737 3051 |
| Kikara Martial Arts Academies | 1727 West Broadway | Fairview | 604 733 9553 |
| Sunrise Kendo Club | 6855 Adair St | Burnaby | 604 420 9088 |

## Mother & Toddler Activities

These days, celebrity mums spring back into shape post-birth with the help of personal trainers and plastic surgery. But what's a typical new mother to do? For mums who want to work their way back to their pre-baby body, there are a number of fitness courses that make you sweat and let you interact with that sweet new addition to your life at the same time.

**3120 Highland Blvd**
North Vancouver
*Map 4 A2* **112**

## CoreBody Pilates & Yoga
*604 916 9335 | www.corebody.ca*

In addition to its yoga, pilates, dance and nutrition workshops, CoreBody also concentrates on prenatal and postnatal women. Adorably dubbed peapod Pilates and peapod yoga, you'll focus on everything from breathing patterns to muscle endurance. There's also mummy and me yoga for mothers who want to take classes with their infants. Keep an eye out for courses like the partner birthing workshop for couples who want to practise relaxation techniques and work on yoga poses.

**Various Locations**

## Fit 4 Two
*604 602 1546 | www.fit4two.ca*

Fit 4 Two is a franchise with a number of locations in community centres throughout Downtown Vancouver and False Creek, East Vancouver, Burnaby, the North Shore and Richmond. Availability of classes vary at each, but ones where you can take your baby include mum and baby fitness, stroller boot camp, postpartum nutrition, tummies for mummies and infant massage. There are also plenty of prenatal programmes for expectant mums. The Downtown location is at the Roundhouse Community Arts and Recreation Centre (see p.275). Call Fit 4 Two or check online for class schedules and specific locations.

**244 East Broadway**
Mount Pleasant
*Map 11 B2* **114**

## The Nest
*778 892 5816 | www.inthenest.ca*

This Vancouver company suggests bouncing, tickling and hugging your baby while enjoying singing and dancing through its 'singing and swinging' programme. It also offers postnatal fitness classes for mums who want to take their babies to a workout session. 'Mummy and babe' focuses on muscular strength, posture and kegel muscles and costs $80 for once a week or $160 for twice a week sessions. Yummy mummy classes, where mothers work out while toddlers participate in 'tots n' motion', cost $120, once a week.

## Mountain Biking

Other options **Cycling** p.288

North Vancouver, surrounded by a quartet of superb biking mountains (Grouse, Seymour, Cypress and Fromme), is known as one of the best places in the world for biking off the beaten path. You will find trails on all these mountains, ranging from smooth sailing to extremely challenging, so make sure you pay attention to where you're going. Maps are becoming more readily available as the popularity of mountain biking increases, and can be found online or purchased in most bike shops. One of the most popular mountains in the area is Mount Fromme, which connects to Grouse Mountain, but Seymour and Cypress are excellent as well. Some areas are not maintained by municipalities and can be used at your own risk, so take a buddy and a first aid kit if you plan on pushing your limits. A good resource for mountain bikers is the North Shore Mountain Biking online magazine (www.nsmb.com), complete with articles on mountain bikers, 'trail tales,' biking gear and a listing of upcoming events.

> ### Mount Fromme
> Located at the south entrance of Lynn Headwaters Regional Park (p.243), this 1,185m mountain has roughly 40 marked trails on it that range from beginner to extreme. To get there, just follow Highway 1, exit on Mountain Highway and then follow that to the top. Parking may be scarce, as it is a popular spot, so it's a good idea to stop a bit lower and pedal up (it will be the easiest part of your ride). Most riders avoid the winter, as torrential downpours make for wet, dangerous ground.

*Various Locations* ◄ ## Burnaby Mountain Biking Association

*www.bmba.ca*

The Burnaby Mountain Biking Association has worked to upgrade and maintain Burnaby Mountain Park's dozens of trails. The website includes information including trail maps, discussion forums, bikes and parts for sale, and updates on trail conditions. The association also encouraged the development of a downhill and uphill trail loop around the soon to be open Barnet Bike Skills Park in Burnaby.

*Various Locations* ◄ ## Freeridetours

*www.freeridetours.com*

If you're keen to explore an area by mountain bike but want someone to guide the way, check out Freeridetours. You can custom make one-day or multi-day trips for $90 to $300 per day, or sign up for an existing trip, such as in Whistler or the BC interior (five-day trips are $1,150, week-long ones are $1,499, and eight days costs $1,600). Go to the website to sign up for an outing.

*Various Locations* ◄ ## North Shore Mountain Bike Association

*www.nsmba.bc.ca*

If you take pride in what North Vancouver has to offer, you're not alone. This non-profit charity has one goal: to ensure good riding on the off-road biking trails in the area. Become a member by donation; $20 is recommended, but the more you give the more of a change you'll make. The website has lots of great links for cycling stores and other organisations, as well as trail maps for various mountains.

## Whistler Mountain Bike Park

*Whistler Blackcomb*
*Whistler*

*1 866 218 9690 | www.whistlerbike.com*

When the snow melts and the ski season draws to a close, Whistler's bike park comes to the fore. Take the lift halfway up the mountain and, instead of gliding down on friction-free snow, ride down all those dirty trails a different way. There are 44 trails to attempt, which vary in difficulty – a map is available online. A day pass up the lift for children aged 10 to 12 is $21, $35 for youths and $40 for adults (the price goes up slightly during school summer holidays). You can rent bikes and safety equipment at the mountain, as well as sign up for camps, lessons or tours. Whistler Blackcomb also offers a seasonal Air Dome (from July to October), and an indoor mountain bike facility at Lot 8 on Blackcomb where you can train for three hours for $15, or buy a season pass for $179.

## Women's Only Mountain Biking

*1135 West 23rd St*
*North Vancouver*
*Map 4 A2* **119**

*604 329 5772 | www.womensonly.com*

This North Vancouver-based company offers mountain biking courses for beginner and intermediate female riders (up to intermediate level 3), as well as clinics and workshops, which range from $50 for one focusing on downhill to $107 for a two-day session called 'exploring the shore'. Other clinics include climbing conditioning and tricks and trials.

Whistler Mountain Bike Park

## Music Lessons

Other options **Dance Classes** p.290, **Ballet** p.276, **Music, DVDs & Videos** p.392

Whether your fingers fly along the piano keys like you were born to play, or you thought the letters A to G were simply part of the alphabet, there are music lessons for you. Try one of the companies below for private or group lessons, or head across the water to the North Shore for the Ava Music and Art Centre (320 West 13th Street, 604 990 3541). Like most centres that offer music lessons, this one has a number to choose from, including piano, guitar, violin, flute, bass, drums, voice and music theory.

**3607 West Broadway**
*Kitsilano*
*Map 5 D1* 120

### Prussin Music

*604 736 3036* | www.prussinmusic.com

Music lessons are available at this store for people of all experience levels and interests, but the focus is on high school students and young adults. Registering in one of four terms gets you a weekly lesson with one of the talented teachers. Payments are made according to duration of lessons, but in general expect rates of about $40 per hour. Prussin Music also sells and rents equipment, including drum kits, keyboards, woodwind instruments, guitars, and folk instruments such as banjos, harps and mandolins.

**929 Granville St**
*Downtown*
*Map 7 E4* 121

### Tom Lee Music

*604 685 8471* | www.tomleemusic.ca

Located in on busy Granville Street, this music store has everything a music aficionado could possibly be looking for. With three floors full of instruments, you will have plenty of options when it comes to picking your new guitar or set of drums. If you still haven't mastered your technique, Tom Lee offers a number of music lessons for a wide range of instruments (think guitar, piano, drums and strings) as well as singing. There are also two School of Rock programmes where you can enrol your kids for a summer of cooperative band-oriented learning. Lessons for young beginners can cost $70 for 10 weeks (for 2 year olds) to $16.50 an hour for ages 4 to 10. Private lessons cost more, depending on the instrument and number of sessions signed up for.

**1270 Chestnut St**
*Kitsilano*
*Map 8 F1* 122

### Vancouver Academy Of Music

*604 734 2301* | www.vam.bc.ca

This highly respected organisation offers two divisions of music training to learners of all ages (from preschoolers to adults) who, one day, may turn their passion for music into a career. The preparation division is open to anyone wishing to partake in group classes, although those students wanting to get some private instruction may have to audition to prove they're serious. Classes run for a minimum of 16 weeks and will cost at least $200; longer lessons and certain instruments can often cost much more. You can also join the College Division and earn a bachelor of music degree through the Thompson Rivers University Open Learning programme. Financial assistance can cover almost half the cost, if you are eligible.

## Netball

Netball has a long way to go before it reaches the popularity it has achieved in Australia and the UK. Currently, it's an unusual sight for a Vancouverite stumbling across this version of basketball without dribbling or three-point shots. That said, there is an organisation called the British Columbia Netball Association (604 293 1820, www.bcnetball.net) that, in addition to hosting development camps and other events to increase participation in the province, also runs the Vancouver Amateur Netball Association. Within this are clubs in Vancouver, North and West Vancouver, Richmond, Burnaby and other parts of the Lower Mainland. Vancouver's team is the Checkers (www.checkersnetball.ca), which practises out of the Dunbar Community Centre (4747 Dunbar Street) on Thursday evenings during the season, and welcomes anyone to come along, even if just to play socially. In North and West Vancouver, the club is the North Shore Comets (www.nsnetball.com).

## Orchestras & Bands

Other options **Music Lessons** p.314

Expats who have moved to Vancouver and brought with them a love of the orchestra or a passion for making music are in luck. There are a multitude of local orchestras for amateur musicians young and old. Some focus on scores from baroque and classical eras, some expand their cultural horizons by tackling music from around the globe, and others aim to uncover unknown gems and bring them into the public eye. Many orchestras require auditions before you can join, so keep practising that flute, horn or violin. Attending a performance can also be a lovely night out; you can spend a few dollars to see a youth orchestra, $20 to $30 for a lesser known professional orchestra, to much more for the city's premier outfit, the Vancouver Symphony Orchestra.

**Various Locations**

### CBC Radio Orchestra

*604 662 6028 | www.cbc.ca/orchestra*

The CBC Radio Orchestra, established in 1938, puts on affordable, professional performances, usually at the Chan Centre for Performing Arts at UBC. CBC is Canada's national public broadcaster, and you can also hear the orchestra live on CBC Radio 2. Afterwards, the audio file is posted on the website.

**7024 Boundary Rd**
*Burnaby*
*Map 6 D3* 124

### Summer Pops Youth Orchestra

*604 430 3820 | www.summerpops.ca*

This is a non-profit orchestral opportunity for musically talented youth. Membership costs $425 and includes a two week (10 day) workshop in July, the music, uniforms and participation in the public concerts performed during the rest of the summer. In 2007 the orchestra performed seven free concerts for the public in Vancouver, the North Shore, Richmond and Port Coquitlam. The group also takes a summer tour to a destination in Western Canada, which costs about $600 if you wish to take part. Teens must audition in the spring.

**601 Smithe St**
*Downtown*
*Map 7 E4* 125

### Vancouver Symphony Orchestra

*604 684 9100 | www.vancouversymphony.ca*

The Vancouver Symphony Orchestra performs 150 concerts and draws more than 200,000 people to its shows each season. It has developed a wide variety of concert series to appeal to those who like traditional classical music (Masterworks), jazz, swing and big band (VSO Pops), or who just want to enjoy an afternoon concert and socialise (Tea and Trumpets). For children, the VSO puts on educational kids' concerts. Prices range from $99 for a symphony sampler (four concerts) to as much as $675 for 10 Masterworks concerts in the best seats. The orchestra plays at many theatres in Vancouver, but mainly the Orpheum Theatre Downtown and the Chan Centre for Performing Arts at UBC.

**3214 West 10th Av**
*Point Grey*
*Map 8 A4* 126

### Vancouver Youth Symphony Orchestra

*604 737 0714 | www.vyso.com*

This training school is for young, talented musicians with a passion for orchestra. Potential players must audition for spots in the various orchestras, which include a strings orchestra for ages 8 to 11, junior strings orchestra, intermediate orchestra for strings, woodwind, brass and percussion players, and a senior orchestra for ages 14 to 22. Auditions are held in May and June, require a $25 fee and are competitive. The VYSO plays a number of concerts throughout its season (September to May) with admission by donation, so attending these performances can be an inexpensive way to support youth in music.

### Orchestras & Bands

| | | |
|---|---|---|
| Ambleside Orchestra | 604 926 3030 | www.vcn.bc.ca/amble |
| Burnaby Symphony Orchestra | 604 205 9199 | www.burnabysymphony.com |
| North Shore Sinfonia | 778 786 3208 | www.sinfonia-orchestra.com |
| Richmond Orchestra & Chorus Association | 604 276 2747 | www.roca.ca |
| Richmond Youth Orchestra | 604 270 4520 | music.ryo.ca |
| Vancouver Chamber Players | 604 731 4661 | www.vancp.com |
| Vancouver Intercultural Orchestra | 604 879 8415 | www.vi-co.org |
| Vancouver Philharmonic Orchestra | 604 878 9989 | www.vanphil.ca |
| West Coast Chamber Music | 604 879 9959 | www.westcoastchambermusic.org |

## Paintballing

Vancouver is running out of open space in the city, which makes it hard to have large, forested paintball fields. But chances are you're looking for an excuse to get out of the crowded city and release some tension the way only firing at your friends can. Tsawwassen Paintball (604 501 9966, www.tsawwassenpaintball.ca), located about 45 minutes south of Vancouver in south Delta, is open at the weekends for private and public bookings, and weekdays for private bookings only. Get a private field for $600 and ensure the attack is limited to your friends for the four allotted hours, or join in on someone else's fun for a $10 field fee (bring your own equipment, or rent all the gear for about $20 extra). You can also venture north to get in on the action at North Shore Paintball (100B Lower Capilano Road, 778 896 7529), where women don't pay entrance fees on Fridays, and Thursdays are half price for everyone. If you do have your own supplies, make sure you call ahead and check if they are allowed as many establishments have strict rules regarding guns and paintballs.

## Photography

Vancouver is situated in such a beautiful environment that it can inspire just about anyone to become a shutterbug. Within the mountains, trees and water, there's so much that you'll want to capture indefinitely, whether it's snowboarders at a terrain park or your kid playing ball. In the city, you can find courses for beginners who have just picked up their first digital camera through to people who want to develop a career behind the lens. Two Vancouver artists who have bolstered the city's reputation for contemporary photo-based art are Roy Arden (www.royarden.com) and Jeff Wall, who are both featured at the Vancouver Art Gallery (p.224) alongside other well-respected local photographers.

*6138 Student Union Blvd UBC Map 5 B1* 72

## AMS Minischool At UBC
*604 822 9342 | www.ams.ubc.ca/minischool*

The Alma Mater Society of UBC created its minischool for students looking for fun, inexpensive introductory courses on non-academic subjects like bartending, pole dancing, cooking, knitting and sign language, all of which are taught by experts in their field at discounted prices. One of the more popular courses offered is an intro to photography, which is $50 for students and $60 for non-students, once a week for five weeks – all you need is your digital camera. Students fill up these courses quickly, so get in line when registration opens.

*4474 West 10th Av*
*Point Grey*
*Map 5 C1* **128**

## Focal Point Visual Arts Learning Centre
*604 224 3636* | *www.focalpoint.bc.ca*

Here you can find both full and part-time photography courses on everything from basic digital SLR to advanced darkroom. If you have basic photography skills, you can also register for lectures and workshops on topics such as starting a small photography business and custom matting and framing your work. Within the part-time programme most 10 session courses, such as basic digital SLR photography, intermediate creative photography and narrative photography, cost $325.

*100 West 49th Av*
*Oakridge*
*Map 6 A3* **2**

## Langara College Continuing Studies
*604 323 5322* | *www.langara.bc.ca/cs*

Langara offers a photography certificate programme for those looking to enter the world of freelance commercial photography or photojournalism. Even if you have no experience, you can take Langara's basic photography course as long as you have your own 35mm camera and tripod. If you're just interested in photography as a hobby, you can take certain courses without pursuing certification, from basic photography and darkroom techniques to travel and advanced black-and-white photography. A 12 week basic photography course costs $359.

*1304 Seymour St*
*Downtown*
*Map 9 D1* **130**

## Vancouver Photo Workshops
*778 898 5256* | *www.vancouverphotoworkshops.com*

Vancouver Photo Workshops offers both one day, multi-day and multi-week courses for beginners, amateurs and professionals. It has a wide variety of programmes, from basic introduction to digital photography courses, studio lighting workshops and point and click photography classes to specialised courses in nude, travel and landscape photography. Prices vary; an all-day workshop such as practical studio lighting costs $150, a fine art black-and-white landscape and long exposure four-day workshop costs $695, and a 10 week introduction to digital SLR photography costs $350.

## Rafting

Thrill seekers looking to cool off in the warmer months can enjoy rafting on several of the rivers to the north and east of Vancouver. There are a handful of different establishments that offer day or overnight trips whenever weather and water levels

*Fraser River
Raft Expeditions*

allow (usually May to September). Rivers such as the Chilliwack vary in difficulty depending on what section you raft, whereas the Cheakamus River is great for more relaxing rides. Excellent guides who know the area ensure that even beginners have a safe and fun excursion. Costs vary from place to place, but you can expect to pay about $100 for a trip that could last several hours. Staying overnight is another option for those who want to extend their time on the water or supplement their trip with some late-night beverages – this is a popular activity for large groups or those on stag dos.

**49704 Chilliwack**
**Lake Rd**
Chilliwack

## Chilliwack River Rafting

*604 824 0334* | *www.chilliwackriverrafting.com*

Chilliwack River Rafting is one of the closest white water rafting options to Vancouver, located in the Fraser Valley past Abbotsford. Rafting trips are run from 1 May to 15 September, and at other times when the weather co-operates. The fun crew has given the rapids nicknames such as Double Whammy and Gun Barrel to add to the anticipation. Where the water is lower you can try an inflatable kayak tour.

**332 East Esplanade**
North Vancouver
*Map 4 B3* **132**

## Elaho Adventures

*604 921 7250* | *www.elahoadventures.com*

Families can opt for an introductory three hour rafting trip on the low volume Cheakamus River, while thrill seekers can take full day and weekend trips down the Elaho and Squamish rivers. Other services offered by Elaho include eagle safaris in the winter to watch the soaring bald-headed birds gorge on salmon, and wilderness floats for those who want to travel along the water and enjoy nature. The office is in North Vancouver, but call or visit the website for directions to its home base in Squamish (where the trips take off from), which is just over an hour's drive north from Downtown Vancouver.

**Highway 1**
Yale

## Fraser River Raft Expeditions

*1 800 363 7238* | *www.fraserraft.com*

For those interested in braving the rapids, skilled guides take groups and individuals of all ages and abilities along the Fraser River and its tributaries. One to seven-day trips are offered alongside tailor-made expeditions, and include meals and safety equipment. Daytrips cost around $130 for adults, $110 for those under 16. Trips depart daily from its base in Yale (dependent on safe water levels). It's recommended that you book ahead. Check the website for full details on appropriate clothing and equipment.

**203-3823 Henning Dr**
Burnaby
*Map 6 D1* **133**

## Hyak Wilderness Adventures

*604 734 5718* | *www.hyak.com*

You can have a wet and wild rafting ride on five different rivers with this company. Join a daytrip or overnight stay on the Chilliwack River in the Fraser Valley, the Thompson River in the interior, or a combination Chilko, Chilcotin and Fraser rivers expedition. Children must be at least 10 years old to partake. The office is in Burnaby, but the website includes directions to rafting centres on the Chilliwack and Thompson rivers.

**845 Spence Way**
Port Coquitlam
*Map 2 C2*

## REO Whitewater Rafting

*604 461 7238* | *www.reorafting.com*

REO Rafting caters to nervous first timers and experienced adrenaline junkies. It claims the Nahatlatch River as its speciality, but also navigates the Thompson, Fraser and the challenging class-five Stein rivers. While there you can fish for sturgeon on the Fraser (you need a BC fishing licence), or rappel rocks and hike along Canyon Trail, register for an intro to inflatable kayaking (children can do the easiest sections), or take a soothing float down the calmer parts of the Nahatlatch. The mailing address is listed, but to get to the resort follow the Trans-Canada Highway past Hope and head for Boston Bar.

## Rollerblading & Rollerskating

Other options **Parks** p.241, **Beaches** p.237

Rollerblading may not be as iconic here as in LA, but that doesn't mean there aren't some great places to go on wheels. The Seawall around Stanley Park allows bladers spectacular views of Downtown and the North Shore as they pass beaches that line Burrard Inlet and English Bay. Skaters can follow the promenade east for another five

*Blading at English Bay*

kilometres, along the outskirts of Yaletown and False Creek, to see the rest of the bay and reach Telus World of Science. An alternative is a tour of the UBC campus, which boasts one of the smoothest, almost car-free road networks in Vancouver. Bolder bladers should visit the relatively new 16,000 sq ft City Skate Park in North Vancouver (at the corner of the Trans-Canada Highway and Lonsdale Avenue, www. cnv.org/default.aspx) for inline skating and skateboarding. While it is not BC law to wear protective gear while rollerblading, some municipalities have enacted bylaws that require skaters to sport helmets (North Vancouver being one; the fine is up to $40). If you are looking to pick up a pair of skates, check any local sporting goods store, such as Sport Chek (p.402). Go in the autumn for clearance sales, where you can pick up a good pair for around $150. If you want to rent, Bayshore Bicycle and Rollerblade Skate Rentals by Stanley Park (745 Denman Street, 604 688 2453) hires blades by the hour or the day.

## Rowing

Other options **Dragon Boat Racing** p.292, **Watersports** p.333

Gliding fluidly across the water takes dedication, teamwork and strength. There's plenty of water around Vancouver and a number of clubs to get you started. It is possible to row as an individual, or in teams of two, four or eight. If you decide to race, you need to be fit; a standard championship race length is 2,000m, but can be much longer. Most regattas are held outside the city at BC lakes, like Elk Lake and Shawnigan Lake on Vancouver Island. Check out Rowing BC (www.rowingbc.ca) for its regatta schedule, and for rowing clubs in addition to the ones below.

**2156 Banbury Rd**
*North Vancouver*
*Map 4 F2* **30**

### Deep Cove Rowing Club
*604 929 4510 | www.deepcoverowingclub.com*

Located by Deep Cove at the south end of Indian Arm in North Vancouver, this club has developed programmes for those aged 13 and up, including learn-to-row, junior and adult competitive rowing and training, corporate rowing opportunities and private lessons. An adult learn-to-row course (eight sessions) for ages 19 and up is $240, while competitive rowers ages 27 and up can take part in the masters programme. The latter involves training four days a week between February and November. The cost to join the squad for a member is $425 ($485 for non-members). Recreational members of the Deep Cove Rowing Club pay $25 a year, while a competitive rowing membership is $60 and includes membership of Rowing Canada.

**7277 River Rd**
*Richmond*
*Map 2 B3*

### John MS Lecky UBC Boathouse
*604 247 2627 | www.ubcboathouse.com*

The UBC Boathouse was created as a home for the university rowing teams and is also used by the city of Richmond to run rowing and dragon boating programmes (see p.292). In addition to dragon boating, the boathouse offers adult and youth learn-to-row programmes, a Richmond junior rowing team, and an adult rowing league for non-competitive adults.

**450 Stanley Park Dr**
*Stanley Park*
*Map 3 F4* 137

## Vancouver Rowing Club

*604 687 3400 | www.vancouverrowingclub.com*

The club's rowing season takes place from April to October, and includes programmes from learn-to-row and junior rowing to masters training. Participants in the open rowing programme (any adult who wants to compete) practise Monday and Wednesday evenings and Sunday mornings; competitive rowers in the masters programme (over 27) practise Tuesday and Thursday evenings and Saturday mornings. While rowing is the club's founding sport, it also offers sessions for field hockey, rugby and yachting enthusiasts. To be an active (rather than simply social) member of the Vancouver Rowing Club will cost you $210 a year. This does not include the fees for participating in club sports, which for rowing is another $238.

## Rugby

While you may not find much in the way of organised drop-in events, there is some serious amateur rugby union happening around Vancouver. There are many club teams to join where you will feel welcomed, regardless of your age or skill level. Within the BC Rugby Union (www.bcrugby.com) is a list of youth, senior and over 40s leagues for both genders. There are 19 clubs in the Vancouver Rugby Union (part of the BC union) including Capilano RFC (www.capilanorfc.com) in North Vancouver, SFU/Burnaby Mountain Rugby Association (www.sfurugby.com), Vancouver Rowing Club RFC (www.vancouverrugby.com) and the ones listed below. Vancouver also has nine rugby pitches where you can practise your rucks and tackling.

**3760 Sperling Av**
*Burnaby*
*Map 6 F2* 138

## Burnaby Lake Rugby Club

*604 294 2572 | http://blrc.bc.ca*

This Burnaby club has three senior men's teams, a senior women's team, a junior rugby development programme for under 14s to under 19s youth and 'mini rugby' for ages 5 to 12. The club offers members use of the clubhouse at the fields. A senior playing membership is $360 for men and women, students pay $270 and social members are charged $150, with fees due in September.

**2390 West 10th Av**
*Kitsilano*
*Map 8 D4* 139

## Meraloma Rugby Club

*604 733 4366 | www.meralomarugby.com*

The Meraloma Rugby Club and its clubhouse in Kitsilano welcome players of all skill levels. It has teams for both genders and a variety of ages. There are three senior men's teams, two women's teams (16 to late 30s), junior rugby for under 12s to under 19s, an over 40s squad and rugby for 'minis', which starts at nursery level up to age 11. Training begins mid-August at Connaught Park in Kitsilano and the season commences in early September. If the season isn't enough, join the club for touch rugby on Tuesday and Thursday evenings in the summer. The Meraloma Athletic Club also has teams for basketball, cricket, field hockey, softball and soccer.

**1725 East 14th Av**
*Grandview*
*Map 12 B3* 140

## Scribes Rugby Football Club

*604 433 2905 | www.scribesrfc.com*

Scribes features a men's team, the over 40s Eastside Gentlemen (made up of older Scribes and some ex-Brits), and an Irish sporting and social club that hosts events such as Friday night men's Gaelic football. Anyone of any skill level can drop in to a practise session, which are held on Mondays and Wednesdays at 18:30 during the season (September to May), a short walk from the clubhouse at John Hendry Park. The Eastside Gentlemen also meet Wednesdays at 18:30.

## Running

Whether your goal is to keep fit or you're training for the Vancouver Marathon every May, running is a simple, cheap, and effective way to stay in shape. Vancouver's climate allows for year-round running – you can spend the winter pounding under the evergreens in Pacific Spirit Regional Park and jog the Seawall that encircles Stanley Park in the summer. There are plenty of running clinics, events and clubs where you can get support if you need some motivation to keep your legs moving. Keep in mind that most of the clubs are members of BC Athletics (www.bcathletics.org) and require at least a 'non-competitive' membership, for about $10.

### Capilano Eagles Running Club

**William Griffin Recreation Ctr**
*851 Queens Rd*
*West Vancouver*
*Map 4 A2* 141

www.capilanoeagles.com

This West Vancouver club offers a variety of training runs guided by the expertise of a personal running coach. Training sessions are on Tuesday evenings and the tempo is set according to the goals of members as a whole. To take part in activities, a $50 yearly membership is required in addition to a BC Athletics membership, both of which you can sign up for online.

### Pacific Road Runners

**False Creek Community Ctr**
*1318 Cartwright St*
*Granville Island*
*Map 9 C3* 32

604 515 2488 | www.pacificroadrunners.ca

Intermediate and experienced runners in the Vancouver area can join this club that emphasises the need for an active lifestyle. Runs are informal – they meet on Tuesday and Thursday evenings at the False Creek Community Centre on Granville Island and head off in all directions from there. To register for the year, singles pay $35 (this includes a BC Athletics membership) and couples get a bit of a deal at $65.

### Running Room

**1578 West Broadway**
*Fairview*
*Map 9 A4* 143

604 879 9721 | www.runningroom.com

If you are going to run a marathon, you'd better have a good pair of shoes. The experts at Running Room can determine your foot type and suggest the best pair for you. You can register online or in person for one of the 10 to 16 week walking or running clinics available. In-store training sessions and group walks or runs are also provided to get you moving, all for about $70.

### Vancouver International Marathon

**BC Place Stadium**
*Pacific Blvd*
*Downtown*
*Map 9 F1* 144

604 872 2928 | www.bmovanmarathon.ca

You don't really get to appreciate how beautiful Downtown Vancouver and False Creek are until you have run through 42km of streets with hundreds of other enthusiasts. Register by 30 April each year to become part of Canada's largest marathon, which takes place in May. Like most major events, the cost depends on how early you sign up – early birds in December pay $85 and the cost rises every couple of months, up to $125 in April.

## Scouts & Guides

Scouting has spread like wildfire from Europe to North America since its inception in 1907 in London by Lord Baden-Powell. His sister, Olave, started guiding for girls shortly after and both movements soon reached Canada. Scouting and guiding programmes aim to teach youngsters life skills and build independence and confidence in a friendly environment. The Girl Guides' fundraising staple, a sandwich cookie stamped with a shamrock, is a well-known feature in family-friendly neighbourhoods and has recently been joined by a chocolate mint variety. The original boys' club, the Scouts, is now open to boys and girls across the country.

**1476 West 8th Av**
*Fairview*
*Map 9 B4* **145**

## British Columbia Girl Guides

*604 714 6636 | www.bc-girlguides.org*

This female-only organisation is for 5 to 18 year olds (divided into Sparks, Brownies, Guides, Pathfinders and Senior branches) and is run by volunteer leaders (called Guiders) ages 19 and up. It's a place girls can go to make new friends, take part in games and crafts when they're little, and move on to camping and other outdoor adventures as they get older. Also check out the Vancouver (604 876 6266, www.vancouvergirlguides.ca) and Burnaby/New Westminster (604 291 1257, www.burnabyroyal.com) Guide programmes.

**664 West Broadway**
*Fairview*
*Map 9 E4* **146**

## Scouts Canada – Pacific Coast Council

*604 879 5721 | www.pacificcoast.scouts.ca*

Like Girl Guides, Scouts is also run by volunteers and has a focus on the outdoors, teamwork and leadership. Kids can join from as young as 5 years old up to age 26 and are divided into Beavers, Cubs, Scouts, Venturers and Rovers. Check with the Pacific Coast Council for more information about scouting programmes in Burnaby, East Vancouver, Pacific Spirit (west of Main Street), Richmond, North Shore and Sunshine Coast areas.

## Skiing & Snowboarding

Other options **Snowshoeing** p.325

BC is well known for its skiing and snowboarding. Of all the mountains, Whistler is the most famous, renowned around the world, and is just a few hours' drive up the Sea to Sky Highway; it's also the most expensive. Nearer to the city, the North Shore has three mountains, Seymour, Grouse and Cypress, which are smaller but cheaper. Many Vancouverites are so passionate about skiing or snowboarding that they make the trip up to Whistler almost every weekend. If you don't own your own equipment, you can rent whatever you need. Make sure to dress warmly and in layers (don't forget your toque and gloves), and helmets are mandatory if you enter terrain parks. Lessons are also available on all mountains for all skill levels, and you can buy a season pass if you know you'll be a frequent visitor and want to save some money. Don't feel bad if you're on a bunny hill and a 9 year old zooms by – you can begin taking lessons from as young as 3 at Grouse. All mountains have snow reports, so check the weather before you make the trek. Stay in bounds and out of avalanche risk areas.

**Cypress Bowl Rd**
*Cypress Provincial Park*
*West Vancouver*
*Map 2 A1*

## Cypress Mountain

*604 419 7669 | www.cypressmountain.com*

Of the three local mountains, Cypress is the largest and the highest. And because it's hosting freestyle skiing and snowboarding events during the 2010 Winter Olympics, money is being put into upgrades (such as a new half-pipe and freestyle site). If you're a good skier who can't make it to Whistler for the day, Cypress is your next best bet, and costs about the same as Grouse Mountain ($50 for a full day adult lift ticket, and the mountain generally opens at 09:00). Evening skiing costs about $40 after 16:00, or $32 from 19:00 until close at 23:00, from 15 December

*Snowsports in BC*

until 23 March. If you don't have a car, you can take a shuttle up for about $18 per adult. For those interested in a season pass, the 2007-08 rates were $1,039 for adults, $764 for ages 13 to 18, $613 for seniors (65 and up) and $568 for ages 6 to 12. The price includes downhill skiing and riding, cross-country skiing, snowshoeing and snow tubing. You can also buy downhill-only or evening-only season passes for less.

## Grouse Mountain

*6400 Nancy Greene Way*
*North Vancouver*
*Map 2 B1*

*604 986 6262* | *www.grousemountain.com*

Grouse is the easiest peak to get to as the Skyride takes you from the base of the mountain to the top, so you can be dropped off or arrive by bus. A full day pass for an adult is $47, while the evening session after 16:00 is $37. The mountain is open from 09:00 to 23:00 every day. The 2007-08 ski and snowboard season passes were $730 for adults, $525 for youths and seniors, $315 for children, $40 for under 4s, and $1,775 for a family of two adults and two children. There is not as much terrain as Cypress, but Grouse does have the most winter activities of the three local mountains. While all have snowshoeing, cross-country skiing and snow tubing, Grouse also has a skating pond, an endangered wildlife refuge, sleigh rides and excursions such as helicopter tours.

## Mount Seymour

*1700 Mount Seymour Rd*
*North Vancouver*
*Map 4 E2* **149**

*604 986 2261* | *www.mountseymour.com*

For beginner skiers and boarders, Seymour is a good option – there's less terrain in general, it's not as high as the other mountains (meaning less snow), and it's the cheapest. Seymour also offers inexpensive access to two terrain parks for those who want to practise tricks and techniques, which appeals particularly to youngsters. When planning your daytrip, keep in mind you'll need a vehicle to get up there. The mountain is open until 23:00 and a full day pass for an adult is $39.50. A season pass for 2007-08 cost $675 for adults, $475 for students and youths, $250 for seniors, $175 for children, $20 for kids under 5, and $1,600 for a family.

## Whistler Blackcomb

*Whistler*

*1 800 766 0449* | *www.whistlerblackcomb.com*

Whistler Blackcomb has more than 8,100 acres of terrain featuring everything an expert skier could want, such as double black diamond runs, tree-gladed skiing, terrain parks, moguls and bowls. You won't get bored on the slopes, and you certainly won't be stuck for things to do afterwards either as there are plenty of dining, clubbing and entertainment options. For beginners, Whistler Blackcomb is an experience in snowboarding and ski culture. The only downside is that its global reputation has led to massive development and rocketing prices. It's expensive to stay on the mountain, and the cost is expected to go up as the 2010 Winter Olympics approach. A one day pass (including lifts) costs $83 for an adult, while an unlimited adult season pass to the mountain is about $1,739 (a mid-week pass is $1,179), $729 for youths, $519 for children, $849 for seniors and $10 for kids under 6. If you purchase your season pass before October you can save between $150 and $340 depending on your age group. Whistler Blackcomb is open from 08:30 to 15:00, so wake up early to get a full day in.

## Slo-pitch

Slo-pitch, also known as 'beer league ball', is a summer pastime for adults. Instead of facing fast and furious pitches, batters hit a softball lobbed in a high arch, 6 to 12 feet in the air, by the pitcher on the mound. Usually unisex, slo-pitch is for the casual ball player of any skill level who is looking to enjoy a cold beer on the sideline, play some ball and enjoy the summer sun. Even the rules have been relaxed (there's no sliding or stealing bases) to encourage all levels of ball players to participate. A few slo-pitch leagues can be found through Crosstown Slopitch Softball (www.crosstownslopitch.com), Urban Rec (www.urbanrec.ca) and The West End Co-Ed Slowpitch League (www.wecsl.com).

## Snooker & Billiards

Snooker, pool and billiards are popular social activities, much like bowling. In fact, many billiards halls are connected to bowling alleys, or you can find them at some pubs and coffee shops. Serious shooters should check out the BC Cue Sports Society (604 833 8151, www.bccursports.com). It's based in Surrey, and a $10 membership fee gets you access to tournaments that are frequently held in Richmond, Burnaby and Vancouver. If you just want to play casually for an hour or two, check out one of the pool locations in the table below.

| Snooker & Billiards | | | |
| --- | --- | --- | --- |
| Automotive Billiards Club | 1283 Hamilton St | Downtown | 604 682 0040 |
| The Cue Club In Burnaby | 101-3787 Canada Way | Burnaby | 604 435 1413 |
| Guys & Dolls Billiards | 2434 Main St | Main | 604 879 4433 |
| Hi-Lite Billiards | 4391 No 3 Rd | Richmond | 604 278 8077 |
| Kitsilano Billiards | 3255 West Broadway | Kitsilano | 604 739 9544 |
| Oscar Billiard | 100-10811 No 4 Rd | Richmond | 604 241 9998 |
| Soho Billiards | 1283 Hamilton St | Yaletown | 604 688 1180 |
| Snooker City | 110-3311 No 3 Rd | Richmond | 604 207 0468 |

## Snowshoeing Tours

Other options **Skiing & Snowboarding** p.322

Want to have fun in the snow, but don't really feel the need for speed? Give snowshoeing a try. All the North Shore mountains offer snowshoe rentals and trail passes, or you can pay more for nature tours that end with chocolate fondue in a warm lodge. It's been said that if you can walk, you can snowshoe. Essentially, snowshoes are footwear that spread your weight over a larger surface area, so you don't sink into the powdery snow. And while skiers and snowboarders have to deal with busy slopes and gondola queues, the less-popular snowshoeing trails are quieter, and you can move along at your own pace.

*Cypress Bowl Rd*
*Cypress Provincial Park*
*West Vancouver*
*Map 2 A1*

### Cypress Mountain

*604 419 7669* | *www.cypressmountain.com*

A day of snowshoeing at Cypress will cost $9.43 without rentals and $25.23 with, for ages 13 to 64 (less for children and seniors). If you'd prefer a guided tour, for a bit more money you can be led through the trails in the day, or in the evening under the stars, for two to four hours (depending on whether you include the cheese and chocolate fondue). Cypress also has cross-country skiing and snow tubing options. A two-hour tube rental costs around $15.

*6400 Nancy*
*Greene Way*
*North Vancouver*
*Map 2 B1*

### Grouse Mountain

*604 986 6262* | *www.grousemountain.com*

At Grouse, take beginner snowshoe clinics (including ladies only), drop-in snowshoeing after 19:00 for all levels, or a one hour guided snowshoe tour that ends with fondue in a bistro. Grouse Mountain also hosts the Yeti Snowshoe Race in February – to prepare for the competition, you can register for weekly lessons to train and learn racing tips. Access to any winter activity on Grouse requires a general admission pass for the Skyride to the top ($32.95 for an adult), plus the cost of the clinic or tour. Adult snowshoe rentals are $15, while for children and seniors it's $10.

*1700 Mount*
*Seymour Rd*
North Vancouver
Map 4 E2 **149**

## Mount Seymour
*604 986 2261 | www.mountseymour.com*

For $26.25, adults and youths can get a snowshoe trail pass and equipment for the day (seniors and children are $21.25). Alternatively, try one of the guided snowshoe outings, which include the family drop-in, evening tours, chocolate fondue tours, and winter workout Wednesdays. A mother and baby drop-in is held on Monday afternoons for $35, while winter workout Wednesdays in January and February cost $30 a session.

*Whistler*

## Whistler Blackcomb
*1 800 766 0449 | www.whistlerblackcomb.com*

At Whistler, snowshoeing tours are available for anyone over the age of 4. Prices range from $39 to $109, depending on the length of tour, age and whether you want to include the gourmet three-course fondue meal. The 'tour of the day', for ages 13 and up, costs $89 for four hours of trekking through the snow, and the destination constantly changes – you could end up snowshoeing through an old growth forest or travelling around a glacier lake. Other winter activities besides skiing and snowboarding run the gamut from snow tubing and dog sledding to snowmobiling and helicopter tours.

## Soccer

By sheer numbers, soccer (or football, as it's known outside North America) is the largest participatory sport in Canada. The game boasts more registered players than ice hockey, the country's beloved national winter sport. Whether this is down to the fact that all you need to play is a ball, posts and a patch of grass remains to be seen, but at any rate there's not enough interest to fill the stands – the most attention the Vancouver Whitecaps have received is in 2007 when David Beckham visited with his MLS team LA Galaxy. Still, there are countless clubs for youngsters (in addition to high school teams) and a few options for adults who want to play recreationally. If you are looking for a casual, unisex indoor league, try Urban Rec (604 879 9800, www.urbanrec.ca), which has a four-on-four winter league starting in January, one evening a week for seven weeks. Leagues are governed by the Canadian Soccer Association (www.canadasoccer.com).

*510-375 Water St*
Gastown
Map 10 A1 **155**

## BC Soccer Association
*604 299 6401 | www.bcsoccer.net*

The British Columbia Soccer Association oversees the long list of youth and senior outdoor 11-a-side soccer leagues in the province. In Vancouver, Richmond and Burnaby, check out leagues run by the Burnaby District Youth Soccer Association (boys and girls, www.burnabysoccer.com), Richmond Youth Soccer (boys, www.richmondsoccer.com), Vancouver Richmond Girls Soccer Association (www.vrgsa.ca), Vancouver Youth Soccer Association (boys, www.vysa.ca), and the West Vancouver Soccer Club (youth and adults, www.westvansoccer.com). For adults, a few to contact include the North Shore Thirty Something Soccer League (women over 30, www.thirtysomethingsoccer.com), Vancouver Metro Soccer (men, www.vmslsoccer.com) and Metro Women's Soccer (www.metrowomenssoccer.com).

*Spanish Banks*
Point Grey
Map 5 C1 **156**

## Beach Soccer Blast
*604 818 2845 | www.mysportstournament.com/beachblast*

More than 150 teams of all ages come to Spanish Banks in Vancouver each August for the Beach Soccer Blast. Since the mid 1990s, male, female and mixed teams have been diving into the sand and showing off their ball handling skills on the variable playing field. Players under 18 must be registered with the British Columbia Soccer Association. Registration costs $160 to $250 per team, depending on age and when you sign up.

## North Shore Soccer Development Centre

**Delbrook Rec Ctr**
*600 West Queens Rd*
*North Vancouver*
*Map 4 A2* **157**

*604 987 7529 | www.nssdc.net*

There is a wide range of soccer development course offered by this centre, including high performance programmes aimed at both boys and girls ages 6 to 12, soccer camps, coach certification programmes for adults, and clinics to teach new goalkeepers how to handle, move and save. The centre was founded by the Mount Seymour Soccer Association (www.mountseymoursoccer.ca), Lynn Valley Soccer Association (www.lvsa.com), North Shore Girls Soccer Club (www.nsgsc.ca) and Lions Gate Soccer Association (www.lionsgatesoccer.bc.ca).

## Richmond Development Centre

**Various Locations**

*604 271 7459 | www.richmonddevcentre.com*

Created by Richmond Youth Soccer and the Richmond Girls Soccer Association (within the Vancouver Richmond Girls Soccer Association), the Development Centre has soccer programmes for kids aged 5 up to adults. For the kids, a programme called FUNdamentals teaches skills to children up to age 11. There's also the opportunity to get your coaching certification or learn beginner and advanced goalkeeping. Many of the programmes are held at Hugh Boyd Secondary's relatively new turf field (9200 No 1 Road).

## Squash

Other options **Sports & Leisure Facilities** p.339

Squash is a fast-paced indoor game for people who don't mind bouncing off the walls – it's a demanding, high-impact racquet sport that can burn hundreds of calories. Novice players might leave their first lesson with some bumps and bruises, but you're welcome to give the game a shot at a nearby community centre. A 45 minute session of squash here can cost you from $5.95 to $11.65, depending on the time you play. At some facilities this includes use of the fitness centre.

## Evergreen Squash Club

**1802 Glenaire Dr**
*North Vancouver*
*Map 3 F2* **159**

*604 985 8638 | www.evergreensquash.com*

No tennis, no badminton, no fitness centres – the Evergreen Squash Club on the North Shore is all about squash. Its singles league competes in the Vancouver Squash League, and it also includes in-house singles senior and ladies' box ladders. Evergreen also enters teams in the Vancouver Doubles League and offers in-house doubles throughout the week. The juniors programme runs on Friday and Sunday evenings. A three month trial membership costs $105.

## Squash BC

**Queen Elizabeth Park**
*4867 Ontario St*
*Fraser*
*Map 6 A2* **7**

*604 737 3084 | www.squashbc.com*

If you're up for a competitive game of squash, check out Squash BC for a team near you. Organisations that play in the Vancouver Squash League include most of the private tennis clubs (Arbutus, Hollyburn, Jericho, Vancouver Lawn Tennis and Badminton, Vancouver Racquets Club, The River Club in Richmond and the North Shore Winter Club). There are also a few fitness gyms you can join that enter teams in the league, such as the Denman Fitness Company (604 688 2484, www.denmanfitness.com), Bentall Centre Athletic Club (604 689 4424, www.bentallcentreathleticclub.com) and Sport Central in Richmond (604 278 8884, www.sportcentral.ca).

## Surfing
Other options **Beaches** p.237

When people think of BC sports, they think of what can be done on powdery mounds, raging rivers and calm lakes. But Vancouverites can be surfers too – just not as tanned as their Hawaiian and Californian counterparts. The country's best-known surfing destination is on Vancouver Island in Tofino (particularly Long Beach), so ferry on over to experience surf culture Canadian-style. Remember, wetsuits are a must, even in the summer. A number of Tofino shops offer lessons, clinics and even camps (some, like Surf Sister, have female-only options) for approximately $75, depending on the length of the lesson, and this often includes equipment.

*6138 Student*
*Union Blvd*
*UBC*
*Map 5 B1* 72

## UBC Surf Club
*604 822 6185* | *www.ubcsurf.com*

The UBC Surf Club is open to both students and non-students, for an annual membership of $20 to $30. The club is located within the Student Union building on campus, and takes a few trips to Tofino on Vancouver Island in September and October at prices from $150 to $200, which includes surfboard rentals, transportation and accommodation (and maybe even beer). Each year the club organises a surfing trip during reading break (UBC breaks in February) to a hot destination such as Costa Rica or Mexico.

| Surfing | | | |
| --- | --- | --- | --- |
| Live to Surf | Tofino | 250 725 4464 | www.livetosurf.com |
| Pacific Surf School | Tofino | 1 888 777 9961 | www.pacificsurfschool.com |
| Surf Sister Surf School | Tofino | 1 877 724 7873 | www.surfsister.com |
| Westside Surf School | Tofino | 250 725 2404 | www.westsidesurfschool.com |

## Swimming
Other options **Sports & Leisure Facilities** p.339, **Beaches** p.237

Knowing how to swim in Vancouver is crucial if you want to participate in many of the exciting water sports, such as kayaking and waterskiing, which take place along the shoreline. Splashing about in the pool or ocean is also a fun recreational activity in itself, or you can take it to a competitive level by joining a swimming club or team. Brave, or crazy, Vancouverites will even swim outside in the winter as a way of bringing in the new year. The annual Polar Bear Swim at English Bay on 1 January attracts about 2,000 swimmers to water barely over 0°C, where they plunge in, regardless of the weather, to celebrate. Most of the city's facilities are accessible for people with disabilities, providing aquatic wheelchairs and lifts. All, both indoor and out, offer swimming lessons for adults and children, and many of the indoor pools feature aquafit classes. The city's five outdoor pools and nine indoor pools can be found at the various community centres (p.341); alternatively call the Parks Board on 604 257 8400 for more information. A few outdoor pools are located right by the ocean: Kitsilano Pool, Second Beach Pool in Stanley Park and New Brighton Pool in East Vancouver. Kits pool is Vancouver's only saltwater pool, a place to dip the kids in preparation for salty ocean swimming.

*1050 Beach Av*
*Downtown*
*Map 9 B1* 162

## Canadian Dolphins Swim Club
*604 684 7928* | *www.canadiandolphin.ca*

This competitive swimming club celebrated its 50th anniversary in 2006. Club members range from those just starting out to those who compete at national and international levels. The club is based at the Vancouver Aquatic Centre, and you can register any time throughout the season. However, you must attend an evaluation session to determine your placement in a training group – assessments take place Tuesdays and Thursdays at 14:30. The club is mainly for youths, but does have a triathlon/masters group for adults, with training two to four days a week.

**6260 Killarney St**
*Killarney*
*Map 6 C3* **163**

## Killarney Gators Swim Club

*604 277 3942 | www.gatorswimclub.ca*

Anyone over the age of 6 can join this East Vancouver club, providing they can swim a 25m length without stopping. Training levels include introductory, development/fitness and competitive; all groups start in September and the season ends in June. Because the club is run by volunteers, parents of swimmers are required to participate at events and in fundraising efforts. Training fees range from $70 a month at the junior fitness level to $220 a month at the elite high competitive level, and membership is $60.

**112a-255 West 1st St**
*North Vancouver*
*Map 4 A3* **164**

## Swim BC

*604 987 2004 | www.swim.bc.ca*

Check out Swim BC for a list of member clubs in various parts of the province, affiliated swim organisations and upcoming competitions. You must be a Swim BC member to join member club teams, with fees of $16 for non-competitive swimmers under 17 to $169 for national level swimmers. Members can also take part in summer camps held from May to August, which are $11 a session. Swim BC hosts Aquatics For Arthritis too, a series of fundraisers to raise awareness and money for the cause.

**Kitsilano Beach**
*Kitsilano*
*Map 8 E1* **165**

## Vancouver Open Water Swim Association

*www.vowsa.bc.ca*

If you're looking for a safe alternative to swimming in the confines of a pool, the Vancouver Open Water Swim Association could be for you. The organisation hosts open water swim practises at Kits beach for a $3 drop in fee, or you can pay $30 for a membership. Each session prepares you for the races; challenge yourself individually or on a relay team at one of the number of competitions organised by the association. Register early as races are limited to 300 swimmers.

**2121 Marine Dr**
*West Vancouver*
*Map 3 E2* **166**

## West Vancouver Otters Swim Club

*604 505 7946 | www.westvancouverotters.ca*

The Otters place newcomers into groups named after other marine life, such as belugas, piranhas, whales and orcas. Once you've developed basic swimming skills and strokes, you can work your way up through programmes that go as high as national and international competition levels. While the Otters focus largely on competitive swimming, it does offer a recreational fitness programme. The registration deadline for the season is usually in June, with a $200 deposit required to secure your spot. The total annual fee for swimmers ranges from $1,100 for the fitness level to $2,900 at the national level.

## Table Tennis

Other options **Sports & Leisure Facilities** p.339

Like badminton, table tennis is a popular sport in countries such as China, Korea and Japan, and as such has experienced a spurt in popularity in Richmond, Vancouver and Burnaby as people emigrate from east Asia. A number of community centres have table tennis equipment for recreational use (Dunbar, Killarney and Marpole have programmes for seniors). There are also a range of clubs to challenge skilled players.

*11660 Bridgeport Rd*
*Richmond*
*Map 2 B3*

## Canada International Table Tennis Institute

*604 278 5100* | *www.bridgeportsports.com*

While the Bridgeport Sports Club has been around for a few years, the table tennis institute was only created in 2006. The club boasts a large facility, offering both table tennis and fencing facilities and training, and is open seven days a week from 10:00 to 22:30. Drop in to play for $5.50 for non-members or $4.50 for members. An annual membership is $68, and while equipment rentals are available it is recommend that you bring your own. All levels are welcome, but part of the institute's aim is to develop professional table tennis players to raise Canada's profile at international level.

*495 Sperling Av*
*Burnaby*
*Map 4 F4* **168**

## Greater Vancouver Table Tennis Association

*604 948 8050* | *www.gvtta.ca*

Beginners and skilled kids and adults can join this association, based in Burnaby, for a yearly membership fee ($20 for adults). The training schedule is posted online for everyone from adult beginners and intermediate players to junior beginners (under 14) and junior intermediate and advanced players (under 18). To train for a month costs $44 for members, $48 for non-members. The club also offers a few drop-in sessions during the week for $2.50 and an annual summer camp and Christmas party.

*877 East Hastings St*
*Strathcona*
*Map 10 E2* **169**

## Vancouver Table Tennis Club

*604 215 0288* | *www.vttc.ca*

This table tennis club is open from 13:00 to 23:00 every day, so you can enjoy late night table tennis, reserve a table for a leisurely evening of ping pong, or take on some intense training. If you're new to the game, you can have lessons here, in a group or privately. Membership is $30 a year, plus the purchase of a monthly ($30) or annual ($300) pass, or a drop-in charge of $3. Bat and ball rentals are available for a nominal fee, or you can purchase directly from the club.

## Tennis

Other options **Sports & Leisure Facilities** p.339

Tennis is no longer just a sport for country club members. There are more than 180 public courts at parks throughout Vancouver; these locations will usually have two

*Tennis courts*

to four courts, but some, such as Kitsilano Beach Park, Stanley Park and Queen Elizabeth Park, have 10 or more. Kitsilano Beach is one of the most popular places to play because of its proximity to the sand and water. The Stanley Park courts are another public favourite. At any court, it's common courtesy to play for a maximum of 30 minutes if people are waiting. All the courts are free of charge, except for a few at Stanley Park in the summer, where you can book a court for a fee (604 605 8224). Five Vancouver community centres (Douglas Park, Dunbar, Killarney, False Creek and Trout Lake) offer lessons. Call the Vancouver Parks Board or visit the website for contact information

(604 257 8400, www.city.vancouver.bc.ca/parks), or see Community Centres on p.341. If you'd prefer to join a country club, see the options in the table.

**280 Lloyd Av** ◄
North Vancouver
Map 4 A3 **170**

## Grant Connell Tennis Centre
*604 983 6483*

This centre is a North Vancouver option for those who want to play tennis indoors but who don't want to join a club. Built in 1999, it features six courts that can be booked up to 24 hours in advance for $14 an hour, rising to $39.20 for two hours, depending on the time of day you want to play. If you wish to book a court a week in advance, you can purchase a booking card for $108 a year for an adult. The centre has also developed well-respected tennis programmes for wheelchair users and youths, and a tennis league for adults.

**204-1367 West** ◄
**Broadway**
Fairview
Map 9 B4 **171**

## Tennis BC
*604 737 3086* | www.tennisbc.org

Here you will find tennis leagues for boys, girls, men and women in different Vancouver communities, as well as in the North Shore, Richmond and municipalities further out. You can also look online at a list of public courts and their addresses and check out upcoming tournaments for a range of levels, including the Stanley Park Open, one of the largest amateur tennis tournaments in North America. Tennis BC has created community programmes too, such as the Groovy Girlz Tennis Camps, a free introductory two-hour tennis session for girls aged 7 to 10. For information on this and other community development programmes, call 604 737 3123.

## Tennis

| | | | |
|---|---|---|---|
| The Arbutus Club | 2001 Nanton Av | Arbutus | 604 266 7166 |
| Burnaby Tennis Club | 3890 Kensington Av | Burnaby | 604 291 0916 |
| Hollyburn Country Club | 950 Crosscreek Rd | West Vancouver | 604 922 0161 |
| Jericho Tennis Club | 3837 Point Grey Rd | Point Grey | 604 224 2348 |
| Richmond Country Club | 9100 Steveston Highway | Richmond | 604 277 3141 |
| Vancouver Lawn Tennis & Badminton Club | 1630 West 15th Av | Shaughnessy | 604 731 2191 |
| West Vancouver Tennis Club | 821 West 21st St | West Vancouver | 604 922 9733 |

## Triathlon

Vancouver has a lot to offer athletes, whether they enjoy doing laps at the Kitsilano outdoor pool, braving the labyrinth of paths in Pacific Spirit Regional Park, or cruising up and down the numerous bike routes in the city. It's no wonder then that so many enthusiasts participate in a triathlon (a 1.5km swim, 40km cycle and 10km run). Many triathlons in BC require you to have a yearly membership with Triathlon BC (604 736 3176, www.tribc.org) in order to participate, which costs $40, or $30 if you're a triathlon club member. Below are some Vancouver-specific triathlons, but don't feel limited by this; you can travel all over the province and country to make this a full time hobby (from March to October, when the events are typically held).

**1226-1124 Lonsdale Av** ◄
North Vancouver
Map 4 B3 **172**

## North Shore Triathlon Club
www.nstc.ca/qs

Members of Triathlon BC can join this club and train with more than 100 other triathletes on the North Shore. Yearly membership takes effect in March, when the club gets out of winter hibernation, and costs $30 (plus $30 to become a Triathlon BC member, if you are not already). Watch out for the North Shore Spring Triathlon, which takes place every May. Junior and adult Triathlon BC members can register before 1 May for $50; children under 16 get in for $35.

**Student Rec Ctr** ◄
*6000 Student*
*Union Blvd*
*UBC*
*Map 5 B1* **173**

## UBC REC Triathlon Duathlon

*604 822 3996 | www.rec.ubc.ca/events/triathlon*

A major event held by the UBC Recreational programme, this is the largest indoor triathlon-duathlon in North America. More than 800 people of all ages and skill levels convene at the UBC campus on the second Sunday of March to compete in this incredible race. Brave souls can attempt the Olympic distance (standard triathlon length, entry costs $67). If you wish to take it a bit easier, give the Sprint (a half-Olympic distance, $62) or Short Course triathlon (roughly one quarter of Olympic length, also $62) a try. If swimming's not your strong point, there's still the duathlon (entry $52), a 5km run and 20km bike ride, ending with another 5km run. Register by January to guarantee a spot and save $5. Registration closes by late February, and the event is in March.

**Ceperley Field** ◄
*Stanley Park*
*Map 3 E4* **174**

## Vancouver Triathlon

*www.multisportscanada.com/vancouver.html*

Put a bright red note on your calendar marking Labour Day – this race is held annually on the first Monday of September at Stanley Park. Compete with similar age groups in either the Olympic or Sprint categories. Triathlon BC members pay $89, and everyone else pays an extra $10. If you attend this event, get there early as parking near the start is only available from 05:00 to 06:30 before the roads are closed and the race begins. You can register online through Multisportscanada.

## Volleyball

Volleyball attracts many youngsters in Vancouver. Those who play in high school often also belong to a club, and many who play indoor volleyball take advantage of the city's beach volleyball facilities as well. Pop down to the beach on a summer weekend and you are likely to see a tournament, such as the Vancouver Molson Open at Kitsilano Beach. Otherwise, start your own casual game. Posts are set up and down Jericho Beach, Spanish Banks, Kits Beach and English Bay, all for free public use on a first come, first served basis (be warned: the beaches are packed on hot summer days). All you have to do is bring a ball, let staff hold on to a piece of identification, and you'll have use of a net for some fun in the sand.

**Various Locations** ◄

## Urban Rec

*604 879 9800 | www.urbanrec.ca*

Urban Rec emphasises having fun with your friends and meeting people while being active. Every league is offered to males and females of all ages and skill levels who want to play recreationally. There are indoor volleyball and beach volleyball leagues, as well as train-and-play, an opportunity to be coached followed by a short game. In addition to volleyball, the organisation offers social leagues in dodgeball, basketball, curling, indoor and outdoor soccer, floor hockey, ultimate, slo-pitch and flag football. Its league games are held at various locations in Vancouver, although you will often find yourself using UBC facilities.

**Harry Jerome** ◄
**Sports Ctr**
*7564 Barnet Rd*
*Burnaby*
*Map 4 F4* **176**

## Volleyball BC

*604 291 2007 | www.volleyballbc.ca*

In addition to clinics and camps offering volleyball opportunities, Volleyball BC has links to youth clubs such as Blues Volleyball in North Vancouver (www.bluesvolleyball.com), Air Attack in Richmond (www.airattack.ca), Action Volleyball in Burnaby (www.

actionvolleyball.com), and Apex Volleyball in Vancouver (www.apexvolleyball.com). Clubs hold try-outs, and practice is held at various gyms within their municipalities. Volleyball BC runs 'atomic volleyball' (in Vancouver and Burnaby) for eight weeks for children aged 9 to 12. Adults who are not already on a team can sign up as individuals and be matched with a side for indoor mixed, women's or men's volleyball. Drop-in play is offered to adults at Harry Jerome Sports Centre in Burnaby and costs $4 to $5 on a first come, first served basis.

## Watersports
Other options **Dragon Boat Racing** p.292, **Rowing** p.319

The stunning blue ocean and body of water that surrounds Vancouver means the area is rife with opportunities for water-based activities such as windsurfing, sailing, water skiing and wakeboarding. A number of companies have set up at Deep Cove to make the most of the peaceful waters at the south end of Indian Arm. Another popular watersports location is the west end of Jericho Beach, where clubs and schools have set up operation inside the Jericho Sailing Centre.

*Panorama Park*
*4349 Gallant Av*
*North Vancouver*
*Map 4 F2* 177

### Cove Watersports Wakeboard School
*604 982 9253* | *www.covewatersports.com*
This seasonal operation (May to October) provides lessons in wakeboarding and wakesurfing, boat rentals and kids camps at Deep Cove, North Vancouver. A learn to wakeboard lesson is $75 for 45 minutes, and after that you can purchase sets of lessons. A four-day kids' camp on wakeboarding is $190 and includes use of equipment. There's also a Women on Water programme on Wednesday evenings for $35 for those who want to learn in a female-only environment. If you're in a group, have the wakeboarding know-how and your own gear, you can charter a boat for $130 an hour.

**4420 Gallant Av**
*North Vancouver*
*Map 4 F2* 178

### Deep Cove Yacht Club
*604 929 1009* | *www.deepcoveyc.com*
Both adults and children can learn to sail at this North Shore yacht club. Potential sailors can take 'wet feet' (ages 5 to 7), while those aged 8 to 15 can learn the basics of sailing, including the theory and how to tie knots, before moving on to learn-to-race courses (a three week learn-to-race course costs $500, which includes participation in a regatta). The entrance fee is approximately $4,500. Socially, the club hosts events such as its Valentines Dinner and St Paddy's Day Shindig.

*Beach volleyball*

*Sailing*

**Jericho Sailing Ctr**
1300 Discovery St
Kitsilano
Map 5 C1 **33**

## Disabled Sailing Association Of British Columbia

*604 222 3003 | www.disabilityfoundation.org/dsa*

Catering for people with a variety of disabilities, this organisation provides recreational and competitive sailing programmes and hosts a number of regattas. The Integration Regatta challenges able-bodied sailors to compete against DSA sailors, and the New Beginnings regatta gives disabled first-time sailors a chance to race. The DSA also holds sailing days for kids, which begin with a hike on land and end with boats on the water. The association runs its programmes out of the Jericho Sailing Centre and also has locations in Victoria, Ladysmith and Kelowna. An annual adult membership is $10.

**Ambleside Park**
West Vancouver
Map 3 E2 **181**

## Hollyburn Sailing Club

*www.hollyburnsailingclub.ca*

This sailing club organises races, offers workshops, and owns a fleet of boats for members who don't possess their own (for an additional $105 per year). Through this West Vancouver organisation you can learn to kayak or sail whether you're a youth or adult. Members are invited to social events and can take lessons at discounted prices. Initiation to the club is $160 for adults over 19, $65 for juniors, $95 for seniors and $195 for a family, with monthly dues ranging from $60 to $150 depending on what category you fall into. Members can also store their boats here for an annual fee.

**1300 Discovery St**
Kitsilano
Map 5 C1 **33**

## Jericho Sailing Centre Association

*604 224 4177 | www.jsca.bc.ca*

Located on the west side of Jericho Beach, this centre is a hotbed of water-related activities. The association is home to three watersports schools that offer lessons and boat rentals in sailing, wind surfing, skimboarding, kiteboarding and kayaking, or you can join an affiliated sailing or canoe club and use the club's equipment. The sailing centre also hosts events year round, from regattas and races to safety seminars and boat shows.

**2401 Point Grey Rd**
Kitsilano
Map 8 D2 **183**

## Kitsilano Yacht Club

*604 730 1646 | www.kitsilanoyachtclub.com*

Adults and youngsters can paddle and sail out of English Bay in the range of programmes offered at this club. Advanced youth sailors (who have earned a white III certificate) can take part in the spring warm-up afternoon sessions for $15. Two-week white sail courses will cost $340. For adults, it's $260 for two weekends or four evenings. An active membership to this club is $350 for adults, students and juniors pay $105.

**5854 Marine Dr**
West Vancouver
Map 3 A1 **184**

## West Vancouver Yacht Club

*604 921 7575 | www.wvyc.bc.ca*

Sailing programmes on offer at the West Vancouver Yacht Club include junior training, adult learn to sail, adult keelboating, and power boating. The club also has a racing team for young people with a competitive streak. If you want to join the team but don't have your own boat, the club loans vessels out to members for $25 to $75 a month, depending on the type and size of boat. Meanwhile, 'Mom's afternoon escape' is a unique course where mothers can learn to sail together on weekday afternoons in June, July and August ($265 a member). The cost of joining the yacht club increases with age, and ranges from $2,350 for ages 19 to 25 and up to $9,950 for those over 40. There is also a monthly due of around $80 for active members.

**Jericho Sailing Ctr**
1300 Discovery St
Kitsilano
Map 5 C1 **33**

## Windsure Adventure Watersports

*604 224 0615 | www.windsure.com*

Windsure is one of the businesses operating out of the Jericho Sailing Centre. It features the usual watersports, such as windsurfing and skimboarding, and the ones you might not even know exist, such as paddle surfing (paddling while standing upright on a board) and kiteboarding (travelling the water by mastering a wind-blown kite). Windsure also offers windsurfing camps for youths.

## Wine Tasting

British Columbia is known for its wineries in the Okanagan Valley, and many bottles make their way to Vancouver liquor stores and restaurants. The urban density and lack of agricultural land means vineyards are not found in Vancouver itself, but there are many wineries once you leave town and enter the Fraser Valley, and even a couple closer by in Richmond and Delta. Check out the BC Wine Institute (www.winebc.com) to get ideas for touring wineries or for grape-related events in your area. Two annual tasting events in the city include the Vancouver Playhouse International Wine Festival (604 872 6622, www.playhousewinefest.com) in late February, which features varieties from around the world, and Taste BC (www.libertywinemerchants.com) in January, which promotes local producers. You must be at least 19 to enjoy BC's lovely wines.

**5491 Minoru Blvd**
Richmond
Map 2 B3

## Blossom Winery

*604 232 9839 | www.blossomwinery.com*

Open since 2001, the Blossom Winery takes advantage of Richmond's ideal climate for producing berries by using local fruit whenever possible. The business is known for its range of fruit and ice wines, and offers tastings and seasonal tours. The tasting room is open Monday to Saturday from 10:00 to 18:00, and Sundays from 11:00 to 17:00. Large groups must book ahead.

**Various Locations**

## Liberty Wine Merchants

*604 739 7804 | www.libertywinemerchants.com*

Sip riesling, sake, champagne or sherry on one of Liberty Wine's many tasting tutorials and courses. A basic wine tasting course costs about $275, or get a group together and arrange a one-time class on port basics or 'the fighting wines of France' for a fee split between friends. One-day seminars can be at a store location of your choice, such as Downtown, in North Vancouver or on Granville Island.

**12791 Blundell Rd**
Richmond
Map 2 B3

## Sanduz Estates Wines

*604 214 0444 | www.sanduzwines.com*

This winery opened in 2006 and is already developing a reputation for its produce, which is made from unusual fruits, such as gooseberries, blackcurrants, rhubarb and apples. The owners attempt to use fruit grown locally, including cranberries and blueberries, in support of Richmond's berry farmers. The winery is open every day from 11:00 to 18:00 for wine tasting and sampling of its jellies, syrups and desserts.

**2170 Westham Island Rd**
Ladner
Map 2 B3

## Westham Island Estate Winery

*604 940 9755 | www.westhamislandwinery.com*

This family operated winery is located on Westham Island (before the George C Reifel Migratory Bird Sanctuary), west of Ladner Village and south of Vancouver. It is available for tours, and the wine tasting room is open daily from 10:00 to 17:00, Monday to Friday, and 10:00 to 18:00 at weekends. Keep an eye open for the owners' various events, such as the Christmas artisan fair, or you can host your own fundraiser, corporate event or anniversary party at the winery.

## Spectator Sports

Ask most Vancouverites whether they'd rather be watching sport or out there participating, the answer is likely to be the latter. However, there are a few events that stir up enough passion to draw in the crowds, most notably ice hockey and local heroes the Vancouver Canucks. Football (the North American variety) is popular with spectators too, with the Canadian Football League season running from July to November, and Vancouver also has a team that plays the round-ball variety (soccer). One-off cycling and running events tend to get people lining the streets to cheer on the suffering participants. If you can't get a ticket for the big game, or prefer the carefully cultivated grooves of your own sofa and serenity of your lounge to hard plastic seats and the big guy jumping up and down in front of you, hockey, football and soccer are widely covered by the major television networks such as CBC, CTV, and TSN.

For those who follow the winter sports, the Telus World Ski & Snowboard Festival (www.whistler.mtv.ca) is a free annual event held on Whistler Mountain which runs for 10 days in April. It's a great opportunity to watch pro-ski competitions, enjoy live music and hang out on the slopes. Whistler also hosts CrankWorx in August, a free nine day mountain biking competition, at the Whistler Bike Park (www.crankworx.com).

No rundown of spectator sports in Vancouver would be complete without mentioning the forthcoming 2010 Winter Olympic and Paralympic Games (www.vancouver2010. com). The event has most definitely been the talk of the town since it was awarded to the city in 2003. Largely centred around Whistler Blackcomb, with other venues scattered throughout the region, the games will be a snow and ice-sports lover's dream – although the seemingly never-ending preparations and renovations for a month-long event have not gone down well with some locals (see The Olympic Odyssey, above). Whatever your view on the actual games, the master plan for the Olympics includes a $580 million budget for the restoration and construction of sporting venues, so Vancouverites will at least benefit from having new and improved venues where they can watch their favourite sports.

### The Olympic Odyssey

In 2003 Vancouver was chosen as the host for the 2010 Winter Olympics – and the pros and cons of staging the games have been a constant topic for debate ever since. While some Vancouverites are enthusiastic about the development, renovation and media attention that result from the Olympics, others believe it will be a threat to the economy by creating debt that will become a burden for residents. There are also concerns about the environmental impact of construction, and some contend that the money could be better spent on social issues such as homelessness. One thing's for sure though – if you're a winter sports fan, you'll love 2010.

## Baseball

**Nat Bailey Stadium**
4601 Ontario St
Cambie
Map 6 A2 **190**

### Vancouver Canadians

*604 872 5232 | www.canadiansbaseball.com*

Canada's only Major League team is the Toronto Blue Jays, located in Ontario. For Vancouverites looking for a fix without travelling across the country, the Vancouver Canadians (the only other professional Canadian team) play in the Northwest Minor League. Games take place at the Nat Bailey Stadium (across from Queen Elizabeth Park), and tend to be entertaining, exciting affairs enjoyed by everyone from first date couples to diehard baseball fans. Games are played in the summer months; tickets range in price from $11 to $15, and are available by phoning the stadium directly, online from the club or through www.ticketstonight.com.

## Cycling

Cycling is a popular, community-friendly, spectator sport in Vancouver, with several notable events taking place throughout the year. The annual Tour de Gastown (www.tourdegastown.com) and Haywood Yaletown Grand Prix (www.yaletowngrandprix.com) draw large crowds who line the streets to cheer on cyclists as they pass some of the city's most iconic landmarks. Events usually include live music, free food and loudspeaker commentary to keep onlookers entertained and informed throughout the day. The Haywood Yaletown Grand Prix is a charity event held in early July, with hundreds of cyclists racing through Yaletown, competing for more than $5,000 in prizes. The BC Cancer Foundation's Tour de Gastown is held in mid-July, during BC Superweek (www.bcsuperweek.ca) – a 10 day cycling event with events across the region. The 1.2km course weaves around Gastown and in past years has featured some of North America's best cyclists, including Lance Armstrong, who has won the race seven times. Live entertainment including BMX bike stunts, an obstacle course, a climbing wall for kids and mobile art studios add to the friendly and fun atmosphere.

## Football

Not to be confused with the round-ball variation of the game ('soccer' in North America), Canadian football closely resembles American football, with a few subtle differences. Both are played on a gridiron field, but the Canadian field is much larger, with posts placed at the front of the zone instead of the back. Canadian teams also have 12 players, whereas American teams have 11, and there is a stronger emphasis on kicking the ball within the game.

*BC Place Stadium*
*777 Pacific Blvd*
*Downtown*
*Map 9 F1* **191**

### BC Lions

*604 669 2300* | *www.bclions.com*

The BC Lions compete in the Canadian Football League and are five-time winners of the Grey Cup – the sport's ultimate prize. Tickets are relatively easy to get if you purchase in advance, but are harder to come by during the season (July to November). Tickets cost $28 to $75 for a single match, or $210 to $550 for a season pass that includes 10 home games. You can buy them through Ticketmaster (604 280 440, www.ticketmaster.ca), or on the day of the game at BC Place, but matches often sell out. Pairs of single game tickets can be bought from some 7-Eleven grocery stores, for $39.98, (excluding tax). These seats are located in a special section, usually at the end zone under the screen or in lower tier seats. Check the BC Lions website for participating store locations and upcoming fixtures.

## Ice Hockey

Known simply as 'hockey', this is Canada's national winter sport. Games are passionate affairs that draw in large crowds of raucous fans, and a trip to see one of the big fixtures is a must for any sports fan living in Vancouver. Canadians have a large presence in the North American National Hockey League (NHL), where Vancouver's side is the Canucks. There are also some smaller, local teams to watch, including the Vancouver Thunderbirds (604 224 5891, www.vancouvertbirds.ca).

*GM Place Stadium*
*800 Griffiths Way*
*Downtown*
*Map 10 A3* **192**

### Vancouver Canucks

*604 899 4600* | *canucks.nhl.com*

The Canucks are the city's biggest, best supported sports team, and a night out to watch them compete in the NHL is one of Vancouver's must-do local experiences. Canucks fans are passionate creatures, and taking in the big game at GM Place makes for a couple of hours packed with excitement and deafening noise. The Canucks have only won the league title (the Stanley Cup) once, in 1915, but this doesn't dampen the

enthusiasm. The hockey season runs from October to June. Single game tickets start at
$49, but can be hard to come by so try to get them well in advance.

## Running

*Various Locations*

### Vancouver International Marathon

*604 872 2928 | www.bmovanmarathon.ca*

The Bank of Montreal Vancouver International Marathon is held in May each year and
attracts runners from around the globe, and spectators from all over BC. The course
starts on Pacific Boulevard at the south end of BC Place stadium, then on to Gastown,
through Stanley Park and across Burrard Bridge, past the crowd-filled streets and cafes,
via the beaches of Kitsilano, finally returning to BC Place. Pick your vantage point and
make a day of it. You can meet international and local athletes at a post-race event
– pre-order tickets on the BMO Marathon website. If you like what you've seen and
fancy challenging yourself, you can always apply to enter the event next year.

## Soccer

Although soccer is a popular sport in Vancouver, the attention doesn't compare to
the fever the beautiful game induces in Europe or South America (where it's more
commonly known as football). The Vancouver Whitecaps are the city's professional men's
team, and play their games in the first division of the United Soccer League (USL).

*Swangard Stadium*
*3883 Imperial Street*
*Burnaby*
*Map 6 D3* **194**

### Vancouver Whitecaps FC

*604 669 9283 | www.whitecapsfc.com*

Soccer season runs from April to September, and home Whitecaps games are played at
the Swangard Stadium (604 435 6862). It's a great setting to watch a match – the crowd
is a mixture of couples, beer-drinking buddies and families, all enjoying a lively game,
surrounded by evergreen trees and a mountainous backdrop. In 2007 David Beckham's
LA Galaxy came to town to play in a friendly, and way back in the early 1980s, in
another incarnation, English stars such as Peter Beardsley and Alan Ball actually
played for the club. Schedules are listed on the Whitecaps website; standard season
passes cost $199 to $449, single match tickets cost $16 to $35 and can be purchased
through the club, online or over the phone. You can also buy from Ticketmaster (www.
ticketmaster.ca) or at the stadium's box office, which opens an hour before each match.
Book early though as games sell out quickly.

*Pick-up soccer*

## Sports & Leisure Facilities

There is an abundant supply of sports and leisure facilities in the city to keep fitness enthusiasts busy. There are differing types of clubs, from prestigious private country clubs to casual and inexpensive community recreation centres. All options offer a wide range of activities and social events. Activities such as kayaking and belly dancing are available at recreation centres and sports clubs, and if you're looking for ways to tone-up and get fit there are a variety of gyms, including large international chains. Some specialised health clubs also offer nutritional support and guidance, although these tend to be costly. There are also four public outdoor swimming pools which are popular during the summer months.

Gyms in community centres are cheaper options if you are on a budget, and facilities aren't necessarily inferior to larger more expensive establishments. Some community centres also offer 'pay-per-play' visits. Shop around when choosing a membership, as benefits vary. It can cost anywhere from $1 for a one-off visit at a community centre to $85 a month for a fitness and health clinic.

## Health Clubs

There are a couple of really good health clubs in Vancouver that cater to overall well-being; both appeal to a broad range of clients and offer many different types of health and wellness therapies. Many services suit a niche problem such as giving up smoking or athletic injuries. If spiritual ease and tranquillity is what you are looking for, you can find this at a health club too, with meditation rooms and massages on offer. Also available is health and nutrition advice, plus medical support such as intravenous vitamin injections and hormone replacement therapy. Costs vary for different types of treatment, and some can get pricey.

*970 Burrard St*
*Downtown*
*Map 7 D4 195*

### Electra Health Floor
*604 685 4325 | www.electrahealthfloor.com*
Electra Health Floor offers many services including massage therapy, chiropractic care, acupuncture, Korean hand therapy, bio-energy healing, psychotherapy and counselling. The relaxation station is a room to bliss out in and escape from the bustle of city life while meditation CDs help to soothe. The club is open from 08:00 until 20:00 seven days a week, making it easy to drop in before or after normal work hours. Prices vary according to the treatment.

*601 West*
*Broadway*
*Fairview*
*Map 9 E4 196*

### EnerChanges
*604 681 8340 | www.enerchanges.com*
EnerChanges focuses on addressing symptoms of both the mind and the body, giving lifestyle guidance and employing anti-ageing techniques. Naturopathic, nutritional and fitness professionals help uncover imbalances and deficiencies in your system and then supply you with fitness and eating programmes (and supplements). A fitness centre with modern exercise equipment, aerobics, Pilates, yoga classes and personal training is also offered at this establishment. Open Monday to Saturday.

## Recreation Centres

There are some great recreation centres in Vancouver that offer a wide variety of activities and programmes. Most are inexpensive to join, and some are even free. For those that aren't, prices tend to range from $12 for a family to as little as $1 for a guest pass. The clientele is diverse, with some establishments skewed more towards singles or the 20 to 40 age range. Activities and sports on offer vary from arts and crafts to squash and woodworking. Some even offer social events such as musical nights, ski trips and wine tastings.

*Delbrook Rec Ctr*
*600 West Queens Rd*
*North Vancouver*
*Map 4 A2* **157**

## North Vancouver Recreation Commission

*604 987 7529 | www.northvanrec.com*

The North Vancouver Recreation Commission offers five categories of programmes: arts and community events; aquatics and arenas; fitness, health and wellness; personal and social development; and sports. There are plenty of activities to choose from, held at various locations across North Vancouver, including gardening, hiking, swimming, soccer, mountain biking, pottery, skating, tennis and visual arts. Free and low-cost classes in aquatics, first aid and martial arts are also available. There's also a fitness centre that you can drop into as you please, or which you can join. Drop-in fees range from $2.50 to $5 depending on your age, and memberships come in one month, three month and annual packages (a year for an adult costs $325).

*181 Roundhouse*
*Mews*
*Yaletown*
*Map 9 E2* **3**

## Roundhouse Community Arts & Recreation Centre

*604 713 1800 | www.roundhouse.ca*

The Roundhouse is the city's oldest building, a former railway terminal dating back to 1888. The centre offers a variety of classes, workshops and courses, including weight and metabolic health programmes, dance, Aboriginal culture, tennis, Afro-Cuban movement, aikido, woodwork, and even childbirth preparation. Events are held throughout the year, such as the winter Nia Jam (a night of dancing, movement and expression), and Symphony at the Roundhouse, an exploration of contemporary music. Roundhouse rooms are also available for social and business events. Adult membership costs $9, teen and child membership is $4, while family membership costs $12. The fee for a guest is $1. Non-members can participate in programmes (including drop-in classes) and are also allowed to use the gym.

*Various Locations*

## Urban Rec

*604 879 9800 | www.urbanrec.ca*

Urban Rec is an establishment that provides social and physical activities for people in their 20s, 30s and early 40s. This is a club that helps you keep fit by running indoor leagues in volleyball, floor hockey, dodgeball, basketball, soccer and curling. Social events such as wine tastings, martini tours, a monthly dinner club, ski trips, adventure activities and parties are on offer, and listings can be viewed on the website. Membership is free and you can sign up online. Once a member, you will receive bimonthly emails with info on events and activities. Once you have registered for your first event you will receive a membership key card that grants you special benefits at local restaurants, retailers and other Urban Rec sponsor outlets.

## Sports Clubs

Joining a sports club or team is a good way to meet new people and extend your social circle, particularly when you're new in town. If you don't want to pay the full membership price, some clubs allow social membership – discounted fees in exchange for enjoying the clubhouse and social events, minus the sports on offer. Some of these places have initiation fees that can be as much as $350. These are usually one-off payments when you first join and from then on monthly or annual fees are applicable. Other clubs, however, are relatively inexpensive, depending on the services and facilities offered.

*3837 Point Grey Rd*
*Point Grey*
*Map 5 D1* **200**

## Jericho Tennis Club

*604 224 2348 | www.jericho.ca*

This is a prestigious and picturesque club located on the shore of Burrard Inlet, with views of English Bay and the North Shore mountains. Facilities include 12 tennis courts, four squash courts, a heated outdoor pool and hot tub, fitness centre and spa.

Events are often held at this club such as sporting tournaments, barbecues and a variety of Friday evening entertainment. New memberships were suspended recently due to the large number of applications, but check with the club for the latest status.

**2390 West 10th Av**
*Kitsilano*
*Map 8 D4* **139**

## Meraloma Athletic Club

*604 733 4366 | www.meraloma.com*

Founded in 1923 and originally known as The Mermaids, this club has helped to develop the sporting talents of several generations of Vancouverites. It boasts a tradition of achievement and teamwork in sports such as basketball, cricket, field hockey, rugby, soccer and softball. Men, women, and juniors of all ages and abilities are welcome. Located in Connaught Park in Kitsilano, the Meraloma clubhouse is a heritage building, containing trophies and old team photographs. To become an associate member costs $50. If you wish to join one of the sports teams, additional fees are payable.

**610 Granville St**
*Downtown*
*Map 7 F3* **202**

## Steve Nash Sports Club

*604 682 5213 | www.stevenashsportsclub.com*

This sports club is considered one of the best in Vancouver due to its state-of-the-art equipment and facilities. Programmes on offer include group exercise classes (included in the membership fee) and yoga and Pilates sessions, while a sauna and steam rooms, TVs to watch while you work out, massages, an internet lounge and juice bar all aid the relaxation process. Two types of month-by-month membership are available. Global Membership includes worldwide access to affiliated clubs and a one-off initiation fee of $349, plus monthly fees of $135. Fast Break membership includes access to one club with an initial fee of $299 and monthly dues of $115. Be sure to ask about any special deals before you join. Free one-week or three-day trial passes are also offered.

## Community Centres

Viewed by Vancouverites as an integral part of the city's cultural life, community centres seek to enhance local values by bringing people from all walks of life together to enjoy a wide range of pursuits, ranging from pottery classes to toy and clothing sales, performing arts and dance. There are several centres located in and around the city, so you'll have no trouble finding one close to home, and they all offer an inexpensive way of meeting new people in your area. All ages and backgrounds are welcome at these places, and they have a sociable and unpretentious feel. Many community centres also offer fitness facilities that can rival some of the major gyms. These come at a much lower price compared with larger establishments – some cost as little as $2.50 per visit, and members can work out for free. Becoming a member is not essential, but annual fees are inexpensive – as low as $2 for a child and $13 for adults. The following entries give details of some of the central community centres, and there's a complete table of centres citywide on p.343.

**1318 Cartwright St**
*Granville Island*
*Map 9 C3* **32**

## False Creek Community Centre

*604 257 8195 | www.falsecreekcc.ca*

False Creek Community Centre is situated on Granville Island and is popular due to its easy access to water activities such as canoeing and kayaking. Other programme categories include creative arts, performing arts, Pilates, pottery, tennis and dancing. Upfront payments can be made for activities or you can drop in as you please. This centre has a well-hidden secret: its fitness room. Treadmills, rowing machines, crosstrainers, resistance and core strength machinery are available for a fee of $3.75 for adults and $2.50 for seniors and youths. You can also purchase a 10 or 20 visit pass, or a three, six, or 12 month pass. Personal training is available for an additional fee. Childcare is offered for pupils who attend False Creek Elementary School, and the internet is also available for use.

**5851 West Blvd**
*Kerrisdale*
*Map 5 E3* `204`

## Kerrisdale Community Centre

*604 257 8100 | www.kerrisdalecc.com*

This centre has everything from an indoor ice skating rink to a play centre for children with inflatable castles, ping pong tables, foosball, musical instruments and a giant slide. Courses and workshops include pottery, dance, tai chi, yoga, Pilates, photography, swimming and skating. There's an indoor and outdoor pool and a fully equipped fitness centre. Exercise room rates are $2.50 for a drop-in visit or $20 for a 10 visit pass. It also offers one month, three month, six month, and yearly passes. A recreational facility for seniors is available for those over 55. Membership of Kerrisdale Community Centre costs $20 for families, $13 for adults, $9 for children and $8 for retired citizens.

**2690 Larch St**
*Kitsilano*
*Map 8 D4* `205`

## Kitsilano War Memorial Community Centre

*604 257 6976 | www.city.vancouver.bc.ca/parks/cc/kitsilano*

Founded in 1951, this is one of Vancouver's oldest community centres. Facilities include a full-size indoor ice skating rink, youth and seniors' lounge, a preschool, fully equipped fitness centre and an outdoor play area. There are plenty of activities such as camps, fashion shows, toy and clothing sales, dance and music classes, education and development opportunities, yoga, soccer, tennis, jewellery making and much more. You can download a full schedule of activities from the website. The exercise room at this centre is one of the most popular fitness centres in Vancouver because of its full range of equipment – it also has personal training programmes, a sauna and a whirlpool. Annual membership fees range from $2 for children to $9 for families.

**870 Denman St**
*West End*
*Map 7 B2* `206`

## West End Community Centre Association

*604 257 8333 | www.westendcc.ca*

This is an association of three closely located centres – the West End Community Centre, the Coal Harbour Community Centre, and the Barclay Manor heritage house. The West End Community Centre features a library, pottery studio, and an ice rink. Rooms are available for rent, and there's a gym, auditorium, preschool and childcare facilities. The Coal Harbour centre has a gymnasium, cafe, craft room and dance studio. Barclay Manor is primarily used for events such as weddings and meetings, but it also plays host to many recreational activities including creative arts, language lessons and driving workshops. Annual membership to these community centres is approximately $12 for adults and $2 for children, however if you sign up for one of the programmes you are granted life membership to the association for free. The main centre is on Denman Street, while Coal Harbour Community Centre is located at 480 Broughton Street, and Barclay Manor is at 1447 Barclay Street.

**4397 West 2nd Av**
*Point Grey*
*Map 5 C1* `64`

## West Point Grey Community Centre

*604 257 8140 | www.westpointgrey.org*

This centre offers a combination of sports, arts, and education for all age groups. Pottery, maths, science, martial arts, languages, outdoor sports, yoga, swimming, dance, fitness and wellness courses are all available. The fitness centre at West Point

Grey has a range of drop-in classes and personal training on offer. Events include an annual craft fair, Breakfast with Santa, Asian Heritage Month, the Aberthau Family Easter with an Easter egg hunt, and the West Point Grey Fiesta – a celebration of the beginning of summer which includes carnival rides. You can register for any of the programmes online, whereby you will automatically become a member of the centre for free for a year. Normal annual membership fees are $10 for adults and $6 for children and seniors.

## Vancouver Community Centres

| | | | |
|---|---|---|---|
| Britannia | 1661 Napier St | 604 718 5800 | Indoor swimming pool, fitness centre, ice rink |
| Champlain | 3350 Maquinna Dr | 604 718 6575 | Fitness centre, squash & racquetball courts |
| Coal Harbour | 480 Broughton St | 604 718 8222 | Arts & crafts rooms |
| Douglas Park | 801 West 22nd Av | 604 257 8130 | Fitness centre, tennis lessons, pottery studio |
| Dunbar | 4747 Dunbar St | 604 222 6060 | Fitness centre, dance studio, tennis & squash courts, pottery studio, lawn bowling |
| False Creek | 1318 Cartwright St | 604 257 8195 | Fitness centre, dance studio, canoeing & kayaking programs, tennis lessons, waterpark |
| Hastings | 3096 East Hastings St | 604 718 6222 | Indoor swimming pool, fitness centre, racquetball courts, games room |
| Kensington | 5175 Dumfries St | 604 718 6200 | Indoor swimming pool, fitness centre, pottery studio, racquetball courts |
| Kerrisdale | 5851 West Boulevard | 604 257 8100 | Indoor swimming pool, outdoor wading pool, fitness centre, ice rink |
| Killarney | 6260 Killarney St | 604 718 8200 | Indoor swimming pool, fitness centre, ice rink, pottery studio |
| Kitsilano | 2690 Larch St | 604 257 6976 | Fitness centre, ice rink |
| Marpole-Oakridge | 990 West 59th Av | 604 257 8180 | Fitness centre, dance studio, racquetball & tennis courts, water park |
| Mount Pleasant | 3161 Ontario St | 604 713 1888 | Outdoor swimming pool, fitness centre, raquetball courts |
| Ray-Cam Cooperative Centre | 20 East Hastings St | 604 257 6949 | Fitness centre, family support programmes, computer lab, dark room |
| Renfrew | 2929 East 22nd Av | 604 257 8388 | Indoor swimming pool, fitness centre, computer lab, martial arts programmes, games room |
| Riley Park | 50 East 30th Av | 604 257 8545 | Indoor swimming pool, fitness centre, ice rink, pottery studio |
| Roundhouse | 181 Roundhouse Mews | 604 713 1800 | Arts & cultural centre with pottery, dance, woodworking, plus gymnasium |
| Strathcona | 601 Keefer St | 604 713 1838 | Fitness centre, games room, food security and child safety social programme |
| Sunset | 6810 Main St | 604 718 6505 | Fitness centre, dance studio, ice rink, arts & crafts room |
| Thunderbird | 2311 Cassiar St | 604 713 1818 | Fitness centre, computer lab, games room |
| Trout Lake | 3350 Victoria Dr | 604 257 6955 | Fitness centre, ice rink, raquetball & tennis courts, games room, pottery studio |
| West End | 870 Denman St | 604 257 8333 | Fitness centre, ice rink, dance studio, arts & crafts room, dark room |
| West Point Grey | 4397 West 2nd Av | 604 257 8140 | Fitness centre, tennis courts, pottery studio, games room; nearby swimming pool and arts centre |

## Country Clubs

Vancouver has a small number of country clubs, which tend to be exclusive members-only establishments that cater to families or couples. The real attraction of the city's country clubs is that they provide a great sense of Canada's landscapes within city reaches. Manicured grounds thrive with native trees, plants and flowers, and many clubs have views of the ocean, mountains, or both. Luxurious facilities are offered, with restaurants to dine at and areas to grab a quick snack or enjoy a cool beverage. Membership prices vary, and initial fees can be extremely steep – as much as $39,000 at the most prestigious. These are one-off payments you make to join the club; annual fees are required to retain your membership. There are other options if your budget doesn't stretch that far, and not all clubs demand such a hefty first payment. Dress codes and etiquette rules are enforced at some clubs.

**950 Cross Creek Rd**
*West Vancouver*
*Map 3 E1* 208

## Hollyburn Country Club
*604 922 0161 | www.hollyburn.org*

This club has a casual and friendly atmosphere and multiple activities to choose from, including music lessons, tennis, badminton, hockey, karate, squash, figure skating, curling, cycling and more. In addition to these, kids are taken care of with spring and summer camps, a homework room, and arranged birthday parties. Spa treatments are also on offer including massages, facials and pedicures, and the Bar & Grill restaurant offers tasty meals and nightly drinks specials. You can choose to eat a meal on the outdoor deck, which is blessed with views of the city, Burrard Inlet and Mount Baker. One of the benefits of being a member of this club is the extended privileges you receive, with over 90 affiliated clubs worldwide.

**3723 Mount**
**Seymour Parkway**
*North Vancouver*
*Map 4 F3* 209

## Seymour Golf & Country Club
*604 929 5491 | www.seymourgolf.com*

This members' club opens up to the public on Mondays and Fridays. The golf course is described as 'challenging', and playing prices range from $27 to $59. Prices also vary for public days, between $13 for juniors and $59 for adults. There are a couple of different membership options and fees range accordingly: from $39,000 (which can be paid over five years) to $400 for a social membership with $100 monthly dues. Social members enjoy limited playing benefits. Golfing lessons are available and can be booked as private, paired, or in groups of three or more. Booking as a group significantly reduces the cost of your lessons. Enjoy a meal at the Grille Room restaurant (only open to the public on Mondays and Fridays) or a beverage on the outdoor heated deck. Reservations are recommended. You can also book rooms for private events, and a shop offers designer brand clothing for wear on the greens.

**4300 SW Marine Dr**
*Southlands*
*Map 5 C3* 210

## Shaughnessy Golf & Country Club
*604 266 4141 | www.shaughnessy.org*

The Shaughnessy Golf & Country Club features an 18 hole course that overlooks the Fraser River and the Strait of Georgia. The grounds are filled with many species of trees and flowers, making this one of Vancouver's most attractive places for a putt. The club is open all year round and, as well as golf, it offers tennis for youths, a fitness centre, and areas you can rent for functions such as weddings or business meetings. The Garden Lounge, Grill Room, and Cedar, Hemlock, and Spruce rooms are also available for meetings and functions, and you can also enjoy a meal at the Dogwood Dining Room. This is an exclusive club and is not open to the public. To become a member you must be invited.

## Gyms

Going to the gym is a popular way for urbanites to stay in shape, and Vancouver's city dwellers are no different. Cardio and weight resistance machines, as well as group classes such as yoga, Pilates and spinning, are available in most places. Personal training is often offered too, usually at an additional cost.

Be careful when signing up – some gyms offer month-by-month contracts, but others lock you into 12 or 24 month plans. Membership prices vary significantly. Many gyms offer free week or day passes, which are a good way to try the facilities without committing for an extended period of time. Try to find a club that has at least a few group classes included in your membership fee too, as these tend to be good value for money. Also be sure to ask about membership specials on offer when you sign up. Most gyms are constantly updating their offers and so prices are not usually fixed.

**81 Kingsway**
*Mount Pleasant*
*Map 11 B2* **211**

### Curves

*604 872 5667 | www.curves.com*

A female-only gym, Curves is a global operation with several locations in and around Vancouver. Its specialism is a 30 minute workout. Currently Curves offers special membership deals (worth looking into if you want to join with a friend or partner), and also provides 'fitness calculations' designed to tailor your exercise programme to your natural weight range and how many calories you aim to burn at each visit. For further details about fees, contact the club directly. The second main branch is in Kitsilano (West 4th Avenue, 604 732 6047); see the website for other locations.

**1214 Howe St**
*Downtown*
*Map 9 D1* **212**

### Fitness World

*604 681 3232 | www.fitnessworld.ca*

Fitness World is one of the most recognised names when it comes to Canadian gyms. With 12 locations across Vancouver and more than 100,000 members in the Lower Mainland and Victoria, it's a popular choice. The gyms tend to get quite busy before and after normal office hours, but outside these times they are generally not too crowded. There are ladies-only facilities, and 1,200 fitness and speciality classes are available. Group classes include spinning, body ball, step, yoga and salsa (although not all of these are included in your membership). Members get a free cardio and body composition test every six weeks. Month-by-month contracts are not offered, but a one-week free trial pass is available. Prices are approximately $40 per month, and the website details the locations of the other branches.

**1845 York Av**
*Kitsilano*
*Map 8 F2* **213**

### Just Ladies Fitness

*604 736 7784 | www.justladiesfitness.com*

This is a women-only gym where all ages and levels of fitness are welcome. A free seven-day trial pass is offered. Group fitness programmes include yoga, Pilates, spinning, step, hip-hop, belly dance, and dance fit. These are all included in the membership fee, which is approximately $40 per month. Nutrition programmes are also available. Childcare services are onsite, so mums can work out while the kids play. In addition to the Kitsilano centre there are several other branches around the city (see the website for further details).

**1923 West 4th Av**
*Kitsilano*
*Map 8 F3* **214**

### Kitsilano Workout

*604 734 3481 | www.kitsilanoworkout.com*

Kitsilano Workout was voted Vancouver's best independent gym in 2006 by readers of *The Georgia Straight*. This recently upgraded facility includes 25 LCD televisions and 65 music channels (for those who bring their own headphones). The club is open 24 hours a day, and offers a month-by-month membership option with prices ranging from $27 to $50 per month. All 75 fitness classes are included in the membership fee. Power yoga, step, belly dancing and Pilates are all available. You can also enlist the services of a personal trainer for an additional fee.

**You Tell Us**

Have we missed anything? If you have any thoughts, ideas or comments for us to include in the Activities section, drop us a line, or if your club or organisation isn't in here, let us know and we'll give you a shout in the next edition. Visit www.explorerpublishing.com and fill in the reader response form in the Feedback section.

## Ron Zalko

*1807 West 1st Av*
*Kitsilano*
*Map 8 F2* **215**

*604 737 4355* | *www.ronzalko.com*

Ron Zalko offers a large selection of up-to-date equipment as well as weight loss programmes, personal training, and a full range of classes such as aerobics, step, cardio, yoga, Latin dance and karate. This quality gym has a ladies-only section, childminding services, and offers a free introductory pass. The club is a member of the International Physical Fitness Association (IPFA), which means that if you join you gain access to other IPFA facilities around the world. Membership costs between $29 and $40 per month, depending on how you pay.

## World Gym On Robson

*1676 Robson St*
*Downtown*
*Map 7 C2* **216**

*604 915 3032* | *www.worldgymvancouver.com*

World Gym on Robson is a stylish establishment offering state-of-the-art fitness equipment. There's a snack bar, juice bar and clothing outlet, as well as professional personal trainers who will devise individual programmes to suit your needs and objectives. You can read about the personal trainers on the World Gym website. Prices depend on how long you sign up for (monthly membership is $100, yearly subscription costs $599). Parking is available. There's another branch in Yaletown (1085 Homer Street, 604 915 3002).

*Ron Zalko gym*

## Well-Being

Preserving the mind, body and spirit is easy to do in Vancouver, with many massage facilities, yoga studios, beauty salons, spas, and nail bars to choose from. The city has drawn inspiration from eastern philosophies when it comes to ancient therapies, and you will find many yoga schools in the inner Vancouver area, and reiki schools in North and West Vancouver.

If outer beauty rather than inner beauty is more your thing, you can keep up appearances with regular manicures, pedicures and facials at outlets across town. Highly skilled hairstylists are also on call to preen your locks to perfection, and when it comes to selecting a spa or masseuse, you'll be spoiled for choice.

If you require a full day of pampering, or just a quick, inexpensive manicure, there are a variety of spas and salons to choose from. There are luxurious spas in expensive hotels, or smaller establishments with just as much pampering but minus the hefty price tag.

Small nail bars have popped up all over Vancouver and each offer fairly inexpensive and quick ways to keep your fingers and toes looking their best. Cleanliness can vary, so it is best to visit before you make an appointment. If you need to alleviate aches and pains, you can also find masseurs in the city that provide basic services. For more specialised treatment, look out for registered massage therapists (RMTs) who are fully qualified and trained to knead away the toughest of knots.

## Beauty Salons

Other options **Perfumes & Cosmetics** p.396, **Health Spas** p.349

Beauty salons are an essential part of many women's routine, and offer a similar range of treatments to the bigger spas. Services provided include facials, manicures and pedicures, waxing, eyelash tinting and eyelash extensions, make-up application, laser hair removal and microdermabrasion. Some also have a hair salon attached. Prices vary, but expect to pay from $40 for a facial and from $190 for beauty packages.

**1028-736 Granville St**
*Downtown*
*Map 7 E4* **217**

### Beauty Matters

*604 681 1557 | www.beautymatters.ca*

This salon offers a multitude of treatments, including aesthetic facial services, hair removal services, hand and nail treatments, spa foot therapies, photo rejuvenation, and microdermabrasion. The signature treatment is clinical anti-ageing therapy – a treatment performed over a four-month period that aims to reduce the appearance of fine lines, scars, hyperpigmentation and blotchiness. Visit the website for a full list of services (including descriptions of what each treatment entails) and prices.

**1001-999**
**Canada Place**
*Downtown*
*Map 7 F2* **218**

### Spa Utopia & Salon

*604 641 1351 | www.spautopia.ca*

This premium salon at the Pan Pacific hotel caters to both men and women. It offers all the expected treatments such as facials (from classic to enzyme and acid peels), microdermabrasion, massage, women's health, hydrotherapy, aromatherapy, hairdressing, makeup application, lash and brow tinting, waxing and men's grooming. Spa packages are also available. Facials start at $90 and go up to $135, and massages start at $100. Although it's not cheap, customers can be assured of highly qualified technicians, many of whom have won awards. The salon is open seven days a week, until late. There are other branches in North Vancouver (604 980 3977) and Langley (604 539 8772).

*1093 West Broadway*
*Fairview*
*Map 9 C4* **219**

## Splash Beauty Studio

*604 736 7500 | www.splashbeautystudio.com*

This small emporium can take care of most pampering needs. Skin services range in price from $35 to $99 and include European, hot stone and collagen facials. All manner of waxing treatments are available, as well as nail care, hairdressing, makeup application, and speciality services such as eye lash extensions and eyelash pulls. Special packages are also available and can be good value for money; the Complete Beauty package costs $190 and includes a European facial, French manicure and pedicure and a shampoo, cut and blow dry. Reservations are not necessary.

## Hairdressers

There are hundreds of hair salons in Vancouver, so you'll have no problem finding one that suits your needs and budget. From big names to training centres, there are great cuts, colour and blow-dries to be had at any price. Be prepared to pay big bucks for the top salons – $300 is not unusual for a cut and highlights. For those on a tighter budget, you can get lucky at some of the academies or training salons where student hairdressers will practise on you for a fraction of the cost of their qualified salon colleagues. Well supervised, it's not as scary as it might sound, especially for a simple trim or similar. Prices usually start at $8. All salons are required by law to follow strict hygiene and safety rules so you'd be hard pressed to find a dirty or unkempt salon in the city.

*1228 Robson St*
*Downtown*
*Map 7 D2* **220**

## Aveda Academy Salon

*604 689 5484 | www.aveda.com*

This is a great salon for those on a tight budget who want a professional look. Aveda is well known for its environmental approach and eco-friendly culture, high-end hair expertise and products. The training academy uses Aveda products, has a lovely interior, and despite the fact that you'll be having your hair done by students, you never feel like you are getting 'second-best' service. Besides, experienced trainers are always on hand to advise, comment, and supervise.

*1150 Hamilton St*
*Yaletown*
*Map 9 E1* **221**

## Blo Bar

*604 909 9495 | www.blomedry.com*

Perfect for busy people who are constantly on the go, Blo Bar offers a shampoo and blow-dry in less than 30 minutes for just $30. The menu of blow drying options includes such intriguingly named speciality hair-dos as executive sweet, red carpet, LA confidential, European chic, Bardot updo, Holly would, sex, sugs and rock & roll, and hidden assets. Extensions, styling, and straightening are also offered. Meanwhile, Blo On The Go will come to your home or workplace for $120 per person. Reservations are not necessary.

*512 West
Broadway*
*Mount Pleasant*
*Map 9 F4* **222**

## Future Hair

*604 709 6055 | www.futurehairtraining.com*

Future hair is a friendly student-training salon, with a relaxed, fun vibe. Services offered include hair consultations, shampoo, cut and blow-dry, styling, conditioning treatments, perms and colour. The salon has been going strong for more than 13 years and for just $8 a cut, you can't go wrong (especially since all students are under strict supervision). The most popular treatment is the 'glossifier' – a clear coat of gloss for your hair that helps to maintain colour. Booking is essential as it can get very busy, especially at weekends. Dog phobes beware, there's a resident pug.

**300 West Pender St**
*Downtown*
*Map 10 A1* 223

## London School Of Hairdressing & Aesthetics

*604 685 4121* | *www.londonschool.ca*

This is a large school with a warehouse vibe. It offers the whole gamut of beauty essentials including cuts, styling, shampooing, colour, chemical straightening, perms and extensions. For an extra treat, facials, waxing, and manicures and pedicures are also available. Cuts start at $8 and colour starts at $25. All services are performed by students, but under the supervision of qualified and trained staff.

**22 East Cordova St**
*Gastown*
*Map 10 B1* 224

## Moustache & Darling

*604 715 5725*

There's only space for one client at a time in this exclusive salon, so a personalised service by Vidal Sassoon-trained owner Nicole Lefaivre is a given. The stylish interior measures just 100 sq ft, making for a small and intimate space tucked away in the backstreets of trendy Gastown. Lefaivre is known to some as the best hairdresser in town, a fact verified by her 500 plus clients and a waiting list as long as your arm. Prices for ladies' cuts start at $70, $40 for men. Colour starts at $70 and highlights at $100.

**206-1030 West
Georgia St**
*Downtown*
*Map 7 E3* 225

## Suki's

*604 687 8805* | *www.sukis.com*

Suki's is a professional brand and a well-known name in Vancouver hairdressing. There are four Suki's salons to choose from, all equally chic, clean, and contemporary (check online for locations). All Suki's hairdressers go through a rigorous interview, and most undergo a two-year apprenticeship. The most popular option is the 'ritual treatment' – a 45 minute conditioning session. Prices are high end, but for those on a tighter budget, the training academy is next door to the Downtown studio.

**1088 Alberni St**
*Downtown*
*Map 7 D3* 226

## Toni & Guy

*604 608 4247* | *www.toniguy.com*

Toni & Guy is probably one of the most recognised hairdressing names in the world. Complimentary consultations will help you determine the cut that will suit you best, while a stylist and colour technician work together to create an individual look. Cuts start at $55 and go up to $90. Colour starts at $70. There's a second location at 2177 West 4th Avenue (604 737 4249).

## Health Spas

Other options **Sports & Leisure Facilities** p.339, **Massage** p.351

The city has a proliferation of excellent health spas, many of which are members of the Leading Spas of Canada (www.leadingspasofcanada.com), an organisation that supports and promotes the country's affiliated spas and regulates hygiene practices and standards. Each spa has its signature treatments and offers a unique experience. Health spas are a one-stop shop for all things beauty; many include a hair salon while others will offer steam baths, saunas and therapies such as acupuncture, reiki and crystal healing. Prices vary, but tend to be high end. Expect to pay upwards of $60 for a massage and $65 and up for body exfoliations and wraps. In addition to the company listings, the award-winning Absolute Spa chain (www.absolutespa.com) and La Raffinage (604 681 9933, www.laraffinage.com) come highly recommended.

**325 Howe St**
*Downtown*
*Map 7 F3* 227

## Breathe Spa

*604 688 4769* | *www.breathespa.net*

Breathe bills itself as one of the city's exclusive spots, and it's frequently listed as one of the top spas in the city by local media. Treatments are tailored to individual needs and pampering packages are popular, including a facial, massage and a pedicure. A two-hour facial can cost around $120. Pedicures are a little pricey at $65, but they last for 75 minutes. Massages come in two different forms: hot stone and Swedish. These range in price from $100 to $120. Discounted packages for a course of six treatments over an extended period are available, as well as add-ons such as waxing and tinting.

## Elements Wellness Spa

*207-2678 West Broadway*
*Kitsilano*
*Map 8 C4* 228

*604 732 9355 | www.elementswellnesscentre.com*

Not just your typical spa, Elements has a strong focus on healing and well-being. From spa day packages including massage, electrolysis, facials and slimming treatments to acupuncture and reflexology, the list of services on offer is astounding. There is also a counselling service, nutritionist and allergist. The ionic footbath is one of the most popular treatments – it's a spa for your feet that cleanses the body of heavy metals and significantly improves blood oxygen levels. A 30 minute session costs $40.

## Eveline Charles Salons & Spas

*1495 West 11th Av*
*Fairview*
*Map 9 B4* 229

*604 678 5666 | www.evelinecharles.com*

This sophisticated spa has won numerous awards. The interior is luxurious chic, with a metallic design and neutral wall tones. Large windows overlook trendy Granville Street where you can watch the passersby as you indulge in a pedicure. For the privacy conscious customer, there's another separate pedicure and manicure section. This spa has all the features of a full-scale hair salon, and offers facials, manicures and pedicures, hair removal, massage, water therapy, and even makeup application. As expected, sessions don't come cheap; one of the signature body treatments, such as the 'white tea antioxidant renewal', costs $185 – but if you can afford it, it's worth it.

## MiraJ Hammam Spa

*1495 West 6th Av*
*Fairview*
*Map 9 B3* 230

*604 733 5151 | www.mirajhammam.com*

This spa offers indulgent and traditional Middle Eastern treatments. The interior is reminiscent of an ancient land with gold marble, water fountains, and handcrafted mosaic tiles decorating the walls. It's also the only authentic hammam in the city. Other treats include massage, facials and crystal healing. Prices range from $40 to $270. Velvet beds, silk cushions, and traditional tea and sweets are all included in a very unique spa experience.

## The Rejuvenating Body Spa

*222 East 25th St*
*North Vancouver*
*Map 4 B2* 231

*604 315 4352 | www.rejuvenatingbody.com*

This small space was specifically designed so that each client feels like they are receiving personalised attention. From luxurious body scrubs, back treatments, detoxifying and anti-cellulite wraps to facials, there's plenty on offer to make sure that both men and women come out gleaming. Facials start at $40. Packages are available for couples and individuals. There is also a separate men's grooming spa menu.

## Spa Ethos

*2200 West 4th Av*
*Kitsilano*
*Map 8 E3* 232

*604 733 5007 | www.spaethos.com*

Focused on the more traditional, tried and tested remedies and treatments, this is both a spa and a centre of well-being. The spa menu includes body toning and polishing, facials, manicures and pedicures, makeup application, massages and more. There is also a eucalyptus steam room. The food menu encompasses chicken, vegetarian and seafood dishes, cheese plates and fruit platters. Facials range in price from $105 to $155, and add-ons such as a soothing eye relief ($25) or a total eye makeover ($85) can bump up the experience to luxury levels. Pedicures come in delicious concoctions of mint and rose, with a lemongrass salt scrub, and cost between $85 and $105. Special treatments are provided for teenagers, such as the clear complexion facial, and there are packages just for men.

## Vida Wellness Spa

**The Sutton Place**
845 Burrard St
Downtown
Map 7 D3 **233**

*604 682 8410 | www.vidawellness.com*

Pristine, pleasantly aromatic treatment rooms (11 in total) and soft lighting exude a strong sense of calm here. The friendly staff are highly proficient and any extra expense is worth the relaxing experience. The menu includes Ayurvedic treatments, body exfoliations, body therapy, facials, body wraps, manicures, pedicures and waxing. Prices start at $20 for a chin or upper lip wax and go up to $295 for the abhyanga swedana treatment. Try one of the popular Ayurvedic massages or facials that cost between $125 and $275.

## Massage

Other options **Sports & Leisure Facilities** p.339, **Health Spas** p.349

Few places cater purely to massage, with most massage centres also offering a full range of relaxation and pampering treats. Massage can have many health benefits and can aid in reducing tension and anxiety, improve blood circulation, relieve muscle pain, stimulate the lymphatic system and help in rehabilitation. Popular types include Swedish, aromatherapy, hot stone, deep tissue, shiatsu, Thai, sports and Ayurvedic. Prices vary, but for a good one expect to pay at least $60 for an hour.
The most reputable massage therapists are the Registered Massage Therapists (RMT). These are strictly regulated and continuing education is a perquisite. Other practitioners can be just as good of course, but there is no guarantee. It is advisable to see an RMT if you need a sports massage or pain relief.

## The Mobile Excape

**Various Locations**

*604 328 8707 | www.mobileexcape.com*

This mobile massage service offers a holistic approach to rejuvenate both mind and body through personalised, traditional therapy and massage. Treatments are available at your home or any other location of your choice. It also offers tailored nutrition programmes, one of a large range of other services. The biggest bonus though is the excellent service – it runs 24 hours a day, seven days a week.

## Serenity Therapeutic Massage

**405-750 West Broadway**
Fairview
Map 9 E4 **235**

*604 879 2257 | www.serenityclinic.com*

This small clinic specialises in therapeutic massage. It's far from flashy, opting instead for a basic, simple decor. That said, it is still inviting and the staff are friendly. There are just two treatment rooms and four professional RMT massage therapists, proficient in a variety of techniques including therapeutic, postural, headache, and prenatal. A one hour massage costs $80 and a 40 minute massage costs $60. Hypoallergenic oils are used and if the pummelling gets too much, you can add on a relaxation massage (this combo is the most popular). Book online to ensure you get a space.

## Meditation

Meditation has long been thought of as a spiritual practice, but the growing awareness of its health benefits is adding to its popularity. These include, among others, increased concentration and mental clarity, relaxation, decreased muscle tension, greater self-confidence and an increase in serotonin production that can help to improve moods. It is also said to aid healing.
Meditation centres are open to everyone, including beginners, and sessions usually carry

minimal charges or are free. Regular practise is the key to meditation but courses are also available (for a fee) for those who want to learn more about it.

## FWBO Vancouver

**1871 East 7th Av**
*Grandview*
*Map 12 B2* 236

604 682 3269 | www.vancouverbuddhistcentre.com

Friends of the Western Buddhist Order (FWBO) is a welcoming centre, open to people at all levels of meditation, including beginners. Regular practise is held at the Vancouver Buddhist Centre every Thursday from 19:00 to 21:00. 'Practise in action' teaches participants how to use meditation in everyday life. Courses such as introduction to Buddhism and meditation (held on a Thursday evening over five weeks) are available.

## The Shambhala Centre

**3275 Heather St**
*Cambie*
*Map 5 F2* 237

604 874 8420 | www.shambhala.org

If you're looking for a calming influence, this centre runs daily meditation sessions. Member practise takes place from 19:00 to 21:30 on Mondays, and most Wednesdays there are open house sessions from 19:00 to 21:30. The open house nights are free and are followed by a talk or video about Shambhala Buddhism, and how to bring meditation into your daily life. Check the website for an up-to-date schedule. Evening classes, children's programmes and one-day intensive practise are also available.

## Siddha Yoga Meditation Centre Of Vancouver

**2780 East Broadway**
*Renfrew Heights*
*Map 12 E2* 238

604 255 7960 | www.siddhayoga.ca

The Siddha Yoga teachings are open to all faiths and beliefs, and are centred around finding the divine presence in everything, even when faced with difficult times. This is done by embracing the spiritual practises of yoga, meditation contemplation and study to gain self-realisation. This centre offers weekly meditation on Thursdays at 19:30. On Sundays, chanting of the Guru Gita starts at 08:00. Meditation and chanting programmes are a regular feature, as are meditation retreats.

# Nail Bars

Fun, relatively cheap and incredibly popular, most nail bars offer an assortment of manicures and pedicures, from a 15 minute special to 80 minute pampering sessions. Choose between gel nails or acrylics, or a simple shape, shine and polish. Walk-ins are pretty standard, but the popular places may require a wait if you haven't got a booking. Prices range from $10 to $75. Tips are not included in the price but are expected at most places. Nail academies offer cheaper rates, from just $10, if you don't mind the practising hands of students.

## Element Spa For Nails

**1151 Homer St**
*Yaletown*
*Map 9 E1* 239

604 687 6245 | www.elementspafornails.com

This bar meets all talon needs and includes treatments such as the 'quickie' manicure and pedicure for $20 and $35 respectively, the 'element' for $30 and $48, and the 'VIP' – described as 'a facial for the hands and feet' for $50 and $75. Nail extensions, hair removal and massage chairs that move in sync to the music of your choice are all offered. Visit the website for more information and promotions.

## Pro-Nails Academy

**837 West Broadway**
*Fairview*
*Map 9 E4* 240

604 872 3882

This is a student academy so the rates are cheaper than at most other nail bars. On Tuesdays, manicures cost just $15, and it often runs mani and pedi combo specials. Despite their trainee status, the students here tend to do a good job, helped by the fact that they are under the constant watchful eye of supervisors. Walk-ins are welcome.

**1282 Pacific Blvd**
*Yaletown*
*Map 9 D2* **241**

## Pure Nail Bar

*604 605 1282* | *www.purenailbar.com*

The pristine state of these chains may have a lot to do with their huge popularity. Sophisticated interiors done out in bright hues and an unpretentious crowd ensure it's a winner every time. Used tools are either discarded or sterilised after use, and all technicians use hand sanitisers before and after every service. Walk-ins are welcome, but be prepared to face crowds, especially on weeknights and at weekends. Surprisingly inexpensive, a manicure costs just $25 and a mani-pedi combo is just $50. A French polish costs $29. Other locations include: West End (604 688 1866), Kitsilano (604 738 8990), North Vancouver (604 988 1150), Metrotown (604 439 7873), Granville (604 730 1178) and Kerrisdale (604 263 9622).

**1288 West Broadway**
*Fairview*
*Map 9 C4* **242**

## Sparkle Nails

*604 739 9269*

This excellent nail bar with friendly staff has a loyal following. Set in an attractive, clean space, massage chairs relax tired muscles as a technician gets to work on your feet, whether it's the $30 spa pedicure or the mini pedicure for $25. Special combos are available too, with add-ons such as the hand paraffin treatment or the mini manicure and pedicure for $35. Walk-ins are welcome, but you may have to join the queue. Waxing and eyelash extensions are also available.

## Pilates

Other options **Yoga** p.356

Pilates focuses on strengthening the core muscles that help to keep the body balanced and support the spine. It isn't an intense cardiovascular activity, rather a slow paced, yoga-like workout that focuses on one muscle at a time for maximum effect. In addition to encouraging a leaner body, the benefits attributed to this workout include developing balance, flexibility, graceful movement and strength. It has also been said to help reduce pain caused by injury, create better posture and aid athletic performance. Pilates can be performed either as a mat workout or on special apparatus. Lessons in Vancouver typically range from $18 for group classes, up to $110 for private lessons. To receive maximum benefits, an ongoing approach is needed. Most Pilates centres suggest that you do at least four private lessons before entering a class, to help you to gain a good understanding of the foundations of the exercises.

**210-2006 West 10th Av**
*Fairview*
*Map 8 F4* **243**

## Boditree Pilates & Healing

*604 736 2634* | *www.boditreepilates.com*

You can take part in private or group lessons at this clinic, but all workouts are designed to meet individual needs. Prior to joining group sessions, you are required to undertake four private lessons of up to 75 minutes ($289 in total). Group workouts subsequently cost $37, or you can buy in bulk which is more cost effective. Private sessions cost $105, again with a discounted rate when you buy in bulk. This clinic also offers massage therapy, chiropractic treatment, and an infrared sauna.

**719 West 16th Av**
*Cambie*
*Map 5 F2* **244**

## Dianne Miller Pilates Center

*604 879 2900* | *www.diannemillerpilates.com*

Beginners can take part in entry level classes at this centre, including a 'discover Pilates' course – a series of eight small group classes over a four week period. Subsequent classes are then scheduled according to individual level of experience. Private sessions are also offered as well mat classes, sessions that use Pilates equipment and a 'well back' clinic.

**2475 Bayswater St**
*Kitsilano*
Map 8 B4 **245**

## Meridian Pilates Studio

*604 730 4094 | www.meridianpilates.ca*

This fully equipped, albeit small, Pilates studio offers a variety of classes that are limited to a maximum of 10 participants. Private lessons, apparatus classes and mixed level groups are some of the options. Intensive workshops are also offered at various times. Mat class rates are $19 per session or you can buy six, 12, or 24 class packages at a discounted rate. Apparatus classes start at $32 and you can also buy these at package rates. Private lessons are $77 (discounted rates are available too if you purchase a bulk amount). There are duet packages, mat and apparatus combos, and private and independent combo packages as well.

**2211 West 4th Av**
*Kitsilano*
Map 8 E3 **246**

## The Movement Studio

*604 732 9055 | www.themovementstudio.ca*

With a friendly, inviting atmosphere, this full service Pilates studio offers mat and apparatus classes in private, semi-private or small group formats. Group classes are available in a variety of packages. They include a well back clinic, which focuses on maintaining and strengthening the back, gyrokinesis, core fusion, mums and babies, and conditioning for dance. Private training is also available, and an introductory session costs just $60. Semi-private apparatus sessions, which include two clients per class, are $39.95 each or $399 for a 10 lesson package.

## Reiki

Reiki is a Japanese technique that is mainly used to reduce stress and promote relaxation. By placing the hands above the 'charkas' of the body, energy fields are passed between the practitioner and the client. The practitioner assesses where there are blockages and then directs 'healing' energy to these places, charging the person with positive energy. It is a fairly simple technique, but is believed to be a very powerful healing therapy. The majority of reiki clinics are located in North or West Vancouver. Clinics typically offer a warm and welcoming environment with experienced reiki masters. Some also offer other services such as BioMat therapy, which is used to create an electrical charge from crystals that are embedded in a ceramic super fibre mat. When the mat is turned on, these charges penetrate the body, helping to ease joint and muscle pain. Other benefits include stress relief, improved blood circulation, better healing time, detoxing qualities and improved skin. Rates vary, but sessions are generally not cheap, costing anywhere from $55 to $85 for one hour. The number of sessions needed depends on the individual.

**Mount Seymour**
**Parkway**
*North Vancouver*
Map 4 E3 **247**

## Holistically Yours

*604 929 2952 | www.holisticallyyours.ca*

This clinic offers reiki treatment in addition to ear candling and Amethyst BioMat therapy. The practitioner is a member of the Canadian Reiki Association, with extensive experience within the field. In-house rates are $55 per hour, or you can pay for three sessions at a discounted fee of $145. You can also opt for off-site visits for $75 per hour. Call for the precise location.

**North Vancouver**
Map 4 B2 **248**

## Inner Focus Holistic Healing

*604 985 7302 | www.innerfocus.ca*

Reiki sessions at this clinic usually take between 60 and 90 minutes. You can also opt for BioMat therapy. Rates are $65 for one hour, or you can select a prepay option, which is three sessions for $175. If you wish to include BioMat healing the price is $85 for one hour. Sessions off-site can also be arranged and cost $75 per hour (the full address is available when you book an appointment).

**Marine Dr**
*Dundarave*
*West Vancouver*
*Map 3 E2* **249**

## Therapeutic Reiki

*604 630 2409 | www.therapeuticreiki.com*

Reiki Master Astrid Lee offers a one hour studio session for $74. For $69 reiki energy can also be sent to you, at a specified time, wherever you are, through the distant healing treatment. Discount packages are also offered if you buy in bulk, and sessions for pets or children can be arranged. Call for the location.

## Stress Management

Other options **Support Groups** p.164

Many people will experience varying levels of stress throughout their lives, but continuing periods of high stress can be problematic, resulting in both emotional and physical symptoms. Sudden feelings of fear, disturbed sleep, poor concentration and exhaustion are all associated with stress. It can also bring on a lack of motivation and poor memory. Popular techniques used to manage the problem include cognitive behavioural therapy, hypnosis, relaxation, meditation, and deep breathing methods. The number of sessions needed really depends on each individual. There are a few clinics in Vancouver that specifically focus on reducing stress, and many offer a variety of methods. In serious cases, however, it is always best to seek professional medical advice at the beginning.

**3126 West Broadway**
*Kitsilano*
*Map 8 B4* **250**

## Alpine Anxiety & Stress Relief Clinic

*604 732 3930 | www.anxietyandstressrelief.com*

This clinic has a holistic approach to its work, practising both mind and body healing. Its services include help with stress, anxiety, depression, insomnia, alcohol and drug use, as well as relationship advice. Methods used include cognitive behavioural therapy, self regulation therapy, somatic experiencing, hypnosis, relaxation, meditation, and deep breathing methods. Free lectures are often held, so check the website regularly for information. Group or private sessions are also offered. Fees vary for each practitioner.

**200-1311 Howe St**
*Downtown*
*Map 9 C1* **251**

## Milardo Wellness Center

*604 669 9699 | www.medhypnosiscenter.com*

Milardo Wellness Center offers hypnotherapy, counselling and life coaching to manage problems such as stress, anxiety and panic attacks. There is an initial free consultation with a certified medical hypnotherapist, counsellor and life coach. The amount of treatment needed varies from four to 12 sessions, which range in price from $140 to $170. There is another branch in West Vancouver (1-1718 Marine Drive, 604 921 7930).

## Tai Chi

Although the tai chi following in Vancouver is relatively small, there are still a few noteworthy schools where you can practise this ancient art form. Tai chi is a type of moving meditation that is believed to relieve stress, improve circulation, balance and posture. It is an exercise that is suitable for nearly all people, regardless of age or level of fitness. Prices start at $15 and you can often buy packages to reduce the price.

**220 Jackson Av**
*Strathcona*
*Map 10 D1* **252**

## Shouyu Liang

*604 255 5149 | www.shouyuliang.com*

A variety of martial arts are taught at this school, including tai chi. Many of the students have been involved in national and international competitions and demonstrations, and all of its instructors also have competition experience. New students and visitors are warmly welcomed. Drop-in classes cost $45, or you can purchase a one month pass for $85. Check online for class schedules.

588 East 15th Av
Main
Map 11 D4 253

## Taoist Tai Chi Society of Canada

*604 681 6609 | www.taoist.bc.ca*

This company is part of the International Tai Chi Society, which has associations in more than 25 countries around the world. Different languages, cultures, and backgrounds are all welcome. In Vancouver, classes in tai chi are offered for seniors, students, youths, low-income earners, and children. An initial fee of $20 is required when you first join, and after that prices vary from $15 to $45, depending on your age and income level. Those who pay in advance are eligible for a discounted rate.

## Yoga

Other options **Pilates** p.353

Yoga is an ancient Indian philosophy that aims to enhance well-being through a series of poses and breathing techniques. Anyone can do it regardless of age, body type, fitness level or experience, and many use it as a calming way to exercise and reduce stress. You'll find a studio in most inner suburbs and you can even join yoga programmes at recreation or community centres. There are many different types of yoga to choose from, including hatha, power, bikram (or hot yoga), yin, iyengar, ashtanga and kundalini. Prices are approximately $15 and up for a drop-in class and some places, mainly the bikram yoga studios, offer a special low introductory fee for your first week only. After that, prices rise significantly, but you can reduce your cost by purchasing monthly passes at discounted rates.

101-1650 Alberni St
West End
Map 7 C1 254

## Bikram's Yoga College Of India Vancouver

*604 662 7722 | www.bikramyogavancouver.com*

This college teaches bikram yoga, also known as 'hot yoga', and as well as this central clinic, has two other handy locations, on Cambie Street (604 876 9642) and West Broadway, Kitsilano (604 742 3830). Bikram yoga is performed in 40°C heat, and is thought to help your muscles ease into positions more effectively. Membership fees are available in different formats, including an 'as you go' option of 10, 20, 40, or 80 classes, and a monthly unlimited pass for one, three, six or 12 months. New students can purchase a one-week unlimited pass for $30, or a one month pass for $99. The website provides schedules for each location, as well as information on upcoming special events.

202-888 Burrard St
Downtown
Map 7 D4 255

## Flow Yoga

*604 682 3569 | www.flowyogavancouver.com*

This modern studio with a simple decor offers ashtanga vinyasa, hatha yoga, ashtanga primary series, yin yoga, and morning flow yoga. The first-time rate is $10, drop in classes are $17, and students get discounted rates. You can purchase passes for 10 classes ($150 for three months) and 20 classes ($275 for six months). There are also one, three, six, and 12 month unlimited passes starting from $150, and a payment plan if necessary. Check the website for an up-to-date schedule.

280-1050 Homer St
Yaletown
Map 9 E1 256

## Yaletown Yoga

*604 684 3334 | www.yaletownyoga.com*

This studio offers a variety of types of yoga, including bikram, power, anusara-inspired and yin yoga. It also runs meditation and programmes for children. Take advantage of the first week special, which offers unlimited yoga for just $20, or a one month special of unlimited yoga for just $99. Thereafter fees range from $15 for a single-hour drop-in class, up to $1,200 for a yearly unlimited yoga pass. Child minding services are offered on Tuesday and Thursday mornings from 09:00 until 11:30.

# When you're lost what will you find in your pocket?

*Item 71. The half-eaten chewing gum*

When you reach into your pocket make sure you have one of these miniature marvels to hand… far more use than a half-eaten stick of chewing gum when you're lost.

## Explorer Mini Maps
Putting the city in your pocket

Therapeutic Feeding    Essential Medicines    Surgery

MEDECINS SANS FRONTIERES
أطـبـاء بـلا حـدود

Providing emergency medical
relief in over 70 countries.

# help us help the helpless

# Shopping

## Shopping

Shopping options in Vancouver cater for every personality; from anti-consumers who will only support local and fairly traded goods, to the diva who only sets foot in the most upmarket boutiques, the 'City of Glass' provides a diverse selection. Particularly unique is the urban trend for sustainability in eco-fashion, home design, food and electronics. Not only is the city consciously 'green,' but so are many of the products being sold. Affordable treasures abound and within each street the most unique shops selling that perfect gift or vintage jacket can be found. Spend a lot or spend a little – either way you'll find something to make you want to part with your hard-earned cash. Although Vancouver ranks highly in international terms for cost of living, this is mainly due to rising real estate prices in the Lower Mainland. When it comes to shopping for essentials such as clothing, furniture, groceries and appliances, you'll find goods available in various price ranges and at a considerably lower cost than in New York or Toronto. Waiting for store sales requires little patience as they occur pretty frequently, and pre-Christmas, post-Christmas, seasonal stock and inventory clearance sales are especially rewarding. Before you merrily place your purchases on the sales counter, bear in mind that price tags can be misleading. On top of the retail price is both a provincial service tax (PST) and federal goods and services tax (GST), adding 12% to most purchases.

### The Shopping Experience

Vancouverites are traditionally a laidback bunch, usually preferring smaller shops to bustling megastores. This is slowly changing, however, and larger stores are cropping up around the city. Sales people are typically cheerful and highly caffeinated, although grumpy clerks with their eye on the clock do exist. For the most part, expect helpful staff. Overly eager employees can be easily defeated by a polite 'I'm just looking and will let you know if I need your help'. Bartering isn't widely practised in the city, and you won't get much chance to utilise your haggling skills unless you head into Chinatown and some of the markets.

When it comes to clothes, although Vancouver doesn't quite have the chic designer status of Paris, London or Milan, local designers such as Yumi Eto and Allison Wonderland have picked up the slack. International brands are on the increase, with Holt Renfrew (p.410), H&M (p.388) and Tiffany & Co (p.388) having all surfaced in the city. Yaletown (p.407) is the place for uber-trendy boutiques, Robson Street (p.406) is filled with high fashion and tourist shops, and Kerrisdale Village (p.408) serves clientele who prefer classic to trendy. Antiques and up-and-coming designers are based out of Main Street (p.407) and Gastown (p.406), while Fairview (p.106) caters to art buyers. Commercial Drive will satisfy the hippy in you (p.408), and you can find the freshest produce on Granville Island (p.406) or discover the city's obsession with yoga wear in Kitsilano (p.408).

### What & Where To Buy – Quick Reference

| | | | | | | | |
|---|---|---|---|---|---|---|---|
| Alcohol | p.364 | Electronics | p.379 | Lingerie | p.390 | Second-Hand Items | p.398 |
| Art | p.365 | Eyewear | p.380 | Luggage & Leather | p.391 | Shoes | p.399 |
| Art & Craft Supplies | p.366 | Flowers | p.381 | Maternity Items | p.391 | Souvenirs | p.400 |
| Baby Items | p.367 | Food | p.381 | Medicine | p.391 | Sports Goods | p.401 |
| Beachwear | p.367 | Gardens | p.383 | Mobile Phones | p.392 | Stationery | p.402 |
| Bicycles | p.368 | Hardware & DIY | p.383 | Music, DVDs & Videos | p.392 | Tailoring | p.402 |
| Books | p.370 | Hardware & DIY | p.384 | Musical Instruments | p.394 | Textiles | p.403 |
| Camera Equipment | p.372 | Health Food | p.386 | Outdoor Goods | p.394 | Toys & Games | p.403 |
| Car Parts & Acc | p.374 | Home Furnishings | p.386 | Party Accessories | p.396 | Wedding Items | p.404 |
| Clothes | p.374 | Jewellery & Watches | p.388 | Perfume & Cosmetics | p.396 | | |
| Computers | p.378 | Kid's Items | p.389 | Pets | p.397 | | |

**Inter-nett Fees ◄**

*There is a $5 processing fee for all packages that enter Canada, in addition to GST and PST if it wasn't charged on the original bill – adding another 12%, on top of the $5 fee, to each shipment.*

## Online Shopping

The online shopping movement has picked up in Vancouver, although it's still not as popular as visiting a real shop. Given that you can buy almost anything in the city, cyber shopping is often a preference for those searching for particular bargains or who prefer the convenience of ordering on the web. Internet-savvy bargain hunters use sites like eBay and Amazon for deals on almost anything, while families with new additions tend to check out Pinky & Company (www.pinkyandcompany.com) for designer items they don't have to leave the house for.

Many Vancouverites tend to buy their electronics, music, DVDs and games online, and stick to shops for fashion, home design and food. Many retail companies in the city also have an online shopping service with minimal delivery costs.

Delivery charges are reasonable, with most websites offering free shipping after spending $39 to $50. The majority of stores accept Visa, MasterCard and PayPal, while American Express is not as widely accepted.

If you purchase something that's being shipped from across the globe, make sure a description of the contents, quantity and value of the item is written on a visible label. Prohibited items include explosives, high quantities of tobacco, firearms, alcohol, drugs, medical or biological materials, perishable items, liquids, plants and dangerous goods.

### Online Shopping

| | |
|---|---|
| www.amazon.ca | Books, music, DVDs, software, games, gifts and more |
| www.chapters.indigo.ca | Rare or out-of-print books |
| www.ebay.ca | Buy and sell rare and everyday items through bidding |
| www.etsy.com | Unique hand-made items and one-of-a-kind crafts |
| www.morethanmilk.ca | Free home delivery of dairy, meat and groceries |
| www.spud.ca | Home delivery of organic local produce and groceries |

## Eco-Shopping

Vancouver is a leader in the green movement; the city is the home of Greenpeace (see p.295), and Vancouverites' respect for nature is beginning to manifest itself in an increased demand for environmentally friendly merchandise. The folks at Bring Your Own Bag (604 605 0685, www.bringyourownbag.ca) have heeded the call and manufacture cloth bags that are being imitated by almost every large shop in the city. The Fashion High organisation (www.fashionhigh.ca) has brought together designers, retailers, manufacturers and other industries to form a hub of local and sustainable fashion, while organically made products from Sparrow Handbags (www.sparrowhandbags.com) sell in various Vancouver retailers. With a city so intent on leaving the smallest ecological footprint possible, there are a rising number of shops that are using sustainable products in every sector. Other eco-friendly companies worth looking into are HTnaturals (604 255 5005, www.htnaturals.com) for organic clothing, Lotuswear (604 738 7168, www.lotuswear.com), which caters for the active and yoga enthusiasts, and m-smart design (778 280 3610, www.m-smartdesign.com) and Upholstery Arts (604 731 9020, www.upholsteryarts.ca), both of which offer sustainable furniture and accessories for the conscious homesteader.

## Refunds & Exchanges

Trying to get your money back for something you mistakenly purchased or had second thoughts about can be a frustrating process. It's a given that if you lose your receipt, a full refund will be unattainable. In general, you have 15 to 30 days to take back an unworn item with the original receipt. Although most stores will happily let you return something, they will only give you store credit or the option to exchange. The sales assistant should warn you if you are buying an item that cannot be returned, and in such cases a 'no returns' note should also be stamped on your receipt. Every once in a while you'll come across a shop like Plum Clothing (p.376) that offers a generous refund policy within 10 days, if you have the receipt and the tag is still attached. From small boutiques to large corporations, the norm has gone from 'the customer is always right' to 'we can't lose your money.' Be sure to ask an employee about the returns policy before you pay; many shops also have this on display near the cash register.

## Consumer Rights

The Better Business Bureau of Mainland BC (604 682 2711, www.bbbvan.org) allows consumers to be proactive about negative experiences. This non-profit organisation regulates complaints in the province. Its services stretch across North America in different branches, and include reports on a company's reliability, scam warnings, consumer information, and assistance in mediating and arbitrating a complaint. Residents can call at any time to retrieve a company's report, or file a complaint through the website.

If there's a serious problem with the way a shop has handled your situation, shoppers are protected by the Business Practices and Consumer Protection Authority of British Columbia (1 888 564 9963, www.bpcpa.ca), the only organisation of its kind in Canada. Its purpose is to protect consumers in BC by enforcing the Business Practices and Consumer Protection Authority Act. Penalties include forcing a retail outlet to reimburse money, issuing a warning or compliance letter, and, in extreme cases, filing criminal charges or taking civil action.

## Shipping

International shipping is straightforward in Vancouver. Canada Post (1 866 607 6301, www.canadapost.ca), which has multiple branches around the city, offers a variety of services. Post offices are scattered throughout all neighbourhoods, usually in pharmacies, and prices are posted along the back wall. The usual delivery time is three business days within the city, four to six business days throughout Canada, and up to 10 business days between major cities such as Toronto and Ottawa. Its Xpresspost and Priority courier services will get your package to the recipient as fast as noon on the next business day.

Other courier options are Fedex (1 800 463 3339, www.fedex.ca), UPS (1 800 742 5877, www.theupsstore.ca) and Purolator (1 888 744 7123, www.purolator.ca), all of which have a range of domestic and international services. Most department stores, including The Bay (p.410) and Sears (p.410), will arrange shipping for you at a cost, charging extra only for bulky and fragile items.

## How To Pay

Cash is accepted everywhere, and some establishments take US or foreign currency – although spending greenbacks this way is not advised as many charge a set rate that is almost always worse than a bank. Debit cards and credit cards are commonly used. Visa and MasterCard are the most widely accepted credit cards, while American Express has more limited use (although most upmarket shops do accept it). Check the entrances to shops or the cash register for stickers displaying accepted credit cards. Some smaller, independent shops may not accept payment by credit card, so it helps to carry some extra cash. Doing so is not unsafe, but common sense must be used at all times if carrying large amounts of money. Personal cheques are rapidly being phased out and require two forms of ID if they are to be accepted. Many visitors still carry traveller's cheques in Canadian currency – while this is a convenient and secure way to carry money, these cheques must be cashed at a bank or foreign exchange broker before heading out on a shopping spree.

*Bargaining In BC*

*Although uncommon, bargaining is not unheard of in the city. While mainstream stores along Vancouver's key shopping streets display final prices on their products, shops along Commercial Drive, and Main Street's second-hand retailers, are the most likely to haggle. They will often throw in a free accessory or give you a discount if they know you want to play the game. The other place where hagglers may be able to practise their bargaining skills is at the markets of Chinatown and Little India.*

*Everything for sale in Vancouver*

## Alcohol

Other options **On the Town** p.457,
**Drinks** p.457

Buying alcohol in Vancouver is a bit trickier than in the US. It's not sold in convenience stores or supermarkets, although there are plenty of government-run and private retailers that have excellent selections, such as the West Coast Liquor Store at Vancouver International Airport.

If you're looking for wine made in BC, try the BC VQA shops (Vintners Quality Alliance, www.bcwine.ca) that sell 100% BC-produced bottles. Speciality wine shops also dot the city and offer produce from all over the world.

Most private shops close their doors at the end of the business day or early evening, so finding a retailer after hours can be a bit of a pursuit. You may be able to buy alcohol to take home at many of the local bars until 23:00, although not all will have permits for this. Prices are higher outside of the BC Liquor Stores, but so is the variety. A six-pack of lager will put you back $11, a decent bottle of white wine $15, and a 750ml bottle of vodka sells for $24. Note that the legal drinking age in British Columbia is 19 years.

*BC Liquor Store*

**Various Locations** ◀ ## Liberty Wine Merchants
*604 633 1922* | *www.libertywinemerchants.com*
With six locations in Vancouver, North and West Vancouver, Surrey and even in Point Roberts (Washington), Liberty Wine Merchants is more than just a retail outlet. On top of carrying almost 5,000 different wines throughout its stores, and exclusive champagnes such as Marquise de Sade 1996 Vintage ($99.99), it holds a wine school with courses, tastings and training. These range from group sake tutorials to four-day basic taste training. Within their classy exterior are essentials such as corkscrews, wine decanters and wine boxes, as well as gift baskets for the wine lovers on your list. It's not just a store for those with surplus cash to spend either – bottles start at $8.99.

## Alcohol

| | | | |
|---|---|---|---|
| BC Liquor Stores | Various Locations | www.bcliquorstores.com | 604 660 9463 |
| Brewery Creek Cold Beer & Wine Store | 3045 Main St | Main | 604 872 3373 |
| Broadway International Wine Shop | 2752 West Broadway | Kitsilano | 604 734 8543 |
| Darby's Cold Beer Wine & Liquor Store | 2001 MacDonald St | Kitsilano | 604 731 8750 |
| Delaney's Cold Beer & Wine | 175-5665 Kingsway | Burnaby | 604 433 2388 |
| Fairview Cold Beer & Wine Store | 888 West Broadway | Fairview | 604 708 2337 |
| Jack Lonsdale's Cold Beer & Wine | 1433 Lonsdale Av | North Vancouver | 604 986 7333 |
| Jimmy's Cold Beer & Wine | 783 Home St | Downtown | 604 689 2827 |
| Liberty Wine Merchants | Various Locations | www.libertywinemerchants.com | 604 224 8050 |
| Okanagan Estate Wine Shop | 3669 West 4th Av | Kitsilano | 604 730 1341 |
| Sutton Place Wine Merchant | 855 Burrard St | Downtown | 604 642 2947 |
| West Coast Liquor Store | YVR Airport | Richmond | 604 207 1127 |

**1034 Davie St**
*Downtown*
Map 7 C4 **2**

## Marquis Wine Cellars

*604 684 0445* | *www.marquis-wines.com*

This friendly store is where professionals go to discover new arrivals, and novices go for expert advice. Long-serving staff are thorough with assistance and always seem to find just the right bottle for your requirements – which is probably because they travel regularly to source wines directly from producers in France, Italy, Spain and beyond, such as the Albert Mann Cremant d'Alsace for $27.90. Not only does it carry hard-to-find brands from all over the world, but it also stocks a nice selection of BC wines that are not found in most shops. If you're really stuck trying to find a gift, ask the staff for their favourite picks and they'll even gift wrap or ship it anywhere in BC. Even more enjoyable are the wine-tasting series, which are held frequently, and the annual winemakers' dinner in November.

## Art

Other options **Art Galleries** p.210, **Art & Craft Supplies** p.366, **Art Classes** p.274

The city is a hotbed for First Nations and Inuit art that showcases indigenous culture, and you're sure to be able to pick something up for a reasonable price. Buyers purchase work right off the gallery walls and the city fosters independent artists in events such as the Eastside Culture Crawl (see p.220). If you're looking for that perfect portrait, try classy Photos By Kathryn (301-70 East 2nd Avenue, 604 488 1254) or romantic images by Randal Kurt Photography (604 266 8145, www.randalkurtphotography.com). Local studios abound in a seven-block radius just south of Granville Bridge. Granville Island and Gastown also have independent galleries worth a look. Significant local artists Charisse Baker (604 537 7313, www.charissebaker.com) and John Ferrie (604 215 0012, www.johnferrie.com) are making their mark on the modern scene. Call to request a viewing or to commission a custom piece.

**3045 Granville St**
*Fairview*
Map 5 F1 **3**

## Bau-Xi Gallery

*604 733 7011* | *www.bau-xi.com*

When Canadian artists needed a west coast space to sell their work in 1965, Bau-Xi Gallery was established. The name means 'great gift,' and the gallery has held hundreds of openings of first-class exhibitions. Today, around 50 artists are represented, working in paint, print, drawing and sculpture, varying from emerging to recognised talent. Reviews have been favourable from the beginning, and a sister gallery in Toronto opened in 1976. By 2002, the owners had also purchased Seattle's Foster/White Gallery. Prices for works usually begin at just under $1,000, but can get as high as $18,000. Open Monday to Saturday from 10:00 to 17:30, and from 12:00 to 16:00 on Sundays.

**1024 Mainland St**
*Yaletown*
Map 9 E1 **4**

## Coastal Peoples Fine Arts Gallery

*604 685 9298* | *www.coastalpeoples.com*

Located in trendy Yaletown, this important gallery showcases the work of the north-west coast First Nations and Inuit people. Since 1996, it has engaged visitors with high-quality art from leading master sculptors in the province. It has a reputation for having 'museum quality' work on display that comes from both emerging artisans and established leading players. The space boasts totem poles, ceremonial masks, glass sculptures, jewellery and original paintings. Custom-made wedding bands can also be ordered for that special day. Paintings start at $125, while a pair of sterling silver earrings is likely to set you back about $250. There is another branch in Gastown, at 312 Water Street (604 684 9222).

*1590 West 7th Av*
*Fairview*
*Map 9 A4* **5**

## Diane Farris Gallery

*604 737 2629* | *www.dianefarrisgallery.com*

This welcoming space features contemporary art from Canada and around the globe. Of particular interest is the glass sculpture courtyard that entices curious passersby with pieces selling for US$4,000 to US$6,600. The gallery has been around since 1984 and continues its reputation for discovering and fostering up-and-coming artists. It's a place to visit often as the exhibits and installations change frequently. It was voted the 'best private art gallery' in 2006 by readers of *The Georgia Straight*, and was awarded with the Queen Elizabeth II Golden Jubilee Medal for the owner's effort to support new artists.

*1359 Cartwright St*
*Granville Island*
*Map 9 C3* **6**

## Gallery of BC Ceramics

*604 669 3606* | *www.bcpotters.com*

Located on the artistic haven of Granville Island, the Gallery of BC Ceramics is operated by the Potters Guild of BC. The gallery helps guide those who are still developing their careers, and a panel judges the shows several times a year. Mediums include tableware, home decor, jewellery and sculpture, which are exhibited almost every month. Learn about the pottery and ceramic scene in this area or release your inner artist. If nothing else, you'll be able to find a hand-made set of serving bowls for around $35.

*308 Water St*
*Gastown*
*Map 10 A1* **7**

## Marion Scott Gallery

*604 685 1934* | *www.marionscottgallery.com*

Three decades of reputation precede this significant gallery. Specialising in fine Inuit works, it brings with it a commitment to showcasing the best from the north of Canada. The Marion Scott Gallery has had a strong influence in establishing a lasting market for this kind of work. Judy Scott Kardosh, the director and daughter of the late Marion Scott, organises two major curated shows each year. Between these large exhibitions, selected Inuit artists fill the space with sought-after prints, drawings, wall hangings and sculptures ranging in price from $550 to $2,800. In conjunction with its exhibitions, the gallery also publishes catalogues and books. It is certified by the Canadian Cultural Property Export Review Board, meaning it can appraise pieces of Inuit work.

## Art & Craft Supplies

Other options **Art Galleries** p.210, **Art** p.365, **Art Classes** p.274

With so many artists living and working in the city, it's no surprise that there are some great deals afloat. Opus Framing & Art Supplies and Loomis Art Store are the two most popular and heavily trafficked art supply stores. They both offer a wide range of products for almost all mediums, from $15 sketchbooks to $40 acrylic paint sets. Monthly sales allow you to bulk up on the essentials like brushes and frames. These shops are where pros gather what they need and where beginners cross the threshold for weekend workshops and helpful advice. Urban Source sells supplies in bulk, averaging $6 for a lunch-bag-sized portion, while The Cloth Shop is your one-stop shop for all things crafty; a quilt set runs from $80 to $170. Head over to Country Beads to snag enough supplies for an $8 bracelet or $15 necklace. On the North Shore, Queen's Stationery provides basic art supplies such as brushes, paints and canvases,

| Art & Craft Supplies | | | |
|---|---|---|---|
| Country Beads | 2015 West 4th Av | Kitsilano | 604 730 8056 |
| Loomis Art Store | 1431 West Broadway | Fairview | 604 733 1331 |
| Michaels Stores | A1-1000 Main St | North Vancouver | 604 913 6145 |
| Opus Framing & Art Supplies | 120 Lonsdale Av | North Vancouver | 604 904 0447 |
| | 1360 Johnston St | Granville Island | 604 736 7028 |
| Queen's Stationery | 3034 Edgemont Blvd | North Vancouver | 604 987 8443 |
| The Cloth Shop | 4415 West 10th Av | Point Grey | 604 224 1325 |
| Urban Source | 3126 Main St | Main | 604 875 1611 |

while Michaels is the crafts shop for home decor ideas, fine art and scrapbooking.

## Baby Items

Numerous boutiques have opened within the last few years that cater to hip families seeking designer labels; these are mostly located along Kitsilano's West 4th Avenue. Whether you visit The Bay, Sears or Zellers (p.410) – all places where you can get everything you need in one go – or visit the many independent shops for special items, the

Opus Framing & Art Supplies

city has it covered. The online Mia Moon store (www.miamoon.ca) makes shopping easy, selling quaint items including personalised bassinet blankets for $35 (shipping is free with a $49 purchase). Crocodile Unique Baby Store can up the style stakes for the ultimate trendsetting family with a $900 pushchair, carriage and the bassinet all in one. Those throwing baby showers can create a gift register at Babies R Us or Baby's World, which also has stores in Burnaby and Coquitlam. Baby food is available at almost every grocery store, usually from its own section of Gerber, Nestlè Baby and Heinz brand foods. Prices are fairly standard in supermarkets and rise as the store becomes more focused.

| Baby Items | | | |
|---|---|---|---|
| Babes On Fourth | 2354 West 4th Av | Kitsilano | 604 739 9870 |
| Babies R Us | Various Locations | www.babiesrus.ca | 604 733 8697 |
| Baby's World | 1948 West 4th Av | Kitsilano | 604 731 3400 |
| Belly & Beyond | 4118 Main St | Main | 604 874 2298 |
| Crocodile Unique | 2156 West 4th Av | Kitsilano | 604 742 2762 |
| Oh Baby! | 3475 Cambie St | Cambie | 604 873 5803 |
| Room For 2 | 1409 Commercial Dr | Grandview | 604 255 0508 |

## Beachwear

Other options **Clothes** p.374, **Sports Goods** p.401

Vancouver is surrounded by beaches – and has the retail space to match. Boutiques that only carry beachwear do well and are open all year round. Sales typically go on before the summer season, starting in May, as well as before and after Christmas. Winter deals can be incredible. American Apparel stocks swimwear, with three stores on Granville Street alone and others on Robson Street, West 4th Avenue, and in Burnaby and Park Royal Shopping Centre. Swimco has two stores in Kitsilano and one in the Oakridge Centre. For sunglasses, Watch IT! has stores in Kitsilano, Robson Street and the Coquitlam Centre. Department stores (see p.409) offer

| Beachwear | | | |
|---|---|---|---|
| American Apparel | Various Locations | www.americanapparel.ca | 604 685 5904 |
| Blue Crush By Swimco | 1854 West 4th Av | Kitsilano | 604 732 7944 |
| Just Swimwear | 890 Howe St | Downtown | 604 688 2030 |
| Karma Athletics | 2066 West 4th Av | Kitsilano | 604 731 7747 |
| Splash Swim & Cruise | 2950 West 4th Av | Kitsilano | 604 736 8868 |
| Sunglass Hut International | 1015 Robson St | Downtown | 604 689 2554 |
| Swimco | Various Locations | www.swimco.com | 604 732 7946 |
| Watch IT! | Various Locations | www.watchit.ca | 604 733 0009 |

**Baby Showers**
*If your partner, sister or relative is expecting a newborn, a baby shower is a must. The tradition began as a way to 'shower' new mothers with practical gifts and advice. Far from the original idea of having one shower for the first born, now women throw these events every time a child arrives. Friends and relatives bring a gift each, ranging in expense from nappies and bibs to high chairs. A baby shower wouldn't be complete without the games, which the hostess creates. These vary from guessing how big the expectant mother's tummy is to having a baby pool, where guests bet a dollar or two and guess the delivery date.*

run-of-the-mill selections, and countless speciality shops carry a full range of sizes. You can find UV protective swimwear, sunglasses, thermal wetsuits and beach clothing for children online at Just Kids Clothes (www.justkidsclothes.com). For expectant mums, talk to the women at Hazel & Co (p.391) for a select range of bathing suits.

## Bicycles

Other options **Cycling** p.288, **Mountain Biking** p.312, **Bike Tours** p.248

Bikes are a serious business in a city with so many cycling paths. Not only are Vancouver streets filled with cyclists, rain or shine, but electric bikes are gaining immense popularity. Both require a helmet by law and can be ridden without insurance or a licence, although you must be at least 16 years old to ride an electric bike. The price for a basic bike is around $350, with helmets ranging from $20 to $50; a bike light costs $10, and the essential lock around $25. Large outlets such as Canadian Tire (p.385) sell a good variety of bicycles for people of all ages. Sports Junkies (p.395) has a large collection of new and used bikes from $300 to $700, as well as parts, accessories, a repair service and a consignment option. If you're heading to English Bay for a cycle, there are a few shops along Denman Street between West Georgia and Robson streets. Here you can rent bikes, tandems, take inline skating lessons and kit yourself with protective gear. Standard rates are $20 per day and $1.50 for knee and elbow pads.

Devoted mountain bikers will be in heaven; the best trails are on the North Shore, around Cypress Mountain, Mount Fromme and Mount Seymour. Maps of the routes can be bought at the local shops along the way. For the best advice on the area and good prices on mountain bikes, visit both Deep Cove Bike Shop and On Top Bike Shop, the former a manufacturer of bikes specifically made for North Vancouver's terrain. A great way to get acquainted with the scene is to contact the North Shore Mountain Bike Association (www.nsmba.bc.ca), which can set you up with events, other riders and good information. Although almost every bike shop in the city is committed to the environment, Our Community Bikes (604 879 2453, www.pedalpower.org) takes things a little further, with programmes designed to educate people about cycling as well as the recycling of bicycles.

**999 Pacific St**
*Downtown*
*Map 9 C1* 8

## Bicycle Sports Pacific

*604 682 4537* | *www.bspbikes.com*

The staff at Bicycle Sports Pacific are fun and know their stuff so well that you may enjoy the buying experience almost as much as the bike you leave with at the end. The store carries brands such as Trek, Giant, Cannondale, Gary Fischer and Lemond, covering full suspension, mountain, road, hybrid, children's bikes and cruisers. Not only do you get a wide variety of bicycles to choose from, but you also get tips on how to select the right one, accessory recommendations and suggestions for finding other bike-minded people. The gift registry offered here is a great way to record items you would like for a special occasion. There's a 10% reduction for those who decide to buy from your list.

| Bicycles | | | |
|---|---|---|---|
| Atomic Bike Shop | 1555 West 6th Av | Kitsilano | 604 714 0158 |
| Coast Mountain Sports | Various Locations | www.coastmountain.com | 1 877 977 2435 |
| Deep Cove Bike Shop | 1389 Main St | North Vancouver | 604 929 2222 |
| Denman Bike Shop | 710 Denman St | West End | 604 685 9755 |
| JV Bike | 955 Expo Blvd | Yaletown | 604 694 2453 |
| On Top Bike Shop | 3051 Lonsdale Av | North Vancouver | 604 990 9550 |
| Simon's Bike Shop | 608 Robson St | Downtown | 604 602 1181 |
| The Bike Gallery | 4443 West 10th Av | Cambie | 604 221 2453 |
| West Coast Sports | 1675 West 4th Av | Kitsilano | 604 732 4810 |

**3317 Cambie St**
*Cambie*
**Map 5 F2** 9

## Cambie Cycles

**604 874 3616** | *www.cambiecycles.com*

This one-of-a-kind shop is famous for its recumbent bikes (bicycles in which the rider is seated in an almost reclining position). It manufactures and sells the Cambie Recumboni, as well as offering a surprisingly large fleet of velomobiles, Rans bikes, Sun Bicycles, Bellandare's HP Velotechnik, Cycle Genius and Hase Spezialrader. Prices range from $700 for a Speedster up to $6,200 for a very sleek Rans Stratus. The store also carries what is probably the leading selection of unicycles in the city. Also available are trailers, trikes, urban bikes, scooters, electric and folding bikes.

**4219 Dunbar St**
*Dunbar*
**Map 5 D2** 10

## Dunbar Cycles

**604 224 2116** | *www.dunbarcycles.com*

You won't get any friendlier than the folks at Dunbar Cycles. They're known for spending as much time with newcomers as with regulars. The shop carries three main brands: Miele, Devinci's and Brodie Bikes. The latter two are Canadian-made and designed and cover bicycle types for every use. Jackets, shorts, jerseys, socks, shoes and gloves are also sold to equip stylish riders. Parts and accessories are available in a wide range of brands, and you can buy gift certificates. The maintenance shop is led by an expert wheel builder who can do repairs, or a basic tune-up for $40. There is free parking at the rear of the store – a real asset in Vancouver.

**3825 Main St**
*Main*
**Map 6-A2** 11

## Green World Electric Vehicles

**604 879 4559** | *www.gwev.com*

Green World supplies top power-assisted electric bikes (also called e-bikes). These look like traditional bicycles but have motors with varying power installed. The cost starts at about $750 and goes up to $1,800 for a mountain bike-styled machine. Most can run for 40 kilometres before having to recharge, and have gears like ordinary bikes. Green World also has a 'scrap' programme that allows people discarding cars built in 1993 or before up to $750 off an e-bike or scooter purchase. Accessories available include lights, speed and distance calculators, waterproof ponchos, bike covers and front-wheel locks.

*Deep Cove Bike Shop*

*Coast Mountain Sports*

**45 East 6th Av**
*Main*
Map 11 B1 **12**

## Jorg & Olif

*604 877 1850* | www.jorgandolif.com

This outlet is all about the Dutch-inspired 'city bike.' Coming in two versions, they've become a huge hit for active city dwellers who crave European cool. The bikes are designed for transport in urban areas and include little extras such as backward-arching handlebars, installed lights on the front and rear, an anti-theft device, a bell, and a coat guard to keep your chic clothes safe – no more shoving your trousers into your socks. These bikes are a tasteful way to get around, and cost between $545 and $1,500. You can also find city bikes at hip boutique Lark 8th Avenue (p.376).

## Books

Other options **Second-Hand Items** p.398, **Libraries** p.309

The laidback spirit on the west coast even finds its way into the world of literature – you'll often see people, book in hand, cosying up by the fire in winter or lying on the beach in summer. Almost every title you can imagine is within reach of the city: if a shop doesn't carry it, it'll order it in for you at no extra cost. Staff tend to be more knowledgeable the smaller the shop; a great niche store is Little Sister's Book & Art Emporium, for gay and lesbian related literature and the latest political debates on censorship rules. Thrifters head over to Pulpfiction Books on Main street or its branch in Kitsilano (3133 West Broadway, 604 873 4311) for great deals on second-hand treasures. For rare books, try local online store AbeBooks (www.abebooks.com), which will trawl thousands of booksellers to help you find what you're looking for.

Shops are spread equally throughout the city, with Chapters, or its sister stores Indigo and Coles, found in all malls. Uniquely, all stores apart from the Chapters chain are independent and have only one or two locations dotted throughout Vancouver (the main branch of each one is listed in the table). The biggest competition is Amazon (www.amazon.ca), where web users shop online to take advantage of discounts.

### The Word On The Street

The city's largest book fair, The Word On The Street (604 684 8266, www.thewordonthestreet.ca), occurs annually on the last Sunday of September, bringing readers and writers together for a day of fun. Publishers and authors set up tables so that visitors can walk through and chat with them for free, and live music and contests keep things hopping. Big names in attendance in the past include David Suzuki, Susan Musgrave and Evelyn Lau.

**3608 West 4th Av**
*Kitsilano*
Map 5 D1 **13**

## Banyen Books & Sound

*604 732 7912* | www.banyen.com

This speciality outlet is a gem for spiritual titles, from self-help and new age to religion and psychology. City dwellers have been flocking here since 1970 for its serene environment and range of books, tapes, CDs, videos and calendars geared towards those seeking personal growth. The shop is packed with wonderful finds and has more than 200 categories to choose from. Sign up to its newsletter to receive the latest info on what is happening – you'll be notified once a month about any presentations, performances and retreats. Special orders are accepted and the staff will do their utmost to accommodate all requests. Although you can peruse over 27,000 books on

### Books

| Blackberry Books | 3-1666 Johnston St | Granville Island | 604 685 4113 |
| --- | --- | --- | --- |
| Kidsbooks | 3083 West Broadway | Kitsilano | 604 738 5335 |
| Little Sister's | 1238 Davie St | West End | 604 669 1753 |
| Oscar's Art Books | 1533 West Broadway | Kitsilano | 604 731 0553 |
| People's Co-op Bookstore | 1391 Commercial Dr | Grandview | 604 253 6442 |
| Pulpfiction Books | 2422 Main St | Mt Pleasant | 604 876 4311 |
| The Comicshop | 2089 West 4th Av | Kitsilano | 604 738 8122 |

its website, the store is in itself a perfect setting for browsing peacefully through books; take your pick from its wide selection and curl up with it on one of the comfy chairs.

**302 West Cordova St**
*Gastown*
*Map 10 A1* **14**

## Biz Books

**604 669 6431** | *www.bizbooks.net*

With such a large film industry in 'Hollywood North', many people are into their movies in Vancouver. Biz Books has been successfully honing its creativity since 1996, acting as the hub of the film, television and theatre community. Classic plays are well represented, as are guides to the many facets of the industry, writing books, career development and photography titles. A lively industry board lists events, classes, shows and news to point people in the right direction. Staff will help find the right book or recommend a product that will inspire your creativity. The store's website makes ordering any book from its catalogue an easy task – but it's definitely worth the effort of meeting these guys in person.

**Various Locations**

## Book Warehouse

**604 683 5711** | *www.bookwarehouse.ca*

With seven locations in Vancouver, most locals have been into a Book Warehouse at one time or another. Branches are found Downtown, on West Broadway, in Kitsilano, Point Grey, Yaletown, the West End and in North Vancouver. As the name implies, the company stocks books with deep discounts. It is still independent and the atmosphere is much more welcoming than a large warehouse. Its roots took hold in 1980 and the stores have since become a familiar sight in almost every neighbourhood. In addition to carrying standard titles in stock at a 20% discount, it sells overstocks, reprints, barely flawed books, samples, imports and even bankruptcy stock at fantastic prices. Just look for the red circular sales tag and know you're going home with a great deal.

**788 Robson St**
*Downtown*
*Map 7 E4* **16**

## Chapters

**604 682 4066** | *www.chapters.indigo.ca*

In addition to its Downtown flagship store, the largest book retailer in Canada has locations in every mall, on West Broadway and in all suburbs. Chapters also has sister stores Indigo and Coles, and an online service. This major bookshop carries the widest variety of titles, from health and fitness to business and self-help, and also ships rare books through its website. Magazines, DVDs, music and gifts are big sellers too, but with higher prices. The chain has a rewards programme for frequent shoppers that gives discounts on almost every purchase. It also features guest authors on book tours who read and sign copies of their latest work. These events are usually advertised online and on signs outside the stores. Chapters' clearance section is also a key draw and is usually found at the entrance.

*Indigo*

2239 West 4th Av
Kitsilano
Map 8 E3 **17**

## Duthie Books

*604 732 5344* | *www.duthiebooks.com*

A Kitsilano favourite, Duthie Books is a popular independent establishment staying true to its roots. It celebrated its 50th anniversary in the city in 2008 and It carries a wide range of categories, from Canadian cookery and gardening to foreign language. Ask staff for recommendations or advice on any title in the store and they'll find it for you; there's a fair chance that they've probably read it as well. The online database of books is large, and special orders are welcomed.

450 West Hastings St
Downtown
Map 7 F3 **18**

## Sophia Books

*604 684 0484* | *www.sophiabooks.com*

This multilingual shop placed neatly in the Downtown core offers books in Japanese, French, Spanish, Italian and German. Staff can also help you in most of the above languages. Not only will you find language books to brush up on your skills or learn something new, but magazines, DVDs and audio are also available in each language. This is the place to find English as a second language kits, speciality Japanese magazines and French movies. Special orders are frequent and it's the only outlet in the city with such a large Japanese magazine subscription base. Particularly interesting are the tattoo photography books from Japan, featuring pictures of body art by world famous artists.

## Camera Equipment

Other options **Electronics & Home Appliances** p.379

Cameras have become so easy to use and inexpensive to buy that most big box stores like Future Shop (p.379) and Best Buy (p.379) have great prices, although London Drugs (p.380) leads the large chains. Prices for a basic point-and-shoot start at under $150, rising according to the quality and features. An adequate, solid camera usually costs $250 (not including tax), and the best place to check on the value is www.consumerreports.org. A one-year manufacturer's warranty comes with camera purchases, and most shops will also offer a two and four-year option for an additional cost.

Dunne & Rundle is a family owned company, with a nice selection of standard cameras. Broadway Camera has a range of specialised equipment and multilingual staff. Leo's Camera Supply provides top-notch advice and has a huge variety of stock, especially Canon. The folks at Kerrisdale Cameras service the surrounding area at prices

### Big Box Stores

Large chain retailers, with stores often covering a city block and having huge carparks, are called 'big box stores' in North America. Examples include Future Shop (p.379), Canadian Tire (p.385), Best Buy (p.379) and Home Depot (p.379). These stores are usually huge and rectangular and the adjoining carparks are enormous. While many residents see them as cheap and convenient, they do have their critics: certain groups believe they ruin local businesses and create excessive pollution, and vehemently oppose any plans to build new big box stores.

### Camera Equipment

| Black's | 700 West Georgia St | Downtown | 604 684 2467 |
|---|---|---|---|
| Broadway Camera | 102-1055 West Broadway | Kitsilano | 604 733 9282 |
| Dunne & Rundle Foto Source | 595 Burrard St | Downtown | 604 681 9254 |
| Kerrisdale Cameras | 2170 West 41st Av | Kerrisdale | 604 263 3221 |
| Lens & Shutter | 2912 West Broadway | Kitsilano | 604 736 3461 |
| Leo's Camera Supply | 1055 Granville St | Downtown | 604 685 5331 |

Babywear p.98
Bank Loans p.22

Written by residents, these unique guidebooks are packed with insider info, from arriving in a new destination to making it your home and everything in between.

**Explorer Residents' Guides**
We Know Where You Live

just over average (and have other shops around the Lower Mainland), while Black's is for those wanting a basic camera for personal use.

## Car Parts & Accessories

Although the trend towards developing and buying greener cars is gathering pace, there are still those who love their gas-guzzling machines. Parts and accessories can be found for all makes and models, although imports usually take longer to bring in. Buy and Sell (www.buysell.com) is a popular way to get your hands on a good deal, although knowledge of parts is essential to ensure you aren't swindled. The safest bet is Canadian Tire (across the city, but with a large branch at 2290 Cambie Street), which has an auto section and knowledgeable staff. See the table for a selection of reputable spots around town to get your car fixed in an emergency or to buy parts that need replacing. Lordco Auto Parts and NAPA Auto Parts are the main service centres in Vancouver and have proven themselves over the years. OK Tires specialises in tyre, break, exhaust and suspension services, and Ralph's Radio is

| Car Parts & Accessories | | | |
| --- | --- | --- | --- |
| Budget Brake & Muffler | 6756 Royal Oak Av | Burnaby | 604 439 0248 |
| Canadian Tire | Various Locations | www.canadiantire.ca | 604 707 2290 |
| Craftsman Collision | 1315 Cotton Rd | North Vancouver | 604 980 4581 |
| Lordco Auto Parts | 1302-56th St | Tsawwassen | 604 943 1599 |
| NAPA Auto Parts | 1-8555 Cambie St | SW Marine | 604 321 4434 |
| OK Tires Store | 1843 Kingsway | Knight Road | 604 879 1457 |
| Ralph's Auto Supply | 12011 Mitchell Rd | Richmond | 604 325 7010 |
| Ralph's Radio | 220 East 1st Av | Mount Pleasant | 604 879 4281 |

the place for security, audio and video needs. In Burnaby, Budget Brake & Muffler offers experienced service and good prices, and Craftsman Collision on the North Shore provides a guarantee on its work, with a high level of service. If you're in Richmond, find Ralph's Auto Supply for excellent used parts.

## Clothes

Other options **Lingerie** p.390, **Tailoring** p.402, **Kids' Items** p.389, **Shoes** p.399, **Sports Goods** p.401, **Beachwear** p.367

Although the reputation for north-west coast fashion is fleece and GORE-TEX, Vancouver is fast becoming a hotbed for high fashion and local designers going on to sell internationally. The city's abundant supply of boutiques features a mixture of designers and brands to satiate the most eclectic fashionista. Department stores (p.409) carry a broad range of items and can be relied on for the basics, while boutiques in Yaletown focus on the season's hottest trends. Hip urbanites turn to shops such as Off The Wall and Aritzia for the latest styles for juniors and teens, while DKNY and Plenty cater to older shoppers. Head over to Fab Clothing in Kitsilano for denim galore, and into Holt Renfrew for designer favourites.

Robson Street is lined with fashion stores and is a perfect strip for a *Pretty Woman*-style shopping spree. Look out for great stores like Banana Republic, Zara, A/X Armani Exchange, lululemon athletica, Below the Belt and Club Monaco.

Vancouver also has a thriving vintage scene that mingles well with its blooming burlesque dancers. Some of the best shops in town sell vintage clothing, and practised shoppers roam the suburbs and auctions for the best in era-specific pieces. Many stores are known for their owners, who almost always have sparkling personalities.

Main Street (p.407) and Gastown (p.406) are home to a large concentration of clothing designers. Some have their own shops, such as Eugene Choo, while others sell their lines in stores like Twigg & Hottie. Wherever you choose, you'll often find a cherished item that you never realised you were looking for.

## Accessories

Finding just the right accessory for an outfit can be a daunting experience, but Vancouver makes it a bit easier with plenty of great boutiques that specialise in the perfect addition to your wardrobe. On top of fashion accessories, you can also find retailers like The Umbrella Shop that help during the city's rainy weather. In the same vein try Gumdrops on a rainy day – its motto is 'get wet in style'. For the largest selection of tights, head over to Ethel's Boutique, where you'll find leggings you never imagined existed. You can find a selection of handbags at shoe stores like Aldo (p.400) and Nine West (604 261 4222, Pacific and Oakridge Centres). Hats can be found at almost every clothing store, with a nice selection at Le Chateau.

**1036 Mainland St**
*Yaletown*
*Map 9 E1* **19**

## Atomic Model

*604 688 9989* | *www.atomicmodel.com*

This Yaletown gem has lots of attitude, and some hot designers that you won't find elsewhere – think Lotta, Sass & Bide, and Oligo Tissew. This is the perfect place to find that unique piece for a special event or a classy jacket to match your new outfit. A visit wouldn't be complete without trying on a pair of Nanette Lepore's vintage-style heels. For that super celebrity treatment, call for a personal shopping appointment. Owner Kristen Pellack specialises in selecting ideal pieces for specific wardrobes and builds style through personality. Prices at this at this end of town, however, usually match the status.

**4393 Main St**
*Main*
*Map 6 A2* **20**

## Bodacious

*604 874 2811* | *www.bodacious.ca*

The playful girls at Bodacious design and sell clothing to make you feel fabulous – their body-positive attitude is always fun and just a little bit cheeky. Catering to women from sizes 10 to 24, Bodacious carries a wonderful collection of local designers including Mitzylaneous Debris and Sweet Soul Designs. Its claim to fame, though, is without a doubt the wrap dresses of its signature line. The many variations are manufactured locally and give women with curves one more reason to celebrate their bodies.

**418 Davie St**
*Yaletown*
*Map 9 D1* **21**

## Brooklyn Clothing Co

*604 683 2929* | *www.brooklynclothing.com*

With more than a thousand pairs of men's jeans, this hip store proves that fashion is not just for girls. You won't find high-end stuff, but you can score with well-made jeans by the bucketful. Sizes range from 27 to 40 and vary within the 50 different cuts. Highlights are the local Ginch Gonch underwear line, Deuce hoodies and Nudie jeans. There are also a few lines of jewellery, belts, shoes and many international designers.

## Accessories

| | | | |
|---|---|---|---|
| Bentley | 1173 Robson St | West End | 604 676 1742 |
| Claire's Stores | 762 Granville St | Downtown | 604 602 4391 |
| Claudia Schultz Hats | Mooncruise Gallery, 235 Cambie St | Cambie | 604 685 9575 |
| Edie Hats | 4-1666 Johnston St | Granville Island | 604 683 4280 |
| Ethel's Boutique | 2346 West 4th Av | Kitsilano | 604 736 0910 |
| Gumdrops | 2029 West 4th Av | Kitsilano | 604 733 1037 |
| HotBox Accessories Inc | 2560 Main St | Main | 604 871 0095 |
| I Love Hats | 1509 West Broadway | Fairview | 604 739 0200 |
| Icing By Claire's | 1024 Robson St | Downtown | 604 408 0733 |
| Satchel Shop | Various Locations | www.satchelshop.ca | 604 261 8713 |
| The Umbrella Shop | Various Locations | www.theumbrellashop.com | 604 669 9444 |
| Tie Rack | 797 Thurlow St | West End | 604 669 7315 |

**2535 Main St**
Main
Map 11 B2 **22**

## Burcu's Angels

***604 874 9773***

One of the most recognisable shop windows in the city, a *Charlie's Angels*-like logo adorns this busy shop. It is know for its 1970s garb and is packed with creative vintage finds. Burcu herself is often the main appeal, but as her 'angels' take over the store, the focus turns back to the clothes. This treasure trove contains some crazy outfits, and you'll often end up buying the items the staff encouraged you to try on 'just for fun'. The store is also known for catering to the movie business, offering a free box outside for people to rummage through, and for accepting trades if it's time to clean out your closet.

**2315 Main St**
Main
Map 11 B2 **23**

## Lark 8th Avenue

***604 879 5275*** | *www.lark8thave.com*

Lark designer Vanya Mcdonell has put together a lovely range that is locally made, and, aside from the signature line, a collection of beautiful items by up-and-coming local designers is worthy of the buzz. Paperbird Clothing adds a whimsical touch to the mix and Kulpa stays cool with tailored cuts. You'll also find the increasingly coveted Nudie jeans from Sweden. Lark carries a larger menswear section than womenswear, stocking hot designers like Victorinox and Fenchurch. The shop is also a distributor of Jorg & Olif city bikes (p.370).

**931 Commercial Dr**
Grandview
Map 6 B1 **24**

## Little Miss Vintage

***604 255 3554*** | *www.littlemissvintage.com*

What it lacks in space it makes up for in personality and pleasure. Hostess Miss Cara welcomes her male and female customers into the shop with a determined attitude,

## Clothes

| | | | |
|---|---|---|---|
| American Apparel | 872 Granville St | Downtown | 604 685 5904 |
| Aritzia | 1110 Robson St | Downtown | 604 684 3251 |
| Armani Exchange | 1070 Robson St | Downtown | 604 488 1668 |
| Banana Republic | 1098 Robson St | Downtown | 604 331 8285 |
| Below the Belt | 1131 Robson St | Downtown | 604 688 6878 |
| Club Monaco | 1034-1042 Robson St | Downtown | 604 687 8618 |
| DKNY | 2625 Granville St | Fairview | 604 733 2000 |
| Eugene Choo | 3683 Main St | Main | 604 873 8874 |
| Fab Clothing | 2177 West 4th Av | Kitsilano | 604 734 0139 |
| Gap | 910-609 Granville St | Downtown | 604 682 5503 |
| Gumdrops | 2029 West 4th Av | Kitsilano | 604 733 1037 |
| H&M | 609 Granville St | Downtown | 604 692 0308 |
| Holt Renfrew | 737 Dunsmuir St | Downtown | 604 681 3121 |
| Le Chateau | 813 Burrard St | Downtown | 604 682 3909 |
| lululemon athletica | 1148 Robson St | Downtown | 604 688 6678 |
| Momentum | 1237 Burrard St | Downtown | 604 689 4636 |
| Off The Wall | 748 Burrard St | Downtown | 604 605 0314 |
| Plenty | 2803 West Broadway | Kitsilano | 604 736 4484 |
| Plum Clothing | 2799 Granville St | Cambie | 604 737 0246 |
| Roots | 1001 Robson St | Downtown | 604 683 4305 |
| Staccato | 1842 West 1st Av | Kitsilano | 604 731 4343 |
| Twigg & Hottie | 3671 Main Street | Main | 604 879 8595 |
| The Block | 350 West Cordova St | Gastown | 604 685 8885 |
| The Original Levi Store | 1068 Robson St | Downtown | 604 331 9960 |
| Wal-Mart | Various Locations | www.walmart.com | 604 597 9169 |
| Zara | 1056 Robson St | Downtown | 604 677 8489 |

set on finding you what you need. Each item of stock has been hand-picked by her, and her speciality is 20th century fashion with a mix of pin-up, sex kitten and new wave mod. Shopping here is like stepping back in time with your own personal adviser.

*44 Water St* ◄
*Gastown*
*Map 10 B1* **25**

## Obakki

**604 669 9727** | *www.obakki.com*

If you're searching for classic chic, look no further than Obakki. This Canadian powerhouse has made its mark in Vancouver while tantalising the international scene. Its focus is on detailed designs that stand the test of time and changing fashions. Both the women's and men's collections are fine examples of the precise consideration each piece is given. All garments are made locally at The Studio Vancouver. Headed up by owner Treana Peake, this is a label to watch out for.

*3634 Main St* ◄
*Main*
*Map 6 A2* **26**

## Smoking Lily

**604 873 5459** | *www.smokinglily.com*

The beginnings were small – Smoking Lily was started by two girls in a spare bedroom and has grown into a 44 square foot shopfront and nearby production studio, with its current position on Main Street. Although now owned by only one of the originators, the company has grown in terms of both staff and products. Throughout, Smoking Lily has maintained its trademark bug prints and now sells male and female clothing, scarves, wallets, belts and tea towels. Definitely a local favourite, it's always a pleasure to step into this petite shop to see what new things it's come up with.

*4483 West 10th Av* ◄
*Point Grey*
*Map 5 C1* **27**

## tenth & proper

**604 222 1115** | *www.tenthandproper.com*

This Point Grey boutique was started by 23 year-old Deanna Dunic in 2007. After launching her neighbouring girly shop, Miss Coquette, three years earlier, tenth & proper was created to fill the gap with casual wear for men and women. The two shops are now combined and contain a fantastic array of feminine dresses, shiny accessories and classic, well-made staples. Local designers are aplenty, with labels such as Dace, Sunja Link, Narcissist, Pink Tartan and its own line, Property. Sign up for the private or group wardrobe consultations and get yourself a whole new look.

Roots

**980 West 15th Av**
Cambie
Map 5 F1 **28**

## Vaudeville Kitten
*604 732 7529*
Come and play in this wonderful celebration of hotchpotch fun. Shari Young has gone from a London Drugs photo lab worker to a fabulous vintage queen. The shop is chock-full of bloomers, garters, lingerie, shoes, jewellery and clothing. Take time to browse the fascinating exhibits on display as you walk through the half-boudoir, half-living room filled with all things old-world and glamorous. What makes this recent addition to the vintage world so great is the owner's passionate presence throughout the store, and the knowledge that you'll be back for something a little more risque next time.

**2248 West 41st Av**
Kerrisdale
Map 5 E3 **29**

## The Velvet Room Boutique
*604 264 8664* | *www.thevelvetroomboutique.com*
On the lookout for the next best Canadian designers? Check out this boutique for a wide range of newer and established lines. Each designer is hand-picked and must design and produce their label in Canada. The owner is careful to choose clothing for a variety of budgets in order to keep the store fresh. More than 35 designers make up the stock of clothing, jewellery, accessories, gifts and skin care. Visit frequently, as new designers are added regularly.

**321 Cambie St**
Gastown
Map 10 A1 **30**

## Woo Vintage Clothing
*604 687 8200* | *www.woovintage.com*
Named after Ms Woo, a Chinese immigrant with impeccable taste for custom-made dresses, this store stocks a wide range of clothing and accessories for the whole family. Run by a 'vintage clothing junkie,' she aspires to 'woo' the city with select vintage picks. You can find everything from a 50s party dress to a 1960s mod suit. Prices are always reasonable, with a pair of children's Baby Mary Jane shoes setting you back a mere $9. Gift certificates are also available and the online shop offers a separate collection that can be brought into the store upon request.

## Computers
Other options **Electronics & Home Appliances** p.379

Computer shops are spread throughout the city. Most are independent outlets selling the latest technology and all the main brands, while some allow you to custom-build your own machine. Heading over to the US can mean cheaper deals, but factor in time spent crossing the border and petrol and you're probably better off shopping closer to home. Manufacturers' warranties are included with all purchases and are standard across the board, usually covering one year on parts and one-to-three years on labour. There's always an option to upgrade for a fee. Repairs and servicing can be done at any computer store, although it's best to take it back to where you purchased it. Most computer stores still sell only PCs, but the two main places for Macs are Mac Station and WestWorld Computers.

| Computers | | | |
|---|---|---|---|
| ATIC Computers | 45 East Broadway | Mount Pleasant | 604 875 8859 |
| CompSmart | 1109-88 West Pender St | Downtown | 604 608 8703 |
| Downtown Computer Centre | 1035 Davie St | Downtown | 604 682 5240 |
| FrontierPC.com | 105-1755 West Broadway | Fairview | 604 739 8060 |
| Kube Computers | 2921 Cambie St | Cambie | 604 873 5823 |
| Mac Station | 101-1014 Homer St | Yaletown | 604 806 6227 |
| NCIX | 1711 West Broadway | Fairview | 604 739 9985 |
| NTCW.com | 1179 Pacific Blvd | Yaletown | 604 899 0328 |
| WestWorld Computers | 1368 West Broadway | Fairview | 604 732 4499 |

# Electronics & Home Appliances

Other options **Computers** p.378, **Camera Equipment** p.372

Other options **Computers** p.378, **Camera Equipment** p.372

Shops in Vancouver carry just about every electronics brand you've ever heard of. Taking a look at the big box stores such as Costco (see p.416), Future Shop and Best Buy is often the best way to go, as they supply all of the top brands and have the widest selection possible. White goods (general appliances) are usually bought at Home Depot, Trail Appliances, or department stores, where the selection is extensive and sales are frequent. And of course everybody knows about Wal-Mart, where you can get a huge range of electronics and almost everything else (www.walmart.com). Even if you decide to go with a smaller retailer, check these places for price comparisons of the models you like. In general, after a new product has been out for a year or two, prices decrease substantially.

Conveniently, all of the listed stores except London Drugs also have payment plans. Another way to score a deal is to check out the classifieds sections in local papers or try Craigslist (vancouver.craigslist.ca), an active, free listings site for everything including electronics and appliances. If you've bought an item and need to take it overseas, you'll have to get a voltage converter to match the country's capacity. For larger purchases such as TVs, it is best to sell them before leaving. In Europe, for example, the broadcast signals will reduce your picture to static.

### *2220 Cambie St*
*Fairview*
*Map 9 F4* **31**

## Best Buy

**604 683 4966** | *www.bestbuy.ca*

Best Buy is the place to find TVs, stereos, recorders, DVD players and mobile phones, and it also carries an impressive stock of electronics. Weekly sales are the norm, and there are frequent last-minute sales online or in store. DVD players range from $50 to $450, and the store says it will beat any competitor's price by 10%. The sales staff here are not commissioned, so they're less pushy than in other stores. Best Buy is home to the Geek Squad, a fleet of computer and home theatre installers and repairers, with a home theatre set-up costing from $199. Delivery is available for an additional charge (delivery of a CD player, for example, costs an extra $10).

### *1740 West Broadway*
*Kitsilano*
*Map 9 A4* **32**

## Future Shop

**604 739 3000** | *www.futureshop.ca*

With an equally good selection as Best Buy, Future Shop carries the widest variety of electronics and home appliances. It has weekly sales that start on Fridays, and every week a new series of items are reduced. This is the place to go for TVs, camcorders, DVD players and appliances, as sales are so frequent. The product service plan here extends the manufacturer's warranty for the typical extra fee. Large items can be delivered, although because the window of delivery is limited to between 08:00 and 17:00, you'll need to pick up your purchase if you are not home when it arrives. There is also a branch at 798 Granville Street (604 683 2502).

### *900 Terminal Av*
*Mount Pleasant*
*Map 10 E4* **33**

## Home Depot

**604 608 1423** | *www.homedepot.ca*

Combining professional services and easy-to-find household appliances, you can get everything from the tools you need for DIY to white goods at Home Depot. Major appliances such as dishwashers, fridges, ovens and washing machines are stocked in a variety of brands. Find a basic Moffat dishwasher for around $250 or a classy Maytag refrigerator for $1,550. These large items are not available for delivery, but you can rent a truck for $19 for an hour and a half. Prices are guaranteed to be the lowest, and it claims to beat a competitor by 10% if you find the same product cheaper elsewhere. Staff can be hard to find after 15:00 and the service you get can be hit and miss – although some employees are ex-contractors with practical knowledge about appliances, others are less knowledgeable about the products. For other locations in the region, check the website.

*Various Locations* ◄ ## London Drugs
*1 888 991 2299* | *www.londondrugs.com*

With nine locations throughout Vancouver (Granville Street, Robson Street and Davie Street to name a few – check online for the full list), you can buy almost anything at London Drugs. It sells everything from computers and electronics to food and beauty products, a great selection of digital cameras, voice recorders, mobile phones and game consoles, and it's a great place to stock up on CDs and DVDs. This is where you'll find a decent voice recorder for $50. A fortnightly flyer goes out and lists all of the sales that week, which makes it easy to plan a shopping trip. Returns are straightforward within 15 days, and the friendly staff work without commission, so tend to be helpful even if you're bringing something back.

*2752 Rupert St* ◄ ## Trail Appliances
*Grandview*
*Map 6 C1* **35**
*604 434 8711* | *www.trailappliances.com*

Holder of the local Consumers' Choice Award seal of approval since 2003, this store carries the widest selection of appliances in the country. It has a reputation for knowledgeable sales staff and providing a complete shopping experience. As well as featuring over 40 different brands, the store also has full displays to demonstrate how an appliance will look and work in each setting. Its sales team can assist with electrical requirements, plumbing and ventilation, and offer advice if you're renovating. It also provides a financing plan through its 'Trail Card', giving you six months interest free before you make the first payment.

## Eyewear
Other options **Opticians & Ophthalmologists** p.158

Whether you need to find the right contact lenses or those frames to last a lifetime, there are more than 100 opticians conveniently scattered throughout malls, in medical buildings and along main streets. The average cost of an eye exam is $90, which isn't usually covered under benefit plans unless there's a medical reason. The most well-known eyewear chains, Iris and LensCrafters, do full exams and offer discounts on frames or sunglasses you buy from them. Most boutiques conduct eye tests

### Eyewear

| | | | |
|---|---|---|---|
| Bruce Eyewear | 219 Abbott St | Gastown | 604 662 8300 |
| Downtown Vancouver Optometry Clinic | 1440-700 West Georgia St | Downtown | 604 681 5351 |
| Eyes on Burrard | 1493 West 12th Av | West End | 604 732 8812 |
| | 775 Burrard St | Downtown | 604 688 9521 |
| Iris | Various Locations | www.iris.ca | 604 873 2448 |
| Kitsilano Optometry | 1813 West 1st Av | Kitsilano | 604 732 5487 |
| LensCrafters | Various Locations | www.lenscrafters.ca | 604 263 2485 |
| Lens Masters | 1456 Lonsdale Av | North Vancouver | 604 985 5367 |
| Mt Pleasant Optometry Centre | 104 East Broadway | Mount Pleasant | 604 874 7302 |
| Optix Eyewear & Contact Lenses | 1685 Marine Dr | West Vancouver | 604 925 2110 |
| Skylight Optical | 102- 1100 Robson St | Downtown | 604 683 8223 |
| Spectus Eyewear | 2259 West 4th Av | Kitsilano | 604 730 0503 |
| Sunglass Hut | Various Locations | www.sunglasshut.com | 604 689 2554 |

and will often offer a deal if you buy two pairs. The trendiest frames can be found at Bruce Eyewear, Eyes on Burrard, Kitsilano Optometry and Spectus Eyewear, while the Downtown Vancouver Optometry Clinic, Mt Pleasant Optometry Centre and Lens Masters offer more in-depth services such as speciality exams. The easiest place to find a wide range of non-prescription sunglasses at fair prices is at Sunglass Hut. All optometrists and eyewear stores listed sell prescription sunglasses in a variety of styles, from unbranded $20 glasses to $330 Dolce & Gabbanas. Keep an eye out in malls for independent stands that sell pairs for $10.

## Flowers
Other options **Gardens** p.383

Flowers are sold in many supermarkets and corner shops, but the most attractive ones can be found at The Flower Box and The Flower Factory, both of which are neighbourhood favourites. They are sourced from all over the world, so varieties are available through all seasons. Full bouquets start at about $25 and prices stay steady all year round.
If you are looking for something particularly elegant, Thomas Hobbs Florist in Kerrisdale provides an excellent selection. It also delivers every day except Saturday and is an expert at wedding arrangements. The folks at Thai Orchid Flowers import the finest orchids from Thailand, including the vanda coerulea, or blue orchid. If you need fast delivery across North America, or within 48 hours overseas, contact Terra Plants & Flowers for a range of options and gift baskets. Lonsdale Florists ships locally and internationally. Most shops also offer a standing order service and can custom-make arrangements for special occasions.

### Flowers

| | | | | |
|---|---|---|---|---|
| Lonsdale Florists | 1211 Lonsdale Av | North Vancouver | 604 980 5048 | www.lonsdaleflorist.ca |
| Terra Plants & Flowers | 228-5300 No 3 Rd | Richmond | 604 278 3921 | www.terraflowers.com |
| Thai Orchid Flowers | 107-1668 West Broadway | Fairview | 604 734 1557 | www.thaiorchid.ca |
| The Flower Box | 1704 Charles St | Grandview | 604 254 3269 | www.theflowerbox.ca |
| The Flower Factory | 3604 Main St | Main | 604 871 1008 | www.flowerfactory.ca |
| Thomas Hobbs Florist | 2127 West 41st Av | Kerrisdale | 604 263 2601 | www.thomashobbsflorist.com |

## Food
Other options **Health Food** p.386, **Supermarkets** p.416

Vancouver is teeming with places to buy groceries, from cheap produce along Victoria Drive and 41st Avenue to delicacies at the Granville Island Public Market. A single person can easily live off a $50 a week grocery bill, given that there are so many options. The large Asian influence makes it easy to buy regional items such as bullhead fish for $3.99 per pound from places like T&T Supermarket (p.417), as well as Indian products at the Punjabi Market (p.413). The main supermarket chains are Safeway, Costco (p.416) and the Real Canadian Superstore (p.417), where you can buy things like pork back ribs for about $3 per pound. Popular independent stores are MarketPlace IGA, Nesters Market and Stong's Market, where prices are a bit higher but the service is more personable. Here, items such as Italian bread go for $2.70 and two litres of milk for $3.40. Save-On-Foods is another chain of stores, with branches throughout Greater Vancouver (www.saveonfoods.com). If you're in the West End, Super Valu has you covered 24 hours a day, providing huge savings on a regular basis. SuperValu on the North Shore (similar names but different companies) is a great family-owned grocer for fresh produce, weekly deals and an excellent bakery. For elderly people and those on the go, see the Online Shopping section (p.361) for companies that deliver right to your door.

| | |
|---|---|
| **606 East Broadway** | ## Anna's Cake House |
| Fraser | *604 876 6532* \| *www.annascake.com* |
| Map 11 D2 **36** | Without doubt the busiest bakery in Vancouver and beyond, this family-run business keeps expanding. Its commitment to using natural products and no chemicals has kept regulars coming back for years. It makes cakes, pastries, bread and buns, in a fusion of European and Asian cooking in its two stores (the other location is at 5510 Cambie Street, 604 325 8214). Weddings are its main business, making more than 300 brides and grooms happy each season. You can be sure you're in for a mouthwatering treat every time you visit Anna's. |

| | |
|---|---|
| **4675 Arbutus St** | ## Finest At Sea |
| Arbutus | *604 266 1904* \| *www.finestatsea.com* |
| Map 5 E2 **37** | Beginning as a fleet of fishing boats in Victoria selling to Asia, Bob Fraumeni waited for the right time to tap into the local market. He finally opened his Vancouver store in 2006, selling fresh seafood and a selection of choice dishes. All products are sustainable, local, and in season. The company has its own fleet of fishing boats docking in Victoria (where there is also another seafood store), and sells fish to local restaurants such as Blue Water Cafe (p.441), Raincity Grill (p.451) and Provence Marinaside (p.432). |

| | |
|---|---|
| **7860 Alderbridge Way** | ## Galloway's Speciality Foods |
| Richmond | *604 270 6363* \| *www.gallowaysfoods.com* |
| Map 2 B3 | With so many of the products you need to buy at your fingertips, there are not many reasons to leave Vancouver. However, the natural foods available at Galloway's are well worth the trip to Richmond. In order to save on commercial packaging, the store sells its products in bulk, making this the perfect place to fill gift baskets with dried fruits, nuts, spices and many varieties of rice. Delicious aromas waft out to the pavements outside, drawing new customers in. With about 10,000 square feet of retail space packed with delicious treats, it's hard to leave without stocking up. |

| | |
|---|---|
| **1729 Commercial Dr** | ## JN&Z Deli |
| Grandview | *604 251 4144* |
| Map 12 B1 **39** | This beloved Commercial Drive deli has been whetting appetites for years. The smell of smoked ham beckons to those who crave traditional eastern European meat. Serbian sausages are a major hit, as are high quality bacon and ham. Its meats are also served to huge acclaim at local eateries such as the Salt Tasting Room (p.440). |

| | |
|---|---|
| **3002 Granville St** | ## Meinhardt Fine Foods |
| Cambie | *604 732 4405* \| *www.meinhardt.com* |
| Map 5 F1 **40** | Another gourmet food store, this one is headed by Linda Meinhardt, the hands-on owner. Her philosophy, that food is sensuous and romantic, is embodied in this centrally located outlet. Meinhardt Fine Foods was set up over 10 years ago, and over the last decade has become a Fairview predilection. Famous for its gift boxes, each is heaped full of fine products in themes such as 'health nut', 'sweet tooth' |

### Food

| MarketPlace IGA | Various Locations | www.marketplaceiga.com | 604 731 5750 |
|---|---|---|---|
| Nesters Market | 990 Seymour St | Yaletown | 604 682 3071 |
| Safeway | Various Locations | www.safeway.ca | 604 873 0225 |
| Stong's Market | 4560 Dunbar St | Dunbar | 604 630 3154 |
| Super Valu | 1255 Davie St | Downtown | 604 688 0911 |
| SuperValu | 3230 Connaught Cres | North Vancouver | 604 987 7917 |

and 'the globetrotter'. Prices range from $20 to $500. Also on sale are delicate flowers such as orchids, daisies and roses.

**177 Davie St**
*Yaletown*
*Map 9 E2* **41**

## Urban Fare

*604 975 7550 | www.urbanfare.com*
Situated in Yaletown, with another location in Coal Harbour (305 Bute Street, 604 669 5831), this is the gourmet megastore for those who love to eat well. With a meat section, deli, bakery, pharmacy, coffee bar, restaurant and florist, it's got all bases covered. Hosting a dinner party? Order one of the many platters starting at $60. Going to a dinner party? Pick up a gourmet gift basket from $60 to $100. If the cost of the imported French cheese is just too much, try the $29.99 gourmet cooking class with the in-house chef.

*Urban Fare*

## Gardens

Other options **Flowers** p.381, **Hardware & DIY** p.384

There are large garden centres in all hardware and DIY stores, with a full range of furniture, accessories, tools, plants and seeds, but for a more in-depth service and staff who can give you advice on your garden, try specialised shops such as Earthrise Garden Store or The Natural Gardener. GardenWorks is a top choice for the North Shore, with locations in Edgemont Village and Capilano. Plant sales are held throughout the year, mostly at the information-rich UBC Botanical Garden (p.246) and the VanDusen Botanical Garden (p.246). These include a manure sale in March, the plant sale in April, and a big compost, spring bulb and indoor plant sale in September.

| Gardens | | | |
| --- | --- | --- | --- |
| Art Knapp Urban Garden | 1401 Hornby St | Downtown | 604 662 3303 |
| David Hunter Garden Centres | 2084 West Broadway | Kitsilano | 604 733 1534 |
| Earthrise Garden Store | 2954 West 4th Av | Kitsilano | 604 736 8404 |
| Figaro's Garden | 1896 Victoria Dr | Grandview | 604 253 1696 |
| GardenWorks | 705 West 3rd St | North Vancouver | 604 988 8082 |
| | 3147 Woodbine Dr | North Vancouver | 604 980 6340 |
| The Natural Gardener | 4376 West 10th Av | Point Grey | 604 224 2207 |

## Gifts

Gifts are a big part of Canadian culture. They're given when someone hosts a party in their home, at birthdays, anniversaries, graduations, christenings and first communions, as well as at Christmas, baby showers and weddings. Usually something of moderate price will do, as people care more about the gesture than the actual item. For example, graduation might tempt you to buy practical houseware, while a host will love a bottle of wine. A few gift shops in the city supply general presents, and department stores (p.409) carry presents and a registry for almost any occasion. If in doubt, flowers are always appreciated.

Obsessions is a safe bet for classy photo albums and clocks, Atkinson's for porcelain vases, Ten Thousand Villages for fair trade jewellery, and L'Occitane en Provence for luxury bath products. If you're on the North Shore, wander through Lonsdale Quay to Favourite for gifts and accessories, it's a boutique gift shop stocking Canadian designed jewellery, clothing, home decor and baby products. All shops listed also take online orders for delivery.

### Gifts

| | | | |
|---|---|---|---|
| Atkinson's | 1501 West 6th Av | Kitsilano | 604 736 3378 |
| Favourite | 219-123 Carrie Cates Court | North Vancouver | 604 904 8840 |
| Gifts Vancouver | 2439 Yukon St | Fairview | 604 877 0100 |
| L'Occitane en Provence | 3051 Granville St | Fairview | 604 734 4441 |
| | 765 Burrard St | Downtown | 604 688 1198 |
| Murata | 15 East Broadway | Mount Pleasant | 604 874 1777 |
| Obsessions | 387 Water St | Gastown | 604 622 7494 |
| Ten Thousand Villages | 929 Denman St | West End | 604 683 0929 |

## Hardware & DIY
Other options **Outdoor Goods** p.394

Home renovations have become all the rage, with DIY a popular activity for people trying to sell a home, moving into a new one or just customising the one they're in. The number of shops within the city boundaries has made 'doing it yourself' easier than ever before. In large shops such as Home Depot (p.379) and Canadian Tire, you can buy everything needed to complete a renovation, as well as hire professionals to install or help design your project. Financing is available in these stores, as are painting supplies, lumber, lighting and garden furniture.

For those in need of plumbing help or bathroom ideas, Hillcrest Plumbing and Heating is the local favourite. It has plumbers who do both emergency and scheduled work, and there is also a showroom at 3272 Main Street. For more upmarket DIY materials, check out Restoration Hardware, which provides everything you need to help restore older buildings. Most of the DIY stores featured are within the city, and located near public transportation. The companies listed in the table opposite tend to have several store locations around the city and the North Shore, so visit their websites or call to find your nearest one.

*Restoration Hardware*

**3900 Main St**
*Main*
Map 6 A2 **42**

## A & B Tool Rentals

*604 879 8633 | www.abtoolrentals.com*

If you haven't got the space to store bulky items then pay a visit to this rental store and choose from a range of hire tools and equipment. As well as using the gear for a set period of time, the fee also includes maintenance costs. You can rent a range of equipment, from a masonry saw for $188 a week to the 20 tonnes-per-hour conveyor belt for $85 a day. Stock is updated each year to maintain safety and quality.

**6191 West Blvd**
*Kerrisdale*
Map 5 E3 **43**

## Kerrisdale Lumber

*604 261 4274 | www.kerrisdalelumber.com*

With its origins dating back to 1921, this pioneering company has been an integral part of the neighbourhood for approaching 90 years. It even sold the paving stones for use in the Downtown core in the early days. Today, it has the same verve and ensures many household and professional projects are satisfactorily completed. Special services include saw sharpening and custom cutting, while a whole gamut of tools are available for every need. It's a great place that generates regulars – once you shop there you'll always make an effort to go back.

**1180 South East**
**Marine Dr**
*South Vancouver*
Map 6 A4 **44**

## Lee Valley Tools

*604 261 2262 | www.leevalley.com*

You will always find a personable service and high-quality tools at the Vancouver outlet of this family owned business, which has a reputation based on good advice and no sales commission. It manufactures its own equipment under the name of Veritas Tools, which has a solid standing in the industry. Staff are knowledgeable and can help you choose products that best suit your project, while regularly scheduled workshops are arranged for those who want to learn how to do it all themselves. In a welcome change from most retail stores, returns with a full refund are accepted up to three months after purchase. Shipping charges are included if you buy online.

**6191 West Blvd**
*Kerrisdale*
Map 5 E3 **45**

## True Value Hardware

*604 261 4274 | www.truevalue.ca*

Selling everything from paint and plumbing supplies to tools and houseware, this independent co-op boasts efficient service and helpful staff. Expect a hassle-free shopping experience if you know exactly what you want, and assistance if you are not yet sure. As it's a franchised company (there's another store at 3121 Arbutus Street, 604 738 3031), different locations may vary slightly. The stores are a neighbourhood essential and serve residents picking up supplies for both large and small jobs.

### Hardware & DIY

| | | | |
|---|---|---|---|
| Benjamin Moore | Various Locations | www.benjaminmoore.ca | 604 872 5275 |
| Canadian Tire | Various Locations | www.canadiantire.ca | 604 707 2290 |
| Cloverdale Paint | Various Locations | www.cloverdalepaint.com | 604 731 5858 |
| Home Hardware | Various Locations | www.homehardware.ca | 604 733 8014 |
| General Paint | Various Locations | www.generalpaint.com | 604 731 6505 |
| Hillcrest Plumbing & Heating | 212 East 17th Av | Main | 604 879 1415 |
| Home Depot | 900 Terminal Av | Mount Pleasant | 604 608 1423 |
| Restoration Hardware | 2555 Granville St | Fairview | 604 731 3918 |
| Rona | Various Locations | www.rona.ca | 604 877 1171 |

*Whole Foods Market*

## Health Food
Other options **Food** p.381,
**Supermarkets** p.416

Speciality food stores are common
in this health-conscious city. They
tend to sell a range of items such
as free-range eggs and organic
produce, as well as natural brands
not common in grocery stores.
Some people choose to do all of
their shopping at these stores since
they carry almost as much stock
as the bigger supermarket chains.
They also sell products for those
with particular allergies and special
diets. Vitamin and supplement
sections usually stock a wide range
of both branded and unbranded
options. Make a stop at Granville
Island Public Market (p.413) and
the Vegetarian Resource Centre. Two big names in organic food, Whole Foods
Market and the well-known Capers, have recently merged, and have several outlets
across town.

Choices is another popular chain, while Eternal Abundance, Mainly Organics and West
Pointe Organic Produce are smaller stores that specialise in organic produce.

### Health Food

| | | | |
|---|---|---|---|
| Capers/Whole Foods Market | Various Locations | www.capersmarkets.com | 604 687 5288 |
| Choices Market | Various Locations | www.choicesmarket.com | 604 875 0099 |
| Eternal Abundance | 1025 Commercial Dr | Grandview | 604 255 8690 |
| Famous Foods | 1595 Kingsway | Knight Road | 604 872 3019 |
| Mainly Organics | 4348 Main St | Main | 604 872 3446 |
| Vegetarian Resource Centre | 2250 Commercial Dr | Grandview | 604 628 7864 |
| West Pointe Organic Produce | 2625 West 4th Av | Point Grey | 604 736 2839 |

*Antique Blockwise* ◀

*Antique Row is located
along Main Street from
King Edward Avenue to
29th Avenue, and there
are also good stores
south of Granville
Island. If you want
to buy second-hand
antiques but can't
afford the prices, try
Able Auctions (1055
Vernon Drive, 604 325
2253) for new and
used items.*

## Home Furnishings & Accessories
Other options **Hardware & DIY** p.384

From upmarket interior stores with custom design services to the shops that carry just
about every knick-knack you'll ever need, there's a huge range of home furnishing
stores available in Vancouver.

Large chain stores such as The Brick in Renfrew Heights and HomeSense in West
Vancouver offer super deals, while shops like The Wood Co-op on Granville Island
can customise sustainable furniture to fit exactly into your space. Country Furniture
and Oscar Grann's Furniture offer upmarket choices, while Koolhaus sticks to
modern designs. In Point Grey, quirky Folkart Interiors sells a range of Canadian and
reproduction furniture. To get an overview of the current trends and designers, even if
you're not buying anything, check out the Interior Design Show West at Canada Place
in spring (604 730 2060, www.dvexpo.ca). Department stores (see p.409) are also often
great hunting grounds for beautiful additions to your home.

**950 Homer St**
*Yaletown*
*Map 9 E1* **46**

## Chintz & Company

*604 689 2022* | *www.chintz.com*

Discover unique items for your home in this large store in Yaletown selling elegant furniture and accessories, lighting and outdoor pieces. Prices are surprisingly reasonable for the upmarket products, and there are also customised window dressings, design consultations and a gift registry service. The store's staff also provides detailed assistance. Whether you're creating a new dining room or an outdoor retreat, you'll find some unexpected delights here.

**3200 Sweden Way**
*Richmond*
*Map 2 B3*

## IKEA

*604 273 2051* | *www.ikea.com*

Take a trip down to Richmond and spend the day at IKEA, the megastore to beat all megastores. Pile your trolley full of modern home decor, furniture, storage, kitchenware and items for children – there are fantastic prices. 'Wacky Wednesday' is the time to stock up on big deals on selected items, while sales are frequent and popular. Items are boxed ready for you to assemble at home. Note that plastic bags now cost five cents.

**1635 West Broadway**
*Fairview*
*Map 9 A4* **48**

## Liberty

*604 682 7499* | *www.libertyinside.com*

For the classic traditionalist looking for exquisite chandeliers, wood fixtures and ornate mirrors, check out this exclusive shop. A classy sofa will set you back about $5,000, while a children's sleigh bed can be found for $2,200. Can't decide which table will match your living room decor? Ask the staff, who are experts at finding corresponding styles and colours. While you are there, pick up original artwork hand-picked for discerning tastes.

**1803 Commercial Dr**
*Grandview*
*Map 12 B1* **49**

## Wonderbucks

*604 253 0510* | *www.wonderbucks.com*

It's almost impossible to walk away from Wonderbucks without something fun in your hand. It sells funky knock-off furniture, lamps, kitchenware and basics, meaning you can revamp entire rooms for under $100. Although the store is large, staff are always

*Inform Interiors*

*Bernstein & Gold*

around to help you find something and it often feels more like an eccentric meeting place than a home decor store. Check out the hot ticket promotions each month, where a popular item is featured at a reduced price.

## Home Furnishings & Accessories

| | | | |
|---|---|---|---|
| Alexander Lamb Antiques | 3271 Main St | Main | 604 876 8713 |
| Antique Warehouse | 226 SW Marine Dr | SW Marine | 604 324 3661 |
| Bernstein & Gold | 100-1168 Hamilton St | Yaletown | 604 687 1535 |
| Country Furniture | 3097 Granville St | Fairview | 604 738 6411 |
| Folkart Interiors | 3651 West 10th Av | Point Grey | 604 731 7576 |
| Guild House Antiques Vancouver | 2121 Granville St | Fairview | 604 739 2141 |
| HomeSense | 1000 Main St | West Vancouver | 604 913 2990 |
| Industrial Revolution | 2306 Granville St | Fairview | 604 734 4395 |
| InForm Interiors | 50 Water St | Gastown | 604 682 3868 |
| INspiration Interiors For Home & Office | 1275 West 6th Av | Fairview | 604 730 1275 |
| Koolhaus Vancouver | 1 Water St | Gastown | 604 875 9004 |
| Liberty | 1635 West Broadway | Fairview | 604 682 7499 |
| Metal To Measure | 103-8410 Ontario St | SW Marine | 604 325 9117 |
| Modern Times Antiques | 4260 Main St | Main | 604 875 1057 |
| Oscar Grann's Furniture | 237 East 1st St | North Vancouver | 604 987 9833 |
| Peking Lounge | 83 East Pender St | Chinatown | 604 844 1559 |
| Pottery Barn | 2600 Granville St | Fairview | 604 678 9897 |
| Second Time Around Antiques | 4428 Main St | Main | 604 879 2313 |
| Sellution Vintage Furniture | 3206 Main St | Main | 604 876 4517 |
| The Antique Market | 4280 Main St | Main | 604 875 1434 |
| The Brick | 2999 Grandview Hwy | Renfrew Heights | 604 433 2000 |
| The Gourmet Warehouse | 1340 East Hastings St | Hastings East | 604 253 3022 |
| The Wood Co-op | 1592 Johnston St | Granville Island | 604 408 2553 |
| Williams-Sonoma | 2903 Granville St | Fairview | 604 330 2581 |

## Jewellery & Watches

All styles, types and prices of jewellery, from celebrated Tiffany & Co and Birks to local boutique Mukado Jewellery, can be found in Vancouver. Locals tend to wear semi-precious stones for formal occasions and costume or sparkling gems to go out. Prices here are reasonable compared to prices around the world and it's possible to find locally sourced diamonds from Canada's north. Canada is the third-largest diamond producer, after Botswana and Russia. With four mines in the Northwest Territories and Nunavut, Canada produces high-quality diamonds sourced without bloodshed – 15% of the world's supply. In order to

## Jewellery & Watches

| | | | |
|---|---|---|---|
| Birks | 698 West Hastings St | Downtown | 604 669 3333 |
| Blue Ruby Jewellery | Various Locations | www.blueruby.com | 604 899 2583 |
| Boutique Cartier | 456 Howe St | Downtown | 604 683 6878 |
| Edgemont Village Jeweller | 3102 Edgemont Blvd | North Vancouver | 604 985-1500 |
| Era Design | 1266 Homer St | Downtown | 604 688 2714 |
| Habsons Jewellers Supplies | 200-76 West 6th Av | Fairview | 604 708 9700 |
| Jeweliette | 692 Seymour St | Downtown | 604 687 5577 |
| Jewellery Artists 3D | 4485 West 10th Av | Point Grey | 604 272 0500 |
| Mizu Diamonds | 55-3195 Granville St | Shaughnessy | 604 681 5573 |
| Mukado Jewelery | 3288 Main Street | Main | 604 874 3887 |
| Object Design Gallery | 4–1551 Johnston St | Granville Island | 604 683 7763 |
| Ragnars Jewellery | 8038 Granville St | Shaughnessy | 604 261 0412 |
| Tara Jewellers | 720 Robson St | Downtown | 604 688 1244 |
| Tiffany & Co | 723 Burrard St | Downtown | 604 630 1300 |
| Time & Gold | 565 West Georgia St | Downtown | 604 683 1812 |

*Souvenirs*

make sure the 'ice' you're buying is Canadian, look for the government-certified logo or the official certificate stating its source. Visit Canada Diamonds (359-5525 West Boulevard, 604 618 6807) for the best selection of local gems. Blue Ruby sells $25 earrings, and you can find cheap jewellery at kiosks in the Oakridge Centre (p.415). Ragnars, Boutique Cartier and Habsons cater to higher end consumers, while Jeweliette and Era Design are for those looking for a boutique experience. Head over to Edgemont Village Jeweller for repairs, custom designs and cleaning. Mizu Diamonds also produces custom-made designs, as does Jewellery Artists 3D (by appointment only). Watches are available by all the well-known designer brands, but less expensive kinds and $10 bargains can be found at mall stands.

## Kids' Items

Other options **Clothes** p.374

Children's clothing and toys have become a big market in Vancouver, making it easy to find specific items. While stores such as Please Mum, Gap Kids (see p.376) and Toys R Us (see p.404) are the retailers that are often turned to, there are a number of smaller shops with fantastic toys, clothing and gifts. For a full day's treat, take the little ones to Kids Market (p.403) on Granville Island, which contains a play area, clothing, sweets and books; it's also a great place to find gifts for children of all ages.

Check out Beansprouts and Dandelion Kids for unique designs, while Modern Kid offers clothes for the most stylish kids on the block. Little feet can be fashionable too, with fancy footwear available from the popular Panda Shoes. If it's a costume you're after, Just Imagine is a great place to play at dressing up, while It's All Fun & Games offers an interactive environment for children so parents can pick out some cool toys. For pushchair repairs, head over to TJ's Kids for help.

| Kids' Clothes | | | |
| --- | --- | --- | --- |
| Beansprouts | 4305 Main St | Main | 604 871 9782 |
| Bobbit's For Kids | 2935 West 4th Av | Kitsilano | 604 738 0333 |
| Dandelion Kids | 1206 Commercial Dr | Grandview | 604 676 1862 |
| It's All Fun & Games | 1308 Commercial Dr | Grandview | 604 253 6727 |
| Just Imagine | 3060 West Broadway | Kitsilano | 604 222 3523 |
| Little Earth | 2643 East Hastings St | Hastings East | 778 737 7004 |
| Modern Kid | 45 Water St | Gastown | 604 662 3181 |
| Panda Shoes | 431-650 West 41st Av | Oakridge | 604 266 0025 |
| Please Mum | Various Locations | www.pleasemum.com | 604 732 4574 |
| TJ's Kids | 88 South West Marine Dr | SW Marine | 604 324 2888 |

# Lingerie

Other options **Clothes** p.374

Underneath Vancouverites' clothing you'll find a variety of styles: plain old cotton, silky satin, provocative lace or naughty fetish. For the latter, go to Dare to Wear (1028 Granville Street, 604 801 5482); otherwise play it safe at any department store (see p.409). The cheapest prices are found in the big box stores, although the selection is pretty basic. Boutiques that specialise in bras and underwear, and many department stores, will have staff that are trained to measure and fit you. Get the basic North American brands at branches of La Senza (604 678 8838, www.lasenza.com) and La Vie en Rose (604 684 5600, www.lavieenrose.com), or hunt down European labels at Scarlet.

## Agent Provocateur

*1026 Alberni St*
*Downtown*
*Map 7 E3* **50**

**604 258 7943** | www.agentprovocateur.com
If you're serious about having fun with lingerie and have the disposable cash to go the whole way, make a visit to this sleek store. Pushing the boundaries between exotic and erotic, the atmosphere of this UK import has women reeling and men speechless. It uses sexy window displays and lush boudoir-inspired interiors to encourage its visitors to go gaga over the garters, knickers, corsetry, shoes and beauty products. To kit yourself in the Francoise bra that Maggie Gyllenhaal models, be prepared to fork out over $165. Sign up online for the steamy monthly fanzine and at least take the opportunity to wander through this provocative store.

## Change

*2815 West Broadway*
*Kitsilano*
*Map 8 C4* **51**

**604 742 0557** | www.change.com
Change carries an array of lingerie, loungewear and swimwear all the way from Scandinavia. Sizes are a remarkable A to J cup, the widest range in the city. Its sports bra line conveniently caters to women of all sizes, a good option for those with a larger cup size. With adjustable straps, open mesh, a double band and high-tension microfibre material, the options help make being active a little easier. There's a new branch at 4416 West 10th Avenue (604 222 2287) and one in Park Royal Shopping Centre, West Vancouver (604 913 7792).

## Diane's Lingerie

*2950 Granville St*
*Fairview*
*Map 5 F1* **52**

**604 738 5121** | www.dianeslingerie.com
Personal care is the name of the game at Diane's. It is known as the place to be fitted for a bra – the expert staff will measure you correctly and help you find a comfortable and stylish choice. Options include bras for the busty, mums to be, active girls, post-surgery as well as eveningwear undergarments. The staff also regularly support the Canadian Breast Cancer Foundation by participating in the CIBC Run for Cure.

## Scarlet

*460 Granville Mall*
*Downtown*
*Map 7 F3* **53**

**604 605 1601** | www.scarletshop.com
Scarlet has probably the largest selection of lingerie for women in Vancouver. It carries designer names such as Betsey Johnson, Elle Macpherson and Hanky Panky. Staff know their brands and merchandise, making the experience a pleasure – and specialities include more than just lingerie. Books to tantalise, corsets to contour and scents to stimulate adorn the shop. If you're feeling insatiable, why not book the store for a private party? It's free, but of course the toys for sale are for adults only.

## Luggage & Leather

Vancouver has a few dedicated retailers and speciality stores for luggage and leather items. Reasonably priced luggage can be found at Zellers (p.410) and Bentley (p.375), while brand names such as Samsonite Black Label are sold at Holt Renfrew (p.410). Leather items are not as popular as they once were, although there are still a few shops that carry exceptional merchandise. The cost isn't cheap but the quality is high. All leather stores listed sell coats and trousers, as well as leather accessories. Danier can be found in Downtown Vancouver and West Vancouver, or head to the branch of Allyado Enterprises in Lonsdale Quay Market (p.408) for a wide variety of luggage, leather bags and wallets.

### Luggage & Leather

| | | | |
|---|---|---|---|
| Allyado Enterprises | Various Locations | www.allyado.com | 604 629 2268 |
| Danier | Various Locations | www.danier.com | 604 689 7330 |
| Kudos Leathergoods | 720 Alexander St | Gastown | 604 254 6900 |
| Marte's Fine Leather | 134-1055 West Georgia St | Downtown | 604 684 6424 |
| Roots | 1001 Robson St | Downtown | 604 683 4305 |
| The Original Leather Factory | 123-2323 Boundary Rd | Collingwood | 604 298 3770 |
| The Travel Bug | 3065 West Broadway | Kitsilano | 604 737 1122 |
| Vancouver Luggage Warehouse | 1014 Robson St | Downtown | 604 266 7679 |
| Wanderlust The Traveller's Store | 1929 West 4th Av | Kitsilano | 604 739 2182 |

## Maternity Items

There are some stylish mothers walking the streets of Vancouver, women who are no longer relegated to wearing baggy sweatshirts and shapeless dresses. Maternity fashion has hit an all-time high, and shops such as Belly & Beyond (p.367) provide not only cute clothing, but also practical items such as nursing wear that are also fashionable. Although the price range is a bit more expensive than ordinary clothing, there are still many affordable options, such as the maternity section at Gap (p.376), for all the basics. Hazel & Co has great service and a welcoming atmosphere, while Vie Maternity Boutique offers a more upmarket setting. Make your way to Thyme Maternity for standard styles such as black stretchy pants, and Motherhood for the best prices on wrap skirts and dresses. Although Jools is a regular fashion store, it has a growing selection of funky maternity styles.

### Maternity Items

| | | | |
|---|---|---|---|
| Hazel & Co | 3190 Cambie St | Cambie | 604 730 8689 |
| Jools | 4255 Dunbar St | Dunbar | 604 221 0721 |
| Motherhood | 2146-2148 West 4th Av | Kitsilano | 604 733 2644 |
| Thyme Maternity | 2119 West 4th Av | Kitsilano | 604 737 2229 |
| Vie Maternity Boutique | 102-1038 Hamilton St | Yaletown | 604 647 0281 |

## Medicine

Other options **General Medical Care** p.148

Medicine must be prescribed by your doctor, except for over-the-counter drugs for pain relief, medicine to reduce a fever, cough, cold and allergy medicine, laxatives and antacids. Pharmacists can give advice on medication but will usually refer you to your doctor for recommendations. You can purchase prescriptions at any pharmacy, which are found in all areas of the city. There isn't an exclusive relationship between pharmacies and insurance companies, so policies are valid in any branch. Most are standalone stores, meaning that they have pharmacists but are not attached to a

larger store like Shoppers Drug Mart (604 669 2424, www.shoppersdrugmart.ca).
Pharmacies can also be found in Zellers (p.410) and the Real Canadian Superstore
(p.417), while over-the-counter products can be bought in London Drugs (p.380). A
good independent company is Garlane Pharmacy, which has three locations: 232 East
Hastings Street, 4101 Main Street and 104-3380 Maquinna Drive. Call 604 873 3527 for
store hours.

## Mobile Phones
Other options **Telephone** p.142

As in other cities across the globe, mobile phones are fast replacing landlines in
Vancouver. Because of the inexpensive deals and fierce competition between
companies, customers can pick and choose between operators. They all offer one to
three year contracts that have fixed monthly fees and provide customers with a 'free'
phone. You can also opt for a pay-as-you-go plan in case you don't want to be tied in.
Hand over a set-up fee of around $50, purchase credit and simply pay for the minutes
you use.

| Mobile Phones | | | |
|---|---|---|---|
| CellCity | 105-950 West Broadway | Fairview | 604 656 2311 |
| Cellmart Commmications | 2691 West Broadway | Kitsilano | 604 736 1813 |
| Celtek | 208 Keefer St | Strathcona | 604 688 3883 |
| Go Wireless | 205-896 Cambie St | Downtown | 604 718 2929 |
| Staples Business Depot | 1322 West Broadway | Fairview | 604 678 9449 |
| The Source by Circuit City | 62 Seymour St | Downtown | 604 331 1402 |
| Wireless Wave | 650 West 41st Av | Oakridge | 604 261 3666 |

Although shopping
around is recommended,
you can buy from stores
such as Future Shop
(p.379), Best Buy (p.379)
or London Drugs (p.380).
Prices don't usually
fluctuate and most
offer similar deals, so
shopping directly from
the providers or from electronic stores yields the same prices. Mobile phone outlets are
spread throughout the city, with several branches in authorised stores and within malls
– accessories are sold at the same locations.

Phones typically come with a one-year manufacturer's warranty, and although some
family members pass their handsets down, there are few second-hand purchases. Sim
cards usually come with the purchase of a phone, but you can buy a new one for $25
or use the one you already have.

Check out www.cellphones.ca for honest opinions from consumers about phones,
brands, rates and operators of the basic services available in Vancouver. Note that
CellCity, Cellmart Communications, The Source by Circuit City, Staples Business Depot
and Wireless Wave are also found on the North Shore. The main branch of each
company has been listed in the table; to locate a store in your area check online or call.

## Music, DVDs & Videos
Local music and film addicts tend to shop at both the well-known megastores such as
Chapters (p.371) and HMV, as well as the fantastic local independent shops. Although the
download trend is on the up, many fans still frequent the shops to get hold of the real
CD or DVD and to support the local industry. Independent CD shops also sell live music
tickets and stay connected to the music scene through selling home-grown bands.
If you want to stock up on your music or movie collection, head to the large stores that
offer savings at peak shopping periods. Alternatively, find somewhere local and pick
up something different. They often stock the best collections of rare records and have
expert staff to help you out. If all else fails, head online to www.amazon.ca and have
your purchase shipped to your door. Prices vary and unless you buy enough to get free
shipping, it's usually cheaper to buy in store.

*819 Granville Mall*
*Downtown*
*Map 7 E4* **54**

## Charlie's Music City

*604 688 2500*

Centrally located on the corner of Robson and Granville, Charlie's is a must for used CDs, DVDs and video games. Two floors of retail space mean you can get lost in the old movies you forgot you loved, the 80s music you want to forget and the brand new box sets of your favourite TV shows. There is something for every taste, and decent prices to match: a second-hand DVD will set you back around $11.99. Also in store are celebrity posters and a currency exchange counter if you're still holding on to foreign money. Best of all, staff will take your old merchandise if it's in pristine condition and give you cash or store credit.

*4340 Main St*
*Main*
*Map 6 A2* **55**

## Cinephile Video

*604 876 3456*

A favourite of the Main Street hipsters, Cinephile has developed from a small rental space into a large supporter of local and international releases. This is where you can rent new films from all over the world for under $5 and older titles for less than $3. The local film-makers section is a treasure trove of interesting and extraordinary releases that you can borrow for free. Independent films are widely covered, as are box office hits from around the world. Get a membership, peruse the collection and cultivate your knowledge.

*432 West Hastings St*
*Downtown*
*Map 7 F3* **56**

## Sikora's Classical Records

*604 685 0625* | *www.sikorasclassical.com*

Classical music fans will enjoy this independent shop, which is filled with both popular and relatively unknown discs. The comprehensive selection of music is slightly overwhelming at first, but the simple layout, proficient staff and friendly atmosphere make calling in here worthwhile. Sikora's has been a Downtown staple for more than 25 years, and holds 25,000 classical CDs, tapes, DVDs, videos and books, as well as a second-hand collection of over 50,000 items. With music playing gracefully in the background, it's a great place for a lengthy browse.

*1855 West 4th Av*
*Kitsilano*
*Map 8 F3* **57**

## Videomatica

*604 734 0411* | *www.videomatica.bc.ca*

Film buffs rely on Videomatica to get their fix. Specialising in foreign films, classics and cult favourites, it has grown over the years to include every possible movie imaginable. It has also been voted 'best video store' by *Georgia Straight* readers; you'll be in film heaven. Not only does it rent and sell videos, it also has a large mail order rental system

| Music, DVDs & Videos | | | |
|---|---|---|---|
| A&B Sound | 556 Seymour St | Downtown | 604 687 5837 |
| | 15-935 Marine Dr | North Vancouver | 604 986 6200 |
| | 732 SW Marine Dr | South Cambie | 604 321 5112 |
| Audiopile | 2016 Commercial Dr | Grandview | 604 253 7453 |
| Black Dog Video | 3451 Cambie St | Cambie | 604 873 6958 |
| | 1470 Commercial Dr | Downtown | 604 251 3305 |
| Happy Bats Cinema | 198 East 15th Av | Main | 604 877 0666 |
| HMV | 788 Burrard St | Downtown | 604 669 2289 |
| | Park Royal North Mall | West Vancouver | 604 926 9711 |
| | Oakridge Centre | Downtown | 604 430 1660 |
| Limelight Video | 2505 Alma St | Point Grey | 604 228 1478 |
| Red Cat Records | 4307 Main St | Main | 604 708 9422 |
| Zulu Records | 1972 West 4th Av | Kitsilano | 604 738 3232 |

*Videomatica*

that delivers movies right to your door. For as little as $11.95 per month, you'll never have to leave the house again. The store also ships stock to collectors worldwide, which means you can send a great gift to your film buff friends across the globe.

## Musical Instruments

Other options
**Music Lessons** p.314,
**Music, DVDs & Videos** p.392

Tom Lee Music and Long & McQuade are the safest bet for music lovers looking to purchase an instrument. Both offer large retail spaces filled with a wide variety of instruments for beginners and pros, as well as prices that can't be beaten by smaller stores. Long & McQuade chain stores are located across Canada, and Tom Lee Music stores can be found throughout BC, providing lessons, rentals and repair services at all outlets. Head over to Westcoast Music if you want great advice, repairs or to rent a vintage instrument, while Commercial Drive accommodates Bone Rattle Music, selling electric guitars starting at $125. Basone Guitars makes customised electric guitars locally. A mahogany, hand-made selection will put you back $1,300. And if it's a grand piano that takes your fancy, Showcase Pianos is the exclusive dealership for Fazioli and Baldwin.

| Musical Instruments | | | |
|---|---|---|---|
| Basone Guitars | 310-2050 Scotia St | Mount Pleasant | 604 677 0311 |
| Bone Rattle Music | 2012 Commercial Dr | Grandview | 604 251 2663 |
| Long & McQuade | 3151 Arbutus St | Arbutus | 604 734 4886 |
| | 412 West Hastings St | Downtown | 604 682 5288 |
| Showcase Pianos | 1224 West Broadway | Fairview | 604 437 5161 |
| Tom Lee Music | 929 Granville St | Downtown | 604 685 8471 |
| Westcoast Music | 3454 West Broadway | Kitsilano | 604 682 4422 |

## Outdoor Goods

Other options **Sports Goods** p.401, **Hardware & DIY** p.384, **Camping** p.282

Make your way to West Broadway between Ontario and Cambie streets or the area around West 4th Avenue and Burrard Street for the biggest outdoor goods shops. The West Broadway stores sell a wide range of hiking, camping and fishing gear, while the shops along West 4th Avenue focus on clothing lines, skiing, snowboarding and skateboarding equipment. Staff are usually active themselves and will give you advice based on their own experience. Sport Mart and Sport Chek are good places to find mid-range hockey, racquet sports and fitness gear (see p.401). Shop in store or get it delivered for a fee; Mountain Equipment Co-op will ship purchases over $150 for free.

**2113 West 4th Av**
*Kitsilano*
*Map 8 E3* **58**

## lululemon athletica

*604 732 6111* | *www.lululemon.com*

If you want to look like a local, you'll need to get yourself a pair of original lululemon yoga pants. More than just a trend, lululemon is a must-have brand – you'll hear the name mentioned everywhere. Quality craftmanship and a commitment to well-being have turned this small clothing line into a world-famous name. The west coast love for staying active has led Vancouverites to look like they've just stepped out of a yoga class, whether that's true or not. Don't expect sales, even though a standard pair of trousers sells for about $100, as shoppers buy clothing, gear and accessories here year-round. Even if you don't plan to buy anything, a visit to the store to see what all the fuss is about is a must.

**130 West Broadway**
*Mount Pleasant*
*Map 11 A2* **59**

## Mountain Equipment Co-op

*604 872 7858* | *www.mec.ca*

Launched in 1971 by a six-member team of outdoor enthusiasts, Mountain Equipment has grown into the largest co-operative in Canada. Lifetime membership of the store is $5, which allows you to buy merchandise and vote in co-op meetings. Members are from around the globe and have grown to more than 2.6 million. Staff are members too; they don't sell on commission and therefore give out great advice. They aim to give you the best experience, whether it's suggesting a new brand or sending you to a neighbouring store. The co-op also believes in protecting the environment and has taken many steps towards lessening its carbon footprint, such as using organic materials, bio-degradable bags, garment recycling and donating to 'green' charities.

**102 West Broadway**
*Mount Pleasant*
*Map 11 A2* **60**

## Sports Junkies

*604 879 6000* | *www.sportsjunkies.com*

Sports Junkies is the most popular sports second-hand store as it's a place where you can find great deals on sporting equipment and clothing. The store runs the gamut of activities from baseball and camping to hockey and soccer. Regulars are kept up to date on the latest sales via email newsletters, and are quite happy to bring in their

*lululemon athletica*

*Mountain Equipment Co-op*

duds for new materials. You have the option of either selling your used equipment to the store for a set price or agreeing to receive 60% of the profit once it is resold. Almost everything is accepted except for bikes, hockey gear and golf equipment, which must be sold entirely to the store. Staff are knowledgeable and will make recommendations on everything you bring in. Along with ski and snowboard rentals and repairs, the shop also has a reputed bike repair service (see Bicycles, p.368).

## Outdoor Goods

| | | | |
|---|---|---|---|
| AJ Brooks Outdoor Outfitters | 147 West Broadway | Mount Pleasant | 604 874 1117 |
| Altus Mountain Gear | 137 West Broadway | Mount Pleasant | 604 876 6044 |
| Coast Mountain Sports | Various Locations | www.coastmountain.com | 1 877 977 2435 |
| Comor | 1980 Burrard St | Kitsilano | 604 736 7547 |
| Eco Outdoor Sports | 2136 West 4th Av | Kitsilano | 778 371 9845 |
| Europe Bound Travel Outfitters | 195 West Broadway | Mount Pleasant | 604 874 7456 |
| Nadex | 307 West Broadway | Fairview | 604 879 3728 |
| Pacific Boarder | 1793 West 4th Av | Kitsilano | 604 734 7245 |
| Sport Mart | 551 West Broadway | Fairviw | 604 873 6737 |
| Taiga Works | 301 West Broadway | Mount Pleasant | 604 875 8388 |
| Three Vets | 2200 Yukon St | Fairview | 604 872 5475 |
| Tilley Endurables | 2401 Granville St | Fairview | 604 732 4287 |
| Valhalla Pure Outfitters | 222 West Broadway | Mount Pleasant | 604 872 8872 |
| Westbeach | 1766 West 4th Av | Kitsilano | 604 732 6449 |

## Party Accessories

Other options **Party Organisers** p.478

Planning or attending a party is a piece of cake. Costumes, accessories and decorations are sold and rented from stores such as The Party Bazaar and Watts Costume Rentals, while The Balloon Shop has you covered for balloon bouquets, deliveries and set ups. You can even order a singing telegram for $105. Another cheap and fun way to decorate is to invade Dollar Giant. It has several stores across Vancouver (including one at 2533 East Hastings Street) where you can stock up on party bags, seasonal decorations and costume accessories. If you need help with the catering, try The Lazy Gourmet (604 734 2507, www.lazygourmet.ca) and The Butler Did It (604 739 3663, www.butlerdiditcatering.com) for all your food preparation.
Dairy Queen (604 876 1818, www.dairyqueen.com/ca) is the place to contact for icecream birthday cakes, or get a full-service birthday party with entertainers, bouncy castles and face painters with Par-T-Perfect (604 987 3365, www.par-t-perfect.com). If all you need are a few lively tunes to go alongside your disco ball, adults can hire a DJ by calling EchoWave DJ Service (604 813 7281, www.echowavepro.com) for a quote.

## Party Accessories

| | | | |
|---|---|---|---|
| Dollar Giant | Various Locations | www.dollargiant.com | 604 255 1008 |
| Lonsdale Events | 100-50 Fell Av | North Vancouver | 604 986 5651 |
| The Balloon Shop | 2407 Burrard St | Kitsilano | 604 684 0959 |
| The Party Bazaar | 215 West 2th Av | Fairview | 604 873 5241 |
| Watts Costume Rentals | 217 West 6th Av | Fairview | 604 876 5611 |

## Perfumes & Cosmetics

Try the major department stores (p.409) for the full range of well-known brands such as Yves Saint Laurent, Clinique and MAC Cosmetics. At the higher end of the scale is Holt Renfrew (p.410), supplying Burberry and Estee Lauder. A wider range of lines such as Gwen Stefani and Fantasy Britney Spears are carried at London Drugs (p.380) and Shoppers Drug Mart (p.392). Local spas sell a small collection of mid-range cosmetic products and fragrances (see p.349). Grooming ranges for men are provided by the specialist services at beautybar and Momentum (see p.376). For problem skin and ethnic complexions, a fairly wide range of products are available in most stores. For personal service on the North Shore, try Merle Norman Cosmetic Studio.

**103-1120 Hamilton St** ◄
*Yaletown*
*Map 9 E1* **61**

## Beautymark

*604 642 2294* | *www.beautymark.ca*

High-quality select brands are represented at Beautymark, and you're likely to find lines not sold at department stores, such as Child perfume, worn by Madonna and Jennifer Aniston, or the scented Art of Shaving cream that retails for $17. Customers range from makeup lovers to professional stylists, and staff are always happy to send shoppers home with samples. On top of cosmetics and fragrance, the store also holds makeup application classes and wedding consultations.

**1020 Robson St** ◄
*Downtown*
*Map 7 E2* **62**

## Lush

*604 687 5874* | *www.lush.com*

If hand-made cosmetics and items that are free from animal testing are your thing, take a peek into Lush. These stores are powerfully fragranced environments in which you'll find soaps, natural makeup, fresh fragrances and plenty of gifts. Perfumes come in cute containers called Karma or Go Green, and cosmetics are made from organic fruits and vegetables. Although most of Lush's products are unisex, all stores include a collection of products for men. There's another branch at 2248 West 4th Avenue (604 733 5874).

**226-757 West** ◄
**Hastings St**
*Downtown*
*Map 7 F3* **63**

## The Perfume Shoppe

*604 299 8463* | *www.theperfumeshoppe.com*

This is an expensive perfume store with exceptional service. The owner will go through a perfume profile with interested customers and recommend a scent that fits their style. Popular brands such as Teint de Neige, Psychotrope and Bois Blond are on sale, averaging around $125 for a 100 millilitre bottle. Niche perfumes are also available, as well as a few scented creams and nice gift packaging. Shopping through its website is easy and costs $5 to ship within Canada.

## Perfumes & Cosmetics

| | | | |
|---|---|---|---|
| beautybar | 2142 West 4th Av | Kitsilano | 604 733 9000 |
| Kiehl's | 100-1025 Robson St | Downtown | 604 408 4182 |
| L'Occitane en Provence | 3051 Granville St | Shaughnessy | 604 734 4441 |
| MAC Cosmetics | Various Locations | www.maccosmetics.com | 604 682 6588 |
| Merle Norman Cosmetic Studio | 935 Marine Dr | North Vancouver | 604 986 9912 |
| Shifeon | Various Locations | www.shifeon.com | 604 263 0708 |
| The Body Shop | Various Locations | www.thebodyshop.ca | 604 688 9777 |
| The Lip Lounge | 3628 Main St | Main | 778 330 6952 |

## Pets

Other options **Pets (Residents)** p.136

Cuddly cats and dashing dogs are a common addition to many households. Almost every neighbourhood has a veterinary clinic (see p.139). The BC Society for the Prevention of Cruelty to Animals (604 879 7721, www.spca.bc.ca) is the organisation from which most people adopt homeless cats, dogs, rabbits, guinea pigs and birds. Animals from here come with vaccinations, spayed or neutered, guaranteed health, a short bio about their history and a welcome info package. All new owners are required to fill out an application form and be interviewed by the organisation. The cost of a dog is $295 and a cat is $145 (not including taxes).

You can also buy animals from pet shops like Pet Habitat, where you can take them home right away. An annual vet visit is mandatory and you need to make sure all shots are done within the first three days. An annual licence is also required and can be obtained from City Hall for $35 to $65 (see p.138).

For that extra-special treat, discover the burgeoning pet bakeries dotted around the city. Owners here like to do more than just take their dogs out for a walk – they also like to buy organic food and healthy treats for their small family members. Favourites include Woofles & Meowz (also a toys and accessories store), and Three Dog Bakery.

## Pets

| | | | |
|---|---|---|---|
| Animal Wellness Natural Foods | 105 East Broadway | Mount Pleasant | 604 708 2327 |
| Barking Babies | 1188 Homer St | Downtown | 604 647 2275 |
| Bosley's | 3502 West 41st Av | Southlands | 604 266 2667 |
| | 1683 Davie St | West End | 604 688 4233 |
| | 6914 Victoria Dr | Knight Road | 604 327 3676 |
| Bow Wow Haus | 67 East Cordova | Gastown | 604 682 1899 |
| Pet Food 'N More | Various Locations | www.petfoodnmore.com | 604 980 0669 |
| Pet Habitat | Various Locations | www.pethabitat.com | 604 986 4812 |
| Petcetera | Park Royal South | West Vancouver | 604 913 1040 |
| | 2876 Rupert St | Renfrew Heights | 604 454 0600 |
| | 170-4255 Arbutus St | Quilchena | 604 733 9812 |
| Three Dog Bakery | 2186 West 4th Av | Kitsilano | 604 737 3647 |
| Tisol | 2738 Arbutus St | Arbutus | 604 730 1768 |
| | 2949 Main St | Main | 604 873 4117 |
| Woofles & Meowz | 1496 Cartwright St | Granville Island | 604 689 3647 |

## Second-Hand Items

Other options **Books** p.370

Vancouver has seriously taken to the second-hand movement. Along Main Street and Commercial Drive are countless second-hand stores, and those run by charities are located in every neighbourhood. You can buy an assortment of clothing, furniture, houseware, jewellery, books and baby items, some almost brand new. Trendy Vancouverites plunge into these shops for cheap finds and also donate to them regularly. Check out the Salvation Army (604 874 4721, www.thriftstore.ca), YWCA Thrift Shop (604 675 9996, 4399 Main Street) and Vancouver General Hospital Thrift Store (120 East Broadway, 604 876 3731).

## Second-Hand Items

| | | | |
|---|---|---|---|
| Changes | 4454 West 10th Av | Point Grey | 604 222 1505 |
| Cheapskates 1 Consignment Sporting Goods | 3644 West 16th Av | Dunbar | 604 222 1125 |
| Colette's Designer Consignment | 109 West 1th Av | North Vancouver | 604 984 3636 |
| Consignment Canada | 171 Pemberton Av | North Vancouver | 604 980 1110 |
| Deluxe Junk Company | 310 Cordova St | Gastown | 604 685 4871 |
| Front & Company | 3742-3746 Main St | Main | 604 879 8431 |
| Tanglewood Books | 2932 West Broadway | Kitsilano | 604 731 8870 |
| Temple Of The Modern Girl | 2695 Main St | Main | 604 630 8656 |
| Value Village | Various Locations | www.valuevillage.com | 604 254 4282 |

Secondhand Savvy (604 222 1945, www.secondhandsavvy. com) runs a 'second-hand safari' throughout the year, taking shoppers on themed trips around the city in search of antiques, home decor and clothing. It also has an online board for garage sales and other second-hand events, as does Used Vancouver (www.usedvancouver.com). Supermarkets, streetlamps and local newspapers also feature sales info, so keep your eyes peeled.

For the ultimate in thrift shopping, head to the many locations of Value Village to

*Robson Street shoes*

explore its warehouse-style stores filled with the good, the bad and the ugly. Sales are frequent and you can walk away with a vintage leather jacket for $50. At the other end of the scale, Changes, Deluxe Junk Company, Front & Company and Temple of the Modern Girl offer boutiques packed with consignment and new items that scream hip. Sports-minded folks can get used gear at Cheapskates 1 Consignment Sporting Goods and bookworms will unearth classics or popular culture at Tanglewood Books. North Shore residents can either visit the showroom or shop online at Consignment Canada, a large shop selling high quality antiques, collectibles and appliances. You can also acquire playful outfits at Colette's Designer Consignment.

## Shoes

Other options **Clothes** p.374, **Sports Goods** p.401, **Beachwear** p.367

Like clothing, shoe shops are widespread throughout the city and come in as many varieties as there are tastes. Head to department stores (p.409) for well-made casual shoes and designer brands, or you can hit the boutiques. All stores cover both male and female styles and accessories, while children's selections are usually found at speciality shops such as Panda Shoes (p.389). There are many stores Downtown on Granville Street, starting at Robson Street and heading south a few blocks. Otherwise, speciality shops are spread far and wide. You'll find experienced staff at Lords, chic lines at Umeboshi and boots for the rain at the Australian Boot Company. As most stores don't do repairs, it's best to find the neighbourhood cobbler, such as Quick Cobbler at 430 West 2nd Avenue (604 682 6354). Big sales can almost always be found at Aldo Liquidation, but for an even better option head to Rino's Shoes where you can customise your own. The main outlets for each store are listed in the table, but many have several branches around Vancouver, so check online for the nearest one to you.

**2675 Granville St**
*Fairview*
*Map 9 B4* 64

### ecco

*604 734 3223 | www.ecco.com*

An assortment of casual, business and sports shoes for men, women and children can be found here. The company's commitment to comfort means that no matter what the style, you can count on happy feet. Accessories include socks, inlays, handbags, business bags and enough cleaning products to keep your new purchases in good condition. The large collection for children and infants makes this a good spot for the whole family.

**837 Granville Mall**
*Downtown*
*Map 7 E4* **65**

## Fluevog Shoes

*604 688 2828* | *www.fluevog.com*

*Fluevog Shoes*

You may be lucky enough to run into a celebrity at Fluevog – stars including Marilyn Manson have been known to buy footwear here. Even if you don't, you'll find a beautifully adorned shop with quirky, hand-made shoes that border on eccentric. New to the mix are Veggie Vogs and Earth Angel, which are eco-friendly lines. Although the innovative designs have high prices to match, such as the women's black pumps at $359, you may be able to restore or resole some lines by purchasing replacement parts.

**2205 West 4th Av**
*Kitsilano*
*Map 8 E3* **66**

## Gravitypope

*604 731 7673* | *www.gravitypope.com*

This ultra-stylish boutique carries a large range of designer footwear for men, women and children. Favourites include Betsey Johnson, Angeli Inquieti and Michael Kors, as well as sporty Reebok, Puma and Converse. Prices aren't cheap, but run parallel to the quality; a pair of Bronx heels averages $135, and Goliaths for men hover at $140. Head next door to the new Gravitypope tailored goods store for independent lines from North America and Europe, which will complement whichever shoes you choose.

| Shoes | | | |
|---|---|---|---|
| Aldo | 1025 Robson St | Downtown | 604 683 2443 |
| Aldo Liquidation | 810 Granville St | Downtown | 604 605 8939 |
| Australian Boot Co | 1968 West 4th Av | Kitsilano | 604 738 2668 |
| Feetfirst Shoes | 1025 Robson St | Downtown | 604 683 1724 |
| Foot Locker | Various Locations | www.footlocker.com | 604 608 1804 |
| Freedman Shoes | 2867 Granville St | Fairview | 604 731 0448 |
| Ingledew's Shoes | 535 Granville St | Downtown | 604 687 8606 |
| Joneve | 2871 West Broadway | Kitsilano | 604 732 6133 |
| Lords | 2932 Granville St | Fairview | 604 730 2914 |
| Pegabo | 1137 Robson St | Downtown | 604 688 7877 |
| Rino's Shoes | 75 West Broadway | Mount Pleasant | 604 876 5316 |
| Ronsons | 2144 West 4th Av | Kitsilano | 604 731 1244 |
| Stephane de Raucourt | 1067 Robson St | Downtown | 604 681 8814 |
| Sterling Shoes | 640 Granville St | Downtown | 604 683 4498 |
| Stone Ridge | 1049 Robson St | Downtown | 778 328 9757 |
| Umeboshi | 3638 Main St | Main | 604 909 8225 |

## Souvenirs

Finding a souvenir that represents the west coast isn't difficult. The city abounds with crafts made by artisans, together with native carvings, stuffed moose, and of course the usual Royal Canadian Mounted Police themed gadgets. For all of the above, walk down Water Street in Gastown from Richards to Carrall. Otherwise, souvenir shops are spread around different areas, in museum gift shops, malls, the airport and some hotels. The least tacky are sold at museums and other city attractions, although Water Street has souvenirs that are equally silly and easy on the wallet. On Robson Street between Howe and Hornby, check out the artisans selling their hand-crafted native designs. Gifts and non-perishable items can be put into your packed luggage without a problem.

| Souvenirs | | | |
| --- | --- | --- | --- |
| Canadian Mementos | 1205-1955 Haro St | West End | 604 609 6639 |
| Clamshell Gift Shop | Vancouver Aquarium | Stanley Park | 604 659 3413 |
| Gallery Store | Vancouver Art Gallery | Downtown | 604 662 4706 |
| The Garden Shop | VanDusen Gardens | Shaughnessy | 604 257 8665 |
| Prospect Point Lookout Complex | 5601 Stanley Park Dr | Stanley Park | 604 669 2737 |

## Sports Goods
Other options **Outdoor Goods** p.394

Finding sports gear is easy in active Vancouver. Head to Sport Chek or Sport Mart, the largest sports store chains in Canada, for a good assortment of athletic shoes and clothing, as well as basics such as footballs, studded boots and even a full range of fitness equipment and free weights. Exercise equipment can be purchased at department stores for reasonable prices, or try Fitness Town for mid to high-range products, such as treadmills starting at $950. If you're in the suburbs, visit Athletes World in most malls for branded workout clothes and sports shoes. A hop over to North Vancouver for hockey and inline skating equipment is worth the effort just for the opportunity to talk to the expert staff at Larry's Sports. A standard soccer ball goes for $19.99 and a pair of 20 pound dumbbells usually costs $29.99. Second-hand baseball gloves, tennis racquets and golf gear can be found at Sports Junkies (see

*Souvenirs*

p.395). See the Outdoor Goods section (p.394) for a large range of outdoor sporting equipment and accessories. A selection of branches have been listed below; for more information on other locations check the relevant website.

| Sports Goods | | | |
| --- | --- | --- | --- |
| Athletes World | 4700 Kingsway | Burnaby | 604 435 7437 |
| Fitness Town | Various Locations | www.fitnesstown.ca | 604 739 8184 |
| Larry's Sports | 2029 Lonsdale Av | North Vancouver | 604 987 6630 |
| Sport Chek | Various Locations | www.sportcheck.ca | 604 874 6530 |
| Sport Mart | 551 West Broadway | Fairview | 604 873 6737 |

## Stationery

Paper supplies are cheap and easy to find at large chains such as Staples Business Depot and Office Depot, with various locations around town (main outlets are listed below – check for your nearest branch). You can gather all you need to kit out a home office with a few extras such as a photocopier. Customer service is cheerful but not always the most knowledgeable. These shops cater to both small businesses and personal use. Also listed here are speciality shops where you will find unique products with more style and a higher price tag. A set of custom designed invitations will cost $2.75 to $6 per card at appointment-only paperqueen, while a Japanese calligraphy paper pack will cost about $7.75.

| Stationery | | | |
| --- | --- | --- | --- |
| Office Depot | 310 West Broadway | Fairview | 604 879 5955 |
| Paper Parade | 283-650 West 41st Av | Oakridge | 604 266 5501 |
| paperqueen fine stationery | www.thepaperqueen.com | na | 604 926 6606 |
| Staples Business Depot | 1322 West Broadway | Fairview | 604 678 9449 |
| The Original Paper-Ya Co | 9-1666 Johnston St | Granville Island | 604 684 2531 |
| zing Paperie & Design | 60-323 Jervis St | West End | 604 630 1885 |

◀ Top Tailors

*The best way to find a good tailor is to ask your neighbour or friends; most people stick with the same one for years and will happily recommend them. Bringing your own fabric is an option and will also save you money – ask your tailor for more information.*

## Tailoring

Other options **Clothes** p.374, **Tailors** p.132, **Textiles** p.403

There are countless tailoring shops littered throughout the city. Locals use their services for alterations, custom-made designs, weddings and specific measurements. Dunn's Tailors and Tip Top Tailors are two of the largest companies and offer a range of casual and formal attire, as well as having a free club for private sales. All you have to do is sign up online to receive sales, promotions and special events emails.

Steve Samson's tailor-made shirts and suits are preferred for those wanting a personalised service. Prices vary from shop to shop and depending on the scope of work to be done, although having a pattern and solid idea of what you want will speed up the process and lower the price. A made-to-measure, high-quality suit will set you back an average of $900, including fabric, labour and fittings.

| Tailoring | | | |
| --- | --- | --- | --- |
| Angelo Tailors | 1501 Commercial Dr | Grandview | 604 253 7633 |
| Ben's Custom Tailors | 6482 Fraser St | Fraser | 604 322 9782 |
| Dunn's Tailors | 480 Granville St | Downtown | 604 681 2836 |
| Johnny's European Tailors | 3258 West Broadway | Kitsilano | 604 734 4748 |
| Kerrisdale Custom Tailors | 2082 West 41st Av | Kerrisdale | 604 266 6422 |
| Olympia Tailors | 2425 East Hastings St | Hastings East | 604 253 4481 |
| Steve Samson | 1240 Seymour St | Downtown | 604 682 7848 |
| Tip Top Tailors | Pacific Centre | Downtown | 604 684 8021 |
| Tozzi Tailors | 102-229 Lonsdale Av | North Vancouver | 604 987 8430 |

## Textiles

Other options **Tailoring** p.402, **Souvenirs** p.400

There are some fantastic fabric stores in Vancouver, overflowing with unique designs at reasonable prices. Materials are sold at a set price per metre (some still measure by the yard) and vary widely depending on quality and design. You can get deals from $2.95 per metre for cotton prints up to $10.95 per metre or more for wool flannel and other home furnishing materials. Fabrictime sells at wholesale prices if you're buying over 20 metres. The best places to find good deals all year round are Dressew Supply, Textile Clearance House and Atex Fabrics, all of which offer huge showrooms crammed with fabric and sewing supplies. Head to The Natural Textile Company and Clothworks of Vancouver for quality home furnishing materials, or Rokko's Fabrics for sarees and exquisite cloths. The only single area selling fabrics is the Punjabi Market on Main Street between East 48th and 51st avenues, where you will find some wonderful materials to haggle for. Whether you're looking for special fabric for a wedding dress or simple material for drapes, make the trip out to Fabricana in Coquitlam and Richmond for expert staff and a huge selection.

| Textiles | | | |
|---|---|---|---|
| Atex Fabrics | 150 West Hastings St | Downtown | 604 669 3455 |
| Clothworks of Vancouver | 2962 West 29th Av | Downtown | 604 263 4493 |
| Dressew Supply | 337 West Hastings St | Downtown | 604 682 6196 |
| Fabricana | Various Locations | www.fabricana.com | 604 273 5316 |
| Fabricland | 1678 SE Marine Dr | Victoria | 604 321 1848 |
| Fabrictime | 1325 East Pender St | Strathcona | 604 630 0822 |
| Jax Fashion Fabrics | 316 West Cordova St | Gastown | 604 684 7004 |
| Performance Textiles | 203-2030 Marine Dr | North Vancouver | 604 990 4415 |
| Rokko's Fabrics | 6201 Fraser St | Fraser | 604 327 3033 |
| Textile Clearance House | 5550 Fraser St | Fraser | 604 321 7188 |
| The Natural Textile Co | 2571 West Broadway | Kitsilano | 604 736 2101 |

## Toys & Games

Other options **Kids' Items** p.389

The behemoth of all toy shops is Toys R Us, the shop where kids rule and parents throw down their credit cards. Price examples include $29.95 for a toy lawnmower and $14.99 for a Play-Doh set. Computer and video games for kids and adults can be found at EB Games, a huge company with stores all over the world, and A-Z Video Games, a busy store for those who want to buy, sell or trade titles. The large warehouse stores such as Future Shop and Best Buy (p.379) also have a selection of games. For hand-made toys and old-fashioned wooden models, be sure to visit Knotty Toys, Kaboodles Toy Store and Voltage, as well as Toy Jungle in North Vancouver.

### Kids Market

*1496 Cartwright St*
*Granville Island*
*Map 9 B2* 67

**604 689 8447** | *www.kidsmarket.ca*
This mini mall accommodates 28 boutiques selling everything from novelty candy to wooden toys, and features a childproof arcade and playground. What's more, there's a pond outside for kids to play around in, as well as a water park. This place is always a kid pleaser as the employees make the atmosphere fun. It's practical for parents too, because shops such as the Granville Island Toy Company take care of toys, while the Hairloft caters to family haircuts, ear piercing and children's parties.

### Knotty Toys

*1496 Cartwright St*
*Granville Island*
*Map 9 B2* 68

**604 683 7854** | *www.knottytoys.com*
You'll find a large selection of old-fashioned treasures such as wooden toys, building sets and traditional hand-made blocks at Knotty Toys. What began as an idea in a family

garage has turned Into a wonderfully imaginative enterprise. You'll find dolls' houses, puzzles, musical instruments, wooden swords and shields, and the Rolli-Rider (a hand-crafted, primitive bike made in the US). The store carries its own line of toys called Buzz Woodcrafts, which consist of about 30 different wooden toys designed by the owners.

## Toys & Games

| A–Z Video Games | 748 East Broadway | Mount Pleasant | 604 874 3919 |
|---|---|---|---|
| EB Games | Oakridge Centre | Oakridge | 604 263 3745 |
| Kaboodles Toy Store | 1496 Cartwright St | Granville Island | 604 684 0066 |
| | 4449 West 10th Av | Kitsilano | 604 224 5311 |
| Toy Jungle | 2022 Park Royal South | North Vancouver | 604 925 0741 |
| Toys R Us | 1154-1174 West Broadway | Fairview | 604 733 8697 |
| Voltage | 4346 Main St | Main | 604 709 8214 |

## Wedding Items

Whether you want a tailor-made dress and shoes or you need someone to plan the whole event for you, there are plenty of services in Vancouver to help. Visit the Vancouver Wedding Show (www.vancouverweddingshow.ca) in spring or autumn for ideas and big prizes, or contact Sweet Beginnings Wedding Consulting & Event Planners (604 738 9552, www.asweetbeginning.com) to make personalised arrangements for you. Gift registries are usually set up at The Bay or Sears (p.410) department stores and overseas guests can purchase items online to be picked up once they arrive.

Dresses can be personalised or made from scratch at shops such as Clara Couture and Manuel Mendoza, the latter with a price starting at around $1,500. There are small clusters of great stores on East Hastings Street around Chantilly Bridal, and also around Bliss Consignment Bridal in New Westminster. Shoes are often bought at regular shoe outlets (see p.399), although you can dye them to match your dress at Charm Wedding & Evening Design.

For full makeup and photography services, try Bello Wedding World. The wedding party can find their own formal wear at Perfecto Formal Wear, while men can rent suits at Black & Lee. The Tux Store, Dunn's Tailors (see p.402) and Tip Top Tailors (see p.402) are great places to rent a tux. On the North Shore, try The Mensroom, a boutique store with a small but classy selection of formal wear. Tailor-made suits average about $1,000 and shirts can be ordered within a week.

For all your invitation and stationery needs, buy your own templates at Staples Business Depot or have classy ones made by a speciality store (see Stationery, p.402). The ultimate cake can be found at Anna's Cake House (p.382), where you can customise your own, buy from its large selection, or do a little bit of both.

## Wedding Items

| Bello Wedding World | 3207 Main St | Main | 604 872 1245 |
|---|---|---|---|
| Bliss Consignment Bridal | 710 Columbia St | New Westminster | 604 522 6930 |
| Black & Lee | 1110 Seymour St | Downtown | 604 688 2481 |
| Chantilly Bridal | 3660 East Hastings St | Hastings East | 604 299 0888 |
| Charm Wedding & Evening Design | 3673 East Hastings St | Hastings East | 604 205 7362 |
| Clara Couture | 2423 Burrard St | Downtown | 604 730 9378 |
| Manuel Mendoza | 692 Seymour St | Downtown | 604 681 0183 |
| Perfecto Formal Wear | 3674 East Hastings St | Burnaby | 604 291 0331 |
| Sandra Sung Bridal | 863 Hamilton St | Yaletown | 604 602 8989 |
| The Mensroom | 1411 Bellevue Av | West Vancouver | 604 925 1812 |
| The Tux Store | 926 West Broadway | Fairview | 604 732 5868 |

# Small but indispensable…

Perfectly proportioned to fit in your pocket, this marvellous mini guidebook makes sure you don't just get the holiday you paid for but rather the one that you dreamed of.

**Vancouver Mini Visitors' Guide**
Maximising your holiday, minimising your hand luggage

## Places To Shop

For bargain hunters and bulk shoppers, boutique seekers and one-of-a-kind fashionistas, Vancouver is a playground with plenty of options. Neighbourhoods are distinct from each other in terms of the types of shop they feature and the level of service, while malls and supermarkets offer a one-stop shop for everything you can think of.

## Areas To Shop

Vancouver can be conveniently split into shopping districts that have developed their own style, attracting similar stores. Robson Street is well known for its high fashion and its tourists, Main Street is the hub of local designers, and Commercial Drive is a haven for organic and cultural food. Head to Chinatown for inexpensive knick-knacks and Gastown for unique styles for your home. Kitsilano is the best place to kit yourself out with trendy yogawear, and Yaletown charms its visitors with brick warehouses filled with designer creations. You can also visit Granville Island for its market and fresh foods.

*Map 7 E4* ◀ *Granville Street*

When you head into Downtown, you'll most likely find yourself somewhere along Granville Street, the main north-south thoroughfare. The north end of the street up to West Georgia is home to well-known names such as Buffalo and Parasuco. Walking south, you'll run into Pacific Centre mall (p.416), The Bay and Sears (p.410) on one side of the street and accessory stores and boutiques on the other. These few blocks are under heavy construction due to the building of the new Canada Line with work planned until late 2008, but all stores are still accessible. Keep going and you'll pass Robson Street, after which more boutiques including John Fluevog Shoes (p.400), Aldo Liquidation (p.400) and Golden Age Collectables (p.412) are located. Once you pass Nelson Street, it's mainly cheap pizza places and grungy storefronts mixed with trendy new restaurants, but keep an eye out for new store openings.

*Map 7 B1* ◀ *Robson Street*

Designer names, quality clothing and high price tags bombard you on this street. This is where you'll find celebrities and tourists mixing with locals with lots of disposable income. Robson is always busy with shoppers, people talking on their mobile phones and plenty of traffic. The three main blocks are between Hornby and Bute streets, which are filled with fashion brands like Shifeon, Esprit, A/X Armani Exchange and Tommy Hilfiger, and a couple of optical stores. Heading further west, you'll encounter hotels, gift shops, luggage stores and currency exchanges. There are many cafes, fine dining restaurants and sushi joints along this street, so spending the day walking its length is not uncommon.

*Map 10 A1* ◀ *Gastown*

Check out the one-of-a-kind boutiques, antique shops and souvenirs in historic Gastown while walking down its cobbled streets. Native art galleries such as the Marion Scott Gallery (p.223), Coastal Peoples Fine Art Gallery (p.365) and Hill's Native Art (165 Water Street, 604 685 4249) have congregated here. You'll find souvenir shops (p.400) for tourists (think tacky moose in a can), and contemporary funiture in stores like Inform Interiors (50 Water Street, 604 682 3868). It's also a ripe area for new and unique fashion. Around the 300 block of Cordova Street at Cambie are local designers, young entrepreneurs and eclectic styles. Shops such as the Deluxe Junk Company (p.398), Richard Kidd (65 Water Street, 604 677 1880) and New World Designs (306 West Cordova Street, 604 687 3443) always have something original, while Ric Yuenn will make you a gorgeous tailor-made gown (315 West Cordova Street, 604 685 8373).

# Places To Shop

*Map 9 E1*
## Yaletown

This small area mixes industrial history with renovated brick warehouses containing uber-trendy lounges and stores. Price points rise substantially here, as celebrities walk among the locals. Niche labels fill the boutique's shelves, while showrooms display ultra-chic furniture to match the neighbouring condos. Street parking is almost impossible to find, so don't waste your time. Slide into the carpark off Davie Street and Mainland, or cross Pacific Boulevard and use the Roundhouse Community Centre's underground carpark. The one community bus in the area is the number C21, but the numbers 6 and 50 stop within a block of Yaletown.

*Map 10 C2*
## Main Street

This area is branded as up and coming, but locals know that the best shops have already arrived. Mix the young artistic professionals with hip boutiques and you have a thriving, eclectic neighbourhood. Start at East 7th Avenue and make your way up to 29th Avenue for local designers, Antique Row (p.386), independent music shops and lots of second-hand choices. Restaurants are fantastic and well priced, so be sure to stay long enough to have a bite to eat. Parking is metered along Main Street, although you can usually find a spot on one of the side streets. Transportation is covered by the number 3 bus which runs every six to 10 minutes daily.

Fluevog Shoes

Yaletown

Robson Street

Club Monaco

**Map 6 B1** ◀ *Commercial Drive*

Affectionately called 'The Drive,' expect funky shop windows and an absence of big box stores. The community is strong and consists of a high percentage of Italian and Portuguese residents, making it one of the most interesting places to eat in the city. You'll also find the neighbourhood cinema and a small theatre space for local companies (see p.477). Shops include vintage clothing, cheap houseware, ethnic decor and unique gifts. Street parking is metered and half of the side streets are strictly for residents – watch out for the 'permit only' sections; visitors should park across the street. The number 20 bus runs along the length of The Drive, although during rush hour it's unfeasibly crowded.

**Map 8 D4** ◀ *Kitsilano*

Kitsilano has shed its hippie image for its new yuppie status. With more than 300 shops to leisurely stroll through, the streets are filled with young professionals with money to spend and young students who pay a high price to live the beach bum life. Yoga retailer lululemon athletica (p.395) has spurred a significant yoga wear industry along West 4th Avenue. As well as hip eateries, you'll find stylish hair salons, travel shops, designer baby items and health food. Parking along West 4th and West Broadway is metered and can be hit and miss; side streets are half reserved for permit holders. Buses number 4, 7 and the 84 express run along West 4th, while the number 9 and express 99 buses cover West Broadway.

**Map 5 E3** ◀ *Kerrisdale Village*

A 15 minute drive from Downtown Vancouver, Kerrisdale Village is a wonderful area to while away the day. With brick-paved walkways, a European feel and classy boutique shops, locals who live nearby often get everything they need in 'The Village.' Most of the shops have been around for many years, with the owners developing personal relationships with regulars. The stores are at the higher end of the scale and sell one-of-a-kind pieces rather than mass-produced items. With streets and pavements that are kept clean and tidy, this is a nice neighbourhood for a day out with the family.

**Map 4 A3** ◀ *Lonsdale Quay Market & Shops*

A short trip across the Burrard Inlet, Lonsdale Quay (www.lonsdalequay.com) on the North Shore is a lively daytrip from Downtown Vancouver. It has more than 90 different shops covering clothing, fresh food, speciality stores and florists. On top of those boutiques are a shiatsu parlour, Flight Centre and banks. Monthly events at the Quay include street sales and community benefits. The biggest hit is the food market, with fresh produce, speciality goods and an aromatic setting. The easiest way to get there is by a 15 minute SeaBus ride from Downtown. By car, cross the Lions Gate Bridge and head east, or over the Second Narrows Ironworkers

*Lonsdale Quay Market*

Memorial Bridge and head west until you reach Lonsdale Avenue. Make your way south to the edge of the water and you can't miss it.

**Map 2 A3**

### Steveston Village

Often overlooked, Steveston Village offers a quaint shopping experience just outside of the big city. Located in Richmond, south of Vancouver, this area is worth a trip to soak up the old-world atmosphere. Here you'll find the remnants of

*Steveston fish sales*

a historic fishing village that has kept a lot of its charm – think picturesque small-town appeal. The small shops are housed in historic buildings and sell everything from fresh flowers and deli products to children's toys and interesting souvenirs. If you become enamoured with the scenery, check into one of the many day spas to prolong your trip. From Vancouver, head south over the Arthur Lang Bridge and then merge right onto Russ Baker Way. You'll cross the Steveston Highway and stop at the Moncton Street intersection. Turn right and drive straight into the village.

## Department Stores

The Bay, Sears and Zellers top the list for department stores across North America that have stood the test of time. In addition to their Downtown flagship stores, you can find these stores in almost every mall in the city. The most well-known department store historically is Woodward's, a legendary building on West Cordova Street with a big red 'W' that was a retail giant in its glory days. Today, it's being redeveloped into a controversial condominium project. On top of finding almost anything in a department store, from underwear to flat-screen TVs, there are also restaurants, cafes, dry cleaning and alteration services. If you're buying appliances, home furnishings or any other expensive items, it is a good idea to do a price check – competition is high and most have a price-match policy that ensures you get a good deal. The stores have varying delivery or set-up services, and most offer a range of financing options and their own credit card.

### Wood You Believe It

Woodward's, one of Vancouver's most famous department stores, closed in 1993 after 90 years, but the heritage building it occupied Downtown is still a major talking point. After being sold to various developers, part of the building was demolished in 2006 to be rebuilt as a multipurpose venue incorporating apartments, offices, shops and community spaces. The original facade, however, remains, and once complete, the store's famous big red letter W will be reinstalled.

**36 West Cordova St**
*Gastown*
**Map 10 B1 69**

### Army & Navy

**604 682 6644** | *www.armyandnavy.ca*

A Vancouver oldie, Army & Navy has been dealing out low prices in the Downtown Eastside since 1919. Nicknamed 'Canada's original discount store,' it has now moved on to sell current fashion, home decor, home and bath supplies, groceries, outdoor goods and a whole room full of shoes. You can snag curtain panels for $14.99 or a fleece hoody for $19.99. Note that its annual shoe sale in April is mayhem, but designer brands start at $9.99. Doors open at 08:00 and queues are the norm.

**674 Granville Mall**
*Downtown*
*Map 7 E3* **70**

## The Bay

*604 681 6211 | www.hbc.com/bay*

Created to capitalise on the new fur trade in Canada in 1670, the Hudson's Bay Company has been an integral part of the country's history ever since. By 1912, the company had transformed into a retailer when fur trading diminished, and The Bay is one of its most recognised outlets. The department store now sells designer clothes and shoes, name brand fragrances and makeup, accessories and home furnishings in the mid to upper price range. Its gift registry is an easy way to set up wedding lists or shower gifts, and there is an HBC rewards system that accumulates points with every purchase – it's worth having that extra card in your wallet if you're a Bay regular. When you're exhausted from shopping, quench your thirst or ease your hunger on the third floor restaurant or sixth floor cafeteria.

**798 Granville Mall**
*Downtown*
*Map 7 E4* **71**

## Canadian Winners

*604 683 1058 | www.winners.ca*

Although not quite matching The Bay or Sears in terms of variety of name brands and product lines, the prices at Canadian Winners are sometimes 60% lower than elsewhere. It carries clothes for men and women as well as children's clothing, shoes, accessories and jewellery, plus home decor from its sister store, Homesense (604 913 2990, www.homesense.ca). There are branches of both companies in North and West Vancouver, Burnaby and Richmond.

**737 Dunsmuir St**
*Downtown*
*Map 7 F3* **72**

## Holt Renfrew

*604 681 3121 | www.holtrenfrew.com*

At the other end of the discount store spectrum from Canadian Winners is Holt Renfrew, which offers a range of premium brand names for those who like to indulge. First opened as a hat shop in 1837, the company then added fine furs to the business before branching out to high fashion for both men and women. These days, it's considered a leader in the world of fashion, offering styles from around the globe, as well as cosmetics, fragrances and concierge and personal shopping services. Check the website for regular events, such as product launches, makeup classes and charity events.

**701 Granville Mall**
*Downtown*
*Map 7 E3* **73**

## Sears

*604 685 7112 | www.sears.ca*

The second-largest national department store, Sears has many unique features. As well as selling fashion, accessories, home appliances, furnishings and electronics, the store also has a travel centre for vacations, renovation services, flower arrangements, a portrait studio, repair services and many more, all of which are conducted by skilled professionals. Visit the outlet store in Burnaby (9850 Austin Road, 604 421 0757) for surplus stock and great deals.

**650 West 41st Av**
*Oakridge*
*Map 5 F3* **74**

## Zellers

*604 261 6234 | www.hbc.com/zellers*

Like The Bay, Zellers is owned by the Hudson's Bay Company. Its focus is on consistently lower prices with less of a designer influence. You will find stylish clothing for all ages, school supplies, toys, accessories, luggage, electronics and home furnishings. There's also a pharmacy in the Vancouver location that will complete prescriptions while you shop. The store is set to introduce higher quality and more popular merchandise to its inventory, including Stuff by Duff, Alfred Sung Home and Cherokee brands. The grocery area carries lots of treats, packaged foods and snacks.

# Places To Shop

The Bay

Holt Renfrew

Zellers

Sears

## Independent Shops

There are a few independent stores that are top picks and deserve a special mention. The most up-and-coming independent fashion boutiques are opening along south Main Street, but also keep an eye out in Gastown. West 4th Avenue is a hotbed of local entrepreneurs concentrating on baby, kids' and maternity items, while Commercial Drive continues to evolve with an interesting variety of shops. Vancouver is packed full of enterprising residents opening up shop, so keep your eyes peeled for the newest stores.

**7860 Alderbridge Way**
*Richmond*
*Map 2 B3*

### Galloway's

*604 270 6363* | *www.gallowaysfoods.com*

With everything you need to buy available at your fingertips in the city, there are not many reasons to leave Vancouver – but Galloway's is the exception to the rule, providing city dwellers with natural food worth the trip to Richmond. In order to save on commercial packaging, the store sells its products in bulk, making this the perfect place to fill gift baskets for your friends. Large families or solitary roamers alike can enjoy shopping for dried fruits, nuts, spices and many varieties of rice. Delicious aromas waft into the walkways, making the store not only a place for regulars but also an interesting stop for those intrigued by tantalising smells. With about 10,000 square feet of retail space, it's hard to leave without buying a few of your favourite treats.

**852 Granville St**
*Downtown*
*Map 7 E4* **76**

### Golden Age Collectables

*604 683 2819*

Visit Golden Age Collectables for a trip back in time. Most items hail from the 1920s onwards and include posters, sports cards, comics, movie memorabilia, Manga magazines and graphic novels. This is probably the largest collection of such a variety in the whole Lower Mainland. Although packed with interesting eye candy, the layout is tidy and items simply categorised. Ask the staff if you have any questions about finding something in particular, they offer lots of information about the business of collecting.

**152 East 8th Av**
*Main*
*Map 11 B2* **77**

### Scout

*604 879 7903* | *scout152e8th@hotmail.com*

This new fashion shop is a welcome addition to the south Main Street neighbourhood, setting itself apart from the rest with its diversity of select brands. There are local favourites such as Ric Yuenn, Sweet Soul and Isabelle Dunlop, and celebrity designer brands including VAVA, Black Halo and Willam Rast Jeans. Alongside these labels are one-of-a-kind garments, hand-picked from cities around the globe. This store is boutique shopping at its best.

**896 Commercial Drive**
*Strathcona*
*Map 6 B1* **78**

### Womyns' Ware

*604 254 2543* | *www.womynsware.com*

Voted 'best sex toy store' by *Georgia Straight* readers for more than a decade, this is a hot shop for men and women to roam in. It sells sex toys in the name of women's empowerment and has been doing so since 1995. The staff are phenomenal and provide a comfortable environment to explore your bedroom behaviour, while offering practical advice. Seminars are a part of the services offered and cover alternative sexuality, product awareness and overcoming disabilities. If you're still too shy to walk into the store you can shop online and products will be delivered in a plain package.

## Markets

Although markets are slowly gaining momentum in Vancouver, they're still not as popular as they are in other parts of the world. The fresh produce markets are operated by Your Local Farmers Market Society and run all year-round in various neighbourhoods, as does the Granville Island Public Market. Setting itself up as the leading fashion market, Portobello West brings local designers and shoppers together. The Vancouver Flea Market provides rare finds and cast-off items throughout the year, and (polite) bargaining is always welcomed.

For Chinese night markets, check out Chinatown Night Market (180 Keefer Street, 604 682 8998) and the Richmond Night Market (12631 Vulcan Way, 604 244 8448). The Vancouver market runs from May to September each year, while Richmond's takes place from May until October and has become quite a bit larger than its Downtown counterpart. It's a fun environment for finding trinkets, cultural food and even live performances. Also interesting is the Punjabi Market, or Little India area, in South Vancouver, which begins at East 49th Avenue and continues for about four blocks south along Main Street. Here you'll find gorgeous fabrics, delicious restaurants and food stores and jewellers ready to bargain for your business.

All the markets are great places to amble around, chat with friendly vendors, and pick up some local goods. Check the websites listed for opening times, as most do not open daily.

**999 Canada Place**
*Downtown*
*Map 7 F2* **79**

## Circle Craft Christmas Market

*604 669 8021 | www.circlecraft.net*

In its 36th year, this seasonal craft fair is a wonderful event for purchasing high quality gifts. Held at the Vancouver Convention & Exhibition Centre, locals return every year in November to stock up on Christmas presents. The show runs over six days, and features about 250 vendors enthusiastically selling their Canadian wares. Gift ideas include handcrafted jewellery and pottery, fashion, glasswork, bath products, toys, art and fine food. Entry is $12 for adults and $8 for seniors, with free admission for children under 12. If you're a serious shopper, be sure to ask for the 'deck the halls' pass, which entitles you to unlimited re-admittance during the fair. There is a main store on Granville Island; visit the website for more details.

**Various Locations**

## Farmers Market

*www.eatlocal.org*

With four regular locations, the Farmers Market has grown as more Vancouverites start to appreciate the abundance of locally grown produce. The Trout Lake market is the largest, and there are other sites in the West End near Nelson Park, the parking lot at Nat Bailey Stadium, and at the Kitsilano Community Centre. Farmers come from all over the Lower Mainland to sell seasonal fruits and vegetables, hand-picked nuts, organic meat, free-range dairy and fresh seafood. There are usually some crafts and preserved condiments and often neighbourhood musicians will jam throughout. In the winter, the market moves to Wise Hall in East Vancouver. Entrance is always free. Trout Lake and West End markets are open Saturdays 09:00 to 14:00, at the Nat Bailey Stadium Wednesdays 13:00 to 18:30, and at the Kitsilano Community Centre Sundays 10:00 to 14:00.

**1689 Johnston St**
*Granville Island*
*Map 9 B2* **81**

## Granville Island Public Market

*604 666 6477 | www.granvilleisland.com*

This market is probably the most frequently visited by out of town visitors, and it's also a place locals flock to for fresh produce, speciality food, foreign spices, cheese and seafood. If you want a tester before digging in, contact Edible BC (604 662 3606, www.edible-britishcolumbia.com) for a walking tour. The tour is a good introduction to the market's welcoming merchants. There are also restaurants and cafes if you need to refuel throughout the day. During spring and summer there's always something going on – you could stumble across a cheese festival, farmer's market, plant sales and much more. Open 09:00 to 19:00 daily, entry to the market is always free – except for the tour.

*1755 Cottrell St*
*Mount Pleasant*
*Map 10 E4* **82**

## Portobello West

*www.portobellowest.com*

This recent addition to the fashion scene is based on format of the famous market of the same name in London, England. Local designers are chosen by director Carly Smith to sell their merchandise directly to the public. But the fair doesn't stop there. The free entrance enticed more than 30,000 visitors last year by providing them with funky DJs, live entertainment and grub to keep them energetic. This is not the place to find tacky souvenirs or cheaply made crafts – the designers are all highly reputable and talented in their field. Portobello West runs on the last Sunday of the month, from 12:00 to 18:00. Check the website for re-scheduled holiday dates.

*703 Terminal Av*
*Mount Pleasant*
*Map 10 D4* **83**

## Vancouver Flea Market

*604 685 0666* | *www.vancouverfleamarket.com*

This curious market has been a thriving community of collectors, unwanted items and hidden treasures since 1983. The statistics are impressive: almost 40,000 square feet of space, 360 tables and about 4,000 shoppers on the weekends. It has also begun to hold antique and collectibles shows to help build its reputation for quality finds. For an old-fashioned $0.75, walk into the huge red building reminiscent of a barn and start rummaging through the stalls. Vendors are generally interesting folk who love to start up a conversation about their wares. Haggling is common, especially if you buy a few things. Prices vary from $2 for a vintage magazine to $200 and up for an antique chandelier. Note that there is also a basic cafeteria on the premises that is a popular stop for breakfast. Open Monday to Friday 09:00 to 17:00 and 10:00 to 16:00 during holidays.

## Shopping Malls

There are a few key malls in the city that are on regular shopping routes. They are favoured by teenagers hanging out after school, parents trying to make the most of their free time and elderly people strolling through for exercise. They are filled with shops of every kind, from large international chains to independent boutiques. Foodcourts offer more than just fast food, and some feature full service restaurants. The Oakridge Centre and Metropolis at Metrotown both have cinemas, and most have a children's play area and push cars for parents to borrow free of charge.

Other than at malls Downtown, parking is free, abundant and easy to find, while the core has ample parking for an hourly fee. You can count on doors opening for business at 10:00 during the week, 09:30 on Saturdays and 11:00 on Sundays, closing at 18:00 Saturday through to Thursday, and at 21:00 on Fridays. To avoid the crowds head there during the day Monday to Friday.

### Smaller Malls & Outside The City

For upscale shops in a gorgeous heritage building, Sinclair Centre is a great choice (757 West Hastings Street, 604 660 6000). City Square (555 West 12th Avenue, 604 876 5165) supplies a balance of grocery stores and inexpensive fashion, and also includes a gym. The Royal Centre (1055 West Georgia Street, 604 689 1711) is an underground mall with a cinema, foodcourt and smattering of stores. The main malls outside of the city are all worth the extra effort for their scope of shops and great deals. Coquitlam Centre, about a 45 minute drive from Vancouver, has one of Vancouver's two H&Ms.

*2929 Barnet*
*Highway*
*Coquitlam*
*Map 2 C2*

## Coquitlam Centre

*604 464 1414* | *www.coquitlamcentre.com*

This suburban shopping mall in Coquitlam has gone from almost insignificant to booming in the last 10 years. It now takes up all of its 57 acres with new shops, megastores and hordes of parking. The big box stores are well represented, covering major department stores like London Drugs, T&T Supermarket and Old Navy. It also holds the only branch of H&M in the area, meaning Vancouverites need to take this small road trip to get their fix. Watch out for the traffic around the mall, which rivals any of Vancouver's busiest streets.

## Metropolis At Metrotown

*4700 Kingsway*
*Burnaby*
*Map 6 D3* **85**

*604 438 4715* | *www.metropolis.shopping.ca*
Probably the most popular mall outside of Vancouver, Metropolis at Metrotown has a SkyTrain and bus station, as well as ample free parking, making it an easy journey from Vancouver. With 470 stores, a separate office complex and a full service cinema, there is literally every type of outlet here. It also boasts the largest foodcourt in western Canada, able to feed more than a thousand people at a time. Striving to make shopping even easier, Metropolis offers gift registries so you can let friends and family know just what you're looking for. Sign up online, choose the gifts you'd like from the many shops and send out a message to your email list.

## Oakridge Centre

*650 West 41st Av*
*Oakridge*
*Map 5 F3* **86**

*604 261 2511* | *www.oakridge.shopping.ca*
Come here for fashion, fashion and more fashion. Rebranding itself with runway shows and fashion events, you'll find quality stores here such as Michael Kors and Edward Chapman Ladies Shop. The mall also has full service office buildings with a Montessori school, opticians and medical and dental professionals, as well as a library, Safeway grocery store and Royal Bank. Children play in the designated 800 square foot area and can be carted around in 'kiddie kruzzers' or regular strollers. Oakridge Centre also has a cinema that plays new movies and a foodcourt that serves a range of healthy options. Parking is not usually a problem here as there is a lot surrounding the building with special needs and expectant mother bays.

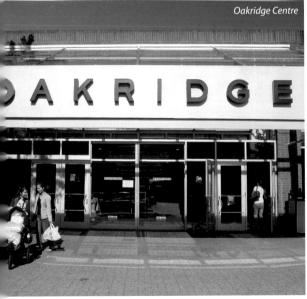

*Oakridge Centre*

910-609
**Granville St**
*Downtown*
*Map 7 F3* 87

## Pacific Centre

*604 688 7235 | www.pacificcentre.com*

Popular for its central Downtown location, Pacific Centre has shops ranging from electronics and sporting goods to high fashion such as Holt Renfrew (p.410). The manned information desk can direct you to specific stores, or suggest shops that are similar to the one you're seeking. For those in need of a wheelchair, ask at the information desk to take one out on loan. Almost half a million visitors shop here each week, but visiting on a weekday will mean fewer crowds. You will find parking underneath the three-block mall at both the Robson Street and Howe Street entrances for around $4 an hour.

**2002 Park Royal**
**South**
*West Vancouver*
*Map 3 F2* 88

## Park Royal Shopping Centre

*604 925 9576 | www.shopparkroyal.com*

Another great afternoon trip from Vancouver, Park Royal Shopping Centre on the North Shore offers a different selection of shops. About 280 stores and restaurants line the mall, with names including Whole Foods Market, Old Navy, New Age Nike and Urban Barn. Services include pushchair and wheelchair access, coat and parcel check in, gift cards and gift wrapping. This is the biggest retail space on the North Shore and combines The Village and The Market at Park Royal. It boasts open-air spaces, fresh foods and a laidback atmosphere.

**6551 No 3 Rd**
*Richmond*
*Map 2 B3*

## Richmond Centre

*604 713 7467 | www.richmondcentre.ca*

Although mostly catering to residents of Richmond, people who live in Vancouver sometimes make their way to the Richmond Centre for a change in scenery. Filled with 240 stores, the mall is family oriented and has many great events including fashion shows, community shows and holiday festivities. You'll also find Sears and The Bay, as well as a Famous Players cinema. The shops are more upmarket, but it also contains boutiques like Morgan and Bluenotes.

# Supermarkets & Hypermarkets

The easiest way to buy groceries is at a supermarket. You can do your weekly shop, buy flowers and plants as well as pick up bulk items and occasionally grab a bite to eat in a cafe. Most have fresh bakeries, fish counters and sections featuring food from around the globe. The Real Canadian Superstore and T&T Supermarket are the two major supermarkets in the city, and also have out of town locations. Safeway outlets (www.safewway.ca) have a nice floral section, while MarketPlace IGA (www.marketplaceiga.com) is a little pricey, but it is known for its abundant produce. Both have several branches around town. Nesters Market (p.382) and Stongs Market (p.382) are two independent options. For inexpensive groceries in a no-frills setting, shop at one of the Buy-Low Foods stores (www.buylowfoods.com) on Alma Street, East Broadway and Fraser Street. They offer a home delivery service and staff who help you out to your car. Dairyland Home Service (1 800 667 1228, www.morethanmilk.ca) or Small Potatoes Urban Delivery (604 215 7783, www.spud.ca) are options for those who want products delivered right to their door.

**605 Expo Blvd**
*Downtown*
*Map 10 A2* 90

## Costco

*604 622 5050 | www.costco.ca*

The Costco store is a membership-based, international club offering major discounts on bulk items. The old main branch on Grandview has recently closed (replaced by a new branch in Burnaby), but a smaller location Downtown gets urbanites in on the action. An individual membership is $55 per year and there are business and executive options as well. Savings are substantial on groceries, appliances, furniture, clothing, home decor and games. Members also benefit from a real estate programme, roadside assistance and insurance benefit plans. For basic photo finishing, prices are $0.16 per print and are ready the next day.

**350 South East Marine Dr**
Oakridge
Map 6 A4 **91**

## Real Canadian Superstore

*604 322 3704* | *www.superstore.ca*

There are a plethora of items in this superstore, which has another location at 3185 Grandview Highway (near Burnaby). Low prices offered every day is the name of the game, and its brand President's Choice offers even higher savings. A bakery, fish counter, meat deli and large produce section are only a small part of this huge chain. Find its highly popular Joe Fresh Style clothing brand for dirt cheap fashion teenagers love, or visit its houseware, footwear, electronics, floral and bed and bath sections, as well as the photo lab, financial services, walk-in medical centre and an outdoor gas station. Load up your trolley, bring your own bags and go home with everything you need, and probably a few things you don't need as well.

**179 Keefer Place**
Chinatown
Map 10 A2 **92**

## T&T Supermarket

*604 899 8836* | *www.tnt-supermarket.com*

Discover speciality products from China, Japan, Taiwan and the Philippines at the largest Asian supermarket chain in Canada. The huge store is always bustling with a lively crowd looking for items from their home country or in search of a special ingredient not found anywhere else. Top of a shopper's list is usually the seafood department, with hauls of fresh fish on display, followed by the Asian deli and bakery, sushi counter and Chinese barbecue delicacies, all of which can be ordered online for special occasions.

Real Canadian Superstore

Pacific Centre

# Going Out

## Going Out

Vancouver has shaken off its reputation as a fresh faced, early to bed city, more concerned about getting on the slopes and trails the next morning than about eking out the evening at a late bar. Having found that there's room in the wardrobe for both active attire and social apparel, Vancouver has finally come out of its shell and emerged as an appealingly energetic and cosmopolitan character, ready to saunter off the slopes or the waves and bound out to play. After all, there's really no better reward for doing the Grouse Grind in record time or kayaking Indian Arm than a perfect martini in a Yaletown hotspot or a few choice small plates at a Gastown izakaya.

The city is home to a bevy of Canada's top tables. The dazzling dining scene boasts a constellation of star eateries, ranging from dining destinations where the decor, clientele and chef get as many column inches as the food, to no-frills ethnic gems. Rarely a week goes by without a new venue opening its doors, compounding the difficulty of choosing a dining or drinking destination in this tasty town; more than 100 restaurants opened in the city in 2007. While they don't all manage to carve an instant niche, Vancouver's inhabitants seem to have a limitless appetite for new places to devour and imbibe.

Alcohol has definitely been seen as a secondary attraction to food until recently, but with the city's new-found confidence and some helpful changes in liquor legislation, the balance has tipped and a plethora of truly exciting lounges, bars and martini lairs has sprung up. It's now as common for Vancouverites to go out, hop on a bar stool and delve into delights from an innovative cocktail menu, or tuck into tapas and a glass of chenin blanc from the Okanagan, as it is for them to book a table in the back. There's a palpable sense of pride in local wines and brews, and a fresh crop of debonair mixologists man the shakers and muddlers.

Where Vancouverites go out to play has diversified too as the stranglehold the boisterous Granville strip has held on the city's nightlife recedes. Focus has shifted to all corners of town – from the stylish and upscale emporia in Yaletown and the grungy dives and swanky lounges of Gastown, to the ever chirpy gay establishments of the West End, the thirty-something bohemian dens in Main and the exuberant student drinking rooms in Kitsilano.

Vancouver has grown up. It's become increasingly sophisticated and it's no longer afraid to stay up after dark.

## Eating Out

Until recently Vancouverites have been able to leave their dining selection to the last minute, but word has now spread that Vancouver has got some seriously hot tables and restaurant-obsessed locals are reluctantly making reservations if they want to guarantee seats in many of the city's popular spots. Now, even on weekdays, you'll often have to wait in line for tables during peak hours (between 19:00 and 21:00), and longer in July and August.

## Cuisine List – Quick Reference

| | | | | | |
|---|---|---|---|---|---|
| African | p.426 | Indian | p.433 | Russian | p.441 |
| American | p.426 | International | p.434 | Seafood | p.441 |
| Brunch | p.427 | Italian | p.434 | Singaporean | p.443 |
| Caribbean | p.427 | Japanese | p.437 | South-East Asian | p.443 |
| Chinese | p.428 | Korean | p.437 | Spanish | p.444 |
| European | p.429 | Latin American | p.438 | Thai | p.444 |
| Fish & Chips | p.429 | Malaysian | p.439 | Vegetarian | p.445 |
| French | p.430 | Mediterranean | p.439 | Vietnamese | p.445 |
| Greek | p.432 | Middle Eastern | p.440 | West Coast | p.446 |

Although you can find pretty much any type of cuisine in any area of the city, there are a few pockets where you should go if you are craving flavours of a particular country. For a wealth of south-east Asian food, particularly Cantonese, the city's two Chinatowns – the official Chinatown Downtown and sprawling Richmond – are key destinations. South Main around the Punjabi Market area thrills with the aromas of north Indian food. A scattering of Vietnamese pho houses are dotted along Main Street. Commercial Drive's Italian cafes and restaurants have been joined by more than two dozen other nationalities of eatery, from El Salvadoran to Belgian. In the West End, Robson's tasty cluster of Japanese izakayas and Korean barbecue places entices posses of ESL students through their doors. Other great areas include Kitsilano's Fourth Avenue, a veritable smorgasbord of eateries that range from budget Chinese cookhouses to some of the city's chicest addresses.

Most restaurants are family friendly, but chains such as Moxie's (www.moxies.ca), Earls (www.earls.ca), Cactus Club (www.cactusclubcafe.com) and Milestone's (www.milestonesrestaurants.com) are excellent options if you've got the kids in tow. Children are made welcome with colouring sheets, games and often special kids' desserts. Restaurants generally welcome young ones, but they are not allowed in any venue classified as a bar.

When you've worked up a major appetite, regular all-you-can-eat promotions are common in Japanese restaurants, as well as a few Indian, Chinese and Mongolian eateries. Many more offer all-you-can-devour buffets on specific days, such as the Chocoholic Bar at Sutton Place (604 682 5511, www.suttonplace.com), the city's only chocolate buffet.

Dine Out Vancouver (p.54) is the main annual restaurant promotion; for three weeks in January and February fixed-price menus can be found at more than 180 restaurants. Details of the event can be found at www.tourismvancouver.com.

## Local Cuisine

With Vancouver being such a marvellously multicultural destination, its flavours are deliciously varied. New residents eager to taste cuisine from home might enjoy a feast of reasonably priced sushi, a sizzling hotpot of Korean bibimbap, or skewers of fish curry balls from the Richmond Night Market (p.413). They might think wistfully of boat-fresh moules frites, or may pine for mutter paneer, samosas and butter chicken from Main Street. Vancouver's contribution to world menus, however, comes in the shape of small plates and in its pronounced emphasis on organic and sustainability-conscious ingredients. An ever-increasing number of restaurants adhere to Vancouver Aquarium's Ocean Wise sustainable seafood programme. Yet for all those politically correct elements, the food can be surprisingly straightforward, letting the ingredients take the spotlight. Local and seasonal produce feature proudly and prominently on the city's menus. Restaurants that specialise in creatively

**Drinking & Driving**
*Police in the cities that make up Greater Vancouver are strict on drinking and driving. Drivers who have a Breath Alcohol Content (BAC) over 0.08, who refuse to give a breath or blood sample, or who drive while impaired, stand to lose their licence for a year on a first conviction, with a minimum fine of $600. A lower BAC reading can lead to a short-term ban if an officer considers you impaired by drugs or alcohol. The city is well served by taxi companies, and night buses cover major bus routes. The last SkyTrains leave Downtown just after 01:00 Monday to Saturday and just after midnight on Sundays and holidays.*

### Dress & Door Policy

In reality, other than some of the more upscale four and five star hotel restaurants, there are few places where you absolutely have to make an extra effort. However, things are beginning to change in this laidback city and there are plenty of places, particularly Downtown and in Yaletown, where you'll be glad you decided not to wear a T-shirt or running shoes. The more popular bars and clubs, especially on the Granville strip, have a stricter door policy than other venues, but this is usually to keep numbers inside within capacity. Surprisingly, only the most upscale and expensive restaurants have cloakrooms. Several clubs allow you to skip the queues at the door by registering for their guest list online. Some gay and lesbian venues have stricter door policies in order to keep venues predominantly male or female.

combining this fresh local fare with the city's spectrum of ethnic influences are usually referred to as 'west coast' (see p.446 for a selection).

Vancouver has grown into an exciting city for all-round dining options. While it is the area's spectacular scenery and surrounds that have traditionally lured visitors, its food scene has now begun to contribute substantially to the city's allure.

## Delivery & Takeaways

There is a wide variety of food delivery options across town. Restaurants specialising in Asian food often offer home delivery, so when you crave Chinese, Japanese, Vietnamese, Singaporean, Thai or Indian food, there is a good choice available from both fastfood outlets and those offering a higher standard of cuisine. Pizza places can be found all over town, with the popular Flying Wedge Pizza (www.flyingwedge.com) having a presence in most areas – you can even order online. Fish and chips on the go are also well catered for wherever there's water; if you're out in the 'burbs, try Pajo's for a particularly fine bundle (www.pajos.com, locations in Steveston, Port Moody and Port Coquitlam). Other delivery possibilities range from Montreal-style chicken and ribs from Rooster's Quarters (836 Denman Street, 604 689 8023) and barbecue from places such as Downtown's Bronco Belle Texas Barbecue (604 696 6088, www.broncobelle.com) to healthy prepared meals from The Specialty Gourmet (604 685 7054, www.thespecialtygourmet.com). Takeaways can be ordered at all but the highest end restaurants.

If you're having a dinner party and want more upscale eats, stock up on Rangoli's (604 736 5711, www.vijsrangoli.ca) perfectly prepared Indian feasts or call the gourmet Sliced Tomatoes (604 254 2545, www.slicedtomatoes.ca) ready-to-cook food delivery service. Other ready-made delights can be found at Granville Island Public Market (p.413).

## Hygiene

Most Vancouver outlets are extremely hygienic. Restaurants and bars legally have to be smoke-free, although some clubs still have separate smoking rooms. Those working in restaurants are required to study for and obtain safe food handling certificates, and restaurants are strictly policed by the Vancouver Coastal Health

*Flying Wedge Pizza*

*Pajo's Steveston*

Authority (www.vch.ca) for compliance with food safety regulations; reports are made available online.

## Special Deals & Theme Nights

Dine Out Vancouver, co-ordinated by Tourism Vancouver (www.tourismvancouver. com), is the city's annual restaurant event. It debuted in 2003 and showcases many of the city's most exciting restaurants. The promotion, which runs for three weeks from mid-January every year, features more than 180 Vancouver restaurants. Each participating restaurant offers a special fixed-price dinner menu with a choice of appetiser, entree and dessert for $15, $25 or $35, depending on the restaurant's reputation.

New Year's Eve is the only other night where a large number of restaurants offer any major promotions. Many places will have set dinner menus and specific seating times. It's a popular night to go out, so reserve well in advance if you want to ring in the new year in a particular venue.

A handful of venues have quiz nights or special ladies' nights in Vancouver; check with your favourite local to see what events it runs. Likewise, keep an eye out for venue-specific happy hours and drinks promotions in pubs and bars. One standout regular event is at The Majestic (p.471), which offers a popular mixed gay/straight bingo night every Wednesday. If karaoke is more your thing, try Tuesdays at the Two Parrots (1202 Granville Street, 604 685 9657) or Wednesdays at the rough and ready Met (320 Abbott Street, 604 915 5336).

## Tax & Service Charges

The majority of menu prices do not include tax. Food items are subject to a 5% goods and services tax, marked on your bill as GST. In BC, alcohol is subject to a 10% provincial liquor tax, or PLT. Some fastfood outlets and smaller restaurants include GST in their prices. Most restaurants add on a service charge once your group reaches a certain size, usually six or eight people. This service charge tends to be 15% or 17% and should be marked clearly on the restaurant's menus and website.

## Tipping

Tipping is expected in Vancouver's restaurants and bars. For good service, 15% to 20% is a fair amount to add; more if service is truly excellent. Restaurants often divide tips between servers, hosts and bus and kitchen staff, so including gratuities on a credit card bill is as effective as leaving cash on the table.

## Independent Reviews

All reviews in this book have been conducted by writers based in Vancouver eager to provide a wide-ranging assortment of the best the city has to offer. Each entry aims to provide an informative view of the restaurant that is honest and unbiased. If you feel that any of the reviews have not hit the mark, or your much-loved local or hidden gastronomic gem has not been included, contact Explorer at info@ explorerpublishing.com.

## Restaurant Listing Structure

Reviews of all the restaurants and bars in Vancouver would take up a whole book in itself so, rather than include every establishment in the city, the Going Out section includes a broad selection of

### Discounts

*The Vancouver Entertainment Book (http://vancouver. entertainment. com) offers discount coupons for more than 400 restaurants, as well as for shops, movies and BC attractions. Food Vancouver (www. foodvancouver.com) offers downloadable coupons for a few city restaurants. Another excellent way to reduce the price of dining out is The Georgia Straight. The restaurant section has more than a dozen two-for-one tokens to tear out in every issue.*

### The Yellow Star

This classy yellow star highlights places that merit extra praise. It might be the atmosphere, the food, the cocktails, the music or the crowd that makes it stand out, but any review that you see with the star attached marks somewhere that's a bit special.

places that are well worth a visit. Each review provides information on the venue's overall character, decor, service and the quality of its food. Restaurants have been categorised by cuisine and are listed in alphabetical order.

## Vegetarian Food

A high proportion of Vancouver's restaurant menus offer vegetarians much more than a token risotto. In fact, the city's vegetarian population is so well catered for that animal rights organisation PETA voted Vancouver the top city in Canada for non-meat eaters. There's even a Vegetarian Resource Centre (604 628 7864, www. vancouverveg.com) to assist with settling into the city or the lifestyle. With the preponderance of vegetable-dish-heavy south-east Asian cuisines in the city, such as east Indian and Thai, vegetarian delights are easily found.

The city also boasts almost two-dozen vegetarian-specific restaurants, from anarcho-hipster hangout The Foundation Lounge (p.445) to the venerable Naam (p.445) and vegan-friendly Café Deux Soleils (p.455). For those who want to steer clear of meat, but want to stay high-end, Lumière (p.431) offers an eight-course vegetarian tasting menu.

## Street Food

**Look Who's Corking**
*Many residents don't know this, but thanks to a recent legislative change, you can now take home that unfinished bottle of wine you ordered in a restaurant or bar. There's just one caveat: it must be sealed up tightly by one of the employees before you leave.*

Strict health restrictions have limited Vancouver's street food scene, which means that it's a rare corner that has a hot dog stand or chestnut vendor. It does mean, however, that the stands that remain tend to be hygienic and worry-free. Chomp on chestnuts from Yv's Chestnuts (Robson Street at Howe Street), delve into a distinctive dog at Japa Dog on Burrard Street at Smithe, or stock up on popcorn and drinks at the cart on the beach at English Bay.

Social strips including Granville Street, Davie Street and Commercial Drive all offer late-night takeaway options, such as cheap shawarma houses, pizza joints or burrito places. If it's fish and chips you crave, try Mr Pickwick's on Denman Street (p.430) or gorge on the catch of the day from Go Fish (p.429), a bright blue shack beside Granville Island.

Vancouver Park Board food concessions run the gamut from upscale restaurants to traditional beachside shacks offering standard fish, fries and burgers. With concessions throughout Stanley Park and at West Side beaches, they offer the best picnic backdrop in town.

The treasure trove of street food stalls, however, is at Richmond Night Market (12631 Vulcan Way, 604 244 8448). Wander amid the bright lights and stalls and sample bubble tea, fish curry balls and barbecued chicken liver. Downtown's Chinatown also offers some thrilling snacking for the adventurous late-night diner on Main Street and Gore Street. Both Chinatown and Richmond night markets are open from 19:00 to 00:00 on Fridays and Saturdays, and until 23:00 on Sundays, from mid-May to early October.

### Restaurant Timings

Peak dining hours are generally from 19:00 to 21:00. Establishments outside Downtown, the West End and Main Street often shut as early as 22:00 on quiet nights. Many venues close earlier on Sunday nights and on major holidays such as Christmas and New Year. However, there is no shortage of dining dens and hidden gems happy to keep turning out the tapas or robata until 01:00. Before venturing out for lunch, check opening times. A surprising number of restaurants remain closed during the day and only open at 17:00 or 17:30 for dinner. Restaurants that do offer lunch usually open at 11:30. Popular bars fill up, even on a weekday, by 21:00. Clubs pick up at 22:30 or later, but lines can form for the hottest spots as early as 21:30.

# Life in the fast lane?

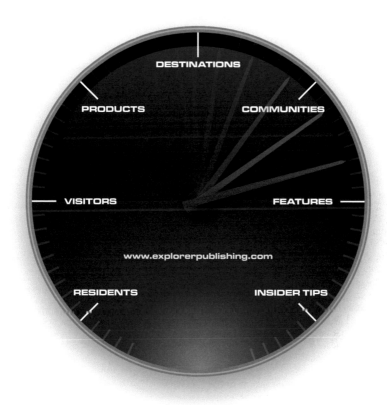

**DESTINATIONS**

**PRODUCTS**

**COMMUNITIES**

**VISITORS**

**FEATURES**

www.explorerpublishing.com

**RESIDENTS**

**INSIDER TIPS**

Life can move pretty quickly so make sure you keep in the know with regular updates from **www.explorerpublishing.com**

Or better still, share your knowledge and advice with others, find answers to your questions, or just make new friends in our community area

**www.explorerpublishing.com** – for life in real time

## African

*52 Alexander St*
Gastown
Map 10 B1 **1**

### Le Marrakech Moroccan Bistro

*604 688 3714 | www.lemarrakech.ca*

A delicious place for a date or a cosy catch-up with your best friend, Le Marrakech tastes good from the first sip of blood orange mojito to the last eked-out morsel of honey and orange blossom pastry. Vancouver's best Moroccan restaurant opened in this culinary hotspot in Gastown in 2007 and delivers plate after plate of upscale north African fare fit for sultans and sultanas. Local, organic and seasonal produce are worked into dishes. The fiery colour scheme makes an exotic backdrop for weekend belly dancers.

*4148 Main St*
Main
Map 6 A2 **2**

### Nyala

*604 876 9919 | www.nyala.com*

Named after the capital of the Sudanese state of South Darfur, Nyala brings the taste of Africa's largest country to Canada. A colour scheme of rich ochre and russet red is the backdrop for an appealing menu of stews, and chicken, lamb and goat dishes. Sample lemon marinated chicken in red pepper sauce, savour beef or lamb with the distinctive flavours of nutmeg, cardamom, ginger and spicy butter, or tuck into an appetising array of vegetarian dishes in spicy berbere sauce. Two inquisitive wooden giraffes peer into the dining area and a collection of African drums hangs on the warm-hued walls. South African treats such as biltong (dried meat) and boerwors (sausage) lure in those missing these distinctive delights. If you go with a larger group, you can arrange in advance to have your after-dinner coffee roasted as you watch.

## American

*871 Beatty St*
Downtown
Map 9 F1 **3**

### Dix BBQ & Brewery

*604 682 2739 | www.markjamesgroup.com*

Practically in the shadow of GM Place, it should come as no surprise that hockey reigns supreme on game nights in this spacious sports brew pub, where a slew of television screens plasters the bar area. In the 85 seater restaurant, however, barbecue is definitely king. Favourites such as pulled pork, ribs and all the fixings star on a cheekily toned, meat-laden menu that would make a staunch vegetarian quail. Soups, salads and wraps are ever so slightly healthier options, but this is not a venue to visit on a diet. Easy going servers amble between tables, whisking off paper table covers after each satisfied group has eaten and drunk their fill. It's a low-key place to add a 'mighty butt rub burger' to your culinary checklist, or grab some applewood-smoked beef brisket, order a pint of the day's special and catch up with friends in low-lit, laidback surrounds.

*1550 Philip Av*
North Vancouver
Map 3 F2 **4**

### Tomahawk Barbecue

*604 988 2612 | www.tomahawkrestaurant.com*

Filling the citizens of the North Shore with oysters on toast, enormous mixed grills (complete with nine slices of Yukon bacon) and fish and chips since 1926, the family-owned and run Tomahawk is a culinary character that is perfect to introduce the kids to. Try some of the burgers that Chick Chamberlain, the grandfather of the restaurant's current owner, named after friends who were First Nations chiefs, and take in the collection of pots, drums, totem poles and masks while you eat. If it's earlier in the day, hearty breakfasts with free-range eggs are what the Tomahawk is famed for. The menu of 'old fashion favourites' lures in expats and older locals for classic feasts such as meatloaf, steak and mushroom pie, and roast beef dinner.

## Brunch

Weekend brunch is a popular option at many restaurants, with Sunday sessions a particular tradition at Downtown's grand hotels. For a special occasion, try the grandiose brunches at Hotel Vancouver (900 West Georgia Street, 604 684 3131), The Sutton Place (845 Burrard Street, 604 682 5511), or the Latin-inspired brunch at The Four Seasons (791 West Georgia Street, 604 689 9333). Hotel brunch usually runs from about 11:30 until 14:30.

When not working their way through such gargantuan buffets, Vancouverites tend to brunch relatively early – after all there are mountains to climb, kayaks to clamber into and trails to be run and biked. Make a reservation, or expect a queue if you arrive between 10:00 and 12:00.

Casual dining chains such as Moxie's (www.moxies.ca), Earls (www.earls.ca) and Cactus Club (www.cactusclubcafe.com) are a popular and relatively inexpensive brunch option – and a good choice if you're bringing the kids or a larger group. Menus feature omelettes, scrambles, eggs benedict and accompanying breakfast beverages from juices to mimosas. The best of these is Milestone's (www.milestonesrestaurants.com), which has 12 Greater Vancouver restaurants. Book ahead if you want to brunch with the backdrop of English Bay at its original address (1210 Davie Street, 604 662 3431). A slew of neighbourhood diners offer basic eggs and bacon breakfast menus at low prices for younger locals, slouching out of bed after nights on the town. For something a bit more upscale, try Provence Marinaside (1177 Marinaside Avenue, 604 681 4444), Crave (3941 Main Street, 604 872 3663) or Nu (1661 Granville Street, 604 646 4668), which does Sunday jazz brunches. Granville Island Hotel (1253 Johnston Street, 604 683 7373) also does a popular open-air jazz brunch in the summer.

## Caribbean

**1212 Commercial Dr**
Grandview
Map 6 B1 **5**

### Havana

*604 253 9119 | www.havana-art.com*

One of around two dozen international cuisines to choose from on the Drive, this funky, arty, graffiti-covered Cuban restaurant has been rustling up rancheros and empanadas and muddling mojitos since 1996. A slew of eastsiders lounge over lattes and enjoy Caribbean flavoured fare from breakfasts such as chorizo hash (served until a generous 14:00) to dinner dishes such as fiery tequila prawns. Havana tops most locals' lists for the city's best nuevo Latino food. The service is always pleasant and the booths and tables fill with some fascinating characters, while the heated patio area that looks across at Grandview Park allows yet more people-watching opportunities. At weekends and every summer evening, there are a dozen or more people mingling on the pavement, waiting for a table. There's a tiny wine bar area, an art gallery and a small theatre attached to the restaurant.

**4172 Main St**
Main
Map 6 A2 **6**

### The Reef

*604 874 5375 | www.thereefrestaurant.com*

The bold flavours of Jamaica are emblazoned all over the menu at The Reef. Start off with deliciously salty plantain chips with tangy jerk mayonnaise, sashay into island thyme chicken or a curry and lime pan-seared mahi mahi fillet, and wash it all down with some Dragon Stout or Red Stripe. The Reef specialises in spicy food, north coast Jamaican style, with scotch bonnet peppers, garlic and ginger bright and strong in almost every dish. Daily specials are crammed with hot and fruity spices, reggae plays in the background and servers are outgoing and helpful with menu choices. Bring a posse of friends and take over the patio, or have a laidback date in the funky, brightly decorated room. For a leisurely way to start the weekend, saunter round for brunch, where crab cakes, frittala and, for kids, the 'wee little pirate' bring the taste of Jamaica to brunch on Saturdays and Sundays from 11:00 until 15:00. Another branch opened recently at 1018 Commercial Drive.

## Chinese

**1339 Robson St**
West End
Map 7 C2 **7**

### Hon's Wun-Tun House

*604 685 0871 | www.hons.ca*

This Chinese cafeteria-style restaurant specialises in cheap, cheerful combo dinners and other such voluminous feasts. Dishes are plastic, service is minimal and lighting is harsh and neon, but this family-style Cantonese diner is a great place to fill up on inexpensive fastfood. Dumplings and the eponymous 'wun-tuns' keep people dashing through the doors. Lemon chicken, congee, beef with udon noodles, and barbecue pork buns are among hundreds of items scattered across the various menus. Separate vegetarian and non-vegetarian counters groan with vast amounts of western-friendly fare, and servers dart about between

*Hon's Wun-Tun House*

the tables. There's even a separate, specific vegetarian kitchen that churns out dozens of meat-free dishes that are sure to keep the non-carnivores in the party happy. Many of these are wheat-gluten based, such as mock-duck and mock-chicken; give them a try and be pleasantly surprised. There's another Hon's outlet at 268 Keefer Street in Chinatown, and branches in Richmond, New Westminster and Coquitlam.

**102-1166 Alberni St**
Downtown
Map 7 D2 **8**

### Kirin Mandarin Restaurant

*604 682 8833 | www.kirinrestaurant.com*

For more than 20 years, Kirin Mandarin, one of Vancouver's original Chinese fine-dining rooms and now one of four Kirin restaurants in the region, has been delighting locals and visitors alike with its decadent northern Chinese cuisine. At lunchtime, dim sum (ordered a la carte, rather than chosen from carts) is the big draw, offering small-plate dishes in the lofty, three-storey high room. For dinner, peking duck with crepes is by far the most popular dish. If you have culinary courage and fancy deviating from the usual Chinese fare, try braised sea cucumber with prawn roe sauce, or the pricy double-boiled Buddhist delicacies soup. Kirin Mandarin is popular with tour groups who delve into fixed-price 10 course banquets, and with those who work Downtown and want to have a lengthy business lunch. Service is slow and deliberate, and the wine list is impressive. The other Kirin outlets are at 555 West 12th Avenue (a seafood specialist), and in Richmond and Coquitlam.

**3888 Main St**
Main
Map 6 A2 **9**

### Sun Sui Wah

*604 872 8822 | www.sunsuiwah.com*

In a city that ranks alongside New York and San Francisco for quantity and quality of Chinese restaurants, Cantonese stalwart Sun Sui Wah rises majestically above the competition. Famed for its signature roast squab and Alaskan king crab, fished live from the restaurant's seafood tanks, these house specialities tend to distract from minor complaints about the service. The volume is always near deafening in the lively, brightly lit room. On weekends it sounds as though half of Hong Kong has descended on Main Street to flag down Sun Sui Wah's dim sum carts. If you're there for dim sum (available daily from 10:00 to 15:00), wave down staff, rather than wait for the carts of potstickers, chicken's feet and congee to trundle round. Even with a reservation you can expect to wait 20 minutes or more for a table. There's a second branch in Richmond (4940 No 3 Road, 604 273 8208).

**3700 No 3 Rd**
*Richmond*
*Map 2 B3*

## Yaohan Centre
*604 231 0601 | www.yaohancentre.com*

Next time you're craving chrysanthemum tea or a quick snack of chicken's feet, head for Richmond's Yaohan Centre. Cheap prices make this a magnet for inquisitive culinary bargain seekers. It may not be a venue for a refined evening out – this is essentially a food court in a shopping mall, complete with plastic seating – but with 15 different outlets, you can be sure to find something to suit your tastes, whether calm or courageous. Food stall feasts range from steam table servings at Golden Rice Bowl to prawn won tons at Wah Yuen Noodle House. If you're inspired to try stirring up your own dishes at home, pay a visit to the frenetic Osaka Supermarket where many Asian-Canadian locals shop.

## European
Other options **Russian** p.441, **French** p.430, **Italian** p.434, **Spanish** p.444, **Mediterranean** p.439

**3250 Main St**
*Main*
*Map 11 B4* **11**

## Budapest Restaurant & Pastry Shop
*604 877 1949*

When you're craving a hearty portion of Hungarian goulash, only Main Street's Budapest Restaurant can satisfy. It's best to call ahead, since the compact and bustling restaurant, run by a husband-and-wife team, has only 28 seats, and they're usually filled with an assortment of older eastern Europeans missing the tastes of home, those with Hungarian ancestry and locals from the immediate area. The fare is better quality than you might expect from the unprepossessing exterior and bright, canteen-like interior. While the thick beef goulash is very definitely the star of the menu, many swear that the generous portion of crispy duck is the city's most delicious. Transylvanian platters are great for an introduction or for the indecisive, and come laden with deep-fried bread (langos), schnitzels, red cabbage with apples, cabbage rolls and sausages. The service is on the slow side, so it's not the place to saunter into expecting a quick dinner, but what's the hurry? The duck and the goulash deserve time to be savoured.

*Go Fish*

## Fish & Chips

**1505 West 1st Av**
*False Creek*
*Map 9 B2* **12**

## Go Fish Ocean Emporium
*604 730 5040*

So close to the water that the fish practically leap on to the plate, this harbourside fish shack is one of the best spots in the city to fend off the voracious seagulls and chow down on perfectly fried, battered and grilled fish. The tasty creation of Bin 941's Gord Martin (see p.447), Go Fish dishes out fish tacos and oyster po' boys within sight of the fishing boats they came in on. Literally a compact kitchen with a take-out window, Go Fish attracts queues of devotees rain or shine, and the few open-air picnic tables and benches are always crammed with families, False Creek locals and surprised tourists who are delighted to have stumbled upon such an unexpected, appealingly priced gem. On a sunny day, there's no better backdrop for feasting on a wild albacore tuna salad: traffic bustles across Burrard Bridge, False Creek Ferries shuttle back and forth from Granville Island, and the city skyline and mountains dominate the horizon.

**1007 Denman St**
*West End*
*Map 7 B2* **13**

## Mr Pickwick's Seafood Bistro Restaurant
*604 681 0631 | www.mrpickwicks.bc.ca*

If the notoriously good fresh cod, haddock and salmon at Mr Pickwick's isn't enough to tempt you to the friendly cafeteria-style restaurant, then British pub fare, from pub pies to bangers and mash, also graces the extensive menu. Ever wondered how they eat their fish in Fiji or how to spice up small fry, Indian-style? Mr Pickwick has the answers. Each day of the week the restaurant features fish and chips made in the style of countries where the dish has some history. Even those on special diets can sidle up to the counter in this West End gem and order a fishy feast; Mr Pickwick's rustles up a mean dairy-free batter, wheat-free chowders, vegetarian mushy peas and other such quintessentially British tastes of home. The tables fill quickly with expats, gay couples who live in the neighbourhood, and camcorder-toting tourists fresh off the Seawall. There's another outlet at 8620 Granville Street (604 266 2340).

## French

**1459 West Broadway**
*Fairview*
*Map 9 B4* **14**

## Cru
*604 677 4111 | www.cru.ca*

There's an air of palpable excitement in this bright, narrow Broadway room, as couples linger over small plates or the thrilling three-course fixed-price menu. Mouthwatering morsels such as duck confit and Moroccan-spiced lamb chops are just some examples of Cru's affordable excellence. The dishes are easily as good as some of the bigger-name culinary draws around the city, but at a far friendlier price. The long, chic room's decor is muted and doesn't distract, giving the food and wine centre stage. Make sure to leave room for dessert: there are five to choose from (plus ice cream) on the fixed-price menu, including the interesting spiced vanilla bean risotto. There are 35 varieties of wine by the glass to wash it all down with. Those with special dietary requirements are accommodated with ease; alerting the restaurant in advance ensures you don't miss out.

**216 Abbott St**
*Gastown*
*Map 10 A1* **15**

## Jules Casual French Bistro
*604 669 0033 | www.julesbistro.ca*

This contemporary Gallic kitchen is an airy emporium in the city's ever-improving cobbled quarter. Within the traditional red brick walls of this Gastown gastronomic destination, the Jules team seems to almost effortlessly impress all who scamper eagerly through the doors. Efficient and smiling waiters sashay across the black-and-white tiled floor, bearing delicious dishes of steak frites, terrine de campagne, beef bourguignon and cassoulet – traditional French working class classics done to perfection. Everyone from older couples to young design-conscious types crowd into the pleasantly noisy room, where a chandelier glitters over the cosy scene. Fixed-price menus and lunch sets present excellent value for money at this comfortable neighbourhood bistro. Only open since mid-2007, Jules is very much the French bistro of choice, so make reservations or expect to go hungry.

### Le Crocodile

**909 Burrard St**
*Downtown*
*Map 7 D4* 🔢

*604 669 4298* | *www.lecrocodilerestaurant.com*

Crisp white tablecloths, bold flowers and bright yellow curtains set the scene for the Crocodile experience. The venerable Crocodile has been conjuring the freshest and best west coast ingredients into timeless French classics for more than 20 years, much to the delight of the procession of celebrities and other devotees who have passed through its doors. Jack Nicholson, Steven Spielberg, Al Pacino and Cindy Crawford have all swooned over chef Michel Jacob's mouthwatering masterpieces. Star attractions at this elegant dining destination range from Atlantic lobster in morel mushroom and white butter sauce to Mediterranean style roasted sea bass and pan-seared veal sweetbreads. The five-course tasting menu offers an exceptional way to experience Le Crocodile's hot haute cuisine, and the staff, many of whom have been here since the restaurant opened, are superb at guiding choices from the rich, decadent menu.

### Lumière

**2551 West Broadway**
*Kitsilano*
*Map 8 C4* 🔢

*604 739 8185* | *www.lumiere.ca*

One of Vancouver's bright lights, Lumière continues to shine despite famed Canadian chef Rob Feenie moving on in late 2007. This refined room, with its focus on the finest and freshest ingredients, has an incredible reputation to uphold after winning everything a restaurant could possibly aim for and more – the honours list is nearly as long as the menu. Bold hues glow in the low-lit room, staff are unobtrusive and on the ball, and the experience is perfect for whenever the occasion demands culinary fireworks. Opt for one of the tasting menus (vegetarian, signature, chef's or cheese), a perfect way to sample the twists on contemporary French and west coast fare, or try some of the a la carte options from the Lumière Tasting Bar. Exquisite wines and bar drinks complement the edible extravaganzas that appear out of the kitchen. Also, watch out for a Vancouver version of New York's DB Bistro Modern, a collaboration between Lumière's owners and chef Daniel Boulud, which was due to open next door in 2008.

Jules Casual French Bistro

Lumière

## Pied-à-Terre

*3369 Cambie St*
*Cambie*
*Map 5 F2* **18**

*604 873 3131 | www.pied-a-terre-bistro.ca*

Although it's only been open since November 2007, Pied-à-Terre has swiftly vaulted to the top of the upscale French bistro category. It's no surprise, as this intimate, inconspicuous room on the Canada Line comes from an impressive stable – it's owned by the people behind La Buca (p.436) and Parkside (p.451). Snack on steak frites with a choice of four titillating sauces, sample new takes on classic fare such as duck à l'orange, or discover unusual French wines by the glass. A set lunch menu pares down the choice for the busy local lunch crowd, and the three-course table d'hote dinner menu is good value (and includes the famed steak). Ingredients are predominantly locally sourced and organic. Simple, elegant black-and-white decor sets a smart tone and the assured staff guarantee your enjoyment of the succession of French bistro classics.

## Provence Marinaside

*1177 Marinaside Av*
*Yaletown*
*Map 9 E2* **19**

*604 681 4444 | www.provencevancouver.com*

A pleasant stop along the Yaletown stretch of the Seawall, Provence Marinaside manages to successfully mimic a hotel dining room ambience, right down to the muted, inoffensive jazz that seems to be obligatory to such venues. Baroque flourishes abound and distressed paintwork creates a retro shabby chic feel. Its charm lies outside, however. The sunny patio gazes out on to flotillas of yachts and boats in the marinas and is the perfect spot to take in the Yaletown comings and goings on a sunny afternoon or summer evening. Staff are down to earth and on the ball. The French fare ranges from good and reliable to really rather good. Try popping in for an early-morning eggs benedict, or a delicious croissant and a wake-me-up coffee, or work up an appetite before delving into the antipasto or oyster selections as the sun is setting. The afternoon menu features an 'antipasti showcase'.

## Greek

## Bouzyos

*1815 Commercial Dr*
*Grandview*
*Map 12 B1* **20**

*604 254 2533 | www.bouzyostaverna.com*

The lifelong dream of a jovial Greek carpet salesman, Bouzyos is a Commercial Drive institution. Hefty portions of affordable classics such as souvlaki plates, moussaka and roast lamb and a welcoming ambience are the reasons this has become a neighbourhood mainstay. Can't make up your mind what you want? Come to a deal with your dining partner and order one of the substantial vegetarian or seafood platters. An enticing patio section is the refuge of smokers and ouzo drinkers on sunny days and provides entertaining views of life on the Drive. Inside, the seemingly non obligatory Greek taverna decor stars, complete with stucco arches, and things can get raucous once the retsina starts to flow. Entertainment ranges from hits of the 80s on the stereo to Friday night's boisterous belly dancing displays and live jazz or Latin music on Saturday evenings.

## Stepho's Souvlaki Greek Taverna

*1124 Davie St*
*West End*
*Map 7 C4* **21**

*604 683 2555*

For those with patience, gargantuan portions of incredibly inexpensive food wait inside Stepho's – hungry diners have been known to queue for up to an hour for a table at this popular joint. The queues of tourists, locals and bridge and tunnel workers are legendary, stretching to the corner of the block seven nights a week. Since reservations are not accepted, the only way to beat the hordes is to opt for lunch at this bustling traditional taverna, or to arrive before 16:00. Things speed up once inside; appealingly priced wine is delivered in record time and dishes from saganaki fried cheese and garlic calamari to smoky roast lamb and enormous mounds of vegetarian lasagne appear in minutes. It might not be the finest Greek food in the city, but with nothing on the menu stretching over $10, it's a winner every time.

## Indian

### All India Sweets & Restaurant

**6507 Main St**
*Main*
*Map 6 A3* **22**

*604 327 0891* | *www.allindiasweetsrestaurant.com*

Vancouver's largest Indian restaurant is the place to hit when you've worked up a serious appetite. The famous daily $6.95 vegetarian buffet packs in droves of local families, visiting vegetarians and Downtowners hungry for a bargain meal. Famed for its creamy rasgulla and sticky sweet gulab jamun desserts, All India Sweets is situated in the heart of the predominantly Sikh Punjabi Market area of the city and provides great meal deals for those looking for quantity as well as good quality. Outside of the enormously popular buffet, butter chicken and tandoori, tikka and biryani dishes satisfy carnivores at this enormous hall of Indian delights. The frenetic food fest is fully licensed and has a patio area. The eponymous sweets are brightly coloured delights available at a vast desserts counter, which will have you scuttling back down Main Street at every opportunity.

### Ashiana Tandoori

**1440 Kingsway**
*Knight Road*
*Map 6 B2* **23**

*604 874 5060* | *www.ashianatandoori.com*

Opulent Indian art and sculptures adorn the walls of this Knight Road classic. The magic combination of herbs and spices that create Ashiana's distinctive tandoori and east Indian curry dishes are used on meat and seafood destined for the clay tandoor oven. Specialities include peshwari chicken tikka, shikampuri kebab and Ashiana's signature dish, the mixed grill, a feast of chicken, lamb and prawn, done tandoori style. The lengthy menu offers all the Indian favourites you would expect and more, including a wide selection titled 'wonderful world of vegetables', which stars the sumptuous eggplant bhartha and keeps vegetarians eagerly coming back for more. Dishes are low in fat and oil and high in flavour. It's an intimate, inviting and calm restaurant, kept busy by a slew of delivery orders. Restaurant portions, however, are considerably smaller than those rushed out the door for home delivery. There's a private banquet room for special occasions.

### Chutney Villa

**147 East Broadway**
*Mount Pleasant*
*Map 11 B2* **24**

*604 872 2228*

The flavours of southern India are served up in an appetising array of thali dishes at this welcoming Mount Pleasant restaurant. The laden silver trays include a main dish, rice, sambar, chutney, salad, a traditional lentil soup and tapioca dessert. Servers in sarees glide between tables, and walls are decorated with Indian wood carvings, which are for sale should you want a souvenir of your visit to this cosy venue. Bold reds brighten the walls and silk curtains soften the lines. Using a very different selection of spices to north Indian cuisine, Chutney Villa's dishes are crammed with the flavours of star anise, cinnamon, cardamom, mustard seeds and tamarind, and accompanied by delicious dosa lentil flour crepes with dollops of fruit chutney, idli rice, lentil cakes and rasam (tomato tamarind soup). There is a rotating selection of chutneys, with four flavoursome varieties on offer each day.

**1480 West 11th Av**
*Fairview*
*Map 5 F1* **25**

## Vij's

*604 736 6664* | *www.vijs.ca*

It's first come, first served at Vij's, Vancouver's standout Indian restaurant. There are no reservations here, as droves of regulars keep on coming back for east Indian fusion delights from the ever-changing menu. Waiting for a table is never a hardship, however, as the enticing dark, hip lounge area is an inviting place to linger over complimentary chai and snacks until seats open up in the contemporary dining room. One dish that doesn't change is the wine-marinated lamb popsicles with fenugreek curry. Other thrillingly inventive dishes are made from organic and locally sourced produce, and vegetarians have some hard decisions to make as the menu offers a wealth of tempting meat-free options. Service is excellent and usually overseen by the charming and attentive owner. If you want your curry in a hurry, head next door to Vij's Rangoli which serves a small lunch menu and offers a selection of Indian dishes to go.

## International

**4434 West 10th Av**
*Point Grey*
*Map 5 C1* **26**

## Burgoo

*604 221 7839* | *www.burgoo.ca*

Upscale comfort food reigns in this warm, stone-flagged room in West Point Grey, the domain of old moneyed homeowners and impecunious grad students. One of a trio of stew and soup houses ('burgoo' is a form of spicy stew) in the city (other locations are in North Vancouver at Lonsdale Avenue, and a new branch in Main), Burgoo's bowls of wholesome goodness range from steaming hot French onion soup and tangy Prince Edward Island mussels mariniere to hefty portions of Irish stew and the eponymous Kentucky burgoo. Fondue and big cup soups are other heart-and-stomach-warming menu options. Candles flicker and a fireplace casts a cosy glow on the old travel posters that line the walls in the two-wood beamed rooms. Sit down at a chunky wooden table amid middle-aged academics, family groups and earnest UBC students, order a Burgoo brew or a louisville lemonade and tuck in. Burgoo doesn't accept reservations, and short lines often form on chilly winter evenings.

## Italian

Other options **Mediterranean** p.439

**1154 Robson St**
*West End*
*Map 7 D3* **27**

## CinCin

*604 688 7338* | *www.cincin.net*

Offering a much appreciated place to drop your shopping and escape the crowds on Robson Street, CinCin sits up a short flight of stairs off the main strip. The heritage wood-fired oven is responsible for a succession of delights from the Italian-inspired seasonal menus, such as sablefish from the Haida Gwaii islands and pizza with fennel sausage. The grill gives subtly different flavours to venison loin, Mediterranean sea bass and Alberta beef tenderloin. For a sweet farewell to the restaurant, leave room for dessert – CinCin's pastry chef is a veteran of a constellation of Michelin star-struck restaurants. Should those bags get too heavy to carry before it's time to eat, the bar opens at 16:00, and *Wine Spectator* heartily commends the wine list.

**1133 Hamilton St**
*Yaletown*
*Map 9 E1* **28**

## Cioppino's Mediterranean Grill & Enoteca

*604 688 7466* | *www.cioppinosyaletown.com*

Classic Mediterranean cuisine lures lovers of food and wine to the elegant Cioppino's. When risotto with Alaskan king crab or roasted rack of lamb with mint and decade-aged sherry vinegar is exactly what you need, choose from the 126 seat restaurant, its adjacent 88 seat Enoteca ('wine library') or one of the five private rooms that seat between six and 26. The wine library is incredibly well stocked, with an inventory of 2,600 bottles to browse, valued at a cool $2.5 million. The decor mixes rustic yellows with crisp white linen and warm, cherry-hued chairs and shutters. This place may not be the cheapest spot to grab a bite to eat, but it's been attracting an ever-increasing number of loyal customers (as well as the odd celebrity) since it opened in 1999. It's not just Canadians who appreciate the food either – in 2005 the restaurant became the only one outside Italy to win an award of excellence from the Accademia Italiana della Cucina. Ambitious diners can buy the Cioppino cookbook to try to recreate the delicious treats at home.

*860 Burrard St*
*Downtown*
*Map 7 D3* **29**

## Don Francesco Ristorante

*604 685 7770* | *www.donfrancesco.ca*

This fine-dining restaurant, located steps away from busy Robson Street, is the best stop for Mediterranean-focused Italian cuisine. There is a decent bar area, and the dining space is casual at the front near the windows, with a more refined air towards the back. For starters, try the wrapped prosciutto (with crushed banana, avocado, and roasted almonds), tuna, boiled egg and avocado salad, or the house-cured wild salmon carpaccio. For mains, there is an extensive list of pastas to choose from, while grilled selections include charbroiled fillet of halibut (perhaps the best tasting regional fish), braised wild quails, or the trio of shellfish neptune (prawns, scallops and oysters sauteed in butter). The streetside patio is fine but Burrard can get a little busy. A smart-casual dress code is in effect.

*Vij's*

*CinCin*

*Cioppino's Mediterranean Grill & Enoteca*

**4025 MacDonald St**
*Arbutus*
*Map 5 E2* **30**

## La Buca

*604 730 6988 | www.labuca.ca*

The creative minds behind the West End's Parkside (p.451) and Cambie Street hotspot Pied-à-Terre (p.432) are responsible for the city's most exciting Italian opening of late, the cosy La Buca. Service is outstanding, food is both hearty and elegant, and the decor is sharp yet rustic. The intimate dining room in this upscale trattoria is sharply tiled in black and white, and the ambience is relaxed and welcoming. Diners come from all over Vancouver to savour osso bucco, scaloppini and pasta done to perfection. You can also order half portions of

*Nachos*

pasta if you want to leave room to try several dishes, and considering the dessert menu features tiramisu and panna cotta to die for, this is definitely recommended. Reserving well in advance is the only way you'll get a table in this intimate West Side den.

**1641 Commercial Dr**
*Grandview*
*Map 6 B1* **31**

## Lombardo's Pizzeria & Ristorante

*604 251 2240 | www.lombardos.ca*

A den of doughy deliciousness on the Drive, Lombardo's dishes out thrilling thin crust pizzas, baked to perfection in its wood-fired oven. Generous pies and calzones, featuring distinctive flavours of basil, capers, fresh dill and hot chilli, have won admirers for more than two decades. Sit in the bright, inconspicuous Commercial Drive location or call ahead and order pizza to go. Lasagne and a slew of spicy spaghetti dishes offer an alternative, and other Italian specialities, such as stracciatella chicken broth with eggs, bulk up the tasty menu. Lunchtime panini are popular with those who work in the vicinity, and the good news for fans of these fabulous fresh slices is that they no longer have to trek over to the Drive every time they have a craving for a slice or a salad – a Downtown branch is now in operation at 970 Smithe Street (604 408 0808).

**1600 Renfrew St**
*Renfrew*
*Map 6 C1* **32**

## Osteria Napoli

*604 255 6441*

There are plenty of west coast fusion-style Italian restaurants around Vancouver, but for something a little more old-school head for Osteria Napoli, decked out with murals of Naples. Tucked into a non-descript block of retail space off of 1st and Renfrew, little has changed for this Eastside eatery over the years. The classic menu of Osteria is a delight; steaming bowls of stracciatella, large plates of salamis, prosciutto and cheeses, snails in wine and garlic, home-made pasta to worship, and, of course, the ample plates of osso bucco and veal done in myriad ways – all delicious. To wash it down, choose from a wine menu of decently priced quality offerings. As you dine, you'll smile (or grimace) to the eclectic background music – Andrea Bocelli, Neil Diamond and the Lambada. The music is not to everyone's taste, but, like the food, it is staple.

## Japanese

**105-375 Water St**
Gastown
Map 10 A1 **33**

### Guu With Otokomae

*604 685 8682* | *www.guu-izakaya.com*

There's only one word of Japanese that you'll need at this irrepressible Gastown izakaya: oishii (delicious). Tucked away off Water Street and upstairs in a large, brick-walled, split-level room, Guu With Otokomae is the best of the Guus in the city. The entire staff shout a welcome to each guest as they arrive, and the volume at the tables and along the bar rises exponentially as pitchers of 'jump around' and other such intriguing cocktails hit their mark. The menu at this vivacious venue features a raft of small plates. Start with onigiri rice balls stuffed with kelp, salty miso and sumptuous maturo (an avocado and tuna mousse), and follow that up with a wasabi-centric bowl of kimchi, skewers of beef and decadent dumplings, washed down with plum wine or shochu vodka. Finish off this decorative feast with a few deep-fried rice balls with strawberry sauce. There are other Guu outlets at 838 Thurlow Street (604 685 8817), 1698 Robson Street (604 685 8678), and in Richmond (604 295 6612).

**1063 Davie St**
West End
Map 7 C4 **34**

### Kadoya

*604 608 1115*

Other than debating the pros and cons of the forthcoming Winter Olympics, there are few topics more contentious among Vancouverites than who does the best sushi. If you want to devour this staple of Vancouver life and don't want to take out a second mortgage to eat at Tojo's (below), a plethora of vocal locals will tell you to head to the West End's tiny Kadoya. It's compact, crammed, and adored for its creative sushi rolls (and for the often entertaining comment cards that decorate the walls). As you tuck into a crab-filled spider roll, the unusual coconut-adorned snow white roll, or savour the yam and unagi in a Stanley Park roll, you might be seated beside ambulance drivers from St Paul's, staff from Davie's gay clubs filling up before their shift, or former Vancouverites who gallop to this pint-sized venue whenever they come back to town. If there's no room to squeeze in, take your rolls to go and hunker down on Sunset Beach a few blocks south.

**1133 West Broadway**
Fairview
Map 9 C4 **35**

### Tojo's

*604 872 8050* | *www.tojos.com*

It's pricey, but then Hidekazu Tojo's Broadway address is the top Japanese restaurant in the city, and quite possibly the continent. It's not uncommon for diners to give the chef a standing ovation here. If you're feeling adventurous, head for the omakase bar (which loosely translates as 'chef, I'm in your hands'), simply tell Tojo of any allergies and food dislikes, and wait for his choice of creative sashimi, thrilling seafood, and other such delights to appear on your plate. Otherwise, choose from the a la carte sushi, sashimi, teriyaki and tempura options that Tojo elevates to an entirely different culinary level. Seating varies from private tatami rooms to some much sought-after stools that offer views of sushi action guaranteed to keep you on the edge of your seat. And don't get so distracted by dishes such as baked oysters and the northern lights roll that you miss out on the amazing choices offered by the sake bar.

## Korean

**1719 Robson St**
West End
Map 7 C1 **36**

### Hal Mae Jang Mo Jib

*604 642 0712*

Hal Mae Jang Mo Jib is the best place in town to snack on delicious, authentic bibimbap, seafood pancakes and hotpot. A plastic vat of barley tea is unceremoniously plonked down on your table when you arrive, and dishes come accompanied by an endless supply of sides (rice, kimchi, radish, potatoes and seaweed), providing you are able to catch the attention of the sometimes disinterested staff. The music is loud and the hubbub of conversation even louder. It's bright, noisy and often chaotic, but it's the closest thing to Seoul that you'll find in the city. To really get the full Jang Mo Jib experience, saunter along in the wee hours of the morning when it cranks up the Korean pop music and the two rooms are teeming with hordes of boisterous, homesick ESL students. There are two other branches, at 518 Richards Street (604 688 0712) and 395 Kingsway (604 872 0712).

*1215 West Broadway*
*Fairview*
*Map 9 C4* **37**

## Seoul House Royal Korean Restaurant
*604 739 9001*
Recommended by Koreans as the best place in the city to tear into an authentic barbecue dinner, Seoul House is most popular for its weekend all-you-can-eat lunch buffets, from 12:00 to 16:00. Since the service doesn't win too many fans, this is the best way to enjoy the tender, perfectly marinated meat dishes that you grill at your own table. Tables fill with large groups of boisterous families, while private booths are perfect for quieter lunching or dining. Other popular Korean dishes star on the menu (and at the buffet), including japchae yam noodle stir fry, pancakes and kimchi. Vegetarians can happily devour the beef-free version of bibimbap, a spicy rice, fried egg and vegetable dish, cooked in a stone pot. Seoul House also offers a selection of beer and wine to while away the time it takes for the barbecue to cook to perfection.

## Latin American

*2535 Alma St*
*Point Grey*
*Map 5 D1* **38**

### Baru
*604 222 9171* | *www.baru.ca*
An appealing neighbourhood bistro, Baru has won plenty of admirers in West Point Grey and its surrounds for its pan-Latin concoctions, well-priced drinks and spot-on service. The menu offers a Latin American culinary odyssey from the tangy tastes of Honduran ceviche all the way down to the salty, spicy flavours of Argentine chimichurri. Created by a trio of Colombians, Baru's small plates rule the warm room, complemented by a South American and Spanish-leaning wine list. Cocktails take on a Latin flavour too – try the refreshing Peruvian pisco and shimmering Brazilian cachaca. The inviting room has both space and grace and its modern design (polished concrete floors, bold colour scheme and open kitchen) contrasts with well-placed religious and indigenous art and artefacts.

*52 Powell St*
*Gastown*
*Map 10 B1* **39**

### Cobre
*604 669 2396* | *www.cobrerestaurant.com*
Nuevo Latino tapas and small plates that range from subtle flavours of Brazil to lively Cuban concoctions grace the menu at Gastown's sexy, two-level eating address. Since it opened in July 2007, locals have been thronging through Cobre's doors for thrills such as wild boar chorizo tacos and an extensive wine list that delivers the very best of Argentine, Chilean and Uruguayan liquid wonders. The rooms' wooden beams and exposed red brick make a cosy backdrop for lingering over a concise but inventive menu of ceviches, soups, empanadas and pupusas. A handy 'Latino lingo' sheet explains any terms that might be unfamiliar to new diners, from achiote to verde. Cobre's assured staff will also explain menu options to patrons who range from hungry tourists to local chefs, couples on dates and youthful, trendy Gastown regulars.

*1326 Davie St*
West End
Map 7 B3 **40**

## Lolita's South Of The Border Cantina

*604 696 9996 | www.lolitasrestaurant.com*

With its warm colours and tongue-in-cheek tiki touches, Lolita's is ideal for sharing 'bocadita' morsels with friends or dates. Don't plan on private conversations; the tiny tables are packed tightly together and on any night you might be crammed alongside models, off-duty chefs or homesick Mexicans. Hipsters and local gourmands perch at the heavy wooden bar that runs the length of the low-lit room and a cheerful hum of conversation provides a vibrant backdrop for Mexican, south-western and Caribbean-influenced dishes. Discerning liquor drinkers also detour to Lolita's to sample the extensive collection of tequilas. Shots run the gamut from the respectable Sauza Blanco at $5.25 to the top notch Patron Anejo at $19.25. To be sure of a seat, visit before 18:00 or after the dinner rush subsides at 21:00.

*2515 Main St*
Mount Pleasant
Map 11 B2 **41**

## Zocalo

*604 677 3521 | www.zocalorestaurant.ca*

A funky contemporary Mexican room near the corner of Broadway and Main, Zocalo is the place to sashay to when you've had your fill of straightforward tacos and enchiladas. Smallish portions of a modern fusion spin on Mexican food encourage slow savouring of dishes such as coriander and jalapeno-rich ceviche, sauteed prawns with guajillo chillies, and decadent chicken mole poblano. You'll be glad you took your time when you have to choose between traditional desserts such as coco de flan and pastel tres leches. Snazzy decor featuring Day of the Dead type skulls, deep blue walls and fun, primary coloured lighting fixtures are the backdrop, and the ambience is upped a notch Wednesday to Saturday nights when live salsa and Latin jazz is the soundtrack, with people often taking to the floor and dancing between tables. Service is decent, and strong margaritas rule the drinks list.

## Malaysian

Other options **Thai** p.444, **Singaporean** p.443, **Chinese** p.420

*1096 Denman St*
West End
Map 7 B2 **42**

## Banana Leaf

*604 683 3333 | www.bananaleaf-vancouver.com*

Step off bustling Denman Street and find yourself in this calm, cool den of Malaysian delights. Even when Vancouver's weather is far from idyllic, Banana Leaf's dark wood and shutters create the illusion that they are keeping out the blazing hot sun outside, creating the perfect setting to savour the lively menu's lemongrass, turmeric and ginger-laced creations. Malaysian food is a joyful collision of Indonesian, Chinese, Thai, Singaporean and even Portuguese influences, courtesy of its strategic geographic location. The Banana Leaf takes all these inspirations and serves them up in the form of fiery Singapore laksa, rich red curry sayur lemak, tangy satays and traditional local street food staples, such as mee goreng fried noodles. These satisfying servings are accompanied by a small yet cheerful wine list. There are also branches of Banana Leaf in Fairview (820 West Broadway, 604 731 6333) and Kitsilano (3005 West Broadway, 604 734 3005).

## Mediterranean

Other options **Greek** p.432, **Italian** p.434, **Spanish** p.444

*1 West Cordova St*
Gastown
Map 10 B1 **43**

## Boneta

*604 684 1844 | www.boneta.ca*

Simple yet elegant decor sets the tone in Boneta, one of Gastown's more recent arrivals. Another brick in the gentrification of the area, Boneta's walls are two tone, with rich wood panelling anchoring crisp white paint, while plain wooden bistro tables and chairs are lined up in the airy room. The gourmand magnet fills with a cheerful crowd of hipsters and the occasional celebrity as night falls. A nightly fresh sheet showcases fine west coast produce, and chef Jeremie Bastien's creativity is on display in the open kitchen. The bar area of this modern bistro fills to capacity most evenings with socialites, laidback locals and those who work nearby. Dishes such as boar bacon lardons or pheasant au vin are accompanied by cleverly crafted cocktails and elusive biodynamic wines. A warm welcome and farewell leaves you feeling like a regular on your very first visit.

**562 Beatty St**
*Downtown*
*Map 10 A2* **44**

## Chambar

*604 879 7119* | *www.chambar.com*

Informal fine dining is what Vancouver's top Belgian address is all about. Chambar's European flavours are cleverly juxtaposed with spicy north African influences and the result is utterly titillating. Moule frites is the star menu attraction here and, when presented in a fresh tomato, smoked chilli, coconut cream and coriander sauce, it is irresistible. But don't miss out on some of Chambar's other excellent offerings, such as bouillabaisse or sweet and delicious cherry duck. Servings here are extremely generous, while the cocktails are slick and inventive, and, naturally for a Belgian hostelry, there's an excellent selection of beers. A trendy, big city ambience prevails in the hip, modern, inviting room, and both the staff and the crowd are almost as decorative as the dishes that come efficiently out of the kitchen. Changing artwork hangs on the walls and an opulent chandelier illuminates the warm red hues and red brick of the room.

**45 Blood Alley**
*Gastown*
*Map 10 B1* **45**

## Salt Tasting Room

*604 633 1912* | *www.salttastingroom.com*

This wine and charcuterie deli is a brilliantly stark and simple restaurant concept, offering an exciting eating experience with a difference. After braving a slightly insalubrious alley (with an equally dark name), diners choose three meats or cheeses and three condiments and wine to accompany them. There's no kitchen, and handwritten menus and a blackboard detail the day's range of locally sourced sausages, salamis, cured meats and artisan cheeses provided by adjacent suppliers, such as Granville Island's famed Oyama Sausage Company, Robert Belcham of Fuel and Seattle's Salumi. Red brick walls and hanging bulbs continue the minimalism and a thrilling wine list offers sumptuous sips by the 2oz taste, glass or bottle. A long communal table hosts so many off-duty chefs and restaurant managers you have to wonder who is helming the rest of the city's dining emporia. Staff are smiling, knowledgeable and welcoming. A limited number of reservations are available, but largely it's first-come, first-served.

## Middle Eastern

**1206 Seymour St**
*Downtown*
*Map 9 D1* **46**

## Nuba

*778 371 3266* | *www.nuba.ca*

Authentic Lebanese cuisine stars at Nuba, a cosy den just off Davie Street. Decor is sparing, without descending to drab. White-painted brick is brightened by splashes of greenery in the corners, and eye-catching photographs of urban scenes punctuate the walls. An eclectic ambience prevails; muffled jazz might ricochet into reverb-heavy trip-hop or soul as youthful staff in ironic T-shirts slouch behind the counter and take orders from purposeful commuters, earnest vegan couples on dates and locals on their days off. Offering an impressive array of vegetarian, vegan and carnivorous fare, Nuba promises – and delivers on its claim – fresh ingredients, as vegetables are hand selected and all produce is certified organic, where possible. All beef on the menu is non-medicated and hormone free. You can taste it in the lively salads, mezzes and falafel and kafta plates. There's another branch at 322 West Hastings Street (604 688 1655).

## Russian

**457 West Broadway**
*Mount Pleasant*
*Map 9 F4* **47**

### Rasputin Russian Cuisine
*604 879 6675*

The hedonistic spirit abounds in this lively room, with larger-than-life owner/entertainer Michael Shinder ensuring spirits (of all sorts) among his beloved patrons are soaring all evening long. Traditional home-style Russian food rules the day, including cabbage rolls, Ukrainian borshch, Russian beet salad, and chicken kiev. The house stand-out is Rasputin's fabulous sword kebab (grilled lamb, chicken or pork), served using a two foot sword. The portions are enough to make any bear dance. Vancouverites are not used to being serenaded at dinner, let alone feeling as if they are in the middle of a joyous peasant wedding in Siberia, so check your inhibitions at the door and prepare for a most memorable party. The vodka list includes 40 different brands. Budem zdorovy!

## Seafood

**1095 Hamilton St**
*Yaletown*
*Map 9 E1* **48**

### Blue Water Cafe
*604 688 8078* | *www.bluewatercafe.net*

Inside the red brick walls of this heritage building sushi knives flash and marvels are created from lobster, sockeye salmon and other recent residents of nearby waters by a team of master seafood chefs. Opt for dining room seating, a 'ringside' seat by sushi deity Yoshi Tabo's raw bar, or out on the sunny patio on Hamilton Street. While entrees are predominantly fish focused, you can also opt for sumptuous beef tenderloin and short ribs. Be sure to leave space for dessert; the extensive menu, with its creative dessert wine pairings, is reason enough to visit the cosy, elegant room. Rare cognacs, tequilas and perfect cocktails keep those at the bar company as they snack on oysters from BC,

Salt Tasting Room

Blue Water Cafe

Washington and the east coast, and the wine list has won numerous awards. As you would expect from such an assured dining destination, the service is impeccable.

C Restaurant

**2-1600 Howe St**
False Creek
Map 9 C1 **49**

## C Restaurant

*604 681 1164 | www.crestaurant.com*
Playful creations such as 'virtual' smoked Kagan Bay scallops and foie gras macaroons feature on the innovative and intriguing menus at C. Tucked away at the foot of Howe, adjacent to the Aquabus dock, the restaurant turned 10 in 2007. The consistently excellent contemporary seafood address has won shoals of awards in its first decade and stands to reel in plenty more with its confident cuisine, an impeccable wine list featuring more than 900 varieties, and those killer False Creek views. Wine-paired tasting menus offer an exciting way to sample a delicious range of C's creations, and there's also a children's menu. The light, bright, airy room's minimalist decor and open kitchen create an upbeat backdrop that doesn't distract from the edible art on the plate. A generous patio area looks out at the marina, the bridges and Granville Island.

**2205 Commissioner St**
Hastings East
Map 4 B4 **50**

## The Cannery

*604 254 9606 | www.canneryseafood.com*
This classic seafood fine-dining destination is located in the middle of a waterfront industrial zone on a road that requires permission from a security guard to drive on to. Established in what feels like the secluded mansion of a weather-beaten skipper, this dimly lit restaurant boasts some of the finest views, service and wines around. Try the fennel and BC octopus salad or dark rum marinated ahi tuna carpaccio for starters. Mains include fresh local Dungeness crab, salmon wellington, and smoked rack of lamb. Wines focus on BC, Pacific west coast and California, but classic Italian and French selections are on hand for traditionalists. On a nice day, order the deluxe take-out picnic basket (equipped with disposable cutlery and plates) and drive further down the road to New Brighton Park and its large waterfront views.

**777 Thurlow St**
Downtown
Map 7 D3 **51**

## Joe Fortes Seafood & Chop House

*604 669 1940 | www.joefortes.ca*
Featuring 'ocean friendly seafood choices', the Ocean Wise-accredited San Francisco style seafood grill and chop house is very much a Vancouver institution. At lunchtime, blue plate specials such as Carolina pulled pork shoulder and seafood jambalaya fill the grand, lofty room with jovial family groups, professional couples in business attire, lone ladies and ESL students. A cheerful hubbub of noise rises up to the brass ceiling fans, skylights and six foot long swordfish models, and chart music plays discreetly when the pianist finishes his set. The acoustics mean that you can have private conversations and not feel like the people at the next table could join in. A central oyster bar and grill sits in the middle of the two-storey restaurant, and banquettes line the walls. The upstairs patio is one of the best places to eat in summer. A hefty wine list is laden with more than 200 varieties, including two dozen by the glass or half bottle.

## Singaporean

**1043 Davie St**
West End
Map 7 C4 **52**

### Kam's Place
*604 669 3389*

Huge portions and speedy service are the star attractions at this quirkily decorated Davie Street Asian food favourite. Bird cages full of toy eggs and decorative elephants seem to have been almost surreptitiously placed about the wide, dimly lit room. Popular with staff from the adjacent St Paul's hospital, gay and lesbian couples from the neighbourhood and tourists from the dozens of Downtown hotels nearby, operations are presided over by the smiling Kam and kept running at a rapid pace by his unobtrusive and efficient staff. Lunch specials bring enough to make do for dinner as well, and two-for-one tokens from *The Georgia Straight* make an evening meal a bargain option too. While Kam's draw is sometimes considered to be more on account of quantity than quality, it does a reliable pad thai, a good spicy nasi goreng (shrimp fried rice) and a snappy red vegetable curry.

## South-East Asian

**2958 West 4th Av**
Kitsilano
Map 8 B3 **53**

### The Flying Tiger
*604 737 7529* | *www.theflyingtiger.ca*

A tantalising array of reconstructed Asian street food decorates a stellar menu at swanky West Side dining destination The Flying Tiger. It's a slender, inviting room of Buddhas and warm hues where westsiders lounge over leisurely feasts. The menu takes you on a tasty culinary adventure through the streets of Mumbai, Seoul, Hanoi, Manila and other delectable, lesser-known corners of south-east Asia. Settle into a banquette or grab a seat on the patio and savour a succession of small plates, from spring rolls nestled in banana leaves and served in bamboo steamers to Saltspring mussels in Panang red curry with chilli-heavy fried bread. This parade of tempting treats not only tastes good, but is good for your conscience – meats are free-range, produce is organic and seafood is sustainable. A lively wine list skims down the west coast, and picks a few classics from further off.

**1026 Granville St**
Downtown
Map 7 D4 **54**

### Sanafir
*604 678 1049* | *www.sanafir.ca*

*Sanafir*

Named after a small town on the legendary Silk Road, opulent Sanafir is where Vancouver's bright and beautiful come to mingle over morsels from a lively menu that steps smartly from Indonesia to India to Korea without faltering. Once you've discovered this sultry social emporium, you'll yearn to return for its platters of tapas trios that present very different takes on a central ingredient, such as chicken or salmon three ways. Decor in the sexy room has an Arabian accent, and the lofty, split-level room sparkles with serious star power, both on account of the sumptuous food and, in no small part, because it's very much a celebrity haunt – you never know who might be lurking in the dimmer corners where the flickering candles and bronze lanterns have cast their shadows. Rich colours, vaulted ceilings and leather beds add to the distinctive spell Sanafir casts over its customers. Upstairs is a lounge featuring eastern-style beds to recline on while you sip cocktails.

## Spanish
Other options **Mediterranean** p.439

**1277 Howe St**
*Downtown*
*Map 9 D1* **55**

### La Bodega
*604 684 8815* | *www.labodegavancouver.com*
Whenever you want to revisit that beloved restaurant you went to on a family holiday back in the 70s, head past the bus stops on Howe and slope through the doors of La Bodega. A fabulous slice of Spain, La Bodega dishes up the city's finest paella, a sumptuous feast of saffron rice, chicken, clams, pork and prawns that will take you to Madrid with every mouthful. Much to the relief of the phalanx of regulars who report to the bar on a seemingly daily basis, the traditional dark interior and lengthy tapas menu remain resolutely unchanged. Thankfully, the prices of those spice-laden patatas bravas, ceviches, chorizos and hefty meatballs, not to mention the sangria and robust red wines that accompany them, have stayed remarkably constant too over the years. Why change a good thing?

## Thai

**2325 Cambie St**
*Fairview*
*Map 9 F4* **56**

### Chao Phraya
*604 732 3939*
Named after the famed 'river of kings' in Thailand, Chao Phraya's colourful exterior lures passers-by with sculptures of elephants and dancers. Once through the doors, blue vinyl banquettes and central circular tables provide comfortable seating from which to enjoy substantial feasts of traditional dishes such as pad thai and the traffic light choices of curry. Lemongrass, lime and galanga flavour the dishes, available in various degrees of spiciness. Just as traditional, but not so common in the western world, are menu items such as boneless chicken's feet spiced with chilli and lime, and a tilapia dish that delivers a super hot spicy kick. Pop in for an elaborate three-course dinner or grab a swift lunch special. Chao Phraya's tangy delights are also available for takeout or delivery. Those feeling like creating their own culinary adventure can stock up on curry sauces and recreate their favourite feasts at home.

**3629 West Broadway**
*Kitsilano*
*Map 5 D1* **57**

### Montri's
*604 738 9888* | *www.montri-thai.com*
A well-dressed cross section of Vancouverites flock to this straightforward yet elegant and tranquil West Side room. Fresh coriander, lemongrass, kaffir lime, kha ginger, strong coconut milk and some of the world's most searingly hot chillies create the tapestry of flavour woven into each of the dishes. To guarantee everything tastes just like home, some of the ingredients are flown in fresh from Bangkok. Five levels of chilli rating warn diners what they are about to bite into. Don't see exactly what you want to have for dinner? Opt for the menu's 'your very own creation' and the chef will happily oblige. Indeed, you'll find all the staff on the helpful side, which contributes to making dinner at Montri's a popular option. An extensive wine list focuses its attention on BC and Pacific north-west wines, but still manages to pay homage to old world vintages as well.

## Vegetarian

**2301 Main St**
*Mount Pleasant*
*Map 11 B2* **58**

### The Foundation Lounge
*604 708 0881*

An edgy, eco-conscious crew in their 20s and 30s frequents Foundation. An eclectic array of the population, from off-duty anarchists to on-the-ball legal types, perch on mismatched retro tables and vinyl chairs as they feast on heart and conscience-healthy fare such as tofu satay salads, veggie burgers, vegan pesto pasta and tofu and mango scramble. Both the funky decor and the politics behind this restaurant lounge are several shades of green, and the menu has an agenda of its own. Make your statement with 'insurgent hummus' or 'sesame society', or other such examples of Foundation's creative and fresh vegan and vegetarian fare. At night, candles flicker and the volume goes up to a din that is sometimes deafening, so you'll have to speak up if you want to make your point or order more local drafts, imported beers, inexpensive wines or the killer sangria.

**2724 West 4th Av**
*Kitsilano*
*Map 8 C3* **59**

### The Naam
*604 738 7151* | *www.thenaam.com*

An authentic old-school haunt left over from Kitsilano's bohemian days as Vancouver's 70s hippy hotspot, The Naam has been sauntering along in its own distinctively unrushed way for more than 30 years. While today's clientele still includes those who spent the summer of love on West 4th, they have been joined by armies of young mums with yoga mats and toddlers under their arms, penny pinching grad students and local new age lesbians. Don't go to The Naam hoping for a quick plate of its famed blueberry pancakes or vast veggie omelette – you'll get the food, but the staff are in absolutely no rush to feed you, so it's a perfect time to catch up on reading up on some new crystals or to dither over which of the five dragon bowl wok dishes you're going to try. It's open 24 hours and has live music on the calendar every night.

## Vietnamese

**4851 Main St**
*Main*
*Map 6 A2* **60**

### Au Petit Café
*604 873 3328*

Delicious iced coffee with condensed milk and a generously stacked, crispy meatball baguette makes a perfect lunch to stay or to go from this small, cosy Vietnamese favourite in south Main. Squeeze into one of the 10 tables crammed tightly together in the tiny pink room and tuck into a bahn mi or Vietnamese spring rolls. The pho is adequate and pleasantly salty. You'll usually have to wait 20 minutes or more to get a seat, but once there, service is speedy. The fact that the homey Au Petit Café is always packed is a sure sign that it's worth the wait. If you're craving a crispy baguette get there before noon – they can sell out before the lunch rush even starts. If there are no meatballs left, try the chicken, coriander and daikon version. Call ahead if you really just can't do without one.

**3388 Main St**
*Main*
*Map 11 B4* **61**

### Pho Hoang
*604 874 0832*

The perfect place to take friends for pho, this nondescript option in the south Main Vietnamese hub dishes out steaming bowls of the country's famed broth. More than 100 items are crammed on the menu, meaning plenty of reasons for returning for more. Standout options include the impossibly cheap lemongrass pork chop on rice. Both the room's decor and the service are decidedly below par, and at times Pho Hoang would win an award for the slowest take on fastfood in the city, but these are not the reason you're here. Slurp a few mouthfuls of the near addictive pho and you'll swiftly forget if the server just slammed down the drinks and stood on your foot.

## West Coast

### Aurora Bistro

**2420 Main St**
Mount Pleasant
Map 11 B2 **62**

604 873 9944 | www.aurorabistro.ca
Every night the very best of modern Canadian fare appears out of the kitchen of this upscale bistro that has become an integral part of the Mount Pleasant neighbourhood. Decor is minimal and retro hip, with swathes of blonde wood panelling. Aurora specialises in local and organic produce and the impressive wine list is kept strictly regional

*Aurora Bistro*

too, with all wines hailing from BC. This commitment to keeping it close pays off and the modern bistro presents a tightly cohesive take on Canadian cuisine. Try the red wine shallot tart tartin, tea smoked Polderside Farm duck or one of the daily takes on Sloping Hill natural pork. Seafood is all sustainable and approved by Ocean Wise. Service from an obviously passionate, courteous staff is impeccable. It's one of those restaurants that you know you can't go wrong in choosing, whether for a casual dinner or an important occasion.

### The Beach House At Dundarave Pier

**150 25th St**
West Vancouver
Map 3 D2 **63**

604 922 1414 | www.atthebeachhouse.com
Join an affluent West Vancouver set for a neighbourhood take on fine dining at this immaculately restored 1912 teahouse at the beach. The heritage building offers the best views of Vancouver that you can get while sipping a desert-dry martini or sampling oysters with mango jalapeno salsa. Its famed weekend brunch attracts well-heeled locals and visiting big names. At night diners get to look up from their wild mushroom cappuccino, spicy wok fried calamari or roasted free range chicken and see lights flicker on the Lions Gate Bridge and across the inlet. A 70 seat heated patio puts you at the water's edge, with perfect Stanley Park views, and a martini lounge beckons inside. On rainy days, a fireplace casts a welcome cosy glow on the room. The 450 vintage wine list has won *Wine Spectator* awards time after time. Book ahead, as this one is always popular.

### Beyond Restaurant & Lounge

**1015 Burrard St**
Downtown
Map 7 D4 **64**

604 684 3474 | www.beyondrestaurant.com
A voluminous venue in the Century Plaza hotel, Beyond offers a cohesive array of distinct dining areas. Whatever pace of meal you want to set there's a section of the restaurant sure to suit your mood: devour a swift breakfast in the voyeuristic zone by the kitchen's glass wall; sink into a cream leather armchair with an after-work drink and an eye on the game in the relaxed lounge; or slink into a horseshoe banquette upstairs for a successful dinner with the clients. The very reasonably priced menu thoughtfully outlines sustainable seafood and health-conscious choices. Breakfasts range from house-made granola to hefty plates of beef hash. Dinner highlights include BC wild

salmon with truffle honey, west coast bouillabaisse, and duck breast with creamed apples. Service runs smoothly and pleasantly, making it tempting to try out all seating areas for successive meals.

**941 Davie St** ◀
West End
Map 7 D4 **65**

## Bin 941

*604 683 1246* | *www.bin941.com*

Every ethnicity of cuisine is invited into former rock singer Gord Martin's kitchen, where flavours ricochet from Moroccan to Mexican to Portuguese to Japanese. A flamboyant small plate menu sees Yucatan spice-rubbed bison flat iron steak nestle alongside mussels steamed with garam masala and baked brie wedges with anjou pear. The menu is as eclectic as the upbeat crowd who eagerly cram into the minute 40 seat tapas parlour's few tables. Bin 941 is a delicious highlight on the otherwise fairly generic Davie Street. The drinks list includes a small but enthusiastic selection of wine, as well as sangria, beer and some choice scotch. It's a hectic, boisterous stop, popular with both an after-work set and the after-bar crowd. No reservations are taken, so prepare to wait outside for at least half an hour and work up an appetite for Martin's unexpected, quirky masterpieces. If you want to go one better, try Bin 942 at 1521 West Broadway (604 734 9421).

**2183 West 4th Av** ◀
Kitsilano
Map 8 E3 **66**

## Bishop's

*604 738 2025* | *www.bishopsonline.com*

Bishop's has achieved almost mythological status in Vancouver for the locally sourced, sustainable creations that it has consistently sent out over the past 20 years, and for the gracious welcome owner John Bishop extends to his guests. Weekly menus highlight the best of the season and might include such seemingly simple options as tarragon marinated Hazelemere Farms beet salad, roasted Cowichan Bay farm duck cassoulet or Mission Hill cabernet-poached pear. Excellent pairings from the impressive wine list are always suggested by the staff to accompany each course. Celebrities and dignitaries dine alongside home-grown food lovers in a modern dining room, bright with splashes of colour from the liberal flower arrangements and with art and sculptures. Leave the mobile phone behind, book ahead to be sure of a seat in the elegant split level space and prepare to pamper your palate.

**1583 Coal Harbour Quay** ◀
West End
Map 7 D1 **67**

## Cardero's

*604 669 7666* | *www.vancouverdine.com/carderos/home.html*

Elevated just above the waters of Coal Harbour, Cardero's has killer views of all the waterfront action against the stunning backdrop of the North Shore Mountains and Stanley Park. The cavernous marina-side room fills at lunchtime and in the evening with work colleagues, visiting couples, ladies who lunch (and dine), and those who ambled in from the Seawall on an off-chance of a table. The menu offers a glimpse into BC's waters and culinary influences, from the First Nations-inspired cedar plank baked wild salmon to Chinese-style wok squid. For those who prefer tastes from dry land, grilled prime rib steaks, succulent burgers and wood oven pizza top the bill. An impressive selection of wines is available by the glass. The adjoining Live Bait Yacht Club Marine Pub is a handy place to while away any time until your table is ready. The pub stays open until midnight.

**3121 Granville St** ◀
Fairview
Map 5 F1 **68**

## Chow

*604 608 2469* | *www.chow-restaurant.com*

Another shining star among the constellation of glamorous hotspots on South Granville, Chow's self-conscious service and decor are somewhat at odds with the simple west coast wonders that emanate from the kitchen. Organic cuisine is translated to the plate in the form of Sloping Hills Farm organic pork and sun choke puree, baby beet salad with Okanagan goat cheese – sweet with candied walnuts, tart with bitter orange puree – and the unexpected delight of contrasting textures of pistachio frozen nougat with vanilla poached pears. A tidy menu presents dining options in easily digestible chunks. Chow attracts a crowd made up of those drawn by the style and those lured by the food, exquisitely cooked and perfectly presented.

**3941 Main St**
*Main*
*Map 6 A2* **69**

## Crave

*604 872 3663 | www.craveonmain.ca*

The very good brunch served here is a compelling reason to make your way up Main Street to this modern bistro with a gallery ambience. With menu sections that include 'cold chillin' and 'hot off the griddle', Crave offers a confident, cool take on breakfast standards from eggs benedict to buttermilk pancakes. Later in the day or on weekdays, appealing lunch sandwiches range from pulled pork and coleslaw to chicken melt with citrus tapenade and a tasty brown rice and roasted veggie burger. The menu also stars retro-chic comfort food put together with a knowing modern twist. Try the sundried tomato and basil meatloaf or poutine with truffle parmesan fries. At night, candles flicker on the dark wood tables and Crave feels cosy and romantic. If you've worked up a thirst, there is Okanagan Springs on tap and a small selection of other bottles. A compact wine list puts pins all over the map of world wines. Seats on the intimate patio are the ones to nab in the summer.

**645 Howe St**
*Downtown*
*Map 7 E3* **70**

## Diva At The Met

*604 602 7788 | www.metropolitan.com/diva*

Diva's dashing three-tier dining room creates a dramatic backdrop for seasonal selections that will make you delighted it's spring – or summer, autumn or even winter; every season tastes delicious at Diva. An award-winning wine list and a comprehensive cocktail menu accompany playfully presented dishes that all sound sweet. It's as if the kitchen was entirely staffed by pastry chefs. Entree choices include the likes of Vancouver Island smoked black cod with lemon and tarragon, cod cake or foie gras with hazelnut, sultana and bittersweet chocolate dust. Conversely, desserts borrow extensively from the herb garden and feature unexpected savoury twists, such as yuzu roulade coriander puree or blackberry verbena sorbet. For an early morning Downtown treat, sample citrus and maple croissants or more substantial fare from the breakfast menu. Diva's pleasant and precise service means you'll be left wanting for nothing.

*Fuel*

**1944 West 4th Av**
*Kitsilano*
*Map 8 F3* **71**

## Fuel

*604 288 7905 | www.fuelrestaurant.ca*

Fuel's high-end food is regional, seasonal and exceptional. Seats at the bar overlooking the open kitchen practically make you feel like you're in the kitchen at a party. The intimate 45 seat dining room attracts big names from sport, TV and politics. If you can take your eyes off who is at the next table, you'll see a stunning silver lightning chandelier overhead, the main feature in an otherwise minimal room. On the plate is a thrilling seasonal showcase of the best of BC in compact portions, of which you'll savour every mouthful. The roasted line-caught ling cod and the dry aged Alberta prime ribeye are perfect, while the chef's menus are delectable opportunities to spoil yourself.

**1079 Mainland St**
*Yaletown*
*Map 9 E1* **72**

## Glowbal Grill & Satay Bar

*604 602 0835* | *www.glowbalgrill.com*

Saunter in off the cobbled streets and choose between the chocolate-toned banquettes or social bar stools of this welcoming room. Polished wood and red brick walls backdrop power lunches, lingering dinners and drinks. Decorative but down-to-earth staff give a warm welcome and attentive service throughout. At the open kitchen, a line of chefs in black hurtles out dishes picked from the weighty blue and gold leather menus. At lunch, the Glowbal signature Kobe beef burger is always a winning choice. Dinner options such as the sumptuous barbecue BC wild salmon and beef tenderloin with butternut squash ravioli create a dining experience that will have you loping back for more. Excellent cocktails and unexpected beer choices abound. The long line of bar stools fills with a fashion-conscious set of Yaletown loft dwellers and creative types from the offices and headquarters in the neighbourhood. A seat at the bar is highly recommended for cocktails and beautiful-people watching. The sultry Afterglow is Glowbal's award-winning martini lounge.

**1118 Mainland St**
*Yaletown*
*Map 9 E1* **73**

## Goldfish Pacific Kitchen

*604 689 8318* | *www.goldfishkitchen.com*

This Yaletown hotspot offers an interior as beautiful as the scenester set it attracts. Sand art and clear chandeliers hang in the bar area. The Starck chairs lounge alongside, filling with decorative denizens as the evening wears on. Frosted glass and aluminium star in a consciously cool kitchen, which sends out excellent fusion fare that casually wears its Asian and European influences on its designer sleeves. Try the mussels with black bean coconut cream, the sweet potato and pork curry with turmeric or the Alaskan king crab with spicy hot sambal. Booths that host genteel ladies and ad execs wooing clients at lunchtime bask below blue-lit walls in the main room, and a sunny patio beckons outside. Staff are pleasant but unconcerned, chosen for their looks rather than their charm. An interesting wine list sits well beside a rake of premium sakes and creative signature cocktails.

**2610 Main St**
*Mount Pleasant*
*Map 11 B2* **74**

## Habit Lounge

*604 877 8582* | *http://habitlounge.ca*

Arguably one of the neighbourhood's hottest hangouts since it took over its small space on Main Street in 2005, Habit Lounge is the easy answer to the question: 'where to eat?'. Situated on the area's hip strip, the narrow space's rec room style recalls the 70s and 80s with its orange vinyl booths and glass orb lights swinging overhead. Though the decor is retro the menu is thoroughly modern, featuring sharing plates that allow for a nibble of this and a taste of that. Standout selections include the smoky Spanish mussels – soak up the broth with the freshly made bread – carrot and brie perogies, and the sablefish-halibut cake made from a sustainable source. Young couples with kids, hipsters, and even Downtown denizens line up to get a spot in this friendly joint that packs a crowd in each evening. Arrive early to snag a seat, or be prepared to cool your heels outside or at The Cascade Room next door (also owned by the same group).

## Lift Bar & Grill

*333 Menchion Mews*
*West End*
*Map 7 C1* **75**

*604 689 5438* | *www.liftbarandgrill.com*

Consistently good food and service have finally caught up with expectations at this cutting-edge architectural wonder on the waterfront. A clever, rich French-Japanese-west coast menu ricochets from excellent sushi to cauliflower soup with stilton and wild salmon with a tobiko-champagne butter. The food is so good it might even distract you from the million dollar views of the North Shore, floatplanes coming and going and other Coal Harbour activity as you dine; from the second you arrive you see why Lift is billed 'Bar. Grill. View.' It's an impossibly sophisticated, sexy spot that makes your heart beat faster. The upper deck patio with its duo of outdoor fireplaces is probably the best summer seating the city can offer. Schedule a stop at Lift into a Sunday Seawall stroll and sample weekend brunch classics such as Belgian waffles with lemon yoghurt and the substantial Coal Harbour breakfast plate.

## Monk McQueens Fresh Seafood & Oyster Bar

*601 Stamps Landing*
*False Creek*
*Map 9 E3* **76**

*604 877 1351* | *www.monkmcqueens.com*

There's really no more quintessential Vancouver experience than a long summer evening spent on a sunny patio with a crisp glass of BC white in hand and a plate of oysters on the table. Monk's, as it's known, is one of the city's top spots for such indulgences. The patio and two storeys of dining room look out over False Creek at Yaletown and the mountains beyond. The extensive menu favours seafood but doesn't overlook four-legged fare. Consider ordering a few 'whet plates' while deciding on entree choices: lobster corndogs with miso mustard or caramelised Baja scallops will see you through until your paella or nori crusted ahi arrives at the table. Upstairs (simply called McQueens Upstairs) is more upmarket and romantic than the downstairs Oyster Bar and offers dinner and dancing to live jazz on weekends. Downstairs, the room fills with a pleasant swell of conversation and kids are actively welcomed with their own menu.

## Nu

*1661 Granville St*
*Downtown*
*Map 9 C2* **77**

*604 646 4668* | *www.whatisnu.com*

Located at ground level, just outside the shadow of Granville Bridge, Nu perches out over the waters of False Creek, a stunning beacon of modern design with food to match. Nu rewards those who persevere in trying to find its rather obscure location with French-tinged takes on west coast cuisine, such as side shrimp fritters and caramelised lamb cheeks. Whether you're sitting inside in the handsome turquoise retro chairs by the floor-to-ceiling windows or lounging outside on the small sleek patio, you'll have front row seats for watching the False Creek Ferries and, during the day, kayaks and dragon boats glide past as you graze. An impressive bar set-up dominates the room and rustles up some truly excellent cocktails. Sunday jazz brunch packs the chic, light room with an affluent set of Yaletown locals and tourists who were determined to hunt this elusive emporium down.

## The Ocean Club

*105-100 Park Royal*
*North Vancouver*
*Map 3 F2* **78**

*604 926 2326* | *www.theoceanclub.ca*

A youthful North Vancouver crowd flock to this casual, sultry Park Royal restaurant and lounge. Upbeat dance tunes pulse through the sexy, suburban space and an exuberant cocktail list is full of flavours of the other coast. While the vibe says Miami Beach, The Ocean Club takes full advantage of its Pacific location. The curvaceous blonde wood panelling, slick white horseshoe armchairs and couches, and glass tables might transport you to sunnier climes, but the menu will bring you happily back to BC. As you delve into Salt Spring Island mussels in chilli and coconut broth, Fraser Valley pork tenderloin, Yukon gold potato cream and Queen Charlotte halibut, you'll be happy to do without Miami's spices. When you live in BC, there really is no taste like home. Closed on Mondays.

## Parkside

**1906 Haro St**
*West End*
*Map 7 B1* **79**

*604 683 6912 | www.parksiderestaurant.ca*

A quaint West End hideaway, nestled in a residential street near Stanley Park, Parkside is out of sight of the bright lights and glitzier rooms of Downtown. Tucked underneath the Buchan Hotel, this sophisticated spot excels at unpretentious classical cuisine with a Mediterranean slant. Assured staff easily explain any menu queries, and the house-made sorbets are exquisite. Despite the restaurant's cosy size, tables don't intrude on one another, and on a warm summer night the courtyard tables outside are the most romantic in the city. Back inside, a sophisticated selection of after-dinner drinks, including lengthy lists of cognac, port and eau de vie, are served up from the dark oak bar. Other interesting flavours are on the menu each October when Parkside hosts a wild mushroom and game festival. Parking is near impossible, so opt for valet parking, walk or take a cab.

## Raincity Grill

**1193 Denman St**
*West End*
*Map 7 A2* **80**

*604 685 7337 | www.raincitygrill.com*

One of the original staunch supporters of the movement to use organic, artisan and regional produce, Raincity Grill continues to proffer inventive takes on the delights that come from farms and waters in the vicinity. Menus teem with local and seasonal ingredients gathered and foraged from a 100 mile radius, from Okanagan berries to Saltspring Island mussels. Sample the highlights with a tasting menu: the three course early bird menu is just $30, and six and seven course fixed-price menus are a steal. Each dish is paired with a suggested grape, and the elegant wine list stretches the length of the west coast from BC to California. The vibrant, warm room with its splashes of colourful art often gets overlooked for the views of English Bay outside. To get even more of a view, try to nab a seat on the patio.

*Nu*

*Raincity Grill*

## Salmon House On The Hill

**2229 Folkestone Way**
*West Vancouver*
*Map 3 D1* **81**

*604 926 3212 | www.salmonhouse.com*

Perched on the slopes of the North Shore, the three-decade-old Salmon House has an eagle's eye view of Burrard Inlet below. Its sea-centric menu delights diners ensconced in upper level booths or gazing out the windows from prime view seats overlooking the vista. To feel in tune with the First Nations-inspired decor and impressive collection of art, masks and canoes, opt for the three course Uniquely BC menu. It takes you on a tasty tour of the province, from Bella Coola clams to Fanny Bay oysters and redcurrants and raspberries picked in Nelson and rustled into a linzentorte. The colour-coded menu shows you exactly where your dinner came from. The helpful, smiling staff add to the enjoyment of each visit, whether you are there for a romantic dinner or with the entire family racing to be front of the omelette bar line at Sunday brunch.

## The Shore Club

**688 Dunsmuir St**
*Downtown*
*Map 7 F3* **82**

*604 899 4400 | www.theshoreclub.ca*

Sibling of the nearby Gotham Steakhouse, this opulent, lofty steak and seafood emporium that dominates the Granville Dunsmuir corner is a striking dining choice. Handsome mahogany fixtures, ample banquettes and efficient servers in crisp white jackets set the tone in the generously proportioned upper level dining room. Like the amount that was spent on creating this destination dining room behind the stately 1928 facade, menu prices are not slight. High-grade Alberta beef shares the bill with an elegant haul of seafood. Steaks range from $36 to $50 and a side of lobster tail will add another $25 to your bill. If you really want to have it all, order the mixed grill (meat or seafood) and sample a cross section of The Shore Club's fare. It's the perfect place to take those clients you're trying to win round or that hard-to-impress in-law.

## Watermark

**1305 Arbutus St**
*Kitsilano*
*Map 8 E1* **83**

*604 738 5487 | www.watermarkrestaurant.ca*

The energy-efficient contemporary restaurant, with its picture windows looking out over Kits Beach, effortlessly delivers a succession of Pacific north-west classics off its confident menu. Try the prawn penne putanesca or crackling pork rack chop. The prawn spring rolls with water chestnuts and wasabi dip are reason enough to visit. Desserts are winners too: the Israeli couscous pudding with citrus compote and the single estate chocolate cake are irresistible. Seasonal specials enhance an already enticing menu and reasonable wine prices impress. The weekend brunch is highly recommended. While the daytime sees the room the domain of lunching ladies, relaxed tourists and animated realtors with their clients, evening attracts a more local set into seats at the wine bar and to the well-spaced four seater tables that stretch the length of the spacious room. Like the concession on the ground floor, Watermark has a dramatic two-way fire place, dividing the restaurant from the chic Fireside Lounge.

## West

**2881 Granville St**
*Fairview*
*Map 5 F1* **84**

*604 738 8938 | www.westrestaurant.com*

Vancouver's top restaurant, West gets everything right. The warm, russet colours, temperature controlled wall of wine and cherrywood bar are the backdrop for long lunches, even lengthier dinners and perfect martinis, courtesy of a stellar team of staff. Impeccable service ties together all the components of West's excellence. The menu informs you precisely which farm your duck came from and who made the goat cheese that accompanies your organic beetroot. Unexpected dishes you won't find anywhere else, such as pumpkin soup with cinnamon marshmallows, lure in locals, visiting moguls and celebrities, and food tourists. Some diners come to Vancouver specifically to eat at West. For an out-of-this-world experience, treat yourself to one of the three tasting menus (seasonal, signature or vegetarian). Every morsel of the west coast contemporary fare is a thrill, from the first taste of an amuse bouche to the petits fours that cap off the night.

### Zin Restaurant & Lounge

**1277 Robson St**
*West End*
*Map 7 D2* **85**

**604 408 1700** | *www.zin-restaurant.com*

Although this West End restaurant and lounge is on Robson Street, when you sink into a plush velvet couch, banquette or striped booth, you feel a world away from the hustle and bustle outside. Situated in the Pacific Palisades Hotel, sultry red and orange walls and dramatic lighting fixtures are the backdrop for Zin's excellent array of merlots, sauvignons and zinfandels. The menu teems with lively takes on west coast cuisine. You wouldn't know it, but a high proportion of dishes are actually gluten free. Hotel guests saunter in to join well dressed westenders as they dally over breakfast, lunch and dinner. An innovative kids' tasting menu gets the young ones to clean their plates. Zin's strength lies in its truly excellent staff, who manage to be warm, friendly and chatty, yet deliver flawless service at all times.

*West*

*Gastown dining*

*Stanley Industrial Alliance Stage*

## Cafes & Coffee Shops

Vancouverites love coffee. You can't walk more than half a block through Downtown without passing a coffee shop, usually sporting a long-but-patient queue. In winter, where most people wear gloves to keep their hands warm, Vancouver residents simply clasp hold of a paper cup full of a steaming brew. Fierce loyalty to specific coffee houses characterises the caffeine scene. Many swear by the latte art swirled out by Caffe Artigiano's award-winning baristas. Others hanker for the perfect roasts and pastries from 49th Parallel, yet others still can't be swayed from their devotion to the ethical blends served up at the many organic options available.

Starbucks, which originated across the US border in nearby Seattle, has sprouted on a vast number of Vancouver blocks, but local chain Blenz gives it a run for its money, with more than two dozen locations throughout the city, as does Canadian caffeine provider Tim Hortons. Smaller coffee chains

*Vancouver Art Gallery Cafe*

and roasters JJ Bean's, Bean Around The World and Waves also offer reliable grinds at various addresses, and many provide wireless internet.

Vancouver's cafes and coffee houses are popular evening meeting places and most fill until closing time with people catching up with friends, meeting for first dates or pouring over laptops and books. Many offer a simple sandwich, soup and pastry menu, but some, such as Main's Soma, serve upscale bistro fare and an inventive wine list in the evenings.

Most cafes are more adult-focussed than family friendly, and facilities specifically aimed at mothers are rare. An exception to this is Café Deux Soleils, which uses its live music stage area as a kids' play area during the day.

*2152 West 4th St*
*Kitsilano*
*Map 8 E3 86*

### 49th Parallel

*604 420 4901 | www.49thparallelcoffeeroasters.com*

This enticing Kitsilano room features a bold, rich chocolate and deep turquoise colour scheme. Decor is minimal but luxurious, and a lofty, high ceiling makes the elongated room feel airy and light. The decadence continues: the coffees roasted by the company, and concocted into mochas and more by the efficient and professional counter staff, are silky smooth, the opposite of Starbucks' more bitter brews, and chocolate croissants that are delivered daily practically melt in your mouth. As well as the affluent local set, 49th Parallel also attracts connoisseurs who make pilgrimages to the elegant coffee house from across the city.

## Café Deux Soleils

*2096 Commercial Dr*
*Grandview*
*Map 12 B1* **87**

*604 254 1195 | www.cafedeuxsoleils.com*

During the day, the booths and tables of Café Deux Soleils (not be confused with Café du Soleil further up the Drive) fill with an assortment of local bohemians, young mothers and their progeny and an array of artistic types. Toys litter the stage and kids seem to run loose throughout the cavernous room. As the afternoon wears on, the little ones disperse and the stage becomes the setting for spoken word, open mic and live music. It's one of the Drive's most popular brunch options. The cafe has kept the same much-loved vegetarian and vegan breakfast items and burgers on the menu for years.

## Caffe Artigiano

*763 Hornby St*
*Downtown*
*Map 7 E3* **88**

*604 694 7737 | www.caffeartigiano.com*

In a bustling block a few steps off Robson, Caffe Artigiano creates the perfect caffeine-based froth. Artigiano's baristas have won almost every award going for their creations. Pasta and grilled sandwiches are on the menu, but are very much a second thought after the exquisite espressos and lattes that appear from behind the counter. More a place for a quick jolt than one to lounge away an afternoon, this branch of the cafe is popular with Downtown workers, and there invariably seems to be a realtor or two proclaiming across a table. There are six Artigianos around town, all owned and run by the Piccolo family, and all guaranteeing the most perfect percolation possible.

## Continental Coffee

*1806 Commercial Dr*
*Grandview*
*Map 12 B1* **89**

*604 255 0712*

A considerable proportion of Vancouverites swear that the compact room on the corner of 2nd serves the city's best coffee. One of the Drive's many Italian cafes, the family-owned Continental fills with local lesbians, visiting bikers and old Italian men who down espresso before their games of bocce in nearby Victoria Park. It's a bustling, no-frills cafe which, despite the modern sign that appeared a couple of years ago, still feels pleasantly faded and comfortable. Huge picture windows are perfect for watching and wondering at everyone passing by. Another thing that hasn't changed much is the price list: Continental brews up some of the best bargains on the Drive.

## JJ Bean House Of Coffee

*3010 Main St*
*Main*
*Map 11 B3* **90**

*604 879 2326 | www.jjbeancoffee.com*

One of the city's most design-conscious coffee emporiums, JJ Bean on Main is one of six stars in the Vancouver caffeine chain's crown. It's a refreshing place to spend time, with its bleached blonde wood and polished aluminium exterior and spacious, bright interior. Its retro decor successfully manages to look and feel impeccably modern. The cafe is popular with the neighbourhood's twenty and thirtysomethings. They fill the tables and perch at counters that line the windows of the corner store, staring intently at their Macs and iBooks. Fast-moving staff keep queues to a minimum and quality high.

## Kits Coffee Co

*2198 West 4th Av*
*Kitsilano*
*Map 8 E3* **91**

*604 739 0139 | kitscoffee@shaw.ca*

The picture windows of this cheerful neighbourhood coffee house allow great views of the comings and goings on busy West 4th. Reliably good coffee is only half the reason Kits Coffee Co keeps its clientele; the cinnamon buns account for another sizeable proportion of its fan base. It's a bright place where pop music plays and local ladies who lunch sit at tables adjacent to business movers and shakers.

Wireless access, amiable and youthful staff, a good selection of newspapers and a sheltered patio (on the west-facing Yew Street side) are additional draws.

## Melriches Coffeehouse

*1244 Davie St*
*West End*
*Map 7 C4* **92**

*604 689 5282*

Crammed with people, even at hours of the day when you think everyone should be busy at work, Melriches is the caffeinated heart of Davie Village. Very much a neighbourhood coffee house, Melriches' edgy, young staff serve up excellent brews of local Bean Around The World coffee. Breakfast options provide many locals with a tasty start to their morning, and substantial sandwiches and cakes are on hand for those who need nourishment later in the day. Grab a paper, take a book or a friend and while away a few hours in this cosy java den.

## Pedro's Organic Coffee House

*1550 Anderson St*
*Granville Island*
*Map 9 B2* **93**

*604 899 0741*

Considering its location alongside Granville Island's Kids Market, it's no surprise that this L-shaped cafe often has rather a youthful demographic. On sunny days, the outside tables, overlooking a pond filled with ducks, are perfect for lingering over a latte in the fresh air. Inside, wireless access lures artistic island workers in. Pedro's also attracts a crowd of regulars from the neighbourhood, as well as a few tourists who have strayed away from the hordes at the island's main attractions. In addition to the always excellent coffees and teas, Pedro's has a range of sandwiches and soups, and a popular gelato counter.

## Soma Coffee Bar/Wine Bar

*151 East 8th Av*
*Mount Pleasant*
*Map 11 B2* **94**

*604 630 7502* | *www.somavancouver.com*

Despite its move to a new location a few blocks from its original home, Soma has held on to its incredibly loyal clientele and rewarded them with the addition of an extensive wine list, bottled and draught beer and a full kitchen. The hip, dark interior of this long room fills with local hipsters and eccentrics during the day, many hunched over laptops or devouring pastries with friends. Lattes are works of art and staff are always welcoming. The kitchen serves a selection of inventive and elegant salads, entrees and fondue. Wireless internet access is available.

## Turks Coffee Lounge

*1276 Commercial Dr*
*Grandview*
*Map 6 B1* **95**

*604 255 5805*

Turks sits opposite Grandview Park and is filled with a motley array of Drive characters, lured back over and over again by the friendly service and the excellent Milano coffee. It's an entirely laidback cafe and an easy place to spend a few hours solo during the day or evening. An appetising array of panini and pastries are on offer. Smokers cram into the two sidewalk spots, which means tables inside the windows are often rather smoky. Local artists' works feature on the walls and change every couple of months.

### Surf While You Slurp

For the many coffee lovers in Vancouver a quiet spot to settle down with a steaming brew isn't too hard to find. For some though, the coffee is not the only draw; many like to surf while they slurp, and can do so for free at a number of coffee shops in Vancouver that offer complimentary wireless for their customers. Vancouver Wifi Mug (vancouver.wifimug.org) is a handy website that lists the city's best hotspots. The site also provides info on opening times, whether you can use VPN and if you can buy fair trade coffee. Check out the site for a place in your area, or add your own Wi-Fi hideout to the list.

# On The Town

Vancouver's nightlife can be literally all over the map, with sexy lounges, rough and ready sports bars and gastropubs that take tired pub grub to tasty new heights. Nightclubs seem to be waning, but the chic cocktail lounge is enjoying a renaissance, especially in the high-end hotels that cater to an international guest list. And almost every establishment has a resident DJ that sets the tone and gets the party in gear.

In recent years, the Downtown Granville Street 'mall' has been designated the city's entertainment zone, and has become the hip strip for the college crowd, tourists and backpackers that stay in nearby hotels and hostels. With so many places packed into a few short blocks, Granville Street is an ideal place to stage a pub crawl, or flit from one nightclub queue to another, but it can get crazy on the weekends with so many people spilling out on to the streets after closing time. There has also been a proliferation of Irish-inspired Downtown pubs and bars, each offering its own brand of culture, whether it is a Celtic sing-along, an exhaustive list of imported beer, or non-stop sports being broadcast to a proud soccer jersey-wearing crowd.

Yaletown's swanky establishments entice a more moneyed and sophisticated clientele, while if you head west to Davie Street you'll find a thriving gay scene, replete with pubs, nightclubs and testosterone fuelled bars. Gastown has finally started to shed its reputation as a T-shirt selling tourist trap, reinventing itself as Vancouver's hotbed of hip. Live music is making a resurgence too. Local and visiting bands help keep the party fresh, and international acts often choose Vancouver as the launching point for world tours.

## Drinks

Other options **Alcohol** p.364

Drinking can be pricy in Vancouver's watering holes, especially in the classy lounges that serve up chic cocktails. Expect a typical 2oz martini to set you back about $8-$12, or more, especially if you're opting for premium liquor such as Grey Goose or Belvedere vodka. If an ice-cold beer is your drink of choice, you'll find plenty of local microbrews and imports on tap, and many pubs have specials so you can enjoy a pint for about $4-$5. Wine aficionados can imbibe some of BC's sought-after varietals, which are hard to come by outside of the wineries, but at $80 and upwards these bottles don't come cheap. Not to worry; many lounges and restaurants have an extensive selection of wines by the glass, so you can sniff, swirl and taste to find your favourite before committing to a pricey choice.

### Drinking & Driving

There's no need to get into your car after drinking, and there's little tolerance for those who do. It's easy to flag down a taxi on the street in central areas, but it can get really busy on rainy nights – pop into a hotel to grab one more quickly. You can cover a lot of territory for about $10-$20, or link up to a night bus or the SkyTrain (see p.47). On New Year's Eve, all public transportation is free, and in outlying communities Operation Red Nose volunteers (www.operationnezrouge.com/en) will drive you and your car home. Visit the website to find out if services are set up in your community. Police operate a year-round roadblock programme, which is stepped up significantly during the holiday season. Though the legal blood alcohol content limit is 0.08%, if you show signs of impairment your licence can be seized for 24 hours, and your car will be impounded or worse. You could get a hefty fine along with a lengthy driving suspension, and even jail time.

## Restaurant Or Lounge?

What came first, the food or the booze? Unless you're at a nightclub, you'll find that these elements have a symbiotic relationship in Vancouver's bars, pubs and lounges. Gastropubs (bars that serve high-quality cuisine) and resto-lounges (a restaurant or lounge, like a supper club) have become ubiquitous in the city, and the lines between food and booze are often blurred.

## Sports Bars

You'd be hard pressed to find a pub or bar without a few TVs, but there are some that truly cater to the spectator scene. The Shark Club (p.464) and Malone's (p.463) are great places to watch hockey, football, basketball, boxing and even golf. For international soccer, the Frog & Firkin (p.461) opens its doors in the early hours (and serves breakfast) so you can watch an international game on satellite TV.

## Bars & Pubs

### The Alibi Room

**157 Alexander St**
Gastown
Map 10 B1 96

*604 623 3383* | *www.alibi.ca*

You don't need an excuse to chill with a group of friends in The Alibi Room's raw industrial space. A crowd of 30 plus urbanites that slurp back cocktails and local microbrews from the ample drinks list dominates this New York-style haunt on the fringes of Gastown. Upstairs, sit amid the action at one of the communal tables in the post-and-beam room or find a perch at the bar and watch trains rush past, their din audible above the hum of lively conversation. Film enthusiasts congregate here to read scripts and host private parties in the digs downstairs. As the evening progresses, the crowd gets younger, and the vibe becomes more energetic. Start the night upstairs, and then move to the basement's rec room-style lounge where you can dance to DJs playing hip-hop, reggae and other genres on Friday and Saturday nights.

### Atlantic Trap & Gill

**612 Davie St**
Downtown
Map 9 D1 97

*604 806 6393* | *www.trapandgill.com*

The Trap, as locals affectionately call it, is a pub done right, east coast style: loud, friendly and a riot of fun. The rowdy masses come to slurp up seafood flown in fresh from the Maritimes and wash it down proudly with a bottle of Moosehead or Alexander Keith's. Picnic-style tables suggest the east coast hospitality and encourage the crowd to mingle and share some stories. The Trap isn't fancy, but it's an energetic escape with toe-tapping, singalong-style bands playing on Thursday and Saturday nights. For a bargain-priced bite, drop by on Tuesday nights for all-you-can-eat fish and chips. Or sidle up to the bar and ask for a double shot of whiskey, rye or bourbon – it's so cheap that before long you'll have earned yourself a spot on the wall of shame.

### Bacchus Piano Lounge

**845 Hornby St**
Downtown
Map 7 E4 98

*604 689 7777* | *www.wedgewoodhotel.com*

Luxury, elegance and grandeur abound at the Wedgewood Hotel, and this extends to Vancouver's favourite piano lounge. Business types, romantics, tourists, and locals who

The Alibi Room

Bacchus Piano Lounge

appreciate an escape to old-world luxury flock to The Bacchus for after-work drinks, business meetings and intimate evenings spent lingering over a cognac. Though the lounge is swathed in silk, velvet and further embellished with gilt-framed art, the lavish decor is neither stuffy nor staid, and the attentive staff ensure everyone feels welcome. Carefully chosen wines and top-drawer liquor are well worth the splurge, especially when you can unwind to the sound of the pianist tinkling away at the baby grand (he starts at 17:00) and bask in the warmth of the fireplace.

**310 Cambie St**
*Gastown*
*Map 10 A1* **99**

## The Cambie

*604 688 9158* | *www.thecambie.com*

Being voted 'best place to get wasted on the cheap' by *Vice* magazine is a proud notch in The Cambie's belt, and the honour certainly suits the modern-day saloon and hostel situated on the seedy fringes of Gastown to a beer-stained T. After all, drinking has been alive and well within these hallowed walls since 1897, and Prohibition in the 1920s wasn't reason enough to go dry. Unsophisticated and gritty, The Cambie is well loved by backpackers, the university crowd and anyone else who wants to come here to blow off some steam and share pitchers of cheap suds with friends old and new. Though your wallet won't suffer too much after a night at the Cambie (where else can you get a burger and a brew for $5.95?), your dignity might be a little worse for wear. In the summer, the corral-like Cordova Street patio fills up quickly, so arrive early and join in the fray.

**2616 Main St**
*Mount Pleasant*
*Map 11 B2* **100**

## The Cascade Room

*604 709 8650* | *www.thecascade.ca*

Stiff drink or smooth brew? You can get both at The Cascade Room, Vancouver's newest lounge that cleverly combines the golden age of cocktails with 70s flourishes. Hipsters from the happening Main Street neighbourhood relax in the casual space and sip Singapore slings, pisco sours and Pimm's cocktails while listening to The Stone Roses, but there's no pomp and ceremony here. The cocktail lounge atmosphere is tempered with quirky-cool touches like large drum shades emblazoned with Queen Victoria's droll mug, which dangle above half-moon shaped leather booths. There's a respectable beer selection too, a fitting tribute to The Cascade Room's Main Street location where Brewery Creek once crafted Cascade, its premier beer. A simple menu of comfort foods that include dressed up versions of fisherman's stew and sausage and mash, plus the expected burger and pizza selections, rounds out the room.

**3611 West Broadway**
*Kitsilano*
*Map 5 D1* **101**

## The Cellar Jazz Club

*604 738 1959* | *www.cellarjazz.com*

Music devotees slip down the stairs to this subterranean jazz joint to take pleasure in nightly performances from much-loved Canadian players and international icons. Purists might protest, though, since music ranges from contemporary jazz to sultry blues and even hip-hop, but the cellar has been awarded countless accolades. Owner Cory Weeds, an alto saxophonist and jazz aficionado in his own right, has started his own label – Cellar Live – and has released full album compilations of the club's live performances, so you can revel in the music long after the band has packed up. Turn up for a set or two any day of the week; cover charges ($5-$15) and minimum food and beverage charges ($10-$15) apply. Visit The Cellar for an evening out on the town, complete with live entertainment, a sumptuous meal of tapas to share or full-on entrees featuring steak and seafood. The beverage selections mirror the music with their diverse appeal. Choose from boozy coffees, champagne cocktails, memorable martinis and more.

*3 Alexander St*
Gastown
Map 10 B1 **102**

## Chill Winston

*604 288 9575 | www.chillwinston.ca*

Eat. Drink. Chill. This Gastown resto-lounge easily fulfils its mantra with its sumptuous menu, imaginative drinks list and sexy decor. A chic crowd fills the ample room outfitted with low leather ottomans for intimate gatherings and sleek tables for glamorous groups that gather on weekends. If you want to see – and be seen – sit at the bar and watch the chefs work their magic, or snag a seat by the windows overlooking the street-level patio. Exposed brick walls and aged honeycomb tiles are offset with luxe curtains and ornate mirrors that give the space a bit of sparkle, and set the mood for a first date or romantic night on the town. Chill Winston's eclectic menu of cocktails and small share plates, like

Chill Winston

venison carpaccio and bok choy with gin broth, outshine the tired selections that turn up on so many menus. But service can be painfully slow, so you'll have to just sit back – and chill.

*1789 Comox St*
West End
Map 7 B2 **103**

## Delilah's Restaurant & Bar

*604 687 3424 | www.delilahs.ca*

Dear old Delilah's, the grand dame of the cocktail crowd, has been one of Vancouver's most celebrated martini lounges for more than two decades. This queen of camp doesn't disappoint, with its plush velvet booths and ornate opium den decor that appeals to a gay and straight clientele. Enjoy a romantic interlude over a candlelit dinner or a raunchy encounter that's well lubricated with bawdy named martinis, such as booty call, foreplay and pearl necklace. The opulent lounge fills up quickly so arrive early and indulge in Delilah's two or four-course dinner ($31 and $43 respectively). On Saturday nights, be sure to make a reservation for Divas at Delilah's, and settle in for an evening of entertainment with female impersonators at centre stage. Closed on Mondays.

*13 Lonsdale Av*
North Vancouver
Map 4 B3 **104**

## The District Social House

*778 338 4938 | www.thedistrictsocial.com*

What do you do when you can't find a decent place to hang your hat without leaving your neighbourhood? Do you drive across town, or open your own place close to home? Luckily, owner Paul Mon-Kau and partners decided to take a leap with the latter choice, so The District's denizens who hail from the area now have a top-notch spot right in their own Lonsdale backyard. And with so much goodness close to home, why tamper with a theme? This was the rationale behind The District's dedication to a seasonal menu that amplifies the best of BC's food. The wine list is also a foray through the region's celebrated wineries, but when it comes to beer, most selections hail from Belgium. But the patrons don't mind the globe-trotting ales, since all draughts are served as a 20oz pour, perfect to wash down an appetiser of fiery chicken satay or spicy long beans.

### Doolin's Irish Pub

**654 Nelson St**
*Downtown*
*Map 7 D4* **105**

*604 605 4343* | *www.doolins.ca*

Irish pub, sports bar, live music venue, restaurant: Doolin's aims to please. It's louder and younger than the smattering of Irish-style pubs that line Granville Street, but this mid-strip spot strikes the right tone with its all-ages clientele. Although it's more shiny veneer than well-aged patina in here, there's plenty of Bushmills and pub grub if you need some convincing. Most weekday evenings it can get downright boisterous with live Celtic music. Friday and Saturday nights trade tradition for 80s, 90s and chart hits spun by local DJs ($8 cover charge). You can still find quaint niches in which to relax and contemplate the slow pour of a perfect Guinness, or watch rugby and soccer. And if you have a hankering to get your kilt on, do it on the first Thursday of the month and your first pint of Guinness is on the house.

### The Five Point

**3124 Main St**
*Main*
*Map 11 B3* **106**

*604 876 5810*

Though this heritage hall hotspot was once a Russian restaurant, all vestiges of the old world have been scrubbed away. The casual pub attracts the typical beer and nachos crowd who like to get comfortable, watch the game and suck back a brew or two. There's an attempt to class up the usual pub fare with amped-up twists, but really you're here for the beer and to hang out on one of the Eastside's largest covered patios. Monday night is open mic, so if you're an aspiring singer, musician or spoken-word poet, you can hit the stage and introduce your act to the local crowd.

### The Frog & Firkin

**1941 West Broadway**
*Kitsilano*
*Map 8 F4* **107**

*604 734 3418* | *http://thefrogandfirkin.com*

If you're hungry for Firkin food or thirsty for good Firkin beer and want to take in some international soccer or rugby at the same time, The Frog scores top honours. The come as you are atmosphere encourages groups to gather for an afternoon gawking at the tube and cheering for the underdog. Though the clientele is comprised mostly of young to middle-aged men, women will feel right at home among the boys, sipping a glass of sangria or munching on a plate of hot wings. The nightly drink specials make this bar a bargain (double highballs are $5.75 on Saturdays), especially on Wednesday's 'customer appreciation day,' when all drink specials are available. Slam back a few to wash down the salty goodness of dry ribs, yam fries and other items from its long list of upscale pub fare.

*Delilah's Restaurant & Bar*

*1137 Hamilton St*
Yaletown
*Map 9 E1* **108**

## George Ultra Lounge

*604 628 5555 | www.georgelounge.com*

George is slick. George is money. George is steaming hot. If George were a real person he'd be a debonair player, a bit of a dandy, and even a little bit randy. Self-proclaimed as Vancouver's first 'ultra lounge', the dazzling room highlighted with a stunning spiral chandelier caters to the high-end after-work crowd who come to catch a buzz with a carefully crafted $12 cocktail. Pair that with posh nosh – perhaps some smoked rainbow trout or a $39 rack of lamb – or pop over to Brix Restaurant & Wine Bar for a more extensive repast; the places are connected by a set of stairs. For an exclusive experience, movie-star types slip back into the titillatingly named G Spot, a private enclave for six, which is off limits unless a staff member is 'summoned' with the G spotlight.

*217 Carrall St*
Gastown
*Map 10 B1* **109**

## Irish Heather

*604 688 9779 | www.irishheather.com*

In Vancouver's sea of emerald-tinged pubs, Irish Heather is arguably the city's only authentic Irish watering hole (Bono and U2 showed up here one St Patrick's Day – it doesn't get more Irish than that). Kegs of Guinness stored in the nooks and crannies at the back, wobbly tables sitting cockeyed on the brick floors, and foamy pints of Guinness recall the weathered pubs of Ireland, with nary a TV in sight. But it's not really just about the stout, shandies and snakebites at The Heather – the self-professed gastropub serves up some serious grub. Chomp on bangers and mash or a hearty steak and kidney pie, and finish it all off with some decadent sherry trifle. After going strong for 10 years, The Heather is rumoured to be pulling up stakes (thanks to a nasty crack in the foundation, which would require a time-consuming renovation) and moving its operation (along with the Shebeen Whiskey House) right across the street. But the tireless staff promises they'll bring The Heather's charm along for the journey.

*4210 Main St*
Fraser
*Map 6 A2* **110**

## The Main

*604 709 8555 | www.themainonmain.com*

There's nothing fussy about The Main, but this live music venue and Greek restaurant has plenty of charm that draws the neighbourhood pub crowd. Find a seat in the cosy bar area and watch hockey while quaffing a $4.50 pint of Storm Black Plague stout

*George Ultra Lounge*

*Opus Bar*

crafted by local brewmasters, or settle into one of the comfy 1980s-style banquettes near the tiny stage and get ear-splittingly close to local and visiting bands that amp up the joint to rollicking levels. With no cover charge and an eclectic assortment of music that ranges from jazzy guitar riffs to folk tunes and 'regressive-passive-aggressive country power' Thursday through to Saturday nights, plus budget-friendly booze (think $3.50 Jägermeister shots and $3.95 rye and coke specials), The Main is a friendly spot you'll visit time and again. The entertainment starts at 20:00, but it can get pretty packed so arrive early and get stuck in to some stick-to-your-ribs Greek favourites.

## Malone's Bar & Grill

**2210 Cornwall Av**
Kitsilano
Map 8 E2 **111**

*604 737 7777 | www.malones.bc.ca*

Whichever location you choose, the party's always under way at Malone's, and both of its laidback bars serve up hearty offerings of NFL, NHL, baseball, basketball, and even testosterone-fuelled Ultimate Fighting Championship boxing. The Kits location is packed during the summer, thanks to its streetside patio overlooking the bronzed bodies across the road at Kits beach. Arrive early to squeeze into a sweet seat on the patio or at the bar, and join the crowd of nubile nymphs and buff dudes who hang out here all summer long. Colder days bring an exodus to the Downtown locale (608 West Pender Street, 604 684 9977), which is more pubby than clubby, but both establishments invite a beer-drinking, sports-watching crowd. And if you like your music fast and heavy, the Downtown branch runs Temptation Tuesdays, offering a cheap ($2.22 pints of draught) night of punk, metal and alternative rock, with no cover charge.

## Opus Bar

**350 Davie St**
Yaletown
Map 9 D1 **112**

*604 642 0557 | www.opusbar.ca*

If you're in search of the beautiful people, or your alter ego, look no further than this swanky hotel bar in the heart of Yaletown. There's an inimitable list of lifestyle-inspired cocktails that each come with a fictional 'bio' to match the hotel rooms' similarly inspired schemes. What will it be tonight? According to the menu, if you're a Billy, the artist/filmmaker playboy type who's into the alternative scene, you'll like the 'long day's night', a cocktail crafted of vodka, Baileys and espresso. Or maybe you're feeling more like Dede, the Los Angeles actress and drama queen whose concoction of choice is a 'some bling beautiful' cocktail, comprised of honey vodka, lime, syrup and gold dust. Well-to-do personas parade in and out of the designer-chic space, which is splashed with hot colours, plush velvet, marble and dangly beadlike chains that provide a little retro shimmer. Nibble on some tempura olives and other 'O' bites with your $12 drink, but beware of being watched: the bathrooms sport tiny monitors so your date can check up on you while your alter ego flirts with the DJ.

*579 Dunsmuir St*
*Downtown*
*Map 7 F3* **113**

## The Railway Club

*604 681 1625 | www.therailwayclub.com*

No, that's not the smell of stale beer that hits you when you enter the Railway Club; it's the aroma of authenticity. This 1930s-era watering hole that was once the exclusive domain of railway workers has earned its rep as a Vancouver institution. Renowned Canadian musicians, including KD Lang, Tragically Hip and Blue Rodeo, tromped up the stairs to this Dunsmuir Street haunt and hit the stage here before they made it to the big time. But it's not all about the stars in the making; many people are content simply to relax amid the bric-a-brac and groove to the beat of bands like Vancouver's venerable Hard Rock Miners. Others practise their hand at chucking darts in the quiet enclaves near the back room. Sure, you can sip an espresso martini but somehow it would seem uncouth in a place that practically beckons you to honour this hard-working bar with a pint of ale or dram of single-malt scotch.

*2427 Marine Dr*
*West Vancouver*
*Map 3 D2* **114**

## Red Lion Bar & Grill

*604 926 8838 | www.redlionbarandgrill.com*

Sometimes a trip across Lions Gate Bridge to the upscale community of West Vancouver feels like a journey to another land (unless you're lucky or rich enough to live there in the first place). The owners of the Red Lion Bar & Grill want to take you even farther afield when you walk through its doors. Stained glass imported from Ireland, snug rooms and stone fireplaces create a welcoming atmosphere in West Van's sleepy Dundarave village. Shake off the chill on the heated patio and watch the world slip slowly by, or repair to the Quinn Room for a spirited game of cards. Grand wing chairs and leather sofas outfit the Lion's Den, a place to sit back and enjoy the satellite feeds of sporting events that can be viewed on the plasma screen. The prices are geared toward the wealthy neighbourhood clientele ($15 for a chicken pot pie), but there are set menus and daily specials to appease your wallet.

*1535 Johnston St*
*Granville Island*
*Map 9 C2* **115**

## The Sandbar

*604 669 9030 | www.vancouverdine.com/sandbar*

Ah, summer love. Perhaps it's the aphrodisiac qualities of the oysters at play, the inhibition-reducing collection of wines, or the pulsating sounds from Granville Bridge above. Whatever it is, when the sun's rays have cast their last glow over False Creek and the heat lamps go on, the crowd on Sandbar's outdoor patio starts to sizzle. Romantically charged conversations over cocktails and tete-a-tetes in front of the fireplace are the mainstay of Sandbar's well-heeled, 30 plus denizens. If you don't find someone to keep you warm on a chilly evening don't worry, attentive staff will supply you with a blanket to cosy up to. Inside, the action is centred on the dancefloor in the Teredo Bar where it's more about body language than talk. Arrive early for a romantic seafood dinner in the restaurant, or show up late and join a lively and well-lubricated crowd.

*180 West Georgia St*
*Downtown*
*Map 7 F4* **116**

## Shark Club

*604 687 4275 | www.sharkclubs.com/vancouver*

With its hot waitresses, cold beer, 36 TVs, pool tables, and all sports all the time, it's no surprise that the Shark Club chain was voted Canada's best sports bar in 2007 by Rogers Sportsnet. The Vancouver location is mere steps from BC Place Stadium and GM Place, making it the premier pre-game spot to soak up some team spirit before heading to the big match. Sports memorabilia and video games add to the atmosphere, but after the game ends, the nightlight shifts into full gear. DJs provide the soundtrack for the youthful clientele who like to tear up the dancefloor in this massive multi-level bar.

## Six Acres

*604 488 0110 | www.sixacres.ca*

You could be forgiven for walking right past this gem of a pub as it's cloistered in the shadows of the Gassy Jack statue. But once inside, the room's quaint lack of pretence and its global selection of beers (and whiskeys, too) are both soothing and compelling. There are no TVs or other garish distractions here, just a few timeworn books and other retro touches of homey character. A narrow staircase skims up the exposed brick walls to the loft-like space upstairs where the sound of lyrical conversation is in sync with the soundtrack of James Brown and other soulful

*Steamworks Brewing Company*

grooves. The youthful clientele that hang here, or tuck themselves into snug seats by the windows looking out onto Gastown's cobbled streets, walk the fine line between hip and bookish. But Six Acres isn't about being the coolest spot. It's about beer, whiskey, a bit of banter and a side of tapas that invites you to linger longer and sample its amber delights.

## Steamworks Brewing Company

*604 689 2739 | www.steamworks.com*

The Gastown steam line that this brewery is named after runs through the building and plays a starring role in the production of its range of lagers, pale ales and stouts. It's a serious beer drinker's paradise, with a changeable and varied range of tipples brewed on site. Those wanting to enjoy conventional pub food alongside their beer won't be disappointed with Steamworks' extensive lunch menu, which includes burgers, pizzas and fish and chips. Beers sell for a budget $15.80 for a two litre pitcher of Lions Gate lager or $3.39 for a 10oz glass. Steamworks has two other locations: The TransContinental (601 West Cordova Street, 604 678 8000) and West Vancouver (900 Main Street, 604 922 8882).

## Stella's Tap & Tapas Bar

*604 254 2437 | http://stellasbeer.com*

Since it hit The Drive a few years back, people have been queuing up along the block to squeeze into this Belgian-inspired tap house and tapas bar. With its cosy corners and warm decor, Stella's feels more bistro than bar, but the staff are especially serious about their Belgian brews, adopting a 10 step pour process that's appreciated by aficionados. The delectable tapas offerings complement the artful pours with their inventive flavours. Choose from dishes such as delicate Thai tea sandwiches or cornets of finger-licking Belgian frites and moules (french fries and mussels) simmered in – you guessed it – Stella Artois. Come for a pint and stay for the evening at this bustling hotspot that's hip enough to draw the Downtown crowd.

**1035 Marine Dr**
North Vancouver
Map 4 A2 **120**

## Taylor's Crossing Restaurant & Brew Pub

*604 986 7899* | *www.markjamesgroup.com*

With six pubs in the region, plus the Lotus Hotel's lounges, The Mark James Group (yes, that's Mark James of the eponymous men's clothing boutique) has painted its midas touch on Vancouver's pub scene, and Taylor's Crossing is no exception. The dressed-up brewpub appeals to all who want to relax with a draught and burger, or steak and wine, while watching the game or enjoying a lively evening with family and friends. Taylor's chalet-style decor meshes well with its North Vancouver location, and TVs and pool tables are on hand in the expansive space. Whet your whistle with a local brew: a hopped-up Two Lions Pale Ale (the name is a nod to the local mountains) or the creamy and slightly bitter but creamy Mad Scow Stout, are both tasty choices.

**1330 Granville St**
Yaletown
Map 9 D1 **121**

## The Yale

*604 681 9253* | *http://theyale.ca*

Although its signature saxophone sign, rendered in neon blue lights, has been removed from its facade, this institution that has hosted legendary musicians for decades is still going strong. The pub that anchors the historic 1880s-era hotel can feel a bit gritty, but its enduring character has won over the hearts of Vancouverites and visitors alike. Jimmy Page and Supertramp have jammed here, and celebs such as U2 and Sheryl Crow have dropped by to hear their favourites belt out the blues. Almost every evening you can hear the wail of a guitar, throb of the drums and soulful vocals that compel the audience to get up, hit the dancefloor and get down to the grooves. And on some days, people simply come by The Yale to shoot some pool, chew the fat, and catch glimpses of the Granville Street traffic outside. Show up on Saturday or Sunday between 15:00 and 19:00 for weekend blues jams, with no cover charge.

**1111 Mainland St**
Yaletown
Map 9 E1 **122**

## Yaletown Brewing Company

*604 681 2739* | *www.markjamesgroup.com*

For those seeking unpretentious fare, this pub brews up its own varieties of lagers and beers for a mixed crowd of regulars uninterested in dressing up for an evening down the local. Although the surrounding area may have been gentrifying at a rapid pace, this bar has kept its cool and continues to offer down-to-earth, quality food and drink for those who come to watch sports on its TVs, play pool or tuck into its 12 inch pizzas and beer battered fish and chips on the spacious outdoor patio. The extensive range of beers includes the strappingly titled Red Truck Ale and Big Bitter Wolf.

**791 West Georgia St**
Downtown
Map 7 E3 **123**

## YEW restaurant + bar

*604 689 9333* | *www.fourseasons.com/vancouver*

If Mother Nature were a glamour puss, she'd look like the swanky YEW restaurant + bar in the Four Seasons Hotel. Stone, wood and other natural materials shine strong in the recently renovated room, which is a fresh addition to Vancouver's resto-lounge scene. Magnificent ceilings stretch skyward, a weighty fireplace anchors the room, and back down to earth, communal tables hand-hewn from hefty maple slabs host a well-heeled crowd of business types, tourists and locals. You

### Shaken Or Stirred?

Exotic liqueurs, pureed fruit, freshly grated wasabi, and even espresso are turning up in glasses at many bars and lounges. The Opus Bar (p.463), always ahead of the curve, has concocted cocktails that match fictional characters, such as Mike, a doctor from New York. The beverage lists at George Ultra Lounge (p.462) and The Cascade Room (p.459) include dozens of cocktails which are elevated to an art form by their accompanying glasses and garnishes. Attention is even paid to ensure the ice is apropos - whether crushed or cubed.

certainly won't go thirsty in this luxurious landscape – oenophiles will appreciate the outstanding collection of wines by the glass, reported to be more than 150 at last count. There's also nothing rustic about these earthy elements either. The gorgeous decor channels the striking splendour of BC, which is emulated in the menu, a homage to the Pacific Ocean's bounty of quality ingredients. Grilled octopus and oysters are just some of the raw bar's seafaring offerings that will tantalise your palate.

**1277 Robson St**
*West End*
*Map 7-D3* 124

## Zin Restaurant & Lounge
**604 408 1700** | www.zin-restaurant.com

Situated amid the hustle and bustle of Robson Street, Zin is an urban oasis for dedicated shoppers, business types, tourists and locals who appreciate its eye-candy appeal. Zin's compact lounge is a soothing retreat from the street, but its high-wattage decor (think electric orange hues, velvet flecked with swirls, sleek booths) and quick-to-please staff create enough energy on their own. Find a seat in front of the fireplace or at the back of the bar and be soothed by the sounds of jazz. The cocktail and wine offers are pared down, but there's plenty to sample, perhaps with an order of chef Richard Tyhy's haute twist on popcorn: it's anointed with truffle oil and sea salt.

*George Ultra Lounge*

*Zin Restaurant & Lounge*

*Yaletown Brewing Company*

## Gay & Lesbian

Other options **Gay & Lesbian** p.28

Vancouver boasts Western Canada's largest gay population. It is one of the gay-friendliest places on earth, with same-sex marriage legal and federal legislation long in place to protect equal rights for gays and lesbians.

The scene is concentrated on a few rainbow-flag adorned blocks of Davie Street, and a large gay population lives in the blocks around the Gay Village. Restaurants, bars, bookstores and clothes shops have a very definite gay slant in this area, with only the occasional deviation from the strip – usually for women's events such as Hershe parties on holiday weekends (www.flygirlproductions.com) and Electric Honey's events (www.electrichoney.ca). Women congregate in small numbers at most Davie Street bars and clubs, the exception being the almost entirely male Pumpjack. Lick (455 Abbott Street, 604 685 7777) in Chinatown is the only predominantly women's venue. While stalwarts such as The

*Davie Street flags*

Fountainhead and The Pumpjack are gay-dominated, the Majestic and Score attract more of a mixed gay and straight crowd. If going out with a large group, the Majestic is the best bet.

---

**1181 Davie St**
*West End*
*Map 7 C4* **125**

### 1181

*604 687 3991* | *www.tightlounge.com*

A modernist gem of a drinking den amid the colourful clutter of Davie Street, 1181 presents the confident, cosmopolitan face of gay Vancouver. This sleek lounge sits subtly in the centre of the strip and serves the gaybourhood's best drinks from a lengthy, leather-bound cocktail menu. Since it opened in 2006, 1181's polished chrome exterior, sexy bartenders and alluring interior have beckoned in the city's most style-conscious citizens. Lean the length of the bar, mingle alongside the cork and mirror walls or lounge on banquettes in the dimly lit back area of the bar. DJs and shows fill up a sophisticated events calendar and both the surprisingly friendly crowd of regulars and the cheerful bartenders swiftly make any solo drinkers feel at home.

---

**1022 Davie St**
*West End*
*Map 7 C4* **126**

### Celebrities Night Club

*604 681 6180* | *www.celebritiesnightclub.com*

This thumping club is packed every night with a hot, young gay crowd, drawn to the 1,000 plus capacity venue by the upbeat vibe, slick lighting and world-class sound system. For years Tuesday nights have been popular with a youthful, budget-conscious crowd of mostly straight students that are unable to resist the lure of cheap drinks. House sounds feature most of the week, except on Sundays when the turntables spin to chart hits and music videos are played. Porn stars, pop stars and drag king shows are regular features on the calendar. A few seating areas and bar stools overlook the small central dancefloor but there are better views to be had from the upstairs balcony, where there are excellent opportunities for staking out the object of your affections. A small smoking room lurks off to one side of the club.

Written by residents, the Los Angeles
Explorer is packed with insider info, from
arriving in the city to making it your home
and everything in between.

**Los Angeles Explorer Residents' Guide**
We Know Where You Live

**1141 Davie St**
West End
Map 7 C4 **127**

## Davie Village Café & Bar

*604 228 1429* | *www.davievillage.ca*

The gay-owned and run Davie Village Café & Bar takes up the main floor of a Victorian house, set slightly back off the main Davie drag. While the service and food is at best ok, this central Village gathering spot is more of a community centre than a restaurant. Kitsch details such as flowery teacups and souvenir spoons are reminiscent of a visit to an elderly relative's house. In the evening, everyone from punky young lesbians to burly older men dally over beers, ciders or high balls. With events ranging from drag shows and women's singer-songwriter nights to reading series and coffee socials, this homey cafe draws every sector of the community. Walls are lined with archived stories from local gay paper *Xtra West*, and signed posters and calendars feature community events. Pop music belts out, sashaying from Tom Jones and David Bowie to Britney Spears remixes.

**1025 Davie St**
West End
Map 7 C4 **128**

## The Fountainhead Pub

*604 687 2222* | *www.thefountainheadpub.com*

Other than the oversized nude paintings and the occasional glimpse of a drag queen on her way to a show at Celebrities across the street, you might not see many other signs that you're in a gay bar at this genial pub. Although the decor may remind you of a hotel lounge from the 70s, The Fountainhead is the most popular of Vancouver's gay pubs. A slew of television screens hang overhead, broadcasting a muted, competing array of sports and entertainment shows while chart hits play on the sound system. At night the pub is packed and noisy. The pool table is the haunt of the bulk of the girls who frequent this mixed venue. Good pub food such as burgers and quesadillas complement the daily drinks specials, but The Fountainhead's main draw is the outdoor patio – the perfect spot in which to see and be seen on a sunny day.

**1202 Davie St**
West End
Map 7 C4 **129**

## Hamburger Mary's Diner

*604 687 1293* | *www.hamburgermarys.ca*

Hamburger Mary's is a long-established diner on the corner of Bute and Davie. Couples and crowds from the neighbourhood's gay and lesbian community flock in for solid fare at the unabashedly retro 1970s diner. It's popular with a slightly older, old-school set, happy to linger in a relaxed environment. Straightforward burgers and sandwiches provide the bulk of the menu, but Mary's all-day breakfasts are also definitely worth waking up for, whether you fancy a healthy fruit salad to keep things light or steak and eggs to keep you going all day. Specials such as meatloaf and perogies add to the choice. Although there are more glamorous places to eat on Davie, the strategic location of Hamburger Mary's, not to mention its shady streetside patio, keep it high on the list of gay-favoured places to dine in.

*Hamburger Mary's Diner*

## The Majestic Restaurant & Lounge

**1138 Davie St**
*West End*
*Map 7 C4* **130**

*604 669 2013* | *www.majesticvancouver.com*

Another relative newcomer to the scene, The Majestic swiftly nabbed the title of the gay strip's roomiest venue. The cavernous space is filled with a generous supply of tables that are crammed with a diverse cross section of the community. A good cocktail menu, a well-stocked bar, and lounge food are part of the draw, but are very much secondary attractions to The Majestic's full entertainment schedule. Bingo, drag shows and a popular Sunday drag-brunch have already carved a place for the venue on the city's social calendar. Staff are friendly, although not the speediest. Luckily there are excellent shows to distract from any delays.

## Oasis Cocktail Lounge

**1240 Thurlow St**
*West End*
*Map 7 C4* **131**

*604 685 1724* | *www.theoasispub.com*

The Oasis is a restaurant and show bar dominated by a baby grand piano. On summer Sundays an outdoor barbecue on the lush, heated patio packs in the crowds and live jazz provides a smooth backdrop. Its laidback style attracts an older crowd for show tunes, jazz duos and competitions such as 'West End Idol' that are on the bill every evening. The decor is warm and cheerful, the service is efficient and friendly and the 200 martinis on offer are enticing. On Saturday nights, house DJs spin for an upbeat crowd. When there isn't a show on the go, old movies play on the bar's flat-screen televisions. The food menu consists of tasty and inventive tapas-style dishes. A warning though: it has unisex bathrooms.

## The Odyssey

**1251 Howe St**
*Downtown*
*Map 9 D1* **132**

*604 689 5256* | *www.theodysseynightclub.com*

Packed with a hard partying crowd of exuberant young gay boys and girls, The Odyssey is a low-lit dance club crammed to capacity on weekend nights. There's an enticing patio area outside for smokers and for those who need an escape from the sizzling dancefloor. Famously anti-women, The Odyssey is a fun venue to go to with a crowd if you're willing to put up with bolshy staff, interminable queues to get in the door and long waits for a drink. Nights feature go-go dancers, strippers who take it all off (behind poles strategically placed by the dancefloor), Vancouver's longest-running drag shows and other such eye candy. Upbeat house, chart and electro dominate the playlist.

## The Pumpjack Pub

**1167 Davie St**
*West End*
*Map 7 C4* **133**

*604 685 3417* | *www.pumpjackpub.com*

If you're into a little bit of debauchery, lots of leather and a heavy dose of brawn, you'll be ready to brave the queues at Davie Street's Pumpjack Pub, where the boys, quite literally, let it all hang out. Before you arrive, familiarise yourself on the 'hanky code' (an orange hanky on the left means the wearer is up for 'anything, anytime'), and share your penchants with the sometimes shirtless and chap-wearing patrons. The long room is pretty stripped down when it comes to decor, but the crazy crowd makes up for it with its own colourful antics. In summer, when it can get kind of sweaty, the windows open wide and the sounds spill out on to the street so passers-by can enjoy the show.

## Score

**1262 Davie St**
*West End*
*Map 7 C3* **134**

*604 632 1646* | *www.scoreondavie.com*

Billing itself as Davie Village's 'sports restaurant', Score has changed its name more often than an indecisive drag queen, but it remains popular with the same down-to-earth lesbian, gay and straight crowd. Its latest reinvention sees stone floors, bright walls and skylights lightening the room. Perfect for meeting with a crowd of friends, you can sample Score's nightly drink specials and catch up on the hockey action – Score shows all Canucks, NHL, CFL and AFL games. Early risers can also grab a $3 breakfast on Sunday mornings and catch an NFL game on screen.

## Nightclubs

When the condos went up in the city, the nightclubs came down and many underground institutions disappeared into the dust and rubble, never to return. Some were muscled over to Granville Street, the city's newly minted 'entertainment district,' where there is still a smattering of dance clubs that entice a young crowd. Nightclubs in Vancouver are in short supply; the handful that are still around mostly cater to a college-age crowd that's chomping at the bit to get beyond that velvet rope. Larger groups can get on the guest list and bypass the queues, but expect to pay $5 to $20 cover at most venues, depending on what's on.

Pulsating lights, ear-splitting sounds and high-energy hip-hop, pop and house grooves spun by resident DJs are the mainstay of many nightclubs on weekends. Though the club scene doesn't hit the big time like New York or even Toronto, Vancouver still manages to draw international DJs, such as Tiësto, Cut Chemist and DJ Shadow. Parties and raves crop up from time to time, but you have to be in the know to tap into the underground scene.

**1222 Hamilton St**
*Yaletown*
*Map 9 D1* **135**

### Bar None

*604 684 3044* | *www.barnonenightclub.com*

Yaletown's hippest nightclub has been drawing urbanites to its industrial space since it opened its doors 15 years ago. Exposed brick walls and hardwood floors lend a lounge-like atmosphere that complements house band Soul Stream's funkadelic and soulful sounds on Monday and Tuesday nights. It gets loud in here, especially when sexy singles put down their cocktails to work it out on the dancefloor. Visiting DJs, such as Chicago's DJ Sneak, and rotating residents (DJs Hedspin, Madness and Dicky Do) bring the noise to this Soho-styled staple, where it's standing-room only on Friday and Saturday nights.

**868 Granville St**
*Downtown*
*Map 7 E4* **136**

### Commodore Ballroom

*604 739 4550* | *www.hob.com*

Old habits die hard, and haunting the hallowed halls of this Downtown institution will put you in fine company. Indisputably Vancouver's best live music venue, this 80 year old art deco landmark has hosted an iconic assortment of entertainers over the years, from Tina Turner, The Supremes and James Brown to The Cure, Nirvana, U2 and

*Commodore Ballroom*

Coldplay. An extensive $3.5 million renovation recently brought this grand dame of Granville Street back to its former glory with its plush seats, sweeping staircases and signature springy floor. Vancouver's bastion for live acts amply accommodates up to 900 locals and visitors of all ages. You can reserve a table to get a spot up close to the stage, but once the music gets going the crowd spills forth. Make sure that you bring along some identification, whatever your age – the bouncers don't make exceptions or listen to excuses.

**1219 Granville St**
*Downtown*
*Map 9 D1* `137`

## Ginger 62

*604 688 5494 | www.ginger62.com*

No effort – no entry. The dress code details sum up the haute-couture crowd that braves the long queues to be granted entrance into this cocktail den. Here, the young and vivacious nibble on Asian-inspired bites while lounging on low-slung couches in the glamorous 1960s-inspired space. Walls are swathed in red and the sultry lighting and extensive list of champagne cocktails and martinis add to Ginger's mythical allure. Saucy cocktails such as the wreck beach blonde and yaletown blowhard show that Ginger has a sense of humour – albeit a mocking one – but this is one sweet spot that's destined to please. When DJ Krown gets behind the decks on Saturday nights, booty-shaking babes hit the dancefloor to strut their stuff to the house hits.

*The Modern*

**2291 West Broadway**
*Kitsilano*
*Map 8 D4* `138`

## Lola's Bar

*604 733 7989*

Though Lola's, formerly the Side Door, has grown up a bit and shed its unpolished youth, Kitsilano's only nightclub still attracts a college-age crowd to its swanky new space. This small enclave is hidden away in a neighbourhood that's not known for nightclubs or bars, but locals are still drawn to the spot. Despite its extensive renovations and new name, Lola's still maintains its laidback vibe. Modern banquette seating flanks the dancefloor, which gets jam-packed with gyrating twentysomethings attracted by the cheap drinks ($3.50 highballs and $4.00 Jägermeister shots). On Tuesdays, resident DJ Lieutenant Dan keeps the party going. Arrive early to beat the queues and cover charge (which usually starts at 21:00) and hustle some pool at one of the two tables.

**455 Abbott St**
*Gastown*
*Map 10 A2* `139`

## Lotus Sound Lounge

*604 685 7777 | http://markjamesgroup.com*

Head downstairs to the dark and grungy space where underground disciples get their late-night groove on in this genre-defying space. Need some extra cash to pay the bills? Show your talent on Tuesday's Rent Cheque nights and you could walk away with half of the door's take. DJs bring the decks; you bring your best booty-shaking moves. Wallflowers can watch the action and indulge in some liquid courage at bargain basement prices. Focus Fridays bring some serious sounds with resident DJs and international guests.

**7 Alexander St**
*Gastown*
*Map 10 B1* `140`

## The Modern

*604 647 0121 | www.donnellynightclubs.ca*

Though this spot just opened in 2007, it's already made its mark on the young and hip. Crowned the new 'it' club in Gastown, this underground venue gets steamy as scenesters rip it up on the lighted dancefloor to a crazy-sexy-cool soundtrack spun by local and international DJs until the early hours. Miles of mirrors, tiles, smoky glass, neon lights and plenty of action draw the crowds like bees to nectar. And this club is certainly sweet thanks to its VIP bottle service and customised cocktail menu. No detail is left to chance, which sets The Modern apart from the rest. On Friday nights DJ Flipout and guests play funk and classic hip-hop, and on Saturdays the Modern goes retro with La Discotheque. Open Thursday to Saturday.

## Republic

*958 Granville St*
*Downtown*
*Map 7 E4* **141**

*604 669 3266* | *www.republicbar.ca*

From the glow of the main floor's backlit bar to the glass-encased patio that soars over Granville Street, Republic has earned its spot as a metropolitan star. Even soccer celebrity David Beckham and his LA Galaxy team-mates have dropped in for a drink, and the VIP bottle service is sure to bring an added cachet for the high-style set. Inventive cocktails command higher prices and a mixed clientele who appreciate a late-night spot where thirtysomethings won't feel past their prime. The downstairs bar radiates with light, mesmerising barflies that perch on the stools to watch urbanites stream through the doors. A dancefloor dominates the main level, and the mod lights that hang down cast a flattering glow on the stylish crowd. Upstairs, people recline in leather club chairs or buzz to the DJs spinning drum and bass on the patio on Tuesday nights.

## The Roxy

*932 Granville St*
*Downtown*
*Map 7 E4* **142**

*604 331 7999* | *www.roxyvan.com*

This Granville stalwart never stops rocking it out and packing the crowds in. On weekends, without fail, scantily clad women, jocks, suburbanites, and anyone that likes to party hard, angle to get inside and listen to house bands Joe's Garage and Troy's R Us perform to an enthusiastic crowd. The longstanding venue is a little time-worn, and the stony-faced bouncers can be a bit intimidating, but that doesn't dissuade diehard Roxy bar stars. On Sunday nights, country music rules the roost but city slicks still come out to play. Unfortunately even The Roxy has a dress code – no bags, backpacks, tracksuits or ripped jeans.

## Shine

*364 Water St*
*Gastown*
*Map 10 A1* **143**

*604 408 4321* | *www.shinenightclub.com*

Dance, drink or lounge, Shine offers up this straightforward mix in its basement locale that is anything but dark and moody. Whether you party in the blue room, or the red room at the back, it's all a youthful playground with sleek seating and subterranean sounds. On Monday nights DJs hark back to the 50s and 60s with The Ice Cream Social, while Tuesday's Laser Dance plays to a disco-crazed crowd that's more Gap than Gucci. Located at the nexus of Gastown's burgeoning nightlife scene, Shine burns brightly.

## Tonic Nightclub

*919 Granville St*
*Downtown*
*Map 7 E4* **144**

*604 669 0469* | *www.thetonicclub.com*

Take some free-flowing drinks, add a heavy dose of hip-hop hits, squeeze it all into a narrow nightclub and you have the elixir for all that ails you; this is another Granville Street watering hole that caters to a casual crowd keen to have a good time. Sunday night is Sin Sexy industry night where waiters, waitresses, bartenders and other bar stars bypass the queues and get some industry perks: tequila shots, Corona, draught beers, and highballs are just $3. The boozy crowd can get a little wild, but there is an easy reprieve in the VIP or Harley Bar upstairs where you can watch the action from above. Get on the guest list and move to the head of the queue at this party central where college kids go crazy.

## Cabaret & Strip Shows

When it comes to women baring it all while swinging around a pole or twisting and contorting on stage, Vancouver's so-called 'peeler bars' have helped get the city a bit of a reputation. As for high-end 'gentlemen's clubs', Brandi's Exotic Nightclub (595 Hornby Street, 604 684 2000) is the only act in town, and it's well known for its affluent clientele (men, women and couples come here). It also has a Hollywood celeb crowd, such as Kurt Russell and Goldie Hawn, who were once part-time Vancouverites. Vancouver has plenty of less-gentlemanly spots too, which have earned the city equal acclaim. On the Granville strip, The Cecil Exotic Show Lounge (1336 Granville Street, 604 683 5029) offers a special secluded VIP room for preferred guests so they can watch dancers up close. A short stroll away, The Penthouse (1019 Seymour Street, 604 683 2111) has been entertaining a colourful clientele since 1947 (including luminaries such as Frank Sinatra, when it was a supper club). Still run by the Filippone family, The Penthouse has exotic entertainment on stage six nights a week, as well as private dancing.

On the seedier side of town, at the No. 5 Orange (205 Main Street, 604 687 3483) women compete with the big-screen TVs for attention. Most of these places are popular with men out on a boys' night, but you can visit some of them in the glaring light of day if you prefer, and have a beer and a burger while the women entertain.

## Casinos

Casinos are very much legal in Vancouver and, though they once were limited to 'games of skill' (like poker and blackjack), legislative changes have relaxed the rules and many now boast hundreds of slot machines, roulette and craps (a dice game) too. Most are luxurious entertainment complexes that feature gaming, live entertainment and fine dining all under one massive roof. Other than the 30,000 sq ft Edgewater Casino (311-750 Pacific Boulevard, 604 687 3343) located in Downtown, most casinos are situated in the suburbs where there's plenty of space and ample parking.

You'll find an assortment of people in Vancouver's casinos, from grannies with blue rinses playing slot machines to young guns with slicked-back hair hunched over tables perfecting their poker faces. Some people don't gamble a dime, or limit their fun to a few bucks on the slots. There are serious gamblers too, and many expat Asians enjoy playing cards at the big-ticket tables.

If being cooped up inside amid the flashing lights and velvet isn't your style, you can place your bet at the racetrack instead. East Vancouver's Hastings Racetrack (604 254 1631, www.hastingspark.com), located in Hastings Park, has been featuring live thoroughbred horse racing since the 1890s. Since Hastings has been taken over by new management, you can now play slot machines here too. But don't expect to hear the rattle of coins signifying a big payout: British Columbia's slot machines don't take coins anymore, there's just a 'ticket-in, ticket-out' system.

Those keen to enjoy a complete gambling getaway should visit Richmond's River Rock Casino Resort, which provides a hotel, spa, restaurants and bars, as well as a theatre and marina. The casino is the centrepiece of the resort, offering the classic card games and more than 1,000 slot machines (8811 River Road, 604 247 8900).

## Cinemas

When you live in a city that can seem unbearably rainy and grey in the winter, it isn't difficult to imagine how packed the movie theatres can get, especially on a Friday night or during a film's new release period – these shows often sell out quickly and queues snake down the street.

You can now purchase tickets online (www.fandango.com) or at one of the automated machines. The best way to find out what's on is to check *The Georgia Straight*, a weekly

---

### Mini Explorers

Don't let the size of these little stars fool you – they're full of insider info, maps, contacts, tips and facts for visitors. From shops to spas, bars to bargains and everything in between, the Mini Explorer range helps you get the most out of a short stay or city break, however long you're there for.

---

entertainment rag, or myTELUS (www.mytelus.com/movies), an online database that lets you search by cinema, city or film.

Major multiplexes can be found in the suburbs, but two of Vancouver's best spots are the Scotiabank Theatre (Downtown), and Cinemark Tinseltown, which is located on the edge of Gastown. Each boasts comfy stadium seats, state-of-the-art sound, and multiple screens so you can catch the new releases with the hordes as soon as they come out. Anywhere you go, tickets cost about $10 to $12, and a few bucks less for matinees (usually shows that screen before 18:00). Students, seniors and kids get a discount too, but the real cost seems to come from the premium-priced, super-sized tubs of popcorn and litres of soda pop. Movie night for two? Expect to spend at least $30 or more – easily.

If you're ready for a romantic night of movie watching under the stars, you'll have to pack up the car and head way out to Langley to the Twilight Drive-In. First-run flicks only cost $11 per person, or you can bring a whole carload (five people maximum) for a family-friendly price of $25.

## Cinemas

| | | | |
|---|---|---|---|
| Cinemark Tinseltown | Gastown | 604 806 0797 | www.cinemark.com |
| Cineplex Odeon Park & Tilford | North Vancouver | 604 985 4215 | www.cineplex.com |
| Empire Cinemas | Various Locations | 604 983 2791 | www.empiretheatres.com |
| Fifth Avenue Cinemas | Kitsilano | 604 734 7469 | www.festivalcinemas.ca |
| The IMAX Theatre | Downtown | 604 682 4629 | www.imax.com |
| Pacific Cinémathèque | Downtown | 604 688 8202 | www.cinematheque.bc.ca |
| Scotiabank Theatre | Downtown | 604 630 1407 | www.cineplex.com |
| Telus World Of Science | Main | 604 443 7443 | www.telusworldofscience.com |

At the other end of the spectrum, Pacific Cinémathèque screens arthouse, foreign and short films in its 210 seater facility (you can even rent it during the day and screen your own masterpiece). Because Cinémathèque is a registered non-profit society, you must be a member, but the cost is cheap: just $3 per year and films are a reasonable $9.50, or $11.50 for a double bill. There's a film reference library and west coast film archives here too.

Film buffs are always in their element come September when the three-week long annual Vancouver International Film Festival (p.59) gets into full swing, and screens about 600 films from over 50 countries. And if you haven't had your fill of flicks yet, just wait a week and then take in a film or two at the Vancouver Asian Film Festival (www. vaff.org), which has been going strong for over a decade.

## Comedy

Comedy clubs in Vancouver can be hit and miss; some host creative, belly-splitting performances while others fall flat with barely a titter or giggle. There are, however, a couple of long-running venues that hit the right note, leaving the audience in stitches. The Vancouver TheatreSports League (604 738 7013, www.vtsl.com), which usually performs at the New Revue Stage on Granville Island (p.203), has mastered the fine art of lampoon and improv performances where the audience gets in on the action. Shows run most evenings and weekends and cost about $10, depending on the performance. At Yuk Yuks' (604 696 9857, www.yukyuks.com) new Downtown digs at the Century Plaza Hotel (p.34), pro comedians share the stage with amateurs on Tuesdays' Crash 'n' Burn Night, which costs just $5. There are drinks specials every night as well as dinner packages that include a two-course meal and admission for $40-$49.

On slow weekday evenings, places including the Jupiter Lounge (1216 Bute Street, 604 609 6665), Maxine's Hideaway (1215 Bidwell Street, 604 689 8822) and the Shark Club (p.464) host a weekly comedy night featuring local jokesters of varying talent levels.

There's generally a $5 admission fee but no drink minimum, so they're all good value and are worth checking out.

## Concerts & Live Music

When The Police and the Spice Girls commenced their respective reunion tours, they used Vancouver's GM Place (800 Griffiths Way, 604 899 7400) as a launching pad, playing sell-out shows. Big-ticket acts generally stop in Vancouver as they travel across the country, but many only make it as far north as Seattle, leaving their Canadian fans out in the cold. But who wants to be lost in a crowd of 18,000 when you can get up-close and personal at the Commodore Ballroom (p.472), Richards on Richards (1036 Richards Street, 604 687 6794) or one of the other live music venues that get indie bands and eclectic acts? Sometimes the Orpheum Theatre (604 665 3050, www. vancouver.ca/theatres) plays concert host for an evening. The venue is the home of the Vancouver Symphony Orchestra, which has been performing classical and popular music since 1919, and has 2,800 seats, but it's hard to rock to Keane when you're cramped in rows of theatre seats. That said, the theatre was due to undergo renovations in 2008.

In May, the music festival season kicks off with New Music West (www.newmusicwest. com), North America's showcase of new and emerging artists who get a chance to show their talent to industry reps and fans over five days and nights. As summer approaches, Vancouverites get jazzed by the sounds of over 1,500 artists performing blues, jazz and funk throughout the city during the two-week long Vancouver International Jazz Festival (p.56). In mid-July, folk music lovers take in a three-day celebration of eclectic musical acts at the Vancouver Folk Music Festival (p.56) held at Jericho Beach Park.

## Theatre

Other options **Drama Groups** p.294

When the few Broadway shows that make it to Vancouver perform, they usually set up shop at the Queen Elizabeth Theatre (649 Cambie Street, 604 665 3050), Vancouver Playhouse (160 West 1st Avenue, 604 873 3311) or the Centre in Vancouver for Performing Arts (777 Homer Street, 604 602 0616), all in Downtown.

*Chan Centre*

Tickets can be pricey, but the big performances don't come often so it's worth a splurge. Granville Island's cluster of venues host smaller theatre productions and plays (www.granvilleisland.com); spaces include The Waterfront Theatre and Performance Works, both run by the Granville Island Cultural Society (604 687 3005, www.giculturalsociety. org). In the summer Stanley Park has Theatre Under The Stars (604 231 7535, www.tuts.ca), with evening performances in its outdoor theatre of classics such as *Jesus Christ Superstar* and *Annie Get Your Gun*. Just across False Creek in Kitsilano, you can take in a Shakespearean performance under the tents in Vanier Park with the Bard on the Beach festival (p.56). The Chan Centre for the Performing Arts (6265 Crescent Road, 604 822 9197) offers a variety of cultural (predominantly musical) experiences, staging theatrical productions like *Socrates on Trial*. The Arts Club Theatre Company (604 687 644, www.artsclub.com) has productions throughout the year in Vancouver (at the Stanley Industrial Alliance Stage and the Granville Island Stage), and was once graced by a young Michael J Fox. Plays with a Christian, spiritual or ethical dimension are performed by the Pacific Theatre (1440 West 12th 604 731 5518). The unique location of a former fire station is the home of the Firehall Arts Centre (280 East Cordova Street, 604 689 0926), which offers a range of theatre and dance performances, and you should also visit Vancouver East Cultural Centre, which recently staged *Frankenstein* (1895 Venables Street, 604 251 1363).

## Caterers

High-end hotels and golf clubs are generally the venue of choice for people who need the space, and each provides its own on-site catering services. Power brokers favour a range of local haunts, including La Terrazza's (1088 Cambie Street, 604 899 4449) private room, Bacchus in the Wedgewood Hotel (p.458), and Quattro on Fourth (2611 West 4th Avenue, 604 734 4444). If you're hosting a late-night soiree or alfresco event, Culinary Capers' (604 875 0123, www.culinarycapers.com) staff will serve up a seasonal menu that showcases the best of west coast cuisine (think Dungeness crab cakes with mango, and sake-cured salmon crisps). Self-described as 'the Renoir of catering,' Critic's Choice (604 980 8516, www.criticschoicecaterers.com) has earned plenty of accolades with its creative approach to feeding corporate executives, movie stars and wedding guests. Uniformed staff will set the tableau whether it is for a hearty brunch, elegant lunch or multi-course meals for a crowd.

If you fancy yourself as a bit of a modern-day Julia Child, you can drop into foodie boutiques such as Quince (1780 West 3rd Avenue, 604 731 4645), The Gourmet Warehouse (1340 East Hastings Street, 604 253 3022) or Meinhardt Fine Foods (3002 Granville Street, 604 732 4405) and stock your larder with high-end eats. Sushi platters to go are always a crowd pleaser, and many of Vancouver's hundreds of sushi spots will put one together for you to take home.

## Party Organisers

Other options **Party Accessories** p.396

With the ever-present Hollywood glitterati supporting Vancouver's billion dollar film industry, and the likes of former US president Bill Clinton and vice-president Al Gore popping into town pitching their post-political pet projects (not to mention billionaire land developers), local party planners have proved they can hold their own. Whether it's an intimate engagement or glamorous gala there are plenty who can lend a hand, including Party Planners (604 551 8887, www.partyplannersinc.ca) and Greenstone Productions (604 628 4441, www.greenstoneproductions.com). If face painting and a rubber-nosed clown who excels in twisting balloons into kid-cool shapes is more your speed, then look no further than www.kidsvancouver.com for an exhaustive list of party people that can pull it all off. If haute cuisine for your prince or princess is de rigueur, then you can hire Travelling Gourmet Personal Chef Services (604 921 1604, www.travellingourmet.com) and serve up puff-pastry wrapped organic sausages alongside a chocolate fountain with fruit skewers. More down-to-earth types are turning to eco-friendly shades of green by hiring Green Print Events (604 782 0448, www.greenprintevents.com), which will make sure your party makes a big impression with a smaller ecological footprint.

---

**Online Communities**

Log on to www.explorerpublishing.com and click on the Communities link. Here you'll be able to connect with like-minded residents, join forums, pose questions and maybe even learn about hot new bar and restaurant discoveries.

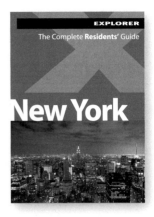
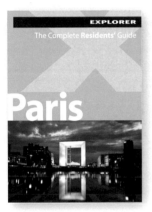

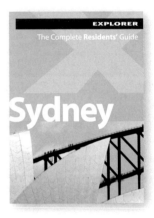

# Tired of writing your insider tips…

## …in a blog that nobody reads?

The Explorer Complete Residents' Guide series is growing rapidly, and we're always looking for literate, resident writers to help pen our new guides. So whether you live in Tuscany or Timbuktu, if writing's your thing, and you know your city inside out, we'd like to talk to you.

Apply online at www.explorerpublishing.com

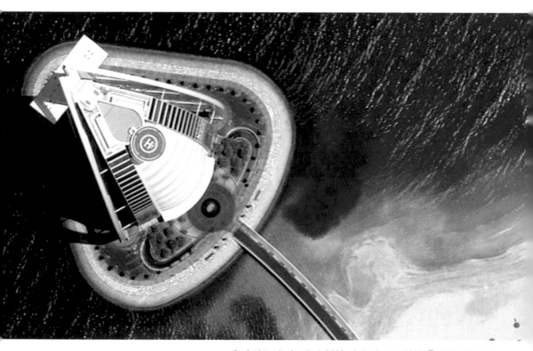

# Maps

## User's Guide

Vancouver's grid-like road network makes the city fairly easy to navigate, and this section of the book should provide you with all the tools you will need to get around town. There are four maps of wider Vancouver, starting on p.488, and six detailed maps of Downtown and its surrounding areas, starting on p.496. There is also an overview map of the surrounding area on p.485 and a TransLink transit map detailing the rail, boat, and bus networks running across the city on the inside back cover.

The overview map on p.486 details which areas are covered on each spread. Maps 3 to 6 cover the city at a scale of 50,000:1. This means that 1mm on the map is equivalent to 50,000mm (or 50 metres). The central areas are covered in more detail, on a scale of 10,000:1 (so 1mm is equal to 10m).

The maps are dotted with annotations marking the location of companies mentioned within the book. Each chapter's annotations are colour coded, and in sequential order where appropriate, so you can reference the map back to the entry (for example, purple for Shopping and blue for Exploring). You can also find the annotations and map references beside relevant entries throughout the book.

As many of Vancouver's streets begin at one end of the city and end at the other, pinpointing a specific address can prove difficult. To help, approximate street numbers have also been included on the maps so you can calculate which end you need to get to.

### Gridlocked?

*Vancouver's streets run north to south, and its numbered avenues run west to east (from 1st Avenue in the north to 75th Avenue in the south). Avenues are also divided into 'east' and 'west', with numbers on each section increasing outwards from Ontario Street.*

## Need More?

This weighty book will provide you with all you need to know to get the most out of Vancouver, but for when you need something a little more convenient in size, you can also buy the Vancouver Mini Map. The whole city can slot in your back pocket, handy

for when you need to travel light but still navigate your way around. The diverse range of mini maps on offer includes cities such as London, Dubai, New York and Barcelona. For details on where to pick up a mini marvel visit www.explorerpublishing.com.

## Online Maps

*If you would like to explore Vancouver online, you can view the city and the rest of Canada on Google Maps (http://maps.google.ca). The site allows you to search by address or business name, or you can zoom in and look around manually. You can also see the city in three different ways: the standard view is a vector map with landmark icons shown, there is a satellite image, and the hybrid view is a blend of the two. Two other sites that provide more detail on building names are http://ca.maps.yahoo.com and http://www.mapquest.com.*

## Map Legend

| | | | |
|---|---|---|---|
| Hotel | | Highway | |
| Education | | Major Road | |
| Park/Garden | | Secondary Road | |
| Hospital | | Other Road | |
| Shopping | | Ferry Route | |
| Heritage/Museum | | Expo Line | |
| Industrial Area | | Millenium Line | |
| Built-up Area/Building | | Canada Line (open 2009) | |
| Land | | Railway Line | |
| Pedestrian | | Fire Station | |
| Beaches | | Police Station | |
| Airport | | Golf Course | |
| | | Churches | |
| | | Parking | |
| | | Library | |
| | | Tourist Info | |

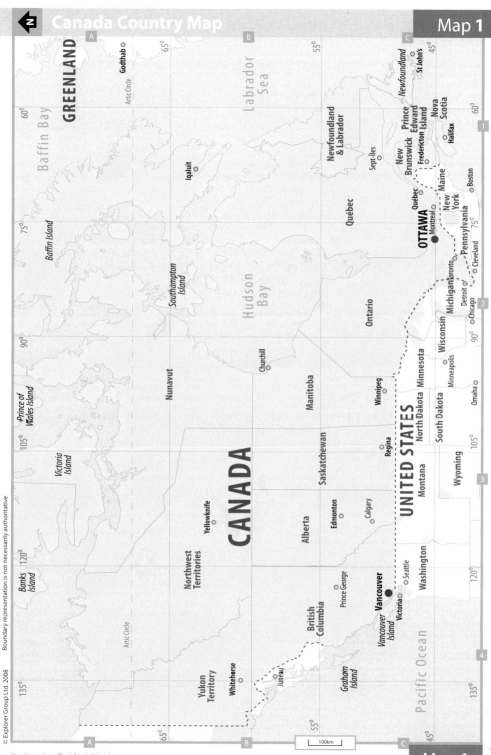

# Street & Area Index

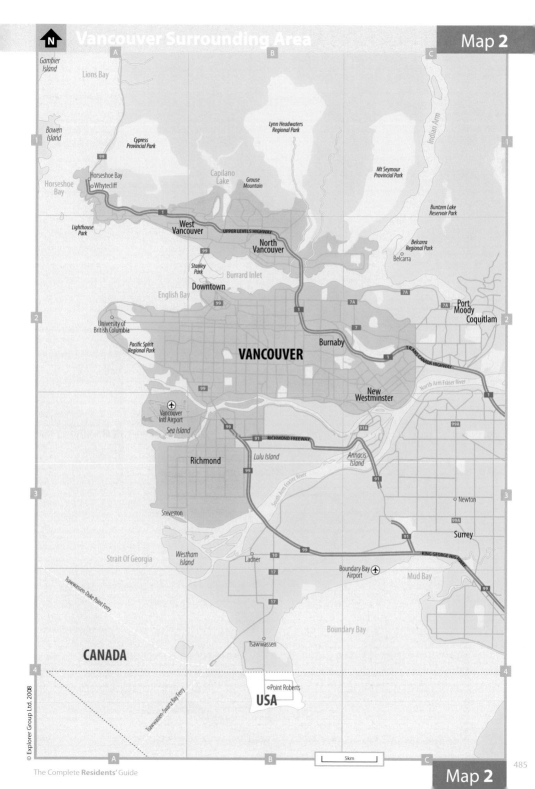

© Explorer Group Ltd. 2008

5km

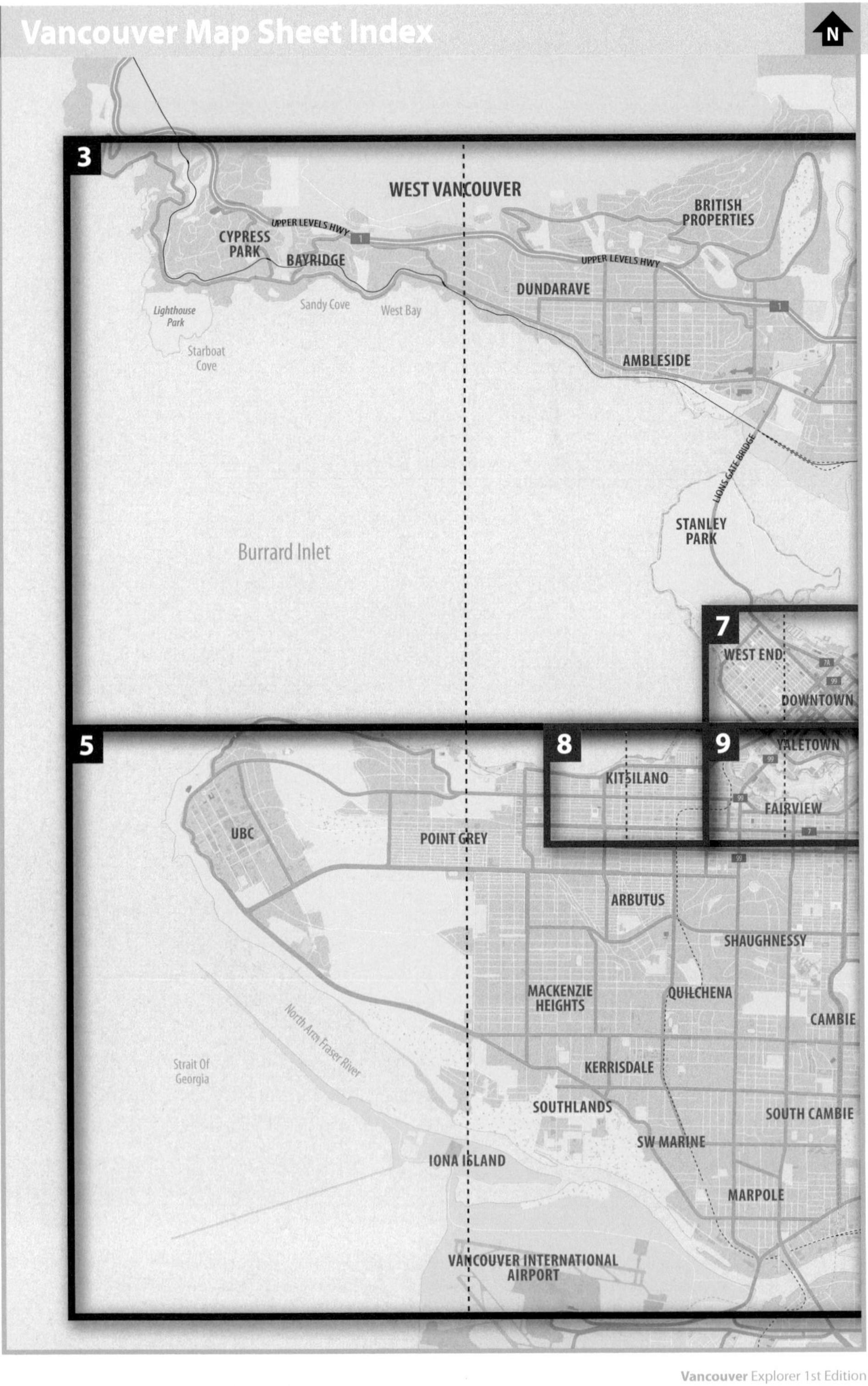

**N**

**3**

WEST VANCOUVER

BRITISH PROPERTIES

UPPER LEVELS HWY
1

CYPRESS PARK

BAYRIDGE

UPPER LEVELS HWY

1

DUNDARAVE

Lighthouse Park

Sandy Cove

West Bay

AMBLESIDE

Starboat Cove

LIONS GATE BRIDGE

Burrard Inlet

STANLEY PARK

**7**

WEST END

7A
99

DOWNTOWN

**5**

**8**

**9**

YALETOWN

KITSILANO

FAIRVIEW

UBC

POINT GREY

99

7

ARBUTUS

SHAUGHNESSY

MACKENZIE HEIGHTS

QUILCHENA

CAMBIE

North Arm Fraser River

Strait Of Georgia

KERRISDALE

SOUTHLANDS

SW MARINE

SOUTH CAMBIE

IONA ISLAND

MARPOLE

VANCOUVER INTERNATIONAL AIRPORT

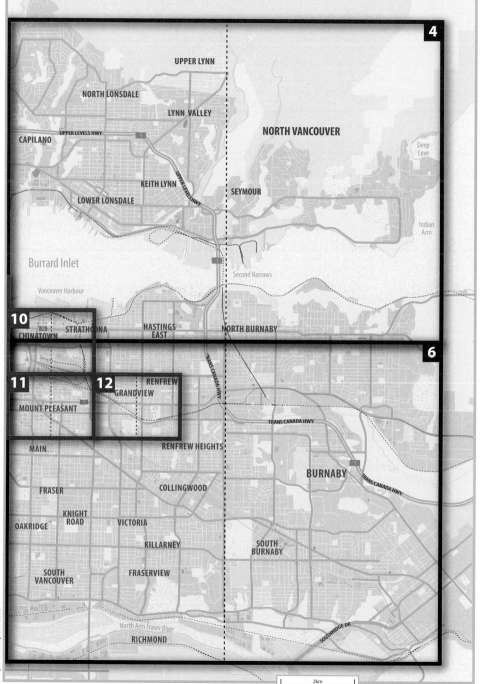

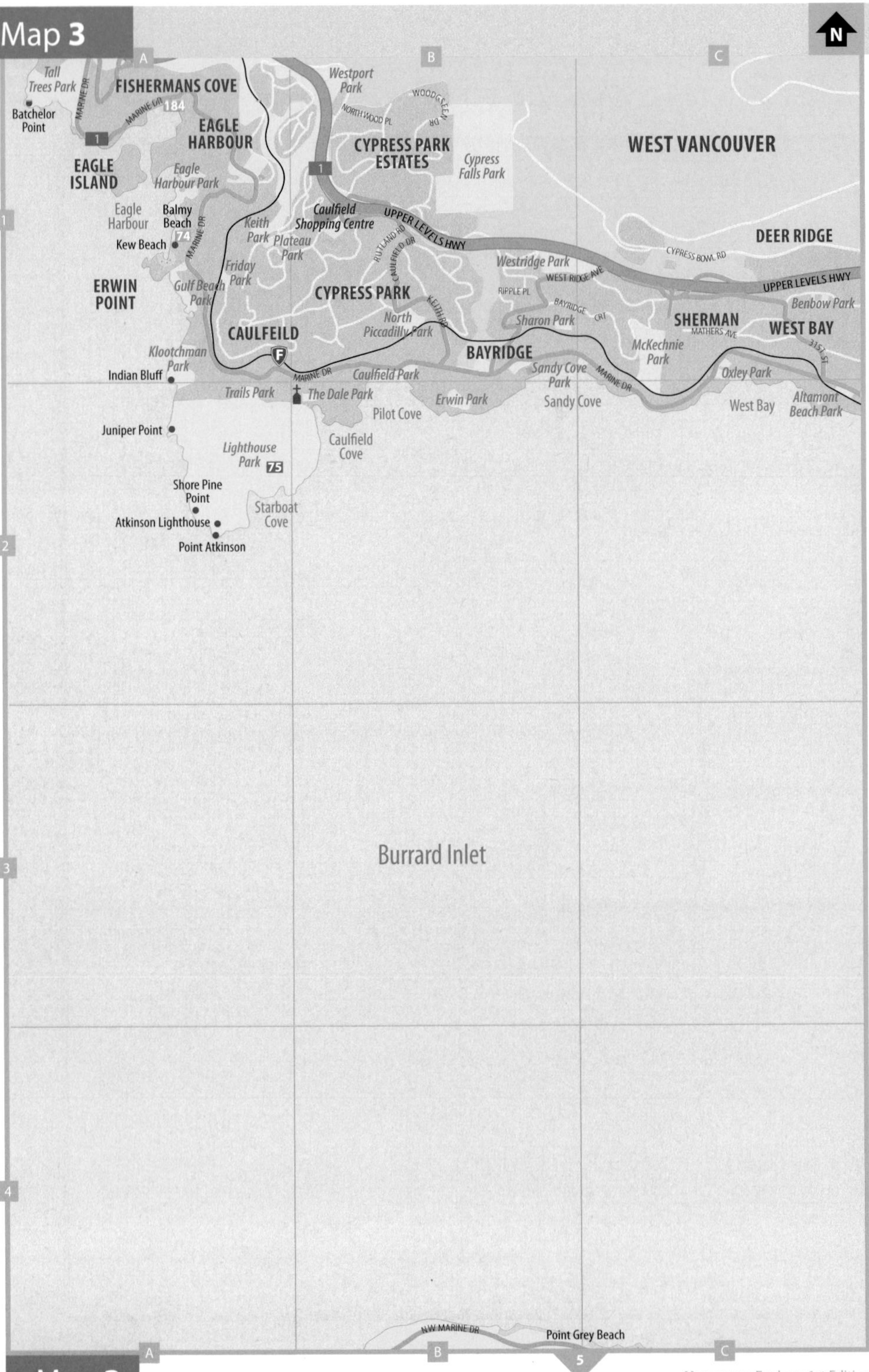

# Map **3**

N

General Information p.1  Residents p.61  Exploring p.183  Activities p.271  Shopping p.359  Going Out p.419

Tall Trees Park

Batchelor Point

**FISHERMANS COVE**

Westport Park

**EAGLE HARBOUR**

184

**CYPRESS PARK ESTATES**

Cypress Falls Park

**WEST VANCOUVER**

**EAGLE ISLAND**

Eagle Harbour Park

**1**

**DEER RIDGE**

Eagle Harbour

Balmy Beach

Keith Park

Caulfield Shopping Centre

UPPER LEVELS HWY

CYPRESS BOWL RD.

74

Kew Beach

Plateau Park

Westridge Park

WEST RIDGE AVE

UPPER LEVELS HWY

**1**

Friday Park

**CYPRESS PARK**

RIPPLE PL

BAYRIDGE CRT

Benbow Park

**ERWIN POINT**

Gulf Beach Park

North Piccadilly Park

Sharon Park

**SHERMAN**
MATHERS AVE

**WEST BAY**

Klootchman Park

**CAULFEILD**

**F**

**BAYRIDGE**

McKechnie Park

Indian Bluff

MARINE DR

Caulfield Park

Sandy Cove Park

Oxley Park

Trails Park

The Dale Park

Erwin Park

Sandy Cove

West Bay

Altamont Beach Park

Pilot Cove

Juniper Point

Caulfield Cove

Lighthouse Park

75

Shore Pine Point

Starboat Cove

Atkinson Lighthouse

Point Atkinson

**Burrard Inlet**

NW MARINE DR

Point Grey Beach

**5**

© Explorer Group Ltd. 2008

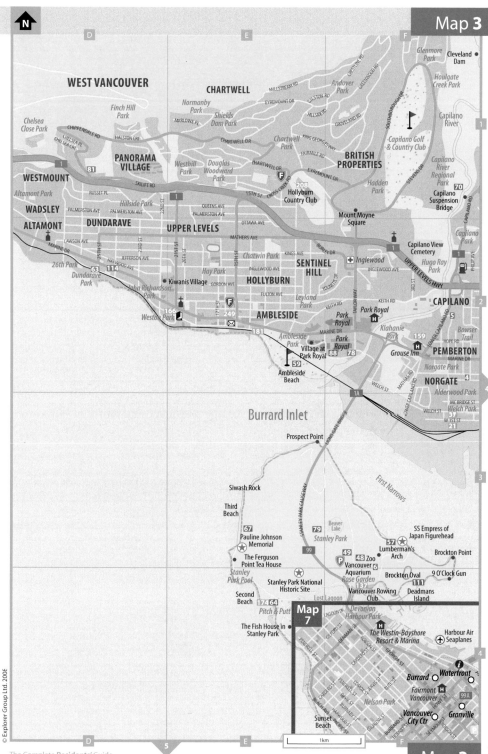

WEST VANCOUVER

CHARTWELL

Cleveland Dam
Glenmore Park
Houlgate Creek Park

Finch Hill Park

Normanby Park
Shields Dam Park

Capilano River

Andover Park

MILLSTREAM RD

CRESTLINE RD

GILSTON RD

EYREMOUNT DR

HILLSIDE RD

Chelsea Close Park

CHIPPENDALE RD

HALSTON CRT

CHELSEA PL
CHELSEA CRT

PANORAMA VILLAGE

81

Westhill Park

Douglas Woodward Park

CHARTWELL DR

Chartwell Park

FAIRMILE RD

Capilano Golf & Country Club

Capilano River Regional Park

BRITISH PROPERTIES

70

WESTMOUNT

SKILIFT RD

15TH ST

CROSS CREEK RD

CHARTWELL DR

EYREMOUNT DR

Hadden Park

Capilano Suspension Bridge

RUSSET PL

208
Hollyburn Country Club

Altamont Park

QUEENS AVE

WADSLEY

Hillside Park

PALMERSTON AVE

PALMERSTON AVE

PALMERSTON AVE

Mount Moyne Square

Capilano Park

ALTAMONT

DUNDARAVE

UPPER LEVELS

OTTAWA AVE

MATHERS AVE

Capilano View Cemetery

Hugo Ray Park

CAPILANO RD

MARINE DR

LAWSON AVE

Chatwin Park

KINGS AVE

BURLEY DR

Inglewood

UPPER LEVELS HWY

PHILIP AVE

26th Park

63

114

JEFFERSON AVE

Hay Park

INGLEWOOD AVE

SENTINEL HILL

Inglewood AVE

Dundarave Park

Kiwanis Village

GORDON AVE

HOLLYBURN

FULTON AVE

Leyland Park

KEITH RD

Park Royal

CAPILANO

5

John Richardson Park

166

17TH ST

F
249

AMBLESIDE

Park Royal

Klahanie Park

KEITH RD

159

Bowser Trail

Weston Park

181

Ambleside Park

MARINE DR

Park Royal

88  78

Grouse Inn

HOPE RD

PEMBERTON

59

Village at Park Royal

Norgate Park

Ambleside Beach

WELCH ST

NORGATE

4

Alderwood Park

1A

MC BRIDGE ST
Welch Park

WELCH ST

W 1ST ST

21

Burrard Inlet

Prospect Point

First Narrows

3

Siwash Rock

Third Beach

67
Pauline Johnson Memorial

79

Beaver Lake

Stanley Park

SS Empress of Japan Figurehead

57
Lumberman's Arch

Brockton Point

The Ferguson Point Tea House

99

49

48 Zoo
Vancouver Aquarium

Brockton Oval

9 O'Clock Gun

111

Stanley Park Pool

Stanley Park National Historic Site

Rose Garden

137
Vancouver Rowing Club

Deadmans Island

Second Beach

174 64

Pitch & Putt

Lost Lagoon

LAGOON DR

Devonian Harbour Park

The Fish House in Stanley Park

Map 7

The Westin-Bayshore Resort & Marina

Harbour Air Seaplanes

Burrard

Waterfront

Fairmont Vancouver

Nelson Park

99A

Sunset Beach

Vancouver City Ctr

Granville

Map **4**

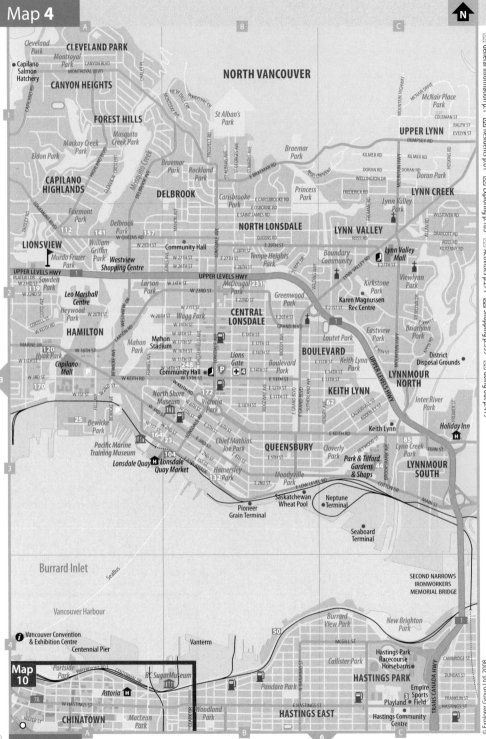

Map **4**

Vancouver Explorer 1st Edition

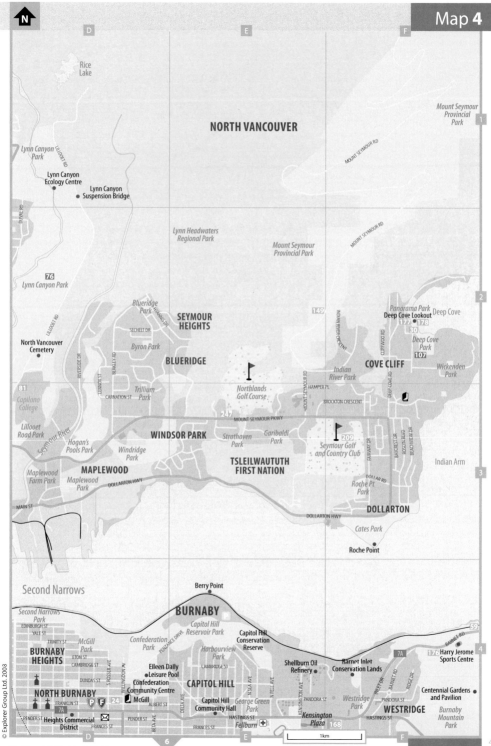

Rice Lake

**NORTH VANCOUVER**

Lynn Canyon Park

LILLOOET RD

Lynn Canyon Ecology Centre

Lynn Canyon Suspension Bridge

DUVAL RD

Lynn Headwaters Regional Park

Mount Seymour Provincial Park

MOUNT SEYMOUR RD

Mount Seymour Provincial Park

**76**
Lynn Canyon Park

LILLOOET RD

Blueridge Park

HYANNIS DR

SECHELT DR

**SEYMOUR HEIGHTS**

North Vancouver Cemetery

RIVERSIDE DR

BERKLEY RD

LENNOX ST

Byron Park

**BLUERIDGE**

CARNATION ST

Trillium Park

**149**

INDIAN RIVER CRESCENT

Panorama Park

Deep Cove Lookout

Deep Cove

**177** **178**

**30**

Deep Cove Park

**107**

CLIFFWOOD RD

Indian River Park

Wickenden Park

**COVE CLIFF**

**81**
Capilano College

Lilloet Road Park

Seymour River

Hogan's Pools Park

Windridge Park

**MAPLEWOOD**

Maplewood Farm Park

Maplewood Park

Northlands Golf Course

MOUNT SEYMOUR RD

HAMPER PL

BROCKTON CRESCENT

**247**

MOUNT SEYMOUR PKWY

**WINDSOR PARK**

Strathoven Park

Garibaldi Park

**TSLEILWAUTUTH FIRST NATION**

Seymour Golf and Country Club

**209**

FAIRWAY DR

DEEP COVE RD

BAYRIDGE DR

BAYVIEW DR

Indian Arm

DOLLARTON HWY

MAIN ST

DOLLAR RD

Roche Pt Park

**DOLLARTON**

DOLLARTON HWY

Cates Park

Roche Point

**Second Narrows**

Berry Point

**BURNABY**

Second Narrows Park

EDINBURGH ST

YALE ST

TRINITY ST

McGill Park

ETON ST

CAMBRIDGE ST

DUNDAS ST

**BURNABY HEIGHTS**

S. ROSSER AVE

WILLINGDON AVE

Capitol Hill Reservoir Park

Confederation Park

PENZANCE DRIVE

Harbourview Park

CAMBRIDGE ST

Capitol Hill Conservation Reserve

Shellburn Oil Refinery

Barnet Inlet Conservation Lands

**59**

BARNET RD

**7A**

**177**

Harry Jerome Sports Centre

BARNET RD

Eileen Dally Leisure Pool

Confederation Community Centre

McGill

**NORTH BURNABY**

FRANKLIN ST

**7A**

PENDER ST

**P** **F** **24**

ALBERT ST

DELTA AVE

BETA AVE

**CAPITOL HILL**

Capitol Hill Community Hall

PENDER ST

FRANCES ST

Heights Commercial District

FRANCES ST

George Green Park

HASTINGS ST

Fellburn

N SEA AVE

N FELL AVE

KENSINGTON AVE

Kensington Plaza

**168**

PANDORA ST

Westridge Park

INLET DR

PANDORA ST

RIDGE DR

BARNET RD

**WESTRIDGE**

HASTINGS ST

Centennial Gardens and Pavilion

Burnaby Mountain Park

1km

© Explorer Group Ltd. 2003

Map **5**

Spanish Banks 65
Locarno Beach Park 156
Locarno Beach 63
Hostelling Intl H

BELMONT AVE

Tower Beach
UBC Museum 42
of Anthropology
Rose Gardens
Pool
Library SUB
Belkin Art Gallery
UBC 173
First Nations 105
Longhouse
Biological Sciences 72
27
UBC Hospital 7
83
68 University of British Columbia
Wreck Beach
Pacific Spirit Regional Park

UNIVERSITY HILL
UNIVERSITY ENDOWMENT LANDS

Westmount Park

W 2ND AVE
W 3RD AVE
W 4TH AVE

QUEENSLAND RD

104

ACADIA RD

UBC

University Golf Course

West Point Grey Park 111

W 7TH AVE
W 8TH AVE
W 9TH AVE
W 10TH AVE 128 26
10 27
W 11TH AVE

POINT GREY

Thunderbird Residences
Logan Track P F

W 14TH AVE
W 15TH AVE

W 16TH AVE

Camosun Park

Matthews Field
UBC Botanical Garden Centre
Thunderbird Stadium
NRC Animal Science
BC Research
84
UBC Botanical Gardens Nursery/Greenhouse
CAMPUS RD S

Pacific Spirit Regional Park 77

Triumf (TRI- University Meson Facility)

North Arm Fraser River

Shaughnessy Golf & Country Club 210

Strait of Georgia

Iona Beach Regional Park

District Sewage Treatment Plant

Duck Pond

© Explore Group Ltd. 2008

Map **5**

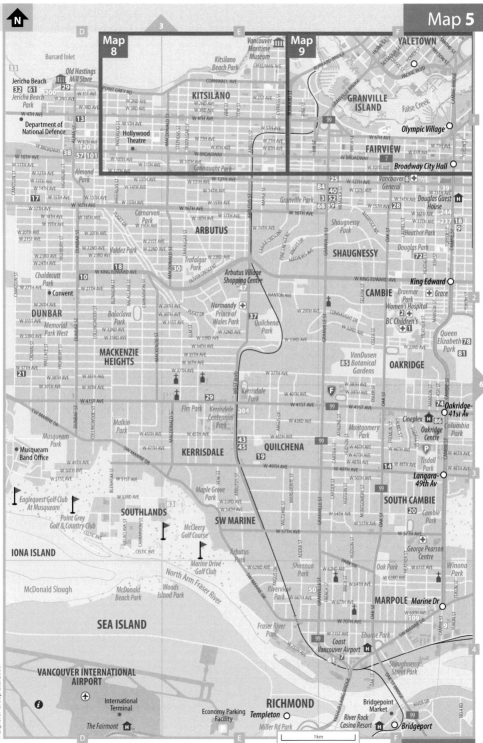

Map **6**

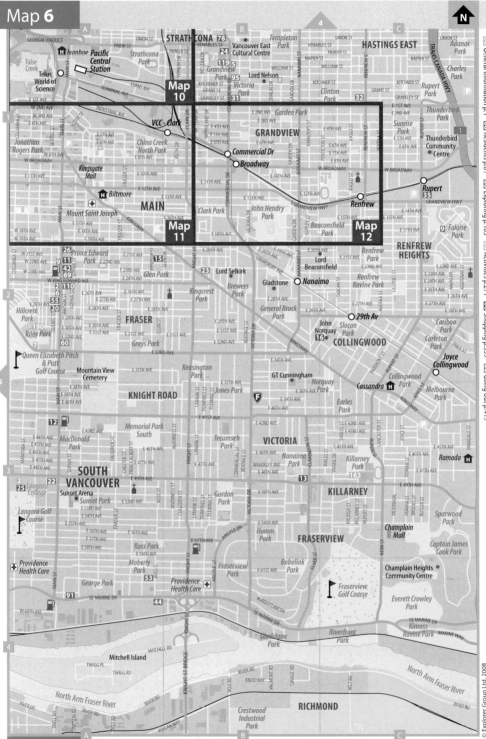

© Explorer Group Ltd. 2008

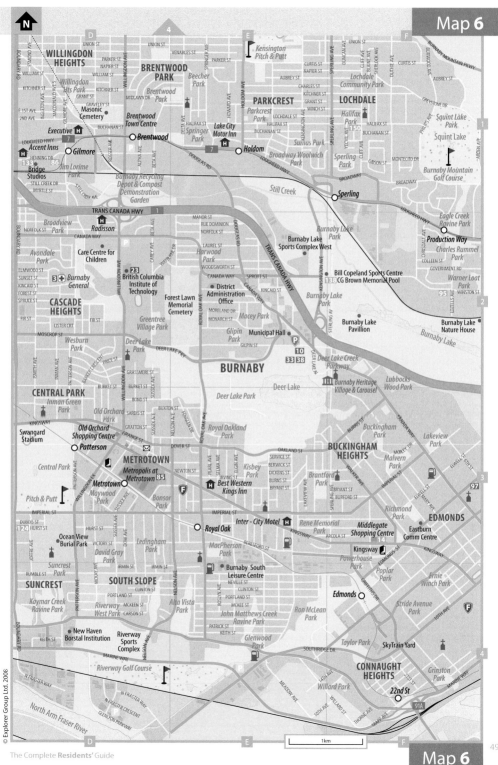

Map **7**

N

Stanley
Park

Lost Lagoon

Devonian
Harbour Park

Harbour
Cruises

95

75

19

The Westin Bayshore
Resort & Marina

Lord Stanley
Suites on the Park

Times Square
Suites

91

General Information p.1   Residents p.61   Exploring p.183   Activities p.271   Shopping p.359   Going Out p.419

LAGOON DR

PARK LN

LAGOON DR

Buchan

79

Robson Suites

36

254

216

11

99

English Bay Inn

King George

206

17

West End
Community Centre

West End

13

The Sylvia

Shato Inn

Empire
Landmark

16

Oceanside

103

Denman
Place Mall

42

Roedde House
Museum

36

Barclay

The Listel

English Bay
Beach

60

80

Coast
Plaza

Lord Roberts

Barclays Manor
Community Centre

English Bay
Apartment

English
Bay Park

Best Western
Sands

WEST END

West End
Guesthouse

RPB & Resort

Alexandra
Park

Pendrell Suites

The Inukshuk

Lord Roberts
Annex

1100

Nelson Park

Empire Towers Inn

40

134

92

35

129
125
133

Park Hill

130

127

11

6

St Paul's Hospital

131

21

Sunset Inn & Suites

128
34   7
52
2

126

Sunset Beach
Park   66

110

Landis Hotel
& Suites

26

Vanier Park

9

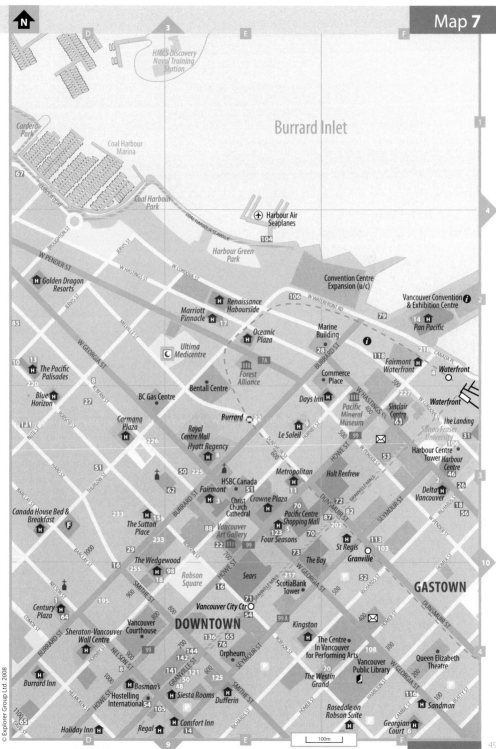

Burrard Inlet

HMCS Discovery Naval Training Station

Cardero Park

Coal Harbour Marina

Coal Harbour Park

67

HARBOUR QUAY

BROUGHTON ST

W PENDER ST

JERVIS ST

W HASTINGS ST

W CORDOVA ST

MELVILLE ST

W GEORGIA ST

ALBERNI ST

JERVIS ST

COAL HARBOUR SEALWALK

Harbour Green Park

Harbour Air Seaplanes

104

Convention Centre Expansion (u/c)

106  W WATERFRONT RD

79

Vancouver Convention & Exhibition Centre

Golden Dragon Resorts

Renaissance Habourside

Marriott Pinnacle

17

Oceanic Plaza

Ultima Medicentre

Marine Building

28

BURRARD ST

118

14
Pan Pacific

218  CANADA PL

85

10

13
The Pacific Palisades

220

Blue Horizon

27

ROBSON ST

BUTE ST

Carmana Plaza

226

BC Gas Centre

7A

Forest Alliance

Bentall Centre

Burrard

Commerce Place

W HASTINGS ST

Days Inn

Le Soleil

9
HORNBY ST

Pacific Mineral Museum

500  99

Fairmont Waterfront

Waterfront

Waterfront

227

Sinclair Centre

63

W CORDOVA ST

The Landing

Simon Fraser University

31

106

Harbour Centre Tower

Harbour Centre

46

HARO ST

THURLOW ST

51

BARCLAY ST

BURRARD ST

Royal Centre Mall
Hyatt Regency

8

50  225

62

HSBC Canada

Fairmont

3

Christ Church Cathedral

Crowne Plaza

88

DUNSMUIR ST

Metropolitan

11

600

HOWE ST

W PENDER ST

Holt Renfrew

70

72

82

87
202

53

GRANVILLE MALL

2

Delta Vancouver

18

56

SEYMOUR ST

RICHARDS ST

W PENDER ST

Canada House Bed & Breakfast

F

233

15
The Sutton Place

233

29

16

The Wedgewood

255

18

Robson Square

Vancouver Art Gallery

22

99

Four Seasons

123

5

70

Pacific Centre Shopping Mall

73

The Bay

St Regis

113
103

Granville

52

10

GASTOWN

DUNSMUIR ST

NELSON ST

Century Plaza

64

195

BURRARD ST

HORNBY ST

NELSON ST

99

Sheraton-Vancouver Wall Centre

Vancouver Courthouse

Vancouver City Ctr

54

71

Sears

16

Robson Square

217

ScotiaBank Tower

99 A

Kingston

RICHARDS ST

500

HOMER ST

400

DOWNTOWN

Vancouver Courthouse

Orpheum

136  65

76

144

142

141

121

50

48

125

Bosman's

Hostelling International

54

105

Siesta Rooms

Dufferin

The Centre In Vancouver for Performing Arts

108

300

Queen Elizabeth Theatre

W GEORGIA ST

The Westin Grand

20

Vancouver Public Library

Sandman

116

100

BEATTY ST

Georgian Court

6

HOMER ST

CAMBIE ST

HELMCKEN ST

HOWE ST

DAVIE ST

Burrard Inn

1000

1100

65

Holiday Inn

Regal

Comfort Inn

14

9

E

Rosedale on Robson Suite

100m

F

Map **7**

# Map **8**

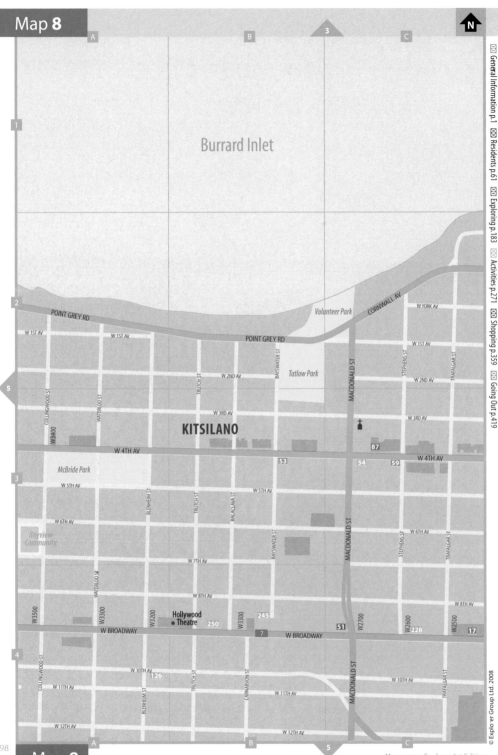

Burrard Inlet

🕮 General Information p.1 🕮 Residents p.61 🕮 Exploring p.183 🕮 Activities p.271 🕮 Shopping p.359 🕮 Going Out p.419

POINT GREY RD

W 1ST AV
W 1ST AV

Volunteer Park

CORNWALL AV
W YORK AV

W 1ST AV

POINT GREY RD

Tatlow Park

W 2ND AV

W 2ND AV

W 3RD AV
W 3RD AV

**KITSILANO**

87

W 4TH AV
W 4TH AV

McBride Park

53

54  59

W 5TH AV
W 5TH AV

Bayview
Community

W 6TH AV
W 6TH AV

W 7TH AV

W 8TH AV
W 8TH AV

Hollywood
● Theatre
250

245

51
7   W BROADWAY

228   17

W BROADWAY

126

W 10TH AV
W 10TH AV

W 11TH AV
W 11TH AV

W 12TH AV
W 12TH AV

W3400
W3500  W3300  W3200  W3300  W2700  W2600  W2500

COLLINGWOOD ST
WATERLOO ST
TRUTCH ST
BAYSWATER ST
MACDONALD ST
STEPHENS ST
TRAFALGAR ST
BLENHEIM ST
BALACLAVA ST
CARNARVON ST

© Explorer Group Ltd. 2008

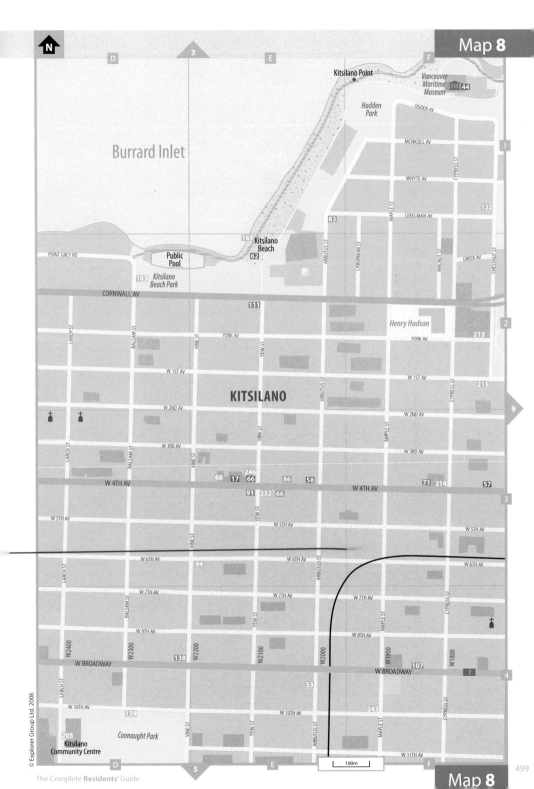

Kitsilano Point

Vancouver
Maritime
Museum  🏛 **44**

Hadden
Park

OGDEN AV

MCNICOLL AV

CYPRESS ST

**1**

WHYTE AV

MAPLE ST

**122**

CREELMAN AV

Burrard Inlet

ARBUTUS ST

LABURNUM ST

WALNUT ST

GREER AV

**83**

CHESTNUT ST

**165**  Kitsilano
Beach
**62**

POINT GREY RD

Public
Pool

**183**  Kitsilano
Beach Park

P

CORNWALL AV

**111**

Henry Hudson

**213**

**2**

LARCH ST

BALSAM ST

VINE ST

YORK AV

YEW ST

YORK AV

W 1ST AV

ARBUTUS ST

W 1ST AV

CYPRESS ST

**215**

**KITSILANO**

W 2ND AV

MAPLE ST

W 2ND AV

**9**

† †

W 3RD AV

VINE ST

VINE ST

W 3RD AV

**66**  **17**  **246**
**66**

**86**

**58**

**71**  **214**

**57**

W 4TH AV

W 4TH AV

**91**  **232**  **66**

W 5TH AV

YEW ST

W 5TH AV

W 5TH AV

W 6TH AV

VINE ST

W 6TH AV

ARBUTUS ST

W 6TH AV

**94**

LARCH ST

W 7TH AV

W 7TH AV

W 7TH AV

CYPRESS ST

BALSAM ST

YEW ST

MAPLE ST

†

W 8TH AV

W 8TH AV

W2400

W2300

W2200

W2100

W2000

W1900

W1800

W BROADWAY

**138**

W BROADWAY

**107**

**7**

**4**

**53**

LARCH ST

W 10TH AV

W 10TH AV

**243**

**139**

VINE ST

YEW ST

ARBUTUS ST

MAPLE ST

**205**
Kitsilano
Community Centre

Connaught Park

CYPRESS ST

W 11TH AV

100m

Map **9**
N

General Information p.1  Residents p.61  Exploring p.183  Activities p.271  Shopping p.359  Going Out p.419

Vanier Park
80

HR MacMillan
Space Centre
47

Vancouver
Museum
45

56    WHYTE ST

Sunset
Beach

False Creek Ferries

Vancouver
Aquatic Centre
162

BURRARD BRIDGE

**WEST END**

BURRARD ST

PACIFIC ST
900
1000

Viva Suites  H  251
Vancouver
Central Lodge

HORNBY ST
DRAKE ST
1300

Meridian
H

HORNBY ST
1400

BEACH AV
1500

HOMER ST
700

ROLLSTON CR

49

99
77

BURRARD ST

CREEKSIDE DR

PENNY FARTHING DR

Molson
Brewery

12

W 1ST AV

False Creek

Granville Island
Public Market
81
79
100
93
31
103    92
65
40    115
Wickaninnish Native
Gallery
Kids Market
68    93
67
96
6    32
1
Sutcliffe
Park
Gallery of
BC Ceramics

Creekhouse Gallery

94
24    Art Club
13    Theatre
55
93

GRANVILLE BRIDGE

JOHNSTON ST

DURANLEAU ST

OLD BRIDGE ST    RAILSPUR ALLEY
CARTWRIGHT ST

**GRANVILLE
ISLAND**

Granville
Island

George
Wainborn
Park

False Creek
Yacht Club

Aquabus

**KITSILANO**

BURRARD ST

W 1ST AV

W 2ND AV

PINE ST

W 3RD AV

FIR ST

86
52

W 4TH AV

41

99

Granville
Bridge
Loop Park

W 5TH AV

LAMEY'S MILL RD

ALDER CROSSING

SITKA SQ

THE CASTINGS

FORGE WALK

LAMEY'S MILL RD

W 4TH AV

W 5TH AV

W 6TH AV

230
16
21
W 6TH AV
W 6TH AV

BURRARD ST

W 7TH AV

PINE ST

Centre Culture
Francophone de
Vancouver

17
5
15
20

W 8TH AV

FIRST AV

W 1600
W 1500

Fairview
Centre

145

14    W 1400

W 1300

HEMLOCK ST

BIRCH ST

**FAIRVIEW**

W 7TH AV

W 8TH AV

SPRUCE ST

W 8TH AV

W 1200

W 1100

W 1700

32

48

W BROADWAY

143

W 8TH AV

171    69    11

W BROADWAY

242

102    37

35

219

W 10TH AV

Vancouver Schoolboard
Administration Office

64
229

W 11TH AV

FIRST AV

H MLOCK ST

W BROADWAY

ALDER ST

SPRUCE ST

W 10TH AV

W 1700

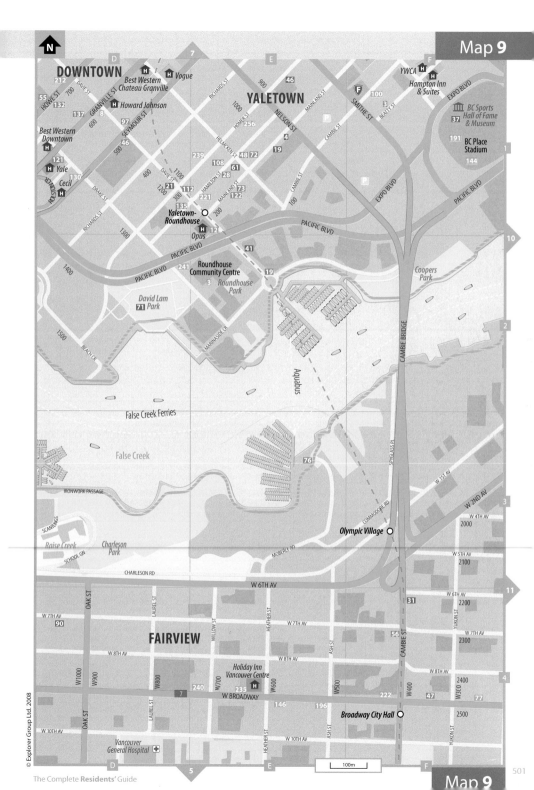

Map **9**

© Explorer Group Ltd. 2008

Map **10**

W WATERFRONT RD

Portside
Park

E WATERFRONT RD

RAILWAY ST

ALEXANDER ST

DURLEY AV

194 118 155 68
143 25 7
**Gastown**

Gastown
Steam Clock 18
99 19
14
30
Dominion

WATER ST

TROUNCE ALLEY

BLOOD ALLEY ST

W CORDOVA ST

33
25
15
24 140
27 102
69 45 117
109

1 39

96 100

MAIN ST

POWELL ST

200

POWELL ST

Oppenheimer
Park

49

**GASTOWN**

43
224

W HASTINGS ST

E CORDOVA ST

300

Firehall Arts
Centre

Lotus Light
Lei Zang Si
Temple

Budget Inns
Patricia Hotel

223
42
Vancouver
Community College
(City Centre Campus)

7A
Regal Place
139

Chelsea

W PENDER ST

West

**CHINATOWN**

Vancouver Police
Museum

43

E HASTINGS ST

GORE AV

E100

E PENDER ST

400

KEEFER ST

500

7

2 Stadium
Chinatown
92

30

39

Dr Sun Yat Sen
Classical
Chinese Garden
82

COLUMBIA ST

CARRALL ST

KEEFER PL

KEEFER ST

MAIN ST

600

90

Andy Livingstone
Park 69

E GEORGIA ST

700

GM Place
192

DUNSMUIR VIADUCT

EXPO BLVD

GEORGIA VIADUCT

UNION ST

GRIFFITHS WAY

PRIOR ST

900

MILROSS AV

1000

STATION ST

3

Plaza of Nations

Ivanhoe

Creekside
Park

NATIONAL AV

1200

MAIN ST

NATIONAL AV

Thornton
Park

116

Pacific Central
Station

EXPO BLVD

9

False Creek

False Creek Ferries

Aquabus

50
Telus World
of Science

QUEBEC ST

Science World
Main Station

1400

TERMINAL AV

120

101

4

1600

W 1ST AV

E 1ST AV

MAIN ST

E100

WESTERN ST

CENTRAL ST

SOUTHERN ST

S KING ST

INDUSTRIAL AV

1700

502

Map **10** **Vancouver** Explorer 1st Edition

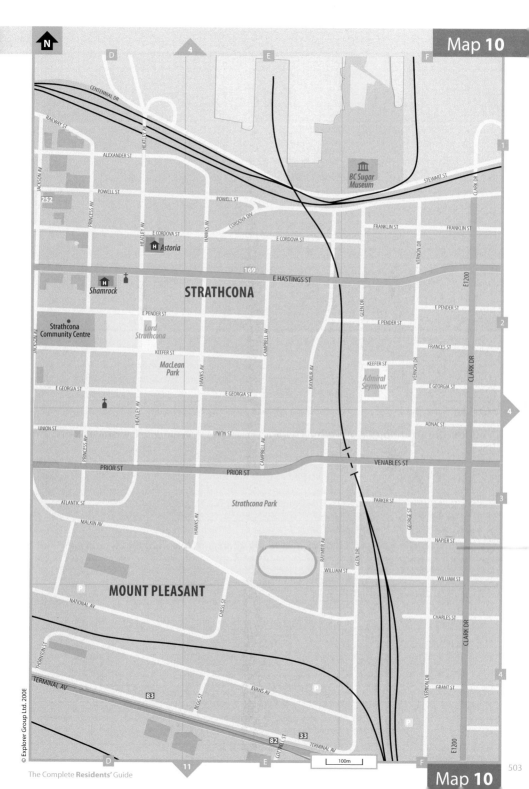

Map **10**

N

CENTENNIAL DR

RAILWAY ST

ALEXANDER ST

JACKSON AV

POWELL ST

PRINCESS AV

HEATLEY AV

POWELL ST

252

BC Sugar
Museum

STEWART ST

CLARK DR

E CORDOVA ST

E CORDOVA ST

HAWKS AV

CORDOVA DIV

FRANKLIN ST

FRANKLIN ST

VERNON DR

Astoria

169

E HASTINGS ST

E1200

Shamrock

**STRATHCONA**

Strathcona
Community Centre

E PENDER ST

E PENDER ST

E PENDER ST

Lord
Strathcona

CAMPBELL AV

GLEN DR

E PENDER ST

FRANCES ST

JACKSON AV

KEEFER ST

MacLean
Park

HAWKS AV

RAYMUR AV

KEEFER ST

VERNON DR

Admiral
Seymour

CLARK DR

E GEORGIA ST

E GEORGIA ST

E GEORGIA ST

HEATLEY AV

ADNAC ST

UNION ST

PRINCESS AV

UNION ST

CAMPBELL AV

VENABLES ST

PRIOR ST

PRIOR ST

ATLANTIC ST

Strathcona Park

PARKER ST

GEORGE ST

MALKIN AV

HAWKS AV

NAPIER ST

RAYMUR AV

GLEN DR

WILLIAM ST

WILLIAM ST

**MOUNT PLEASANT**

NATIONAL AV

CHESS ST

CHARLES ST

CLARK DR

VERNON DR

THORNTON ST

TERMINAL AV

83

BEGG ST

EVANS AV

GRANT ST

82

33

TERMINAL AV

E1200

COTTRELL ST

100m

© Explorer Group Ltd. 2006

Map **11**

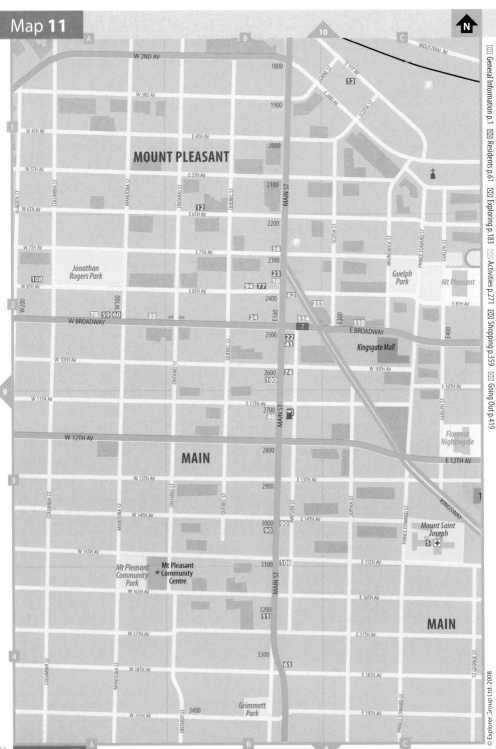

**MOUNT PLEASANT**

Jonathan Rogers Park

Guelph Park

Mt Pleasant

Kingsgate Mall

Florence Nightingale

**MAIN**

Mt Pleasant Community Park

Mt Pleasant Community Centre

Mount Saint Joseph

**MAIN**

Grimmett Park

Map **11**

© Explorer Group Ltd. 2008

**Map 11**

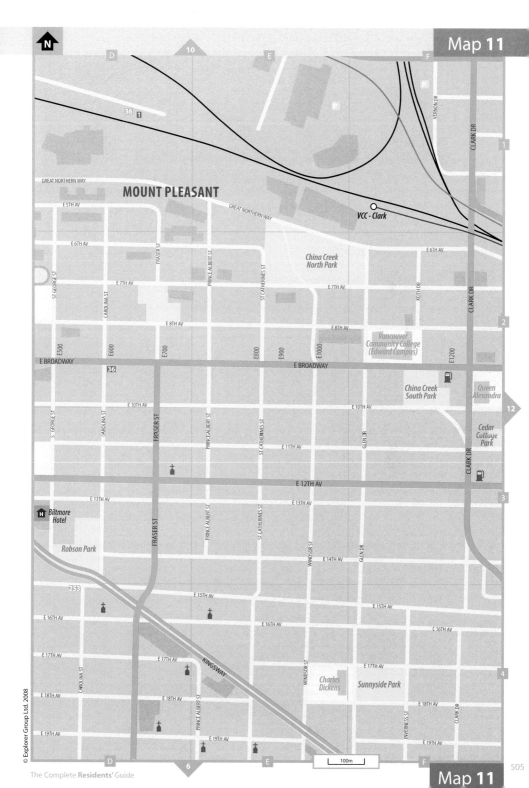

N

10

D

E

F

Map 11

VERNON DR

CLARK DR

36  1

GREAT NORTHERN WAY

**MOUNT PLEASANT**

GREAT NORTHERN WAY

VCC - Clark

1

E 5TH AV

E 6TH AV

FRASER ST

PRINCE ALBERT ST

ST CATHERINES ST

China Creek
North Park

E 6TH AV

KEITH DR

CLARK DR

ST GEORGE ST

CAROLINA ST

E 7TH AV

E 7TH AV

E 8TH AV

E 8TH AV

Vancouver
Community College
(Edward Campus)

2

E500

E600

E700

E800

E900

E1000

E1200

E BROADWAY

E BROADWAY

36

China Creek
South Park

Queen
Alexandra

12

S. GEORGE ST

CAROLINA ST

FRASER ST

E 10TH AV

PRINCE ALBERT ST

ST CATHERINES ST

E 10TH AV

GLEN DR

Cedar
Cottage
Park

E 11TH AV

CLARK DR

E 12TH AV

E 13TH AV

E 13TH AV

3

H  Biltmore
Hotel

FRASER ST

PRINCE ALBERT ST

ST CATHERINES ST

WINDSOR ST

GLEN DR

Robson Park

E 14TH AV

253

E 15TH AV

E 15TH AV

E 16TH AV

E 16TH AV

E 16TH AV

E 16TH AV

CAROLINA ST

E 17TH AV

E 17TH AV

KINGSWAY

E 17TH AV

Charles
Dickens

Sunnyside Park

4

E 18TH AV

E 18TH AV

PRINCE ALBERT ST

WINDSOR ST

INVERNESS ST

E 18TH AV

CLARK DR

E 19TH AV

E 19TH AV

E 19TH AV

E 19TH AV

D

6

E

F

100m

Map 11

# Map **12**

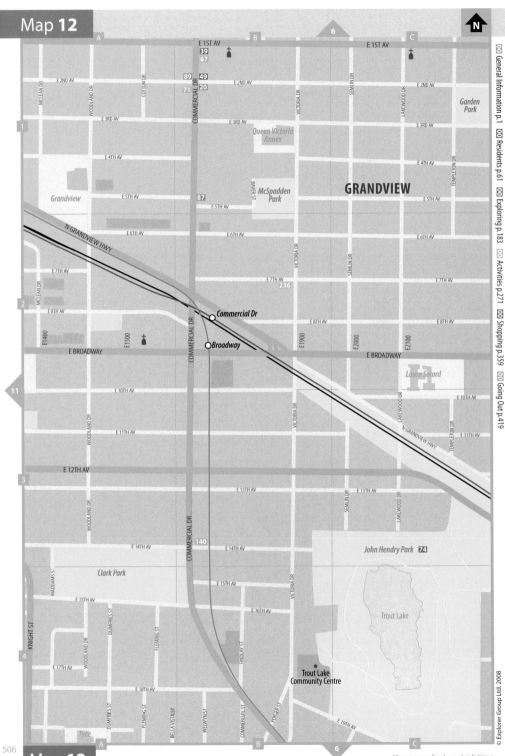

E 1ST AV

E 1ST AV

E 2ND AV

**39**
**67**

**89** **49**
**71** **20**

E 2ND AV

E 2ND AV

E 3RD AV

E 3RD AV

E 3RD AV

*Garden Park*

McLEAN DR

WOODLAND DR

COTTON DR

COMMERCIAL DR

VICTORIA DR

SEMLIN DR

LAKEWOOD DR

TEMPLETON DR

*Queen Victoria Annex*

E 4TH AV

E 4TH AV

*Grandview*

E 5TH AV

**87**

E 5TH AV

BAUER ST

*McSpadden Park*

**GRANDVIEW**

E 5TH AV

E 6TH AV

E 6TH AV

E 6TH AV

N GRANDVIEW HWY

McLEAN DR

E 7TH AV

E 7TH AV
**236**

VICTORIA DR

SEMLIN DR

E 7TH AV

E 8TH AV

E 8TH AV

E 8TH AV

E1400

E1500

COMMERCIAL DR

**○** *Commercial Dr*

**○** *Broadway*

E1900

E2000

E2100

E BROADWAY

E BROADWAY

E BROADWAY

*Laura Secord*

E 10TH AV

E 10TH AV

E 10TH AV

WOODLAND DR

VICTORIA DR

LAKEWOOD DR

E 11TH AV

E 11TH AV

E 11TH AV

N GRANDVIEW HWY

TEMPLETON DR

E 12TH AV

E 13TH AV

E 13TH AV

E 13TH AV

WOODLAND DR

COMMERCIAL DR

SEMLIN DR

LAKEWOOD DR

*John Hendry Park* **74**

E 14TH AV

**140**

E 14TH AV

*Clark Park*

MADDAMS ST

E 15TH AV

E 15TH AV

DUMFRIES ST

FLEMING ST

WOODLAND DR

E 16TH AV

VICTORIA DR

*Trout Lake*

KNIGHT ST

E 17TH AV

E 18TH AV

DUMFRIES ST

FLEMING ST

BELLA VISTA ST

WELWYN ST

COMMERCIAL ST

FINDLAY ST

POPLAR ST

*Trout Lake Community Centre*

E 19TH AV

*Tyee*

© Explorer Group Ltd 2008

Map **12**

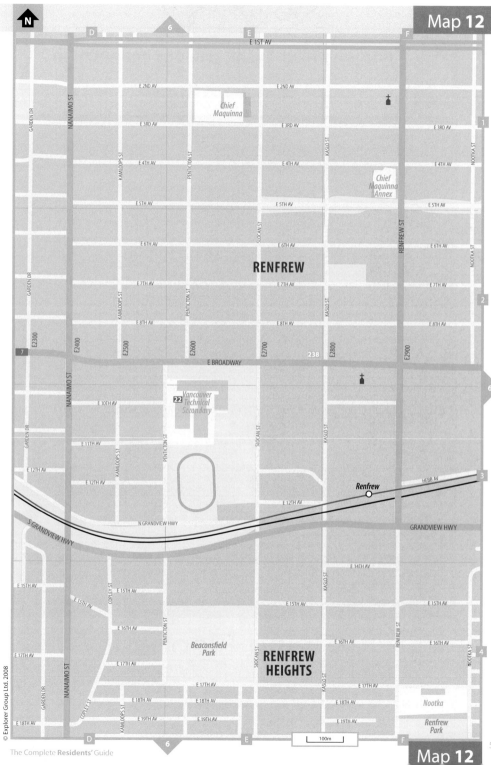

# Index

# Index

# Index

# Index

# Index

# Residents' Guides

All you need to know about living, working and enjoying life in these exciting destinations

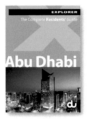   

Coming in 2009: Bangkok, Brussels, Mexico City, Moscow, San Francisco, Saudi Arabia and Taipei

## Mini Guides
The perfect pocket-sized
Visitors' Guides

Coming in 2009: Bangkok, Brussels, Mexico City, Moscow, San Francisco and Taipei

## Mini Maps
Wherever you are,
never get lost again

**Check out www.explorerpublishing.com/products**

## Photography Books
Beautiful cities caught through the lens

## Calendars
The time, the place, and the date

# Maps
Wherever you are, never get lost again

# Activity and Lifestyle Guides
Drive, trek, dive and swim... life will never be boring again

## Retail sales
Our books are available in most good bookshops around the world, and are also available online at Amazon.co.uk and Amazon.com. If you would like to enquire about any of our international distributors, please contact retail@explorerpublishing.com

## Bulk sales and customisation
All our products are available for bulk sales with customisation options. For discount rates and further information, please contact corporatesales@explorerpublishing.com

## Licensing and digital sales
All our content, maps and photography are available for print or digital use. For licensing enquiries please contact licensing@explorerpublishing.com

**Check out www.explorerpublishing.com/products**

## Ahmed Mainodin
AKA: Mystery Man
We can never recognise Ahmed because of his constantly changing facial hair. He waltzes in with big lambchop sideburns one day, a handlebar moustache the next, and a neatly trimmed goatee after that. So far we've had no objections to his hirsute chameleonisms, but we'll definitely draw the line at a monobrow.

## Andrea Fust
AKA: Mother Superior
By day Andrea is the most efficient manager in the world and by night she replaces the boardroom for her board and wows the pants off the dudes in Ski Dubai. Literally. Back in the office she definitely wears the trousers!

## Ajay Krishnan R
AKA: Web Wonder
Ajay's mum and dad knew he was going to be an IT genius when they found him reconfiguring his Commodore 64 at the tender age of 2. He went on to become the technology consultant on all three Matrix films, and counts Keanu as a close personal friend.

## Bahrudeen Abdul
AKA: The Stallion
Having tired of creating abstract sculptures out of papier maché and candy canes, Bahrudeen turned to the art of computer programming. After honing his skills in the southern Andes for three years he grew bored of Patagonian winters, and landed a job here, 'The Home of 01010101 Creative Freedom'.

## Alex Jeffries
AKA: Easy Rider
Alex is happiest when dressed in leather from head to toe with a humming machine between his thighs – just like any other motorbike enthusiast. Whenever he's not speeding along the Hatta Road at full throttle, he can be found at his beloved Mac, still dressed in leather.

## Ben Merrett
AKA: Big Ben
After a short (or tall as the case may have been) career as a human statue, Ben tired of the pigeons choosing him, rather than his namesake, as a public convenience and decided to fly the nest to seek his fortune in foreign lands. Not only is he big on personality but he brings in the big bucks with his bulk!

## Alistair MacKenzie
AKA: Media Mogul
If only Alistair could take the paperless office one step further and achieve the officeless office he would be the happiest publisher alive. Wireless access from a remote spot somewhere in the Hajar Mountains would suit this intrepid explorer – less traffic, lots of fresh air, and wearing sandals all day – the perfect work environment!

## Cherry Enriquez
AKA: Bean Counter
With the team's penchant for sweets and pastries, it's good to know we have Cherry on top of our accounting cake. The local confectioner is always paid on time, so we're guaranteed great gateaux for every special occasion.

## Annabel Clough
AKA: Bollywood Babe
Taking a short break from her successful career in Bollywood, Annabel livens up the Explorer office with her spontaneous dance routines and random passionate outpouring of song. If there is a whiff of drama or a hint of romance, Annabel's famed vocal chords and nifty footwork will bring a touch of glamour to Al Quoz.

## Claire England
AKA: Whip Cracker
No longer able to freeload off the fact that she once appeared in a Robbie Williams video, Claire now puts her creative skills to better use – looking up rude words in the dictionary! A child of English nobility, Claire is quite the lady – unless she's down at Rock Bottom.

### Darwin Lovitos
AKA: The Philosopher

We are firm believers in our own Darwinism theory at Explorer – enthusiasm, organisation and a great sense of humour can evolve into a wonderful thing. He may not have the big beard (except on weekends), but Darwin is just as wise as his namesake.

### David Quinn
AKA: Sharp Shooter

After a short stint as a children's TV presenter was robbed from David because he developed an allergy to sticky back plastic, he made his way to sandier pastures. Now that he's thinking outside the box, nothing gets past the man with the sharpest pencil in town.

### Derrick Pereira
AKA: The Returnimator

After leaving Explorer in 2003, Derrick's life took a dramatic downturn – his dog ran away, his prized bonsai tree died and he got kicked out of his thrash metal band. Since rejoining us, things are looking up and he just found out he's won $10 million in a Nigerian sweepstakes competition. And he's got the desk by the window!

### Enrico Maullon
AKA: The Crooner

Frequently mistaken for his near-namesake Enrique Iglesias, Enrico decided to capitalise and is now a regular stand-in for the Latin heartthrob. If he's ever missing from the office, it usually means he's off performing for millions of adoring fans on another stadium tour of America.

### Firos Khan
AKA: Big Smiler

Previously a body double in kung fu movies, including several appearances in close up scenes for Steven Seagal's moustache. He also once tore down a restaurant with his bare hands after they served him a mild curry by mistake.

### Grace Carnay
AKA: Manila Ice

It's just as well the office is so close to a movie theatre, because Grace is always keen to catch the latest Hollywood offering from Brad Pitt, who she admires purely for his acting ability, of course. Her ice cool exterior conceals a tempestuous passion for jazz, which fuels her frenzied typing speed.

### Hashim MM
AKA: Speedy Gonzales

They don't come much faster than Hashim – he's so speedy with his mouse that scientists are struggling to create a computer that can keep up with him. His nimble fingers leave his keyboard smouldering (he gets through three a week), and his go-faster stripes make him almost invisible to the naked eye when he moves.

### Helen Spearman
AKA: Little Miss Sunshine

With her bubbly laugh and permanent smile, Helen is a much-needed ray of sunshine in the office when we're all grumpy and facing harrowing deadlines. It's almost impossible to think that she ever loses her temper or shows a dark side... although put her behind the wheel of a car, and you've got instant road rage.

### Henry Hilos
AKA: The Quiet Man

Henry can rarely be seen from behind his large obstructive screen but when you do catch a glimpse you'll be sure to get a smile. Lighthearted Henry keeps all those glossy pages filled with pretty pictures for something to look at when you can't be bothered to read.

### Iain Young
AKA: 'The Cat'

Iain follows in the fine tradition of Scots with safe hands – Alan Rough, Andy Goram, Jim Leighton on a good day – but breaking into the Explorer XI has proved frustrating. There's no match on a Mac, but that Al Huzaifa ringer doesn't half make himself big.

### Ieyad Charaf
AKA: Fashion Designer

When we hired Ieyad as a top designer, we didn't realise we'd be getting his designer tops too! By far the snappiest dresser in the office, you'd be hard-pressed to beat his impeccably ironed shirts.

### Ingrid Cupido
AKA: The Karaoke Queen
Ingrid has a voice to match her starlet name. She'll put any Pop Idols to shame once behind the mike, and she's pretty nifty on a keyboard too. She certainly gets our vote if she decides to go pro; just remember you saw her here first.

### Ivan Rodrigues
AKA: The Aviator
After making a mint in the airline market, Ivan came to Explorer where he works for pleasure, not money. That's his story, anyway. We know that he is actually a corporate spy from a rival company and that his multi-level spreadsheets are really elaborate codes designed to confuse us.

### Jake Marsico
AKA: Don Calzone
Jake spent the last 10 years on the tiny triangular Mediterranean island of Samoza, honing his traditional cooking techniques and perfecting his Italian. Now, whenever he returns to his native America, he impresses his buddies by effortlessly zapping a hot dog to perfection in any microwave, anywhere, anytime.

### Jane Roberts
AKA: The Oracle
After working in an undisclosed role in the government, Jane brought her super sleuth skills to Explorer. Whatever the question, she knows what, where, who, how and when, but her encyclopaedic knowledge is only impressive until you realise she just makes things up randomly.

### Jayde Fernandes
AKA: Pop Idol
Jayde's idol is Britney Spears, and he recently shaved his head to show solidarity with the troubled star. When he's not checking his dome for stubble, or practising the dance moves to 'Baby One More Time' in front of the bathroom mirror, he actually manages to get some designing done.

### Johny Mathew
AKA: The Hawker
Caring Johny used to nurse wounded eagles back to health and teach them how to fly again before trying his luck in merchandising. Fortunately his skills in the field have come in handy at Explorer, where his efforts to improve our book sales have been a soaring success.

### Joy Tubog
AKA: Joyburgh
Don't let her saintly office behaviour deceive you. Joy has the habit of jumping up and down while screaming 'Jumanji' the instant anyone mentions Robin Williams and his hair sweater. Thankfully, her volleyball team has learned to utilize her 'uniqueness' when it's her turn to spike the ball.

### Juby Jose
AKA: The Nutcracker
After years as a ballet teacher, Juby decided on mapping out a completely different career path, charting the UAE's ever-changing road network. Plotting products to illuminate the whole of the Middle East, she now works alongside the all-singing, all-dancing Madathil brothers, and cracks any nut that steps out of line.

### Kate Fox
AKA: Contacts Collector
Kate swooped into the office like the UK equivalent of Wonderwoman, minus the tights of course (it's much too hot for that), but armed with a superhuman marketing brain. Even though she's just arrived, she is already a regular on the Dubai social scene – she is helping to blast Explorer into the stratosphere, one champagne-soaked networking party at a time.

### Kathryn Calderon
AKA: Miss Moneypenny
With her high-flying banking background, Kathryn is an invaluable member of the team. During her lunchtimes she conducts 'get rich quick' seminars that, she says, will make us so much money that we'll be able to retire early and spend our days reading books instead of making them. We're still waiting...

### Katie Drynan
AKA: The Irish Deputy
This Irish lass is full of sass, fresh from her previous role as the four leaf clover mascot for the Irish ladies' rugby team. Katie provides the Explorer office with lots of Celtic banter and unlimited Irish charm.

### Kelly Tesoro
AKA: Leading Lady
Kelly's former career as a Korean soapstar babe set her in good stead for the daily dramas at the bold and beautiful Explorer office. As our lovely receptionist she's on stage all day and her winning smile never slips.

### Matt Farquharson
AKA: Hack Hunter
A career of tuppence-a-word hackery ended when Matt arrived in Dubai to cover a maggot wranglers' convention. He misguidedly thinks he's clever because he once wrote for some grown-up English papers.

### Kiran Melwani
AKA: Bow Selector
Like a modern-day Robin Hood (right down to the green tights and band of merry men), Kiran's mission in life is to distribute Explorer's wealth of knowledge to the fact-hungry readers of the world. Just make sure you never do anything to upset her – rumour has it she's a pretty mean shot with that bow and arrow.

### Mathew Samuel
AKA: Mr Modest
Matt's penchant for the entrepreneurial life began with a pair of red braces and a filofax when still a child. That yearning for the cut and thrust of commerce has brought him to Dubai, where he made a fortune in the sand-selling business before semi-retiring at Explorer.

### Laura Zuffa
AKA: Travelling Salesgirl
Laura's passport is covered in more stamps than Kofi Annan's, and there isn't a city, country or continent that she won't travel to. With a smile that makes grown men weep, our girl on the frontlines always brings home the beef bacon.

### Michael Samuel
AKA: Gordon Gekko
We have a feeling this mild mannered master of mathematics has a wild side. He hasn't witnessed an Explorer party yet but the office agrees that once the karaoke machine is out, Michael will be the maestro. Watch out Dubai!

### Lennie Mangalino
AKA: Shaker Maker
With a giant spring in her step and music in her heart it's hard to not to swing to the beat when Lennie passes by in the office. She loves her Lambada… and Samba… and Salsa and anything else she can get the sales team shaking their hips to.

### Mimi Stankova
AKA: Mind Controller
A master of mind control, Mimi's siren-like voice lulls people into doing whatever she asks. Her steely reserve and endless patience mean recalcitrant reporters and persistent PR people are putty in her hands, delivering whatever she wants, whenever she wants it.

### Mannie Lugtu
AKA: Distribution Demon
When the travelling circus rode into town, their master juggler Mannie decided to leave the Big Top and explore Dubai instead. He may have swapped his balls for our books but his juggling skills still come in handy.

### Maricar Ong
AKA: Pocket Docket
A pint-sized dynamo of ruthless efficiency, Maricar gets the job done before anyone else notices it needed doing. If this most able assistant is absent for a moment, it sends a surge of blind panic through the Explorer ranks.

### Mohammed Sameer
AKA: Man in the Van
Known as MS, short for Microsoft, Sameer can pick apart a PC like a thief with a lock, which is why we keep him out of finance and pounding Dubai's roads in the unmissable Explorer van – so we can always spot him coming.

### Najumudeen Kuttathundil
AKA: The Groove
If it weren't for Najumudeen, our stock of books would be lying in a massive pile of rubble in our warehouse. Thankfully, through hours of crunk dancing and forklift racing with Mohammed T, Najumudeen has perfected the art of organisation and currently holds the title for fastest forklift slalom in the UAE.

### Noushad Madathil
AKA: Map Daddy
Where would Explorer be without the mercurial Madathil brothers? Lost in the Empty Quarter, that's where. Quieter than a mute dormouse, Noushad prefers to let his Photoshop layers, and brother Zain, do all the talking. A true Map Daddy.

### Pamela Afram
AKA: Lady of Arabia
After an ill-fated accident playing Lawrence of Arabia's love interest in a play in Jumeira, Pamela found solace in the Explorer office. Her first paycheque went on a set of shiny new gleamers and she is now back to her bright and smiley self and is solely responsible for lighting up one half of the office!

### Pamela Grist
AKA: Happy Snapper
If a picture can speak a thousand words then Pam's photos say a lot about her - through her lens she manages to find the beauty in everything – even this motley crew. And when the camera never lies, thankfully Photoshop can.

### Pete Maloney
AKA: Graphic Guru
Image conscious he may be, but when Pete has his designs on something you can bet he's gonna get it! He's the king of chat up lines, ladies – if he ever opens a conversation with 'D'you come here often?' then brace yourself for the Maloney magic.

### Rafi Jamal
AKA: Soap Star
After a walk on part in The Bold and the Beautiful, Rafi swapped the Hollywood Hills for the Hajar Mountains. Although he left the glitz behind, he still mingles with high society, moonlighting as a male gigolo and impressing Dubai's ladies with his fancy footwork.

### Rafi VP
AKA: Party Trickster
After developing a rare allergy to sunlight in his teens, Rafi started to lose a few centimeters of height every year. He now stands just 30cm tall, and does his best work in our dingy basement wearing a pair of infrared goggles. His favourite party trick is to fold himself into a briefcase.

### Richard Greig
AKA: Sir Lancelot
Chivalrous to the last, Richard's dream of being a medieval knight suffered a setback after being born several centuries too late. His stellar parliamentary career remains intact, and he is in the process of creating a new party with the aim of abolishing all onions and onion-related produce.

### Roshni Ahuja
AKA: Bright Spark
Never failing to brighten up the office with her colourful get-up, Roshni definitely puts the 'it' in the IT department. She's a perennially pleasant, profound programmer with peerless panache, and she does her job with plenty of pep and piles of pizzazz.

### Sean Kearns
AKA: The Tall Guy
Big Sean, as he's affectionately known, is so laid back he actually spends most of his time lying down (unless he's on a camping trip, when his ridiculously small tent forces him to sleep on his hands and knees). Despite the rest of us constantly tripping over his lanky frame, when the job requires someone who will work flat out, he always rises to the editorial occasion.

### Shabsir M
AKA: Sticky Wicket
Shabsir is a valuable player on the Indian national cricket team, so instead of working you'll usually find him autographing cricket balls for crazed fans around the world. We don't mind though if ever a retailer is stumped because they run out of stock, he knocks them for six with his speedy delivery.

### Shan Kumar
AKA: Caped Crusader
Not dissimilar to the Batman's beacon, Explorer shines a giant X into the skies over Al Quoz in times of need. Luckily for us, Shan battled for days through the sand and warehouse units to save the day at our shiny new office. What a hero!

### Steve Jones
AKA: Golden Boy
Our resident Kiwi lives in a nine-bedroom mansion and is already planning an extension. His winning smile has caused many a knee to weaken in Bur Dubai but sadly for the ladies, he's hopelessly devoted to his clients.

### Shawn Jackson Zuzarte
AKA: Paper Plumber
If you thought rocket science was hard, try rearranging the chaotic babble that flows from the editorial team! If it weren't for Shawn, most of our books would require a kaleidoscope to read correctly so we're keeping him and his jazz hands under wraps.

### Tim Binks
AKA: Class Clown
El Binksmeisterooney is such a sharp wit, he often has fellow Explorers gushing tea from their noses in convulsions of mirth. Years spent hiking across the Middle East have given him an encyclopaedic knowledge of rock formations and elaborate hair.

### Shyrell Tamayo
AKA: Fashion Princess
We've never seen Shyrell wearing the same thing twice – her clothes collection is so large that her husband has to keep all his things in a shoebox. She runs Designlab like clockwork, because being late for deadlines is SO last season.

### Tom Jordan
AKA: The True Professional
Explorer's resident thesp, Tom delivers lines almost as well as he cuts them. His early promise on the pantomime circuit was rewarded with an all-action role in hit UK drama Heartbeat. He's still living off the royalties – and the fact he shared a sandwich with Kenneth Branagh.

### Sobia Gulzad
AKA: High Flyer
If Sobia's exam results in economics and management are anything to go by, she's destined to become a member of the global jet set. Her pursuit of glamour is almost more relentless than her pursuit of success, and in her time away from reading The Wealth of Nations she shops for designer handbags and that elusive perfect shade of lipgloss.

### Tracy Fitzgerald
AKA: 'La Dona'
Tracy is a queenpin Catalan mafiosa and ringleader for the 'pescadora' clan, a nefarious group that runs a sushi smuggling operation between the Costa Brava and Ras Al Khaimah. She is not to be crossed. Rival clans will find themselves fed fish, and then fed to the fishes.

### Sunita Lakhiani
AKA: Designlass
Initially suspicious of having a female in their midst, the boys in Designlab now treat Sunita like one of their own. A big shame for her, because they treat each other pretty damn bad!

### Zainudheen Madathil
AKA: Map Master
Often confused with retired footballer Zinedine Zidane because of his dexterous displays and a bad head-butting habit, Zain tackles design with the mouse skills of a star striker. Maps are his goal and despite getting red-penned a few times, when he shoots, he scores.

The *Vancouver Explorer* Team
**Lead Editor** Tom Jordan
**Deputy Editor** Pamela Afram
**Editorial Assistant** Ingrid Cupido
**Designer** Rafi VP
**Cartographers** Juby Jose, Noushad Madathil, Ramlath Kambravan, Ruksana Peruvankuzhiyil, Sunita Lakhiani
**Photographers** Pamela Grist, Pete Maloney, Tom Jordan, Mark Grist
**Proofer** Jo Holden-MacDonald

## Publisher
Alistair MacKenzie
**Associate Publisher** Claire England
**Assistant to Associate Publisher** Kathryn Calderon

## Editorial
**Group Editor** Jane Roberts
**Lead Editors** David Quinn, Katie Drynan, Sean Kearns, Tim Binks, Tom Jordan
**Deputy Editors** Helen Spearman, Jakob Marsico, Jenny Lyon, Pamela Afram, Richard Greig
**Senior Editorial Assistant** Mimi Stankova
**Editorial Assistants** Grace Carnay, Ingrid Cupido

## Design
**Creative Director** Pete Maloney
**Art Director** Ieyad Charaf
**Design Manager** Alex Jeffries
**Junior Designer** Jessy Perera
**Layout Manager** Jayde Fernandes
**Designers** Hashim Moideen, Rafi VP, Shawn Jackson Zuzarte
**Cartography Manager** Zainudheen Madathil
**Cartographers** Juby Jose, Noushad Madathil, Sunita Lakhiani
**Traffic Manager** Maricar Ong
**Production Coordinator** Joy Tubog

## Photography
**Photography Manager** Pamela Grist
**Photographer** Victor Romero
**Image Editor** Henry Hilos

## Sales & Marketing
**Media Sales Area Managers** Laura Zuffa, Paul Santer, Pouneh Hafizi, Stephen Jones
**Corporate Sales Executive** Ben Merrett
**Marketing Manager** Kate Fox
**Marketing Executive** Annabel Clough
**Marketing Assistant** Shedan Ebona
**Digital Content Manager** Derrick Pereira
**International Retail Sales Manager** Ivan Rodrigues
**Business Relations Manager** Shyrell Tamayo
**Retail Sales Coordinator** Sobia Gulzad
**Retail Sales Supervisor** Mathew Samuel
**Retail Sales Merchandisers** Johny Mathew, Shan Kumar
**Sales & Marketing Coordinator** Lennie Mangalino
**Senior Distribution Executives** Ahmed Mainodin, Firos Khan
**Warehouse Assistant** Najumudeen K.I.
**Drivers** Mohammed Sameer, Shabsir Madathil

## Finance & Administration
**Finance Manager** Michael Samuel
**Junior Accountant** Cherry Enriquez
**Accountants Assistant** Darwin Lovitos
**Administrators** Enrico Maullon, Kelly Tesoro
**Drivers** Rafi Jamal, Mannie Lugtu

## IT
**Senior IT Administrator** Ajay Krishnan
**Senior Software Engineer** Bahrudeen Abdul
**Software Engineer** Subbu Lakshmi

# Contact Us
## Reader Response
If you have any comments and suggestions, fill out our online reader response form and you could win prizes. Log on to **www.explorerpublishing.com**

## General Enquiries
We'd love to hear your thoughts and answer any questions you have about this book or any other Explorer product. Contact us at **info@explorerpublishing.com**

## Careers
If you fancy yourself as an Explorer, send your CV (stating the position you're interested in) to **jobs@explorerpublishing.com**

## Designlab & Contract Publishing
For enquiries about Explorer's Contract Publishing arm and design services contact **designlab@explorerpublishing.com**

## PR & Marketing
For PR and marketing enquiries contact **marketing@explorerpublishing.com** **pr@explorerpublishing.com**

## Corporate Sales
For bulk sales and customisation options, for this book or any Explorer product, contact **sales@explorerpublishing.com**

## Advertising & Sponsorship
For advertising and sponsorship, contact **media@explorerpublishing.com**

**Explorer Publishing & Distribution**
PO Box 34275, Dubai, United Arab Emirates
www.explorerpublishing.com

**Phone:** +971 (0)4 340 8805
**Fax:** +971 (0)4 340 0000

# Quick Reference

## Emergency Numbers

| | |
|---|---|
| Emergency services (police, fire, ambulance) | 911 |
| ICBC Dial-A-Claim | 604 520 8222 |
| TransLink Lost Property | 604 682 7887 |
| Vancouver Police Department | 604 717 3321 |

## Public Holidays

| | |
|---|---|
| New Year's Day | 1 January |
| Good Friday | Friday before Easter Sunday |
| Victoria Day | Monday on or before 24 May |
| Canada Day | 1 July |
| British Columbia Day | First Monday in August |
| Labour Day | First Monday in September |
| Thanksgiving | Second Monday in October |
| Remembrance Day | 11 November |
| Christmas Day | 25 December |

## Medical Services

| | |
|---|---|
| Shoppers Drug Mart (24 hour) | 604 669 2424 |
| St Paul's Hospital | 604 682 2344 |
| Ultima Medicentre | 604 683 8138 |
| Vancouver General Hospital | 604 875 4111 |

## City Information

| | |
|---|---|
| www.canada.com/ cityguides/vancouver | CanWest Media |
| www.city.vancouver.bc.ca | City of Vancouver |
| www.tourismvancouver.com | Tourism Vancouver |

## Airlines

| | |
|---|---|
| Air Canada | 1 888 247 2262 |
| Air China | 604 685 0921 |
| Air New Zealand | 1 800 663 5494 |
| Air Pacific | 1 800 227 4446 |
| Air Transat | 1 877 872 6728 |
| Alaska Airlines | 1 800 252 7522 |
| All Nippon Airways | 1 800 235 9262 |
| American Airlines | 1 800 433 7300 |
| British Airways | 1 800 247 9297 |
| Cathay Pacific | 604 606 8888 |
| China Airlines | 604 682 6777 |
| China Eastern Airlines | 604 689 8998 |
| Continental Airlines | 1 800 231 0856 |
| Delta Airlines | 1 800 221 1212 |
| Japan Airlines | 1 800 525 3663 |
| KLM | 1 800 447 4747 |
| Korean Air | 1 800 438 5000 |
| Lufthansa | 1 800 563 5954 |
| Mexicana | 1 800 531 7921 |
| Northwest Airlines | 1 800 225 2525 |
| Qantas | 1 800 227 4500 |
| Singapore Airlines | 604 689 1223 |
| United Airlines | 1 800 241 6522 |
| WestJet | 1 800 538 5696 |

## Airport Information

**Vancouver International Airport:**

| | |
|---|---|
| Lost & Found | 604 276 6104 |
| Enquiries | 604 207 7077 |

## Landmark Hotels

| | |
|---|---|
| Century Plaza | 604 687 0575 |
| Delta Vancouver Suites | 604 689 8188 |
| The Fairmont Hotel Vancouver | 604 684 3131 |
| The Fairmont Waterfront | 604 691 1991 |
| Four Seasons Hotel Vancouver | 604 689 9333 |
| Georgian Court Hotel | 604 682 5555 |
| The Granville Island Hotel | 604 683 7373 |
| Hyatt Regency Vancouver | 604 683 1234 |
| Le Soleil Hotel & Suites | 604 632 3000 |
| The Listel Hotel | 604 684 8461 |
| Metropolitan Hotel | 604 687 1122 |
| Opus Hotel | 604 642 6787 |
| Pacific Palisades | 604 688 0461 |
| Pan Pacific | 604 662 8111 |
| Sheraton Vancouver Wall Centre | 604 331 1000 |
| The Sutton Place | 604 682 5511 |
| The Syliva Hotel | 604 681 9321 |
| Vancouver Marriott Pinnacle Downtown Hotel | 604 684 1128 |
| The Wedgewood Hotel | 604 689 7777 |
| The Westin Bayshore Resort & Marina | 604 682 3377 |
| The Westin Grand | 604 602 1999 |

## Embassies & Consulates

| | |
|---|---|
| Australia | 604 684 1177 |
| Austria | 604 687 3338 |
| Brazil | 604 696 5311 |
| China | 604 734 0704 |
| Finland | 604 687 8237 |
| France | 604 681 4287 |
| Germany | 604 684 8377 |
| Greece | 604 681 1381 |
| Hungary | 604 730 7321 |
| Iceland | 604 922 0854 |
| India | 604 662 8811 |
| Ireland | 604 683 9233 |
| Italy | 604 684 7288 |
| Japan | 604 684 5868 |
| Korea | 604 681 9581 |
| Netherlands | 604 684 6448 |
| New Zealand | 604 684 7388 |
| Norway | 604 682 8376 |
| Philippines | 604 685 7645 |
| Poland | 604 688 3530 |
| Singapore | 604 669 5115 |
| South Africa | 604 688 1301 |
| Sweden | 604 683 5838 |
| Switzerland | 604 687 1143 |
| UAE | 613 565 7272 |
| United Kingdom | 604 683 4421 |
| USA | 604 685 4311 |

# VANCOUVER TRANSIT MAP

English Bay

Vancouver

Downtown Vancouver

**PARK ROYAL**
239.246.250.251.252
253.254.255.257.258

**UNIVERSITY LOOP**
4.9.17.25
41.43.44.49.84
99.258.480
C20.C22.N17

**CAPILANO UNIVERSITY**
28.130.239

**IRONWORKERS MEMORIAL BRIDGE**
28.130.210.211.212
214.290.292

**PHIBBS EXCHANGE**
28.130.210.211.212
214.229.232.239.C15

**PNE PARK & RIDE**
10.135

**SUBURBAN BUSES ON HASTINGS STREET**
135.160.190

**KOOTENAY LOOP**
C1.C10.27.28.123
130.135.160.190.N35

**KOOTENAY**
10.16.N35
N16

**COMMERCIAL DR**
9.20.99.N20

**NANAIMO**
7.25

**BROADWAY**
9.20.99.N20

**MAIN STREET**
9.20.99.N9.N20

**VCC-CLARK**
16.20.135.N20.N35

**MAIN STREET-SCIENCE WORLD**
3.8.19.22.C21
C23.N8.N19

**WATERFRONT**
WCE.44.50.98

**STADIUM-CHINATOWN**

**BURRARD**

**GRANVILLE**

**STANLEY PARK LOOP**
19

**AirCare**
1333 MCKEEN AVE

**BOUNDARY LOOP**
9.N9

**GILMORE LOOP**
28.129.N9*

**RENFREW**
16.26
29.N16

**RUPERT**
27

**29th AVE**
16.26
29.N16

**JOYCE-COLLINGWOOD**
26.27.28.41.43

**PATTERSON**
129

**LONSDALE QUAY**
228.229.230.236
239.242.246.N24

**SEABUS**

**DUNBAR LOOP**
7.22.32.41
43.49.480.N22

**TO AIRPORT STATION**
98.100.491.496.N10

## Legend

- Transit Exchange
- Shared Station
- SkyTrain Expo Line
- SkyTrain Millennium Line
- West Coast Express (WCE)
- SeaBus Route
- Bus Route
- Bus/HOV Lane
- **123** B-Line Route & Stop
- **123** Regular Route
- **123** Peak Hour Route
- **123** Limited Service * refer to timetable
- Central Valley Greenway
- Park & Ride Lot
- Bike Locker
- Travel InfoCentre
- Transportation Link
- Point of Interest
- Park and Open Space
- Hospital

Map courtesy of TransLink